By 2/5   45/-

Y0-BDZ-175

THE HOLSTEIN PAPERS

THE MEMOIRS, DIARIES AND
CORRESPONDENCE OF
FRIEDRICH VON HOLSTEIN
1837–1909

II
DIARIES

BISMARCK IN 1885

THE
HOLSTEIN PAPERS

EDITED BY
NORMAN RICH & M. H. FISHER

VOLUME II
★
DIARIES

CAMBRIDGE
AT THE UNIVERSITY PRESS
1957

PUBLISHED BY
THE SYNDICS OF THE CAMBRIDGE UNIVERSITY PRESS
London Office: Bentley House, N.W.I
American Branch: New York
Agents for Canada, India, and Pakistan: Macmillan

Printed in Great Britain by
Western Printing Services Limited, Bristol

CONTENTS

Preface . . . . . *page* vii

Introduction xi

Diaries: 1881, 1882 . . . 1

        1883 25

        1884 42

        1885 170

        1886 274

        1887 330

        1888 360

Appendix I 385

      II 388

Index 395

The frontispiece shows Prince Bismarck
in 1885

PREFACE[1]

WHEN Holstein began his diplomatic career as Attaché in St Petersburg, Bismarck warned him that keeping a diary was incompatible with diplomatic discretion. For this reason, Holstein says, he kept no diary during the early part of his career.

In 1881 Holstein jotted down some of Bismarck's anecdotes in a bound notebook. By 1882 he had begun to use this notebook to record day-to-day events. There are large gaps in the entries. Nothing was written from April to November 1882, and there are no entries at all in the bound notebook after 27 March 1883. Only about half of the notebook was ever filled.

In 1884 Holstein began the custom of sending his diaries to his cousin, Ida von Stülpnagel.[2] These diaries were written on loose sheets of paper, and continue reasonably consecutively from January 1884 through 1887, when they gradually thin out. There are no entries after 11 November 1888. In the letters written by Holstein to Ida von Stülpnagel during the years 1884 to 1888, references are made to these diaries.[3] After 1888 these references cease, and it seems probable that no entries were written after that date.

The Holstein Papers contain a second set of what might be called diaries, dating from 10 December 1901 to 13 November 1902, and 27 October 1906 to 14 December 1907. These are much more fragmentary than the earlier diaries and consist largely of political jottings. Since they lack all continuity in themselves, they have not been published as a body, but, in so far as they are of historical interest, under the appropriate dates with the correspondence.

The diaries form the largest body of Holstein's own writing in the Holstein Papers. They are especially valuable because it is probable that Holstein never revised or cut them. The bound notebook in which he began his diaries is intact, and the loose sheets sent to Frau von Stülpnagel remained in her possession

---

[1] For a full discussion of the Holstein Papers, see the Introduction to vol. I (*Memoirs*).

[2] See pp. 42–3.

[3] Helmuth Rogge, *Friedrich von Holstein. Lebensbekenntnis in Briefen an eine Frau* (Berlin, 1932), pp. 135, 144, 148.

until Holstein's death.[1] A few days before he died he asked for the suitcase with papers which he had left at Karlstein, his cousin's estate, with the purpose of looking through them, but he died before they had been sent.[2] Unlike his memoirs, Holstein's diaries therefore represent his contemporary appraisal of daily events without the glosses of hindsight. It is indeed remarkable that Holstein wrote his memoirs without making use of his diaries.

In his earlier diary entries, Holstein remained faithful to Bismarck's warning about diplomatic discretion, with the result that they reveal very little about German diplomatic activity or Holstein's own ideas. Even after Holstein began sending his diaries to his cousin, he noted in his entry for 16 February 1884 that he preferred not to speak in his diaries of 'current policy'. Happily for the historian, Holstein's discretion fell away as his disapproval of German policy mounted, so that by 1886 he was not only writing freely about German foreign policy but about his own secret diplomatic activity. On 4 August 1885 he had written to his cousin: 'Your question as to whether I have written my [diary] notes solely for my own satisfaction I interpret as wondering whether I ever intend to publish them. You can calm yourself on that score. Publication is out of the question for by far the greater part of the contents.'[3]

The editors have cut the diaries very little. Some of the Bismarck anecdotes recorded by Holstein have been omitted because they are already well known through Bismarck's own publications. A number of Holstein's anecdotes about historically unimportant people, some repetitions, and a few unintelligible jottings have also been omitted. All omissions have been marked thus: [...]. Spelling and punctuation have been standardized. Wherever necessary, the text has been elucidated by reference to the files of the German Foreign Ministry, to printed documents or memoir literature, or to works based on unpublished documents.

Microfilms of the full manuscript text of the diaries, together with a corrected typewritten transcript, will be placed at the disposal of scholars by the Foreign Office in the Public Record Office in London, and by the Department of State in the National Archives in Washington with the publication of this volume.

[1] Holstein did, to be sure, pay a quick visit to Karlstein in September 1906, the first such visit in twenty-four years. Before his arrival he asked his cousin to have the 'suitcase with papers' placed in his room. (Rogge, *Friedrich von Holstein*, p. 263.) As he was at this time collecting evidence to counter attacks made against him in the Press, which related to a later period of his career, he probably looked through his correspondence, not through his diaries which show no sign of having been tampered with in any way.

[2] Rogge, *Friedrich von Holstein*, pp. 340, 343, note 2.

[3] *Ibid*. p. 136.

The editors wish to express their warmest thanks to Mrs Joan Spencer for preparing the English translation of the present volume and to Mrs Joan Rich, who made the index.

We also wish to thank Professor Werner Frauendienst for his generous co-operation in the publication of the German edition. Professor Frauendienst has written a separate introduction to volume I of the German edition, and has made many valuable suggestions which have been incorporated in the present volume. Every effort has been made to preserve the maximum uniformity between the two editions.

NORMAN RICH
M. H. FISHER

January 1956

INTRODUCTION[1]

DURING the years covered by his diaries, Friedrich von Holstein served as Senior Counsellor (*Vortragender Rat*) in the Political Division of the German Foreign Ministry in Berlin. Holstein had entered the Prussian diplomatic service in 1860 under the aegis of Otto von Bismarck. In succeeding years Bismarck furthered his career in numerous posts abroad, and it was Bismarck who brought him to Berlin in 1876.

Whatever special influence Holstein enjoyed during his early years in the Foreign Ministry resulted from his personal relations with Bismarck. On numerous occasions he served as the Chancellor's secretary during his extended sojourns in the country, and in Berlin he was called on for personal reports more frequently than most Counsellors. Holstein had a capacity for work extraordinary even by Prussian standards. In a short time he mastered the files of the Ministry, remembering what he had read with astonishing accuracy. With the Chancellor's approval, he maintained an extensive private correspondence not only with members of the diplomatic service, but with officials of other Ministries and influential figures in court, parliamentary, financial and Press circles. This correspondence often enabled him to provide the Chancellor with information about delicate political or personal questions which did not ordinarily find its way into official communications. Bismarck had in Holstein not only a tireless, but an unusually well-informed assistant.

Holstein's ability to get on with Bismarck was perhaps even more unusual than his capacity for work. He seems to have been one of the few men who never bored the Chancellor. Part of his success with Bismarck undoubtedly lay in his unique ability to draw him out. Another frequent guest in the Bismarck household described it as 'a particular art, which led to some of the most gripping descriptions of the Chancellor's life'.[2] Holstein was himself a lively raconteur, and was particularly stimulating when talking about political subjects. Indeed, his political conversation is said to have been considerably more persuasive than his writing.

[1] When not otherwise stated, all quotations in the introduction are taken from the diaries.
[2] Ernst von Dryander, *Erinnerungen aus meinem Leben* (Bielefeld and Leipzig, 1922), p. 166.

With Bismarck's family, Holstein was on the friendliest terms. He was a great favourite with Princess Bismarck and the boon companion of the Chancellor's sons. His close relationship with the two sons was especially significant, for Herbert and Wilhelm von Bismarck were to become increasingly important political figures in their own right. They alternated with Holstein as their father's personal secretary, and while Bismarck lived in the country their correspondence with Holstein in Berlin often served as the main unofficial link between the Chancellor and the Foreign Ministry.

The origin of the gradual change in Holstein's personal relationship to the Bismarck household may be found in the marriage of Marie, the only daughter of Otto von Bismarck, to Count Kuno zu Rantzau on 6 November 1878. Rantzau became a *Vortragender Rat* in the Foreign Ministry, and soon joined the trio of Herbert, Wilhelm (Bill) and Holstein on temporary service as the Chancellor's personal secretary in Varzin and Friedrichsruh. The appointment of Herbert and Bill to posts outside Berlin and the birth of children to Marie Rantzau—the first Bismarck grandchildren—were to make her husband something of a fixture on Bismarck's staff in the country. This in itself would not have been important had Holstein maintained the same relationship with him as he did with Herbert and Bill. But Holstein never felt drawn to Rantzau and did not ordinarily correspond with him while the Chancellor was in the country. Herbert complained about the situation in a letter of 22 February 1884: 'When I was with my father in the past years, you for the most part kept me informed; you don't seem to be doing this with Rantzau. Thus only the regular incoming documents reach my father, and at best short numbered political reports, though even these are rare. In this way contact, not to mention an intimate acquaintance with affairs, cannot be maintained when he stays away for six or seven months. [...] How is my father to form a correct estimate of certain situations, when it is often a question of the shading of specific points, if he only receives official communications? The countless nuances, which can be decisive, cannot be expressed in them, but they can be expressed in private letters to the acting secretary.'[1]

Herbert's letter had no effect on Holstein's attitude to Rantzau. By 1884 he had almost given up his visits to the Bismarcks' house because of his distaste for their son-in-law. In May of that year he took offence at Rantzau's manner and challenged him to a duel.

[1] *Holstein Papers. Correspondence.*

Holstein's quarrel with Rantzau does not seem to have affected his personal relationship with the Chancellor or his sons. His status in the Foreign Ministry itself had meanwhile greatly risen with the appointment of his friend, Paul von Hatzfeldt, to the State Secretaryship in 1881. From 1881 to 1885, when Hatzfeldt gave way to Herbert von Bismarck, Holstein was the most influential adviser to the head of the Ministry. This did not mean that Holstein, or Hatzfeldt himself for that matter, in any sense directed German foreign policy, for in this realm Bismarck excluded every other initiative, but Holstein did play a steadily increasing part in its execution. He also established a political partnership with Hatzfeldt which was to have considerable significance in the future.

When Herbert von Bismarck became head of the Foreign Ministry in 1885, Holstein's status did not appreciably change, but his day-to-day contact with Herbert made him increasingly critical of his old friend's arrogant and inconsiderate behaviour in his high position. It was at this time that Holstein began to have serious reservations about the conduct of German foreign policy. Until now he had done his share of carping, yet in 1884 he could still write: '[Bismarck's] little foibles would dwindle to nothing if they could be set against his great qualities.'[1] During Herbert's first months as acting State Secretary, Germany suffered what Holstein considered to be a humiliating diplomatic defeat by Spain in a dispute over the ownership of the Caroline Islands. Holstein did not regard this setback as serious in itself except as an indication of the decline of the Chancellor's powers and an inspiration to Germany's enemies. What he did consider potentially disastrous was Herbert's pro-Russian policy.

Holstein rejected out of hand Bismarck's plans for solving the Balkan problem by dividing the region into spheres of influence between Russia and Austria. The firm establishment of Russian power in Bulgaria would not end the agitation of the Russian Pan-Slavists, but only give it added momentum. Any increase in Russian power or prestige, Holstein felt, might make the eastern colossus an irresistible magnet to neighbouring weaker Powers, including Turkey. With the whole of south-eastern Europe and the Near East in her sphere of influence, Russia could seize any favourable opportunity to crush Austria, while the greater portion of the German army was bound to the line of the Vosges. Even if Germany succeeded in eliminating France as a major Power, she would in the end find herself alone facing the Russian might in the east.

[1] Diary entry for 16 February.

In Holstein's opinion, every extension of Russian power had to be prevented, and Austria given every support. Since Germany, with the French menace on her flank, could never throw her entire weight on the side of Austria, Holstein used his influence to build up a diplomatic coalition against France and Russia which would include Austria, Italy, Great Britain, and perhaps even Turkey, the Balkan States and Spain.

Aided by Count Hatzfeldt, now the German Ambassador in London, Holstein secretly tried to stiffen the backs of Austria and Britain against moves by Russia to extend her sphere of influence. In pursuing a secret policy with Hatzfeldt, Holstein reasoned that he was doing no more than establishing a counterweight to the pro-Russian influence of Herbert, and that he, not Herbert, was conducting policy in accordance with the real intentions of the Chancellor. 'Whereas Herbert would go through thick and thin with Russia and would gladly sacrifice to Russia every other alliance', Holstein wrote on 3 November 1885, 'his father told Hatzfeldt that the links now being forged between the House of Orleans, Denmark and Russia, combined with the increased royalist temper in France, were such as to make us cautious. We should have to arrange things so that, if the worst happened, we could play off an Austro-Anglo-Italian alliance against a Franco-Russian alliance. Well, we will not remain in a position to do so for very long if Herbert has his way.' On 13 January 1886 Holstein wrote: 'For the first time in twenty-five years I mistrust Bismarck's foreign policy. The old man is led by his son, and the son is led by vanity and the Russian Embassy.'[1]

By 1887 a loose entente between Britain, Austria and Italy had in fact been established, and Holstein claimed no little credit for its inception. On 8 May of that year he wrote in his diary: 'Now that the Austria-Italy-England bloc has been welded together, the sooner this grouping comes to blows with Russia the better.' Holstein reverted frequently to this idea in succeeding months. 'If I seem to be talking lightly about war', he wrote on 11 January 1888, 'it is because I regard it as inevitable. The only question is whether it will break out at a moment favourable to us or to our enemies.'

As in his personal relations, Holstein's preference in diplomatic affairs lay in clearly defined, precise alignments. Other Powers should be regarded and treated as either friendly or hostile. In

---

[1] The criticisms Holstein made in 1898 of Bismarck's pin-prick policy towards Russia (*Memoirs*, Chapter vii) may be interpreted as an attempt to show that German-Russian antagonism antedated the dropping of the Reinsurance Treaty with Russia in 1890 after Bismarck's dismissal.

Holstein's opinion, Bismarck's method of encouraging now Russia, now Austria, now Britain, or even France, only exposed Germany to the suspicion of all parties.

Holstein's commentaries on Bismarck's policy after 1886 not only reveal his increasing disagreement with the Chancellor's diplomacy, but his failure to understand it. Now, as later, he lacked the feeling for the *imponderabilia* of international politics. Bismarck's intricate network of alliances represented for Holstein nothing more than an old man's love of finessing and intrigue, and his fear of taking clear-cut decisions. Even before the conclusion of the Reinsurance Treaty with Russia, Holstein wrote on 11 January 1887: 'Our policy with its criss-cross of commitments [...] resembles the tangle of lines at a big railway station. The chief pointsman thinks he can click everything into its proper place and hopes particularly that the greater the confusion the more indispensable he is.'

With all his criticism of the Chancellor's failings as a statesman and a human being, Holstein wanted Bismarck to remain in office. He fully appreciated the continued value of his prestige for Germany's international position, but the primary consideration was the prospect of the imminent death of the old Kaiser and the succession of his liberal-minded son. Crown Prince Friedrich Wilhelm was well known to favour a more liberal form of government for Germany, and had frequently expressed his dislike of Bismarck's authoritarian methods. The Crown Prince received firm support for his political views from his wife, the eldest daughter of Queen Victoria of England, an outspoken champion of liberalism and a passionate partisan of her native land. To German liberals, the coming reign represented the hope of the future, the opportunity to see their theories at last translated into practice. For this very reason men of conservative views like Holstein were filled with apprehension about the future.

In 1881 Kaiser Wilhelm I was eighty-four years old, and the succession came to dominate German political activity with daily increasing insistency. Holstein's concern with the problem is revealed in his earliest diary entries. He was convinced that Bismarck would have to stay in power at least during the first years of the new reign to avoid domestic upheaval or prevent Germany from waging war on behalf of Britain. Holstein therefore favoured the Chancellor's various moves to strengthen his political position within Germany: the negotiations to end the struggle with the Catholic Church (the *Kulturkampf*), to make it at least possible to gain the backing of the powerful Catholic

Centre Party; the establishment of a German colonial empire, in order to undercut a popular item in the liberal programme; the contact with moderate Liberals, who might form a Ministry under Bismarck acceptable to the next Kaiser. 'I have no illusions about the Chancellor's humanity', Holstein wrote on 16 April 1884, 'but as an institution I think he is the best thing the German Reich possesses, and neither one man nor many could replace him. A proof of this is the way he has made all preparations to steer the ship of state through the stormy days of the succession that lies ahead.'

Holstein's efforts to smooth the personal relations between the Crown Prince and the Chancellor, to remove at least the minor sources of irritation, form a prominent theme in his diaries. He established working relationships with like-minded members of the Crown Prince's court, and used his influence and ingenuity to get allies into key positions there. His most notable success was the appointment of his friend Count Hugo von Radolinski as Court Chamberlain.

Holstein's knowledge of the views of the Crown Prince added to his fears about Herbert von Bismarck's pro-Russian attitude. 'If this is not changed we shall in a couple of years have, not a Three Emperors' Alliance, but a Two Emperors' Alliance, and Austria will seek support elsewhere', he wrote on 24 October 1885. 'That will certainly not accord with the Crown Prince's policy.'

A policy favourable to Russia accorded still less with the views of the pro-English Crown Princess, whose antagonism to Bismarck was a good deal more intense than that of her husband. The tension was further heightened in 1884, when the Crown Princess began a campaign to marry her second daughter to Alexander von Battenberg, the Prince of Bulgaria. In this project she faced the steady opposition of Bismarck. As ruler of Bulgaria, Prince Alexander had incurred the active hostility of Russia. His marriage to a Prussian princess would have implied German support for his policies and might well have forced Germany to take up an anti-Russian position. Bismarck had no intention of allowing such a policy to be thrust upon him. Holstein tried to turn this situation to advantage. He secretly encouraged British and Austrian support for Prince Alexander as part of his programme to block an extension of the Russian sphere of influence. At the same time he worked with Hatzfeldt for closer co-operation between Germany and Britain, leaving the way open for possible accord between Bismarck and the Crown Princess over foreign policy.[1]

[1] This programme is revealed in Holstein's correspondence as well as his diaries for 1886.

Count Radolinski wanted to go a step further. He asked Holstein whether he should advise Herbert von Bismarck to advocate the Battenberg marriage, which in Radolinski's opinion would come to pass sooner or later anyway. Herbert would thereby establish for himself an impregnable position at the Crown Prince's court. Failing that, Radolinski wondered what was to prevent the Crown Prince from sanctioning the marriage despite the objections of the Kaiser and the Chancellor.[1] Here Holstein drew the line. He thought there was no chance of the Chancellor conceding the marriage voluntarily. 'Your question about the pros and cons of the possible creation of a *fait accompli* I would prefer not to answer', he wrote on 6 October 1886. 'Put yourself in my position. I have sometimes gone beyond the intentions of the Big Chief, have occasionally even used *my* ways in reaching *his* goals. But I have never consciously gone directly counter to his intentions. And since I don't know in advance how my advice would turn out—in case I should sit myself down to think the matter through thoroughly—I prefer to keep my hands off.'[2]

All this activity suggests that Holstein may have intended to secure a safe niche for himself in the next reign whether Bismarck remained in office or fell, but there is no actual evidence on this point. Holstein of course avoided all outward signs of currying favour with the Crown Prince in order not to arouse the antagonism of the Bismarcks. Yet even in his diaries and personal letters there is no mention of personal hopes for the future. Nor is there a hint of any plan, which might have been expected under the circumstances, to groom a favourite candidate for the Chancellorship in the event of Bismarck's sudden dismissal by the next Kaiser. Holstein appears to have remained convinced, even in the days of his bitterest criticism, that there was no alternative to Bismarck.

What Holstein's activity does reveal is an overpowering urge to play a creative part in German politics, a role that ill accorded with his own views of the position he occupied. 'The responsible *Vortragender Rat* has so far not been invented', he wrote in an essay on Heinrich Abeken in 1898.[3] 'The Minister alone bears all the responsibility. The *Vortragender Rat* who knows his place and does his job well is not concerned with the direction of policy, but must justify the policy framed by his Minister with the most valid arguments available.' It is clear that Holstein, from whatever

---

[1] Letters to Holstein of 2, 4 and 5 October 1886 (*Correspondence*).
[2] *Correspondence*.
[3] *Memoirs*, p. 54.

motives he may have acted, did not know his place. He wished to concern himself with the direction of policy, although after Bismarck's dismissal he stated that he would not accept promotion to a post which would have given him the concomitant responsibility.

All the planning, the bargaining, the intrigue that had taken place in preparation for the reign of Crown Prince Friedrich Wilhelm were suddenly reduced to futility when it was learned in 1887 that the Crown Prince was mortally ill with cancer of the throat. As Kaiser Friedrich III, he was to rule his country for only ninety-nine days. His heir, Prince Wilhelm, proclaimed a warm admiration for Bismarck and gave every sign of continuing in the traditions of his grandfather.

Holstein did not share the initial unbounded enthusiasm of the Bismarck party for Prince Wilhelm, fearing that he was under the pro-Russian influence of Herbert. 'Now, when a young Kaiser will join with Herbert in sometimes forcing old Prince Bismarck's hand', he wrote on 17 May 1887, 'the situation is fraught with great danger.' Holstein was much relieved when he learned that the Prince was by no means dominated by Herbert, but had a will of his own. 'However strange this may sound coming from me', he wrote on 4 February 1888, 'I hope sincerely that the Prince's "backbone" will also make itself felt in our foreign policy. We may perhaps strike a good middle course between his policy and the Chancellor's policy of backing down.'

Wilhelm II came to the throne on 15 June 1888. The diaries carry the story only into the early months of his reign, but Holstein's letters from numerous document collections show that he continued to hope for this 'middle course'.[1] His criticism of Bismarck went on unabated, and he freely admitted to his cousin that his sympathies were all on the side of the young ruler.[2] But he was forced to recognize that Bismarck's prestige value for Germany remained enormous, especially in this time of transition, and that he still had the occasional great idea. Holstein also began to have doubts about the Kaiser's judgment and seriousness of purpose.

Long before Prince Wilhelm became Kaiser, Holstein had seen the hope for future collaboration between him and Bismarck menaced by the Chancellor's inconsiderate, schoolmasterish

---

[1] Especially Holstein's letters to Karl von Eisendecher, found in the Foreign Ministry files (*Correspondence*), and his letters to Ida von Stülpnagel (Rogge, *Friedrich von Holstein,* pp. 148–52). Even Holstein's letters to Waldersee admit this interpretation. (*Aus dem Briefwechsel des Generalfeldmarschalls Alfred Grafen von Waldersee,* edited by Heinrich Otto Meisner, vol. I (Berlin and Leipzig, 1928).)

[2] Letter of 15 October 1888. Rogge, *Friedrich von Holstein,* p. 151.

methods in dealing with the young man. In Berlin he saw support for the Bismarcks melting away on account of Herbert's arrogant and overbearing manner towards all people with whom he came into contact. Holstein urged Bill to come to Berlin to act as a moderating influence on his brother.[1] As late as January 1890 he warned Herbert of the forces undermining his father's position and advised him not to draw the bow too tight in relations with the Kaiser.[2] For if it came to a test of strength between the Kaiser and Chancellor, Holstein was in no doubt about which power would be victorious.

It was soon obvious that all warnings had been in vain. In a letter of 5 March 1890 to Prince Reuss, the German Ambassador in Vienna, Holstein mentioned the inconsiderate way the Chancellor was speaking about the Kaiser before a group of foreign diplomats. 'In the beginning I argued and wrote as best I could to ameliorate matters. Now I refuse to meddle any longer. I don't think the two powers will ever again be on cordial terms, but I don't believe in an imminent crisis, either.'[3] Holstein's prediction was wrong. Bismarck was dismissed on 18 March 1890, and a new phase in Holstein's career began.

[1] Letter of 18 October 1887, from the Varzin archives. Quoted in Hans Goldschmidt, 'Mitarbeiter Bismarcks im aussenpolitischen Kampf', *Preussische Jahrbücher*, vol. ccxxxvi, pp. 48–50.
[2] Letter of 24 January 1890, from the Friedrichsruh archives. Quoted in part in Arnold Oscar Meyer, *Bismarck* (Stuttgart, 1949), p. 639. A copy of the letter was found in the Holstein Papers (*Correspondence*).
[3] *Berliner Monatshefte*, vol. xv, part 1, pp. 327–8.

DIARIES

1881, 1882

August, Count zu Eulenburg. Negotiations with the Curia. Gambetta. Bismarck on the *Kulturkampf*. Bismarck and Schorlemer. Bismarck and Orlov. Hatzfeldt. Russian resentment against Austria. The Egyptian question. The position of the Minister for War. Radowitz in Constantinople. Austria and the Turkish railways. Attacks on Hatzfeldt.

28 *March* 1881

[...] The trouble about politics is that you can never be certain when your policy has been correct.[1] Perhaps our policy after 1866 was in fact mistaken. The Federal Diet had greater means of checking revolutionary movements and tendencies to disaffection in individual states than the modern Reich with its Federal Council and its Reichstag. [...]

9 *February* 1882[2]

[...] Eulenburg,[3] the Court Marshal, recently showed the Crown Prince a letter from His Majesty to Baron Cohn,[4] in which the Kaiser confers upon him the Order of the Hohenzollern. Amongst Cohn's services deserving recognition is mentioned the way he straightened out the H[atzfeldt][5] affair.[6] Eulenburg's comments as he showed the letter are said to have been far from kind. I told [Seckendor]ff[7] that nothing could be easier, in view of H.'s touchiness, than to get rid of him. The Crown Prince and Princess, by their treatment of H., could do much to determine whether he went or stayed.

[1] Holstein is quoting Otto von Bismarck, Chancellor of the German Reich, 1871–90.

[2] Here Holstein begins his own narrative.

[3] August, Count zu Eulenburg. Chamberlain and Court Marshal to the Crown Prince, 1868–83; Chief Master of Ceremonies from 1883.

[4] Baron von Meyer-Cohn. Court Banker to the Kaiser and many members of the German nobility, including Holstein.

[5] Paul, Count von Hatzfeldt-Wildenburg. Attaché in Paris, 1862–6; Secretary of Legation at The Hague, 1866–8; *Vortragender Rat* in the Foreign Ministry from 1868; on Bismarck's personal Foreign Ministry Staff, 1870–1; head of the French Section in the Foreign Ministry, 1872–4; Minister in Madrid, 1874–8; Ambassador in Constantinople, 1879–81; State Secretary in the Foreign Ministry, 1881–5; Ambassador in London, 1885–1901.

[6] Financial difficulties for a time prevented Paul von Hatzfeldt from accepting the post of State Secretary in the Foreign Ministry.

[7] In his diaries, Holstein occasionally used the final letters of a name to identify a person. 'ff', a much-used abbreviation, seems to stand for Götz, Count von Seckendorff, Chamberlain to Crown Princess Victoria.

I did in fact learn the effect of this piece of advice when a few days later H. told me that the Crown Prince and Princess had been extremely kind to him.

I had advised H. to report to the Crown Prince from time to time. He told me the other day that the Crown Prince seemed reluctant, probably to forestall any false interpretations on the part of Their Majesties.[1] He said that His Imperial Highness,[2] each time he suggested coming to see him to report, always replied with another question: 'So other papers have come in, besides those I have seen?'

[Seckendor]ff confirmed that the Prince felt he had exposed himself too much to the criticism of public opinion in his dealings with the Foreign Ministry over the Eulenburg affair.[3] (Probably means, pushed the affair too vigorously.)

10 *February* 1882

[...] Schlözer[4] has now been in Rome some days.[5] How will he get on? Will he still be able to scrape off the thick crust of laziness that has gradually formed during all these years of slacking? Puttkamer[6] and Friedberg[7] (the latter only yesterday) both expressed doubts to me on his professional seriousness. At any rate he has an extreme aversion to reading files. I met him in the Central Bureau the day before his departure, glancing through files. When I asked whether he had read the Chief's[8] dictated memorandum to Busch[9] yet, he asked in his turn: 'What was in it?'[10]

[1] Kaiser Wilhelm I and Kaiserin Augusta.

[2] The Crown Prince.

[3] In order to relieve Count August Eulenburg of his post as Court Marshal, the Crown Prince wished to have him appointed to a Legation. Eulenburg did in fact apply for the post of Minister at The Hague, but the Kaiser decided he was to continue in his present office. See pp. 3–4.

[4] Kurd von Schlözer, Secretary of Legation in St Petersburg, 1857–62; temporary Chargé d'Affaires in Copenhagen, 1863; Secretary of Legation to the Holy See, 1864–9; Consul-General of the North German Federation in Mexico, 1869–71; Minister in Washington, 1871–82, to the Holy See, 1882–92.

[5] For negotiations with the Holy See to end the conflict between the Roman Catholic Church and the Prussian Government (the *Kulturkampf*).

[6] Robert Viktor von Puttkamer. Prussian Minister of the Interior, 1881–8.

[7] Heinrich von Friedberg, Prussian Minister of Justice, 1879–89.

[8] Otto von Bismarck.

[9] Dr Klemens August Busch. Under State Secretary in the Foreign Ministry, March 1881–5; Minister in Bucharest, 1885–8.

[10] In a memorandum from Bismarck to the Under State Secretary of 30 November 1881, Busch was instructed to open preliminary discussions with the Curia before the projected establishment of a Prussian Legation to the Holy See. He was to explain in particular that the modification of the May Laws (the 1873 laws directed against the Catholic Church in Prussia during the *Kulturkampf*) must be carried through by means of the discretionary powers conferred on the Prussian Government by the Landtag. Bismarck continued: 'The Prussian Government needs greater freedom of action in its decisions relating to those areas with a

I told him the main points. 'Oh', said he, 'I've heard lots about that already, verbally and in writing.'

Yesterday Schlözer reported that he had negotiated on questions of principle and had naturally met with a refusal. An assembly of fourteen Cardinals had turned down Prussia's offers and instead made fresh demands of their own. The Chief had written on the telegram alongside their refusal the words 'so they won't' and alongside their demands he put 'cowards'. The gist of his reply was: 'We can bide our time.'[1]

11 *February* 1882

[...] The other day I had just had a meal with Brauer[2] and Heyking.[3] As we were standing outside an art dealer's window, one of them accidentally brushed his cigar-butt against the hand of a poor youth who was also standing there. B. and H. laughed; the boy looked first at his hand, then at the two men, a dejected smile on his pale face. Were they just thoughtless or are their feelings concentrated on their own interests? I must find out.

Princess Bismarck said to-day that the Kaiserin was now most gracious to her on every occasion, but the Crown Prince and Princess were chilly. This last can of course be traced to the failure of the Eulenburg affair, because, according to [Seckendor]ff, Eulenburg told the Crown Prince that the Chancellor was primarily to blame for the misunderstanding. On the contrary the latter had stated from the outset that he was prepared to take on Eulenburg despite the effect on regular promotions, and would bring the matter to the Kaiser's personal attention; he could not, however, exert pressure on the Kaiser; His Imperial Highness must do that himself. Then the Kaiser, on the advice of the

Polish or mixed population, because there Catholicism is bound up with and in part dominated by nationalist and revolutionary aspirations.' (From the Foreign Ministry files.) On 2 December Bismarck dictated a long supplementary memorandum to Busch on which to base negotiations with Jacobini (the papal State Secretary). It contained a biting attack on the leaders and political attitude of the Centre Party and on the attitude of the Catholic clergy in the Polish districts. A continuation of this state of affairs would oblige Bismarck to advise the Kaiser to seek a fresh understanding with the Liberals, with all the consequences for the Catholic Church that would ensue. Bismarck was therefore of the opinion that the Curia should be prepared to reach a *modus vivendi* with the present government. See Otto von Bismarck, *Die gesammelten Werke* (Berlin, 1923–35), vol. VI c, no. 231, pp. 236–40, also no. 233, p. 241; *Memoirs*, pp. 63–4, and Busch's letter to Holstein of 9 December 1881 (*Correspondence*).

[1] In a telegram of 9 February, Schlözer reported that the commission of fourteen Cardinals convened by the Pope demanded revision of the May Laws. Bismarck telegraphed in reply that the refusal by the Progressives and the Centre Party to vote discretionary powers would have no results other than the continuation of the *status quo*, i.e. of the May Laws. (From the Foreign Ministry files.)

[2] Arthur von Brauer. *Vortragender Rat* in the Foreign Ministry, 1881–8.

[3] Edmund, Baron von Heyking. German diplomat.

Kaiserin, Stillfried[1] and others, had declared that Eulenburg was indispensable in the Ceremonial office (which in fact would seem to be the case). In any event the Chancellor would probably have preferred to take on Eulenburg some time ago rather than now. On his brother's[2] departure from office, Eulenburg had tried to persuade the Crown Prince to make some gesture in his favour. Not until he found that his brother had no following did Eulenburg drop the affair; all hopes of finding a place for him further to the Left have no doubt long since evaporated and Eulenburg (the Minister) would probably be encroaching on someone else's well-earned rights. In addition the Chancellor suffered a further disappointment in August Eulenburg as a result of the conversation they had recently about Eulenburg's expectations and pretensions as a diplomat. He had said he sincerely hoped he would not forfeit his status in the change-over. When asked 'What status?' he explained he was on the brink of becoming a *Wirklicher Geheimer Rat* and hoped this would be taken into account. The Chancellor gave an evasive answer; but afterwards he said he had been greatly surprised by this attitude, which showed what a thorough-going courtier Eulenburg had become.

At any rate August Eulenburg carried through the affair with the greatest aplomb; in the evening he handed the Crown Prince his resignation; the next day at noon he appeared jauntily before the Crown Prince and Princess and said, as I mentioned above, that it was all the Chancellor's fault.

[Seckendor]ff thinks Eulenburg himself was at the back of all this intrigue, since he did not think The Hague good enough; in his view the Crown Prince on becoming Kaiser will have to provide an embassy for him. I know for a fact that [...],[3] who actually told it to the Chancellor, said to Eulenburg: 'You're a fool to be so easily satisfied—you should have waited for the Crown Prince.' [...]

13 *February* 1882

[...] To me the most characteristic feature in the development of the *Kulturkampf* has always been the fact that the Chancellor

---

[1] Rudolf, Count von Stillfried-Alcantara. Chief Master of Ceremonies at the Prussian Court and President of the Prussian College of Heralds.

[2] Botho, Count zu Eulenburg. Head of the Administration of Hanover, 1873–8; Minister of the Interior (in succession to his uncle Friedrich zu Eulenburg), March 1878–February 1881; later Head of the Administration of Hesse-Nassau; Prussian Minister-President under Caprivi, 1892–4.

[3] The abbreviation Holstein used here could not be deciphered by the editors.

sent a memorandum from Varzin *condemning* civil marriage.[1] The
Prussian Cabinet (presided over by Roon[2]) ignored the memorandum and proceeded with its agenda, sent no reply to the Chancellor and introduced the matter in the Landtag! As a result
Bismarck relinquished the post of Prussian Minister-President in
favour of Roon;[3] admittedly he took it on again a year later because
Roon apparently allowed all kinds of things to be removed from
his control. Many people have since maintained that compulsory
civil marriage has proved harmful to the State in so far as without
it the Church would have found itself in still greater embarrassment in those districts where the clergy were suspended.[4]

15 *February* 1882

Hatzfeldt said the Kaiser told him that at Augustovo[5] Tsar
Alexander complained bitterly of the Austrian occupation of the
two provinces. To the objection that such a contingency had
surely been provided for at Reichstadt,[6] the Tsar replied: 'Ah,
but on the express condition that Kaiser Franz Joseph support me
in the war.'[7]

Friedberg said the other day that the Crown Prince had a
morbid fear of attempts on his life. 'Whenever I get out of my
coach I wonder whether the shot will come from the right or from
the left.'

16 *February* 1882

On the 14th the Chancellor told the new French Ambassador,
Courcel,[8] during their first meeting, that he had been worried
lest France and England should fall out over Egypt. It was far
better for them both to have behind them *les burgraves de l'Europe*
as a tranquillizing element.

He went on to say that it was time to go all out to establish

[1] In June 1872 the Reichstag adopted a resolution calling for the introduction of compulsory civil marriage. It was not introduced in Prussia until 1874, and in the entire Reich
until 1875.

[2] Albrecht, Count von Roon. Prussian Minister of War, 1859–73; Prussian Minister-
President, 20 December 1872–3.

[3] See Bismarck, *Die gesammelten Werke*, vol. vi c, no. 36, p. 29.

[4] A large number of Catholic priests in Prussia had been forbidden to carry out their
pastoral duties because they failed to observe the laws introduced during the *Kulturkampf*.

[5] Holstein probably means Alexandrovo, where a meeting took place between Alexander II
and Wilhelm I on 3 and 4 September 1879. See *Die Grosse Politik der Europäischen Kabinette,
1871–1914* (Berlin, 1922–7), vol. iii, nos. 457 and 460, pp. 36–9, 47–51.

[6] Austrian and Russian sources give divergent versions of the Reichstadt agreement of
8 July 1876. Not until the Budapest Convention of 15 January 1877 did Russia recognize
unequivocally Austria's claim to occupy Bosnia and Herzegovina.

[7] Against Turkey, 1877–8.

[8] Alphonse, Baron de Courcel. French Ambassador in Berlin, 1882–6.

friendly relations with the Sultan. Tissot[1] had probably made rather a hash of things in that direction. Then, pointing to the conference[2] photograph, a present from Hatzfeldt, he said: 'Look how highly strung that bald-headed fellow (Tissot) must be to have lost all his hair already.'[3]

I mentioned yesterday evening that the *République Française* was adopting a tone similar to that of the Emperor Napoleon after 2 December 1851. Both turned from the elected representatives, who had failed in their duty, to the electorate, i.e. the masses.

The Chancellor thought the Emperor Napoleon was in a far better position. He had the Napoleonic Legend and thus he had the support of a party; he stepped into something ready-made. But what does Gambetta[4] have and who is he? A coarse, pot-bellied, one-eyed fellow, self-willed and vain. He has a number of supporters who speculate on his future in the belief he'll pay dividends. He could only have a party if he took up a position on the extreme left wing of the Radicals. He would then have the support of all who hope the future will bring an improvement in their lot—which is always the majority. While he was at the helm he showed that he had no idea of his job, almost like Gladstone.[5] Instead of starting by showing the Chambers the utmost cordiality and co-operation, he offended them straight away.

If I[6] had been in charge of Russian policy during the Russo-Turkish War, I should have come to an agreement with Austria over the partition of Rumania and settled our friend Karl[7] in Bulgaria. The Russians are pushing on towards the Danube in the belief they will thereby come nearer to their final goal. The whole thing is a foolish undertaking; they can't even govern the territory they already possess.

18 *February* 1882

In the summer of '48 I[8] had arranged to spend some time with

[1] Charles Joseph Tissot. French Ambassador in Constantinople, 1880–2, in London, 1882–3.

[2] Probably a photograph of the ambassadorial conference held in Constantinople early in 1881 on the territorial dispute between Greece and Montenegro and Turkey.

[3] A memorandum of 16 February 1882 in the Foreign Ministry files confirms Holstein's account of the conversation between Bismarck and Courcel. Bismarck stressed that in the case of a disturbance of the peace in Egypt the Sultan, as sovereign of the country, was primarily responsible for restoring order. Any isolated action by France or England would constitute a threat to peace between the two countries.

[4] Léon Gambetta. French Prime Minister, 1881–2.

[5] William Ewart Gladstone. British Prime Minister, 1868–74, 1880–5, January–July 1886, 1892–March 1894.

[6] Holstein is still quoting Bismarck.

[7] Prince Karl von Hohenzollern-Sigmaringen. Prince of Rumania, 1866–81; King, 1881–1914.   [8] Bismarck.

my wife and family at the home of my parents-in-law in R[einfeld].
It so happened that Gerlach[1] wrote to say I was needed in Potsdam
to make up the King's mind for him. When I proceeded to
comply with the request my mother-in-law was furious. 'I'd
rather my daughter had married a swineherd, at least he'd stay by
her side.' 'My dear Mama, that profession is still open to me.'

I[2] asked him whether he was going to attend the debate on the
Kulturkampf in the Landtag.[3]

Why should I?[4] The more undecided things are the better.
The question is by its very nature an open one, and the conflict
will never be resolved because ever since Colchas there has been
a group of people in every nation who hold as an axiom: 'We
know God's will better than the rest of you.'

If I had been able to conduct the *Kulturkampf* entirely in
accordance with my own ideas I should have been satisfied with
the inspection of schools and the suspension of the Catholic section
of the Ministry for Ecclesiastical Affairs. But the attitude of the
Conservatives obliged me to reckon with a majority which liked
to beat the *Kulturkampf* drum as loudly as possible.

22 *February* 1882

A short time ago Schorlemer[5] inquired through P[aul] H[atz-
feldt] whether the Chancellor would see him. Yes. Then followed
a letter begging audience. 'In deepest respect' and 'Your most
obedient servant'. Turned up in white tie and tails. Surprised
the Chief by his well-bred, almost timid behaviour.

Schorlemer began by apologizing for his former attacks.
Answer: In such cases there's bound to be plenty of sharp-
shooting. He then expressed a lively wish to reach some agreement and in future to ignore confessional differences and vote
with the Conservatives.

The Chief also wished to come to an agreement, but said that
such an agreement would have to be acceptable to the Free Conservatives and if possible to the National Liberals; he had not yet
enough faith in the Centre Party to rely solely on them. The
main thing was for the Centre Party not to disintegrate. Sooner
or later the time would come when a Progressive government
would have to be reckoned with, for a change of ruler would mean
a change of system. If the Chancellor wished to remain in office,

---

[1] Leopold von Gerlach. Prussian General; Adjutant-General to King Friedrich Wilhelm IV
from 1850.   [2] Holstein.
[3] On the second bill designed to mitigate the *Kulturkampf* legislation.   [4] Bismarck.
[5] Burghard, Baron von Schorlemer-Alst. Member of the Prussian Chamber of Deputies
(Centre Party), 1870–89; of the Reichstag, 1875–85.

things would still go 'fairly well'. But he had lost that combative spirit that enabled him to work with colleagues he could not respect, and who were suspicious of him; men who, like the Kaiser himself,[1] would watch him in the hope of seeing him blunder. At such times it would be useful to have a Centre Party a hundred strong; a purely parliamentary government, prepared to barter honour and salvation for the sake of a majority, would come to terms with the Centre and perhaps make greater concessions to it than the present government. In such circumstances flexible regulations would be of more use than fixed laws, which would make any agreement considerably more difficult.

Schorlemer objected that it was imperative for the Centre Party to be *plus royaliste que le roi*, since the reproach of being lukewarm would lose them many seats, particularly to the Conservatives. It was therefore urgently desirable that the necessary negotiations should be conducted and concessions made in Rome itself. He had great hopes that the State would show leniency in the matter of obligatory registration [*Anzeigepflicht*].[2]

The Chancellor replied that he set no particular store by obligatory registration. He shook hands with Schorlemer when he left, a thing he had not done when he came in.

Just before this, also yesterday evening, Bleichröder[3] told me that Windthorst[4] had called on him after a long interval. He expressed the fear that if the government made too heavy demands on the conservative elements of the centre, the party might split, and one section of it go over to the Progressives.

I failed to see the connexion until the Chief told me later of his conversation with Schorl. [...]

27 *February* 1882

Orlov[5] and I were dining with the Chancellor yesterday. The conversation turned on Vereshagin.[6] The Chancellor thought the painter's opinions were made clear in his *Alexander II at Plevna* by the attitude of the Tsar, who sits watching the battle like someone asleep at the opera.

In a private interview beforehand Orlov had asked the Chan-

---

[1] That is, when the present Crown Prince should become Kaiser.
[2] The May Laws of 1873 required the registration of the candidates with the secular authorities before the installation of clergy.
[3] Gerson Bleichröder. Head of the Berlin banking firm of that name.
[4] Ludwig Windthorst. Leader of the Centre Party in the Reichstag.
[5] Nikolai, Prince Orlov. Russian Ambassador in Paris, 1872–84, in Berlin, 1884–5.
[6] Russian painter.

cellor what he would advise to be done about Skobelev.[1] The
Chancellor replied that it was dangerous to give advice in a
domestic matter of this kind; and it would probably be best not
even to mention that Orlov had asked him. But if he, Bismarck,
were Tsar of Russia, he would dismiss Skobelev and intern him—
dismiss him at any rate. If he still wanted to go to Herzegovina,[2]
let him go; he would then be regarded as a rebel against his own
Tsar as well as against the Austrian Kaiser and would probably
lose his following. The point at issue between Tsar Alexander
and Skobelev was essentially a trial of strength. By his speech[3]
the General had challenged his sovereign to personal combat. It
now remained to be seen whether the Tsar was strong enough to
throw his opponent.

Orlov hadn't much use for Ignatiev.[4]

Bl[eichröder] tells us that last Friday the Chancellor said to
him: 'Our relations with the Russian Government are as good as
they have ever been, but—the Austrians ought to hurry up and
crush the revolt in Herzegovina, even if it meant sending along
another 40,000 troops.' Bl. passed this on. Got the reply: on
that terrain it was impossible to deploy effectively more than a
given number of troops.

At any rate in the last three days, either *post hoc* or *propter hoc*,
Austrian troop movements have become far more lively. There
are daily encounters. [...]

They say the Crown Prince has a permanent grudge against
the Chancellor. The reason given is that the Prince was offended
because his opinion had not been sought beforehand on the decree
of 4 January[5] (conduct of civil service officials at elections). When
the Chancellor heard of this recently, he remarked that on the

[1] Michael Skobelev. Russian General, national hero in the Russo-Turkish war of 1877–8,
and a convinced Pan-Slavist. His violent speeches denouncing the Germans were interpreted
in many quarters as a bid for popularity against the Tsar himself.

[2] The resistance in Bosnia and Herzegovina to the military service law of 4 November
1881 led at the end of the year to an outbreak of armed revolt against Austrian rule. The
revolt was supported by Montenegro and it was widely assumed that Montenegro was in
turn supported by Russia, where at this time Ignatiev (see below, note 4) was the most
influential Minister.

[3] An address to Serbian students in Paris on 16 February. Bismarck commented on it in
a report to the Kaiser of 18 February. 'He [Skobelev] threatens the Germans in Russia in
his Paris speech. The Russian revolutionaries, to whom Skobelev essentially belongs, always
regard the Imperial Family, the house of Holstein-Gottorp, as chief among those Germans
who are enemies of Russia. [...]' (From the Foreign Ministry files. Quoted in Wolfgang
Windelband, *Bismarck und die europäischen Grossmächte. 1879–85* (Essen, 1940), pp. 354–5.)

[4] Nikolai Pavlovich, Count Ignatiev. Russian Minister of the Interior, May 1881–
June 1882. Pan-Slavist and a supporter of Skobelev.

[5] The decree stipulated that it was the sovereign's task to direct the policy of his government personally, and that civil servants were bound by their oath of office to follow the
government line at elections.

contrary the Crown Prince ought to be grateful to him because the policy of the future Kaiser thus remained completely free from commitments.

2 *March* 1882

[...] In 1854,[1] during the Crimean War, Gerlach, who was talking over various matters with Friedrich Wilh. IV, had prevailed on the King to send a stiffer reply than usual to the insistent demands by Austria and the western Powers.[2] Manteuffel,[3] who originally had all the sentiments of a Prussian patriot but was now under Austria's thumb, made objections, but the only result was that Bismarck was summoned from Frankfurt and entrusted with the drafting of the note.

Lewinstein, Manteuffel's banker, also acted as Schleinitz's[4] business adviser later on. During the Italian War in 1859, Lewinstein called on Bismarck, who happened to be in Berlin on leave. Introduced himself by means of a recommendation from [   ][5].

Explained that he wanted to interest Bismarck in an important financial undertaking, but one which would only succeed if Austro-Russian relations remained cordial; if so, then there would certainly be a profit of twenty or thirty thousand taler annually for Bismarck. No deposits were required. At first Bismarck gave a polite refusal, at which the other remarked: 'Think it over; it's not healthy to make an enemy of the Imperial [Austrian] Government.' Bismarck pointed out that the steps where they were standing were high and steep; Lewinstein withdrew, still threatening Bismarck with the hostility of the Imperial Government.

5 *March* 1882

[...] The day before yesterday Hatzfeldt, who has been ill for some weeks and is now going on leave to convalesce, had an interview with the Chief. Hatzfeldt seemed very pleased with the Chief's friendliness; he had advised him not to worry his head over details but merely to determine the main lines governing policy and affairs both at home and abroad, and to leave the execution of his orders to some trusted person. As he said this H.

---

[1] This story comes from Bismarck.

[2] Bismarck is referring to the demands that Prussia adopt at least a diplomatic position hostile to Russia.

[3] Otto, Baron von Manteuffel. Prussian Minister-President and Foreign Minister, 1850–8.

[4] Alexander, Baron von Schleinitz. Prussian Foreign Minister, summer 1848, 1849–50, 1858–61; Minister of the Royal Household, 1861–85.   [5] Gap in the text.

looked at the Chief in such a way as to insinuate that H. himself would be a suitable candidate for the post—that is what he told Radolinski[1] afterwards. The Chief appears to have given no sign of having understood. I am really at a loss to know who could one day succeed Bismarck. So far as H. is concerned, he certainly has the ability but it will take time to dim the memory of his family affairs and he himself will have to show a somewhat greater interest in his work than hitherto. He only likes field-days; the daily grind repels him.

7 *March* 1882

[...] Berchem[2] told me yesterday that Andrássy[3] had done his best to become Foreign Minister again in succession to Haymerle.[4] At first Andrássy expected to be sent for; when that did not happen, he went himself and called on the Kaiser, but the vital word he hoped for remained unspoken. The court clique, Hohenlohe[5] and others, had been exultant all along when they saw that Andrássy would not be given office; but we may take it that Taaffe[6] had declared at the outset that he could not work with Andrássy.

Andrássy's friends, according to Berchem, regret that he did not show greater restraint.

Incidentally, Kálnoky[7] is said to be annoyed already with Taaffe's policy towards the Czechs.

[Seckendor]ff: The Crown Prince has often declared of late that he must cut down his expenses, e.g. give up hunting at Spandau. No doubt he said something of the kind to Eulenburg. Just recently the latter wrote and told him the Kaiser had made known his intention of giving the Prince a present of money for his silver wedding. It was then stated, or hinted, that His Majesty desired His Imperial Highness to get in touch with Eulenburg and Cohn to discuss the sum he would find acceptable.

[1] Hugo Leszczyc, Count von Radolin-Radolinski; from 1888 Prince von Radolin. *Hilfsarbeiter* in the Foreign Ministry, 1881–2; Prussian Minister in Weimar, October 1882–May 1884; High Chamberlain of Crown Prince Friedrich Wilhelm, 1884–8.
[2] Maximilian, Count von Berchem. First Secretary in the Vienna Embassy, 1878–83; Director of the Economic Policy Division of the Foreign Ministry, 1885–6; Under State Secretary, 1886–90.
[3] Julius, Count Andrássy. Austro-Hungarian Foreign Minister, 1871–9.
[4] Heinrich, Baron von Haymerle. Austro-Hungarian Foreign Minister, 1879–81.
[5] Konstantin, Prince zu Hohenlohe-Schillingsfürst. Lord High Steward at the court of Franz Joseph.
[6] Eduard, Count von Taaffe. Austrian Minister-President and Minister of the Interior, 1879–93.
[7] Gustav, Count Kálnoky von Köröspatak. Austro-Hungarian Ambassador in St Petersburg, 1880–1; Foreign Minister, 1881–95.

The Prince, also in writing, expressed his profound gratitude for his illustrious father's favour, but refused to negotiate with any one over the amount of the gift.

The Crown Prince and Princess are said to be most annoyed over this fresh intrusion by Eulenb. into their daily affairs. [...]

The Chancellor told a story the other day which illustrates the Russian resentment of Austria.

In 1859, when it was still uncertain whether other Powers would become involved in the Italian War, our Minister,[1] then in Moscow, was visiting some public building and being shown round by a learned Prince Galitzin, Director or Curator of this library (or something of the sort). One of the caretakers was wearing the Kulm Cross. The Minister asked him, probably through an interpreter: 'Who'd you prefer to fight if Russia went to war?' To which he replied: 'Oh, Austria every time.' 'But', interjected the Minister, 'surely it was the French who burned down Moscow?' 'An honourable foe', said the old man, 'is better than a friend that leaves you in the lurch.' Galitzin was so delighted with the answer that he embraced the old soldier.

11 *March* 1882

A couple of days ago the Chancellor sent for me. He asked how it had come about that a *note* had been sent to Paris regarding the Egyptian affair, referring to the possibility of a conference.[2] Such action showed ignorance of ministerial practice. A note sent direct to any foreign government was an act of state for which the Chancellor's personal agreement would have been needed in any event. In this case such a step ran directly counter to his, Bismarck's, intentions.

Prominence and importance were being given to a question which we ought on the contrary to have handled with the greatest *laissez-aller*.[3]

---

[1] Karl, Freiherr von Werther. Prussian Minister in St Petersburg, 1854–9.

[2] The increasing interference by European nations in Egypt's government and finances had fostered the development of a powerful nationalist movement with the army as its focal point. On 5 February the Khedive was obliged to appoint a nationalist ministry. The European Powers were considering whether to convene a conference to deal with the Egyptian situation.

[3] Prince Hohenlohe had reported on 28 February that he had, according to his instructions, delivered a note to the French Government which stated: 'The Government of His Majesty the Kaiser is perfectly willing to enter upon the exchange of ideas on the Egyptian Question which was suggested in M. de Freycinet's note of 12 February, provided the other Great Powers also take part.' A similar note in reply to Lord Granville's note of 11 February was delivered in London. On 9 March Bismarck ordered an instruction to be sent to Paris stating that Germany, in dispatching this note, had not intended to make a formal proposal for dealing with the Egyptian Question. (From the Foreign Ministry files.)

Why had I not remonstrated with Busch? There was always something petty about the way he handled affairs; he had nothing of the grand manner.

I told him I had indeed written a very different version at first, but from the way Busch replied to my remarks I had gathered that, through some misunderstanding or other, he was dead certain that the Chancellor intended to send a *note*.

Prince Bismarck said that in that case the document should at least have been submitted to him. But here he was once more up against this mania for initialling. Even the late State Secretary, Bülow,[1] had not been free from it. Bötticher,[2] too, liked to see the ink glistening on his initials. By all means let them sign, but at least let them show him documents of such importance as this present one. Because of this note we were now in a false position *vis-à-vis* France. The French were surprised and dismayed by our intention of pinning them down; now they were wondering: 'What underhand trick are the Germans plotting against us?' Instead of using a sledge-hammer, as we had with this note, we should have gently touched on the subject by asking simply: 'Do you want to have a conference? Or do you want some other form of discussion? It's all the same to us.'

I said Busch was doing his best and was very scared already. I hoped the Chancellor would deal kindly with him.

Prince Bismarck said I was not to say anything to Busch; he would himself say what was necessary.

Prince Bismarck discussed the whole affair with statesmanlike calm. But he was obviously convinced that the note had done real harm. He only became more lively when he started to talk about Hatzfeldt, who had left him behind here sick, allegedly because he himself needed to convalesce. 'A molly-coddle, a pregnant woman, an egoist through and through. Wraps himself immediately in cotton-wool. Doesn't even read files when he's sick.'

After dinner yesterday I told Prince Bismarck that I could not imagine, once we had the war with Russia behind us, how we should continue to get the necessary army estimates voted.

'We'll never have that behind us', replied the Chancellor, 'because that, like the war with France, is going to be not just one war but a series of wars.'

[1] Bernhard Ernst von Bülow. State Secretary in the Foreign Ministry, 1873–9.
[2] Karl Heinrich von Bötticher. Prussian Minister of State; State Secretary of the Ministry of the Interior, 1880–97.

12 *March* 1882

Kusserow[1] is to be employed on a temporary basis in the Political Division. I took the opportunity of getting rid of my Balkans responsibilities. As things are at the moment, the official responsible is bound to find himself in an anomalous position between Busch's views and those of the Chancellor. Busch, that conscientious hypochondriac, says, 'I'm very sorry, but we must keep strictly to what the Chancellor says.' But I have myself heard the Chancellor declare: 'If they only put down what I've said, I may as well dictate the document and have done with it.'

Busch has no sympathy with the idea that, once the Chancellor has indicated the subject-matter of an instruction and advanced one or two arguments from memory, it is the task of the Foreign Ministry and particularly of the official responsible to produce further arguments from the files or from treaties so far as is practicable. Busch ruthlessly crosses out any such elaboration. The responsible official, particularly in important matters, has simply to ink over Busch's pencilled notes.

That is why I asked Hatzfeldt just after the New Year to relieve me of my Balkans responsibilities, and I told him then: 'It's not that I think myself someone important, but for the sort of work that's now required you can use even humbler folk than me.' Hatzfeldt declined to take up my proposal. Now I let the flood waters rush by me and restrict myself to a small insignificant department. Things will be different some day.

16 *March* 1882

[...] Waldersee[2] has just asked me if I knew what the Kaiser discussed with the Chancellor when he last visited him. The question was of interest because the visit had been occasioned by military matters. When, shortly after Skobelev's speech, the idea of adopting preventive measures against Russia had been put to the Kaiser, His Majesty had agreed in principle. But when, some days later, Albedyll[3] asked the Kaiser to fix a time for a conference to discuss the measures to be taken, he declared he would not hear of a war against Russia; for him the only war that could possibly be considered was a war against France.

This conversation, he said, took place the day before the Kaiser's visit to the Chancellor, and it could be assumed that it occasioned the visit.

[1] Heinrich von Kusserow. *Vortragender Rat* in the Foreign Ministry, 1874–84.

[2] Alfred, Count von Waldersee. Quartermaster-General and Vice-Chief of the General Staff, 1882–8; Chief of the Army General Staff, 1888–January 1891.

[3] General Emil von Albedyll. Chief of Wilhelm I's military cabinet, 1871–88.

The conference on security measures would be held in two days' time, on Saturday. Originally the War Minister,[1] Albedyll, and he, Waldersee, were to have attended as well as Moltke,[2] but in view of the Kaiser's excited state Moltke would be going alone because he could say more during a *tête-à-tête* than in front of other people.

I asked Waldersee whether it had occurred to any one in such times as these to appoint a more able War Minister. He said it was a ticklish question. You needed a man able to deny himself the luxury of behaving too much like a constitutional minister who issued all instructions. The direction of military affairs must remain in the King's hands as before.

17 *March* 1882

Yesterday Lord Ampthill[3] told a lady that the Crown Prince and Princess were grieved at Prince Wilhelm's behaviour. The Crown Princess had had eye trouble for some time. Prince Wilhelm came and went without ever asking after his mother's health. His father reproved him, but his son replied—according to Ampthill—that he didn't wish to hear such language again. Both his parents are said to be deeply hurt, 'the father at the lack of respect, the mother at the lack of love'.

18 *March* 1882

Holleben[4] told me yesterday that he was once discussing sea voyages with the late State Secretary von Bülow. When Holleben told him he had bathed every day while at sea, His Excellency looked thoughtful and said after a short silence: 'But however did you get back on board?' [...]

28 *March* 1882

Yesterday Dolgoruki,[5] the Russian Military Plenipotentiary, told Wilhelm Redern[6] that Germany had it in her power to preserve the Russian dynasty and save Russia from the otherwise inevitable Pan-Slav or Nihilist revolution. Germany need only propose a revision of the Treaty of Berlin and so direct things that Herzegovina and Bosnia went definitely to Austria, Eastern

---

[1] General Georg von Kameke. Prussian Minister of War, 1873–83.
[2] Helmuth, Count von Moltke. Chief of the Prussian General Staff, 1858–88.
[3] Odo Russell, first Lord Ampthill. British Ambassador in Berlin, 1871–84.
[4] Theodor von Holleben. Minister-Resident in Argentina and Uruguay, 1875–85; Minister in Tokyo, 1885–91.
[5] Nicholas, Prince Dolgoruki. Military Plenipotentiary in Berlin, 1879–85.
[6] Wilhelm, Count von Redern. First Secretary in the Embassy in St Petersburg, 1881–2.

Rumelia to Bulgaria, and the two fortresses on the northern end of the Bosphorus to Russia. Whether at the same time the Dardanelles fell into English hands was immaterial to Russia. Such a success for Russian government policy would cripple all attempts to overthrow the dynasty for a considerable time. Otherwise, if nothing were done for Russia's prestige abroad, the prospect was gloomy.

The idea of drawing the sting of the Pan-Slav opposition by successes in foreign policy can now be observed everywhere. Giers[1] himself has this idea and is trying to put it into effect by peaceful means.

29 March 1882

[...] Early this month the *Börsenzeitung* published an article on the occasion of Hatzfeldt's departure. He would probably not return. Despite his great talents he lacked the specialized knowledge required for his post here. The only possible candidate for Berlin was the Under State Secretary.

Pol. Kr.,[2] appointed to investigate the matter, reports that all the evidence points to [...].[3] His belief is strengthened by the fact that former articles also directed against Hatzfeldt were traced to the same source. There is no definite evidence.

Radolinski says that the day before his departure, Hatzfeldt wrote to Busch to ask his opinion of this proposed period of leave. Busch was whole-heartedly in favour of it. This reply does not quite tally with Busch's knowledge of the affair. A couple of days earlier he had informed me that the Chief had repeatedly expressed himself in the strongest terms on Hatzfeldt's proposed leave, because it would throw an even greater burden of business on to the Chancellor's shoulders when he too was in poor health.

That frivolous piece of advice later brought its retribution for Busch, and indeed for other people who were quite blameless. But for Hatzfeldt's departure there would have been none of the annoyance experienced on the 9th of this month.[4]

Bleichröder has just called on me and discussed the proposed Russian decree providing that the Jews shall in future not be allowed to live in the open country, to acquire land or to rent it. Ignatiev introduced the measure; most of the ministers are said to be opposed to it, but the Tsar is in favour. The deliberation in the Council which was fixed for yesterday has been put off for a few days.

[1] Nicholas von Giers. Russian Foreign Minister, 1882–95.
[2] Probably *Polizeirat* Krüger.   [3] Gap in the text.   [4] See the entry for 11 March 1882.

Bl. wrote to Bunge,[1] the Finance Minister, asking him to bear in mind that in 1868 Rumanian bonds fell by 30 per cent because after the first persecution of Rumanian Jewry a committee of Berlin Jews called on their co-religionists throughout the world to discontinue their transactions in these bonds. [...]

11 *April* 1882

Waldersee said to me to-day: 'You can tell the Chancellor he need not believe *all* the bad things he will hear about me in the next few days. The War Ministry has regarded me as an intriguer for the past three days.[2] I stood out against the abuse whereby the War Minister thinks he is Supreme Commander, as in France. Kameke imagined he was General Farre[3] and almost refused to take advice from the Kaiser, let alone from the Field-Marshal. The latter puts up too feeble resistance to these encroachments. But at my suggestion an issue of some importance was recently used to demonstrate clearly the principle that the Kaiser both in peace and war is Supreme Commander. Moltke, in defiance of more recent practice, had audience of the Kaiser *alone*; the outcome of this meeting was communicated to the War Minister through an imperial order, whereby he was commanded to call a halt to one or two schemes already in progress in view of their dangerous character, and instead to put into effect immediately other measures hitherto neglected. Kameke, seething with rage, went to see Albedyll, who simply told him: "Well, you know where to find the Kaiser; go and see him." Kameke is always like that. If he cannot get what he wants by blustering, he gives in. He wants to remain in office at all costs.'

The Minister-Resident, Holleben, told me to-day that Bötticher, the Minister, had expounded to him his views on emigration and colonial policy in a speech lasting an hour and a half. Bötticher would first like to found trading settlements such as exist in Brazil, and to make their relations with the home country as close as possible. Future development was to be based on them.

This project is certainly more in line with the Crown Prince's and Stosch's[4] views than the Chancellor's. So it affords a glimpse into the future and also into the mind of the State Secretary for the Interior.

[1] Nicholas von Bunge. Russian Finance Minister, 1881–7.
[2] See *Denkwürdigkeiten des General-Feldmarschalls Alfred Grafen von Waldersee*, edited by H. O. Meisner, 3 vols. (Stuttgart and Berlin, 1922–3), vol. I, p. 220.
[3] Jean Joseph Farre. French General; War Minister in the Ferry cabinet, 1880–1. He adopted strong measures against the monarchist officers.
[4] Albrecht von Stosch. Prussian Minister of State and Head of the Admiralty, 1872–83.

27 November 1882

[...] Bleichröder was telling me yesterday evening how annoyed he was with Hatzfeldt for failing to support him in his dealings with the Chancellor. Bl. would like to do a deal in Turkey but wants the Chancellor to state that it is his particular wish, and to give him special safeguards. Hatzfeldt had refused to concern himself in the affair, so Bl. asked Radowitz,[1] who was paying a visit to Varzin before leaving for Constantinople, to tell the Chancellor that Bl. was prepared to purchase shares in Hirsch's[2] railways, and participate in the construction of the railway linking Turkey with Austria,[3] provided he were given the same protection as formerly in Rumania.

The Chancellor, to whom the Rumanian affair[4] is a far from pleasant memory, turned down Radowitz's suggestion. [...]

28 November 1882

[...] Windthorst has said that in the Chamber and in fact in any public appearance the Chancellor was relatively harmless because then he let himself go too much; but in a *tête-à-tête* he was the most dangerous adversary imaginable. He could charm you to such an extent that after half an hour you had forgotten what opinion you actually held when the interview began.

Mrs Tyrrell:[5] The Crown Princess was discussing the habit specific to Berlin society of indulging in slander and backbiting. 'And yet, you see, Mrs T., I've grown old and fat under such treatment.'[6]

3 December 1882

Hatzfeldt was talking about King Alfonso of Spain. Just before Hatzfeldt left for Constantinople the King sent for him and asked him his opinion on various political matters. H. advised him above all to give the army closer attention than hitherto. 'Yes', said the King, 'you're right, but it's such a bore. I am longing for the day when I have a twenty-five-year-old son, so that I can shift the whole burden on to his shoulders.'

[1] Joseph Maria von Radowitz. Minister in Athens, 1874–82; Ambassador in Constantinople, 1882–92.

[2] Moritz von Hirsch, Baron Hirsch auf Gereuth. Banker and financier.

[3] In 1869 Baron Hirsch took over the contracts to lay a trunk line linking Constantinople with the Austrian Southern Railway and thus with Vienna.

[4] The German firm Strousberg had undertaken to build a Rumanian railway network with primarily German capital. Unable to pay the interest due in January 1871, it asked the Rumanian Government, which had given a guarantee, to do so. The Rumanian Government fell over this issue, and anti-German riots took place in Bucharest. Bismarck settled the matter by enlisting the financial support of Bleichröder and the *Deutsche Diskonto-Gesellschaft*.

[5] Lady-in-waiting to the Crown Princess; sister-in-law of Count Radolinski.

[6] In English in the original.

Hatzf. says the King is most thrifty. He balances his accounts every day—which is probably unique amongst sovereigns. [...]

4 December 1882

The Chancellor arrived yesterday evening suffering from neuralgia and very depressed. Said he felt like a convict who has to return to his cell.

8 December 1882

The Chancellor said a couple of days ago: 'Believe me, Bl[eichröder], this is a great saying from an ageing diplomat: There'll be no war in 1883.'

I told this to P[aul] H[atzfeldt], who commented: 'Yes, it's not only a great saying, it's a bold one too.'

Bl[eichröder] had also inquired on Poschinger's[1] behalf whether it might not appear indicated, in view of the great success of *Preussen am Bundestage*,[2] to proceed now with the publication of the St Petersburg reports (1859–62).[3]

The Chancellor replied that he would be very inclined to do so, but the Kaiser did not wish disclosures from his own reign to be made public so soon.

9 December 1882

I dined with the Chancellor yesterday. Quite apart from his white beard, I thought he seemed older and in a state of nervous depression. He said his constitution resembled Friedrich Wilhelm IV's.[4] He has been haunted for a long time by the fear of softening of the brain.

In the course of the conversation he compared the character of Fried. Wilh. IV and the Kaiser. The former a most talented orator who, had he not been King, would have annihilated all his parliamentary opponents. The latter, capable of writing an agreeable letter, but a feeble orator. But he possessed one quality lacking in the other: the courage of a soldier. ('I had the moral courage for him.') Once a decision was taken—though often preceded by a long struggle—there was never one word of reproach *afterwards*. A noble character.

[1] Heinrich, Ritter von Poschinger. Historian.

[2] *Preussen im Bundestag, 1851 bis 1859. Dokumente der k. preuss. Bundestags-Gesandtschaft*, edited by Dr Ritter von Poschinger, 4 vols. (Leipzig, 1878 ff.).

[3] They were not published until 1920. *Die politischen Berichte des Fürsten Bismarck aus Petersburg und Paris*, 1859–62, edited by L. Rashdau, 2 vols. (Berlin, 1920).

[4] Friedrich Wilhelm IV, King of Prussia 1840–61, was adjudged insane in 1858 and succeeded by his brother Wilhelm as regent and then as King.

12 *December* 1882

Hatzfeldt had a long conversation with the Crown Prince to-day about one thing and another. The Prince said he had hesitated to call on the Chancellor because he had been told that it hurt the Chancellor to talk, and naturally their first interview would be a long one. Hatzfeldt noticed no trace of that annoyance with the Chancellor reported by Bötticher (probably on the strength of Friedberg's testimony). [...]

13 *December* 1882

Strange symptom. When the courier arrived recently bearing the first dispatches sent by Radowitz from Constantinople, the contents of the reports, taken together, gave the Chancellor the impression that Radowitz seemed bent on destroying every vestige of Hatzfeldt's personal influence still persisting in Constantinople. The Chancellor framed his answer in the light of this interpretation.[1] [...]

Prince Bismarck has been examined by a dentist, Dr Petsch. He stated that he could not say definitely that the removal of a tooth would cure the neuralgia. Bismarck is very depressed and says it is now quite clear he will have these pains till the end of his days. He says there is now nothing else he can do except vegetate in the country.

When Schweinitz[2] was recently in Varzin, Prince Bismarck said: 'Schweinitz's intelligent silence really gets on your nerves.'

15 *December* 1882

Bl[eichröder] was talking to Prince Bismarck yesterday about the repayment of a mortgage—in forty-one years. Bl. remarked that he laid down one condition, namely that Prince Bismarck pay the final instalment in person. Bismarck replied: 'Yes, I'd like to live a good long time yet if only for my children's sake, because I've sunk a great deal of capital in both my estates.'

Another thing Prince Bismarck said: 'I guarantee peace for 1883, though not for 1884.'

Once Russia starts a war, France must join in at the end of six

---

[1] In a dispatch of 10 December Radowitz was instructed to counter the Sultan's condemnations of German policy which he had reported by saying that the German Government had always made it clear to the Sublime Porte that Germany could not afford an open break with the Powers friendly to Germany on Turkey's behalf. Germany would 'in future strive to promote everything that contributed to the consolidation of conditions in Turkey, in so far as vital German interests and above all the preservation of peace in Europe were not endangered'. (From the Foreign Ministry files.)

[2] Hans Lothar von Schweinitz. Prussian General; Ambassador in St Petersburg, 1876–92.

weeks no matter whether the government of the day wants war or not.

17 *December* 1882

[...] Rottenburg[1] had sent a paragraph to the *Norddeutsche Allgemeine Zeitung* a couple of days ago proposing an increased duty on French sparkling wines. The demand was based not on economic but on political grounds.

The French Ambassador lodged a complaint with Hatzf[eldt], not because of the possible raising of the duty but because politics had been dragged into the argument. Hatzfeldt reported to the Chancellor, who replied: 'Tell the Ambassador not to insult me by assuming that the paragraph came from me.'

Waldersee told us that he heard from P[rince] W[ilhelm] that Crown Prince Rudolf of Austria has lived at such a pace that already he has no nerves left. The thought of war, possibly with Russia, is extremely distasteful to him.

22 *December* 1882

P[aul] H[atzfeldt]: The Chancellor has stated that he feels in duty bound to direct foreign affairs, whatever the circumstances, for as long as his strength permits it, because his Kaiser and his country have claim on his experience. But if he finds he cannot agree with his next sovereign on domestic policy, he will withdraw from this and from the presidency of the Council of Ministers as well.

23 *December* 1882

Yesterday over dinner the Chancellor was criticizing some engraving or other of Diana as inaccurate, because the forehead was too rounded. He said the goddess of the hunt should have a receding forehead like Frederick the Great, for example. A sign of daring. He then went on to speak of Fred. the Gt. whom he called a dare-devil and a witty *poseur*. In particular his affectation of frivolous cynicism was well calculated to alienate people's sympathies. One could understand a man saying to himself: 'I will play Ziethen[2] to such a King and stand by him through thick and thin.' 'But', added Bismarck, 'as an ordinary citizen and subject I should not have liked to live during the reign of Frederick the Gt.'

---

[1] Dr Franz von Rottenburg. Member of the Reich Chancellery Staff, 1881–90.
[2] Hans Joachim von Ziethen. Prussian general who served under Frederick the Great in the Silesian and Seven Years Wars.

After Hatzfeldt went on Christmas leave yesterday, Under State Secretary Busch to-day took the opportunity of turning out Humbert, the official in charge of personnel, on account of some trifling incident in the office, which cannot be regarded as the cause but merely as the pretext. Busch said to Humbert: 'Well, if that's the way things are run, then I don't like it.' Which left Humbert only one possible reply: 'In that case I shall resign my post as Counsellor for Personnel and prefer to return to the Second Division.'[1]

There was also an article in to-day's *Börsenzeitung* which aimed at blackening Hatzfeldt in the Chancellor's eyes. Bucher[2] submitted the article to Bismarck; it says that illness prevents the Chancellor from working, and that Hatzfeldt has taken over. But the Chancellor, as is obvious from his remarks to Rott[enburg], is perfectly well aware of what was intended.

Struck[3] told me to-day that yesterday's examination of Princess Bismarck revealed a condition of incipient arteriosclerosis. Result of deterioration, usually found in an older person. Condition serious, but no immediate danger.

Frerichs,[4] discussing the Chancellor's condition with Struck, said that his pain was caused either by a tooth or else by senile decay. It provoked states identical with hysteria in women.

Under the influence of his illness the Chancellor is becoming quite unsociable. He has stipulated that his wife is not to invite any one to a meal to whom he will be obliged to talk.

29 *December* 1882

[...] Bl[eichröder]: The Chancellor stated that when his son Herbert[5] last went to Vienna he was on no particular mission. 'I'm even sorry that he wasn't; I'd rather he had been.'

Two days ago I asked the Chancellor whether he approved of the appointment of the notoriously incompetent Count Behr[6]

[1] The economic and legal division of the Foreign Ministry. On 2 April 1885 it was split into Division II (economic) and Division III (legal). See *Memoirs*, Appendix II.

[2] Lothar Bucher. *Vortragender Rat* in the Foreign Ministry, 1864–86.

[3] Dr Heinrich Struck. *Geheimer Sanitätsrat*; later Director of the Office of Public Health.

[4] Professor Friedrich Theodor Frerichs. From 1859 Director of the medical section at the Charité hospital.

[5] Herbert, Count von Bismarck. From 15 January 1874 in the Foreign Ministry; attached to several Legations, but principally employed as private secretary to his father; First Secretary in the German Embassy in London, 1882–4; Acting First Secretary in St Petersburg, January 1884; Minister at The Hague, 11 May 1884–5; Under State Secretary in the Foreign Ministry, 10 May 1885–6; State Secretary, 1 May 1886–90; Prussian Minister of State, 1888–90.

[6] Ulrich, Count von Behr-Negendank. Free Conservative Deputy; Head of the Administration for the province of Pomerania.

(incidentally a man I did not know personally) as Head of the Administration of Pomerania.

He replied that he was glad enough to have placed his own candidate—Count von Haussonville[1]—in Köslin. He could not worry his head about the rest. He was happy if he could get through his Foreign Ministry business during his three or four hours' work each day. Behr, he gathered, was the Kaiser's candidate and certainly the Crown Prince's. Puttkamer could not be blamed for looking for ways and means of drawing closer to the Crown Prince, for he, Bismarck, could not now promise the Minister of the Interior that they would have another ten years in harness together with the same degree of probability as he could ten years ago, so Puttkamer must find his way for himself.

30 December 1882

Yesterday the Austrian Ambassador[2] handed Busch two instructions sent him from Vienna concerning the Turkish railways. The gist of them was that Bleichröder was to be the dominant partner; it was hoped Bismarck would support the undertaking.

The Chancellor, indignant at this association of their names, sent for Bleich. and asked him to withdraw from the affair completely to prevent a further outburst of scandalous gossip such as appeared in the *Reichsglocke*[3] some time ago.[4]

Despite his assurance that he was interested in the scheme only for political reasons, Bleichr., who told me all this, is obviously very unhappy about the attitude the Chancellor has adopted. He wants to ask the Chancellor whether his reason is really the one he states, or whether it is his intention to damage Austria. In the former case Bleichröder could get some bank, like the Darmstädter Bank, to act in his stead.

[1] Maximilian, Count von Haussonville. *Oberregierungsrat* in Köslin.
[2] Imre, Count Széchényi. Austro-Hungarian Ambassador in Berlin, 1878–92.
[3] The *Reichsglocke*, an organ of the Conservative Opposition, had attacked Bismarck during the '70's because of his connexion with the Jewish banker Gerson Bleichröder.
[4] The two Austrian instructions had been handed over to the Foreign Ministry on 27 December. The Austrian Government expressed in them its wish that the German Government would support the formation of a consortium consisting of the Ottoman Bank, the Creditanstalt and the firm of Bleichröder, which by agreement with Baron Hirsch (see p. 18, notes 2 and 3) would undertake to carry out the railroad construction necessary to link Turkey with Austria-Hungary. Bismarck's comment was that Germany would gladly support the project on the political level. 'But the German Foreign Ministry cannot concern itself with the financing of it, nor can it use its political credit with the Sultan to further the scheme.' In an instruction sent to Vienna on 30 December it was further stated that the Chancellor must 'observe the greatest caution with regard to the negotiations touched on in the Austrian communication, precisely because it contains the name of his own banker, and because His Highness [i.e. Bismarck] unfortunately knows from his own experience how readily the scandalmongers would exploit such a circumstance'. (From the Foreign Ministry files.)

Although several people advised him not to, Hatzfeldt went to Sommerberg over Christmas and will not be back until 2 January.

At a court banquet on the 27th the Kaiserin told Lord Ampthill how sorry she was that Hatzfeldt was not there: '*Je regrette de ne pas voir le Cte. Hatzfeldt: je ne connais pas M. Busch.*'

Redern,[1] the old High Chamberlain, went to Hatzfeldt's rooms to inquire personally when H. was due back. He hoped he would at any rate be in time to attend the New Year reception for the diplomatic corps. Would they please write and tell him so.

Radolinski and I wrote to him, but I think it is very doubtful whether he will come. I'm afraid he takes life too easy. In fact Ampthill recently told Rad. that H. was a most delightful person provided you did not talk shop with him; but the moment you began to talk about work you immediately had the impression you were boring him dreadfully: '*Alors il est insupportable et il lui arrive de répondre*: "*Oui, c'est possible, du reste je n'en sais rien, Busch doit savoir cela.*" ' Of course this only happens with topics of secondary importance—Chinese or Pacific questions etc. The ambassadors are delighted with his handling of more important affairs. What a pity that these minor weaknesses offer material for the attacks of the many enemies he has both inside and outside the Bismarck family (Princess Bismarck, Rantzau).[2]

[1] Wilhelm, Count von Redern. Lord High Chamberlain to Wilhelm I, 1861–83.
[2] Kuno, Count zu Rantzau. *Vortragender Rat* in the Foreign Ministry 1880–8; Prussian Minister in Munich, 1888–91. Married to Marie, Otto von Bismarck's daughter.

1883

The Gablenz mission. Gambetta's death. Bismarck's ministerial colleagues. Crisis over Kusserow. Crown Prince Friedrich and Crown Princess Victoria. Count and Countess Hatzfeldt. Bismarck and Bennigsen. Gorchakov. Bismarck's health.

1 *January* 1883

F.W. on the strength of information from a well-known source, has the impression that Prince Bismarck's real reason for appointing Hatzfeldt was to observe his suitability as a possible successor to himself—an idea he appears to have given up, 'because H. is not a conscientious official'.

Yesterday over dinner (with Lehndorff[1] and Wedel[2]) the Chancellor told us again the story of the well-known Gablenz mission of 1866. Gablenz,[3] because of his brother or cousin who was a general,[4] had been ushered immediately into Kaiser Franz Joseph's presence. The latter had read Prince Bismarck's memorandum very attentively.

The document proposed that Prussia and Austria should assume the hegemony of North and South Germany respectively, and resist external aggressors, particularly France.

The Kaiser referred the negotiator to his Ministers.

Mensdorff,[5] who should have been the leading Minister, but was not, referred Gablenz to the War Minister.[6] The latter said it would be time enough to discuss the proposals after the first battle (which he assumed they would win). The Finance Minister[7] said there could at the moment be no question of proposals for an agreement: in six months' time Austria must have either five hundred millions in Prussian war reparations or else some respectable reason for going bankrupt.

---

[1] Heinrich August, Count von Lehndorff. Adjutant-General of Wilhelm I.

[2] Karl, Count von Wedel. Prussian Lieutenant-Colonel; Military Attaché in Vienna, 1877–87.

[3] Anton, Baron von Gablenz. Member of the Prussian Chamber of Deputies.

[4] Ludwig, Baron von Gablenz. Austrian General; Governor in Holstein. Anton's brother.

[5] Alexander, Count Mensdorff-Pouilly. Austrian Foreign Minister, 1864–6.

[6] Karl, Ritter von Franck. Austrian War Minister, 1864–September 1866.

[7] Count von Larisch.

And that is how the Gablenz mission failed.[1]

2 *January* 1883

Retrospect: Hatzfeldt told me one day last summer that he had advised the Chancellor not to burden himself so much with details but to restrict himself to formulating the main lines of policy and to delegate some trusted person to put them into effect.

I think it possible that this suggestion made an unfavourable impression on the Chancellor's distrustful nature and gave him ground for suspicion. At all events Prince Bismarck leaves far less to the discretion of the present State Secretary than was left to Bülow when he was alive. [...]

On New Year's Eve the Chancellor, speaking of Gambetta's death—which occurred a few hours later—said he took a favourable view of the event in that one of the mainstays of a sound republican government had thus been removed. It would probably take some time for a firm system of government to emerge from present conditions. And the Orleanists, with whom Gambetta might have joined forces some day, had also lost a great deal by his death.

6 *January* 1883

The Chancellor said yesterday:

'The only one of all my ministerial colleagues—and I've had a good many—who really supported me, was Roon. But it's only recently that I have even managed to have colleagues who go along with me. Had I been surrounded in the early days by people like Bötticher, Scholz,[2] Maybach,[3] things would have been quite different.

'The first Eulenburg[4] did too little work; when we were reorganizing the *Kreise*[5] and he actually sat down for six weeks to do some hard slogging, he suffered a nervous attack.

'Meyendorff[6] governed in Berlin during the period of reaction in 1848 and '49. He was a fine-grained statesman to whom experience had given what timber-merchants call "fine rings"'.

[1] For Gablenz's mission, see Bismarck, *Die gesammelten Werke*, vol. v, nos. 348, 368, 371, pp. 502–3, 521–2, 524–6.

[2] Adolf von Scholz. From 1880 State Secretary to the Treasury; Prussian Finance Minister, 1882–90.

[3] Albert von Maybach. Prussian Minister of Public Works, 1878–91.

[4] Friedrich, Count zu Eulenburg. Prussian Minister of the Interior, 1862–78. Eulenburg resigned because of a difference of opinion with Bismarck over the new local government organization.

[5] In 1872 Eulenburg introduced a reform of the rural districts (*Kreise*), the smallest unit of the Prussian system of administration, with the aim of developing greater local autonomy.

[6] Peter, Baron von Meyendorff. Russian Minister in Berlin, 1839–50, in Vienna, 1850–4.

'Budberg,[1] his successor, was an irascible, boorish *Chinovnik.* He had once, because of some newspaper article or other, sent an uncouth note to Manteuffel in which he expressed his amazement *que le criminel que tout le monde connaît et qu'on se montre au doigt* was not yet under arrest. Manteuffel, in his anxiety to prevent disclosures about his private life, did not like to make more enemies than he could help, so he asked me to explain his views to the Minister. I did so at a court ball in the White Room, without the least difficulty, for Budberg's vehemence made my task an easy one.'

11 *January* 1883

Yesterday we had a sort of Kusserow crisis. From last March K. had been in the Political Division. The Chancellor had already told Hatzfeldt last summer that K. was not suited for political work, and that it would be better to return him to Division II. Hatzfeldt was reluctant to do this, preferring to put off action until some small foreign post could be found for Kusserow.

Since then there were more and more indications that the Chancellor wanted to remove Kusserow from this Division. In the autumn, when Bucher happened to be on a few days' visit to Varzin, the Chancellor had said in his presence something to the effect that K. had not stood the test and so must go back where he came from.

And so, after learning of that remark, I told Kusserow in November that I did not think he would stay here long, so he'd better look around in good time for a recommendation for a foreign post. I added that if he repeated my remarks to Bucher he could also tell him I had said that Bucher was in the best position to appreciate the accuracy of my opinion because of what he had heard with his own ears.

Since then I heard nothing from Kusserow himself. But the Chancellor, after repeatedly raising the question of Kusserow's transfer with Hatzfeldt, finally sent Bill[2] to Hatzfeldt six days ago to inform him it was high time to remove Kusserow from the Political Division and Holleben from the Foreign Ministry altogether. (Holleben, who had been here since the spring on leave from La Plata, had, on Radowitz's recommendation, managed to

[1] Andreas, Baron von Budberg. Russian Minister in Berlin, 1851–6, in Vienna, 1856–8, in Berlin, 1858–62, in Paris, 1862–8.

[2] Wilhelm, Count von Bismarck. In the Prussian Judiciary Service, 1874–9; temporarily attached to the office of the Governor of Alsace-Lorraine, September 1879–80; an official in the Reich Chancellery, 1881–2; *Regierungsrat*, mostly on the staff of the Chancellor, October 1882–4; *Vortragender Rat* in the Prussian Ministry of State, May 1884–5; *Landrat* in Hanau, August 1885–9; Head of the Administration of Hanover, March 1889–95; of the province of East Prussia, 1895–1901.

get himself employed by Busch first in the Political Division and then in Division II, when Busch took over as Hatzfeldt's deputy at the end of August. Holleben was very keen on staying here to be able to scheme for a more important post outside Europe.)

Hatzfeldt asked the Chief whether Kusserow could be given the post just fallen vacant at Oldenburg, or whether he could be fixed up somewhere abroad.

The Chief asked Hatzfeldt whether he would assume responsibility for Kusserow's tactless behaviour. The safest place for a tactless person was Division II. Moreover there was still time to think over the question of Kusserow, there was no hurry over the Oldenburg appointment. In any case the order relating to his transfer back to Division II must first be made out. The Chief was prepared to sign the document himself if Hatzfeldt did not want to—an offer Hatzfeldt gratefully accepted.

As soon as he received this order Kusserow reported himself sick. Two days later a lengthy document reached the Chancellor, written by Kusserow and accompanied by a note from Bucher in which he stated that the enclosed memorandum had been drawn up by *Geheimer Rat* von Kusserow on the occasion of his transfer back to Division II. It was because Bucher had observed the entire course of events from the day Kusserow was appointed to the Political Division, that he now submitted this document to His Highness.

Kusserow, in his memorandum, took the line that his transfer back was a *capitis diminutio*; he had not deserved it; it was the result of malicious gossip; he was prepared to challenge the people concerned; there was also some mention of an official who had worked under him, K. (i.e. Rantzau). The tone was apparently openly threatening. In conclusion Kusserow expressed his expectation that the Chief would retain him in the Political Division.

The Chancellor sent for Bucher and told him what he thought, in particular that he took K.'s letter to mean his resignation. Bucher produced the monstrous explanation that he had not known the contents of this letter (which had no envelope and was folded inside his own) and that K. had shown him a different document. Bucher could tell by the Chief's manner what he might well have realized before if he'd used his common sense, namely that the Chief was not disposed to yield to threats, and that the whole affair was turning out badly for its instigators. And so he had not a moment's hesitation in leaving in the lurch that fool of a Kusserow, whom he had intended to use as a weapon against Hatzfeldt, and in making him appear deceitful by the explanation given above. It cannot for one moment be supposed that Bucher really had not read the document sent him, or he would be an even bigger fool than Kusserow. As soon as his interview with the Chief was over he hurried round to call on Kusserow. The unexpected account of the effect of his stroke of genius resulted in Kusserow's sending a fresh letter to the Chancellor a few hours later, in which, cap in hand, he begged his pardon and requested a short leave at the end of which he hoped to feel sufficiently restored to undertake the work the Chief had assigned to him.

The Chancellor stated in his reply, which was comparatively mild, that Herr von K. had no doubt already been informed of his amazement at his first letter. Moreover the Chancellor did not share the view that a transfer to Division II constituted a *capitis diminutio*.

The man most furious over the expression: 'Division II equals *capitis diminutio*', is Bojanowski.[1]

This incident has shown me a new side of Bucher, whom I have known for sixteen years. Up to now I had thought him morose, malicious to people he disliked, and unusually capricious. But on this occasion he played a thoroughly mean trick on the unfortunate ill-balanced Kusserow when he said the latter had shown him a different letter.

I forgot to mention above that when Kusserow referred to intrigue in his first letter he said that not even the most senior and most esteemed official in the Foreign Ministry could escape it, and the position of Under State Secretary would soon become untenable.

Rantzau showed amazing persistence, worthy of a better cause, in the way he maintained that Bucher really had not known of the contents of the enclosed letter. Rantzau regards Bucher as a spade with which to undermine Hatzfeldt's position; this useful tool must not be worn down needlessly. In any case the affair has now been dropped.

Brauer has assumed responsibility for Balkan affairs in our Division; he worked on them for six weeks last summer under me.

16 *January* 1883

Stumm[2] told us yesterday that the Crown Prince had given vent to his indignation at the widespread feeling of hostility against

---

[1] Director of Division II in the Foreign Ministry.

[2] Ferdinand, Baron von Stumm. First Secretary in the Embassy in London, 1881–3; Prussian Minister in Darmstadt, 1883–5; Minister in Copenhagen, 1885–7; Minister, later Ambassador, in Madrid, 1887–92.

England. One heard it regretted in army circles—and his own sons shared this view—that England had not taken a beating in Egypt. But this feeling, he said, went deeper: this antipathy sprang from the consciousness that England was the home of liberal institutions.

The remark is interesting because it reveals that the democratic men of the future pose as the friends and the repositories of English ideas of liberty.

Lieutenant-Colonel Sommerfeld,[1] who has just been appointed to succeed Normann,[2] told me all about the difficulties of his position. He said he would resign at once in either of the following situations: if he became aware that the Crown Princess was against him or else that he was being kept in the dark about certain things.

Besides, he must for the moment steer clear of party politics because he felt certain there was an attempt being made to discredit him for being an adherent of Bismarck's.

He said the Crown Princess was very clever; she only touched on subjects she thought her hearer could understand; that was why Seckendorff's influence was limited.

Seckendorff was violent and stubborn. So far his pigheadedness had enabled him to force through a good deal; whether he would force through anything else was doubtful. Pressure evokes counter pressure.

In any case he, Sommerfeld, could not take Seckendorff's behaviour as a pattern. He wished not only to seem impartial but to be so, and simply wanted to do his job.

Whether Normann stood as far over with the opposition as was said, he could not yet judge. Just recently the two men had been discussing the future. When Sommerfeld remarked: 'You know, there are only two broad alternatives before the Crown Prince when he's Kaiser: to rule with Bismarck or without him', Normann replied: '*With*, of course.'

(Presumably Normann meant foreign policy.)

19 *January* 1883

Count Werthern:[3] King Ludwig[4] wrote a letter to Richard Wagner recently in which he said: 'You'd never believe how difficult it is at times to be a Prussian Prefect.'[5]

---

[1] Private Secretary to Crown Prince Friedrich Wilhelm.
[2] Karl von Normann. Court Chamberlain to Crown Prince Friedrich Wilhelm.
[3] Georg, Baron von Werthern-Beuchlingen. Prussian Minister in Munich, 1867–88.
[4] Ludwig II, King of Bavaria, 1864–86.
[5] The letter to which Holstein refers is not included in *König Ludwig II und Richard Wagner. Briefwechsel*, 5 vols. (Karlsruhe, 1936–9).

Yesterday the *Kleine Journal* and the *Volkszeitung* again carried a notice saying that Hatzfeldt's daughter[1] had come here to marry one of Bleichröder's sons. This is quite without foundation, since there is absolutely no social intercourse between the two families. The aim is obviously to make Hatzfeldt's stay here unpleasant.

24 *January* 1883

The Chancellor, speaking the other day about the Crown Prince, said that he understood the art of personal relations, like all the Hohenzollern. Bismarck cited some case or other, but then added: 'It's only a pity the Prince has no confidence in his own popularity; his father has.'

25 *January* 1883

[...] A couple of days ago I dined with Seckendorff and Sommerfeld. Both passed unfavourable judgments on the German Princes, starting with Coburg,[2] who had wanted to become German Kaiser, then moving on to the Grand-Duke of Weimar,[3] the would-be King of Thuringia, who would have been *le plus plat de tous* in an unsuccessful war. (The Grand-Duke is proud of his Russian descent, has pronounced Russian sympathies and thus is *persona minus grata* at the Crown Prince's court. Brincken[4] describes him as a discreet, reliable man, a decided adherent of the Chancellor's.)

Both So. and Se. came out strongly against the retention of sovereign armies; admittedly the feeling in these armies, especially in Bavaria and Württemberg, was imperial. But moods change and the Reich could not allow its security to depend on them in any degree whatsoever. The Princes could be allowed to continue to rule, but *after* they had been deprived of all power to harm.

Typical of the oultook in the Crown Prince's court. No wonder the Princes in question are becoming more demonstrative each year in their display of affection for the Chancellor. [...]

30 *January* 1883

Waldersee said to-day that after the recent debates in the Chamber on the army estimates he thought it impossible to retain Kameke any longer as War Minister. Apart from the fact that

---

[1] Helene Suzanne von Hatzfeldt.
[2] Ernst II, Duke of Saxe-Coburg and Gotha, 1844–93.
[3] Karl Alexander, Grand-Duke of Saxe-Weimar, 1853–1901.
[4] Prussian Minister in Weimar, 1881–3.

he gave most unsatisfactory replies to the various attacks on the army, it was inconceivable for a Minister to remain in his position when he declared in public that our artillery was the best, whereas every artillery officer knows it is on the contrary the worst in the world except for the English. Waldersee believed it was necessary for Albedyll to take steps with the Kaiser against the Minister of War. He also asked whether the Chancellor would do anything? I told him that Bismarck would let well enough alone to avoid unpleasantness between himself and the old gentleman.

8 *February* 1883

[...] Kusserow (see my entry for 11 January) informed Hatzfeldt that he expected some sort of amends to be made him. He should either be allowed to stay on in the Political Division, however humble his duties, or else he should be given some other post.

Hatzfeldt wrote in reply that since he had no wish to ruin Kusserow completely [he] would put no such suggestions to the Chancellor at present.

15 *February* 1883

[...] Hatzfeldt has just gone to Dresden for a few days with his daughter. Countess Hatzfeldt[1] was there and had insisted on their joining her. For three days father and daughter did their utmost, in letters and telegrams, to get out of it. But finally they went, for fear the Countess might otherwise come here. She has now one aim: re-marriage.[2] To this end she is striving to create as false a situation as possible, so that people can say afterwards: 'If they're living together it would be better for them to re-marry.'

That is a miscalculation. Not only the Chancellor but also the Crown Prince and Princess think that the Countess will be unacceptable in official circles for a long time to come. Hatzfeldt has only the choice of remaining at his post alone or else, if he wants to be with his wife, of resigning. The Chancellor has wanted for some days to have a talk on this subject with Ignaz Landsberg.[3] Seckendorff has already stated the position in a letter to Prince Nicholas of Nassau so that the Countess can decide whether it would suit her to live on a slender pension at Sommerberg with her husband, who in fact gets on her nerves because she has no understanding whatever for his good and sterling qualities. The question of money is the only one that counts for this woman. She

---

[1] Helene, Countess Hatzfeldt, *née* Moulton.
[2] Paul von Hatzfeldt and his wife were divorced.
[3] Cousin of Paul von Hatzfeldt.

is quite heartless, and her children's future is a matter of indifference to her. Instead of leaving the eldest daughter of about eighteen with her father where she would have a good social position and the possibility of marrying, her mother forces the girl to stay with her for most of the year; she trails her around Swiss and Italian hotels, where the older woman prevents the younger one from enjoying a satisfactory social life. This happens because the mother realizes that the father can be coerced into re-marriage only when he sees there is no other way of having his children near him.

He could of course command her to give up their daughter, since he was given legal custody of her after the divorce. But he is like a sensitive, rather timid elderly man being henpecked by a determined housekeeper.

The Countess has an unusually repellent character. After dragging her husband's name through the mud in every country in Europe, she is now sacrificing even her children's existence to her selfish desires. I don't think she will stand her quiet life in Sommerberg much longer. When she realizes that there is no hope of marriage this year, she will break loose from there and make for Paris or Italy. Where Hatzfeldt will find the money to satisfy her whims then, I don't know. She will make debts out of sheer fury.

17 *February* 1883

The day before yesterday I was talking to Bennigsen[1] who had called on the Chancellor the previous day and seemed very pleased with his interview. He told me they had discussed a wide variety of topics including the Roman question.

I reminded him of what I had told him on previous occasions, namely that he was one of the few people to whom the Chancellor felt instinctively drawn, and so I warned him not to burn his boats. B. declared that he certainly had no intention of doing so.

I said it was a pity he had adopted such an uncooperative attitude over the tobacco monopoly.[2]

B. replied that such was his opinion, and he could not alter it. The proposal came thirty years too late; nowadays it was impracticable in view of the development of private enterprise. But in

---

[1] Rudolf von Bennigsen. Leader of the National Liberals in the Reichstag. In June 1883 he resigned his seat and did not return to the Reichstag until January 1887. See Hermann Oncken, *Rudolf von Bennigsen*, 2 vols. (Stuttgart and Leipzig, 1910), vol. II, p. 495, note 1.

[2] Bismarck had hoped to solve the financial problems of the Reich by a government monopoly on tobacco. The resulting revenue would have reduced the Reich's dependence on the contributions from its member states. The proposal had been repeatedly rejected by the Reichstag.

any case the Chancellor was no longer keen on the idea and had given it up.

Kameke made himself seem more and more ridiculous during the recent debates. On Stosch's persuasion (according to Waldersee) he said he would agree to make regular officers liable for the payment of local taxation.[1]

Albedyll had a violent argument with Stosch over this business and flung the coarsest insults at him in the Kaiser's presence, but without incurring the royal reproof.

So then Albedyll went to the Chancellor, who told him that even if the Kaiser sanctioned the bill, he, Bismarck, would refuse to countersign the document. Naturally the Kaiser entirely agreed with the Chancellor and instructed the War Minister to that effect.

It was hoped in army circles that now the War Minister would go. But I hear that yesterday he told Köller, the President of the Chamber of Deputies, that he wasn't going to resign on account of the blockheads in the Reichstag. Apparently he wants to wait another year at least, to celebrate his golden jubilee as a Minister.

18 *February* 1883

To-day I told the Chancellor of my conversation with Bennigsen. Prince Bismarck was obviously less edified by his talk with Bennigsen than the latter had been.

'B. can never be really decisive. He's constantly wondering: "Am I still protected by the party umbrella?" He always reminds me of the Russian proverb: I sit on the bank waiting for the wind.'

From this I conclude that Bennigsen has turned down some proposal or other.

A few weeks ago the Crown Prince said to General Blumenthal:[2] 'See how life treats me. Just look at my son, the complete Guards officer.'

The General replied: 'Your Royal Highness must not take too much notice. The Prince is still young.'

Waldersee, who told me this, commented: 'The Crown Prince's statement is not true. Prince Wilhelm is certainly not what one understands by "Guards officer".'

[Seckendor]ff: In less than five years' time Prince Wilhelm will exert a decisive influence on his parents—both of them. He knows what he wants, is very self-willed, and one could even say hard.

---

[1] See Bismarck, *Die gesammelten Werke*, vol. VI c, no. 264, pp. 273–6.
[2] Leonhard, Count von Blumenthal. The Crown Prince's Chief of Staff in the wars of 1866 and 1870; later Field-Marshal.

I saw the Chancellor to-day for the first time for six weeks or more. I had never before been so struck by the signs of old age. After the meal Rantzau and Bill slept quite openly in their arm-chairs for a good hour and a half. At the same time Bismarck does not wish 'strangers', i.e. people outside the family circle, to be invited. This must have an adverse effect on his intellectual life.

11 *March* 1883

Dined yesterday with Rottenburg at the Chancellor's. Bill and Rantzau were dining with Saburov.[1] How much the old gentleman likes company was apparent, for when I left at half past eight after the return of the two diners-out, he was still sitting at table. And Bill told me to-day his father had remarked to Rantzau that he liked having people for dinner. (Rantzau's favourite question, on the other hand, is: what sort of swine or dogs are coming to dinner to-day?) I noticed yesterday more than I had before the interruptions to which the Chancellor is exposed from one section of his family, to such an extent that it is scarcely possible to embark on a conversation. Princess Bismarck and the Countess Rantzau pay not the slightest attention to what Prince Bismarck happens to be saying, but constantly interrupt him, either with remarks about household topics or anecdotes from the *Fremdenblatt*.

With regard to the new War Minister, Bronsart,[2] the Chancellor said in answer to my question that he hoped there was more to him than was apparent at first sight; the man had no chin.

After dinner I informed the Chancellor that Sommerfeld had been anxious to know the Chancellor's attitude towards the question of the purification of the language,[3] because the Crown Prince was now in a position to formulate his reply to a memorandum he had received on the subject. This memorandum had recommended particularly a clean-up of official jargon.

After having audience of the Chancellor I informed Sommerfeld of his views in the following *résumé*.

No Puttkamer business, please. Language purifies itself. This is obvious when one compares modern modes of expression with the German of Luther and Frederick the Great. Any regimentation in that direction leads to particularism because we have no

[1] Peter von Saburov. Russian Ambassador in Berlin, 1880–4.

[2] Paul Bronsart von Schellendorf. Prussian War Minister, 1883–9. See p. 37, note 1.

[3] By a decree of 21 January 1880, Robert von Puttkamer introduced a reform in German orthography to overcome the inconveniences arising from the divergent spelling in North and South Germany (the so-called Puttkamer Orthography).

means of forcing the broad stream of popular speech along official channels. Official and popular language, which have become almost identical in recent times, greatly to their mutual advantage, would after such a reform be running parallel once more as they did at the time of the *Reichskammergericht*. If we attempted to force the purification of the language in a hothouse atmosphere instead of letting it grow naturally out of doors we should again produce results like Jahn's[1] '*Reithalbschaargehülfe*' (*Schaar* = regiment, *Halbschaar* = battalion, *Reitgehilfe* = adjutant), and should probably, now as then, drive the popular wit to the aid of linguistic reaction.

13 *March* 1883

Yesterday the Chancellor happened to mention Gorchakov.[2]

When King Victor Emmanuel was in Berlin during the autumn of 1873 the Press got hold of the news that he intended to present the Chancellor with a snuff-box of unusual value—the figure of 55,000 francs was mentioned. Prince Bismarck drove to see the Kaiser and begged his permission to refuse this present if it were offered. The Kaiser raised objections: 'You cannot refuse to accept a snuff-box bearing the image of a monarch.' Prince Bismarck replied: 'Would Your Majesty, for example, give Prince Gorchakov such a valuable present just at a time when we wished Russia to do something for us?' The Kaiser thought for a moment, then said: 'No, you're right.'

The following spring the Kaiser and Chancellor went to St Petersburg. While there they had to decide what to give Prince Gorchakov, who had long since possessed every imaginable distinction. Should it be a picture or a bust? Prince Bismarck was asked to sound him and found himself obliged to report to the Kaiser next day: 'Your Majesty, we've both misjudged Gorchakov. He replied to my hint at once with: "Oh, give me a decent snuff-box."'

Normann, replying to someone's comment that Caprivi[3] would surely be more suitable as War Minister than Bronsart, said: 'We must save Caprivi for *ourselves*.'

W[alderse]e: Albedyll recently had quite a long interview with

---

[1] Friedrich Ludwig Jahn. An early nineteenth-century German educator who played a prominent part in the revival of German national feeling.

[2] Alexander, Prince Gorchakov. Russian Foreign Minister, 1856–82; Vice-Chancellor, 1862–71; Chancellor, 1871–82.

[3] Leo, Count von Caprivi. Head of the Admiralty, 1883–8; General commanding the 10th Army Corps in Hanover, 1888–90; Chancellor of the German Reich, 1890–4; Prussian Minister-President, 1890–2.

the Crown Prince about the Stosch-Kameke affair.[1] The Prince
had been primed by the opposition and seemed indignant at the
departure of the two men who, in his opinion, were asking nothing
unjust in making officers liable to this tax. It was the only liberal
way of looking at the affair, and he was himself a liberal-minded
man.

The Crown Prince is still confusing the 'liberal' aspirations of
the bourgeoisie, i.e. aspirations springing from vanity, with the
hungry desires of the masses. It is to be hoped that once he has
learned from experience the difference between them there will
still be time to call a halt.

22 *March* 1883

[...] P[aul] H[atzfeldt]. Two days ago the Crown Prince said:
'My son Wilhelm is a good lad, but utterly tactless. Without
asking anyone beforehand he told the Austrian Military Attaché
Steininger that he would very much like to be invited to the
Austrian manœuvres this year. Of course the invitation came, but
that was not the right way to set about it. And there might very
easily have been political reasons against his going.'

The Crown Prince spoke most indignantly about our sending a
Prince to attend the coronation in Moscow,[2] chiefly with reference
to the unsatisfactory treatment of precedence. Prince Albrecht,[3]
as the representative of the thousand-year-old German Empire,
ought by right to *precede* the Archduke[4] who represented the
modern Austrian Empire.

Everything I hear about the Crown Prince's consciousness of
his royal rank strengthens my conviction how right the man was
who told me just recently that the Crown Prince's estrangement
from the Chancellor arose more from trifles than matters of
importance. 'My future subject has a private railway-carriage
and I have not!' Or, 'He is given an order in diamonds, and I
am not!'

I am most curious to see how this sense of royalty will one day
shake down with liberalism, *in practice*.

[1] Stosch belonged to the Crown Prince's party and his relations with Bismarck had been
strained for years, particularly since Bismarck's attack on him during the debate on naval
estimates in the Reichstag on 10 March 1877. In February 1883 the problem of the liability
of the military to local taxation provoked a disagreement between Wilhelm I on the one
hand and Stosch and Kameke on the other. On 26 February 1883 Kameke handed in his
resignation, which was accepted on 3 March with Bismarck's approval. On 7 March Stosch
also handed in his resignation, which the Kaiser at first refused, but then accepted after Stosch
had offered a further explanation of his reasons.
[2] The celebrations for the coronation of Tsar Alexander III were held in Moscow from
20 May to 9 June.
[3] Albrecht, Prince of Prussia.   [4] Albrecht, Archduke of Austria.

23 *March* 1883

The Chancellor told us the other day that in 1862, when his transfer to Paris was mooted, he once said in conversation with the Tsar that he hoped he would use his good offices with the King so that Bismarck could remain in Russia. The Tsar understood that Bismarck wished to enter the Russian service and showed himself very ready to oblige, until Bismarck enlightened him.

24 *March* 1883

I went to see Frerichs to-day to talk to him about the Chancellor, at Bill's request. Bill and Frau von Wallenberg[1] thought it would be advisable to tell Frerichs that the Chancellor's health had not improved since Frerichs treated him, that Frerichs' position was bound to become less and less secure unless he found something to relieve Bismarck's neuralgia and that it might therefore be a good idea to call in another dentist or else Professor Bergmann,[2] the surgeon.

The Chancellor had in fact been complaining of pain a good deal throughout the past week, and had been cursing Frerichs. His family were at their wits' end. He sat or rather lay down all day with the temperature at 20 degrees.

Frerichs' reply to my statement was a categorical refusal. If he was no longer wanted, he really did not care, for in his line he was as big a man as the Chancellor. He had taken on this responsibility because he liked and respected the Chancellor as a man and he was happy to serve him because he was not only a noble but also a likeable person. Sometimes the Chancellor kept him for as long as two hours.

Prince Bismarck, he said, was actually in good health except that at the moment he had catarrh, which would be gone in a week. This neuralgia of his was a very odd business. It caused Prince Bismarck far less pain than people supposed. When Frerichs was present he never had pain. 'So you think he is shamming?' 'No, no, but in his case it depends on his mood. There's something about his family which makes him uneasy. I have no desire to know what it is. His family has no idea how to handle him. I can tell that when I'm there and he's having his solitary cup of tea in the morning. A long lean individual pours it out for him and then goes away.' 'That is Princess Bismarck.' 'Princess Bismarck? Well, in that case it's very wrong of him

---

[1] Marie von Wallenberg, *née* von Rochow, wife of the President of the Royal Exchequer.
[2] Dr Ernst von Bergmann. Professor of surgery in Berlin.

not to say "My wife", and also for her to ignore me, because I was once introduced to her many years ago. But I don't mind. I don't mind anything from him. But if his family thinks that Bergmann, a mere nobody, is better suited to the job, let them send for him; I shouldn't set foot in the house again. It's not a surgical case. You could pull out every tooth in his head and sever every nerve in his face, he'd still be no better. Compared with Bergmann even Leyden[1] is a genius. I tell you there's nothing wrong with the Chancellor, it's just that he's showing signs of wear.'

I asked how Frerichs could allow the Chancellor to live in a room temperature of 20 degrees Réaumur.

'That does him no harm; I sit in a temperature of 21 degrees myself.'

There was only one point we agreed on; Prince Bismarck must see more people. Frerichs promised to do what he could about this, observing that Prince Bismarck had once invited him to dinner but he had declined on the pretext: 'I'm a solitary man and am not fond of society.' His real reason was that he didn't wish to have anything to do with the Chancellor's family.

Wedell-Malchow[2] told us that Stirum[3] is beginning to seem almost sinister to the Conservatives because of his antagonism towards the Chancellor, which is constantly breaking out. Wounded ambition. Bucher is no doubt sowing discord as much as he can.

25 March 1883

[...] The Chancellor once remarked last summer: 'Sometimes I'm fairly spoiling for a fight. If there's nothing to annoy me in my work, I'm quite capable of getting annoyed about a tree and having it cut down.'

27 March 1883

The rumour had gone round Berlin that the Kaiser had been taken ill as a result of the Crown Prince's remonstrances over the Stosch affair. I am told this is not the case. On the contrary, the Crown Prince avoided speaking to the Kaiser. To take the initiative in a case like this when you can be certain of an explosion

[1] Ernst Viktor von Leyden. Professor of medicine in Berlin.

[2] Friedrich von Wedell-Malchow. Conservative Member of the Reichstag, 1871–3, 1877–81.

[3] Friedrich Wilhelm, Count zu Limburg-Stirum. Interim Head of the Foreign Ministry, 1880–1; in 1881 he was given indefinite leave of absence; Member of the Prussian Chamber of Deputies, 1871–1905 (from 1893 leader of the German Conservative Party); of the Reichstag, 1893–1906.

from the old gentleman, requires a degree of determination not everyone possesses.

Yesterday the Chancellor was most annoyed with Stephan.[1] The negotiations with Bavaria about postage stamps have so far produced no result, and Crailsheim[2] therefore complained to Werthern. The Chancellor informed Stephan that if it came to choosing between King Ludwig and Stephan there could be no hesitation over his choice. He therefore requested Stephan to adopt a gentler tone.

Some weeks ago, in this same connexion, the Crown Prince expressed himself most bitterly to Hatzfeldt against particularist tendencies. He (i.e. H.I.H.) is of course an out-and-out unitarian.

I remember his once saying to me in the autumn of 1873, 'The German Princes, with the exception of my brother-in-law,[3] are all like wasps with one wing pulled out; so long as they can crawl, they will sting.'

Even so, somebody who knows the Crown Prince said the other day how very different it will be once he is at the helm. Then there will be constant consideration for a cousin here and a niece there.

W[alderse]e: The Crown Prince and Princess recently inquired of Prince Wilhelm why he went to see the Chancellor so often. 'You're still too immature.'

Prince Christian of Augustenburg wrote a short while ago to Prince Wilhelm asking for information on the Stosch affair. The Prince, who is reluctant to commit his political views to paper, passed on the contents of this letter to his father, who eagerly set about replying forthwith.

The foregoing is based on remarks made by Prince Wilhelm, who also added that all mention of Stosch to his parents was now taboo—it was a sore point.

The Crown Prince, who after all knows what it feels like to be too strictly held in check, is now treating his son in exactly the same way as he himself was treated.

The Crown Prince's taste and his liking for the arts are formed by the Crown Princess. And on other matters too, e.g. agriculture and the navy, the Crown Princess is better informed than he.

The Crown Prince by his foolish outbursts falls an easy prey to any one who has a firmer grip on himself.

[1] Heinrich von Stephan. Postmaster-General.

[2] Christoph Krafft, Baron von Crailsheim. From 1880 Bavarian Minister of the Royal House and Foreign Minister.

[3] The Grand-Duke of Baden.

27 *March* 1883

I learned to-day from Professor Lewin[1] the reason why Frerichs has such a grudge against Bergmann. Frerichs is president of the 'Society for Internal Medicine' whereas Bergmann is a member of the rival medical society. To the latter belong all the medical authorities, whereas the former is composed mainly of Frerichs, Leyden, and their assistants. In addition, Bergmann did not bow to Frerichs.

The Chancellor now has to suffer for miserable things like this. He is very unwell again to-day. Frerichs does not seem to be doing him the slightest good. [...]

[1] Director of the Charité Hospital.

The Crown Prince in Spain and Italy. Rantzau's inefficiency. Schlözer. Normann, Stosch and the Crown Prince. Bismarck's isolation. Manteuffel's regime in Alsace-Lorraine. The Crown Prince and Bismarck. Schweinitz. Domestic politics. Bleichröder. Bismarck on Gladstone. Limburg-Stirum. Bismarck's lack of trust. Saburov's intrigues. Lasker's obsequies. The Crown Princess and Germany. The King of Bavaria and his debts. Mischke's removal. Bleichröder's personal difficulties. Bismarck and the United States. Hatzfeldt's position. Dolguruki's ambition. Holstein's dislike of Rantzau. Saburov's departure. Herbert von Bismarck's future. Bismarck's return to Berlin. His decline. Bismarck to retire from Prussian affairs. The Council of State. The Battenberg marriage plan. Relations in the Bismarck family. Bismarck and the National Liberals. Repercussions of the Battenberg marriage plan. Holstein dines with Bismarck. Moltke's succession. Difficulties in the Foreign Ministry. Bismarck's moods. Herbert von Bismarck's appointment to The Hague. Queen Victoria. Bojanowski. Bismarck and the Kaiser. Prince Alexander's visit. The London embassy. The Crown Prince's entourage. Radolinski's new post. Holstein's quarrel with Rantzau. Prince Wilhelm in Russia. Courcel. Caprivi. Bismarck and Courcel. German colonial policy. The Crown Prince and Prince Wilhelm. Bismarck's scheming.

Holstein to Ida von Stülpnagel[1]

Berlin, 3 January 1884

My dear Ize,

Some time ago I began to keep a diary. The only trouble was that I did not feel that my flat was quite safe, and I also made some strange discoveries about internal security here at the office.

And so I have now hit upon the idea of sending you the loose sheets the same day as they are written. It might amuse you to glance through them occasionally if you have time. You are sufficient guarantee for your husband,[2] but apart from him *don't tell a soul* I am keeping a diary of this nature. Any odd detail you think harmless you can make use of in conversation, e.g. the story about the Kaiser and Kameke. I leave all this entirely to your judgment. But never mention anything bearing on the relations

---

[1] A cousin of Friedrich von Holstein, *née* von Holtzendorff.
[2] Alfred von Stülpnagel-Dargitz.

between Chancellor and Crown Prince, particularly the party relationships in the Crown Prince's entourage (or the Chancellor and his family).

Every good wish for the New Year,
Fritz

3 *January* 1884

At the New Year reception the Kaiser paid all kinds of compliments to the Cabinet as a body, and to many of its individual members, saying amongst other things that he had never before been surrounded by such good Ministers (which I think hard on old Roon, Eulenburg senior and Heydt).[1] To Hatzfeldt he said: 'So the Prince (Bismarck) was right yet again. I had my doubts about the journey to Rome,[2] but look how well it turned out. I must thank you too.'

The Kaiser had been afraid that the Pope would refuse to give audience to the Crown Prince if he were to stay in the Quirinal. And so both the Kaiser and the Crown Prince wanted the question settled by Schlözer before the Crown Prince reached Rome, whereas the Chancellor, acting on Hatzfeldt's suggestion, put forward and carried through the proposal that Schlözer should not announce the Prince's intention of visiting the Vatican until *after* the Crown Prince's arrival in Rome. Thus it would be delicately pointed out that his main purpose in coming to Rome was to see the King.

In addition, the Kaiser thought an audience with the Pope was a 'tremendous concession'. The Chancellor judged it perfectly harmless so long as the Crown Prince firmly refused to touch on questions of fact. Just polite conversation.

The Pope asked *several times* what message the Crown Prince had brought, and was unwilling to believe that H.I.H. had no commission whatsoever. In spite of that the old gentleman was most amiable, and made a very agreeable impression on everyone. Loë[3] kissed his toe and the other members of the royal suite, except Sommerfeld, kissed his hand, which seems to me ridiculous for Protestants.

The Crown Prince greatly pleased the Chancellor by his behaviour in public throughout his journey. On his return H.I.H.

---

[1] August, Baron von der Heydt. Prussian Finance Minister, 1862, 1866–9.

[2] In November 1883 Crown Prince Friedrich Wilhelm paid a state visit to the King of Spain, who had visited Germany the previous summer. The Crown Prince returned home via Rome, where he called on the King of Italy and the Pope. See Wolfgang Windelband, *Berlin-Madrid-Rom. Bismarck und die Reise des deutschen Kronprinzen 1883* (Essen, 1939).

[3] Walther, Baron von Loë. General in command of the 8th Army Corps; later Field-Marshal.

wrote a long account for Prince Bismarck, who sent a reply of fourteen sheets of quarto.[1]

Just before the New Year the Kaiser gave audience to the former War Minister Kameke. H.M. was very communicative and told the General he was glad to say that Prince Bismarck had observed in the Russian Minister, Giers, nothing but peaceful intentions.[2] 'Mark you, my dear Kameke, you know what Ministers are, here to-day and gone to-morrow.'

During Puttkamer's recent visit to Friedrichsruh the Chancellor was complaining bitterly of Kosierowski, the head of his local district, who had nevertheless been selected with great care. Prince Bismarck had been called on to pay 5,000 marks in local taxes, thought this too high and complained in particular of not having been warned in advance. Puttkamer replied that he knew for certain that the district head had drawn the Chancellor's attention to the assessment in question.

Prince Bismarck sent for Rantzau. The latter was obliged to admit that the relevant notification had been received five or six weeks before. H.H. said nothing to Rantzau but kept an embarrassed silence, then remarked to Puttkamer: 'Still, Kosierowski *is* an old carp' (a new expression).

I advised to transfer the district head as soon as possible, because reasonable relations could never be re-established between them.

Rantzau's inefficient work has caused a great deal of annoyance and confusion in the last few months. He is not equal to his job, and in addition he does, or rather, omits to do, all kinds of things

[1] In September 1883 the King of Spain, who was visiting Wilhelm I in Homburg, had proposed to Count Hatzfeldt an agreement, verbal in the first instance, for mutual support in case France made war on Spain or Germany. On 20 October Bismarck suggested to the Kaiser that the question be discussed with the King of Spain during a return visit of the Crown Prince to Madrid. In a report of 23 December to Bismarck on his journey to Spain, which was combined with a trip to Rome, the Crown Prince stated that resistance in the Spanish Cabinet stood in the way of a written agreement between Germany and Spain. On the other hand King Alfonso had given 'verbal assurances of mutual assistance—moral support at first, but then, according to circumstances, material support as well—in case either of the two countries we represent should be threatened by the French.' In Rome Pope Leo XIII had expressed his desire for an understanding with the Prussian Government (abandonment of the *Kulturkampf*). Bismarck replied to the Crown Prince's memorandum on 27 December. The failure to conclude a treaty with Spain, he said, was not a bad thing in view of the unreliability of the Spanish Cabinet; good relations with Spain would usually, perhaps always, remain one of the goals of German policy. As regards the visit to the Pope, Bismarck wrote that there was for Germany no question of a Concordat, which the Pope apparently desired, because the state had to preserve its legislative freedom. He, Bismarck, had never counted on success from the negotiations with Rome, but they must be carried on formally so as to avoid giving rise to the impression amongst Germany's Catholic population that the Prussian Government was irreconcilable. (From the Foreign Ministry files.)

[2] Giers visited Bismarck at Friedrichsruh on 14 November 1883. See *Grosse Politik*, vol. III, nos. 611–12, pp. 302–7.

on purpose to annoy people he dislikes; Hatzfeldt leads the list. [...]

Oddly enough the Crown Prince came back with a good opinion of Schlözer. But Keudell[1] is regarded by H.I.H. and his entourage as bordering on lunacy.

His good opinion of Schlözer is doubtless connected with the fact that he is secretly in opposition [to Bismarck] and one of Normann's adherents. [...]

Bismarck always treated him kindly, although he said: 'Schlözer is one of those people I've never quite fathomed.'

Schlözer's cleverness consists in leading many people, on the strength of a superficial acquaintance, into believing that his clown's mask conceals the seriousness and penetration of a Rigoletto. People who fall for this are indeed being taken in, at least so far as politics are concerned. Of politics he knows nothing; he has neither political sense nor political knowledge. When he had been in Rome almost a year—and he had formerly spent several years as Secretary of Legation to the Vatican—he called the Archbishop of Cologne in the course of a report 'Primate of Prussia'.

The Chancellor has on occasion a certain weakness for people of modest political gifts, and that is how Schlözer has made his way, though he would still like to become Ambassador or State Secretary. [...]

5 *January* 1884

The journalists forming part of the Crown Prince's suite caused all kinds of scandal during his journey, the effects of which have not yet died down.

The reporters made the crossing from Genoa to Valencia on the same boat as H.I.H. The latter could not resist the temptation to let his tongue wag to the Press. As a result readers of the *National-Zeitung* learned that H.I.H. had declared the King of Spain to be the most intelligent sovereign he had ever met. How pleasant for the other sovereigns.

In Madrid Solms,[2] probably on Normann's suggestion, procured for the journalists an audience with the King of Spain. The King, naturally talkative and imagining also that the members of the Crown Prince's suite were tactful people, as English journalists so often are, indulged in some very plain speaking which gave

[1] Robert von Keudell. Minister, then Ambassador in Rome, 1873–87.
[2] Eberhard, Count zu Solms-Sonnenwalde. Minister in Madrid, 1878–87; Ambassador in Rome, 1887–93.

rise to dispatches of such indiscretion that the Spanish Council of Ministers met in order to disavow some of the more disastrous of His Majesty's statements as 'misunderstandings'. I hardly think it can have done much good. The Crown Prince was in no way to blame for the audience given to the journalists; he said later: 'I was very surprised to see the gentlemen in white ties standing in front of the King; if I'd known of this audience beforehand I should have advised him against it.' [...]

There are many indications to suggest that Normann and his followers are trying by every possible means to bring about a split between H.I.H. and Prince Bismarck. For example Normann had at one stage prevailed on the Crown Prince to take Stosch to Spain with him. The letter in which H.I.H. expressed this wish to the Kaiser was already in the post when the Crown Princess came to hear of it and obliged the Crown Prince to send to the post office to retrieve it. She perceived the results of such a suggestion, even supposing the Kaiser had refused it: it would have aroused ungovernable resentment in the Chancellor, who would have felt it was a slap in the face. [...]

Normann was a captain in Magdeburg when Stosch was Chief of Staff there. Stosch, so they say, paid court to Frau von Normann, and Normann used his wife as a stepping-stone.

Stosch recommended Normann to Herr von Stockmar,[1] the first private secretary, when he became a cripple and had to give up the post; then Stockmar recommended Normann to the Crown Prince.

These two, Normann and Stosch, have stuck together ever since, each pushing the other. If ever Stosch were to become Chancellor, Normann could pick whatever suited him.

Normann, with a sense of greater security, recently began attempting to influence the Crown Prince without, or even against, the Crown Princess. He thus created for himself in the person of the Crown Princess a formidable enemy. *Après ça, fera-t-il de vieux os* at the Crown Prince's court? It may be doubted, and it will not be a bad thing if he does disappear.

Please treat the whole of to-day's entry as secret.

6 *January* 1884

[...] Prince Wilhelm views the political scene quite differently from his father. So the Crown Prince regards him with disapproval and suspicion. Last winter he once told somebody: 'See what luck I have with my son; he's the complete Guards officer.'

---

[1] Ernst von Stockmar. Private Secretary to Crown Princess Victoria.

And just before his journey to Spain he was talking with General Albedyll about Prince Wilhelm; the sorrow he was already causing him and how much more he would cause later on, and he became so upset that he burst into tears.

Prince Wilhelm is said to have a determined character; at any rate he is self-willed, devoid of all tenderness; an ardent soldier, anti-democratic, anti-English. He shares the Kaiser's view on everything and has the greatest admiration for the Chancellor.

Among his staff Bülow[1] represents the good element in politics, but Liebenau, the Court Chamberlain, is allied with Normann. [...]

Liebenau's strength, apart from his efficiency as Court Chamberlain, lies in the fearless energy with which he has carved out a place for himself not so much with his own Prince but with the Crown Prince. The Crown Prince has that in common with a sheet of paper that no idea, no matter how well expressed, will penetrate without pressure—and even then it soon fades. His attitude towards Stosch is also strongly intermingled with fear, the *metus reverentialis* of Roman law. I have heard from so many people that I am compelled to believe it, that Stosch used to fly out at his master and often treated him 'like a stupid boy'.

'The Crown Prince is afraid of so-and-so' is an expression often on the lips of the initiated, particularly when talking of Stosch, and Normann too, in which case they add, 'because he's poked his nose into so many things'.

Bülow, First Adjutant to Prince Wilhelm, has a very good influence on him and will go far. He possesses considerable prudence and tact as well as natural intelligence. The late State Secretary told me he thought him the cleverest of his six sons, which I well believe. The brother in Paris[2] shows great ease and skill in appropriating and using other people's ideas, but Captain Bülow has more originality and initiative.

Last winter, when Normann with great regret exchanged his post as Private Secretary to the Crown Prince for the office of Court Chamberlain, Albedyll wanted to push this Bülow into the vacant post, but he declined.

The Stosch-Normann bloc has a burning hatred for Albedyll. During the Christmas holidays or possibly early in the New Year, Liebenau told the Crown Prince it was Albedyll who set Prince

---

[1] Adolf von Bülow. Adjutant to Prince Wilhelm.

[2] Bernhard, Count von Bülow, Prince from 1905. Secretary in the Paris Embassy, 1878–84, in St Petersburg, 1884–8; Minister in Bucharest, 1888–94; Ambassador in Rome, 1894–7; State Secretary in the Foreign Ministry, 1897–1900; Chancellor of the German Reich and Prussian Minister-President, 1900–9.

Wilhelm against his parents. By touching on this sore point, he may have counted on a certain success, but he was disappointed. The Crown Prince was not convinced and the Crown Princess, next time Liebenau called to see her, sent a message to say she had nothing to discuss with him.

Albedyll holds a position of trust with the Crown Prince and Princess, for the moment. [...]

7 *January* 1884

Schweninger,[1] who had been spending a fortnight at Friedrichsruh, broke his journey here recently on his way to Munich. He regards his constant visits as necessary in order to keep a watch on the Chancellor's diet; the latter's inclination to transgress is reinforced by Princess Bismarck, who is never happier than when watching her husband eating one thing on top of another.

At the moment the Chancellor's health is good. He walks and rides better than he has for years, gets up at eight and weighs 196–8 pounds instead of his former 245 pounds.

The Chancellor's inner isolation has notably increased. He never used to drive out alone, but took with him either one of the family or else some guest who happened to be staying. Nowadays the guest, even people like Puttkamer or Orlov, is pushed off on to Bill or some other person 'because it is a strain on the Chancellor to talk during his ride'. Thus he becomes more and more cut off, his contact with contemporary ideas becomes less and less complete. In spite of this he still has the right feel for the When and the How in diplomatic affairs; the way he foresees events is positively amazing. Of domestic affairs, which I do not understand, I can only judge by the results. I think that here too, in the past few years, he has usually hit the nail on the head as regards the method, but his timing has often been less sound. The tobacco monopoly, crudely introduced into the 1881 election campaign, worked in the Opposition's favour, and the question of open voting in the Reichstag elections, which has just been mooted, will, it is generally believed, yield a similar result.[2]

The Chancellor works on the system of hurling an idea at the public to let it germinate and grow, either at once or later. I am certain his ideas will mould the future, but at the time they are released they often have a harmful effect, for which his life as a recluse is chiefly to blame. If the Chief had more contact with people he would be better able to gauge how and when to act.

[1] Dr Ernst Schweninger. Bismarck's physician from 1881.
[2] See Bismarck to Puttkamer, 3 December 1883. *Die gesammelten Werke*, vol. VI c, p. 288.

A few days ago Prince Bismarck said: 'A childless marriage makes it imperative for both man and wife to possess considerable resources if they are to avoid boredom. Actually a woman always needs something to play with, even by the time she's a grandmother.' By this of course he meant Princess Bismarck, whose only amusement now is her grandchildren. We were discussing over Christmas whether it would be practicable to transfer Rantzau, whose work for the Chancellor is below standard both in quality and quantity, to some minor post, such as Karlsruhe or Darmstadt. Herbert said: 'That would never do; mother would then have nothing left to give her pleasure.' And he is probably right. Meanwhile this last week, during which Rantzau has been away to attend his mother's funeral, seems to have afforded Bismarck's sons and Rottenburg an astonishing glimpse into his methods of work. It became particularly obvious to them that Rantzau was withholding from the Foreign Ministry a number of important pronouncements by the Chancellor, so as to make us, i.e. Hatzfeldt, look silly.

I received to-day a most affectionate reply from Rantzau[1] to my unavoidable letter of condolence, signed 'Your faithful friend R'. That is not a line I should care to pursue.

Count Waldersee has just called and told me all kinds of things, chiefly details I already knew about the Manteuffel[2] regime in Alsace-Lorraine. The fact that M. has employed only Alsace-Lorrainers on the railways—not even men subject to do military service—constitutes the danger that in the event of mobilization some of our own employees may take part in hindering the deployment of troops by disrupting communications.

A further danger arises from the retention of the French system of granting shooting rights in the state forests. Many of these forests are set on hills affording a clear view far and wide. The tenants are partly Alsatians, partly Parisians. The General Staff has already been informed of a so-called 'deer-stalking hut' on top of a hill where there was nothing to stalk but plenty to see.

Neither in the Forest Service nor elsewhere is an official willing to run the risk of punishing offences committed by Alsatians or French. Last summer a carter was crossing a square after the men on guard had piled arms, and drove straight over one of the piles. The sentry shouted at him, at which the carter nimbly dismounted, boxed the sentry's ears, and then drove off unmolested. This story was told in Kissingen by a Herr von Blumenthal of

[1] Letter of 6 January 1884 (*Correspondence*).
[2] Edwin, Baron von Manteuffel. Field-Marshal; Governor of Alsace-Lorraine, 1879–85.

the 15th Uhlans, and it was repeated to the Chancellor, who also happened to be there. The Chancellor officially requested Manteuffel to give an explanation and it turned out that the story was absolutely correct. But no further steps were taken.

There may be various reasons behind this lenient treatment of Manteuffel. Scholz, the Minister, once told me that in his opinion the Chancellor worked on the assumption that Manteuffel would at least be less of a thorn in the flesh at Strasbourg than in Berlin. I attach no importance to this motive. Nowadays Manteuffel is morally a spent force and consequently harmless. A successor, equal to his task and somewhat younger, would on the other hand easily entertain the idea of stepping into Bismarck's shoes. But in any case no suitable successor has been found, and it is far more probable that all the influences at court would combine to push some thoroughly inefficient princeling into the post. This view was recently asserted by the Chancellor, and one can readily understand that he has gradually come to have had enough of such intrigues. And finally he has been friendly with Manteuffel since 1870, when Bill was on his staff, and kept up good relations in the years immediately following when a core of resistance against the Chancellor had formed in the army, especially amongst the high-ranking officers.

The story just related recoiled on poor Blumenthal's head. When he realized that investigations were afoot to find out which officers from Alsace had been in Kissingen at the same time as the Chancellor, he denounced himself to his captain and as a result received from the commander a most crushing reprimand in front of his fellow-officers together with the information that his hitherto certain prospects of becoming regimental adjutant had now vanished.

9 *January* 1884

Yesterday the Crown Prince made quite a long speech to Hatzfeldt, the gist of which was that although his journey had passed off satisfactorily on the whole, he really would appreciate it if on future occasions the Chancellor and his entourage would see that he, the Crown Prince, was not chivvied around again so aimlessly. It was not his job to chase across the globe as Prince Bismarck's courier, which was after all what it amounted to in Spain when, without the slightest preliminary consultation or agreement, he suddenly received instructions to proceed to Rome. In the first moment of annoyance he had actually drafted a telegram of refusal but had then thought better of it. His one surprise in Rome was that no further instructions came telling him to go to Bucharest immediately. Nor had the Chancellor briefed him for his audience with the Pope, as if he meant to say, it doesn't really matter if you put your foot in it.

Hatzfeldt pointed out that the brevity of the message instructing him to proceed to Rome was explained by the fact that it had been drafted by His Majesty himself. The Chancellor did not think himself entitled even to transmit such commands to the Crown Prince over his signature. As regards the lack of instruction for the visit to the Pope, the Chancellor had thought it would place the Crown Prince in a pleasant position if it were made possible for him to state that he had no instructions for any detailed discussion of an official nature. In the Chancellor's view it would be a great mistake to involve the Crown Prince in negotiations which held out no prospect of success, etc. etc.

The main reason for the Crown Prince's annoyance has probably not been mentioned, namely the Press feud which has been prolonged as a result of the recent article 'Crown Prince and Chancellor',[1] and in which the Prince is naturally being involved. He is constantly harried by Normann and his cronies, who stop at nothing. They are, for example, spreading the rumour that Krüger, the police officer, who had to accompany the Crown Prince at the last minute because Count Münster[2] had received news in London of a socialist plot to assassinate him, had been sent simply as a spy. We have in fact seen not one single report by Krüger at the Foreign Ministry on any subject whatsoever.

If there is another way in which the Chancellor fails to understand society, or vice versa, it is on the question of courtesy, particularly towards royal persons. Hatzfeldt told me he was once invited to some official banquet at the Chancellor's and found him awaiting his guests in the ante-room, obviously in pain. On

[1] An apparently authentic report of the interview between the Crown Prince and the Pope appeared in the *Nationalzeitung*. The *Reichsfreund*, commenting on this report in an article entitled 'Crown Prince and Chancellor', said: 'The Crown Prince, for his communications to the Press, evidently selects newspapers which are not organs of the Chancellor or dependent on him.' The article concluded with the words: 'The more eagerly the Chancellor's friends strive to commit [...] the Crown Prince to the Chancellor's present policy [...], the more frequently does the Crown Prince utter pronouncements which make it clear to the German people that one may have a different conception of the tasks of the future from that held by the Conservatives and the Chancellor, and that above all the German heir to the throne refuses to be associated in any way with the Chancellor's present policy as a whole, or to accept moral responsibility for it in the eyes of the nation.' On 5 January an article in the semi-official *Norddeutsche Allgemeine Zeitung* attacked both the *Nationalzeitung* and the *Reichsfreund*.

[2] Georg Herbert, Count zu Münster. Ambassador in London, 1873–85, in Paris, 1885–1900.

Hatzfeldt's arrival the Prince stood up with some difficulty. Hatzfeldt scolded him for subjecting himself to the agony of standing up for such an old acquaintance as himself. Prince Bismarck explained to him in detail that he was a firm believer in politeness at all times and seasons, e.g. he would never dream of keeping his hat on even when visiting his sons. Hatzfeldt's comment was: 'Keeping his hat on isn't the trouble', and he is right. Bismarck, merely by removing his hat, cannot remedy the excessive harshness he sometimes displays towards his sons. As a result of this harsh behaviour Bill has withdrawn into an attitude of reserve towards his father, from which he hardly ever emerges.

It is the same with the Crown Prince. Prince Bismarck always tries to treat him with the greatest consideration and whenever they meet face to face the Crown Prince remains under his spell for a week. But when they are apart they get on less well. Bismarck wished to make clear his appreciation of the Crown Prince's royal status by issuing no instructions for the Italian visit himself, but asking H.M. to do it instead. But H.M. did it very brusquely, and for this the Crown Prince blamed the Chancellor, saying, 'My father only does what Bismarck wants.' The Chancellor would have thought it improper to send the Crown Prince an explanatory telegram to supplement the Kaiser's instructions, but the Crown Prince thought it inconsiderate that this was not done. The Chancellor enabled the Crown Prince to go on an exceptionally interesting trip, a triumphal journey through Spain and Italy, but now the Crown Prince thinks the Chancellor ought to be exceptionally grateful to *him*, instead of which he has treated him, the future Kaiser, inconsiderately. His democratic friends of course keep fanning the flames, and Professor Holtzendorff[1] was here recently to lend a hand.

Talking of courtesy reminds me of one of the Chancellor's *bons mots* which is a year or two old now. We were talking about the Minister Patow,[2] whose ineptitude he had long despised. Patow, then Administrative Head in Saxony, had just committed some blunder or other and one of those present called him an ox. 'That', said Prince Bismarck, 'seems to me rudeness to animals. I'm certain that when oxen want to insult each other they call each other "Patow".'

---

[1] Franz von Holtzendorff. Professor of jurisprudence in Munich and Berlin.
[2] Erasmus Robert, Baron von Patow. Former Prussian Finance Minister; Head of the Administration of the province of Saxony, 1873–81.

10 *January* 1884

Herbert Bismarck arrives here to-day from Friedrichsruh on his way to St Petersburg where he will spend a few months as interim Counsellor of Embassy; during this period Plessen[1] will be in Vienna.

Herbert has already a very sure grasp of his profession, works very hard and, being his father's son, will make numerous contacts at once; we shall certainly obtain a clearer picture of events from him than from the lazy and doddering Schweinitz.

Schweinitz, whose father was head of the Military Academy in Liegnitz, rose from quite humble circumstances by observing all his life the maxim 'not merely *being* but *seeming*', and while he was a bachelor he kept these two qualities more or less in balance. He endeavoured to keep up appearances and to learn at one and the same time. His career was materially helped by his outstanding stylistic gifts, because Prince Bismarck, more than he himself realizes, judges people by their style.

Schweinitz engineered his entry into the diplomatic service by a spectacular effort. He said—or rather wrote—to the Minister-President at that time, 1864 or 65, that he sought employment abroad. He hoped primarily that he would be of some use abroad, but he confessed he had also a private reason, namely the desire to escape certain attentions of which he was the object. He then hinted at his meaning somewhat more openly than I wish to do.

As Military Attaché in St Petersburg he was competent and industrious. His reports, rich in content and particularly elaborate in form, did at any rate show to advantage against the feeble efforts of old Redern.[2] In addition Schweinitz supported the Chancellor's policy, whereas Redern, who was dominated by an Austrian wife, came out one day in the Chancellery with the famous saying, 'Yes, gentlemen, your Herr von Bismarck may be a quick-witted orator in the Chamber, but he's no statesman.' That was just before the outbreak of the war against Austria.

Schweinitz was always on the winning side. He became head of the mission in Vienna and continued to distinguish himself by hard work and stylish prose. Whether he ever understood the relation between cause and effect in politics sufficiently clearly to enable him to act upon his own ideas and let other people do the

---

[1] Ludwig, Baron von Scheel-Plessen, from 1898 Count von Plessen-Cronstern. First Secretary in the Embassy in Constantinople from June 1883, in St Petersburg from August 1883, in London, 1884–8.

[2] Heinrich, Count von Redern. Prussian Minister in St Petersburg, 1863–7.

same, I rather doubt because of one stupendous blunder he made at one of the most dangerous moments in our history.

Bismarck has often told me how during the siege of Paris he asked himself the same question every single morning on waking: 'Will the day pass without intervention?' He expected it to take the form of a very polite telegram in which one or other of the Great Powers expressed the desire to earn the gratitude of mankind by helping to bring about an armistice. The other Powers would immediately have joined in. The fact that we stood to gain nothing from negotiations carried on by the European Powers, ruled as they were by envy, was not exactly difficult to perceive, but Schweinitz never saw it. One day—I think it was the second half of October—Beust[1] was uttering the usual formulae about friendly support for bringing about peace, halting the bloodshed, etc. when Schweinitz, instead of declining the overture in some form or another, had it telegraphed to Versailles and was actually under the impression that the offer might be quite well meant. Completely blind to the fearful implications of the matter. The replies he received from Versailles were some of the rudest things the Chancellor ever wrote.[2]

In the meantime the fall of Metz had improved our military position, while Beust's attention was diverted towards Russian policy in the Middle East (tearing up the Treaty of Paris),[3] so that we got off with just a scare; but it was not Schweinitz's fault that there was no mediation. By this act, Schweinitz passed the high-water mark in the Chancellor's estimation.

A few years later Schweinitz, now a married man, was transferred to St Petersburg at Andrássy's request. He never forgave Andrássy. From that day he went rapidly downhill. He had not the dignity or the resolution his position required. In vain did the Chancellor give him explicit messages for the Tsar and Gorchakov—Schweinitz never delivered them. Bismarck once said to him during an interview: 'When you're in front of the Tsar of Russia you always stand stiffly to attention, which is unsuited to your position.'

Since his marriage Schweinitz also grew disgustingly mean, despite his salary of 50,000 taler, never entertained, lost all his connexions, squabbled with his secretaries and did nothing. He

[1] Friedrich Ferdinand, Count von Beust. Austrian Chancellor, 1867–71; Ambassador in London, 1871–8, in Paris, 1878–82.

[2] Compare *Denkwürdigkeiten des Botschafters General v. Schweinitz*, 2 vols. (Berlin, 1927), vol. I, pp. 280–1; Bismarck, *Die gesammelten Werke*, vol. VI b, nos. 1892, 1902, pp. 564–5, 573–4.

[3] On 31 October 1870 Russia had seized on the favourable opportunity offered by the Franco-Prussian War to abrogate the Black Sea clauses of the Treaty of Paris of 1856. See *Grosse Politik*, vol. II, Chapter IX.

once had the impertinence to say to the Chief: 'If it weren't for hunting, nothing would force me out of the nursery.'

His style, always sententious, gradually became oracular, so that Busch calls him 'the mighty Magus of the north'.

This autumn he asked permission to come to Friedrichsruh, was invited, saw the Chief for a few moments in the evening and then wanted to take his departure next morning. The Chief said: 'But we've not talked politics at all so far.' 'Well, I've nothing to report', replied Schw., 'but my position in St Petersburg requires me to have been here.' 'Yes, but I've all kinds of things to tell you about my interview with Giers.'[1] 'I'm very sorry, but His Majesty has invited me to go hunting in the Göhrde forest, so I must leave.' 'In that case I must beg you to return.' Thus Schweinitz had to make a second trip to Friedrichsruh and the Press racked its brains to know what was going on.

Schweinitz had only one close friend in St Petersburg, the Military Attaché, General von Werder,[2] a man who despite his *Pour le Mérite* earned at Sadowa can be regarded as Prussian only with reservations; completely Russianized. The Chancellor once reproached the General because his letters to His Majesty contained so little of interest. The General replied: 'The things the Tsar tells me as a friend I cannot repeat, even to my King.' We may assume that the Chancellor did not fail to answer this incredible statement; at any rate Werder thoroughly detests him.

11 *January* 1884

Yesterday, at the dinner-party given by Lord Ampthill, Hatzfeldt at my suggestion explained to the Crown Prince why Krüger, the police officer, was detailed to accompany him on his journey. Now the Crown Prince is even prepared to suggest decorating Krüger.

During lunch to-day I was observing Herbert Bismarck's behaviour towards one or two Foreign Ministry officials he does not know particularly well. To my regret I could see yet again how he makes himself so generally disliked; the moment someone doesn't happen to suit him he becomes peevish and ill-tempered and starts a row with the waiter. This latter peculiarity, almost inexplicable in a well-bred person, was already evident when I toured Bavaria with him in autumn '74.

At yesterday's banquet the Crown Princess was still letting off

[1] See p. 66.
[2] Bernhard von Werder. Military Plenipotentiary in St Petersburg, 1869–86; Governor of Berlin, 1886–8; Ambassador in St Petersburg, 1892–5.

steam to Hatzfeldt about the journalists who accompanied her husband on his journey. 'Unfortunately I was not in Berlin when they left, otherwise they would only have gone with him over my dead body.' [...]

12 *January* 1884

The moves on the chess-board of domestic politics are sometimes amazing.

This autumn Scholz introduced in the Landtag a plan for the taxation of unearned income. The Chancellor had of course declared himself in agreement with the principle beforehand. Subsequently Rottenburg was instructed—just a week ago to-day—to propose secretly an amendment to the Conservatives whereby *foreign* bonds were to be taxed more heavily than German bonds. When Rott. in turn asked whether he should tell Scholz where the amendment originated, he received the reply, 'Yes.' The idea met with no sympathy; those deputies who wished to see the law on the statute book were afraid this amendment would lead to a defeat of the motion because the obligation to declare how many bonds of each category one owned would further increase the unpopularity of the motion and would certainly ensure a majority against it.

This was not all; it became known at the same time that Bleichröder was going around telling people publicly that the Chancellor had declared himself indifferent to the passing of the unearned-income-tax bill in its present form. Suspicious natures are now supposing that the Chancellor only proposed the amendment so as to be the more certain of wrecking the motion.

Rottenburg told everyone who asked him that Bleichröder's widely publicized version of what the Chancellor said is either a mistake or a lie. At the same time Rottenburg sent a report to Friedrichsruh, but received a reply stating that the Chancellor had discussed the tax on unearned income with Puttkamer and Lehndorff and may well have expressed the opinion to one or other of them that he did not agree with the proposal in every particular.

Rottenburg, horrified at this hint of a *volte-face*, wrote again to-day and said that Bleichröder's rumour had influenced the Landtag to such an extent that the motion would certainly be defeated unless Prince Bismarck published a statement in the *Norddeutsche Allgemeine Zeitung* that he was in agreement with the scheme as a whole.

We now await the reply. The change of front—if it exists—is explained simply by the fact that on purely financial questions, particularly those relating to the Stock Exchange, the Chancellor has no fixed opinion of his own, but bases it on the expositions of Scholz and Bleichröder. The two men are hardly ever in agreement and Prince Bismarck almost invariably sides with Scholz as for example over the currency question. Scholz advocated the gold standard and Bleichröder, like all bankers, advocated the bimetallic system because it creates more work for the international money exchanges.

In this income-tax business there is no doubt that Bleichröder wrote to the Chancellor drawing his attention to real or imagined failings in the motion, and probably himself proposed the more incisive amendment.

Puttkamer cannot bear Scholz, and Lehndorff is said to be a bosom friend of Bleichröder's. Thus any criticisms made by the Chancellor reach the public they were intended for.

14 *January* 1884

I have just driven Herbert Bismarck to the station, where he leaves for St Petersburg. It is now twenty-three years and about ten days since I set out from this very place.

Herbert was only twelve then and wore a little child's-size cuirassier's cap. On being asked, 'What do you want to be?' he replied, 'A soldier! Diplomats haven't enough to do.'

Things turned out differently. His father's endowments enabled Herbert to become a diplomat and no one can deny that he has made a really capable one.

Bleichröder called on Rottenburg two days ago and asked in great excitement how it was that *he*, Bleichröder, had been told nothing about H.B.'s transfer. According to his private information Herbert was being transferred because he had wanted to marry his mistress in London.

There's not a grain of truth in this story. Bleichröder hates Herbert because he knows he has no more implacable enemy. Herbert, like Bill, thinks Bleichröder compromises the Chancellor. I am curious to see how the struggle will end. When the Chancellor grows still older and his sons make it clear to him that they refuse to set foot in their father's house so long as there is a risk of meeting Bleichröder there, then indeed Bleichröder may be in danger. Rantzau and Princess Bismarck do not enter into it because they always hunt with the pack, she from narrow-mindedness, he from self-interest.

Prince Bismarck cultivates Bleichröder out of gratitude, habit and self-interest.

In 1866, just before war broke out, the Finance Minister Bodelschwingh[1] announced that he had no money left with which to pay the troops—already mobilized. Thus Bismarck saw looming ahead the day when he would have to send the men back home. Then Bleichröder suggested entering upon some operation with the Köln-Minden railway which would yield some ten million taler. Bismarck sent Bleichröder with this proposal to Heydt, who declared that he would be prepared, as Finance Minister, to carry out the transaction without parliamentary sanction. That very day Bodelschwingh was dismissed and Heydt appointed Finance Minister. He did indeed carry out this transaction and paid the troops up to the outbreak of war, and later received from the Kaiser in recognition of these services the order of the Black Eagle.

But most of the credit in the affair was no doubt Bleichröder's; it does indeed atone for many misdeeds.

In addition Bleichröder is useful to the Chancellor, much as the Jewish dealer who 'arranges' everything is to a Pomeranian squire.

Finally Bl. administers Prince Bismarck's estate very well, but then every banker does that for a Minister-President.

The harmful feature of their relationship is that Prince Bismarck cannot keep quiet about politics when talking to Bl. any more than Bl. can when talking to other people.

16 *January* 1884

[...] Concerning the tax on unearned income, the *Norddeutsche* did in fact carry the article yesterday in which the Chancellor comes out in support of the motion, though he adds there are one or two things he would have liked altered.

They say that in spite of this the motion will not receive a majority. [...]

Prince Friedrich Karl[2] leads a somewhat sordid existence, does nothing at all, and in the opinion of high-ranking officers no longer possesses the degree of intellect and nerves requisite for a high command in time of war.

Prince Friedrich Leopold, his son, also earns scant praise. Intimidated, hang-dog, malicious and spiteful.

Prince Karl, who died recently, had gradually become a sworn enemy of the Chancellor's for personal and political reasons.

Oil and water cannot mix. One day, many years ago now, the

---

[1] Karl von Bodelschwingh. Prussian Finance Minister, 1851–8, 1862–6.

[2] Friedrich Karl, Prince of Prussia. Son of Prince Karl, the brother of Friedrich Wilhelm IV and Wilhelm I; Commander of the 2nd Army during the war of 1870–1.

Prince drew the Minister-President's notice to the fact that he had affixed one of his decorations incorrectly. 'I will speak to my valet about it, Your Royal Highness', answered Bismarck, at which the Prince dropped the subject and ended the conversation.

But the Prince was wounded in his most sensitive spot when Bismarck introduced 'the institution of first-class and second-class Princes', whereby only the Crown Prince received the title of 'Imperial' Highness. I remember how miserable Keudell and Abeken[1] were during the latter part of the Versailles period because they no longer received invitations from His Royal Highness; his resentment embraced the entire Foreign Ministry.

Later there arose a further political reason for their antipathy. The Prince was always a Russophile and never forgave the Chancellor for putting German interests before Russian interests, and for reacting sharply at times to Gorchakov's diplomatic encroachments.

The Kaiserin recently expressed to her son her regret that in allowing journalists to travel with him he had given rise to so many incidents and misunderstandings. And Her Majesty cited, typically enough, an article in the *Germania*,[2] in which Normann —quite rightly I may say—was made responsible for the journalistic scandal. The Crown Prince, as usual, could think of no reply there and then, but next day he consulted Normann who argued thus: 'Don't allow yourself to be worried by the attacks of the clerical Conservatives. *You* pin your faith on the great liberal and national party; it is perfectly proper for it to be more accurately and more promptly informed than the other parties.' And so the Crown Prince went straight to his mother and justified himself on these lines. She has in fact no right to reproach him; she was a liberal for many years, and even now her sympathies are with the opposition—all from cowardice.

18 *January* 1884

The Chancellor has an unspeakable contempt for Gladstone's political gifts, particularly his diplomatic achievements. Münster in a personal letter to me on official business had, amongst other things, touched on Egypt and mentioned that the British public had a deep distrust of France's Egyptian policy but that Gladstone and Granville[3] refused to believe in the possibility of French

---

[1] Heinrich Abeken. *Vortragender Rat* in the Foreign Ministry, 1853–71.

[2] A daily paper, organ of the Centre Party.

[3] George Leveson-Gower, second Earl Granville. British Foreign Minister in the Gladstone Cabinet, 1880–5.

intrigues. The Chancellor, to whom parts of Münster's letter had been read,[1] remarked at this point: 'Palmerston[2] said of Gladstone: "If that man ever gets to the head of affairs he will drag his country through the mud and end in a madhouse." '[3]

The Chancellor, speaking of Gladstone, once told Prince Wilhelm: 'The silly chap can do nothing but make speeches and hew wood.' Many people in England think so too, but the Conservatives lack the courage to throw Gladstone out. They are afraid things would then go from bad to worse.

A few years ago Lord Dufferin[4] said to me in Varzin: 'All the measures proposed by the Radicals, in so far as they were put into effect, have had a beneficial effect; the man in the street is aware of this and so the Radicals will be assured of still further successes. We have no peasant class, only landed gentry and tenant farmers. When things go badly for the farmer he does not curse American imports and free trade, but his high rent. To us the idea that rents should cease to be paid seems as impossible as that the sun should cease to shine; even so the tenant-farmer system is probably on its way out.'

Dufferin's words revealed the deep discouragement of the moderate liberals. They feel powerless to check the course of events and have lost nearly all hope of directing it. [...]

25 January 1884

Yesterday I heard something I knew already, namely that Limburg-Stirum is going about complaining of the ill-treatment he had suffered at the hands of the Foreign Ministry. He thinks that but for our machinations he would be State Secretary to-day.

Stirum is a queer bird. Of good average ability in most respects, his one outstanding feature is his fickleness. Any one he happens to trust at the moment can twist him round his little finger. He picks his confidants according to time and circumstance, i.e. he takes as adviser someone he hopes will be of use at a given moment. His views change with each adviser.

I first started a regular correspondence with him during the Danish War.[5] He then kept up a lively correspondence with me so

---

[1] Münster's letter of 14 January. An extract summarized by Holstein above is in the files of the German Foreign Ministry. The original was not found among Holstein's papers.

[2] Henry John Temple, Viscount Palmerston. British Prime Minister, 1855–8, 1859–65.

[3] In English in the original.

[4] Frederick Blackwood, first Marquess of Dufferin. British Ambassador in St Petersburg, 1879–81, in Constantinople, 1881; at Cairo he helped reorganize the Egyptian administration, 1882–3; Governor-General of India, 1884–8; Ambassador in Rome, 1888–91, in Paris, 1891–6.

[5] See Memoirs, p. 26.

as to be able to show my letters to the Chief. Old Wagner,[1] under whom I was Secretary at that time, agreed to my conducting the correspondence, which saved him much trouble. But when I was sent to London I judged it wisest not to include any political news, whereupon Stirum dropped the correspondence with a promptitude which did at any rate bear witness to the sincerity of his egotism.

Between '64 and '76 we seldom met. Some time after Stirum had been made Minister in Weimar I took over his post at the Foreign Ministry on a temporary basis and was able to help him in the increasing difficulties into which he was plunged by his wife's excesses. She lived by the principle *où il y a de la gêne, il n'y a pas de plaisir*, and gave enemies and envious rivals every ground for believing the worst. The court at Weimar was scandalized, the Princesses were forbidden all contact with Countess Stirum, and the Kaiser himself told State Secretary Bülow that Stirum must be warned that his wife must be more careful. Finally poor Stirum, who did not wish to divorce the mother of his four children but seems to have behaved rather spinelessly towards her various admirers, hesitantly and reluctantly handed in his resignation, to the great delight of Bülow and Radowitz.

The Chancellor instructed Bülow to write a friendly note to Stirum and advise him to wait a little; somehow or other things might improve; he could perhaps take a holiday. These instructions were not carried out in the way intended; in the particular instruction to Stirum the emphasis was laid on the idea that the Chancellor would deplore Stirum's departure but could not overlook the consideration that Stirum himself must know best what he ought to do. The tone was not calculated to make Stirum withdraw his resignation.

The same evening that the instruction was prepared I called on Bismarck, turned the conversation on Stirum and elicited from the Chief one or two friendly remarks about him. I at once passed them on to Weimar, where they arrived at the same time as Bülow's hostile note and neutralized its effect. Stirum withdrew his resignation and after some time, when the hoped-for vacancy elsewhere failed to materialize, he went on indefinitely extended leave, or put himself on the reserve list—at all events he did not resign.

In the autumn of 1880 he was called upon to replace Hohenlohe[2]

[1] Foreign Ministry representative on Field-Marshal Wrangel's staff.
[2] Chlodwig, Prince zu Hohenlohe-Schillingsfürst. Ambassador in Paris, 1874–85; interim State Secretary in the Foreign Ministry, 1880; Governor of Alsace-Lorraine, 1885–94; Chancellor of the German Reich and Prussian Minister-President, 1894–1900.

during his six weeks' leave—Hohenlohe himself was only acting as interim State Secretary. The six weeks grew to eight months, for Hohenlohe caught typhus and went off altogether, i.e. he returned to Paris, while Hatzfeldt, for whom Hohenlohe was supposed to have been keeping the place warm, had not yet put his finances into satisfactory order and was in addition kept in Constantinople by the Montenegro question.[1]

Busch, already acting as interim Under State Secretary at the time, was deeply hurt by Stirum's appointment. The first thing he did was to go on leave when Stirum arrived. Consequently I was left with the task of propping up Stirum. I had also just taken over the direction of Balkan affairs after Radowitz's departure, so I had no easy task, for it was just at the time of the Montenegro crisis. Even so we cannot have done our work too badly, for when Stirum went to Friedrichsruh some months later, about Christmastime, the Chief let slip expressions which Stirum construed as meaning that he had prospects of becoming permanent State Secretary. In vain did I tell him time and time again: 'Now the Chief has offered Hatzfeldt the job, it is up to Hatzfeldt to accept or decline. Until the offer has been turned down the Chief can't dispose of the job elsewhere, even if he wanted to.' Stirum would not see this but insisted that the Chief was a power unto himself, and that he was not bound by his offer to Hatzfeldt.

Meanwhile things were gradually going less well with Stirum. The Ambassadors complained of his brusque manner towards them, and after Busch came back the written consultations with Friedrichsruh also appeared less satisfactory. When I asked Herbert, who was assisting his father, whether in view of Hatzfeldt's financial situation and Hatzfeldt's wife Stirum might not be more suitable as State Secretary, I was told that the Chancellor would first try his utmost to get Hatzfeldt.

When the Chancellor returned to Berlin Stirum's verbal consultations were a complete failure. The Chancellor grew irritable and made it known through Herbert that he was prepared to receive in audience individual officials from the Political Division as well. Which meant that Stirum was through. It was a good thing for him when Hatzfeldt finally did arrive.

Right up to his last day Stirum never realized where he stood with the Chancellor, in fact he was wondering whether, in the

[1] During the summer of 1880 the British Government attempted to gain the support of the European Powers for a policy of coercing Turkey into granting the territorial concessions to Montenegro and Greece which had been provided for by the Treaty of Berlin. The Montenegro problem was complicated by the Albanian tribes' opposition to the proposed territorial concessions.

event of Hatzfeldt's really becoming State Secretary, he himself ought to accept the post of Ambassador in Constantinople or not. We should all of us, including Hatzfeldt, have preferred to see this post occupied by Stirum rather than by the erratic Radowitz, but the Chief had already given the latter his promise in writing.

Radowitz had declared he would be unable to live on a mere Minister's salary. If he did not remain in Berlin, he would expect to be offered an Ambassadorship.

The Chief stood rather in awe of Radowitz's character and somewhat exaggerated the harm Radowitz might be able to do him if pushed to extremes. In the winter of 1880 he once said to me in Varzin when we were speaking of Radowitz: 'In certain circumstances he'll become a second Harry.'[1]

In short, Stirum came away empty-handed and was gradually worked up by Bucher into his present attitude of fury against the Foreign Ministry and especially against Hatzfeldt, Busch and myself. Stirum's association with Bucher is a pointer to Stirum's character. Before his period of interim duty here he had Bucher as his confidant; this association turned Stirum into a fanatical supporter of the *Kulturkampf*, whereas at its outset he had voted with the extreme Conservatives against the School Bill.[2] During his eight months' duty here Stirum sought advice from no one but me, after discovering on his first day that Bucher is too cowardly ever to proffer advice when there is any risk that the recipient may give him away if things go wrong. Stirum and I took our meals together and discussed things freely, though after Busch's return I kept in the background a little more to avoid putting him in a false position.

After Stirum left the Foreign Ministry and the risk of responsibility for his advice was removed, Bucher wormed his way back into Stirum's confidence and probably has him as completely under his thumb now as in the first phase of the *Kulturkampf*. Bucher, whom I do not wish to discuss in detail to-day, has doubtless retained a good deal from his revolutionary past, certainly the ability and skill in stirring people up. In his younger days he

[1] Harry, Count von Arnim-Suckow. Minister, then Ambassador in Paris, 1871–4. The Imperial Government instituted criminal proceedings against Arnim for refusing to return some documents he had appropriated from the archives of the Paris Embassy. He was first condemned to three months' imprisonment for crimes against public order and then to nine months' for abstracting official documents. After his conviction Arnim fled to Switzerland where he published the pamphlet *Pro Nihilo* (Zürich, 1876) in which he utilized his knowledge of official secrets to launch a virulent attack on Bismarck's policy. As a result he was condemned to five years' penal servitude for high treason, *lèse-majesté*, and criminal libel of the Chancellor.

[2] In March 1872 the Prussian Chamber of Deputies passed a law placing the supervision of all schools in the hands of the State.

worked on me, with some success. I still remember his telling me such tales about the character and conduct of Frau von Hansemann,[1] Kusserow's sister, whose home we both visited, that I stopped going and never doubted he would do the same. On the contrary, from that moment he began to visit there very frequently. The Hansemann and the Kusserow homes are his headquarters to this very day. I must have cramped his style.

Stirum fell an easy prey to his wiles. He is now firmly convinced that but for the intrigues of the Political Division he would be State Secretary.

25 *January* 1884

It is a pity the Chief's mistrust—he calls it pessimism—grows steadily greater.

On the question of the unearned-income-tax he disagreed with Scholz over the question of differential taxation. Prince Bismarck wanted a higher levy on foreign bonds, but Scholz was opposed to this, saying that in that case the motion was sure to be defeated. As a result of this the Chief said Scholz was probably consulting his own interests and doubtless held Russian bonds. I assume this comes from Bleichröder who for his part may well have proposed differential taxation precisely in order to wreck the motion.

The Chief's uncharitable way of judging people and his inability to attach himself to other human beings were partly inherited from his mother,[2] partly fostered by her. A pleasure-loving woman, she sent him when he was six or seven to a boarding-school, of whose severity he often speaks. He has brought his wife to such a pitch of bitterness against his mother by telling these stories, that Princess Bismarck often speaks of her with characteristic lack of restraint. Last winter during a meal, I forget in what connexion, she broke into imprecations rather like this: 'I hope the worthless creature is now being suitably tortured for it.' An old lady, Frau von Tiesenhausen from Courland, who was also at table, asked her: 'Whom do you mean, Princess?' 'His mother.' '*Whose* mother?' 'Bismarck's mother.' A silence fell, to be interrupted by the Chancellor's remark: 'Yes, my pessimism can be traced back to my mother and the training she gave me in my childhood.'

I mentioned just now his inability to make friends. The principle 'be to his faults a little blind, be to his virtues ever kind'[3] is the opposite pole to the Chief's attitude. Suspicion, boredom,

---

[1] Wife of Adolf von Hansemann, Berlin banker and head of the *Diskonto-Gesellschaft*.
[2] Wilhelmine von Bismarck, *née* Mencken.   [3] In English in the original.

neglect, are the acids which would corrode any attachment between him and other people. I have no personal grounds for saying this. I know he once stated in the presence of witnesses (Tiedemann[1] was one) that if things went really badly for him he would entrust his family to my care, for there was no one else he could rely on. Even so I am convinced from what I have seen happen to other people that he would by no means be proof against any kind of suspicion even against me, whether implanted by Bleichröder, Rantzau or anyone else.

Ce que j'en ai vu mourir de jeunes filles! How many close friendships have I seen born only to die, with how many people have I seen him on intimate terms when things were going badly. But it was the contact of the rolling stone. When Roon died in the Hôtel de Rome and the obsequies were held there, Princess Bismarck attended alone. Meanwhile her husband was with me smoking his after-dinner pipe.

And yet you cannot say he is intentionally a bad character. He kills his pleasure in other people by analysis and suspicion, by feeling annoyed when they contradict him, and by wearying of them. His relations with men must be judged by the principle that governs the sentimental liaison: the newer the better.

26 *January* 1884

I am curious to see what will become of discipline in the diplomatic service once the iron hand and the magic sway of Prince Bismarck are removed. Other countries already present some very pretty examples of independence.

I will not dwell on the French Ambassador in Constantinople, Fournier,[2] who wanted to help his Foreign Minister to succeed in spite of himself and so treated his instructions high-handedly. Republic means revolution.

But Russian diplomacy has an independent life, like mites in cheese. Last summer Lobanov[3] suggested to Count Kálnoky in Vienna that it would be very nice if the Tsar, on the occasion of his forthcoming trip to Poland, could also meet the Austrian Kaiser. Admittedly Lobanov put this forward as entirely his own idea. Kálnoky, doubtless supposing that Ambassadors do not usually have entirely independent ideas in matters of this kind,

[1] Christoph von Tiedemann. *Vortragender Rat* in the Prussian Ministry of State from 1876; Head of the newly constituted Reich Chancellery, 1878–81; Head of the Administration in Bromberg, 1881–9.
[2] Hugues Fournier. Ambassador in Constantinople, 1877–80.
[3] Prince Alexei Lobanov-Rostovski. Russian Ambassador in Vienna, 1882–94, in Berlin, January–March 1895; Foreign Minister, 1895–6.

asked if he might submit the plan to his Kaiser. Lobanov said yes. Now the Austrians no longer doubted that Lobanov had been instructed to make inquiries. Kaiser Franz Joseph told Kálnoky to say he very much looked forward to this meeting, but the Austrians were anxious lest there might be Nihilist attempts on Tsar Alexander's life in Austrian territory. Prince Bismarck, who had been consulted on this matter by telegram, advised that the meeting take place on Russian soil. And so the Austrian Kaiser followed up his original expression of pleasure by saying that he left the choice of place to Tsar Alexander, and that he himself was perfectly prepared to enter Russian territory. Then came the cold douche from St Petersburg: Giers told the Austrian Ambassador he had drawn his master's attention to the *Austrian proposal* for a meeting of the two Emperors, and the Tsar had replied that he would indeed be very glad to meet Kaiser Franz Joseph, but that he had at the moment no intention of visiting Poland. The Austrians were extremely annoyed, and a certain ill-feeling sprang up between the two Cabinets.[1]

Saburov behaved in a similar fashion here, but got his fingers burnt in the process.

He came here last summer with a very far-reaching project relating to the Eastern Question. The Cabinets in Berlin and in Vienna were both rather taken aback, particularly the latter.[2] However it gradually appeared that Saburov was pursuing his own policy independently of Giers, or rather in opposition to him. After Giers had been to Friedrichsruh and discussed things with the Chancellor,[3] Saburov called on Hatzfeldt to explain that Giers' conception of the problem differed from his own, perhaps because Giers was older and Saburov was younger and more spirited.[4] Saburov was in fact saying he had cheated, for, unlike Lobanov and his plans for a meeting of Emperors, he had not even put forward his suggestions as his own idea, and had therefore given rise to the belief, quite deliberately, that he spoke on behalf of his government. To avenge himself for this humiliation he went to St Petersburg and took advantage of Giers' absence to work against him; he also outlined his political programme to the Tsar during an audience lasting an hour and a half. But the Tsar said he would discuss the matter with Giers on his return.

[1] Compare Windelband, *Bismarck und die europäischen Grossmächte*, pp. 475–6.
[2] Compare *Grosse Politik*, vol. III, nos. 605–6; 608–10, pp. 292–5; 297–302.
[3] In November 1883. *Grosse Politik*, vol. III, nos. 611–12, pp. 302–7.
[4] Holstein has accurately summarized Hatzfeldt's memorandum of 2 December 1883 on Saburov's visit. According to Saburov, he and Giers differed only on how to pursue their common aim of an agreement with Germany. (From the Foreign Ministry files.)

Giers had an anxious time in Vienna, particularly during the first few days, when he learned of Saburov's stab in the back.[1] But this time he got off with no more than a scare; news came over the wires to-day from St Petersburg that his position is unshaken.[2] Saburov is to leave Berlin, perhaps for London, where he can't do much harm. But he came within a hair's breadth of ruining Giers; it was in exactly the same way, with letters to the Kaiser and personal interviews with him, that Arnim began. There is something about the status of Ambassadors—personal representatives of the sovereign—which makes them look down on other citizens, including the Foreign Minister, and which tends to expose them to delusions of grandeur. That is why the Chancellor has such a loathing for the whole ambassadorial system.

27 January 1884

Scholz called on Rottenburg yesterday morning to tell him that in his opinion the entire Cabinet could not cut Lasker's[3] obsequies; he said some of the Ministers would be going, otherwise the absence of the whole Cabinet would demonstrate even more clearly Lasker's political importance. Bötticher said much the same. Maybach, Friedberg and Lucius[4] were also inclined to attend.

Rottenburg said he felt certain the Chancellor would be opposed to the idea. When Rottenburg made inquiries in Friedrichsruh he received the reply: most certainly not. Otherwise the Cabinet would also be obliged when the situation arose to attend the funerals of men like Richter[5] and Bebel[6] (who, after all, also stand within the framework of the legal Opposition). The Chancellor also informed Rottenburg in writing that he was quite shattered to think that a section of the Cabinet were not clear where their

[1] Compare *Grosse Politik*, vol. III, no. 615, pp. 311–14.

[2] Schweinitz telegraphed from St Petersburg on 25 January that the Tsar's attitude towards the forthcoming negotiations (i.e. renewal of the League of the Three Emperors) and towards the personal question (of Giers' position) remained unchanged. (From the Foreign Ministry files.)

[3] Eduard Lasker. Member of the Prussian Chamber of Deputies, 1865–79; Member of the Reichstag, 1867–83. Until 1866 he belonged to the Progressives; then founder and leader of the left wing of the National Liberal Party; in 1880 he left the National Liberal Party and joined the so-called Secessionists in 1881. Died in New York on 5 January 1884. See below, p. 72.

[4] Robert Lucius, later Baron Lucius von Ballhausen. A leader of the Free Conservatives in the Reichstag, 1870–9; Prussian Minister for Agriculture, Crown Lands and Forestry, 1879–90.

[5] Eugen Richter. Member of the Reichstag from 1867; of the Prussian Chamber of Deputies from 1869; one of the leaders of the German Progressives and later of the German Radicals.

[6] August Bebel. Member of the Reichstag from 1867; leader of the Social Democrats.

duty lay, even *after* the Kaiser had expressed his wish that no officials should be present at Lasker's funeral. (I certainly share the Chancellor's opinion. The incident showed which way the wind is blowing.)

When I arrived at the office this morning and saw the telegram from Friedrichsruh, my first thought was: 'I wonder whether the Crown Prince will lend his support to some sort of demonstration?' If he did he would cause a breach between himself and the Chancellor which would not be healed for a long time, if at all; even if the Crown Prince merely sends a representative to the funeral the Chancellor will take it as a personal slight.

I called on Friedberg, who already knew the contents of the Friedrichsruh telegram, and said: 'Your Excellency, you must prevent the Crown Prince from taking any part at all in the obsequies. I desire this in the common interest, which would suffer from a rift between the Crown Prince and the Chancellor, but I am also thinking of your interest. You know you have enemies, even amongst the Chancellor's entourage. If given the chance, they will not fail to say that your influence on H.I.H., which is an established fact, was either not used at all in this case or was used against the Chancellor.'

Friedberg is a good-natured, intelligent man, more or less a Free Conservative in politics, but a man whose character is marred by an immense anxiety. He does not fear the Crown Prince much, but he fears all the more the Chancellor, the Crown Princess and Normann, a man whose politics are too leftist for his taste, but with whom he would not care to quarrel.

Friedberg, with the insight born of fear, at once appreciated all the possibilities I laid before him. He said it was impossible to go and see the Crown Prince solely on that account, but if the Prince should chance to ask him he would certainly advise as I suggested. The dear old gentleman was quite distraught, rather like a civilian who finds himself during manœuvres in the path of two cavalry charges. Which was the lesser danger? I think his awe of the Chancellor proved the stronger. But time will tell.

As soon as I had returned from seeing Friedberg I wrote to another person[1] explaining the position and the danger of a quarrel between Crown Prince and Chancellor and advising him, in case the Crown Prince had already taken the wrong decision, to urge the Prince to ask Friedberg's opinion.

---

[1] Probably Sommerfeld, with whom Holstein corresponded at this time and whom he used in order to bring delicate questions to the attention of the Crown Prince.

I had finished all this by a quarter to eleven, and now I can do nothing but wait. There is no doubt that Normann will try his utmost to persuade the Crown Prince to make some gesture of opposition. If the Crown Prince refrains, the credit will be Friedberg's.

I was given a very interesting explanation to-day of the attitude Normann has recently adopted towards or rather against the Crown Princess. (Dr M.)

The Crown Princess actually hates Germany and the Germans, and says so quite often. It is not usual in a mother to show a greater interest in her native land than in the land where her children's future lies. But her sentiments are those of an English-woman; she does not merely think English things are best, but in every conflict between English and German interests she stands up for England. For example there was a question some time ago of purchasing some very valuable paintings which had been in England until then. She told the expert who came to ask her opinion: 'Yes, they're beautiful paintings, but don't count on my assistance during the negotiations.' She has shown more than once that the transfer of works of art from England to Germany distresses her.

This anti-German attitude, which she actually delights in flaunting, is beginning to be exploited by Normann in order to damage her, above all in the eyes of the Crown Prince. The Prince has a strong national pride, in Germany rather than in Prussia, and Normann is trying to undermine the Crown Princess's influence by showing that she feels no affection for Germany. We may well be curious to see the outcome of this duel.

Lucius had written to the Chancellor to obtain his approval for the conferring of a decoration on one of his ministry officials, Schröder, who had in the past voted for Rickert.[1]

The Chancellor replied that he felt the fact of having voted for Rickert was too great a barrier to be passed over; and Herr Schröder could take comfort from the thought that when his party, the party of the rosy future, came to power, he could be certain of his reward.

In conclusion the Chancellor remarked, in reply to some observations of Lucius', that at any rate he agreed with him that Herr von Bennigsen possessed far more political acumen than all the Conservatives.

[1] Heinrich Rickert. National-Liberal, later Radical Member of the Prussian Chamber of Deputies from 1870; Member of the Reichstag from 1874. Opponent of Bismarck's protectionist economic policy.

Lucius has in his time behaved treacherously towards Bennigsen. The Chancellor wanted the Conservative parties to make a concession to the National-Liberals and to elect Bennigsen as President of one of the parliamentary bodies, either the Chamber of Deputies or the Reichstag. The Chancellor thereby hoped to pave the way for better relations between the three parties mentioned, since he would have much preferred to push through his economic proposals with the help of all three than merely a Conservative-clerical alliance.

I can still clearly remember the letters the Chancellor wrote or rather asked me to write at that time—the winter of '79–'80— to Stolberg,[1] Lucius and others. Both Stolberg and Lucius kept the Chancellor's letters secret and told their politician friends they had no instructions from the Chancellor (and in fact they were not official instructions). Lucius then canvassed and voted, not for Bennigsen but for Arnim Boitzenburg.[2] Stolberg and Lucius, like the other Ministers, were afraid the Chancellor might yet choose Bennigsen as Vice-President of the Cabinet or as Vice-Chancellor. These mean little Ministers felt that the dry, pedantic Stolberg would dominate the landscape less than Bennigsen might have done.

I have since broken off relations with Lucius. [...]

31 *January* 1884

I hear that the supplementary law on local taxes which is to be brought before the Landtag has provoked differences of opinion between the Chancellor and the various responsible Ministers.

The Chancellor wanted a lower assessment on forests. The question is still undecided.

He also demanded that the railways should pay local taxes not only in the districts where there are railway stations but also in those where the railway runs straight through. Maybach has refused this, and since every one handles him with kid gloves the matter has been dropped.

The Chancellor is particularly annoyed by the church-tax because under the present undoubtedly severe provisions his entire income is assessed several times, and thus he has to pay about 500 marks more than he thinks he ought. In consequence he

---

[1] Otto, Count zu Stolberg-Wernigerode. Vice-President of the Prussian Ministry of State, 1878–81; Lord High Chamberlain, 1884–94.

[2] Adolf, Count von Arnim-Boitzenburg. Member of the Reichstag, 1867–84; President of the Reichstag, 1879–80; from 1878 first Vice-President of the Prussian Upper House; President of the General Synod, 1879.

frightened Gossler[1] with a threat to leave the established church unless there were some alteration. Gossler might have given in, but Lucanus[2] explained that His Highness would still have to pay this year; as soon as the supplementary law on local taxation was passed it could be applied so as to alter the liability to pay the church-tax so that in future his income would be taxed only once. [...]

2 *February* 1884

Von Rauchhaupt, the Deputy,[3] who comes of a family with inherited insanity, recently told his constituents in Delitzsch a cock-and-bull story about a breach of courtesy shown by a French warship to the *Prinz Adalbert* on her way to Spain, and said we came within an ace of war.

The Crown Prince demanded that the Chancellor should publicly refute Rauchhaupt's statement. The Chancellor said he was opposed to this after Hohenlohe had made it clear that Rauchhaupt's story, though it had been mentioned in one or two newspapers, had scarcely attracted any notice. I may say the Crown Prince was less interested in correcting a factual error than in reprimanding Rauchhaupt. H.I.H. has already reached the stage of saying yesterday: 'Of course if Herr von R. were a Liberal they would have got at him long ago, but he happens to be a Conservative, so he takes precedence over me.'

At my suggestion Hatzfeldt to-day wrote the Chancellor a private letter drafted by me in which he said that if Rauchhaupt came off scot-free after drawing the public's attention to the person of His Imperial Highness by means of a set of fabrications, the Opposition would certainly exploit this fact. At the same time he offered to discuss with Puttkamer any verbal instructions the Chancellor might send. For a practising district head Rauchhaupt, as so often, has behaved incredibly badly, and I am surprised Puttkamer has not reprimanded him before. It is typical that the Crown Prince did not go direct to Puttkamer; the fact is he can't bear the man. During the last Landtag elections Puttkamer showed H.I.H. a secret circular calling on the [provincial] Presidents and district heads to exert all their influence to bring about a Conservative victory. The Crown Prince 'as a Liberal' was horrified and has treated Puttkamer like dirt ever since. Puttkamer might have realized that would happen, but his vanity

[1] Gustav von Gossler. Prussian Minister for Ecclesiastical Affairs, 1881–91.
[2] Hermann von Lucanus. Under State Secretary in the Ministry for Ecclesiastical Affairs.
[3] Leader of the Conservatives in the Prussian Chamber of Deputies.

could not bear the idea of depriving the Crown Prince of an example of his prose.

Puttkamer gave further proof of his deficient sense of occasion last year when he had an interview with the Kaiser about pensioning off Madai.[1] Instead of saying: 'The man's got apoplexy from gorging and guzzling', which would have settled the matter, he put it to His Majesty that Madai had reached the age at which one no longer possesses the capacity for work necessary for such a position as his! Since Madai is about sixteen years younger than H.M. the latter stated very curtly that Madai was to remain in office as long as he wished. Consequently we have as our Superintendent of Police a doddering old man; let us hope he goes after his jubilee in April.

At the recent Ambassadors' dinner given by the Crown Prince there were also one or two other privileged guests, protégés of Normann: Forckenbeck,[2] the former Finance Minister Hobrecht[3] (a nonentity), Friedberg and Scholz. Someone very familiar with affairs at court asked me how on earth Scholz managed to be in favour now. It occurred to me that he was the very man who a few days ago proposed that a section of the Cabinet (himself included, of course) should attend Lasker's funeral.

If only the Chancellor were not so violent over trifles. It is all the same to him whether his opponent is alive or dead, 'no peace to the wicked'[4] is his maxim. Indignant at the liberal obituary notices of Lasker, he ordered the *Norddeutsche* to say that Lasker, after making a mess of things in Germany, had then gone to America to be fêted by the friends of the American swine and trichinæ. These friends of the American swine and trichinæ now constitute the greater part of the mourners; for that reason alone the Prussian Council of Ministers would have been out of place at the obsequies.

The Chancellor was informed that the *Norddeutsche* refused to accept the article, and so, fortunately, it was never printed.

In all such affairs Rantzau eggs him on.

Normann is unfortunately restored to the Crown Princess's favour. She recently declared that his departure would be a triumph for Prince Bismarck.

Absolutely confidential.

---

[1] *Landrat*; Superintendent of Police in Frankfurt-am-Main and later in Berlin.

[2] Max von Forckenbeck. Member of the Prussian Chamber of Deputies from 1858, of the Reichstag from 1867; one of the founders of the Progressive Party, 1861, of the National Liberal Party, 1866; Mayor of Breslau, 1873, of Berlin, 1878.

[3] Arthur von Hobrecht. Prussian Finance Minister, 1878–?

[4] In English in the original.

As a result of his craze for building, the King of Bavaria has contracted a debt of five and a half million marks, and wishes to raise a loan. The Ultramontane Party in Bavaria is willing to raise the sum required—as a loan if he changes his Cabinet, and a far greater sum if he abdicates. A Jewish banker has actually offered him *French* money.

Werthern, our Minister, had corresponded direct with Rantzau on the matter. We heard of this two days ago by accident. Yesterday a laconic note from Rantzau arrived for Hatzfeldt: the Chancellor instructs you to ask the Kaiser whether he is prepared to lend his Bavarian fellow-monarch, who is in debt, a sum of about a million taler. Compared with the importance of the affair the letter was so arid and uninteresting that I had the impression at once that it was merely a feint, and that in fact the Chancellor did not care whether H.M. lent the money or not. I learnt in the course of the day that the Chancellor had already asked Bleichröder whether he would undertake the transaction, if necessary. Bleichröder had consented with delight, his eye on a Bavarian decoration, a Bavarian title or something of the kind.

Meanwhile to-day Hatzfeldt, instead of asking His Majesty for a definite reply at once, took my advice and merely explained to him the political significance of this aid. He finally asked and obtained His Maj.'s permission to discuss the financial side of the question with the Kaiser's Court Banker, Baron Cohn, with particular reference to the securities offered. Unfortunately Cohn is away. We sent a telegram to Dessau. The whole thing may fall through because of his absence. I should be very sorry, because there is a very great difference between having the Kaiser as creditor (backed by a Jew, for all I care), and having Bleichröder, backed by Bismarck. I should particularly deplore the second combination for the Chancellor's sake: naturally people would say he had put his banker on to a good thing; while he himself would think, 'Well, I'm doing nothing wrong.' But it is not just a question of actions but of appearances too. Well, I expect it will be decided to-morrow.

I was amused to hear that the Kaiser, on being asked by Hatzfeldt whether he might perhaps discuss this highly confidential matter with Cohn, first looked thoughtful and then replied: 'Hm, yes, he's a thorough Jew, of course, but he looks after my affairs very well.' H.M. is a strong anti-Semite. [...]

I noted here some days ago that the Crown Prince wished Rauchhaupt to be corrected, i.e. reprimanded because of his speech. The Chancellor sent a detailed reply to the Prince. He said he could not allow a *factual* refutation because it was undesirable to revive the incident which had in the meantime already been forgotten. Administering a *personal* reproof to *Landrat* von Rauchhaupt was the province not of the Minister-President but of the responsible Minister. The Prussian Minister-President could only ask his colleagues to do something in the form of a request, a tedious process which nowadays, in view of his age and his state of health, he turned to only in emergencies, or for matters of primary importance like parliamentary bills. Since he no longer felt equal to such exertions he intended, the moment he arrived in Berlin, to ask H.M.'s permission to restrict himself in future to national affairs, particularly the direction of foreign policy, and to retire from his position as Prussian Minister-President. If His Imperial Highness permitted, he would pass on his letter to be dealt with by the responsible Minister. The Crown Prince consented by telegram, so H.I.H.'s letter was sent to Puttkamer with the request that he should regard it as addressed to himself.

Puttkamer is not particularly pleased, first because he is to admonish his faithful Rauchhaupt, and secondly because H.I.H. originally passed him over. And the Chancellor's letter to Puttkamer was very laconic. Puttkamer has already reached the stage of 'boring' the Chancellor.

During the past year the Chancellor has often spoken of this plan of restricting himself to the Reich and to foreign policy. There are two sides to this. He will certainly lose some influence, but he will make it extraordinarily hard for the Crown Prince to oust him when he comes to power; the majority even of the democrats want him to retain control over *foreign* policy. But so long as Bismarck still remains in office the next Kaiser will have to be rather wary in his choice of the people he appoints as Prussian Ministers to work alongside him. I think the Forckenbeck type would be impossible, but not men like Bennigsen.

Saburov announced to-day very modestly that he had been recalled, and asked whether Orlov would be *persona grata*. Of course. The affair had been settled ever since Giers' visit to Friedrichsruh.[1] The Kaiser was not over-enthusiastic about Orlov, to whom he attributes strong Polish sympathies, but the Chancellor smoothed him down. This was all done by means of direct correspondence between Kaiser and Chancellor.

Orlov is a man of sterling character, rendered sickly and driven further into himself as a result of severe wounds. He is also very

---

[1] See p. 44, note 2.

much of a Russian. Whether he too, like almost all Russians, ties a permanent understanding with Germany to the condition that we should allow them to hack their pound of flesh from Austria, remains to be seen. I rather think so.

8 *February* 1884

So Baron Cohn was with Hatzfeldt this morning. When Hatzfeldt informed him he was about to discuss on His Majesty's behalf matters for which he must beg the utmost secrecy, Cohn interrupted him: 'His Majesty never said *that*! He didn't mention secrecy! On the contrary, I know that the phrase "As discreet as Cohn" is proverbial with him.' Hatzfeldt laughed as he told me this, for H.M. had been far from showing a blind faith in Cohn yesterday.

Cohn is itching to arrange this Bavarian loan. He already holds a Bavarian Grand Cross and thinks it his duty to do something for it. Needless to say some secret hope lurks in the background, but the important thing is that he gets the Kaiser to arrange the matter, so that Bleichröder cannot drag the King of Bavaria through the mud as he once dragged poor Hatzfeldt.

I am delighted with the way Hatzfeldt's character comes out of this affair. He knows it will turn Bleichröder into friend or foe, but he goes calmly on his way even though Bleichröder, as a 'crony' of the Chancellor's, is a force not to be despised. I have always liked this gipsy independence shown by Hatzfeldt despite his poverty. It was no doubt the reason why Bleichröder, with his shrewd knowledge of human nature, for a long time did his utmost to push Radowitz into the post of State Secretary. I heard from a source I regard as perfectly reliable that Frau von Radowitz had financial connexions with Bleichröder's partner, Schwabach.[1] But I will write of the relations between Hatzfeldt and Bleichröder another time, perhaps.

The Bavarian affair will not now be decided before to-morrow.

The Chancellor was asked yesterday whether he would see Saburov once more before he left; he replied to-day that he would.[2]

This civility is likely to do more harm than good. Giers, who fears and hates Saburov, and the Kaiser, who despises and distrusts him, will probably be surprised or annoyed at this favour, but

---

[1] Julius Schwabach. Co-director of the banking firm of G. Bleichröder.

[2] Bismarck sent Schweinitz a telegram the same day: 'Herr von Saburov has expressed the wish to take his leave of me before his departure. So long as he is Tsar Alexander's Ambassador I cannot refuse, but I know enough about his shameful conduct not to talk business with him.' Quoted in Windelband, *Bismarck und die europäischen Grossmächte*, p. 535.

certainly not pleased. In addition the Chancellor is running the risk of being misrepresented—a risk he is perfectly well aware of, for everybody knows what a liar Saburov is.

But here we come up against another of Bismarck's peculiarities; he refuses to be influenced and *will never allow his actions to be anticipated*. His incomprehensible decisions—and they are many —can always be explained by one or other of these motives. It is the same with his style; a liking for unusual expressions. But it is only fair to say that this pettiness becomes apparent in minor matters, particularly the internal running of the Ministry. In important matters there has probably never been anyone so self-controlled and objective as Bismarck. Let us hope he remains so until the end.

9 *February* 1884

To-day a person who is a close acquaintance of mine and also of Normann's made a determined attempt to bring us together, a thing I had hitherto avoided. He pointed out that the acquaintance would be of use to me professionally because N. was the shrewdest and best-informed man in the Crown Prince's entourage, and despite all the stories told about him he was a decent fellow who had spoken most kindly and appreciatively of me; of my unselfishness, of the forthrightness I showed in my dealings with friend or foe, though admittedly I went too far and regarded people as absolutely black or absolutely white, etc. etc.

This meant: take a closer look at me and you'll find I am not so bad as people say.

I simply replied that Normann was an enemy of the Chief's, or at least (since the go-between disputed the fact) he was commonly regarded as such. Once in my life I had acted as buffer between two enemies and that was quite enough for me, so I judged it better not to embark on an acquaintance with Herr von N.

I was strengthened in this decision by my knowledge that Normann was also a determined enemy of Hatzfeldt's. No doubt the post of State Secretary in the Foreign Ministry in the coming Stosch-Forckenbeck Ministry has already been allocated to someone else. [...]

11 *February* 1884

Absolutely secret, as usual.

After conferring with Schleinitz and the Court Banker, Cohn, the Kaiser had told Hatzfeldt yesterday that though he was not prepared to advance the sum of three million marks direct to the

King of Bavaria he would furnish the lender with a guarantee.

The affair seemed settled. Cohn would have procured the money and the Kaiser would have remained behind the scenes. The King of Bavaria's Privy Councillor had already told Hatzfeldt he preferred it to appear that the creditor was a private individual.

Hatzfeldt reported all this to Friedrichsruh, where the Privy Councillor had gone in the meantime, under an assumed name. This morning a note from Rantzau arrived, saying the Chancellor, from the account the Privy Councillor had given him of the circumstances, thought it advisable for the King of Bavaria to be made to manage his income better before help were given. And so it was best for the Privy Councillor to return empty-handed for the moment. Hatzfeldt was to inform the Kaiser of this, but if the Privy Councillor reported to Hatzfeldt on the way home he should not be told that the Kaiser had been prepared to furnish a guarantee.[1]

In other words, the Chancellor had not expected that Hatzfeldt would get so far with the Kaiser and is now unwilling to let Hatzfeldt, and to a lesser extent Schleinitz and Cohn, take the credit. And so the whole affair is being dropped or so it seems, for I suspect that within a very short time, perhaps even to-day or to-morrow, the Chancellor will ask Bleichröder to arrange the whole thing in closest secrecy.

Hatzfeldt was beside himself: 'Where do I stand with the Kaiser now? First I oblige him to hold lengthy consultations with Schleinitz, Cohn and myself, and to-day, after he has reached a decision in accordance with what I supposed were the Chancellor's wishes, I am to tell him it was nothing but an academic discussion, and that it's all different now. The Kaiser will throw me out on my neck the next time I go to him with a proposal.'

I advised him simply to show Rantzau's letter to H.M.—which he had not been forbidden to do—and then to leave the Kaiser and the Chancellor to compose their differences, which should not take them long.

But I find this incident a disturbing sign; and by no means the first that the Chancellor is jealous of Hatzfeldt's standing with the Kaiser and the Crown Prince. Last autumn when the Crown Prince expressed a wish for Hatzfeldt to accompany him to Spain, there was this same feeling, which was noticeable at once

[1] The accuracy of Holstein's account of this incident is borne out by the Foreign Ministry files. There is also in the files an instruction issued by Bismarck to the Finance Department of the Foreign Ministry to pay out the sum of one million marks to the Bavarian Privy Councillor Pfister. Pfister's receipt is dated 11 February. It is not possible to determine whether this sum was a loan.

in the rudeness and heightened irritability of all instructions issuing from Friedrichsruh. And yet how useful Hatzfeldt would have been on the trip. I will pass over the main reason and merely point out that Normann's newly increased influence comes from his having been entirely surrounded by nonentities, Solms included—a circumstance which the Chancellor may yet feel to his cost.

I do not think the idea that he might obtain a Bavarian Grand Cross or a Bavarian title for Bleichröder was of any great importance in the Chancellor's decision. He merely wished to prevent any one else from placing the King of Bavaria under an obligation and was disagreeably surprised to find that Hatzfeldt's approaches to the Kaiser and Schleinitz had not failed.

At the beginning of Bismarck's career as a Minister this jealousy was not without foundation. I remember how round about 1863 even a man like Itzenplitz[1] thought quite seriously that it was his vocation to supplant Bismarck in the control of Prussian policy. But the longer Bismarck remained Minister, the further did the idea of replacing him during his lifetime recede from the minds of officials and diplomats. So far as I know Arnim was the last to entertain it.

But Bismarck's mistrust grew in inverse ratio to the danger of being supplanted. To-day his mistrust is livelier and more morbid than ever and is increased not only by solitude and age but by the influence of Rantzau, who detests Hatzfeldt in particular more than anyone else he knows.

I imagine that if ever Hatzfeldt leaves this position in disgust or is obliged to give it up for financial reasons (here he earns 50,000 marks, as Ambassador he would earn 120,000), the Chancellor will choose some insignificant person—Busch, Stirum, Le Maistre.[2] This policy of alternating between the intelligent and the less intelligent has been followed in the appointment of our Ambassadors in Paris. Between Goltz[3] and Arnim, who admittedly both tried to oust Bismarck, one openly, the other secretly, we had Werther, wooden and completely devoid of talent, of whom Bismarck said when appointing him: 'Provided an Ambassador can obey that's all he needs.' Hohenlohe is a good Ambassador, but as a Bavarian he is excluded from becoming a rival for the position of Chancellor even if he aspired to it, which he does not.

[1] Heinrich, Count von Itzenplitz. Prussian Minister of Trade, 1862–73.
[2] Rudolf Le Maistre. Minister in Rio de Janeiro, 1879–85, in Darmstadt, 1886–7.
[3] Robert, Count von der Goltz. Prussian Minister, then Ambassador in Paris, 1863–9.

I should be sincerely sorry if Hatzfeldt, in whom the Chancellor has a thoroughly reliable, highly talented assistant, and who is prevented by indolence and his ignorance of domestic affairs from being a dangerous rival, were to disappear from the scene. But these are trifling considerations in comparison with the chief danger which emerges from the Chancellor's increasing intractability. Would the Crown Prince ever put up with such treatment as was shown the Kaiser over the Bavarian loan?

The Chancellor's intractability derives not merely from his mistrust but also from his lust for battle. 'You see', he once told somebody, 'I'm sometimes spoiling for a fight, and if I've nothing else to hand at that precise moment, I pick a quarrel with a tree and have it cut down.'

This love of a fight is often apparent in his day-to-day conduct of business. He actually looks for trouble—though, one must always add, only when this involves no danger to the Reich.

Last spring I was talking with him about Frederick the Great, whom he does not really like, and whom he reproaches with having often risked everything, e.g. at Hochkirch, out of vanity, ostentation and self-will. The Great Elector is Bismarck's hero.

I pointed out in Frederick the Great's favour the great devotion to duty he showed right up to the end, by undertaking long and tedious journeys every year throughout the realm when he was a childless old man. 'Yes, but his country, the Prussian State which he had made, *that* was his child', exclaimed Bismarck with flashing eyes and a sudden burst of animation which showed me he attributed this feeling to Frederick the Great because of his own parallel case. And it cannot be denied that in serious matters the Reich always comes first. Like an old huntsman he avoids all the jumps that are unnecessary. But he sometimes rides through puddles just for fun, splashing everything, including himself, only to change his coat (i.e. change his friend) later on.

12 *February* 1884

So I was right after all. Bleichröder called on Hatzfeldt yesterday evening and informed him that the Chancellor had sent Rottenburg to ask whether Bleichröder would arrange the Bavarian loan. But it would have to be done with the utmost speed and secrecy. He, Bleichröder, had told Rottenburg he was prepared to do this and Prince Bismarck had immediately conveyed to him his most sincere thanks. Bl. added that there was nothing to be gained by doing this, he was only doing it to be of use to the

Chancellor. When Hatzfeldt observed that surely all kinds of other distinctions would result from it, Bl. replied: 'What's the King of Bavaria got that he could give me?' In other words Bl., always conspicuous for his lack of modesty, would like tokens of recognition from both sides. So far as the Prussian side is concerned he might well be disappointed, for the Chancellor is loath to suggest any reward for his services. In any case Bl.'s attitude is just a hollow pretence. I learned from Rottenburg when I questioned him, that Bleichröder, speechless with delight, embraced him the moment he revealed his mission.

The Bavarian Privy Councillor also took his leave of Hatzfeldt just before his departure and told him he had come to an agreement with Bleichröder and was certainly not returning 'empty-handed', but was taking with him Bleichröder's written statement that he would arrange the matter.

I deplore the whole incident because it adds yet a few more important individuals to the number of those who have an exaggerated picture of the relations between Bismarck and Bleichröder. All this would probably never have happened if one of Bismarck's sons had been at Friedrichsruh instead of Rantzau. But Rantzau, in his blind hatred of Hatzfeldt and perhaps—who knows?—in the hope of a Bavarian Grand Cross, presumably pushed Bismarck the wrong way.

Meantime Herbert, as I gather from a letter of his to-day,[1] is taking great pains to impress on the new Ambassador, Orlov, and the Military Attaché, Prince Dolgoruki, that they, unlike Saburov, are not to stoop to have any dealings with that 'dirty Jew' Bleichröder. Herbert says that Dolgoruki, who has been here for two years already and knows the lie of the land, first looked astonished and then took on an expression of smug contempt. I can believe that.

I remember Eberhard Stolberg[2] saying thirteen years ago at Versailles: 'If it were humanly possible to blacken Bismarck's reputation, Bleichröder would manage it.'

I heard a few days ago that Bleichröder wants to get his youngest son into the diplomatic service. He will not succeed.

14 February 1884

General Mischke, at the same time the Crown Prince's comrade and whipping-boy, has for many years led an idle, carefree exis-

---

[1] Letter of 8 February 1884 (*Correspondence*).

[2] Eberhard, Count zu Stolberg-Wernigerode. From 1853 Member, from 1857 President of the Prussian Upper House; Head of the Administration of Silesia, 1869–72.

tence in his service, first as adjutant, then as Chief of the Army Inspectorate. During the autumn manœuvres in Homburg Mischke had finally convinced the Crown Prince of a fact the rest of the army knew already, namely that the so-called Chief of his Staff was without knowledge or ability. One day when Mischke, in the presence of foreign princes, had misinformed and misled the Crown Prince, H.I.H. reprimanded him, but took it all back later in a *tête-à-tête* with Mischke who drove back with him in his carriage. Since this incident the authorities concerned, in particular Albedyll, had suggested to the Crown Prince that Mischke was perhaps better suited as a Commandant than as a Chief of Staff; recently this idea acquired a concrete form when Loucadou's resignation left vacant the Commandantship at Frankfurt-am-Main.

So Mischke, who had also done his best to bungle things during the Spanish journey and had been malingering ever since, was informed by H.I.H. a few days ago that there was the prospect of the most attractive sinecure in the world for him. Mischke, at first speechless with amazement, then protested most bitterly. He, the Crown Prince's closest friend, had counted on ending his days at his side and was now expected to bow before an intrigue mounted by General Albedyll. The Crown Prince, he said, was surrounded by intriguers, which was precisely the reason why they wished to send away his best friend (Mischke of course). When the Crown Prince remarked that there was nothing to prevent him from recalling General Mischke after a certain time, the General blocked his ears and shouted: 'You've fallen for a pack of lies, all put about by Albedyll and the other intriguers. They want to get rid of me just because I tell you the truth.' Finally he threatened to resign, and refused to go to Frankfurt. The Prince pointed out to the General—who spent a considerable part of last year in Pegli and Montreux—how good for his nerves and general health a period of rest would be. 'Stuff and nonsense!' said Mischke, 'my nerves are as good as those of the rest of the General Staff put together.' But the attack was repulsed. The Crown Prince, no doubt greatly to Mischke's astonishment, held his ground, so that it is certain Mischke will leave his present post; whether he will go to Frankfurt or, in view of his independent means, will stay in Berlin remains to be seen. Normann loses in him his best ally and collaborator. Mischke has no right to talk of intrigues, for he helped Normann in *his* intrigues more than the outside world was aware, because his status as intimate friend gave him an influence that must not be under-estimated, together with the right to touch on every subject he pleased. He was of course also an enemy of the nobility. [...]

16 *February* 1884

Difference of opinion between the Chancellor and Gossler over the *Emeritierungsverordnung* (clergymen's pension scheme). Gossler wants the burden to be borne by the parish, Prince Bismarck wants to transfer it to the State, and in his capacity of Minister-President he voted that way. Gossler was extremely annoyed and said: 'It would almost appear that Prince Bismarck consults his purse before voting', and is toying with the idea of handing in his resignation.

It cannot be denied that in matters like the duty on wood, spirits etc. the Chancellor does take into account his own interests, and this fact has been used against him before now. But in every one of these questions his interests are identical with those of a great mass of citizens, so he is by no means taking up the cudgels just for himself.

We had recently a typical little instance of the Chancellor's refusal to allow his actions to be influenced or guessed in advance. Two versions of a document were submitted to the Chancellor for selection. The head of the department concerned (not the Foreign Ministry) said in a covering note that text A appeared adequate except for one sentence, which might with advantage be replaced by the version in text B.

The Chief replied that text B suited his purpose, except for the sentence mentioned in the covering note, which was more suitably rendered in text A.

Just the exact opposite. I saw both versions and venture to disagree with the Chief's opinion. But this is just one of his innocent pleasures; the security of the Reich is not affected by the matter in question.

These little foibles would dwindle to nothing if they could be set against his great qualities. I cannot do this, since his greatest achievements lie in the domain of current policy, which I prefer not to speak of here. But I do want to mention the most recent move against the Curia, because I think it superb: the Pope has been informed that if, by the time the Law of Dispensation[1] has

---

[1] On 19 May 1880 Bismarck had brought before the Landtag a bill empowering the Cabinet, with royal consent, to fix the principles whereby the Minister for Ecclesiastical Affairs would in future be permitted to grant 'dispensation' from the provisions of the law of 11 May 1873 relating to the training and appointing of the clergy. The bill was eventually passed with the additional provision that the new law should be periodically renewed.

expired,[1] Ledochowski[2] and Melchers[3] have not been obliged to give up their archbishoprics, the government will not ask the Landtag to renew the law, because the representatives can hardly be expected to confer powers which could conceivably be used to recall these same archbishops. It is now for the Pope to decide.[4]

At the Crown Prince's court *l'affaire* Mischke is still producing repercussions. Mischke and Normann stirred up Friedberg to make representations to the Crown Prince against the banishment of his 'friend'. In particular Friedberg advised him to discuss the matter with Normann. This the Crown Prince has so far failed to do.

Mischke played his cards very clumsily, particularly when in the first flush of anger he told the Crown Prince, among other things, that the plan for his removal emanated not from the Prince, who had always been kind to him, but from the Princess. Since then the General has pursued different tactics; he has had recourse to weeping and even told the Princess with tears in his eyes that he would die if he had to leave the Prince. In short, he is still hanging on; it would be a pity if he remained.

18 *February* 1884

Bleichröder is spreading 'in the strictest confidence' that Orlov, the new Russian Ambassador, has sent to inquire whether he would lend him a million marks or francs.

Anything is possible, but at first glance this story seems improbable, for Orlov is a very rich man and I have never heard of his being extravagant.

The first question to be considered is whether Bleichröder is lying, either from boastfulness or a wish to compromise Orlov. Saburov's going was a great loss to Bleichröder because the two men were always together; probably Bl. is already wondering how to gain a hold over Orlov.[5]

[1] The law was due to expire on 1 April 1884.
[2] Miecislaw, Count Ledochowski. Cardinal-Archbishop of Posen and Gnesen, leader of the Polish nationalists during the *Kulturkampf*; on account of his defiance of the May Laws he was condemned in 1874 to two years' imprisonment and deprived of his office; in 1876 he was released and went to Rome. He did not renounce his archbishopric until 1885.
[3] Paulus Melchers. Archbishop of Cologne from 1866. During the *Kulturkampf* he was condemned to six months' imprisonment in 1874, and in 1876 was deposed by the Court for Ecclesiastical Affairs. He renounced his archbishopric in 1885.
[4] Dispatch to Schlözer of 10 February. Schlözer communicated its contents to the Pope on 28 February, but found him adamant. The Pope declared that he refused to deal with this personnel question until his wishes with regard to the seminaries were fulfilled. (From the Foreign Ministry files.)
[5] See also Herbert von Bismarck's letter of 3 March 1884 (*Correspondence*). In a letter of 22 April 1884 Hohenlohe informed Holstein that Count Henckel-Donnersmarck had told him Prince Orlov's agents had inquired whether he was prepared to advance the Prince a loan of

A few weeks ago, the subject came up during a session of the Council of Ministers that Bleichröder had invited the entire Cabinet to dinner. Puttkamer had already declined without giving any reason, but Lucius said he intended to go.

Friedberg then said that though he regretted it he felt obliged to warn people off Bleichröder for the moment, because a discreditable case against him was pending. Friedberg told it as follows:

Bleichröder had had an affair with a married woman who got a divorce on account of him and who gradually became more of an expense than he liked. He turned a deaf ear to her claims, and she threatened him with a public scandal. So early one morning she was hauled out of bed by a police inspector, and transported to Copenhagen where she was set down and informed that unless she kept quiet all kinds of other unpleasant things would happen to her.

The woman raised a storm of protest, lodged a complaint against the police—which I can well understand—and brought an action against Bleichröder for breach of his promise to pay her 25,000 talers.

The complaint against the police was suppressed, and Bleichröder swore on oath that he had never made the woman any promise.

She then accused him of perjury. According to her statement, which is said to have been given an impressive appearance of plausibility by witnesses and a wealth of evidence, Bl. had not promised her the sum in person, but through an intermediary.

The Department of Public Prosecutions pleaded some technical reason for refusing to concern itself in the affair. (Friedberg and Bl. are distantly related.) The plaintiff, who incidentally is said

two million francs. Holstein replied on 2 May that he thought the best course would be for Count Henckel to deal with the matter through a German bank, 'the worst course would be to deal with Frenchmen. Midway between these two extremes stands Bleichröder.' Holstein advised Hohenlohe to write to Bismarck to this effect. Hohenlohe replied on 8 May: 'On receipt of your letter I have spoken to Henckel and informed him of its contents. He was surprised "that they took the matter so seriously in Berlin", was not particularly anxious to give proof of his patriotism in hard cash, but declared himself willing to act as go-between to conclude the loan and then to pass it on to a bank to be indicated to him. I told the Chancellor all this to-day in a letter I wrote myself.' Bismarck's reply to Hohenlohe of 11 May, in the files of the Paris Embassy, reads: 'I am most obliged to you for your communication of the eighth. I do indeed earnestly desire Count Henckel to deal with the matter. Before doing so I should like him to get in touch with the President of the *Seehandlung* bank, *Wirklicher Geheimer Oberregierungsrat* Rötger; he is well-informed and discreet; he will inform Count Henckel on the solidity of the securities and the further course of his negotiations as regards method and persons. In the present political situation I regard the matter as sufficiently important to justify, if need be, a contribution out of the state coffers, perhaps as much as half the required amount, secretly of course. The interested party must regard the matter as a private one between himself and the Count.'

to be a crafty baggage, succeeded in instituting the preliminary inquiry through the courts, independently of the Director of Public Prosecutions, which is possible by the terms of the latest legal procedure.

That is how things stood on the day when Friedberg warned the other Ministers.

A week or ten days later Bleichröder invited the Ministers again for Sunday, the 24th of this month. The day after the invitation was sent out a man of some standing called on Friedberg to ask him what stage had been reached in the preliminary inquiry into the Bleichröder case.

Friedberg told him: 'I shall accept this time, because the reason which prevented me before has been removed: the woman has withdrawn her accusation. But this method of settling the dispute is purely formal, and does not clear up what actually happened. Presumably the plaintiff has been bought off, but I think it possible we've not heard the last of her and her case. She's living now with a former police inspector of Schwerin who may, if he sees any advantage in it, egg her on again.'

Friedberg's anxiety emerges very clearly from all this business.

First of all, for fear that Bleichröder, a Jew, might cause a scandal in this age of anti-Semitism, the Public Prosecutor's office is prevented from functioning. Then, when the preliminary examination is instituted in spite of this, Friedberg privately warns his colleagues, for fear that *they* might reproach him with keeping the affair quiet. After money has been instrumental in bringing the preliminary examination to a standstill—without clearing Bl.'s character—Friedberg hastens to accept Bleichröder's invitation, lest Bl. should take offence and become hostile in his turn. And finally his only reason for telling his influential inquirer: 'Yes, I shall accept, I can't very well do otherwise now the affair has been legally settled, but in fact nothing has been cleared up, for the plaintiff has been made to withdraw her action' —was his fear that the latter might subsequently complain he had been insufficiently informed.

But it is also typical of Bleichröder to wait until prison is staring him in the face before paying up. That is really why I think he is guilty, and that he did promise the 25,000 talers and subsequently committed perjury. Had he been innocent he would have paid before legal proceedings began or after they concluded.

22 *February* 1884

The Chancellor has seized an opportunity of giving vent to the mounting dissatisfaction he has felt for some time with the Americans, their Government and their representative. His behaviour during the Lasker affair can surprise no one who has had an opportunity of seeing the unexampled rudeness which American diplomats and even the Cabinet in Washington display on every occasion when communicating with foreign representatives and governments.

In 1876 [sic][1] Lord Salisbury proposed that Germany and England be joint mediators in the war which had just broken out between Chile and Peru. The Chancellor was willing, but first suggested as an act of international courtesy that the United States should be invited to participate. The Anglo-German invitation met with a blunt reply: the United States had no objection to mediation in principle, but reserved the right to decide on the suitable moment. They advised against any kind of collective mediation in that it was apt to hamper the free self-determination of the belligerents.

Bismarck informed London he was prepared to co-operate with the British Cabinet even in such measures which did not have the approval of the gentlemen in Washington.

But Lord Salisbury did not touch on the affair again. When Münster asked him what he thought of the American reply, Salisbury replied that though it had made a disagreeable impression on him he was nevertheless glad to know for certain where he stood. And so the matter rested. England made no further overtures after Washington's refusal, and since we could not dream of putting into effect an English proposal without England, we too silently pocketed our share of insults.

The tone of American communications, always uncivil, became positively boorish in recent years. The Government in Washington had got its own way because to the European chancelleries it appeared like a cabby with whom no one wished to have words. I remember saying one day to Stirum, who had just received from the American Minister[2] a copy of a note sent him by his Secretary of State:[3] 'Why didn't you hand back this insolent document?' Stirum said he had not understood it properly when it was read to him.

Sargent,[4] the present Minister, adopted such an excessively insolent tone that the Chancellor, in a dispatch signed by himself,

[1] Should read: 1879.
[2] Andrew D. White. Minister in Berlin, 1879–81.
[3] Frederick T. Frelinghuysen. Secretary of State, 1881–5.
[4] A. A. Sargent. Minister in Berlin, 1883–4.

instructed Eisendecher[1]—this would be about May last year—to complain in Washington and to hint confidentially that Sargent was hardly the right person to maintain relations between the two countries on a cordial footing. Eisendecher had carried out his instruction rather ineffectually, as usual, so that the American Government let his protest go in at one ear and out at the other. Sargent stayed on.

In the Lasker affair[2] the Chancellor took a firm stand. To say his patience gave way would be inaccurate; in foreign policy, when questions of any moment are concerned, his patience never gives way. But he had gradually reached the opinion that the Government in Washington must be taught a lesson and he thought the present occasion favourable for a fight.

The dispatch for Eisendecher was drawn up entirely by the Chancellor; and bears evidence of the fact.[3] A masterpiece. His newspaper articles attacking Sargent are unrestrainedly vehement; it would not surprise me if Sargent brought a libel action. But one of the Chancellor's maxims is: courtesy in diplomacy, rudeness in the Press.

Congress cannot do much beyond abuse us; that is about the extent of its power to harm.

The King of Bavaria has declined Bleichröder's offer, because the letter, in which Bleichröder made the ordering of the royal finances the condition of his intervention, seemed to His Majesty impertinent—which may well have been the case. It began like this: 'No reputable firm of bankers would . . .' etc.

This was hardly the way to talk to the King of Bavaria. His awareness of his own dignity increases daily. For example, one of his peculiarities is his refusal to allow any of his officials to be seated in his presence; they are sometimes obliged to remain stiffly at attention while H.M. walks up and down the room giving orders. His former Privy Councillor, Bürkel, chose a moment when the King's back was turned to restore the circulation in one of his legs by giving it a few jerks backwards. The King, observing the movement in a mirror, said curtly: 'I thank you', dismissed

---

[1] Karl von Eisendecher. Minister in Washington, 1882–4.

[2] Bismarck had refused to inform the Reichstag officially of the resolution in Lasker's honour passed by the American House of Representatives.

[3] In a dispatch of 9 February 1884 Bismarck instructed Eisendecher to return the official communication of the House of Representatives' Lasker-Resolution to the American Secretary of State. Bismarck had not felt able to recommend to the Kaiser that the Reichstag be informed of it. The resolution of 9 January stated that Lasker's 'firm and constant exposition of free and liberal ideas has materially advanced the social, political and economic condition of those people' (i.e. the Germans). Bismarck was utterly unable to share this view. See Schulthess, *Europäischer Geschichtskalender 1884*, pp. 20–1.

him and appointed his successor, Pfister. One day during an audience a high Court official ran his hand through his hair. At the time the King said nothing but the man had scarcely gone before the King gave orders that he should never again appear in the royal presence. 'The fellow has no manners.'

Hohenlohe calls the King 'Caligula', for he said that if time and opportunity offered, King Ludwig would behave in exactly the same way; he is heartless, cruel and has delusions of grandeur.

Nevertheless the removal of this King, so ardently desired by the Ultramontanes, would be a misfortune for the German Reich.

Now that the King has turned down Bleichröder's proposal, the Privy Councillor will try his luck in Hamburg, and thinks that if he gets no satisfaction there the King will eventually fall back on Bleichröder. Of course Bleichröder is longing for this, for Pfister has intimated that after the transaction has been completed it will be an easy matter to make Bl. a Bavarian Baron or even a Count.

22 *February* 1884

The doubts I constantly entertained about Hatzfeldt's remaining for long in his present position have unfortunately received further confirmation in the last few days.

Hatzfeldt told Radolinski, who was here on a visit from Weimar, how very indignant he felt that last autumn in Wiesbaden the Crown Princess did not feel herself called upon to take any notice of Countess Hatzfeldt. The Crown Princess used to be different, but she had changed in the last two years. Countess Hatzfeldt wrote to Count Seckendorff in Wiesbaden to say that if the Crown Princess wished to see her daughter Nelly she was always at her disposal. Seckendorff had coldly and politely acknowledged receipt of her letter, but nothing further had come of it. Hatzfeldt declared he was tired of seeing his wife ill-treated. He felt like cutting loose from the whole business and living quietly with her in Sommerberg etc. etc.

Radolinski asked him whether the Countess herself would be satisfied with that kind of life, and also what they proposed to live on? Hatzfeldt had only puerile replies.

Of course the real reason for Hatzfeldt's anger is that he is nagged by his wife. She is bored, she is becoming impatient, and she would like to appear again at his side as his spouse as soon as possible. She cannot endure Sommerberg any longer, so she has moved to Wiesbaden, where she is spending money like water.

It was there, last autumn, that she expected to resume relations with the Crown Princess, but the Princess cut her dead.

I cannot say whether the Crown Princess holds such very strict views. Many people doubt it. But she has no wish to share the burden of contempt which Countess Hatzfeldt has drawn upon herself, for she is aware of her own unpopularity and is loath to increase it.

Countess Hatzfeldt kept her daughter with her as long as possible—I am referring to the elder one, the younger[1] one is still a child—and it was only after putting up considerable resistance that she sent her to her father in January. Now the mother is furious because her daughter is treated well here, particularly by the Crown Prince's entourage.

Hatzfeldt's irregular relations with his wife, his long sojourns in Sommerberg, are being used to turn the Chancellor, the Kaiser and the Crown Prince against him. The other day, when Hatzfeldt was intending to give a little ball, the Crown Prince said that Princess Victoria was not to enter a house in which such a reproach could be levelled at the host.

Hatzfeldt thinks he is more indispensable here, more firmly set in the saddle, than is actually the case, and will be very astonished when one day he meets with some disagreeable surprise bringing his activity here to a close. He is a diplomat of *very* considerable intellectual calibre, but he is one of the weakest and most characterless men I have ever met. Since he is his mother's[2] son I can indeed see why he is so easygoing and indifferent about his wife's public flouting of decency over a period of years. But I find it hard to understand how he can be so blind to the disadvantages and dangers to which his daughter and his entire family, *including* his wife, are exposed by his compromising his home and his position, i.e. his daily bread.

I do not think he can be acting blindly; I believe he is being bullied. His wife knows how much he hates scenes and scandal, and so she creates scenes and threatens him with worse ones. Last year, when Hatzfeldt was taking his daughter back to Berlin *against* her mother's wishes, his wife accompanied them as far as the Frankfurt station. Suddenly, while the train was still stationary, she threw herself across the line in front of the engine. There was not the least danger in this piece of tomfoolery, because of course the railway officials immediately dragged her off, but just imagine Paul Hatzfeldt in such a scene before a large public. He did in fact say to her on that occasion, thus offending her by his 'heartlessness', '*Mais ne faites donc pas de bêtises devant le monde*',

[1] Marie Augusta von Hatzfeldt.
[2] Countess Sophie Hatzfeldt was notorious for her unorthodox behaviour.

so he did retain his outward composure. But if he later gave way to her on many occasions when he ought not to have done so, it was undoubtedly for fear of similar scenes. She has the upper hand because her nerves are steadier.

Some twelve years ago, in Paris, she once said to me: '*Est-ce que vous ne trouvez pas que je serais bien comme cocotte?*' I protested. '*Mais comment*', she said, disappointed, '*on m'a toujours dit que j'aurais été une parfaite cocotte.*'

She has the strong nerves and brazen character of a concierge's prostitute daughter, and that is why she wins every time.

It will be hard to make them see that they are trifling with their children's daily bread. They have both had so much good luck in their lives, and have emerged reasonably well from such difficult circumstances that they will not believe in Nemesis until it can no longer be averted. Hatzfeldt's frivolity and his gipsy-like independence of outlook, good qualities sometimes, are in this case a liability.

But it will be a *great* loss if this man comes to grief. He is to my knowledge the *only person*, after the Chief has gone, capable of surveying the diplomatic situation as a whole and of continuing calmly and skilfully the game on the chess-board of diplomacy. I know no one who could even come near him.

23 *February* 1884

Friedberg, the Minister, told me the other day: 'The Falk legislation,[1] which is now being taxed with more crimes than it was ever guilty of, at least bears the blame for the fact that the King of Prussia, who was hitherto an absolute monarch over the Evangelical Church, is now, after the introduction of local and national synods, a constitutional monarch.[2] Many of the inconveniences in the administration of divorce cases and taxation can be traced to the granting of self-government to the Church.'

So far I have not concerned myself with ecclesiastical questions, but Friedberg's words prejudice me *in favour* of this part of the Falk legislation, for it seems to me that it knits together the structure of the Church rather more. It is precisely because it is under-organized that Protestantism is losing ground.

These catchwords of 'absolute monarch, constitutional monarch' sound positively comic on the lips of a Liberal minister.

Friedberg, like most Jews, has an analytical, negative approach

---

[1] The 1873 May Laws of the *Kulturkampf* drafted by Dr Adalbert Falk, Prussian Minister for Ecclesiastical Affairs, 1872–9.
[2] Falk reconstituted the Evangelical established Church on a synodal basis.

to religious matters. Rottenburg, the responsible official in the Reich Chancellery, is unfortunately not a good influence in this respect either; he is an adherent of the Positivist, Comte, and consequently believes in nothing at all. In addition he bears a personal grudge against Gossler because the latter once said to Frau Rottenburg: 'When your husband has made good with the Chancellor for a year or two he'll be able to count on a consulship, won't he?' Rottenburg saw in this admittedly uncivil remark an intentional impertinence and since then in all the problems he has had to settle between the Chief and Gossler he has acted against the latter's interests, the more so because their principles are diametrically opposed.

It is a pity that the Chief, who at the very beginning of the *Kulturkampf* allowed himself to be influenced by Bucher more than is usual with him, is now absorbing from Rottenburg many ideas which work as Bucher's did, i.e. against religion.

Rottenburg and Bucher differ in every other respect.

Bucher, whom many people imagine to have undergone a political conversion because he treats liberalism with a certain ostentatious contempt, is in my view still a Social Democrat, regarding the destruction of the churches and the undermining of belief as a weapon which will bring about the social revolution.

Rottenburg, a very rich man, has no desire for the sharing out of wealth; he is an anti-clerical only because in his early years as an author he was interested in philosophy and wrote a book on Comte.[1] He is also respectable, industrious, intelligent, ambitious, and past master in the art of keeping away or sending away from the Chancellor anyone who might prejudice his own position. I get on well with him, since our paths—foreign and domestic—never cross. In everything but ecclesiastical affairs he is a good influence.

24 *February* 1884

The Russian Military Attaché, General Prince Dolgoruki, who was recently at Friedrichsruh,[2] put up a far from brilliant showing when he was put to the test as a leader of troops. He held a command during the first ill-fated expedition against the Turkomans, and was to blame for the failure of the assault on Gök-Tepe. Instead of obeying orders and attacking at five in the morning, he

---

[1] Rottenburg wrote a book entitled *Vom Begriff des Staates. I. Einleitung und Geschichte der französischen Staatstheorien bis 1789* (Leipzig, 1878). No second volume or special book on Comte appears to have been published.

[2] See Herbert von Bismarck's letter to Holstein of 5 February (*Correspondence*).

marched at four in the hope of taking the position before the other assault columns arrived. Instead his troops were defeated and almost wiped out. As a result of this performance D. was relieved of his command and given his present post, the sort of treatment which shows he is in good favour with Alexander III. And I hear from Herbert that D. recently danced the mazurka (cotillion) with the Tsarina.

D. is a sort of Russian Lehndorff, but slimmer, more agile, more intelligent. A handsome man with a black beard and light grey roving eyes. A cross between a lady-killer and a beast of prey. Herbert, who has got to know him better, says he is conservative and ambitious.[1] This latter quality is usually regarded by the Chancellor as a virtue, in that an ambitious man with his aim clearly in view is easier to handle and also more patient than the next man.

D. wants to become Ambassador here. It can be assumed from the Gök-Tepe incident that he will have no scruples in his choice of methods. He has been useful so far in that he used his influence to have that dangerous rogue Saburov removed.

D. embarked on this ambassadorship campaign last summer by informing our Kaiser and a few high-ranking army officers that he had very recently discovered to his dismay that his government, completely against the wishes of Tsar Alexander and Giers, was drifting towards war with Germany as a direct result of massing troops in the Russian frontier provinces. This provoked counter-measures on our part, and thus a state of permanent unrest was maintained. He, D., intended to inform Tsar Alexander, who happened to be in Copenhagen at the time, of the true state of affairs.

When Waldersee repeated this conversation with D. to me just before the autumn manœuvres I said to him: 'You'll see, D. is doing his best to become Ambassador here.'

And now Herbert confirms my impression that Orlov will not stay here long.

It was a good thing D. was in St Petersburg at the very moment when Saburov intended to take advantage of Giers' absence to engineer his downfall.

27 *February* 1884

Tiedemann, who is just back from Friedrichsruh, found the Chancellor in surprisingly good health, slender, good-tempered,

[1] See Herbert von Bismarck's letter to his father of 27 January 1884 (*Grosse Politik*, vol. III, no. 617, pp. 315–18).

but more irritable than he used to be. That is said to be a result of the Banting cure.

Prince Bismarck was particularly indignant with Gossler, whom he called the 'mad suckling'. He said Gossler takes on a great many things he knows nothing about, and then as soon as problems become serious he always crawls behind the Chancellor.

Tiedemann, who has a high opinion of Gossler, did his best, though with little success, to modify Bismarck's attitude. He did not see that the actual facts sufficiently warranted such excessive indignation, but thought someone must have been agitating the Chancellor against him.

Rantzau gave the impression that he felt very uncertain where he stood with his father-in-law, and was obviously anxious lest Tied., to whom the Chancellor submitted one or two documents for his opinion, might be invited to assist him in his work.

The Chancellor discovered, in Tiedemann's presence, a spelling mistake made by Rantzau in the final draft of a document awaiting his signature. 'Ah', said the old gentleman, 'I see I must even be on the watch for that kind of mistake', but in a tone of calm resignation. He makes do with Rantzau because Princess Bismarck needs the society of her daughter and grandchildren. The conviction has gradually been borne in upon Rantzau that the Chancellor has had the bad taste to class him as a *non-valeur*, hence his anxiety lest someone or other, Rottenburg or Bill, might supplant him.

General resentment against Rantzau prevails amongst the Ministers. I think I have already said that Maybach, Puttkamer and Gossler, independently of each other, were all on the point of resigning because of muddles caused by Rantzau. Rottenburg prevented Puttkamer from going, and Maybach was prevented by the Chancellor the moment he heard what was happening, while Gossler, I think, decided to stay on after thinking things over.

There must be something strangely satisfying about being a Minister. I should think one of its greatest pleasures is to go for a stroll along the Wilhelmstrasse and be acknowledged by Chancellery officials and *Geheimräte*. [...]

Rottenburg, as was his duty, wrote to Rantzau about the recent incident in the Council of Ministers over the judicial inquiry into Bleichröder's perjury, so as to put the Chancellor in the picture. This was particularly important because the scandal is bound to break out again as soon as the accuser has got through all her compensation money.

Rantzau replied that he had not shown the Chancellor this

letter 'for fear of annoying His Highness'; he would do so only if Rottenburg insisted.

Rottenburg, a cautious man, was unwilling to insist, but will very shortly be going to Friedrichsruh, where he will deliver his message in person.

Rantzau, who formerly behaved as if he hated the sight of Bleichröder, now seems to want a closer acquaintance with him, perhaps to use him to undermine various individuals.

Rantzau, with the same jealousy as he had shown towards Tiedemann, had hitherto prevented Rottenburg from going to Friedrichsruh. He wrote to Rottenburg that his presence in Berlin set the Chancellor's mind at rest, whereas his story in Friedrichsruh was that Rottenburg had so much to do in Berlin that he could not get away.

Princess Bismarck at last wrote to Rott. to-day to ask 'whether it was really true', as Rantzau always claimed, that Rott. was never available even for a single day. As a result Rott. will suggest going on Friday.

I have myself declined three invitations from Princess Bismarck,[1] because I find Rantzau's society so distasteful.

Bleichröder has succeeded in getting himself invited to Friedrichsruh. He leaves early this morning and will be back late this evening. Since Prince Bismarck is returning to Berlin within the next fortnight, the only purpose of this visit is to show off. Bleichröder wants to use it to bolster up his prestige.

28 *February* 1884

Bleichröder has come back radiant from his visit to Friedrichsruh. He left yesterday morning, laden with toys for the little Rantzaus, and stayed there from three until nine.

He achieved only two of the three things he set out to achieve. The third was an attempt to persuade the Chancellor to send Rottenburg to Bavaria to hold consultations with the King's Privy Councillor and to press for the acceptance of Bleichröder's offer by the King of Bavaria. I have already said that the King, offended by the tone and some of the conditions of Bleichröder's offer of a loan, had declined it, observing that he had already received an offer of ten millions from another quarter (though at the rate of 85 for 100 nominal value). Bleichröder, seeing his titles and decorations fade into the distance, is very disconcerted and would like the Chancellor to intervene. But this he could not be prevailed

---

[1] An invitation of 24 February 1884 is published in the *Correspondence*. There are several undated invitations from Princess Bismarck among Holstein's papers.

on to do; he said Rottenburg was too directly connected with him officially to be used for such a purpose.[1]

It was most significant that Bleichröder thought Rantzau had changed for the better, and become more sociable and talkative. This bears out my suspicion that Rantzau sees Bleichröder as a force to be reckoned with, and since he himself commands no following (he has no friends, only a few toadies from outside) wants to make an ally of him, and so turned on the amiability. Formerly, as a concession to his brothers-in-law, and because he thought it the dashing thing to do, he appeared as an anti-Semite, and directed his fury in particular against Bl. His reception yesterday would perhaps have been less cordial if Rantzau had shown Bismarck Rottenburg's warning letter at the proper time.

Another characteristic detail was that while Bleichröder sat telling me about yesterday's visit he was called away, because General Prince Dolgoruki was waiting in his office! And yet dear Herbert imagines he has convinced Dolgoruki that Bleichröder is 'filthy scum no respectable person could touch with a barge-pole'.

The visit to Friedrichsruh was also aimed at restoring Bleichröder's tottering prestige in the eyes of foreign diplomats.

Princess Bismarck, who under her sons' influence used to think no expression strong enough for Bleichröder, also adopts a milder tone in a letter to-day;[2] she says he talked scandal about everybody and was really entertaining. This may be the effect of the toys for the Rantzaus, or it may be due to Rantzau himself.

3 March 1884

The Crown Prince is again coming under strong Liberal pressure with regard to domestic questions. Georg Bunsen,[3] for example, has drawn up a memorandum about (i.e. attacking) the government proposals for accident insurance.

But in recent years, and again at the present moment, the Prince has had fits of gloom and depression, the causes of which can be summed up by saying he regards himself as a 'defeated point of view'. It is gradually dawning on him that the Liberal regime he had hoped to establish would not now ensure him *general* popularity. He intended to rule with and for the bourgeoisie, and is

[1] In March the Bavarian Privy Councillor, Pfister, paid another visit to Berlin and delivered a note from King Ludwig of Bavaria to Bismarck, in which the latter's 'intercession' was sought in the negotiations to be held between Pfister and Bleichröder concerning a loan of six million. Bismarck replied on 2 April that he had hopes of at least a partial success, provided the necessary securities were offered. (Bismarck, *Die gesammelten Werke*, vol. XIV/2, pp. 949–50.) These were not forthcoming and the negotiations between Bleichröder and Pfister broke down. (From the Foreign Ministry files.)

[2] Not found.   [3] Georg von Bunsen. Liberal Member of the Reichstag.

thrown into perplexity by the more and more rapid emergence of the workers; his formulæ do not cover this new situation.

Sometimes he even talks of abdicating his claims—an idea he will never act upon as long as the Princess is alive.

What I wrote the other day about Dolgoruki is already beginning to be proved right. After his visit to Friedrichsruh he sent a dispatch to St Petersburg as if he were Ambassador already and inquired whether he should continue negotiations in some very important matter. Tsar Alexander, who has a high opinion of Orlov, informed Dolgoruki that the handling of this question was for the Ambassador alone. When Dolgoruki suggested that he might at least be acquainted with the contents of all of Orlov's dispatches, he was told that it was left to the Ambassador's discretion which dispatches he wished to show his Military Attaché.[1]

First consequence of Dolgoruki's pushing: Tsar Alexander, Giers, and Orlov will be greatly annoyed with Dolgoruki *and* with the Chancellor, who will be suspected of having negotiated with the Military Attaché as if he were Ambassador, and of giving him big ideas, thus making the new Ambassador's position difficult. In hostile quarters the affair will be interpreted as interference by Bismarck in Russian domestic affairs.[2] [...]

5 *March* 1884

I was told again recently by several people who have returned from Friedrichsruh that Rantzau is doing his utmost to stir up the Chancellor against the Crown Prince. In the first place Rantzau dislikes the Prince, probably because the latter ignores him. And secondly, it is said that Rantzau's dearest wish is to stay on at Friedrichsruh with the Chancellor after his retirement, and to live there year in year out with no work and no expenses. Rantzau would undoubtedly have a clear field, because Bismarck's sons would certainly not endure living with their parents in the country, still less as married men. Rantzau realizes that his father-in-law will not make much out of him. Under these circumstances he prefers to be left in peace to play with his children. It would be hard to find a lazier couple than the Rantzaus in the whole of Germany, even after a long search.

[1] Holstein's account is based on a dispatch from St Petersburg by Ambassador von Schweinitz of 27 February 1884. (From the Foreign Ministry files.)

[2] In a letter of 1 March Herbert von Bismarck wrote: 'Dolgoruki, as you will see [from Schweinitz's dispatch], has shown too great a passion for the chase; the Tsar has no doubt been told: "*Il veut vous forcer la main*", hence a momentary annoyance which will quickly pass. I should like to send Dolgoruki a warning hint to lie low so long as Orlov is about—but how?'

The Rantzaus are now pressing the Chancellor for all they are worth not to return to Berlin yet, and in fact if he does not appear in the Reichstag now his presence here is not at all necessary. But then the Kaiser, and still more the Crown Prince, would again be influenced against him. People say to the latter: 'When you're Kaiser, Bismarck will expect you to go to Friedrichsruh to receive his instructions.' But the Rantzaus, whose town residence is too small for them and who are reluctant to take a bigger one, shelter behind Princess Bismarck and oppose with all the force of their combined inertia any suggestion of leaving.

But the Chancellor, I am convinced, wants to be on good terms with the future Kaiser. For example, an inquiry has just been received from Friedrichsruh whether the Crown Prince would be travelling to Kiel via Hamburg; which means that the Chancellor intends to go to the station to greet him. [...]

Prince Wilhelm is said to be not entirely sincere (a trait inherited from his mother). Rather heartless. He wept on relinquishing command of his company, but only wiped his eyes when his brother Waldemar died.[1]

In '78, the beginning of the new economic era,[2] he quarrelled violently with his father, who thought this policy absurd and maintained there was no such thing as a working class. Nowadays the Crown Prince's conviction is said to waver at times; he will never hold any view *firmly*.

9 *March* 1884

According to the latest news from Friedrichsruh, the Chancellor, though suffering from no specific complaint, has aged considerably over the last few months. His capacity for work is less, his energy has diminished, even his anger, though easily kindled, fades more quickly than in his prime; 'querulous old age'.[3] He is more susceptible to the influence of those about him. Rantzau's influence is limited by his personal insignificance; his strongest means of exerting pressure is his wife, who immediately flares up the moment anything happens that does not suit him. The Bismarcks know that both their sons loathe living in the country, and that consequently they are thrown back on the two Rantzaus for company. And Rantzau has no scruples about strengthening this impression by reminding the parents that it is only at home that their sons are ill and disagreeable, whereas away from home

---

[1] Prince Waldemar died in 1879.
[2] Holstein refers to the abandonment of free trade and the adoption of a protective tariff by Germany. [3] In English in the original.

they are healthy and contented. An exaggerated picture, but not without some truth. The Chancellor, who has a horror of very large families, said recently when someone observed that the Rantzaus ought to have a little daughter to go with their three sons: 'The desire for a little daughter is often father to several sons.'

Eisendecher will not be kept on in America much longer. The Chancellor asked his father-in-law, Eickstedt, to advise him to request a transfer. Judging by the complete incompetence Eisendecher showed both in the Lasker affair and in the question of pork products,[1] this is the least that could happen.

The Kaiser told Hatzfeldt how delighted he was to notice that, for the very first time, the Crown Prince was completely at a loss to understand the British Government and British policy. This led H.M. to express a wish that H.I.H. be shown a communication from the Chancellor to Schweinitz criticizing the 'crass stupidity' of British policy. The reason why he had not already seen it was precisely because it was feared H.I.H. would be offended by the uncivil tone adopted towards England.[2]

Saburov said to Hatzfeldt: '*Je fais le plongeon quant à présent.* But my time will come when relations between Russia and yourselves, at present so good, one day deteriorate. Then I shall be the man of the moment who sets everything right.'

I do not believe Saburov wants to 'set things right'. Instead I think that, finding the Germanophile roles already filled by Giers, Orlov and Dolgoruki, he will choose as his speciality a rapprochement with France. I find it most suspicious that he shows no inclination to accept the Chancellor's invitation to Friedrichsruh. Presumably he wants to pose in Russia as a martyr, crowded out by Bismarck's creatures.

---

[1] Germany had banned the import of American pork products on the ground that they were unhygienic.

[2] The reference is to a dispatch from Bismarck to Schweinitz of 25 February 1884. On 18 February Schweinitz had reported that the Russian Cabinet wished to show due consideration to the Gladstone Ministry in its handling of the Afghan question so as to avoid increasing Gladstone's difficulties with the House of Commons. Bismarck in his dispatch embarked on an extraordinarily biting attack on Gladstone with the words: 'I can hardly imagine that the idea of sparing Gladstone because he is a Russophile in the hope that he will remain in office was the deciding factor, and am more inclined to think that Gladstone's notorious inability to govern a country like England is regarded as useful for Russian interests. Because an incompetent British Government is useful to Russia, the prolongation of the present Cabinet's existence is regarded favourably.' Bismarck went on to say that the continued existence of the Gladstone Ministry threatened to bring about England's downfall, which would endanger the peace of Europe and monarchical interests in general. According to the files, this dispatch was shown to the Crown Prince on Bismarck's instructions. Herbert von Bismarck replied to the dispatch in a private letter of 4 March, Schweinitz in a dispatch of 3 March. Both stated their opinion that nowhere in Russia could you find a real understanding of English conditions. Herbert von Bismarck wrote: 'I do not think Russian policy is far-sighted enough to wish to use Gladstone to ruin England.' (From the Foreign Ministry files.)

He told Hatzfeldt his reason for not going to Friedrichsruh was that Dolgoruki had already been on a mission to Friedrichsruh, which left him, Saburov, uncertain what he ought to say or how he ought to behave, seeing that he was no longer Ambassador.

These are mere excuses. Saburov had a letter from Friedrichsruh to-day in honour of the Tsar's birthday; I wonder if it contained any further mention of an invitation.[1]

Whether it was right to invite him at all is another question. It was one of those polite actions that can easily be regarded as two-faced, and no doubt Saburov thinks it is in his own interest to make it appear that he had first been supplanted and then doled off with empty politeness. It would be very clever of him to assume an air of indignation and refuse to go to Friedrichsruh. For this very reason they must try to get him there.

We have probably not heard the last of Saburov. A man of his intelligence and ability might one day become Foreign Minister. He will adopt a policy—for or against us—which suits his own personal interest. At the moment, as I have said, he has better prospects with our enemies. He is aware of this too, for he told the Tsar that as a result of Giers' policy France was being 'left to (*livrée*) herself, and us'. On that occasion the Tsar stuck to Giers' programme, but the Tsar is weak and indolent. All is quiet at the moment at any rate. [...]

The Chancellor was talking recently of the Crown Prince's melancholy, and said he did not believe he would renounce his claims while he was still Crown Prince, if only because the Princess would prevent it. But when he was Kaiser his abdication was not improbable, once the ship of state was heading straight for the reefs of liberalism and he was unable to stop.

Ah well, if the Chancellor is still alive and retains some of his vigour, things may not get nearly so far, because the Crown Prince is already a prey to misgivings both on foreign affairs (England) and on domestic policy.

10 *March* 1884

General Mischke has gone to join the Army officers, and has been replaced in the post of Chief of Staff of the 4th Army Inspectorate by General von Winterfeld, until now Chief of Staff in Strasbourg. This change means a loss to the Stosch-Normann group.

[1] The last paragraph of Bismarck's letter to Saburov of 8 March reads: ' *Mon départ prochain de Friedrichsruh à mon regret me fait perdre la chance du plaisir de vous revoir ici, mais me fait espérer de vous revoir en tout cas avant votre départ.*' In his reply of 10 March Saburov said he would await Bismarck's arrival in Berlin and take leave of him there. (From the Foreign Ministry files.)

The Kaiser wants Prince Heinrich[1] to do a period of military service with the army and to get to know Prussia. The Crown Prince takes the opposite view. He wishes his son to be trained exclusively as a sailor.

The Chancellor's letter to Saburov contained the remark that the Chancellor hoped to see Saburov soon in Berlin.

Prince Bismarck's arrival had in fact definitely been announced for to-morrow, Tuesday, but at the last minute it became uncertain. He is becoming more and more capricious.

The Chancellor really seems in earnest now about leaving the Prussian Council of Ministers and confining himself purely to national affairs. He has already prepared the Ministers for this, thereby provoking different reactions. On the one hand relief, on the other hand anxiety—not without foundation—lest Scholz, whom they all detest, should be made President. The other Ministers have said that if that happened Maybach would resign, because as senior member he would feel passed over in favour of Scholz. If this threat looked like being carried out, the Chancellor would definitely have to seek an arrangement other than Scholz's Presidency, because Maybach is irreplaceable. [...]

About a week ago a letter arrived for Hatzfeldt from Rantzau in which he requested Hatzfeldt to hold a consultation with the Kaiser about filling the Karlsruhe post again. Candidates to be considered were, first, Derenthall,[2] who however already has wider scope in Alexandria than is possible in Karlsruhe; second, Berchem, who was a Bavarian and would therefore be better suited for a German rather than a Prussian appointment; next in order of seniority would be Count Herbert Bismarck.

The tone of the letter was so lukewarm that Hatzfeldt asked me whether it was known for certain that the Chancellor wanted the Karlsruhe post to go to Herbert. I said that from what I had heard I felt sure he did, but that Rantzau, who had written the letter, was jealous of his brother-in-law.

Hatzfeldt laid the matter before the Kaiser, who raised all kinds of objections. Herbert was very young, and would probably never be present at his post; moreover a wider sphere of activity, such as the post of Chargé d'Affaires at an Embassy, would be more suited to his capabilities. In any case the Kaiser would first write to his daughter, the Grand-Duchess.[3]

The latter's reply has arrived and can be summed up thus: Both

[1] Heinrich, Prince of Prussia. Second son of the Crown Prince Friedrich Wilhelm.
[2] Eduard von Derenthall. First Secretary in the Rome Embassy, 1876–83; Consul-General in Cairo, 1883–4, in Alexandria, 1884–7; Prussian Minister in Weimar, 1887–94.
[3] Luise, Grand-Duchess of Baden.

Berchem and Herbert would be acceptable, but the former would be the more acceptable.

The Kaiser therefore wrote at once to Prince Bismarck, who will not be exactly pleased.

Hatzfeldt called on the Kaiser again to-day to suggest that he inform the Chancellor of his wish to help Herbert to obtain a post as Minister soon, possibly using a *revirement* if Eisendecher is leaving Washington and someone from here is going to America. The Kaiser said he agreed in principle, but wants to see what Prince Bismarck replies first.

The whole business was set about the wrong way. If Hatzfeldt had followed my idea and his original intention of suggesting to the Kaiser that he might care to give the Chancellor a surprise for Christmas or for his birthday by making Herbert a Minister, the old gentleman would have entered into the thing far more eagerly. As it is, Rantzau will seize this opportunity to agitate against the Kaiser and against Hatzfeldt.[1]

I made an unpleasant discovery to-day. Bleichröder voiced doubts as to whether Hatzfeldt was giving the Chancellor satisfaction. And he added: 'Ah, if only we could get Radowitz here.'

Those are the first-fruits of the tacit agreement between Rantzau and Bleichröder. Bleichröder will never really have much time for Hatzfeldt, because he keeps him at arm's length and does not pass on so much information as Bleichröder regards as his due. In view of the Chancellor's antipathy towards Radowitz, the latter's return to Berlin was hitherto regarded by his supporters as hopelessly improbable. But now Bleichröder and Rantzau are probably thinking secretly of setting it in motion by exploiting to the full the follies Hatzfeldt's wife sometimes drives him to commit.

12 *March* 1884

The Chancellor arrived to-day. I thought he looked older, but extremely well. The bubbling energy of former days was perhaps less in evidence, but the old gentleman still gives a decided impression of competence. He is eager for the fray and wants to attend the Reichstag tomorrow with the intention of seizing the first opportunity to speak again on the Lasker resolution.[2]

He is definitely inclined to make Scholz Minister-President; he

[1] Holstein gives a divergent account of this affair in his entry of 4 May 1884. See below.
[2] See Bismarck's Reichstag speech of 13 March 1884 (Bismarck, *Die gesammelten Werke*, vol. XII, pp. 406–16).

was sorry to learn from me that Scholz and Maybach did not get on well.

Speaking of Puttkamer, he said he could not even hold the heads of the regional administrations together, and would succeed even less with Ministers. One of his numerous grounds for complaint against P. is that he refused to make Bennigsen Head of the Administration of Hanover. Hanover, said Prince Bismarck, could be governed only on National-Liberal lines. The Guelphs could then be completely routed. Instead, a handful of non-Guelph Conservatives, some of them civil servants, had been painfully scraped together and nothing could be done with them.

Someone remarked that Lucius had said that although the position of Minister had its darker side, the brighter side was such that it was difficult to endure the idea of sinking back into obscurity.

'I'm sorry to have exposed him to *that* possibility', said the Chancellor with that grim smile of his.

That makes me feel sure he is looking for a way of getting rid of Lucius, but it will not be easy to find one; Lucius will hang on as long as possible. [...]

I had advised Princess Bismarck in a letter to ask the Chancellor to write a few lines to the Crown Prince on the occasion of Prince Heinrich's return.

I touched on the matter again at table, without being overheard by the others. Prince Bismarck said he had written but was very afraid the Crown Prince would think him guilty of tuft-hunting. I laughed at this idea, which can undoubtedly be traced to Rantzau's nagging.

The fact that Prince Bismarck has written at all seems to me to show that he *does* wish to be on good terms with the Crown Prince.

After dinner Bötticher, the Minister, came and raised all kinds of official questions, but made no headway with any of them, so Rottenburg told me—he was sitting near them.

How crude Bötticher's methods are. He follows with slavish attention everyone who happens to be speaking to the Chancellor, noting what is said and how it is taken, so as to regulate accordingly his treatment of the person concerned.

In response to the Kaiser's letter about the Karlsruhe appointment the Chancellor replied, in a communication which the Kaiser sent to Hatzfeldt to read, that he did not set particular store on the Karlsruhe post in itself. His only reason for wanting promotion for his son was that he could then employ him in the Foreign

Ministry, just as formerly he employed the Minister von Rado-witz. But, if H.M. approved, this could be brought about in other ways.

Herbert will then virtually be State Secretary. Since I am on good terms with him, I shall no doubt come off well and find my niche, but for the great majority it will be wormwood and gall, especially Rantzau and Bleichröder, whose intrigues and low-down conduct will be quickly brought to a stop. Apart from Bleichröder, Herbert is the only influence that counts. [...]

15 *March* 1884

Since the Chancellor's return several of us have been struck by the way Schweninger has become the object of particularly marked attentions on the part of the Rantzau family. And we soon per-ceived the motive for these exertions. Schweninger was to be bullied into ordering the Chancellor back to the country as soon as possible.

I therefore made an appointment with Schw. yesterday and put the position to him as follows:

'I have no intention of taking upon myself one particle of your *medical* responsibility; you must bear that alone. And if you feel the Chancellor's health requires a stay in the country, you must of course be guided by no other consideration when giving your instructions. *But* I am not blind and, like several others, have noticed that you are the object of particular attention on the part of the Rantzau family, and every one knows that they would like to have the Chancellor back in the country year in year out if possible. The inconveniences which would arise if the Chancellor were to leave Berlin again at once—possibly this month—are such that they can be subordinated only to considerations of health, but to *no other consideration*. And you know that Bismarck's sons, both of whom are unfortunately away, think exactly as I do.'

Schweninger admitted by a smile that the Rantzaus had been trying to influence him. However, he said that living in Berlin did the Chancellor no harm in itself, but the consumption of large quantities of alcohol certainly did. For example, the previous day during the Lasker debate in the Reichstag Prince Bismarck had drunk one and a half bottles of Moselle, and then a further assort-ment of wines during and after dinner. Alcohol was really dan-gerous for him since it had a weakening effect on the heart, already weakened as a result of a four months' attack of jaundice.

I said it was not surprising Prince Bismarck was so greedy about eating and drinking, because it was the only distraction he had left. Was it really necessary to cut him off so completely from people's society, and would a Reichstag *soirée* do him very much harm? Schw. said no, a few quarts of beer, unless taken daily, would do no harm. He said he would do his best to see that Prince Bismarck entertained more.

I am curious to see who wins, Schw. or Rantzau. The latter has a horror of any kind of social activity—except a game of *Skat*.

Schw. also said Prince Bismarck might get rid of this heart affection, but at the moment it was still there.

I informed Herbert of my conversation with Schw. I should not have interfered anything like so directly if one of the Chancellor's sons had been here. Rantzau has acquired a really shifty expression.

One of the Chancellor's remarks about the Crown Prince, made some years ago: 'The Crown Prince wants to be left in peace to enjoy his constitutional bread and butter with his wife.'

16 *March* 1884

The Chancellor's speeches[1] reveal occasional flashes of remarkable political insight, but the old fire is lacking, his vigour has diminished, old age is gradually asserting its rights. I do not think he is so proof against outside influence as he used to be, and for that very reason it is important to have Herbert here as an element of integrity to withstand the influence of Rantzau and Bleichröder. Even a man of genius cannot escape family tyranny in his old age. That is why Rantzau wants to have the Chancellor by himself in the country again as soon as possible.

17 *March* 1884

I have not seen anything of Schweninger during the last few days. Since our recent conversation he has probably been wondering, like a good diplomatist, which side is the stronger—Rantzau or myself—and has decided in favour of Rantzau. And people are already saying that in a very short time, possibly still this month, Prince Bismarck will be going to Varzin.

At yesterday's session of the Council of Ministers the Chancellor announced his retirement from Prussian affairs.[2] He gave as reasons for this step his age and his health, and expressly declared that dissatisfaction with any one of his colleagues had played not the slightest part in this decision. But in any case he thought it an advantage for the Chancellor to stand in an independent relation to all the member states, including Prussia.

[1] Of 13 and 15 March (Bismarck, *Die gesammelten Werke*, vol. XII, pp. 406–29)
[2] See Hans Goldschmidt, *Das Reich und Preussen im Kampf um die Führung* (Berlin, 1931), pp. 303–6.

The reintroduction of the Council of State[1] was also discussed at yesterday's sitting. Its task would be to work out all the draft Bills before they came before the Prussian Landtag.

The advantage of having such a body has often been spoken of by those who were dissatisfied with the style and wording of the draft Bills in the last few decades.

The Chancellor had even mentioned that he thought it might be a good thing if the Council of State gradually evolved into an Imperial Council, to strengthen the Bundesrat and counterbalance the Chancellor and the Reichstag. The genuine underlying aim is to create a further check to prevent both the Prussian and the German Parliaments from rushing into the abyss. The Chancellor said in this connexion that the Princes were the conservative element, i.e. the force that held the Reich together, and the Parliaments were the disintegrating element.

I think both Prince Bismarck's retirement from Prussian affairs and the formation of a Council of State are useful measures.

The Kaiser and the Crown Prince have both expressed their agreement, the Crown Prince probably without enthusiasm; the Council of State cannot exactly be called a liberal idea.

The Crown Prince found it a particularly distasteful idea that a separate office of Foreign Minister would now have to be created to deal with Prussia's relations with the other German States.

19 *March* 1884

The son of the late Consul-General von Jasmund, an assistant judge, wishes to enter the consular service. Since the family is living in straitened circumstances I shall do nothing to prevent him but nothing to help him either.

Some ten years ago his father was Consul-General in Alexandria, where he made things impossible for himself by unduly violent behaviour in a matter in which he was actually in the right. He was then employed for some years (until the autumn of 1879 I think) here at the Foreign Ministry, in the Political Department, and died just after obtaining the post of Minister in Bucharest through the good offices of the Crown Prince.

[1] The Prussian Council of State of 1817, composed of the Princes who had attained their majority and the highest civil and military officials, had in fact ceased functioning since March 1848. In June 1884 there was an attempt at reviving it in a different form by the formation of definite departments, the nomination of the Crown Prince as President and the Chancellor as Vice-President, and the appointment of seventy-one new members, most of them Conservatives. (Forty-one civil servants and officers, twelve owners of large estates, six merchants and industrialists, four clergy, four representatives of provincial and local government.) See Goldschmidt, *Das Reich und Preussen*, pp. 83–7, and Bismarck, *Die gesammelten Werke*, vol. vi c, no. 278, pp. 290–1.

All the time he lived in Berlin he was in great penury, but this did not prevent him, any more than his wretched state of health, from having affairs with ballet dancers.

The Crown Prince makes an allowance to his widow to this very day. The alleged reason is that during the constitutional conflict (Danzig journey, Winter, etc.)[1] Jasmund had been employed in writing all kinds of opposition pamphlets attacking the government, and had been in a position to cause unpleasantness for the Prince by making 'disclosures'—that nightmare of all royal personages.

I need scarcely add that Jasmund belonged to the Stosch-Stockmar-Normann faction. J. made use of his time in Berlin and the insight into the workings of the political machine afforded him by his post in the Political Division, to submit to the Crown Prince a constant stream of memoranda attacking Bismarck's policy. This was immediately before, during, and after the Russo-Turkish war.

The Chancellor's policy in those very years is one of his greatest achievements. Russia was in a mood to deliver an attack in any quarter, and at any rate it was better to deflect it on to the Turks. But of course that ran counter to the stereotyped tenets of English liberalism.

21 *March* 1884

The Crown Princess has said: it is stated in the Press that the Crown Prince was consulted before the German Radical Party[2] was formed, and that he gave his approval to the step. It was a lie which could only have been invented with the object of alienating the Kaiser and the Chancellor from the Crown Prince.

The Crown Princess said of the Grand-Duke of Weimar: 'He comes of a treacherous family. I say this even though it is my husband's family. But nobody has suffered more from this treachery than I.'

The Austrian Kaiser has the greatest confidence in Prince Bismarck. The Kaiser said recently to the reigning Prince Reuss (nicknamed 'Zulu'):[3] 'May God preserve Prince Bismarck for many years to come.' Kaiser Franz Joseph is also keenly interested in our domestic measures, such as accident insurance.

[1] On 5 June 1863 the Crown Prince made a public speech in Danzig in the presence of the Mayor, Leopold von Winter, in which he declared he was opposed to the most recent Press decrees in Prussia and to the way in which the Prussian constitution had been interpreted.

[2] The German Radical Party was formed in March 1884 by the union of the Progressives and the National Liberal secessionists. It supported the development of the Reich constitution along parliamentary lines and opposed Bismarck's protectionist, social and colonial policy.

[3] Heinrich XXII, Prince Reuss. Prussian General.

I heard the foregoing yesterday from Lieutenant-Colonel Count Wedel and repeated it to the Chief over lunch. He then related a number of Austrian reminiscences. One story tells how in 1865 Kaiser Franz Joseph, hearing someone abuse Bismarck in his presence, muttered: 'If only I had him.'

I remarked that according to my information the Kaiser had no self-confidence at all, and was convinced he lacked the right touch.

'He certainly does', replied Prince Bismarck.

I told him how once in the 'sixties Kaiser Franz Joseph was discussing Napoleon III with Oswald Fabrice, the present Saxon Minister in Munich, at a time when Napoleon's star was still in the ascendant. Fabrice, who had spent some time in Paris, had all kinds of things to say and concluded with the remark that the Emperor Napoleon showed great good sense in never forgetting a service rendered.

'I see', said Franz Joseph. 'So you want to teach me a lesson?' and turned his back on him.

Bismarck said that ingratitude was certainly to blame for many of the misfortunes which had befallen the Kaiser, but Buol,[1] his Foreign Minister, is really responsible, not the Kaiser. Buol became Minister by accident. One day Prince Felix Schwarzenberg,[2] who had been overworking, was ordered a long rest by his doctor. The question now arose, who should deputize for him during his leave. Schwarzenberg said to himself: 'I must find my Ministry and my policy exactly as I left them, just like leaving my overcoat in the cloakroom at the theatre.' In short, he was looking for a puppet.

Prompted by this idea, he wrote to the Kaiser and said he thought Count Buol a suitable person to deputize for him. A few hours after writing this note Schwarzenberg died of a stroke. The Kaiser now regarded his advice as a political testament and appointed Buol as Minister.

Count Buol, who as Austrian Minister in St Petersburg had been badly treated by Tsar Nicholas, entered upon his office with feelings of personal vindictiveness against the latter. And yet Tsar Nicholas had a few years previously[3] restored to Kaiser Franz Joseph his lost territory of Hungary, mobilizing 200,000 troops for the purpose and then departing when his work was done without demanding a farthing.

[1] Karl Ferdinand, Count von Buol. Austrian Ambassador in St Petersburg, 1848, in London, 1851; Foreign Minister, 1852–9; in 1855 he presided over the Vienna Conferences and in 1856 he represented Austria at the Paris Peace Conference.
[2] Austrian Minister-President, 1848–52.
[3] At the time of the Hungarian Revolution, 1848–9.

In these circumstances the policy of ingratitude inaugurated and carried out by Buol was thoroughly stupid, but then Buol was a man of very limited outlook.

When Bismarck informed the Austrian Minister to the Federal Diet, Count Thun,[1] of Buol's appointment, he laid his head on the table, burst into tears and cried out again and again: 'Oh, my poor Austria, what will become of you now?'

In fact Austria stood alone from then until 1879.

22 *March* 1884

The Chancellor is indignant with the President of the Reichstag, von Levetzow.[2]

At one of the recent sittings the Social Democrat, Grillen-berger, had said there were a number of secret police in the public galleries (which is perfectly correct).

Instead of giving one of various sensible answers open to him, Levetzow replied he knew nothing of the matter and regarded the allegation as false, since *he* was responsible for the policing of the House and the galleries. He would look into the matter and inform the House of his findings in due course.

In actual fact the Reichstag is allowed by law only the right to regulate its internal discipline. The provision that the police in the public galleries are also subordinated to the President is merely a clause in the internal *standing orders* of the House, and thus cannot claim to have the force of law.

Bismarck read Levetzow's idiotic statement yesterday, flew into a rage, and made an appointment with him for 9.30 this morning. Levetzow, it seems, had not realized at first the folly of his statement.

When Prince Bismarck returned he said: 'You know, he's such a fathead that it's almost an insult—and he's a conceited fathead too. I said to him: "You claim to be a jurist, Mr President, and you attribute the force of law to the internal rulings of the House? But quite apart from the technical aspect, have you concerned yourself at all with the question of internal security? Have you ever given it a thought? And what have you done about it? Are you also prepared to accept responsibility for any outrages which may occur as a direct result of your supposed police supervision?" In short I gave him a piece of my mind. And in the end he climbed

[1] Friedrich, Count von Thun-Hohenstein. Austrian Minister to the Federal Diet in Frankfurt, 1850–2; Minister Extraordinary in Berlin, 1852–7; from December 1859 Minister in St Petersburg.

[2] Albert von Levetzow. German-Conservative Member of the Reichstag; President of the Reichstag, 1881–4, 1888–95.

down and promised to correct his statement on the legal position in a forthcoming sitting of the Reichstag.'

I have long felt surprised that Levetzow's various little blunders have always escaped censure. He is a man of sound views, but his spinelessness outweighs his conservatism. Rather than give a forthright answer, he will sacrifice the government position to the Social Democrats.

The Chief's anger is understandable, for it is principally *his* person that is endangered. As a result of repeated warnings from outside there are policemen posted above his seat, not solely to prevent attacks on his life but to prevent people in the gallery from using opera-glasses to see what he is reading or writing, a thing they have often been seen doing.

In addition to dressing down the culprit in a personal interview, the Chief sent a long communication to Puttkamer, stating the government's legal position and protesting against Levetzow's statement.

It really looks as if Gossler will be dropped. The man is indeed behaving foolishly.

The schools tax question was recently made the subject of an interpellation.

Gossler thought it beneath his dignity to reply to the interpellation himself (and it is certainly exceptional for the Minister himself to do so), but got a junior judge, von Bremen, to reply, who according to the Chancellor spoke utter nonsense, i.e. he defended the *present* policy. The point at issue was as follows. An ancient law dating from feudal times states that the lord of the manor shall pay the school fees and school expenses of 'destitute' villagers. In a foolish decision which will hardly be made a second time, the Appeal Court pronounced that the obligation of the lord of the manor *still* persists even though the feudal relationship has ceased. The responsible officials, who desire above all things to avoid any liability arising for the Treasury out of this, base their decision on this judgment of the Appeal Court. At the same time, by raising the issue of their competency in every single case that occurs, they prevent the problem from again reaching the courts, particularly the Appeal Court, because many jurists think it probable that the Appeal Court would not uphold its earlier decision.

The main reproach the Chancellor levels at Gossler is precisely that he always raises this question of competency instead of giving the courts an opportunity to correct the situation.

The education taxes are said to be so crushing nowadays that

109

some owners of heavily mortgaged estates pay out nearly half their net income for schools.

In addition to actual blunders arising from an exaggerated fear of involving the state financially, Gossler is also spoiling his position by his tactless behaviour.

He was lunching with Rottenburg recently. The R.'s keep a little Bolognese terrier which they pamper to compensate for having no children, and Gossler began by expressing his surprise and displeasure that this animal was allowed in the room during meals.

He went on to remark to Frau Rottenburg yet again that her husband would no doubt soon be rewarded by a consular appointment.

Why behave like that? He should either not lunch with people or not insult them.

After the speech made by the junior judge, von Bremen, the Chancellor said: 'Gossler will really have to go. I must look around for someone else.' [...]

25 *March* 1884

Princess Bismarck is ill, and I regard her condition as serious, even though she is only suffering from a bronchial affection. Her heart is so weak that even with slight disorders one can never be sure she has enough vitality to overcome them.

Princess Bismarck is being treated by Schweninger. She herself would prefer Struck, and Schweninger is quite prepared to make way for him because she is not an easy patient. But Rantzau, who hates Struck, will not allow it.

It was in fact Princess Bismarck who unintentionally caused the break between Prince Bismarck and Struck in 1881. Struck wanted the Princess to spend six weeks in the Bavarian mountains for the sake of her heart while Prince Bismarck was at Kissingen. Both sons were most eager for this plan to be carried out; Princess Bismarck herself, however, went to her husband and told him that Herbert had thought up this scheme so as to be alone with his father in Kissingen and to wrest from him his consent to his marriage with Princess Carolath.[1]

The Chancellor, always ready to entertain suspicions, gave Struck such an excessively rude reception when he mentioned Princess Bismarck's cure that Struck walked out. He wrote next day that his health did not permit of his exposing himself any

[1] Princess Elizabeth von Carolath, *née* von Hatzfeldt-Trachenberg. In April 1881 she obtained a divorce from Prince Carolath-Beuthen in order to marry Herbert von Bismarck.

longer to the painful incidents involved in attending the Bismarck
family.

The Rantzaus would have liked to keep Struck, and the
Countess wrote begging him to remain their family doctor. But
Rantzau had often been rude to him, so Struck refused to go on
attending them and sent in his account for the past two years.
Rantzau had never paid him a farthing.

Since then Rantzau has felt a burning hatred for Struck and has
tried to make trouble for him wherever he can. At the moment
he is insisting that Schweninger attend Princess Bismarck. If
Herbert, himself one of Struck's patients, were here, things would
be different. Schweninger's chief merit lies in the diet he pre-
scribes for his patients, but the Princess has already declared she
cannot follow it. She dislikes the things she is supposed to eat,
and so she either eats nothing at all or else the things she is
forbidden. And so nothing can be done with her in this direction,
whereas in strictly medical treatment Schweninger, so far as I can
judge, is inferior to Struck.

The nursing of Princess Bismarck is as good as non-existent.
At night she is all alone. Her daughter and son-in-law go off to
their flat in the Dorotheenstrasse, and no nurse has been engaged
even though some of the Princess's own relatives are nurses.

The invalid said to Schweninger to-day: 'Tell me whether I'm
going to die. I should like to live a little longer, but if that cannot
be, I should like to be given warning.'

Schweninger told her that provided she took matters quietly
there was no danger, but as soon as she moved about a lot she ran
the risk of congestion of the lungs.

14 *April* 1884
(*Absolutely secret*)

The Crown Princess is very eager to marry her daughter
Victoria to the Prince of Bulgaria.[1] She expects opposition from
the Kaiser and Kaiserin and is counting on the Queen of England
to overcome Their Majesties' resistance, for the Kaiserin would
do anything for Queen Victoria, and the Kaiser almost anything.
With this end in view the Crown Princess has even submitted
with good grace to the humiliating treatment recently meted out
to her by her mother. For in reply to a communication stating
that the Crown Prince and Princess would attend the Duke of

---

[1] Alexander von Battenberg, nephew of Alexander II, Tsar of Russia. On 29 April 1879,
under Russian auspices, he was elected Prince of Bulgaria. By his refusal to play the part of
a Russian satrap he soon incurred the active hostility of the Tsarist Government.

Albany's[1] funeral, Queen Victoria said the Crown Prince might come, but the Princess not before summer. Two telegrams of protest did nothing to alter Her Majesty's decision. The Crown Princess was beside herself, for the dead man had been her favourite brother, the only one with whom she had kept up a continuous correspondence. But she did not consider it advisable to oppose her mother and so she prevailed on the equally indignant Crown Prince to go to England alone, with a single adjutant.

The Bulgarian marriage would be a political mistake. Even if we do not support Prince Alexander, the Russians will still suspect us of doing so. In any case it is still highly probable that the Prince will very shortly be driven out. This, so they say, is exactly what the Crown Princess wants, so that the Prince can be put in command of a brigade of Horse Guards here and can then live with his wife under his mother-in-law's wing, just like von Meiningen.[2] Princess Victoria—or her mother—turned down the hereditary Prince of Anhalt[3] last autumn.

The Chancellor is very much opposed to the Bulgarian marriage because of the political complications that would ensue. But I would not mind betting that Her Imperial Highness gets her own way, unless, contrary to all expectation, a better suitor is found. The Crown Princess is obstinate and calculating. If [she] says to herself: 'The time will come when I shall need that person I have treated badly hitherto', then she changes her tone very gradually. She can be very charming if she wishes, and truth is not a thing she pauses to consider, whereas her husband never lies.

Relations between the Crown Prince and the Chancellor seem quite good at present. The Chancellor called on H.I.H. on Saturday to confer with him on the proposed Council of State, with H.I.H. as President.

The Prince was very frank and cordial, consented to accept the Presidency and expressed his approval of the Chancellor's decision to retire from the Prussian Ministry of State. After the Kaiser's death, which might come any day, the Crown Prince would be very glad to have Bismarck as his Chancellor; he would then appoint Bennigsen and Miquel[4] to direct Prussian affairs.

Prince Bismarck replied that he had no objection to H.I.H.'s making an attempt to govern with the National Liberals; the

[1] Leopold, Queen Victoria's youngest son.
[2] Charlotte, the eldest daughter of Crown Princess Victoria, was married to Bernhard von Meiningen.
[3] Friedrich II, Duke of Anhalt, 1904–18.
[4] Dr Johannes Miquel. Lord Mayor of Frankfurt-am-Main, 1879–90; Prussian Finance Minister, 1890–1901; co-founder of the *Nationalverein*; one of the leaders of the National Liberals in the Prussian Chamber of Deputies and in the Reichstag from 1867.

attempt might succeed. But if H.I.H. wanted to go one step further towards the Left, to Forckenbeck and his friends, he would soon be rushing headlong down the slope to republicanism.

Crown Prince and Chancellor parted on the best of terms. The Prince accompanied Bismarck a considerable way home. Let us hope nothing disturbs this harmony. So long as Bismarck is in office, nothing like the same follies can be committed as when he is gone. It will be most entertaining when, as a simple onlooker, he criticizes the conduct of the Prussian Ministers from the standpoint of the Reich; useful for the Reich as a whole but dangerous for the Ministers concerned, because Bismarck's criticisms will carry great weight not only with the public but also with the future Kaiser.

Prince Bismarck's tendency to criticize everything (with *few* exceptions), regardless of who may be listening, has reached the stage at which it would make life impossible for anyone but himself.

A short while ago he was criticizing members of the Ministry of State to a man he had never seen before; e.g. 'Maybach, excellent for routine but without the least understanding for overall policy.' Quite true, but if Maybach, with his touchy nature, hears of it, he will resign, and Prince Bismarck says himself that Maybach is the only Minister he cannot replace.

Prince Bismarck not only censures what he *must*, he censures everything he *can*. But his initiative is less firm, his actions less ruthless than formerly.

Recently I went to confer with him just after he had got angry with the State Secretary, Burchard.[1] 'Wants to show he's a Minister of the Reich, and can think of nothing better than to have an immediate row with the War Minister about their respective spheres of authority, and then I must suffer the consequences. Burchard is a good chap, but very soon I shall be rude to him, particularly if he contradicts me again, and then he will soon have to go.'

Burchard was recommended for this post by Scholz for the very reason that he is so insignificant and can never be a rival to such a thoroughly seasoned official as Scholz.

'In diplomatic affairs', the Chief said recently, 'I fully recognize people's right to contradict me and resist my plans. The bear has a right to defend itself against me. It is quite a different thing if the bear (i.e. a foreign power) bites me or if my dog bites me.'

---

[1] Emil von Burchard. *Vortragender Rat* in the Reich Chancellery, 1878; Head of the Reich Treasury, 1880; State Secretary, 1882–6.

Whether Lucius, who was also listening, felt happy in the dog's role, I cannot say.

It is very amusing to watch how differently the other Ministers behave according to whether the Chancellor is present or not. The other day, in Scholz's presence, someone referred to the Chancellor by the name we all use, 'the Chief'. 'Chief, Chief', said Scholz, bridling. 'My colleague.' In contrast it is worth watching Scholz's behaviour, not only to the Chancellor, but even to Rottenburg or Bill.

The Chancellor told me a few days ago that when he was in Paris in 1857 to settle the Neuenburg question[1] Napoleon III outlined to him his plan for attacking Austria, with Prussia's help. Bismarck, who regarded Austria as Prussia's arch-enemy so long as she remained in the Germanic Confederation, replied: 'I am glad for Your Majesty's sake that you have imparted this information to the only Prussian diplomat who will not use it to Your Majesty's disadvantage. I decline to pass it on, because I am convinced in advance that my Government will do nothing and might even prejudice Your Majesty's plans by being indiscreet. I should not like to requite Your Majesty's confidence in that way.'

A peculiar grouping has gradually formed in the Chancellor's family. Rantzau and his wife would like to squeeze out the two sons.

Herbert's influence on his father is so firmly rooted that he can only be ousted in a spatial sense, i.e. by being persuaded that his chances are better abroad than in Berlin. Rantzau has been fairly successful in this, and has also wormed his way into Herbert's favour by flattery and admiration.

But Bill, who is not so easy to get round and is also a cool observer, was particularly inconvenient. In order to get rid of him Rantzau dropped hints for quite a long time that Bill's illness this winter was chiefly imagination, a means of obtaining leave. In addition his father was told 'accidentally' what a wonderful time Bill was having in Italy, instead of coming back to his sick mother. No mention was made of the fact that Bill had not been told *one word* about her illness.

Bismarck spoke his mind about his son with his usual frankness.

---

[1] The canton of Neuenburg, a member of the Swiss Confederation but subject to the suzerainty of the King of Prussia, became a republic in March 1848. In 1856 a Conservative revolt attempted a restoration of the monarchy. War between Prussia and Switzerland was averted through the intervention of Napoleon III. In May 1857 the King of Prussia renounced his rights in return for the promise of a financial settlement, which he also subsequently renounced.

Rantzau was waiting for that: 'Bill doesn't feel happy here. I think he'd like to go into the diplomatic service.' 'We can easily arrange that', said the old man indignantly, and things seemed to be going well for Rantzau.

Even Schweninger, whom the Rantzaus had won over by all the means in their power, urged Bill on his return to go over to the diplomatic service, for the sake of his health.

But there were several people who warned Bill: Rottenburg, Frau von Wallenberg and I. He waited a few days to see which way the wind was blowing, then said: 'Now I am certain they want me out of the house; now I shall stay for sure.' He is now trying to win back his father's favour after several years' estrangement. May he succeed, for he is a man of integrity, in contrast to Rantzau, who follows *nothing* but his own interests and whims.

Rantzau, by the way, is furious at the moment because for the last two days it has been almost certain that the Chancellor will remain in office when the Crown Prince becomes Kaiser. He expressed his disapproval to-day at great length.

He would like to sponge on his parents-in-law and do nothing, year in, year out, and for that reason the Chancellor should retire. An arrant knave is Rantzau.

15 *April* 1884

Dryander,[1] the Superintendent, dined with the Chancellor yesterday. The latter said he would like to be Minister of Education for a few years, for he would then make many changes. 'Would you oppose the present overworking of schoolchildren?' asked Dryander.

'Yes, particularly learning by heart, more especially in religious instruction. There's too much learning of the catechism and passages from the Bible. That's no use. I am more for prayer, hymns and church-going. It's not knowledge you want, but faith, and *that* cannot be forced on a person. If that person later becomes an unbeliever, he only turns what he has learned by heart into mockery at religion.'

Dryander, who seems more tactful than the average Protestant minister, did not become involved in an argument, although he probably approved of His Highness's views as little as I do. It seems to me like saying that a soldier is ruined by drill and by learning the various exercises, because victories are won by sheer

[1] Ernst von Dryander. Evangelical theologian; Superintendent-General of the Evangelical Church in Berlin from 1882.

enthusiasm. In religious matters H.H. is not authoritative; in that sphere, he has sought and *not* found, like so many others.

One day at the end of March, just before the Reichstag was prorogued, the Chancellor requested Miquel, the Lord Mayor, to call on him. But Miquel had already left the previous day.

It was clear from Prince Bismarck's first Reichstag speech of the year, in which he referred to 'his personal and political friend Bennigsen',[1] that he was anxious to make contact with the right wing of the National Liberals. When I spoke to him that day over lunch about this very statement, expressing agreement, he replied: 'Yes, I was trying to encourage the National Liberals. Unless they regain their former spirit the ship of state will once more be on the rocks.' The Chancellor has come round to this view recently because he has become convinced the Conservatives alone can never obtain a majority in the Reichstag, and also because the Conservatives have no one of outstanding political ability.

I thus felt I knew the Chancellor's intentions and felt even more sure of it when I heard he had just sent for Miquel. Bleichröder, who will tolerate no financial gods besides himself, has for years systematically poisoned the Chancellor's mind against Miquel, who is the most intelligent of the right-wing National Liberals. The fact that Bismarck now wishes to confer specifically with Miquel shows that he is earnest.

I spoke to Dietze-Barby[2] about this matter and we both felt sorry Miquel had already left Berlin. Dietze, when I requested him to write to Miquel, said it would attract too much notice, because the Chancellor had often employed him on similar semi-official tasks in parliamentary circles. He advised me to write, which I did, telling myself somebody had to do it. So I told Miquel the Chancellor had sent for him and that I wished to let him know, because I should be glad if he and Prince Bismarck could get together again after a long interval. I had not been instructed to write, and the affair was neither definite nor urgent.

Several days went by before I had a reply. Miquel had obviously first written to Bennigsen and come to some agreement. I then received the following reply: he was very glad, and was prepared to come at any time, but asked me to let him know if he ought to be back before 15 April. He would be back about the 15th in any case.[3]

Of course I did not reply because I could see that my letter had

[1] Speech of 13 March 1884 (*Die gesammelten Werke*, vol. XII, pp. 406–16).

[2] G. A. von Dietze. Member of the Reichstag (Free Conservative party).

[3] Miquel's letter of 30 March is among the Holstein Papers, and has here been accurately summarized.

already produced the desired effect. I had further proof of this when rumours suddenly appeared in the Press that Miquel had been offered, and had declined a portfolio.[1] The Chief, reading this, and knowing nothing about it, was most astonished and issued a denial. I should probably have been reprimanded had he known that I had dared to have an idea of my own. The fact that I do occasionally show any initiative at all, after more than twenty years of Bismarck's discipline, shows how dogged I am.

Of course I kept very quiet, and I knew that the two others in the secret, Dietze and Rottenburg (to say nothing of Bill), would say nothing.

And to-day there is an account in the Press of a policy speech Miquel has just made in Neustadt a.d. Haardt. His aims are—to unite in a group the scattered National Liberal elements in *support* of the Chancellor and to *oppose* the German Radicals. I think the speech will please the Chief. Would Miquel have made such a speech but for my letter? I do not know, but I doubt it. The rapprochement with the National Liberals and Bennigsen has already been proclaimed from the rostrum by the Chief himself, but Miquel had retired from political life with the feeling that *he personally* was unacceptable to the Chancellor. My letter at least disposed of that idea, and I feel I have done some good behind the scenes.

If the Chancellor now reaches an agreement with the Bennigsen-Miquel bloc, and if they later come to power in Prussia under the new reign, his action will have prevented violent upheavals. For supposing the Bennigsen cabinet were overthrown, while Bismarck still had a say in Reich affairs he would certainly have enough influence on the Kaiser and the nation to prevent Forckenbeck, Bamberger,[2] Richter and their associates from seizing power.

The good fight is more than half won provided the Stosch-Forckenbeck group is not swept into power *in the first moment of intoxication* with the change of government.

16 *April* 1884

Friedberg told us yesterday that the Crown Prince was delighted with the outcome of his discussion with the Chancellor,

---

[1] Miquel wrote to Holstein on 16 April: 'After this senseless gossip in the Press—and in this connexion I need hardly assure you that I told nobody of your kind letter—I thought it right, and in [accordance] with the Chancellor's wishes, not to come to Berlin for the present.'

[2] Ludwig Bamberger. National Liberal Member of the Reichstag from 1871; as an opponent of Bismarck's protection policy he took part in the so-called secession in 1880, and in 1884 he joined the German Radical Party.

and with the latter's retirement from the Prussian Ministry. The Prince intends to 'send packing' all the present Ministers except Maybach, who is irreplaceable. And of course Friedberg quietly excepts himself too.

The Crown Prince, he said, then intends to have a shot with Miquel and Bennigsen.

On Saturday Friedberg met the Chancellor in the Tiergarten. Bismarck roundly abused the Crown Prince for not asking to see him until eight p.m. simply because he has spent the whole day hunting at Spandau. The Chancellor said, among other things, that Easter Saturday was particularly unsuitable for hunting; it was not the practice of the country, and the same thing could be said to the Crown Prince as Ziethen said to Frederick the Great: 'Your Majesty, if ever the whole country believes what *you* believe, then everything will go to rack and ruin.'

Friedberg said he was embarrassed to hear all this, and was in doubt whether the Chancellor intended his remarks to reach the Crown Prince's ears or not. But he thought it best to say nothing.

And he was quite right. If all the Chancellor's abuse were repeated, even he would be ruined. At the moment I can recall no instance of his having praised a man during his lifetime. After his death, maybe, but even then it was not from respect for the dead, but to humiliate the living by the comparison.

He even utters harsh opinions of his younger son, Bill, and has done so for years, even to strangers. Only Herbert is spared; he is a younger edition of his father, and never contradicts him, whereas Bill occasionally has ideas of his own.

I have the impression that Bismarck has recently felt a certain jealousy of Hatzfeldt, who, though a pitiably weak character, is yet the cleverest diplomat after Bismarck whom I have come across in twenty-three years. Hatzfeldt is far from entertaining any thought of opposition. He does all he can to please the Chancellor, but sometimes he obtains the Kaiser's and the Crown Prince's consent to things with greater ease than the Chancellor had anticipated; the latter then becomes uneasy and tries to browbeat Hatzfeldt at the earliest opportunity.

The Chancellor's great weakness, the point where even mediocre people surpass him, is the handling of people. He lumps them all together and mistrusts them all. This contempt of mankind is of a piece with his vanity; it suits him to be like that.

I have no illusions about the Chancellor's humanity but as an institution I think he is the best thing the German Reich possesses, and neither one man nor many could replace him. A proof of this is the way he has made all preparations to steer the ship of state through the stormy days of the succession that lies ahead. The Crown Prince can make one or two little liberal experiments in Prussia, and Bismarck will be there to advise in case of need should disappointments arise, as they did for King Wilhelm after the New Era[1] began.

17 *April* 1884

The opponents of the new Council of State have been working on His Majesty, not without success. Yesterday the Chancellor had a four-page letter from the Kaiser full of objections, all of which oddly enough make great play with liberalism.[2] H.M. had absorbed all the arguments of the liberal Press, but there was one he did not mention, the very one which had proved decisive. The *Berliner Tageblatt* had said that by having the Crown Prince as President of the Council of State, the Chancellor retained full control of Prussian affairs. It sounded rather as though the Chancellor and the Crown Prince wanted to govern Prussia without the King. The relevant passage was printed in heavy type to be sure of catching the eye. There are many indications that the Kaiser had been shown this article, which had touched him in his most vulnerable spot. Wilmowski[3] may also be behind this. Both Bismarck and Hatzfeldt are suspicious of him. He is not a bad man at heart but a somewhat advanced Liberal, egged on by *Wirklicher Geheimer Legationsrat* von Wilke, with whom he is closely related by marriage in some way; I think Wilmowski's son married Wilke's daughter. Wilke is very rich; his wife is the Treu and Nuglisch[4] heiress. After his marriage Wilke decided that his position as *Vortragender Rat* in Division II—from which at the time he conducted the Arnim trial with incredible stupidity—was no longer worthy of him, and declared that unless he were made Minister or at least *Vortragender Rat* in the Political Division, he would hand in his resignation, and this was accepted. But he was still treated very kindly, with promotion to first-class *Rat* and elevation to the nobility. But he is bored, he is bursting with vanity, and has repeatedly asked to be made a Minister; once he asked for Berne, once for Athens. Because he is given nothing (for there is no reason why an indifferent counsel should make an efficient Minister), he is furious and invokes curses on

---

[1] The term applied to the Government of moderate Liberals appointed by Prince Wilhelm as Regent of Prussia in October 1858.
[2] See Goldschmidt, *Das Reich und Preussen*, pp. 306–8.
[3] Karl, Baron von Wilmowski. Head of Wilhelm I's Civil Cabinet.
[4] A soap and perfume factory.

the present government, from the Chancellor down. So it is possible that Wilmowski has been up to some mischief. At any rate it is hard to see who else but Wilmowski could have shown the Kaiser the Progressive newspapers from which he took his arguments. Certainly His Most Serene did not produce *that* type of Radical consideration out of his own head.

But the Kaiser's letter was very polite. He merely expressed his wish that the points he raised should be given further consideration.

The Chancellor inquired to-day whether His Majesty would grant him an audience. H.M. replied he was still too exhausted, yet at the same time he held lengthy consultations first with Bronsart, then Albedyll.

I need hardly say that the Chancellor is indignant at this behaviour. He summoned a Ministerial Council and held forth for a whole hour about nothing else. Since he abuses everything, he abused the Kaiser too, and let it appear that he thought His Majesty's letter of yesterday, though certainly dated the 13th, was antedated; on the 13th His Majesty had not been aware of all the considerations he adduced in his letter.

The Chancellor called the refusal to receive him to-day, while consenting to receive other people, an attack of feminine nerves: 'His Majesty is as nervous as a woman.'

It is of course a fact that the old gentleman only wanted to avoid an unpleasant discussion, but the Chancellor would not have damaged his cause by picking his words more carefully. But then, he cannot help being what he is. All this abuse is so pointless, in that he is certain to put the matter through with the Kaiser when next he sees him. But he, the Chancellor, still feels the need of some resistance to overcome.

I am curious to see what attitude the Chancellor will adopt in future towards Hatzfeldt and the Foreign Ministry. Hatzfeldt, who gave up his 40,000-taler post as Ambassador to please the Chancellor, cannot live on 50,000 marks in Berlin; if they want to keep him they must give him an increase. The forthcoming appointment of a Prussian Foreign Minister (in addition to the Imperial State Secretary) would present an opportunity for arranging an additional salary. But the Chancellor has so far seemed averse to any one's drawing two salaries. Since he knows Hatzfeldt's position, this is as good as obliging him to give up his post here and to accept the first Ambassadorship that falls vacant—if one does.

The Chancellor may be intending to restore his former close

connexion with the Foreign Ministry, and may therefore prefer as State Secretary a man of less political ability and social standing. He would certainly like Herbert most of all as an intermediary between himself and the Ministry.

So long as the Chancellor is alive this will work, in fact any arrangement will work. But once he is gone I am firmly convinced that Hatzfeldt is the only man who can direct our foreign policy. He has a quick and comprehensive grasp of a situation, and *great* skill in handling it. Whether he would also display resolution at the vital moment, is another question.

18 *April* 1884

When I told General Caprivi yesterday that the cordial relations at present existing between the Chancellor and the Crown Prince led me to suppose the Chancellor would probably still stay in harness in the coming reign, he said: 'I'm glad to hear it, particularly as I had recently begun to think the Crown Prince was an even lesser man than I had supposed.'

The Kaiser himself has no great opinion of his son. When His Majesty and the Chancellor were recently discussing the Council of State (on which of course they saw eye to eye), and also the Crown Prince's presidency, the Kaiser said: 'I'll be interested to see how soon he gets tired of it.'

The Chancellor said that in the '60's the Crown Prince used to attend the Council of Ministers, but he almost dislocated his jaw with yawning, and gradually stopped going.

When discussing the persons who may be using the Kaiser as a stalking-horse in order to oppose the Council of State, the Chancellor mentioned the name of Roggenbach,[1] who had always been ill-disposed towards him.

I asked: 'Is Roggenbach intelligent?'

'No, but he has great self-assurance and a glib tongue, and he has a way with noble ladies. He takes the credit for being the first to devise the idea of a Reich. That's nonsense. What *he* had was not an idea, but merely the dream of German unity shared by a score of other charlatans. But nobody in that assemblage knew how to set about achieving it.

[1] Franz, Baron von Roggenbach. Foreign Minister of Baden, 1861–5; Member of the Reichstag (German Reich Party), 1871–3; as a confidant of Grand-Duke Friedrich I and of the Prussian Crown Prince, he worked for the creation of a *kleindeutsch* liberal Reich under the leadership of Prussia. In 1865 he resigned as Foreign Minister because he disapproved of Bismarck's policy in the constitutional conflict and the Schleswig-Holstein question. Later he was often mentioned as the Crown Prince's choice to succeed Bismarck as Chancellor.

'Simson,[1] the President, is another of them. I did not congratulate him on his jubilee last year because in order to satisfy him I should have had to tell lies: he too imagines he founded the German Reich, and does me the honour of regarding me at most as a collaborator. "Men like you and me", he thinks, and that's the style I should have had to use if I had written.'

'The Austrian-Germans', said the Chancellor, 'are wine-bibbing Bavarians, without, however, distended stomachs, and therefore more light-headed and volatile. If Charles V and Ferdinand I had gone over to Protestantism, the Austrian nation would be intellectually more able than it is.'

21 *April* 1884

[...] The proposed Battenberg marriage, of which I wrote the other day, is already having all kinds of repercussions. A few days ago the Chancellor, in a conversation with the Kaiser, warned him of possible interference by Queen Victoria. His Majesty was indignant at the idea of such a possibility. 'She can do what she likes with her own Princess Beatrice,[2] but she'd better leave my Princess[3] alone.'

And yesterday the Crown Princess sent for the Chancellor—a most rare occurrence. I asked him to-day how his interview with the Crown Princess had gone. He said it went very well; the lady was now sweetness itself, but he was still rather suspicious. No doubt she wanted something; perhaps she wanted him to win over the Kaiser to a marriage between the Prince of Battenberg and Princess Beatrice or maybe Princess Victoria.

I told him I had heard it was the latter, and that the Crown Princess was not particularly anxious for the Prince to remain in Bulgaria; on the contrary she would rather have him here as brigade commander. 'I see', he said with a laugh, 'a second Meiningen.' I observed that in my opinion it might be better not to oppose the marriage, because the Crown Princess took more interest in these personal matters than in factual problems. An affair of this nature would certainly affect relations between her and the Chancellor, for better or for worse.

Prince Bismarck thought for a moment, then said: 'I have already done her several favours, such as obtaining the Kaiser's

[1] Martin Eduard von Simson. President of the Frankfurt National Assembly, 1848; President of the Prussian Chamber of Deputies, 1860–1; President of the North German and German Reichstag, 1867–73; President of the *Reichsgericht*, 1879–91.

[2] Princess Beatrice, youngest daughter of Queen Victoria. In 1886 she married Heinrich von Battenberg, brother of the Prince of Bulgaria.

[3] Princess Victoria, second daughter of the Crown Prince Friedrich Wilhelm.

consent to the Augustenburg marriage,[1] but always to no effect.'

I said she had recently grown very much estranged from those persons who had influenced her against the Chancellor, and for more or less personal reasons: they had wanted to run the Crown Prince without her or in opposition to her. My impression was, from what I had heard, that the Chancellor could easily manage the Crown Princess if he occasionally did her some favour in personal matters, and talked politics with her in detail from time to time.

The Chancellor said in conclusion that the Kaiser would never be persuaded to consent to the marriage of his granddaughter with the grandson of a Polish-German doctor (Haucke).[2]

I have the impression that the Crown Princess made direct reference to this marriage yesterday and asked for Bismarck's support. He in his turn probably sheltered behind the Kaiser. He could not admit this to me in so many words, since he had undoubtedly promised to say nothing.

When I advised him to have a talk with the Crown Princess occasionally, he said: 'Yes, if I were ten years younger, but now I've lost my enthusiasm. Now that I've lost my passion for hunting I can't stir up enthusiasm for anything.'

'Well', I said, 'that may all come back. You would never have thought you'd ride again, but you ride now, to the amazement of the Berliners.'

'But without the least enthusiasm', he said.

I knew this tone and immediately went on to tell him—and it is perfectly true—that his enemies, Stosch and Co., are completely thunderstruck now they realize that the present Chancellor is not so near fading out as they thought. 'And', he said, this time with no trace of melancholy, 'they've not even begun to realize the implications of my retirement from Prussian affairs. This is the price for my remaining under the Crown Prince, who is quite extraordinarily keen to keep me on as *Chancellor*.'

We went on to discuss Waldersee. The Chief spoke very disapprovingly of him. 'He's become a terrible fire-eater. He talks to everyone passing through Berlin about military operations, now against Russia, now against France, and occasionally he also discusses the possibility of our being obliged to violate Swiss

[1] Augusta Victoria, daughter of Duke Friedrich von Augustenburg (the former Pretender to the Duchies of Schleswig and Holstein), married Prince Wilhelm of Prussia (the future Kaiser Wilhelm II) in 1881.

[2] Prince Alexander von Hesse-Darmstadt, father of Alexander von Battenberg, married Countess Julie Haucke in 1851. Countess Haucke was the daughter of a Polish General and granddaughter of a German doctor who had emigrated to Poland. See the entry for 5 May 1884.

neutrality. The people he talks to are not always discreet, and then we get endless scandals in the Press. These considerations in peace-time do no good at all, there's time enough for that later.'

Waldersee has already received two sharp notes from the Chief on account of his liking for academic war councils. I do not think Waldersee has the mind to direct a million soldiers in the event of war.

The Chancellor was dissatisfied with the Foreign Ministry officials to-day because of their rude manner. He expressed his displeasure to Bojanowski, the Director, and said there were only two well-bred people in the Ministry, Hatzfeldt and myself. 'I don't count you, of course', he remarked to Bojanowski, as an afterthought. He was particularly outraged by Bucher's rudeness and Kusserow's pompous insolence.

After the conference he asked me whether I would come and dine with a couple of wild Holsteiners. I asked who they were. He said, Rantzau's brother-in-law *Brockdorff* and his son. I said in that case I would rather come another time.

21 *April* 1884

The Chancellor sent for me to-day at eleven, when I was with Hatzfeldt, and then again at four.

When I asked after his health he immediately complained about annoyances. The Kaiser, after their last conference, had promised to let him have the signed Cabinet order on the Council of State. The whole of yesterday he had waited for it in vain and as a result had passed a sleepless night wondering what to do now. To-day he had been on the point of going to see H.M. to remind him of his promise when it had suddenly come to light by pure chance that the order, duly signed, had already been received at the Reich Chancellery yesterday afternoon, whence it had been sent to the Ministry of State by a stupid Chancellery clerk without one word being said to the Chancellor. 'It's not Rottenburg's fault. He can't sit in the Reich Chancellery twelve hours on end. Bill takes far too much advantage of a father's leniency. I shall have to depend on strangers if I want Reich Chancellery business done properly.' Bill and the Under State Secretary, Homeyer,[1] were both blown sky-high. Homeyer is a slow, wealthy old bachelor, an insignificant figure. Moreover Prince Bismarck thinks he is secretly an enemy, an adherent of free trade and horse-drawn street-cars (two of His Highness' *bêtes noires*), and he believes that

[1] Gustav Homeyer. Under State Secretary in the Prussian Ministry of State.

Homeyer once told Camphausen[1] a secret—the very man he should not have told.

Reprimands have been flying about a good deal lately. Busch, who admittedly lacks a thorough grasp of his position, being originally a philologist and knowing nothing of law or economics, also blundered recently in a matter of some importance concerning Division II. It was certainly a grave error. Busch, whose courage is not his strong point, tried hard to throw the blame on to someone else, and did in fact succeed in creating serious embarrassment for another official, but did not himself escape an unpleasant interview with His Highness, from which he emerged very white and shaken. Immediately afterwards he took several weeks' sick leave. I think he will probably be pushed off into a Legation after a while, and be replaced by Herbert.

Eisendecher has also been misunderstanding things again. Prince Bismarck asked to see his instructions for the matter in question, pork products, and noted that the draft was fifty-nine pages long. So he said to Bojanowski this morning: 'No wonder such instructions are misunderstood. I can hardly understand them myself, let alone a mendicant Minister like him, who thinks it his duty to go around begging the Americans to maintain cordial relations, whereas they don't matter at all.'

In all this the old gentleman is unquestionably right as regards the facts, but everything could be settled just as well, or even better, without any fuss; but then he is like that.

25 *April* 1884

I dined with Prince Bismarck yesterday. After the meal we were left alone for a while.

I mentioned that according to a telegram in the Press the Prince of Bulgaria was coming to Darmstadt to attend his brother's[2] wedding.

'Yes', said the Chancellor, 'and Princess Victoria will be there too. If they want to marry the Princess to the Prince of Battenberg after he has ceased to be Prince of Bulgaria, then it's simply a poor match, which affects nobody but the parties concerned. But so long as the young Prince remains in his present exposed position between Austria and Russia, he cannot possibly marry our Princess. We cannot jeopardize our relations with Russia merely to please a hysterical female.'

The last time I spoke to him on the subject he was not nearly

[1] Otto von Camphausen. Prussian Finance Minister, 1869–78.
[2] Prince Ludwig von Battenberg married Princess Victoria of Hesse on 30 April.

125

so determined. But now that he has thought the matter over and reached his decision the marriage will hardly take place under the Bismarck regime.

The Chancellor told me that Schweinitz had come to dinner the other day. When he had gone Dietze-Barby, who had been quietly watching him, delivered the following opinion of him: 'It seems to me that our friend would like to appear cleverer than he is.' 'That opinion', said Bismarck, 'is absolutely correct. In order to keep up an appearance of superiority, Schweinitz has accustomed himself to a degree of taciturnity which is a positive insult to the people he is talking to. Andrássy, who wanted to get rid of him, told me: "He always looks as if he were trying to say: I know an awful lot, but I'm not going to tell you because you wouldn't understand."'

'Even so', went on Prince Bismarck, 'although Schweinitz has been rather too engrossed in his children recently, he is someone you can count on when you need him. He still has the Prussian spirit. But Werder is out to feather his own nest, has little sense of honour and is cast in the mould of the generals of Jena, who were doubtless dashing fellows in their youth, but had lost their drive since then.'

The word Jena prompted me to bring up the subject of Moltke's successor. I said I liked Waldersee as a person, but hardly imagined he was intelligent enough to manœuvre a million troops across the chessboard of world history.

'I think I agree', said the Chancellor, 'but in the first place I know the others too little, and secondly the Kaiser would hardly allow me any say in the matter. Years ago I once made the suggestion that the army chiefs were too old, without mentioning names, but even so I met with a poor reception. "The commanders are all younger than I am", said H.M. "So you think I should resign too?" I replied: "Your Majesty cannot resign, and in any case a monarch is always younger than other people." But that did me no good. H.M. was offended and remained so, and the famous young man who could have taken Paris in September 1870, if he had thought of trying, remained commander of his army corps.

'The army has always been so jealous of me that I should have them all against me if I pronounced an opinion. In 1866 when it was proposed to besiege Vienna, thereby losing valuable time, I suggested instead that we should mass our troops lower down the Danube as if we wanted to cross the river at Pressburg. All the generals were furious, but the King supported me and orders were given for the movement downstream. When we emerged from the war council all the generals, including Roon, walked away without speaking to me. But I was justified by the result. The moment the Austrians saw we were showing signs of marching on Vienna from the south, they asked for an armistice.

'During the siege of Paris in 1870 Moltke again acted weakly by giving way to the feminine intrigues aimed at preventing a bombardment, and thereby infinitely increased the hazards of the war. I will not dwell on the fact that both in '66 and in '70 individual commanders like Bonin[1] and Steinmetz[2] were thoroughly incompetent. We owe the greater part of our success to organization and discipline.

'I don't know much about Waldersee, either for or against. But the army chiefs accept him. And I know nothing about any one else I might try to put in his place. Bronsart and Lehndorff speak favourably of Waldersee. The thing I complain of in Waldersee is that he's too fond of talking to all kinds of unreliable people about military plans which then leak out and arouse the mistrust of the general public. But old Blücher[3] also talked ten to the dozen, and was a good leader nevertheless, because of his dash and mettle.'

This argument seemed to me to rest on an imperfect knowledge of human nature. Blücher was a field general, whereas we need a mathematician and a strategist as Moltke's successor.

I was discussing the matter with Bill Bismarck this morning and he said that his father's remarks on the subject simply meant he did not want to bother about it. The Chancellor was more worried about his health than he pretended, and he was therefore firmly resolved to limit the scope of his activities.

On the subject of foreign policy the Chancellor said: 'We can't go on treating England badly or else she and France will again form a nucleus which will then attract other nations to it.'

He said this with reference to the fact that we had just received England's invitation to the Egyptian Conference[4] and had by our acceptance probably brought about the acceptance of those Powers which might otherwise have proved difficult.

'Whether the Conference will be of any advantage to the

---

[1] Adolf von Bonin. Prussian General. He was defeated by Gablenz at Trautenau on 27 June 1866.

[2] Karl Friedrich von Steinmetz. Prussian General. As Commander of the First Army in 1870 he was unwilling to subordinate his personal initiative to Moltke's over-all strategy. On 15 September 1870 he was appointed Governor-General of Silesia and Posen.

[3] Gebhard Leberecht von Blücher. Prussian General during the Napoleonic Wars.

[4] In April 1884 England invited the Powers to attend a conference in London to discuss Egypt's financial position and in particular to consider the possibility of altering the law relating to the liquidation of Egyptian debts.

English is doubtful. Once they are sitting round the conference table they cannot prevent the representatives of other Great Powers from speaking, even if they make inconvenient suggestions.'

I asked whether a community of ideas and interests between France and Russia could result from the Egyptian question.

'Well', he said, 'provided it were aimed against England it wouldn't be a bad thing.'

He shows his greatness in his cool appraisal of diplomatic situations. Here his emotions do not come into play. He hates Gladstone but does not wish to include England in this hatred. And perhaps he suspects that Gl. will commit worse blunders at the Egyptian Conference than he would have done without it.

27 *April* 1884

After to-day's Ministerial Council Prince Wilhelm paid a call on the Chancellor just as he was going to see the Kaiser. The Prince offered to drive the Chancellor there in his own carriage, which he did to the great edification of the thousands of Sunday strollers. If the Crown Prince reads about it in the papers he will be less edified.

Yesterday I wrote a private and confidential letter to Seckendorff in Darmstadt to say that in my opinion the idea of a Bulgarian marriage would come to nothing. I pointed out that it was less a question of opposition from one or two individuals, but rather the attitude of the general public, which would be very loath to see the German Reich caught up in the Bulgarian question because of family interests. Personal attacks on royal ladies would undoubtedly be launched by certain sections of the Press.

It is of course uncertain whether Seckendorff can do anything to prevent it, but it is possible. The Crown Princess is aware how unpopular she is in Germany and so is really afraid of damaging comments by the Press.

After dinner to-day the Chancellor again spoke of the army and its leadership, and again maintained that it was the soldier, i.e. the officer at the front, always at the head of his troops, who won the wars; the upper and the supreme command made countless mistakes. I refused to be drawn into a discussion, because I had only recently said at length all I thought necessary. I merely observed that up to now we ourselves had only had to pit our strength against second-rate commanders; one might speculate on the course of events if ever an outstanding figure came to the fore in France or Russia—which was quite conceivable. The Chancellor said that with their troops against ours, even a man like that would achieve nothing.

I said no more, for it is best not to press him. I should be surprised if he had not taken the point and if he did not make a few inquiries about our army leaders. On Thursday I had mentioned Caprivi and Brandenstein[1] and said Verdy[2] was perhaps the most intelligent of all, but stout, lazy and without the requisite traits of character.

I am sorry the Chancellor is in fact cutting himself off more and more from men or rather from mankind. He said a couple of days ago that the number of people he liked having to dine with him was so small it would not be right to have many at one time. And so he usually invites just one guest daily, rarely two.

It was less interesting to-day because Schweninger was there and I had to be careful what I said and what questions I asked. And Bismarck spoke less freely than on Thursday.

I am reluctant to take steps against Waldersee as a person, because we are on good terms and I hope he will always enjoy a good position. But I do not think he is a strategist, and the mere thought of everything collapsing after a single battle is intolerable.

29 *April* 1884

Internal official relations at the Foreign Ministry are somewhat confused at present. Much of the trouble lies in the fact that Hatzfeldt, though remarkably talented, is also a remarkably weak character and incapable of saying anything unpleasant to any one.

The Under State Secretary, Busch, a former philologist, crafty and adroit, but without the first idea of law or economics, blindly follows the advice of a certain *Wirklicher Geheimer Legationsrat* Göring.[3] This Göring, an advocate of free trade, a democrat, an enemy of the aristocracy, counted on becoming Director the last time the post fell vacant. Instead Bojanowski was appointed. Now Busch and Göring are doing their best between them to squeeze out Bojanowski. Busch is Bojanowski's immediate superior. Busch requests Göring's opinion on every suggestion coming from Bojanowski. Göring then invariably pronounces against the suggestion, whether it is a question of consulate staff, or an innovation in the handling of business in Division II, and Busch adopts his view. Bojanowski is becoming disheartened, and his

---

[1] Karl von Brandenstein. Prussian General; Section Chief at headquarters, in charge of the army railway system during the War of 1870–1.

[2] Julius von Verdy du Vernois. Prussian General; Minister for War, 1889–90.

[3] *Vortragender Rat* in Division II of the Foreign Ministry.

senior officials, who of course notice that he never pushes anything through, are themselves becoming more enterprising than is proper.

A few weeks ago a blunder was committed in Division II which made the Chancellor furious—and no wonder (Mendelssohn Affair).[1] Hatzfeldt was not involved; the offending document was signed by Busch. Busch did his utmost, as usual, to throw the blame on someone else, but even so he suffered a good deal of unpleasantness and is now going on leave to recover. Bojanowski is now directing his Division himself independently, and *pro forma* is also running Division I. Nothing has been happening here, but in the last few days two more incidents have occurred one after the other in Division II, annoying the Chancellor and proving how lax the discipline is. Hatzfeldt very much wanted me to say something to Bojanowski; but at my insistence he decided to do it himself. Bojanowski was beside himself with rage —let us hope it may help. He does his best, is very able and unusually well-informed on economic policy, about which he knows more than Busch and Göring put together. But he is also weak and unable to stand up for himself against his officials or the Under State Secretary. I have just been seriously reproaching him and telling him that, together with many good qualities, he shares with Hatzfeldt the inability to say anything unpleasant.

Business really is made far more difficult by the Chancellor's method of work. He sends first for one man, then for another, sometimes works on the same question with different people, and despises on principle any organic division.

1 *May* 1884

The Russian loan which has just been floated owes its enormous success (eighteen times over-subscribed) mainly to the participation of the *Seehandlung*.[2] I have already mentioned that the Minister, Scholz, who had been circumvented, subsequently spoke unfavourably of the co-operation of a state organization and the influence such co-operation would exert on the public, and that

---

[1] The editors did not have access to the files of Division II. From a Bismarck memorandum of 31 March 1884, a copy of which is in the files of the Political Division, it appears that a pardon had been granted to a Russian Socialist named Mendelssohn without Bismarck's knowledge. Schweinitz was instructed to inform Giers that steps would be taken to prevent similar cases occurring.

[2] Prussian State Bank. Founded by Friedrich II in 1772 as the '*Seehandlungsgesellschaft*' (Merchant Shipping Company) to 'encourage shipping under the Prussian flag'. In 1820 the company was reconstituted as an independent state banking and trade institute under state guarantee. Raising money for the state became its main function. In 1843 it also took over the State Loan-office.

the Chancellor was annoyed with him and had spoken disparagingly about him.[1]

Since then Rötger, the President of the *Seehandlung*, has quarrelled with Bleichröder because he refuses to show Rötger the originals of his correspondence with the Russian Government about the loan, and has sent the *Seehandlung* only a few extracts. One can only suppose that Bleichröder has privately stipulated that the Russians pay him a few hundred thousand roubles or so as a special fee, and that he does not want to share these with the *Seehandlung*.

Bleichröder called on the Chancellor yesterday to complain, and thus to forestall Rötger's complaint. In the Chancellor's ante-room, in front of Bötticher, Rottenburg and others, Bl. cursed the 'arrogance of these Prussian officials', and 'this man Rötger's cheek . . . but I won't be treated like that' etc.

When Bl. had gone in to the Chancellor, Bötticher said to Rottenburg: 'You are largely responsible for this insolence. You've given Bl. a swelled head, he used not to be like *that*.' Of course Rottenburg protested but Bötticher is right. Rottenburg privately hates Bleichröder, but fears him still more, and thinks he will be ruined if ever Bleichröder says a word to the Chancellor against him. Only yesterday he said to me: 'Yes, Bleichröder is a first-rate grave-digger.' As a result Rottenburg is full of little attentions for Bl. A year and a half ago in Scheveningen he went walking with Bleichröder for hours on end, a fact which Bl. made the most of to impress the public, and this winter he actually danced (something he normally never does) with Bleichröder's daughter, who is being socially ostracized.

Well, if Bleichröder's influence is as great as that, I shall not last long, because I broke with him completely six months ago, precisely because I thought he was getting too big and in particular was meddling with politics.

I have noticed nothing yet, on the contrary I am on very good terms with the Chancellor at present. Recently, on my birthday, he drank the health of 'the pillar of the Foreign Ministry', which made a deep impression on Rottenburg, who was present. But —things can change, and I think the only person whose influence might be strong enough to counteract Bleichröder's is Herbert.

The Grand-Duke of Hesse[2] is about to marry a divorcée Russian of the worst possible repute, who was involved some

---

[1] No previous mention of this incident has been found.
[2] Ludwig IV, Grand-Duke of Hesse-Darmstadt.

years ago, together with Michael Gorchakov and a French Secretary of Legation, in an unusually sordid affair. The Grand-Duke's eldest daughter, who has just married the Prince of Battenberg, encouraged her father's relationship with the aforesaid Mme Kolemine, presumably because she thought even the latter was preferable to a royal stepmother. The members of the family now assembled in Darmstadt have only just smelt a rat, but do not expect the marriage can be prevented now. The person most infuriated is the Queen of England who wanted to marry the widower[1] to her youngest daughter, Beatrice. There is in England a law whereby a widower may not marry his deceased wife's sister. This law would first have to be repealed, and the Queen succeeded in having a bill to this effect introduced in Parliament, 'the deceased wife's sister's bill'. But the people called it 'Princess Beatrice's bill'. The bill was regarded with hostility, presumably because there are very many spinsters in England living with their married sisters, and it was feared that the innocence of their relations might be endangered.

But the Queen had not given up hope, although the bill had already been thrown out once, and she came to Darmstadt with her daughter, probably with the intention of keeping the acquaintance from flagging—and now she has to experience this. [...]

2 *May* 1884

The Chancellor feels moody, probably on account of his health. He used to commit indiscretions of diet only when Schweninger was not there, but he has been back now since the beginning of the week, and it is precisely in these last few days that His Highness has committed gross indiscretions of diet, the effects of which have been felt yesterday and to-day by him and by those around him.

Why has Schweninger allowed this? He is usually very firm. Perhaps he wants to spoil the Chancellor's stay in Berlin. At any rate Rantzau wants to have the Chancellor all to himself in the country again as soon as possible, and there is a mutual assistance pact between Schweninger and the two Rantzaus.

Before Prince Bismarck had even been back a fortnight Schweninger told me he had discovered a heart affection which showed that His Highness must return to the country as soon as possible.

I asked what was the cause of this weakness. Schw. said it was drinking; Prince Bismarck drank more here than in the country. I said it was because he left Prince Bismarck to sit all alone in his

[1] Ludwig von Hesse had been married to Alice, Queen Victoria's second daughter. The Grand-Duchess Alice died on 14 December 1878.

room, instead of persuading him to see more people. He drank because he was bored.

But it did no good. Bismarck is still left to sit alone. And as for this 'heart affection', I do not wish to deny that it is present intermittently, but I am not blind to the possibility that an unscrupulous person, as I regard Schweninger to be, will stoop to any kind of mischief to gain his ends. Bill, who discovered Schweninger and thought him absolute perfection, is now on bad terms with him and says he is disappointed with Schweninger because of all kinds of things he has noticed about him. I foresee that once Schweninger feels himself indispensable, and is firmly settled in, he will give the family something to think about. Bojanowski called him the Kaspar doctor, and he does in fact resemble the Kaspar in the *Freischütz*. But he is an unusually skilful physician as well.

His Highness, then, is in a bad mood. He wanted to discuss with Bötticher a question connected with finance. Bötticher wrote to say he wished first to confer with the Reich Treasury on the matter. His Highness burst out: 'He wants to discuss it with the Reich Treasury? What's the meaning of this? He shows his ignorance of the way things are run. *I* am the Reich Treasury.'

In another question concerning the import of petroleum His Highness wished to see a certain treaty. The responsible official sent the treaty, but without clearly indicating the relevant passage. 'They shove documents under my nose as if they were giving an animal its fodder', remarked His Highness, and issued a reprimand to the person concerned, Richthofen.[1] It was certainly careless of him, but we all do these things sometimes, and excessive severity makes work a misery.

Poor Bill also came in for a good scolding yesterday for taking up some matter with Bötticher without instructions. The Chancellor said to him: 'If people follow up your ideas it's only because they think I'm behind them, not on your account.' To make it still clearer that he was not behind Bill, he disavowed him by arranging the affair differently. But it must be admitted that this resentment of other people's encroachment on his authority sometimes has its advantages, although in this case Bill had done nothing wrong. Bill took the affair much more calmly than usual. He is quite right. Despite all his angry outbursts, his father has lost his unflagging energy and is easier to influence than he was.

---

[1] Oswald, Baron von Richthofen. Permanent Assistant in the Political Division of the Foreign Ministry, 1877–86.

4 May 1884

As a result of the Grand-Duke's marriage the Crown Prince and his family have returned from Darmstadt sooner than they intended. The fact leaked out through a Hessian official who told it to Stumm, our Minister, as a close secret. The latter requested an audience of the Crown Prince and told him. The Prince did not think it worth concealing the informant's name, but mentioned it in his explanation to the Grand-Duke. And so the man's career is ruined (i.e. the Hessian official's).

The Grand-Duke, whose civil marriage had taken place the same day as his daughter's wedding, wanted to keep it a secret for a few more weeks, i.e. until he had been married in church. He can hardly hope to now.

The Prince of Wales will soon be here as canvasser for the Prince of Bulgaria, who arrives with him.

The Crown Princess is for the marriage but the Crown Prince, who has a sovereign disdain for all Battenbergs, is against it, and the Kaiser told Hatzfeldt yesterday that he too was most decidedly against it. H.M. spoke his mind on the Prince's origins and deplored the fact that every time the Crown Princess arranged a match she kept it quiet until the only thing remaining was to say 'I do'.

The Kaiser then compared the present marriage scheme with the Hohenzollern candidature of 1870, in so far as this might also give rise to jealousy and complications. The accuracy of this view, which is shared by Prince Bismarck in particular,[1] is shown by the fact that Courcel called on Ampthill about a week ago to inform him a marriage was being arranged between the Prince of Bulgaria and Princess Victoria. He said Prince Bismarck was the originator of this scheme which he regarded as a means of establishing German influence permanently in the Balkan peninsula. Ampthill says he replied that he knew nothing about it.

Of course the French are bound to welcome an event which would drive a wedge between the three Imperial Powers. I wonder who will win the day, petticoats or politicians.

Bötticher, who had, like a slimy eel, hitherto wriggled his way into the Chancellor's favour, has annoyed him in the last few days by one or two blunders.

First, the Chancellor is very interested in Koch's[2] cholera com-

---

[1] See Bismarck's letter to Wilhelm I of 3 May 1884 (Bismarck, *Die gesammelten Werke*, vol. VI c, no. 287, p. 297).

[2] Robert Koch. Bacteriologist. As a member of an official expedition to Egypt and India to study the ætiology of Asiatic cholera, he identified the comma bacillus as the carrier of the disease.

mission and now wishes to confer high distinctions on all its members upon their return, perhaps partly to annoy Struck. The Chancellor had himself conferred with the Kaiser about these proposals, but in spite of this Bötticher, ostensibly to save the Chancellor trouble, had signed the relevant report to the Kaiser and countersigned the Cabinet Order. Meanwhile Bismarck waited more or less impatiently for the documents in question, and when he learned afterwards that Bötticher had seen to everything, he was considerably annoyed. His Highness likes to sign important documents himself, he does not like other people to steal the credit, which apparently happened in this case, in that the documents conferring the honours were countersigned by Bötticher although the idea really originated with the Chancellor. So that was one thing His Highness held against Bötticher.

And then at the last Ministerial Council Bötticher started to discuss with the War Minister a South German railway problem of strategical interest, and mentioned that he had already opened negotiations on the subject with Crailsheim, the Bavarian Minister. The Chancellor interrupted the discussion to remark that his own opinion differed from that of the two Ministers, and in any case such a question was mainly the province of the Prussian Foreign Minister, and not of State Secretary von Bötticher.

Bronsart maintained a prudent silence, but Bötticher embarked on explanations, without success. It was a lack of *savoir-faire* on Bötticher's part to discuss with the Bavarian Foreign Minister, entirely on his own authority, a question which was undoubtedly the prime concern of the Chancellor as Foreign Minister. Still worse was his desire to make this interview, of which he had told the Chancellor nothing, the starting-point for a complacently independent discussion in the Council of Ministers. Admittedly the Chancellor himself does not respect departmental boundaries, but Bötticher is not Bismarck. The duck (for Bö. is no goose) was playing at being a swan, and for his pains he had his wings clipped.

As a result of these and one or two other of Bötticher's mistakes the Chancellor has said he is again wavering in his decision to free himself from Prussian affairs, because to do so he would need to leave behind at least one person in the Cabinet on whose judgment and tact he could rely absolutely. Hitherto he had supposed Bötticher was that person, but now he had doubts.

The Chancellor told Hatzfeldt yesterday: 'The English want to make use of us everywhere. We don't mind letting them use us, but not for nothing.' He means H[eligoland].[1] I will return to this later. Caprivi.

The Kaiser yesterday approved the following transfers: Eisendecher becomes Minister in Karlsruhe, Herbert Bismarck becomes Minister at The Hague and Alvensleben[2] Minister in Washington. It took a long struggle with the Kaiser and with the Chancellor to accomplish this. I do not think any one but Hatzfeldt with his exceptional skill could have pushed the matter through. I was behind it all.

I asked Herbert at Christmas whether he would like Hatzfeldt to suggest him to the Kaiser for the post of Minister in Karlsruhe. It was easier for a third person to propose him than for his own father.

Herbert, who knows his father very well, asked me to wait. But in Friedrichsruh he spoke to the Chancellor about Karlsruhe and wrote to tell me his father had said *he* wished to suggest his son to the Kaiser. He did not know whether H.M. would approve his choice, but at least he, Bismarck, would have done his best for his son.[3]

About six weeks later Hatzfeldt received written instructions to discuss with the Kaiser the filling of the Kalsrruhe vacancy. The two most senior candidates were Derenthall, who already held an important post as Consul-General, and Berchem, who as a non-Prussian was less suitable for a *Prussian* mission. Next after these came Count Herbert Bismarck.

Count Hatzfeldt went to see the Kaiser, but met with little co-operation over Herbert's appointment. H.M sheltered behind his daughter, saying he must first ask her.[4] A fewdays later he told Hatzfeldt he would prefer Berchem, but Herbert was also agreeable. We were led to assume that the opposition came from the Grand-Duke and Grand-Duchess, but in fact it came from the Kaiserin, who had cut Herbert dead during her summer holiday in Baden. She would have preferred a Catholic Count with an Austrian wife to the son of her old enemy. The Grand-Duke and Duchess of Baden have since made an official statement in Berlin that *they* had all along expressed their desire to have Herbert.

Meanwhile I had devised another even more suitable arrangement, namely the one approved yesterday. It did not suit the Chancellor. He had one aim only: the possibility of employing

---

[1] See below, p. 175, notes 1 and 2.
[2] Friedrich Johann, Count von Alvensleben. Minister at The Hague, 1882–4, in Washington, 1884–6, in Brussels, 1886–1901; Ambassador in St Petersburg 1901–5.
[3] Letter of 25 December 1883 (*Correspondence*).
[4] See pp. 100–1.

Herbert *here provisionally*. For this purpose he would have preferred a less important or less agreeable post than The Hague. His choice was Athens, Oldenburg or Budapest. Hatzfeldt had far more trouble with him than with the Kaiser. Hatzfeldt has just told me that when he asked the Chancellor just now whether he was in agreement, and whether the relevant dispatches and orders could be sent, Bismarck replied: 'I will not tamper with fate.' He is very fond of his children, but this affection has a strong admixture of selfishness. He would have preferred to appoint his son simply as Consul-General in Budapest, because then he would have seen more of him than if Herbert becomes Minister at The Hague. Oldenburg is deadly dull, and Herbert would never have been able to live in Athens because an old head wound makes it difficult for him to endure heat.

My opinion, which I confided to Hatzfeldt, Herbert and Bill (the only people who knew about this business), was the following: 'The Chancellor can make his son Under State Secretary as soon as he wishes. Nobody can feel hurt if Bismarck's son obtains more rapid promotion than other people. But appointment on a temporary basis, with Herbert sharing Busch's work, is most definitely to be avoided, unless Busch goes on leave for quite a long period. That's why it is better for Herbert to go to The Hague now. He can then trade places with Busch when Busch has exhausted his usefulness, which probably won't be long now.'

A few days ago Bill was talking to his father about Herbert. His father reverted to his pet idea of 'temporary appointment'. He always prefers to do things on a provisional rather than a definitive basis, because the former is more elastic.

Bill said he thought it would be better to appoint Herbert definitively as Under State Secretary now or later.

'That wouldn't do', said the old man, 'he's still too young. Bucher would resign and Holstein would go off to Schlachtensee.'[1]

Bill was in a position to reply that he knew for certain that I would do no such thing.

5 *May* 1884

[...] I have learnt a further detail about the marriage of the Grand-Duke of Hesse. Queen Victoria, who knew of his 'flirtation', created an appalling scene with Mme Kolemine immediately upon arriving, and demanded that the Grand-Duke should banish her from court. His answer was to marry her. As soon as she heard of it Mama Battenberg rushed to find the Crown Princess,

---

[1] A suburb of Berlin.

flung her arms round her neck and cried: 'To think such things should happen to *us*.'

I like that 'us'. The present Princess Battenberg, formerly Countess Haucke, daughter or granddaughter of a German doctor who emigrated to Poland, was lady-in-waiting to some Grand-Duchess or other when Prince Alexander of Hesse, brother-in-law of the Grand-Duke heir-apparent (the later Tsar Alexander II), made her acquaintance. The fruits of this acquaintance caused Tsar Nicholas to use moral pressure to bring about a marriage. The title 'Battenberg' was conferred by the Grand-Duke of Hesse.

The Crown Princess absolutely refused to leave Darmstadt because she wanted to see the Bulgarian marriage settled. She behaved 'like a virago', but was finally dragged away.

As for the Chancellor, he declared he would resign if there were any more talk of the (Bulgarian) marriage. If it happened he could assume no further responsibility for the foreign policy of the Reich.

The Chancellor has recently changed his foreign policy in one respect. He had told me repeatedly, and said so again quite recently: 'So long as I'm Chancellor we shan't pursue a colonial policy.' And yet he has now begun, in West and South-west Africa.

That reminds me of a conversation Bismarck had with Jules Favre[1] at Versailles in late January or early February 1871.

Favre said: 'When you realize your opinions are mistaken it is your duty to resign.' Bismarck replied: 'Not at all. That would be setting one's own convictions above the welfare of the country. Whenever I see that my opinion is mistaken I alter it.'

He was by no means mistaken to eschew colonial expansion hitherto. In 1871 the whole of Europe regarded us with suspicion and was prepared for us to snatch everything we could lay hands on. Out of this same mistrust, coupled with envy and hatred, grew the danger to us of a European coalition. We were saved from it first by the isolation of republican France and secondly by the Russo-Turkish War. But since Bismarck preserved the peace at the Congress of Berlin the mistrust disappeared in many quarters and Germany has become more powerful each successive year, inasmuch as the number of those wishing to rely on us to preserve the peace has steadily grown.

Cautious reserve, which was a condition of our existence ten years ago, is therefore no longer necessary to-day. No one will

[1] French lawyer and politician; member of the provisional French Government and peace negotiator, 1871.

make war on us if we occupy one or two islands or barren tracts of land.

The Chief realized this, and so he is now quietly advancing upon the Little Popo. Charming name.

7 *May* 1884

In the last few days I have heard some remarkable details of the way the Queen of England alarmed and tyrannized over her family in Darmstadt. A quarter of an hour before dinner, without fail, she would say which of the royal personages was to dine with her. The rest of them ate elsewhere. She completely ignored the attendants of the various princes and princesses. Our Crown Prince simply did not dare to present to the Queen those of his adjutants who had not already been presented. In the end the Crown Princess made up her mind to do so. The ceremony can hardly have been a pleasure. The Queen did not even raise her eyes, and there was no question of her addressing even a single word to them.

Somebody told me he had hitherto [regarded] as affected or exaggerated the anxiety which the Crown Princess always shows at the mention of her mother, but now felt convinced that the Crown Princess was petrified in Queen Victoria's presence. Whenever the Queen withdrew, the effect was 'like an ascension to heaven', those left behind stared after her, transfigured.

During the whole of her stay in Darmstadt the Crown Princess is said to have been summoned to dine with her mother only twice.

I asked whether perhaps the secret of the Queen's authority lay in her personality. On the contrary, he said she was an undersized creature, almost as broad as she was long, who looked like a cook, had a bluish-red face and was more or less mentally deranged.

But she is very rich. Not only is she extremely thrifty, but she has considerably increased her income by a transaction she made a few years ago with a Belgian bank or life-insurance company. She paid in several millions (of pounds, I was told) and bought an annuity which was given at a very high rate, because just at that time very pessimistic rumours about her health were current. Since then Her Majesty's health has improved and there is every prospect of her drawing this income for many years to come, unless the effects of alcohol prevent it.

The Queen's relatives are poor. The Crown Prince and Princess never make both ends meet, and the Hesses depend entirely on the civil list and have no private means.

What the Bulgarian couple would be supposed to live on is a mystery. Queen Victoria may have been thought of, but negotiations in that quarter will not be necessary now the Chancellor has said he would resign if the marriage went through.

The Kaiserin wants to go to Baden, but since it is a point of vanity with her to nurse the Kaiser, it does not suit her to leave him behind. And so she has made the doctors prescribe for the Kaiser a short stay in Wiesbaden. But H.M. detests Wiesbaden. He therefore wrote to ask the Chancellor whether he did not regard it imperative for the Kaiser to remain in Berlin in view of the forthcoming debate on the Socialist Law.[1] His Highness drove to see the Kaiser this evening at seven and told him the political situation certainly made His Majesty's presence appear desirable.

8 May 1884

Herr von Bojanowski, Director of Division II, starts several weeks' sick leave to-day; Berlin does not agree with him. He was Consul-General in London, discharged his duties ably and managed to save part of his salary. He has no private income, because as a young man he gave all he possessed to pay off debts of honour contracted by a brother. He is less suited for his post here; he is too weak. If Busch stays here much longer Bojanowski will be finished in under two years, but then I do not think Busch for his part will hold out much longer. The change from Busch to Herbert would mean a deliverance for Bojanowski.

The Chancellor has not much use for Bojanowski, whom he insists on calling 'Ledochowski', just as he insists on calling Gossler 'Mühler'.[2] In both cases the *qui pro quo* bodes ill for its subject. Bojanowski is long-winded in conference and the Chancellor dislikes his voice, but apart from that, the Chancellor always has the feeling that there was once something fishy about Bojanowski.

There was indeed. Twelve or more years ago, when Keudell was still at the Ministry here, Bojanowski was one day instructed to conclude an agreement with a journalist called Schlesinger whereby we would pay him to publish in London a series of lithographed news-letters, which would naturally have a pro-German slant. The agreement was concluded, but Schlesinger continued to attack us with as much hostility as before, and it was soon discovered that he obtained his information not from

---

[1] On 10 May the Reichstag approved the proposal to keep the anti-Socialist Law in force for another two years.
[2] Heinrich von Mühler. Prussian Minister for Ecclesiastical Affairs, 1862-72.

Münster but from Beust, who was Ambassador in London at the time. Schlesinger actually passed on to Beust the instructions he had received from Münster but had not carried out.

The Chancellor failed to see why we should finance a periodical to disseminate Beust's ideas, and asked what hold the contract gave us over Schlesinger in a case like this. It turned out that no provisos, or inadequate ones, had been incorporated in the contract. His Highness, justifiably indignant, inquired who had concluded the contract. Keudell was mean enough to say it was Bojanowski, suppressing the fact that he had merely acted upon written instructions drafted by Keudell.

The Chancellor soon formed his opinion: 'Bojanowski—a Pole —brother killed manning the barricades on 18 March [1848]—no money—allowed himself to be bribed by Schlesinger or Bleichröder' (who showed a lively interest in Schlesinger and in this contract).

Keudell saw that Bojanowski was ruined so far as Prince Bismarck was concerned, but still he said nothing, although had he confessed that the instructions were drawn up by him, people would at most have reproached *him* with stupidity, not with corruption. By 'people' I mean the Chancellor, for others thought differently and maintained the contract had been concluded in that way because Bleichröder had wished it. They said he had a hold over Keudell dating from the period before he married his wealthy wife. A man I can believe, now a *Geheimer Kommerzienrat*, told me he heard with his own ears how Schwabach, Bleichröder's partner, irritated at some unsuccessful speculation, exclaimed: 'And for that kind of information Keudell bleeds us of 30,000 taler a year.'

From that moment Bojanowski was in complete disgrace with the Chancellor, who had hitherto spoken very appreciatively of his work (so far as His Highness ever does).

I had known the real state of affairs all along, but being in Paris I could do nothing about it and it subsequently slipped my memory. In one of the early years of my Berlin appointment I learnt one day that the Chancellor had struck Bojanowski off the honours list, where he was suggested for the Red Eagle, Third Class. So I called on the late State Secretary, with whom I was by no means on familiar terms, and informed him of the reasons for the Chancellor's dislike of Bojanowski; at the same time, as a proof of Bojanowski's innocence, I referred him to the instructions to be found in the files, written in Keudell's own hand.

The next day the State Secretary told me he was most grateful to me for giving him an opportunity of setting right an injustice. After consulting the files he had explained to the Chancellor the real state of affairs, and Bojanowski would receive his decoration.

Since then the Chancellor has even made Bojanowski a Director. But, as rheumatism is felt in wounds long since healed, so the Chancellor, when someone fails to please him and the storm-clouds gather, comes up with the vague sensation: 'There was once something fishy about that fellow.'

Whenever in the tablets of Bismarck's memory there has been a blot on someone's name, it always, even at best, leaves a faint trace behind. The Chancellor is not interested in erasing the blot entirely.

12 *May* 1884

The Kaiser's personal physicians insist on his leaving Berlin because his homesickness for the Kreuzberg is adversely affecting his health. The day before yesterday, when the standards were being lowered, he said he was ashamed to go to the window, and sat for some time looking the very picture of misery. Riding is now strictly forbidden. He will probably never be able to ride again, unless perhaps for some big review.

It would be interesting to compare the various opinions Bismarck has passed on the Kaiser. They differ completely according to mood and circumstance.

'You can always be sure of the Kaiser if you appeal to his honour.' 'He's got a corporal's bravery, but no moral courage in the face of unpopularity.' 'He has the greatest talent for governing that a monarch ever possessed.'

This last pronouncement is only a few weeks old.

As soon as Bismarck notices contradiction or hesitation in H.M., his tone becomes hostile. When the Kaiser recently wished to have more detailed information and explanation about the Council of State the Chancellor condemned him as an 'illiterate'.

But on the whole the Chancellor has a high opinion of H.M. and precisely for that reason is more annoyed over friction with him than with any one else.

As I have already had occasion to note, the Chancellor's impulses and indignations are not so persistent as they were. This is shown once more by the question of the Bulgarian marriage. The first time I spoke to him he was still undecided—that was after the Crown Princess had spoken to him. The second time he blustered, expressed his complete disapproval and even instructed Hatzfeldt to tell Ampthill that the Chancellor would resign unless the marriage were prevented—which Hatzfeldt, after talking things over with me, omitted to do.

The Chancellor has since heard that the Crown Princess is determined to bring about the marriage and to confront the Kaiser with a *fait accompli* which he cannot ignore. He therefore told Hatzfeldt yesterday that if the marriage took place he, the Chancellor, would be obliged in view of our relations with Russia to cause 'a scandal'. He would hand in his resignation and keep it in force until he received guarantees which would prove to the Powers concerned that he had no part in the intrigue.

He then instructed Hatzfeldt to represent to the Crown Prince and Princess at a suitable opportunity that 'the political interests of the Reich were being swept aside by a Princess's petticoats'.

The way Hatzfeldt will carry out his instructions will be to point out to Their Imperial Highnesses that as soon as the Prince of Bulgaria has married a Prussian princess, and precisely because she is Prussian, the German Government will be obliged to disavow him publicly, thus endangering his position even further.

The Chancellor made no further reference to resigning.

12 *May* 1884, *evening*

Well, even if there is no more talk of resigning, the Chancellor has not come round to the idea of the Bulgarian marriage to the degree I imagined this morning. Yesterday afternoon he spoke to the Prince of Bulgaria and explained to him that he must marry a wife who was wealthy and Greek Orthodox. There were rumours that the Bulgarian wished to marry a Prussian Princess. The Chancellor would regret this, because, although he had every possible sympathy for the Prince of Bulgaria as a man and as a German, it simply was not possible to jeopardize the position of 45 million Germans for the sake of *one*. To obviate this danger, the German Government would be obliged, *if* the marriage took place, to withdraw its support entirely from the Prince of Bulgaria, and to repudiate him publicly.

The young man listened to all this with dissatisfaction but with apparent resignation, said he could well understand the Chancellor's point of view but that in any case he was not contemplating this marriage.[1]

[1] On the same day Bismarck dictated a memorandum on this interview. Before the question of marriage was raised, he had told the Prince that he could under no circumstances count on German help against Russia. 'The German nation's need for peace and the harm, at very best the uselessness, of a war with Russia were absolutely decisive for [German] policy.' (From the Foreign Ministry files. See Egon Corti, *Leben und Liebe Alexanders von Battenberg* (Graz, 1950), pp. 176–9.)

The Bulgarian had told Hatzfeldt he had come to Berlin merely to pay his respects to the Kaiser and to clear himself of the slander put about by the Russians to the effect that he kept a houseful of women, spent money that did not belong to him, was up to his ears in debts and was not even capable of getting himself a respectable wife.

At the banquet in the New Palace two days ago the Crown Prince, who was sitting between the Prince of Wales and the Prince of Bulgaria, treated the latter with quite unusual cordiality, and embraced him several times when taking leave, whereas only a few days earlier he had spoken with the loftiest disdain of all Battenbergs. So the Crown Princess had got round him once again.

The fact that the Prince of Bulgaria told the Chancellor the very next day that he was certainly not contemplating such a marriage, lends colour to the view that this young man, like many Poles and others, lies like a trooper.

In an interview with Hatzfeldt and Busch he did not mince his words when speaking of the Tsar of Russia, who broke his word of honour to him three times in one year, whereupon he, the Prince of Bulgaria, sent the Tsar an open telegram which the latter would certainly not frame and hang on the wall, etc.

Busch was impressed and told me he was convinced the break between them was final. Hatzfeldt took the affair less seriously and said no Russian ever bore you an undying grudge just for saying he was a card-sharper.

The remarkable thing about all this is the Crown Prince's complete powerlessness against his wife. She on the other hand is held in check only by fear of the Press. She is particularly anxious about this because she knows how unpopular she is.

13 *May* 1884

To complete my account of the Chancellor's interview with the Prince of Bulgaria. Bismarck said there were two ways in which the Prince of Bulgaria could extricate himself from his present difficult position. First there was the course of ambition which would probably end in violence; second there was the utilitarian course—and the Chancellor hinted at the possibility of accepting from the Russians a settlement of a few million. The Prince rejected the idea, but I am not at all sure his mother-in-law will not say when the occasion arises: 'Why don't you take it?' Obviously the Chancellor thinks so too, and will probably try to arrange things so that the Russians buy off the Prince of Bulgaria if the marriage cannot be prevented.

At the moment the Kaiser is still firmly opposed to it. Yesterday morning he said: 'I must wait for the wave to break over me, but when it does it will find me "*comme un rocher de bronze*".'

But what will the Kaiser and the Chancellor do if the Crown Princess allows her daughter to be compromised by the Prince of Bulgaria? The Chancellor has apparently considered this question himself and so hit on the idea of a settlement.

The Prince of Wales, who is here as matchmaker-in-chief in the Bulgarian affair,[1] has at the same time been trying to have Münster recalled. He was getting old, paid too much attention to club gossip etc.

In a conversation with Hatzfeldt the Prince suggested Count Brandenburg,[2] now in Brussels, as Münster's successor. When Hatzfeldt reported this interview to the Chancellor and was about to name the possible successor, Bismarck interrupted him: 'I know, they want to have my son Herbert.' 'No, not at all', replied Hatzf., 'they want Brandenburg.' 'I see', said His Highness, 'yes, I can well believe it. I'd be glad too if all the foreign Ambassadors I had in Berlin were as stupid as Brandenburg. The Prince of Wales told me my son was the man for the post. I observed he was too young, but H.R.H. said that did not matter. He spoke to me about "club gossip" too. Münster has probably passed on a piece of gossip concerning the Prince of Wales. Münster's no genius, but he fills our requirements for London.'

Münster is in fact thoroughly insignificant. But here again, as in my recent conversation about Waldersee and the army leaders, can be seen the curious way the Chancellor discounts the fact that some men are less talented than others, unless he has constant personal contact with them, i.e. in conversation.

But it is a remarkable fact that the Prince of Wales suggested two different candidates to Count Hatzfeldt and to Prince Bismarck, and only one to each. He could only do that if he assumed, first that Herbert's candidature would be unacceptable to Hatzfeldt, and secondly that the latter would say nothing to the Chancellor about his conversation with the Prince. Since the Prince has certainly been primed by his sister, it can accordingly be assumed that Hatzfeldt is not identified with the Chancellor and his policy in the eyes of the Crown Prince's entourage. Probably Paul has let out an occasional discreet grumble when feeling

---

[1] In his memorandum of 12 May (see p. 143, note 1) Bismarck said further: 'The discussion I had at the same time with His Royal Highness the Prince of Wales, left me with the impression that British policy has made it its business to implicate us in the Bulgarian interest in opposition to Russia.'

[2] Gustav, Count von Brandenburg. Minister in Brussels, 1875–86.

annoyed; I am absolutely certain he is incapable of intriguing against the Chancellor. But in view of the lack of discretion at the Crown Prince's court it is extremely risky to have the reputation there of finding fault with the Chancellor, because you can never tell how soon the rumour will get back to him, reinforced by the powerful voice of calumny. I warned Hatzfeldt at once of this danger yesterday.

17 *May* 1884

My guess that Herbert's appointment to The Hague is unacceptable to the Chancellor has received confirmation during the last few days.

Stumm, our Minister in Hesse, the first to bring the news to the Crown Prince of the Grand-Duke's foolish marriage, had been involved in a quarrel with the Duke, so that the Duke said he would request the Minister's recall. Stumm had informed me of this in a personal letter.[1] I had laid the matter before Hatzfeldt and told him in my opinion the right thing to do would be to inform the Grand-Duke through his Minister in Berlin that there could be no question of recalling Stumm; at the most we would close the Legation. Hatzfeldt also spoke to the Chancellor along these lines, but the latter merely remarked it might be a good thing to send Stumm to The Hague and Herbert to Darmstadt.

Meanwhile the Legation question became even more complicated.

The Crown Prince sent for the Chancellor the day before yesterday 'to discuss with him a Prussian Legation problem'. The Chancellor was most intrigued to know what it could be. I informed him through Bill that it was the question of finding a post for Normann, whom the Crown Prince and Princess wanted to get rid of, decently though, for they were afraid of him. I said they had asked him on what conditions he would go, and he had stated that a post as head of a provincial administration would not suit him, but he would accept the post of Minister at a small German Court. They thought of Radolinski as Normann's successor.

The Chancellor was frankly amazed and doubted whether Radolinski would feel inclined 'to get involved in this nasty mess'. (I may say that we have already persuaded him.)[2]

His Highness said that finding a post for Normann was a

---

[1] Stumm wrote on 10 February 1884: 'The Foreign Ministry could never allow it to appear to the public that one of His Majesty's Ministers, who had done his duty, was being transferred simply because a Grand-Duke of Hesse had spoken disparagingly of him.'

[2] See Holstein's letter to Radolin of 31 March 1884 (*Correspondence*).

matter of great importance for which he would gladly make the sacrifice of letting Stumm have The Hague and Normann have Darmstadt, and letting Herbert be appointed to Weimar. He spoke to the Crown Prince and Princess on the same lines, and both sides parted on the best of terms.

Through all this, like a scarlet thread, ran the fact that Prince Bismarck would not like to see his son in an important post, but would prefer to use him as his private secretary.

That is how things stood when Hatzfeldt pointed out to the Chancellor that it was not worth while getting rid of Normann from Berlin only to send him to Darmstadt, where he would remain in touch with the Crown Prince's clique, and be only an hour's journey from Östrich, where Stosch lives. Moreover the Crown Prince and Princess were in the habit of staying in that part of the country several weeks each year.

The Chancellor, who had already sent his son a telegram to say he was not to count on The Hague because obstacles had arisen which made an alteration seem probable, was taken aback at this idea. Hatzfeldt touched on the subject again to-day, but both times he only mentioned the subject briefly and did not reply with one syllable to Prince Bismarck's objections. The latter began by claiming that Hatzfeldt's anxiety about Darmstadt was unfounded and that Normann could do no more harm there than at Oldenburg. (Hatzfeldt proposed sending Normann to Oldenburg, and Thielau from there to Weimar.) Moreover, His Highness went on, there was no great hurry over the appointment. The Crown Prince had stated that the transfer could wait until the first of October, so in any case Herbert's appointment to The Hague (which the Kaiser signed a week ago now) could first be published. If reasons appeared later on which made it desirable to appoint someone else to the post, Herbert could always resign.

And so the campaign for Herbert is won; a great testimony to Hatzfeldt's skill. In this kind of discussion with the Chancellor, in which every word, every intonation counts, Hatzfeldt displays his sureness of touch as a diplomatist.

I am glad he has succeeded, both for Herbert's sake and for the principle of the thing. As Minister in Weimar, Herbert would have been constantly with his father (the latter said: 'The post of Minister in Weimar is a sufficient pretext for travelling to and fro'), and his task in Berlin would have been to supplant Busch, who is completely out of favour with the Chief. This very day Prince Bismarck asked someone: 'Who recommended the silly chap to us anyway?'

Busch himself is heartily sick of the post and will be glad to leave it if he is given a nice little job. All this can be arranged by a little juggling, and then Herbert can become Under State Secretary. But we must have nothing provisional.

The Chancellor, in a most courteous telegram, has requested Radolinski to visit him in Friedrichsruh. It is important for Radolinski, who approaches his new post with the feelings of a lamb being led to the slaughter, to extract an assurance from the Chancellor that he will be given a better diplomatic post when he wishes to leave the Crown Prince. He can depend on a promise, but not on gratitude.

The way in which Normann has left his post, or rather will leave it, is typical of relations at the Crown Prince's court. I have probably mentioned this already so I will be as brief as I can.

He had been pushed into prominence and kept there by the anglophile clique. Stockmar, to whom he had been recommended by Stosch, had recommended him to the Crown Princess.

But when Normann saw he had the great democratic party behind him, he gave himself airs and tried to run the Crown Prince without the Crown Princess's help. He, as an ambitious climber, and she as a woman, were both more interested in people than in facts and it was precisely on these personal matters that they failed to see eye to eye, as they had done on liberal slogans.

From last summer Normann decided to go his own way, i.e. he made proposals to the Crown Prince without first coming to an understanding with the Princess. First there was a quarrel over the membership of the Ischia Committee,[1] then Normann tried to get Stosch included in the Spanish tour.[2] The aim of this latter step is very obvious, namely to make the Crown Prince and the Chancellor permanent enemies. The letter which the unsuspecting Crown Prince wrote from Wiesbaden to ask this favour of the Chancellor was already in the post when the Crown Princess heard of it. She sent at once to the post office and retrieved the letter—without consulting her husband. Stosch's name was then struck off the list of those who were to accompany the Crown Prince. For an open breach with the Chancellor in the form of an unprovoked act of defiance seemed to Her Imperial Highness most dangerous.

And then the Princess was furious because Normann had persuaded the Crown Prince to take with him the four journalists

[1] A committee set up by the Crown Prince to organize a relief fund for the victims of the earthquake at Ischia.
[2] Of November 1883. See p. 43.

whose tactless behaviour was to cause so much trouble. 'If I'd been in Berlin at the time they'd only have gone with him over my dead body', the Princess kept on saying.

Nor were such clashes isolated incidents. Normann, secure in the knowledge of his numerous following, did nothing to avoid quarrels, did not become more docile, but made it known that he represented the German element at the Crown Prince's court in contrast to the Crown Princess's English interests. He may also have taken into account her fear of being criticized in the Press. Even so the net result of all his efforts was that measures against him are being speeded up and he is being removed even before the Crown Prince becomes Kaiser.

Normann will be given a small Legation in Germany. He would like Darmstadt, where, an hour's journey from Stosch and surrounded by the Crown Prince's family, he could carry on his intrigues. Let us hope he gets Oldenburg.

Stosch, Eulenburg, Mischke, Normann, all gone—a great improvement in the political situation. Two years ago nobody would have thought it possible. Eulenburg was untrustworthy because he was exclusively for the Eulenburgs and East Prussia.

21 *May* 1884

The Chancellor had noticed when out walking or riding in Berlin that, whereas the rest of the public acknowledged him, the postal officials systematically ignored him. As Head of the Postal Services he found this behaviour improper but did not make it the occasion for an official pronouncement. Towards the end of his stay he met a couple of postmen who failed to salute him, and addressed the elder of the two as they stood gaping at him. 'I take it from your uniform that you are a postman?' 'At your service, sir.' 'Since we are members of the same organization, it would be proper for us to acknowledge each other when we meet. But if you prefer, I will make the first move.' And with that he left the man standing.

General Count Lehndorff, as is well known, received from the Kaiser a plot of ground by the Spree in the Karlstrasse neighbourhood, as a present or at least at a nominal price. During the *Gründerzeit*[1] he asked an exorbitant price and as a result was left with it on his hands. During the lean years that followed he suffered great poverty and was obliged to burden himself with all kinds of liabilities to enable him to find the money to pay

[1] The term applied to the period of rapid expansion of business activity and speculation following the Franco-Prussian War.

mortgages, interest and other expenses. Now his affairs prosper. The city railway bought a strip of ground from him for a million marks, and he has for years been nursing the hope that the rest would be bought as a site for the Reichstag or the Landtag building at two-and-a-half million marks. He must have repeatedly pestered the Chancellor with requests on the subject; when the question arose of purchasing Radzynski's plot for the Reichstag His Highness remarked to a small group of people including, among others, Rötger, President of the *Seehandlung*: 'We'd better hurry up, or else we shall fall into the clutches of my lanky horse-trader friend.'

Lehndorff has probably been worrying the Chancellor again recently to buy this plot of land for the Chamber of Deputies. Although the Chancellor voted for the motion in the Council of Ministers, along with all the other Ministers except Gossler (the motion has since been rejected by the Chamber of Deputies), he said at about the same time, when discussing Radolinski with the Crown Prince and Princess as a possible Court Chamberlain, that Radolinski was a distinguished, wealthy, right-thinking person, with whom their Imperial Highnesses 'would not run the risk of such trickery as they would, e.g. with Lehndorff'.

Radolinski was given a most cordial reception by the Chancellor at Friedrichsruh. His Highness asked him to take on the post of Court Chamberlain as an act of political self-sacrifice for a year, or for six months, as he wished. The Chancellor said that during his recent conversations with the Crown Prince and Princess, particularly the latter, he had become convinced that they were by no means as wedded to democratic ideas as he had formerly supposed. Once Normann's bad influence was removed, a change for the better could be expected. When Radolinski had had enough of court life, he could count on the best possible diplomatic appointment 'even if I had to kill someone to make room'.[1]

22 *May* 1884

When I arrived here eight years ago I discovered Eulenburg was the intermediary between the Crown Prince and the Chancellor, who had the deepest distrust of each other. I gradually realized that Eulenburg did his utmost, personally and through the East Prussian clique (Lehndorff, Radowitz), to increase this mutual distrust. He wished to be used to bridge the gap, and was naturally not keen to see the gap close. I can still remember Radowitz telling me during the first few months after my arrival, that Eulenburg was the only member of the Crown Prince's

[1] Compare Bismarck, *Die gesammelten Werke*, vol. VI c, no. 289, pp. 298–9.

entourage you could depend on, and who could be expected to mitigate somewhat the democratic influence of all the others.

In fact Eulenburg constantly fanned the flame of this distrust, particularly with the Chancellor, while Normann concentrated on the Crown Prince.

So long as such bacteria were at work in the body, the fever could not abate. Now we have reached the end of a chapter. Perhaps the fever will abate, perhaps fresh bacteria will be discovered. We must wait and see.

I wonder whether Normann will refuse to go to Oldenburg? Surely he must realize he is being shaken off. [...]

24 *May* 1884

I was dining with Princess Bismarck a couple of evenings ago; I had asked her to invite me some time when she would be quite alone but for Fräulein Reckow, who is here to nurse her. Actually I wanted to avoid the Rantzaus.

So we had our meal alone except for Schweninger. Frau von Spitzenberg, whom Princess Bismarck had told I was coming that day, asked if she might be invited too. The Princess replied, no, I had stipulated that no one else should be there.

We were all very merry. The Rantzaus arrived at eight. He had probably taken offence at my stipulation that we should be alone, for on entering he merely acknowledged me with a nod and when I left after a while he said good night without standing up or even looking round.

I said to myself: 'You wait, I'll teach you your manners!' On calmer reflection I decided it would be better to draw his attention to the impropriety of his behaviour through a third person. But it was not easy to find this third person. I pictured the expressions of my friends, both civilians and soldiers, on learning that they were to deliver an unpleasant message to Bismarck's son-in-law.

Finally I hit upon an elderly retired Colonel, von Wehren. I went to see him and he consented at once, his only condition being that I would state my message in writing. 'You never know what may happen in this kind of business; somebody might be shot, and then there'd be a lot of fuss.'

I cannot say I regarded this danger as imminent, partly because my remarks were very moderate, and also because I had my doubts about Rantzau's spirit.

This is the message I sent: His behaviour of the previous evening, when he had not so much as turned his head when I left, struck me as discourteous and I could not help wondering whether he intended to provoke a duel. If so, I should like to bring the matter to a decision as soon as possible.

Armed with this note, the Colonel set off for the Ministry, where the unsuspecting Rantzau received him with his customary urbanity, i.e. twice refused to see him and sent word that he should come back that afternoon.

After being turned away a second time the Colonel wrote a card couched in very plain terms, with the result that on his third visit Rantzau received him with the utmost cordiality.

The Colonel's personal irritation made my message several degrees fiercer than I had intended. When he concluded his statement with these words: 'So Herr von Holstein throws down his glove and asks if you intend to take it up', Rantzau, he says, started violently. Then Rantzau began protesting his amazement, and sang a long panegyric of me and of my good qualities, in particular my loyal devotion to the Chancellor. Of course he would never have dreamed of wishing to offend me, etc. He meekly swallowed the term 'discourteous' which the Colonel repeated.

And that settles the affair, so far as the shooting is concerned. The good Rantzau will no doubt strew dynamite in my path wherever he can, but he was doing that already.

26 May 1884

I told Bill about this affair and sent him Wehren's account of it,[1] to which he replied: 'Generally speaking I am in favour of showing one's teeth occasionally. I should have to have been on the spot to hold an opinion on this particular case.'[2] Which is as good as saying he thinks I was in the right.

Poor Bill himself has still a great deal to put up with as a result of his brother-in-law's scheming. It appears from his letter that he enjoys no status whatever with his father, who treats him badly. Naturally the old man still remembers Rantzau's accusation that Bill felt unhappy in his parents' house and wanted to leave it. Rantzau could have thought of nothing more harmful to Bill's standing with his father, and that is exactly why he did think of it. If this treatment continues Bill will in fact be driven from home; I must speak to Herbert about it some time.

Two days ago the Crown Prince called on Hatzfeldt to ask whether it was true, as was thought in England, that we had recently adopted a less friendly attitude, and in particular that we had given anti-English advice to the French. Hatzfeldt replied

[1] Wehren's letter of 23 May (*Correspondence*).
[2] Wilhelm von Bismarck replied by a letter of 25 May (*Correspondence*).

that we had on the contrary advised France and Turkey to attend the Conference,[1] and had thus done England a service. But in any case, he said, it was bound to affect the policy of the German Reich, in so far as the Chancellor determined its direction, and also public opinion in Germany, when people realized that the British Government's way of thanking us for our countless good turns over the last two years was to disregard German interests wherever it came across them—in Fiji, Angra-Pequena, the Congo etc.—and to ill-treat German nationals.

The Crown Prince remarked: 'I see, colonial questions', and walked out without further comment.[2] He had obviously come on behalf of the Queen of England to work for English interests. I see a great many difficulties ahead in that direction, because England is the Crown Prince's blind spot.

Some time ago a Russian Grand-Duke and an English Prince, neither in direct line of succession, were in Berlin at the same time. It was almost amusing to see the Kaiser's annoyance, when in answer to an inquiry he declared: 'Of course the Grand-Duke takes precedence.' The Crown Prince's indignation knew no bounds: how was it possible for anyone to have the slightest doubt. Of course the English Prince was far more distinguished.

6 *June* 1884

On his return from St Petersburg[3] Prince Wilhelm met with a surly reception from both his royal parents, who asked him nothing about his experiences. Partly jealousy of the role he played, partly anger that he came out in support of Russia and against the Bulgarian marriage. After the Chancellor had explained to the Prince before his journey that this marriage project was an Anglo-Polish-Ultramontane intrigue aimed at reopening the rift between ourselves and Russia, the Prince in turn prejudiced his sister Meiningen[4] and Prince Heinrich against the marriage, so that the Crown Princess and her daughter Vicky now stand alone. The marriage may yet come about if the Russians pay the Prince of Bulgaria a settlement in exchange for his abdication, say, one or two million roubles.

The question of a marriage between Grand-Duke Nicholas

[1] The Egyptian Conference. See p. 127, note 4.
[2] Compare Hatzfeldt's report to Bismarck of 24 May on this conversation with the Crown Prince. (*Grosse Politik*, vol. IV, no. 742, pp. 57–9.)
[3] Prince Wilhelm was sent to St Petersburg to represent the Kaiser at the celebrations of 18 May in honour of the coming of age of Grand-Duke Nicholas, heir to the throne. See *Grosse Politik*, vol. III, nos. 631–4, pp. 339–42.
[4] Charlotte, Grand-Duchess of Meiningen.

Alexandrovich and the Crown Prince's third daughter[1] has been in the air recently.[2] The Tsarina, as a Dane,[3] is opposed to the idea and would prefer a Hessian Princess. I do not blame her, in view of the ridiculously anti-Russian attitude displayed by the Crown Prince. Two days ago at the court banquet he sat there the whole time with a face like an angry Jove, and said afterwards to H[atzfeldt?]: 'Did you see? Just like the good old days. They have graciously condescended to honour us with a visit.'[4] And then, turning to Prince Heinrich: 'I suppose we will change back into Prussian uniforms for the theatre.' 'No', was the answer, 'the Kaiser has commanded that Russian uniform should be retained at the theatre.' 'It's disgraceful!' exclaimed H.I.H. indignantly. 'Our uniform's not good enough for them.' And so on. He treated the Tsarina with extreme formality, whereas the Crown Princess was kind to her.

The Crown Prince's character is a compound of weakness and pettiness. H[atzfeldt?], who has often been for walks with him in his garden, was struck by the Prince's annoyance when, on turning round, H. happened to walk on his right.

Even H.I.H.'s affability when he wants to be gracious bears an oddly artificial stamp.

The day before yesterday, as he was handing cigarettes to someone whom he had summoned to an audience, he said: 'Shall we stand or shall we sit down?' Naturally the man replied that it was for H.I.H. to decide. 'Yes, of course, but if *you* had to decide, what would you prefer?' So his guest chose to sit down.

In the very near future the Chancellor will indulge in some plain speaking to the English for their ill-treatment of us in colonial affairs. The Crown Prince is sure to be used as a catapult by the English. It has happened once already—I must surely have mentioned it. About ten days ago the Crown Prince called on Hatzfeldt and said that recently the English had found our attitude unfriendly. Was there any truth in this?

During his Russian trip Prince Wilhelm stated quite openly that his mother, whom he always refers to as 'the Crown Princess', has never become a Prussian, but has always remained an Englishwoman. It was therefore almost inevitable that during the coming reign matters would come to a crisis between her and the Chan-

---

[1] Princess Sophie.

[2] Compare Windelband, *Bismarck und die europäischen Grossmächte*, pp. 570–3.

[3] The Tsarina of Russia, Maria Feodorovna, was the daughter of King Christian IX of Denmark.

[4] The Tsarina visited the German Court on 4 June when she passed through Berlin on her way from Denmark to St Petersburg.

cellor—not merely Bismarck, but any other *German* Chancellor. The Kaiser, i.e. the present Crown Prince, might even feel obliged to 'be separated from his wife'.

The remark sounded as if the threat of imprisonment lurked in the background. By what means this weak man, now completely under his wife's thumb, is to be brought to such a monstrous decision is not clear.

Bismarck would not instigate such a step, but Prince Wilhelm himself might. He is said to be heartless, fiercely determined, obstinate and cunning, and moreover penetrated with the idea that *every* personal consideration should be subordinated to the interests of the state. The Crown Prince is afraid of his son already; if this fear increases it may render possible much that seems inconceivable at present.

The colonial question, now in its early stages, may bedevil our relations with England for a considerable period, even though an actual conflict is out of the question. The problem is likely to pass over unsolved into the new reign. But should a conflict arise, no other question is so liable to put the future Kaiserin, with her Anglophile tendencies, in a false position *vis-à-vis* the German nation. For it is precisely the liberals and democrats who want colonies.

I am far from supposing that this is the reason why the Chancellor has suddenly made the colonial question, to which he was so long opposed, a part of his political programme. But I am firmly convinced that, if the need arises, he will use it as a means of combating foreign influences, and I am also convinced that he will succeed.

Reuss[1] had sent in a report of a conversation between Kálnoky and the Prince of Bulgaria, during which Kálnoky had told the Prince he could not expect Germany or Austria to be involved in war with Russia on his account. Bismarck had written in the margin at this point: 'As if the rascal cared.'[2]

Everything depends on the Chancellor's remaining in good health a few years longer.

27 *August* 1884

Courcel, the French Ambassador, has gone to Varzin to see

---

[1] Heinrich VII, Prince Reuss. Ambassador in Vienna, 1878–94.

[2] Reuss reported on 30 May 1884 that Kálnoky had also advised Prince Alexander to get on good terms with Russia. Kálnoky pointed out that German and Austro-Hungarian neutrality had been to Prince Alexander's advantage. Bismarck commented in the margin: 'Certainly it was to *our* advantage and that is the main thing.' (From the Foreign Ministry files.)

whether joint action can be arranged in one or two matters—e.g. freedom of trade along the unclaimed coastal strips of West Africa, and compensation for the bombardment of Alexandria. Bismarck had suggested these two points. Courcel went to Paris and came back with more far-reaching proposals, most of which related to Egypt.[1]

Now we are pursuing a colonial policy, such an agreement with France would be most useful for intimidating the English, who might otherwise give us some nasty surprises one day. How long the agreement remains binding is by the way—the shorter the better. It will have served its purpose if Gladstone is overthrown.

Courcel and I are old acquaintances. We were Attachés together in St Petersburg and he was later in the Foreign Ministry in Paris. It was in the nature of things that we should not become close friends. On his appointment here he made approaches to me, but I did not respond. He is an honest fellow, talks a lot, has a habit of interrupting (once even much annoyed the Chancellor by doing so), and is shallow rather than profound.

The Chancellor disliked him at first. 'An excitable person who is perfectly capable of saying something quite infuriating, so that we might fly at each other's throats without knowing how it happened.' I put in that Courcel was far more honest than St Vallier.[2] 'But St Vallier was better in that he had a firmer grip on himself', said His Highness. Needless to say, he had the last word.

At first Bleichröder was opposed to Courcel and conducted a powerful intrigue in Paris for St Vallier's re-appointment. Meanwhile Hohenlohe and particularly Bülow, with his great skill, successfully worked to prevent it. Bleichröder is now reconciled to Courcel; so is the Chancellor. Last week Bleichröder called on Hatzfeldt and told him of all the negotiations and schemes relating to a Franco-German rapprochement. Courcel had gone to see Bleichröder on the morning of his departure and had told him all about this.

I sent a note to Courcel saying I should be very glad to see him before he left for Varzin and would call on him unless perhaps it suited him better to come to me straight after seeing Hatzfeldt. He did the latter. I gave him some good advice, warning him particularly not to interrupt the Chancellor. Then, moving from one thing to another, we came from the practical to the academic.

---

[1] See *Grosse Politik*, vol. III, no. 688, pp. 424–6; *Documents Diplomatiques Français*, Première Série, vol. v, no. 385, pp. 390–5.
[2] Charles, Count de St Vallier. French Ambassador in Berlin, 1877–81.

He said: 'The main bone of contention between Germany and France is Charlemagne. We say he was a Frenchman, you make him a German. There's no doubt he spoke some Germanic dialect (*idiome allemand*), but that did not prevent him from being French. France is not, like Germany, constructed on the principle of linguistic unity. Under Louis XIV a great number of French regiments used German as the language of command. When the King was asked whether this should be stopped, he said no, because he regarded German as one of the languages of his country. And so it is in fact. You'll never get a Frenchman, particularly if he's from the centre or the north, to believe that the real France does not lie between the Rhine and the Seine. What you call France nowadays—*Gascons, Provençaux et quelques Champenois avec*—is not France at all. We northerners regard the south of France as conquered territory. The present group[ing] has the disadvantage to us that the southerners run the country because they are more lively and persuasive. The dwellers between the Rhine and the Seine have qualities we need for our political equilibrium. *Aujourd'hui la France a perdu son équilibre.*' For an Ambassador about to go to Varzin to reach agreement on concerted political action, such candour is rather unusual. He spoke in great detail to me because he met with no surprise and only very moderate contradiction. I was indeed not surprised, because I had known for a long time that the French held this opinion. In any case he observed that all this was an academic question, for he was in fact striving to bring our two countries closer together and to divert French attention from such considerations.[1]

I have written down what he said, because if I live a few more years I shall probably witness the attempt at realizing this idea of 'French equilibrium'. With precisely that in mind we ought to use the present moment to embroil France and England. But we can only do this if we give the French moral support; we shall not infuse spirit into them by repeating the usual clichés. On the contrary, that would make them seek an understanding with England. England and France combined can, as naval powers, always count on Italy and Spain, Turkey also, as well as the revolutionary elements in every country.

I should place a blind faith in the Chancellor's decisions if he were ten years younger, but his former vigour is gone. The autocratic tendencies in *internal* policy have increased, whereas the trenchancy and resolution in *external matters* have decreased. Worry is destroying the fruits of thought and threats are replacing

[1] See *Memoirs*, pp. 110–11.

action. So long as the world believes that Bismarck will fulfil his threats, they will have the force of actions. Once there is any hitch over their fulfilment, then Bismarck's and Germany's stock will slump.

The Gladstone Ministry have made fair sport of us, and been suitably threatened, but I am still waiting for action, i.e. a grouping of anti-English Powers. The Chancellor has been on the point of acting several times but Herbert has stayed his hand.

Herbert, usually a sound politician, has been somewhat thrown off his balance by the reception he met with in England. He suffers from the very common fault of imagining he can lead the people who flatter him, whereas on the contrary the essence of flattery consists in its not being cashed in at face value. Herbert thinks skilful diplomacy could neutralize the effects of English self-interest, the most tenacious in the world, and win England's support for our colonization plans, which would take the bread out of the mouths of hundreds of thousands of English workers. That will happen only when the English fear us, and when someone other than Gladstone is at the helm. In fact we have actually strengthened Gladstone by the half-measures we adopted at the Conference.

Three days ago Granville wrote a letter to Herbert[1] in the Taunus Mountains in which, according to Herbert,[2] he cried *pater, peccavi* and hoped he might be forgiven. Of course Herbert sent the letter straight to Varzin. We shall see what comes of it.

The Crown Princess is terrified of attempts on her life. She recently discussed with somebody in great detail the further security measures which might be taken. She demanded a considerable increase in the police estimates and the formation of a large and efficient secret police.

Someone told me yesterday how very unpopular the Crown Prince was making himself with his jokes. On some festive occasion, when he was travelling by steamer from Rolandseck to Cologne, he offered cigarettes to the members of the festival committee, who were all ladies from the cream of Cologne's financial aristocracy. Frau Joost, a stout elderly lady, said: 'I don't smoke, but will Your Imperial Highness allow me to keep this cigarette as a souvenir?' 'By all means', said H.I.H. 'Sit on it, press it nice and flat and paste it in an album.' A frozen silence, but of course abuse later on.

I keenly regret that relations between Hatzfeldt and Caprivi are

---

[1] *Grosse Politik*, vol. IV, no. 751, pp. 79–80.
[2] Letter to Holstein of 26 August 1884 (*Correspondence*).

at present strained. By their very natures the two men are not the types to get on very well, but in addition the two points at which their departments overlap, namely colonial and naval questions, are being dealt with by Kusserow, who has a most unfortunate touch.

Caprivi wrote an official letter recently requesting that Kusserow's visits to the Admiralty should cease, because his conversations with staff officers led afterwards to accusations of alleged discrepancies between the officers' pronouncements and Caprivi's. Caprivi said he could no longer put up with this situation.

Hatzfeldt requested Kusserow to draw up his version of the incidents censured by Caprivi, and both documents, Caprivi's and Kusserow's, were then sent to Varzin.

The Chancellor decided in favour of Caprivi, reproved Kusserow and required him to justify himself on one or two counts. Kusserow then committed the folly of sending direct to Varzin an additional memorandum as well as the official documents transmitted by Hatzfeldt. The Chancellor, already annoyed, took offence at this breach of etiquette and commanded that Herr von Kusserow be forbidden direct communication not only with the Admiralty but also with Varzin. In addition Hatzfeldt was to exercise strict supervision over his drafts, and the Chancellor himself demanded to see the more important ones. Kusserow was also to be forbidden direct contact with Herr Lüderitz[1] (who is at the moment founding the colony at Angra Pequena). Either Hatzfeldt is to speak to Lüderitz or else a letter will be sent.

Kusserow, as official in charge of colonial affairs, is thus placed in a situation which is untenable in the long run. He should be put in charge of a different department, or better still be given the post of Minister in a small Legation. He cannot commit nearly so many blunders in a minor post as he does now, superintending colonial affairs, and I think it cruel simply to make things so unpleasant for him that he resigns, as the Chief apparently intends to do. But it will be difficult to persuade Herbert, an anti-Semite, to allow Kusserow to become a Minister, and Prince Bismarck himself, who unfortunately for Kusserow worked with him a good deal this spring, once said of him: 'He works hard and knows a thing or two. But I shouldn't sleep quietly a single night if he were a Minister, even in Lisbon.'

I regret that Caprivi, instead of getting Waldersee's job, is now neither one thing nor another. Caprivi is admittedly very brusque,

[1] Adolf Lüderitz. Bremen merchant, whose extensive territorial holdings in Africa were to form the nucleus of Germany's colony of South-west Africa.

and the tone of his communications with the Foreign Ministry is not polite. The officials, headed by Busch, say Stosch was far easier to deal with, which I am prepared to believe, though it did not affect me personally. I smoothed out one of the earliest disputes, but this time Caprivi's outburst was from the start so violent that we had to let things take their course.

30 *August* 1884

Courcel called on me yesterday and to-day I called on him. He is delighted with the reception he had.[1] 'Perhaps I'm seeing everything through rose-coloured spectacles. I'm still completely under his spell', he said. He is particularly glad he was not pinned down, e.g. by a demand that France should once again recognize Germany's present frontiers. Any suggestion of a major agreement, such as a treaty of alliance, would have been unacceptable to the French Government because of the state of public opinion, which must first become gradually accustomed to the idea of reaching political agreements with Germany.

Prince Bismarck made no offer of any kind, but simply accepted what the French offered with respect to concerted action on the coast of West Africa, in which we come off best because French sea power is very much stronger than ours. Bismarck made no corresponding concession with regard to Egypt, where the French might well have hoped that we would take the initiative; when Courcel began to speak of the Suez Canal, a joint guarantee, etc., the Chief said: 'These agreements are not worth the paper they are written on. Whoever is master of Egypt is also master of the Canal.' In other words [he] would have nothing to do with an agreement which laid him under an obligation. Courcel thought it a magnificent pronouncement. Never has an evasive reply been received with such enthusiasm. I shall be surprised if Ferry[2] sees it in that light. The impression will not last long in any case, because even if our caution can be interpreted at present as a desire to leave time for French public opinion to get used to us, it will not be for long. In a few months they will notice that we are giving them no support and that England is pursuing her plans undisturbed.

I grow more and more afraid of the moment when the world realizes that Prince Bismarck has lost his punch and lost his nerve. It will be a sad day for him and for Germany too.

[1] In Varzin. See entry for 27 August.
[2] Jules Ferry. French Minister-President, September 1880–November 1881, February 1883–March 1885.

This time the Crown Prince has returned from England rather annoyed. To begin with he disliked the familiarity shown him by the English; apparently the Prince of Wales introduced this tone, but it does not suit the Crown Prince at all to be treated as an equal by people not of royal blood. And then he disliked the way his wife and mother-in-law joined forces to snub him. 'No, Fritz, you can't do that', said one. 'Oh no, Fritz, you mustn't do that', the other would echo. In the end His Imperial Highness grew heartily sick of it.

Caprivi has already found another cause of complaint with the Foreign Ministry. The Chief, to whom matters of this kind are always referred, is so far showing the utmost forbearance. Let us hope all ends well.

19 *September* 1884

Prince Bismarck told Tsar Alexander in Skierniewice[1] that the sole aim of German colonial policy was to drive a wedge between the Crown Prince and England. The Tsar, who had just been saying how anxious he was about the fate of Russo-German relations after the death of Kaiser Wilhelm, remarked: '*Voilà qui est intelligent.*' I think for my part that all this colonial policy was undertaken simply as an election stunt. First came our victories, then the *Kulturkampf* and liberalism, then the economic revolution, and now colonies. Prince Bismarck said recently to Bötticher (who cannot hold his tongue): 'All this colonial business is a fraud, but we need it for the elections.'

Some years ago Prince Bismarck said to me, and to many others: 'So long as I remain Minister we pursue no colonial policy.' Whether he has decided to do so for one or other of the reasons mentioned above, it is nevertheless a fact that he does not

---

[1] Bismarck described the ministerial talks at Skierniewice in a report to the Kaiser of 29 September 1884: 'Concerning the conference of Ministers in Skierniewice, it did not frame or intend to frame any resolutions. As I took the liberty of stating during the brief audience I had of Your Majesty in Your Majesty's antechamber in Skierniewice, the discussion was restricted mainly to the expression of mutual satisfaction, and the summing up of the existing relations between the three Powers which required no further elaboration; in addition my two colleagues again put forward their case, each in support of *his own* protégé, in the dispute between Serbia and Bulgaria and expressed their intention to send expert reports to Berlin shortly for Your Majesty's decision. Count Kálnoky took less part in the discussion of security measures against Socialist plots, and the discussion between my Russian colleague and myself was entirely concerned with matters about which I had already informed Your Majesty in Skierniewice; namely that the Russian proposal handed to me before the interview in Berlin seemed to me to be too diffuse, too legalistic and not sufficiently political, and that I reserved the right to seek Your Majesty's approval for a more simple agreement which we could put into effect *without a parliamentary resolution*, and the draft of which I could then pass on to St Petersburg for examination.' (Bismarck, *Die gesammelten Werke*, vol. VI c, no. 295, pp. 304–6. Cf. *Grosse Politik*, vol. III, no. 645, p. 369, note*.)

pursue this colonial policy with his former vigour. Otherwise he would have adopted, i.e. would still adopt, far more decisive measures against England. His most recent habit is to clench his fist more often than he used to, but without dealing a blow. He is 'amazed', 'astonished', threatens the worst if there is a repetition, but goes no further. The Gladstone Ministry has treated us shamefully both in word and deed, but we stick to the formula: 'Until England treats us with greater friendliness over the colonial question we shall not be any more friendly to England', which means that the moment England smiles we fling ourselves round her neck.

I cannot be suspected of being a Francophile, but I think it a grave error, and so do Hatzfeldt and Bill Bismarck, not to give France our firm support now in Egypt and in the colonies generally; this constant change of front—Haugwitz's policy in 1805—will only result in an agreement finally being reached between France and England. Admittedly Egypt is a bone of contention between them, but for two states which regard the entire non-European world as their hunting-ground, there will be many more. Once England and France have come together, Italy, Greece and North America will soon join them. Whereas if *we* support the French in Egypt and West Africa we shall reap the double advantage of their naval support and of dissuading them from other alliances. *But*—the Chancellor has lost his former logical consistency and Herbert is very fond of England.

The latter is now off to England on the Prince of Wales's invitation. He was also intending to stay with Lord Granville in the country. I hope I have talked him out of this latter idea, and I have also persuaded him to return via Paris and call on Ferry.

Another bad feature is the way the Chancellor, more than he used to, contradicts what he has already said and keeps on changing his mind.

For months I have been doing my utmost to prevent a quarrel between His Highness and Caprivi. They are both hard rocks, even so the Chancellor does make things difficult for Caprivi by changing his mind so much.

Recently they had reached agreement on a naval exercise off the African coast, then, a few hours later, His Highness decided it should all be done differently.

I had noticed that the Chancellor was annoyed with Caprivi for 'taking a Baltic cruise' just at this moment, while the Chancellor is in Berlin. So I wrote privately to Caprivi, telling him he had

162

better come back. His letter,[1] which I enclose, shows he is not an easy man to persuade.

'King Lüderitz' is a very apt name for the shameless Hanseatic who 'founded' Angra Pequena under German auspices, i.e. he set up a trading base and now considers himself a King.

'Princess Rüte' is a wretched Moorish woman, the Sultan of Zanzibar's sister, who married a German merchant and became a Christian. Her husband died, she is now in want, and there was a question of sending a warship to Zanzibar to enforce a demand in her favour. Caprivi has the one-sided aim of equipping the navy exclusively for naval engagements, and so he is unwilling to send single ships on distant expeditions. That is the constant point of friction between him and the Chancellor.

23 September 1884

I found Caprivi's card at home yesterday and returned his visit to-day. He had also called on the Chancellor yesterday and was satisfied with the result of his visit, even if somewhat astonished at it. His Highness had forgotten the contents of his recent ordinances and had asked Caprivi, among other things, whether it was really necessary for three warships to be sent to the South Seas. But that was just what His Highness had been demanding hitherto. He also told Caprivi—as he had already told Bötticher—that all this fuss about colonies was only being made because of the elections. If His Highness tells so many people it will soon be an open secret and its much talked-of effect on the elections will be lost.

I then asked Caprivi his views on the future relations between the Admiralty and the Foreign Ministry. I said he had emerged victorious from the recent dispute and so could either let things go on as they were, in which case the conflict would become permanent, to the delight of Stosch's faction; or else, as victor, he could make the first move and say to Hatzfeldt: 'Oh well, it was a misunderstanding for which neither of us was personally to blame, so let's forget it.' Caprivi received this latter idea with approval, and half an hour later when I called on Hatzfeldt he asked me: 'What do you suppose Caprivi wants? He's just sent to inquire when he can see me. I said I would go and call on him.' I said nothing of my visit but merely observed that Caprivi probably wanted to talk about his recent interview with His Highness, and also that he had perhaps had enough of this eternal bickering with the Foreign Ministry.

[1] Of 17 September 1884 (*Correspondence*).

Two hours later Hatzfeldt told me he had found Caprivi most cordial. They had both expressed the opinion that neither of them had an easy task and had agreed to support each other as far as possible. Caprivi also told him that it was quite true that the present colonizing phase was a complete surprise to him. He said that when he had called on the Chancellor for the first time after being appointed, the Chancellor had asked him: 'I hear you're against colonies too?' 'Yes.' 'So am I.'

On the whole I think the Chancellor is right to pursue a colonial policy; had he not embarked on it, it would have remained a slogan of the opposition. If only he would take a sufficiently vigorous line with England. Hatzfeldt's chief endeavour is to persuade Bismarck to do so. [...]

24 *October* 1884

[...] On the 26th the Crown Prince is holding an evening reception with a stand-up buffet, for the Council of State. It is with all kinds of misgivings that he has decided to do so; apparently Her Imperial Highness had been stirring him up against the Council of State and many other things besides. He emphasized anxiously: 'Be very careful not to use any of my wife's English silver or porcelain. That must not be touched.'

Every one is agreed that the Crown Prince's character grows weaker year by year. And it seems certain that his wife's influence is increasing every year. The only point on which opinions vary is whether the Chancellor will restrain her influence when she is Kaiserin. Formerly I should have felt convinced he would. Now I hope for the best, but without any certainty, for the Chancellor is growing old. A disproportion is apparent in him between his genius, which is markedly diminishing, and his vanity, which is on the increase. Similarly, when the level of water in a pond falls, it becomes overgrown with weeds. He has an uneasy compulsion to allow no talents, even of an everyday kind, to exist beside him, i.e. beneath him. But while this autocratic need for infallibility increases, his trenchancy in his relations with the outside world diminishes. He is nevertheless the only man who can for a time guide the new Kaiser's first hesitant steps in such a way as to avoid a political crisis. And the Crown Prince has such a weak character, combined with such good nature, that I think Bismarck will succeed, provided his own Olympian assurance (in many respects more highly developed than the Crown Prince's) does not influence adversely the unerring certainty of his well-nigh infallible instinct. I am less afraid of the things Bismarck does than of the things he omits to do. The Crown Prince would rather be ill-treated than ignored—a feminine temperament.

The relations between the three generations of our royal family are remarkable, not to say comic. The Kaiser ignores the Crown Prince completely and so far as possible never informs him of anything. The Crown Prince, in turn, ignores Prince Wilhelm in the same way. At this year's Rhine manœuvres, at which the Crown Prince represented the Kaiser for the first few days while his son was on the General Staff, the father treated his son as though he didn't exist. Only once, in the Schloss Benrath, was there a sort of scene between them. The day of the great reception when everyone was assembled, both soldiers and civilians, the Crown Prince and Crown Princess appeared. The former, without looking to left or to right, shot through the room towards Prince Wilhelm and said a few words to him. Prince Wilhelm then bowed, went up to his mother and kissed her hand. The bystanders had heard the Crown Prince say to his son: 'Go and kiss your mother's hand.' It was of course Her Imperial Highness' idea.

The Crown Princess fears her son; she knows that nothing can deflect him from his purpose. The same character as his mother, but a greater contempt of mankind and consequently a greater independence *vis-à-vis* public opinion.

The Chancellor has returned in good health. But after a couple of hours' work he loses his temper and gets tired.

If he only concerned himself with important matters he would easily have enough time, but—and this is connected with the old man's increasing jealousy—he has a morbid compulsion to dabble occasionally in quite trifling matters, so that he can then shout out: 'I have to look after everything.' And then he is constantly issuing orders contradicting the ones he issued some time ago. He has no use for Ministers who are touchy. Bötticher is the best in this respect. He lets Bismarck blow off steam from time to time, but in between times he goes on with his work as best he can. Not a delicate nature, but a willing horse.

26 *October* 1884

At the Kaiser's table yesterday *Kommerzienrat* Bahre (Bochum) said to the Crown Prince during the meal: 'I was really delighted to hear Your Imperial Highness had consented to be President of the Council of State. And does Your Imperial Highness know what pleased me particularly? May I speak quite freely? What pleased me was the knowledge that Your Imperial Highness must have broken with Forckenbeck and his friends.'

The Crown Prince, rather red in the face, replied: 'Yes, you certainly are speaking freely.'

His Imperial Highness is pulled two ways. On the one hand it gives him pleasure to be President of something, on the other hand he is being very much goaded at present by his English wife.

His pronouncements on the Brunswick[1] question do not hang together either. In one breath he repeats what the Chancellor has just told him in conference, in the next breath he repeats Her Imperial Highness' English views. She wants Cumberland to be given Brunswick. She would very much like the private fortune for herself.

Despite all her meanness her domestic staff trick her into enormous prodigality. The way the kitchen is run is reminiscent of Russia; for example the chef, knowing her liking for stewed peaches, cooks a dozen peaches every day throughout the summer and autumn, at three marks apiece. The Crown Prince's domestic staff has the worst possible reputation with all the tradesmen and craftsmen.

Once the old Chancellor is gone I can imagine the state finances will be run in the same slapdash way.

On his return from the opening of the Council of State the Chancellor told me the Crown Prince had read his speech without the slightest comprehension, raising his voice for no reason in all the wrong places, making pauses, looking round for applause, in fact showing he had no idea of the contents.

The Kaiser's health has now improved. When he went to Baden after the manœuvres he was rather run down. The manœuvres had exhausted him very much because riding on horseback, and to a lesser extent driving in a carriage, caused hæmorrhages. And so a special carriage has been built which reduces the jolting to a minimum.

The Kaiser speaks of the Crown Prince with great irritation, saying he has no idea what goes on in the world.

9 November 1884

The Crown Prince has refused to represent the Kaiser at the court hunt at Springe. His Imperial Highness is in a state of

---

[1] Ernst August, Duke of Cumberland and Brunswick, became Crown Prince of Hanover on his father's accession in 1851. In 1866, after the annexation of the country by Prussia, he had to go abroad, but on his father's death (1878) he clung to his rights as heir to the throne. In 1884, after the death of Duke Wilhelm of Brunswick, he was unable to assume his hereditary title and rule over the Duchy because he refused to obey the Prussian demand that he renounce his claims to Hanover; he received only Duke Wilhelm's private fortune.

thoroughly disgruntled resignation and takes a pessimistic view of everything.

'I'm a back number. The liberal views in which I was brought up and which I cannot renounce, have been brushed aside. The best thing for me is to give up my claims to the throne in favour of my son, who is a devotee of modern ideas. He can represent me in Springe too.'

The Crown Prince sits through the Council of State sessions from the very beginning to the very end and listens with delight to the liberal speeches of Bennigsen, Miquel and their friends. When referring to the 'almighty Chancellor', the 'majordomo', His Imperial Highness also adds that Bismarck renders him superfluous.

There is no danger of his abdicating—the Crown Princess will see to that.

The Crown Prince has been cracking some more unfortunate jokes recently. At the party he gave for the Council of State he said to Herr von Helldorf-Bedra[1] who had turned up in the dress uniform of a Chamberlain: 'Chamberlains ought to be at the door. You should really have received me as I came in.' Helldorf, furious, swore loudly and distinctly and declared: 'You won't see me wearing livery again in a hurry.' [...]

17 *November* 1884

The Crown Prince's attitude to the Council of State has gone through various phases. First, opposition to it as a liberal, then interest in the work, but now complete rejection of it again. A completely superfluous institution. Why did the Council of State exist? What was the point of making him, the Crown Prince, its President? It would have been enough if the Chancellor had simply decided in every case: 'That's what I want done', because nothing happened in the Council of State against his wishes.

The cause of this bad temper is that in last week's plenary session the Chancellor delivered a biting attack on the liberal, i.e. independent, speakers, who were displaying their oratorical virtuosity before the Crown Prince, and gave them to understand that there was no question of amendments but simply of accepting the Government motion.

The Chancellor's megalomania renders him incapable of enduring contradiction. It must unfortunately be admitted that his vanity increases in proportion as his talent diminishes, just as a pond, when it dries up, becomes overgrown with weeds. The former dissimilarity between Bismarck and Gorchakov in this

---

[1] Otto Heinrich von Helldorf-Bedra. Leader of the Conservative Party in the Reichstag.

respect is fast disappearing. His jealous anxiety lest there should be any one coming after him who might be capable of entering upon his political heritage or even a part of it, is on the increase. Unfortunately this fear is groundless; at any rate I cannot yet see how things will be managed after Bismarck has gone.

One man alone cannot bear Bismarck's burden; to do that Bismarck's immense prestige is required. But how can the work be divided? If German politics, i.e. the politics of the German states amongst themselves, were assigned to the Ministry of the Interior instead of the Foreign Ministry, then Hatzfeldt would make a good Foreign Minister. As a Rhinelander he has perhaps some German spirit, but no trace of the Prussian spirit. He fails to appreciate the good qualities in the Prussians and magnifies their faults. If his character were even half as outstanding as his intellect he would be a great statesman; but his character is weak. Ill-suited to the position of Chancellor.

It is possible that when Bismarck is gone actual *business* will run more smoothly than at present, when awe of him paralyses all initiative in the other Ministers. But who will perform the greatest task of all, namely stemming the tide of revolution? No one can replace him here, look where you will.

The Crown Prince's conversation with his confidants consists almost entirely of uninterrupted criticism of the Kaiser, Prince Wilhelm, and the Chancellor. This spring, just before Bamberger had his big quarrel over the steamship bill,[1] the Crown Prince sent for him, discussed political questions with him in some detail and soundly abused Prince Wilhelm. Bamberger of course repeated everything.

Prince Wilhelm for his part does not hesitate to say to other people the most outspoken things about his father, as he did recently to the War Minister. When the latter replied it was improper to criticize the royal family in front of one of their subjects, the Prince pointed to the example of his father, who is constantly criticizing the Kaiser. A cosy family life.

The Crown Prince and Princess are both afraid of their son because he is obstinate and heartless. But he may be a good ruler some day.

One of the bones of contention between the Crown Prince and the Chancellor will shortly be removed: we are once again drawing closer to the English.

---

[1] A bill for the subsidizing of steamships travelling to the Far East and Australia. In the Reichstag debate of 14 June, Bamberger declared himself against it. The Reichstag approved the bill on 23 June.

Ferry, who has been under fire from many quarters in France because of his rapprochement with Germany—the Rothschilds in particular have launched a Press campaign against him—is intimidated and may well fail to implement the concessions he had proposed, particularly those relating to free trade in the Congo Basin. The English on the other hand, intimidated by our rapprochement with France, are now like wax in our hands, and will probably outbid the French.

I am not happy at this turn of events. First, a diplomatic success on Gladstone's part will strengthen his anti-monarchical regime; secondly the republican regime in France which is so very useful to us as an example to be avoided will be dealt yet another blow by Ferry's defeat.

The only good thing about it, as I have said, is that the Crown Prince and the Chancellor have now one bone of contention less.

13 *December* 1884

[...] The Chancellor's behaviour during the Conference[1] is peculiar. The whole thing bores him; to him it was scarcely more than an election stunt. He has in fact no interest in the colonial question. He does not follow the progress of the negotiations and as a result when he speaks to the French or English Ambassador he tends to contradict his earlier statements. Consequently both parties distrust him more and more. I am afraid the reputation of dependability which he had earned since the Congress [of Berlin] will not come out of this Conference intact. If he only schemed with A. against B. he would only have one person against him. But now he finesses and plays a double game so that he has both A. and B. against him. For example, whereas he told the French Ambassador that Germany had no interest in the Congo Association, he asked the English Ambassador to inform his Government that he would be glad if they recognized the territorial integrity of this Association as a personal favour to Prince Bismarck. The English did so, to the fury of the French, but at the same time declared it was done to please Prince Bismarck. But the next time they wanted concessions from Germany in return for this favour, Bismarck declared he was dissatisfied with England for various reasons, and that concessions were quite out of the question.

Malet,[2] the English Ambassador, told Hatzfeldt: '*Nous nous sommes mis à genoux devant le Prince Bismarck. Mais c'est fatigant à la longue de rester à genoux, quand cela ne sert à rien.*'

---

[1] The international Conference on Congo affairs which was opened in Berlin on 15 November. [2] Sir Edward Malet. Ambassador in Berlin, 1884–95.

1885

The Crown Prince's pettiness. Hatzfeldt's position. The Crown Princess and the Bismarcks. Bismarck's seventieth birthday. The Crown Princess and Geffcken. Holstein urges Bismarck to stay on good terms with the Crown Princess. Herbert von Bismarck in the Foreign Ministry. Berchem and Bernhard von Bülow. British-Russian relations. Lignitz. Herbert von Bismarck's character. End of co-operation with France. The Portuguese marriage project. British policy. Seckendorff. Diplomatic *revirement*. The Crown Princess's rapprochement with Bismarck. Holstein advises Bismarck. Bismarck's conversation with the Crown Princess. Hohenlohe to Strasbourg, Hatzfeldt to London. Holstein asked to enter into closer relations with the Crown Prince. The Portuguese marriage turned down. Bleichröder criticizes Bismarck. Bleichröder in Varzin. Prince Wilhelm. The Caroline Islands affair. Kopp and the *Kulturkampf*. The Drummond-Wolff mission. Bismarck yields over Caroline Islands. The Battenberg marriage plan. The Crown Prince and Herbert von Bismarck. The Pope to mediate in Caroline Islands affair. Herbert von Bismarck and Austria. His leanings towards Russia. Hatzfeldt's departure. Holstein on the Bismarcks and Hatzfeldt. Bismarck and Prince Alexander. Albedyll. Shuvalov and Herbert von Bismarck. German policy in the Balkans. Holstein dines with the Bismarcks.

3 *March* 1885

The Crown Prince expects every one in Berlin to know him by sight. On several occasions he has narrowly escaped being run over, because when he crosses the road he will under no circumstances stand still or hasten his step to get out of the way of the traffic. Once, on the Bendlerstrasse, he actually made a cabby draw rein for him, and roundly abused him. He gets particularly annoyed when an unfortunate sentry fails to recognize him. He makes his adjutant go at once and take the fellow's name. A short while ago His Imperial Highness was walking towards the royal sentry and was already wondering whether the sentry would call out the guard in time, but a little cobbler's apprentice ran ahead and called out to the sentry: 'The Crown Prince, the Crown Prince', which of course elicited a calling out of the guard. But the Prince resented the way his experiment had been spoiled. The adjutant still had to go and ask the sentry whether he would have recognized His Imperial Highness even without the help of the cobbler's boy.

The Crown Prince suffered a similar vexation from Serpa, the Portuguese delegate to the Congo Conference and Minister of State. The two men met at the Kaiser's dinner-table. It had not been possible to introduce Serpa to the Prince beforehand, but all through dinner they talked about the Prince's Spanish journey.[1] The latter spoke a great deal about his experiences. After the meal Serpa went up to His Imperial Highness and asked confidentially: 'Do you know what impressions the Crown Prince brought back from his trip?' His Imperial Highness told this story afterwards with unfeigned resentment.

The Crown Prince often strikes the wrong note in his contacts with people.

On the occasion of a banquet given by the First Regiment of the Guards he snubbed an officer who was about to pour him out some wine, saying: 'I'll let you know when I want my glass filled' —which the officers took in very bad part.

Last autumn at a big reception in Halle he said to Rauchhaupt, the Deputy: 'Are you our parliamentary windbag?' to which Rauchhaupt is said to have replied: 'You need to do a lot of talking to keep the monarchical spirit alive in the nation.'

The Crown Prince finds it most inconvenient that the Kaiserin, his mother, still feels she must appear in society. 'The moment *she* is there nobody takes any notice of my wife and myself. My dear mother wishes to dominate until she's in her grave. And so, with her so-called sense of duty, she gives the Kaiser no peace. She forces him to give small receptions, whereas he would much rather take his little nap at the theatre and go to bed at ten.'

A certain Count Kesselstadt from Bohemia, who had inherited considerable estates at Trier, was introduced to the Kaiser at Wiesbaden at a party given by Wurmb.[2] The Kaiser had quite a long talk with him. Afterwards Kesselstadt asked someone: 'Who was that nice old man?' It has since become a stock expression.

7 *March* 1885

Little Saldern[3] has been summoned here from Sofia to receive personal instructions concerning an unpleasant errand to the Prince of Bulgaria.[4] Saldern signed the customary written

[1] See p. 43, note 2. [2] Head of the Administration in Wiesbaden.
[3] Konrad von Saldern. Chargé d'Affaires in Sofia.
[4] Saldern returned to Sofia on 25 March bringing Prince Alexander a letter from Kaiser Wilhelm I of 18 March. The Kaiser wrote that his good will depended on the Prince's public renunciation of all thoughts of a marriage with Princess Victoria, and that the Prince must try to regain the good will of the Tsar.
From Saldern's report from Sofia on 27 March, it is evident that Bismarck had instructed

announcement of his arrival with a very large S. I said to myself when I saw this, I wonder whether the Chief will let that pass without comment? He's very susceptible to signatures, and to handwriting in general. I was right, Saldern did catch it. 'Herr von Saldern', said His Highness, 'you write your name with a very large S. It's all the same to me, but there are many senior civil servants who regard such externals as indicating the extent of the writer's pretensions. So if you want to remain on good terms with the civil service you must make allowances for this peculiarity.' Of course nobody but His Highness would have thought of mentioning little Saldern's large S.

I spoke to Ratibor[1] to-day about the Bismarck fund.[2] I told him I thought it hardly fitting if people in my position were to subscribe a donation of perhaps one hundred marks. But Ratibor disagreed, and urged me to do so. Rottenburg had also urged me yesterday. As a result I have already sent off to-day one hundred marks to Rötger, the President of the *Seehandlung*.

Ratibor also told me that the appeal for donations had met with a poor response in America. Gneist[3] had advised to appeal to the 'patriotic' instinct of the German-Americans, because great things might be expected of them. But instead their answer was, oh no, the Lasker affair[4] of the previous year had created bad feeling for a long time to come and they were also (as might be expected) not in agreement with Germany's present policy of protectionism. And so they did not expect any spectacular result from collections, in fact they would not even try. Ratibor had not even a rough idea what the sum total would be. The general opinion is that the fund is not doing brilliantly. [...]

In answer to this letter from Hatzfeldt which I enclose, I told him that even if he did want to leave Berlin and become an Ambassador again, as I observed to my sorrow from the tone of his letter, I strongly advised him to return now (i.e. on the 15th), because powerful intrigues were afoot during his absence aimed at

him to recommend a pro-Russian policy to Prince Alexander, and had compared the Prince's position to that of a hereditary viceroy.

In a letter to Kaiser Wilhelm of 8 April, the Prince made the desired renunciation of the marriage with Princess Victoria. Regarding his relations with Russia, the Prince requested the Kaiser to intervene, but expressed his wish to abdicate if he was expected to convert his position into that of a puppet ruler. (From the Foreign Ministry files. See Corti, *Alexander von Battenberg*, pp. 216 et seq., where Prince Alexander's letter is incorrectly dated 14 April.)

[1] Victor, Prince zu Hohenlohe-Schillingsfürst, Duke of Ratibor. President of the Prussian Upper House from 1877.

[2] This fund was being collected to express the gratitude of the German nation for Bismarck's achievements.

[3] Rudolf von Gneist. Jurist; Member of the Prussian Chamber of Deputies, 1858–93; of the Reichstag (National Liberal), 1868–84. [4] See p. 87.

discrediting him with the Chief.[1] In particular it was being stated that Hatzfeldt was not ill at all, but simply wished to avoid tedious audiences, and would therefore not return until the Chief went into the country. (What I did *not* write, was that the Chief himself says Bucher told him the foregoing.) I urged Hatzfeldt to return from leave on the right day *this time*, and said that his tendency always to stand a little above the laws and to take rather more liberties than other people had, so far as I knew, not had fortunate results hitherto.

Hatzfeldt probably wants an Ambassadorship to get more money. He keeps up an expensive way of life, keeps four horses here and seven in Wiesbaden, and yet pays the small tradesmen and servants most irregularly.

His wife—who is said to be having an affair now with Prince Egon Ratibor—recently suffered the indignity of being informed by the Crown Princess through Prince Nicholas of Nassau that she would never receive the Countess, either now or when she is Kaiserin. Whereupon the Countess declared she would cease to consider any one's feelings, and that her patience was at an end. From now on her daughter's visits to Berlin would cease and she would be given a husband of her mother's choosing. I should be most curious to know what sort of husband *that* mother will dig out.

Hatzfeldt, poor soul, is cracking beneath the weight of these women. I think he sees most things clearly enough, but behaves as if he did not, because he is intelligent enough to realize that blindness is more respectable than slackness. No amount of support or pushing is any use with him. You can't make a backbone out of a towel.

11 *March* 1885

The Chancellor is now, touch wood, in extremely good health. He keeps a diary of what he eats and drinks each day, and has Schweninger listen to his heart and palpate him every morning. He trusts Schweninger implicitly and obeys him almost as implicitly. His Highness is also weighed every morning by Schweninger. On these occasions Schweninger may sometimes ask: 'What did Your Highness eat and drink yesterday?' 'After those three extra glasses of old Rhine wine you will weigh two pounds more', or: 'Your pulse will be seventy-two to-day.' To Prince Bismarck's astonishment the prophecy is always fulfilled.

[1] Hatzfeldt wrote on 5 March that he was returning on the 15th, although his doctors were of the opinion that he would not be able to cope with the work in Berlin in his present state of health.

Recently the Crown Princess during a conversation about the Chancellor said that when the Crown Prince became Kaiser the Chancellor would not be able to treat a monarch of fifty-three, not yet in his dotage, like a monarch of eighty-seven (she must think the succession is not far off).

The reply to this was that the Crown Prince would have some difficulty in preventing the Chancellor from resigning. He had, from all accounts, no overpowering desire to remain during the new reign.

With visible alarm (she is in particular very afraid of bomb outrages and is also generally aware of her unpopularity) she remarked that it was out of the question for Bismarck to leave his Kaiser in the lurch. The answer she got was that the best way of avoiding this would be to see that Prince Bismarck came into greater contact with Their Imperial Highnesses, particularly the Crown Princess whom he regards as an outstanding woman. 'He has never said that', observed Her Imperial Highness bitterly. 'I beg your pardon', came the answer, 'he actually said so to me.'

The Crown Princess was obviously very flattered by this remark. According to someone who knows her very well, she would endure anything, submit to being called a bad mother and a heartless wife, without turning a hair, but would attack with the ferocity of a tigress anyone who disputed her political capabilities.

Prince Bismarck's attitude to England is said to have infuriated her so much that she wept with rage.

I had written to Hohenlohe to say the Paris dispatches were rather thin just now. He himself is becoming prematurely aged because he pursues pleasures unsuitable for his age, and Rotenhan,[1] his Counsellor of Embassy, will never learn to be a skilful diplomatist. The Second Secretary, Kiderlen,[2] a typical Württemberger with a gauche exterior and a crafty mind is more likely to make a success of it.[3]

Among the South Germans the Bavarians and Badeners always hang together against the Württembergers. I have met more intelligent Württembergers than Bavarians or Badeners but I think the reproach of unreliability levelled at the former is not

[1] Wolfram, Baron von Rotenhan. First Secretary in the Embassy in Paris, 1884–5.

[2] Alfred von Kiderlen-Wächter. Secretary of the Embassy in St Petersburg, 1881–5, in Paris, 1885–6, in Constantinople, 1886–8; in charge of Balkan and Near Eastern Affairs in the Foreign Ministry, 1888–94; later State Secretary.

[3] Hohenlohe replied on 8 March: 'I am most grateful for your friendly warning. I think that Kiderlen, who takes a good deal of trouble, will soon know the ropes sufficiently to perform useful services in the collecting of information. He is admirably qualified for it and I find him very congenial. [...]'

without foundation. In this respect Kiderlen is also *de son pays*.
He has however no reason to be against Hohenlohe, and can be
of more use to him than Rotenhan.

14 *March* 1885

The Crown Princess is most indignant at the way the Chancellor treats England. She said yesterday: 'Poor Münster, now *his*
career will be ruined because of the note of 5 May last year.[1]
They're reproaching him with failing to read out or to deliver the
note;[2] he never even received it.' That he *did* receive the note
can be easily shown from the files. But for a woman of that stamp
historical fact is of secondary importance.

On his return from England[3] Herbert Bismarck had expressed
a wish that the Crown Prince and Princess be asked whether they
would receive him.

The Crown Princess's reply to the request was: 'No. He did
not ask to see me before he left, so I don't see why I should see
him on his return.'

The Crown Prince's reply to the request was: 'Oh no, I've so
much to do in the next few days.' And when asked a second time:
'I really haven't time. I'll speak to the Crown Princess about it.'
My advice was to let the matter drop.

Hatzfeldt returns this evening. Struck says he ought by rights
to have recovered long before this. From all one hears, his family
relationships were not calculated to create *du bon sang*.

Hatzfeldt's behaviour was so odd that I wrote to him to say he
seemed to wish to leave Berlin again and become an Ambassador,
but that in this case I advised him not to annoy the Chancellor
by staying away any longer.

His reply, which I enclose, makes it clear beyond a doubt that
he does *not* want to leave Berlin,[4] perhaps because he feels in less

---

[1] Not a note, but Bismarck's dispatch to Münster of 5 May 1884. In it the idea was developed that Germany must make her continued support of England conditional upon reciprocal concessions, such as the protection of German nationals in the South Seas, a greater
consideration for German trade interests and possibly the cession of Heligoland to Germany
by treaty. (*Grosse Politik*, vol. IV, no. 738, pp. 50–2.)

[2] Bismarck wrote to Münster on 1 June 1884: 'Judging by your later dispatches, your
inquiries have been confined to Heligoland, and I am in some doubt whether you carried out
your instructions of 5 and 11 May to their *fullest extent* or whether you allowed a fear of
causing a disagreeable impression to deter you from presenting Lord Granville with the
alternative either of securing our political support by at least a just, though perhaps not a
benevolent attitude, towards our overseas interests, or else of seeing us further our interests
by co-operating with other Powers. [...]' (*Grosse Politik*, vol. IV, no. 743, pp. 59–62.)

[3] Herbert von Bismarck had gone to London on 4 March to bring about a settlement of
the differences between England and Germany. (*Grosse Politik*, vol. IV, p. 100, note *.)

[4] Hatzfeldt wrote on 10 March 1885: 'I will, as I said, resume my duties and perform them
as far as my health and strength permit. [...]'

danger from his wife here than he would as an Ambassador. I am afraid she will ruin him despite all our efforts.

Their eldest daughter, Nelly, was originally very inclined to depend on her father, but he gave her no support. When her mother demanded the daughter's return, Hatzfeldt forced his daughter to go, against her will. Her mother then let her feel who was master, and ever since the daughter has been lost to her father and will not be easy to win back.

During Herbert's recent stay in London the English went out of their way to be pleasant to him. The Prince of Wales proposed him as an honorary member of the Marlborough Club, i.e. Herbert became a member a few years earlier than he would have done by waiting his turn; in addition he was elected without a vote.

The first Herbert heard of it was that he was sent a receipt for a bill of £52 sterling. He returned the receipt, without paying the money, and declined all idea of membership on the grounds that he was leaving London soon, perhaps for ever. Curtain!

16 *March* 1885

The Chancellor's speech to-day[1] about dynastic interests and their disastrous effect on politics will be taken as an attack on the Crown Princess, which indeed it probably is.

Yesterday in response to Hatzfeldt's inquiry how things had been going with Her Imperial Highness since his departure, Prince Bismarck said: 'Oh, quite well but for the fact that she's ill-treated my Herbert.' So the refusal of the Crown Prince and Princess to receive Herbert in private audience had not passed unnoticed and may well be connected with this speech, even though Richter was its immediate cause. But the Chancellor had obviously been watching his opportunity; the style of his reply shows he had the subject all ready in his head.

Some time ago I should have regretted this incident. But after all I have learnt gradually of the idiosyncrasies of our future Kaiser and Kaiserin, I think the Chancellor is right to join issue with them openly. He has the nation behind him in this question more than in any other. The Crown Princess knows it too, and is aware of her unpopularity. She will never like Bismarck, so it is better that she should fear him. She must be made to realize that '*à bas l'étrangère*' is the most dangerous rallying cry in a revolution. For months now I have been talking along these lines to Bismarck's sons, and expressing my conviction that the Chan-

[1] In the Reichstag. (*Die gesammelten Werke*, vol. XIII, pp. 29–40.)

cellor would never make any impact on Her Imperial Highness without resorting to moral pressure.

So far as the Crown Prince is concerned, I was told by a shrewd woman who had the opportunity to observe him: 'He is contemptible. He would not dare to stand up for his own children against his wife.' [...]

17 *March* 1885

A General told me to-day he knew from a reliable source that the Crown Prince and Princess had quite made up their minds that it would be possible to govern even without Bismarck. They would make no serious attempt to keep him if he seemed inclined to go.

I was told something similar some time ago now by a person well-disposed towards Bismarck. The one thing the Chancellor should avoid is tendering his resignation to the new Kaiser; it would be accepted with a few fine phrases and with great satisfaction.

I hold the same opinion: the Chancellor must not tender his resignation, but simply ask the new Kaiser whether he feels himself in agreement with Prince Bismarck's policy, i.e. co-operation with all parties, which may be expected to promote the national interest. Friedrich Wilhelm V has not the nerve to say no to his face, and the rest will then take care of itself, especially if Bismarck retains the slogan—Germans against foreigners—he hurled at the nation yesterday.

The personal breach between the Chancellor and the Crown Prince must probably be regarded as irreparable after yesterday's two speeches. And the speeches in themselves show that the Chancellor himself sees things in that light.

A few weeks ago the Crown Prince saw in the Press that Duke Günther of Augustenburg[1] had been visiting the Chancellor. His Imperial Highness lashed out furiously at Prince Wilhelm that same evening at the opera ball and, *coram publico*, hurled all kinds of crude insults at him for having persuaded his brother-in-law to make this visit.

The young Prince, in his turn, vented his spleen on Sommerfeld, intimating that he, Sommerfeld, was partly responsible for his father's outburst. Sommerfeld, vain and resentful, will take this to heart and will hardly contribute towards bridging the gulf between father and son.

Some time ago, when father and son were at open war, Albedyll

[1] Brother of Augusta Victoria, Prince Wilhelm's wife.

advised the Crown Prince to make peace, giving as his reason that, being a man of sensitivity and sentiment, he was no match for his son who possessed neither of these qualities. The Crown Prince appears to have taken that to heart.

One of the Crown Prince's hobby-horses is the question of decorations. During the siege of Paris the Chancellor once noticed a Bavarian regiment which, though it had been through many battles, showed very few Iron Crosses in the ranks. So Bismarck mentioned this to the Crown Prince. 'That is so', he replied. 'I have deliberately given the Bavarians fewer crosses than the others; the King of Bavaria has not yet conferred on me the Order of St Hubert.'

Just before Prince Wilhelm's visit to St Petersburg last year his father sent for him to give him some final instructions. 'What did he talk to you about?' some one asked Prince Wilhelm. 'Why, decorations, of course, as usual. I'm to wear the Black Eagle and the St Andrew's Cross and occasionally the Danebrog.'

At the ball given recently by the Austrian Ambassador, Széchényi, Prince Wilhelm, according to written instructions from his father, was to wear the Order of the Garter, as well as his Austrian decoration, in honour of Princess Christian.[1] Prince Wilhelm, who may not have received his father's letter, appeared without the Garter. The Crown Prince was furious. But he said: 'I didn't dare say anything to my son because I ran the risk of his replying that it was by order of the Kaiser.'

26 March 1885

[...] Prince Bismarck, according to Bleichröder, is indignant at the prosposal to present him with Schönhausen with a mortgage on it.[2] I must explain that the committee, to put an end to the clamour of the South Germans and other Progressives, set aside half the total sum of about 2,300,000 marks for charitable bequests. Thus the Prince's share is only 1,150,000 marks, whereas Schönhausen costs 1,500,000 marks. Bleichröder consoled him with the assurance that more money would still come in, and that he hoped to reduce the mortgage to a minimum.

The Crown Prince's court is scandalized at Prince Bismarck's idea of accepting the gift for himself. This may be a mere pretext, or it may be envy. To this very day they resent the fact

---

[1] Helena, Queen Victoria's third daughter, was married to Prince Christian of Schleswig-Holstein.

[2] On 24 March the Central Committee for the Bismarck fund decided to spend half the amount contributed on purchasing the old Bismarck family estate of Schönhausen.

that Prince Bismarck got his own private railway carriage some time ago. This railway carriage has often been mentioned to me as one reason for the Crown Prince's ill-will.

The Crown Prince's set regard Hatzfeldt as *their* diplomatist. The Crown Princess, who went to play lawn tennis with him a few days after his arrival, said on leaving: 'Times are difficult just now. Well, we'll talk about it another time.'

A few days later the Prince of Wales[1] said to him: 'It's a difficult situation here at the moment. I suppose it is best to keep still.'[2] And that is just what the Prince did. The Chancellor said that a stenographer could perfectly well have been present at his interviews with the Prince (who paid him two visits), they were so harmless. The Prince was probably waiting to see whether His Highness would discuss topical questions, but His Highness took care not to.

Hatzfeldt's behaviour in all this has been exemplary. He has absolutely nothing of the intriguer. [...]

29 *March* 1885

The Crown Prince is half demented at the honours now being showered on the Chancellor for his birthday. 'A Minister, what's a Minister? Nothing but one of the King's officials. But this man's not a Minister, he's a dictator. This means the overthrow of the monarchy', and so forth. The Crown Prince is also furious at seeing portraits of his father and of the Chancellor everywhere, but his own far less often. The torchlight procession is anathema to him. But what enrages him most is that the Sultan is sending a Pasha here to congratulate the Chancellor, and bestow on him *and* on the Crown Prince the highest Turkish decoration. That the Chancellor should be thus placed on the same level as the heir to the throne goes far beyond His Imperial Highness' idea of a joke. He strides up and down his room like a madman. 'And I suppose they'll expect me to call on Prince Bismarck in full court dress to congratulate him. What's he done anyway? *I* was the man who first had the idea of a Reich.'

I think that if the Kaiser died now, the Crown Prince and the Chancellor would part company and we should then be able to indulge in a war with Russia side by side with England.

The Chancellor did not return the Prince of Wales' visit in person but sent Herbert instead. I do not think this was unintentional. The Russians were very jealous of the English Prince's

---

[1] The Prince of Wales and his son Albert Victor were in Berlin to take part in the celebrations for the Kaiser's eighty-eighth birthday. [2] This sentence is in English in the original.

visit to Berlin. It was probably to allay their suspicions that the Chancellor showed the Prince of Wales this slight discourtesy. It is in the English interest (but by no means in ours) to let the world believe in German-English friendship. The English Press naturally discussed this unreturned visit with indignation.

Prince Bismarck was much more cordial than usual towards the German Princes here for the Kaiser's birthday, i.e. the King of Saxony, and the Grand-Dukes of Weimar and Baden. And they in turn see in him their one salvation from the centralizing tendencies of the Crown Prince and the liberal parties.

Waldersee said again yesterday he was convinced that the Chancellor and the Crown Prince would not work in harness later on, and adduced all kinds of reasons for his assertion. I think, on the contrary, that they probably will, at least for a time. Whether Waldersee himself is still hoping to become Chancellor some day who can tell? I am beginning to think he has such an idea.

30 *March* 1885

Amongst a pile of begging letters the Crown Princess passed on to Seckendorff, there was also a letter which, although signed simply 'G', was recognized as having been written by the former Minister, Geffcken,[1] now a Professor at Strasbourg. The letter, after savagely attacking the Chancellor, went on to outline a scheme whereby the Crown Prince, when he became Kaiser, would be able to get rid of Bismarck. He must of course avoid the odium of having dismissed Bismarck, but it should not be difficult so to provoke him that he tendered his resignation. Then the Crown Prince need merely take him at his word. But until then he must always say he regarded the Chancellor as indispensable. Seckendorff had a furious scene with the Crown Princess. He told her that unless she took care she would be stoned in the streets when the nation learned how she was intriguing against Bismarck. Seckendorff demanded from the Princess a promise not to indulge in such correspondence in future. She refused to comply, but told Geffcken, who happened to be in Berlin, to call on Seckendorff and discuss the matter with him. When Geffcken wished to visit Seckendorff he was informed the latter was not at home. The Crown Prince and Princess, by going behind the Court Chamberlain's back, got Geffcken invited to Saturday evening's reception: Seckendorff stayed at home. His behaviour

[1] Dr Heinrich Geffcken. Professor of jurisprudence and publicist; formerly Hanseatic Minister-Resident in Berlin and London.

has been exemplary, but that will not stop the Crown Princess from further plotting.

Hatzfeldt conferred with the Chancellor yesterday on the question of these Turkish insignia, and asked him to consider what could be done to appease the Crown Prince. The Chancellor was very calm but very bitter. He said there was nothing to be done about it, because whenever he met the Crown Prince halfway, the Prince imagined he was currying favour. Once the Crown Prince actually went so far as to hint as much openly, at which the Chancellor replied: 'I can only hope that Your Imperial Highness may find many such loyal servants as your father has found in me, but *I* shall not be one of them.'

The only arrangement made in this insignia affair is that the Sultan's envoy shall bestow the decoration *first* on the Crown Prince and then on the Chancellor. That will not materially pacify His Imperial Highness.

During his conversation with the Chancellor, Hatzfeldt said he would regard it as a very great misfortune if the Chancellor did not direct at least the early stages of the transition from the old regime to the new. The Chancellor replied it did not depend on him but on the Crown Prince. He said that he had given the same reply to the Kaiser when he asked him, on the 22nd, to remain in office under his son. In any case, said Bismarck, the Kaiser foresaw with a certain satisfaction the possibility that his son's reign would compare unfavourably with his own.

The 350,000 marks mortgage on Schönhausen has been paid off by a group whose main contributors are Bleichröder and Mendelssohn.[1] It is a pity, but that is Bismarck's weakest point.

31 *March* 1885

When Hatzfeldt asked the Crown Prince when he could confer with him on the over-all political situation, His Imperial Highness declined. 'I am well enough informed on the general situation. That's enough for me. Colonial affairs don't interest me. And the war between Germany and England won't break out yet, will it?'

On Saturday somebody heard the Crown Prince asking Hatzfeldt: 'Have you good news from Sommerberg?' The question surprises me because the Crown Prince has hitherto adopted a sharply hostile attitude towards Countess Hatzfeldt. I expect the Prince is trying to flatter Hatzfeldt through his wife, because he thinks he will be unable to dispense with his abilities as a diplomatist after Bismarck's retirement.

[1] Ernst Mendelssohn-Bartholdy. Banker.

After avoiding the Chancellor for personal reasons ever since last autumn (i.e. declining his invitations), I went with the entire Foreign Ministry staff to congratulate him on 1 April. I could not have avoided going without creating a stir in very many quarters. His Highness was very friendly in spite of the crowd, gripped me firmly by the hand and said, after thanking me for my congratulations: 'Well, I'm very glad to see you again after such a long time. What's been the reason for it?' I made some non-committal reply, we said a few more words to each other and there the matter ended. Princess Bismarck was also very pleased to see me and said to several people who wondered why she was looking so astonished: 'Have you seen Holstein? He's here.' After presenting my respects to them both, and savouring to the full the vexed expression on the Rantzaus' faces, I stayed only a short time.

In the course of the afternoon I heard all kinds of gossip about the Crown Prince's views and behaviour. On his return home from the ceremony of congratulation he said he had tried to express to the Chancellor the Crown Princess's congratulations but he had not heard them. The Crown Prince then tried to tell him that the Crown Princess had decorated the frame of the picture presented to the Chancellor by the royal family, but the Chancellor did not catch that remark either.

I thought this a matter of some importance, and so, lacking any confidence in the elegant indifference of Bismarck's sons, I called on Bismarck himself next morning at ten, worried lest I should find him with a bit of a hangover. Not at all. The old gentleman was sitting at his desk in his dressing-gown writing all kinds of letters of thanks to royal and imperial personages.

A letter to Princess Wilhelm was just being taken out.

I told him that in the Crown Prince's opinion Bismarck had twice failed to hear what he said, that the suspicious and touchy mood of the Crown Prince's family might lead them to think this deliberate, and that it might be a good idea to write a short note to the Crown Princess, who did after all put in a few hours' work on the picture frame. The Chancellor thought he had acknowledged the Crown Prince's expression of Her Imperial Highness' congratulations, but he really did not know anything about the frame, so he took a large sheet of paper immediately and plunged straight into a letter to the Crown Princess. At the same time he handed me the letter from the Kaiser which had accompanied the picture, and which he thought, justifiably, very fine.

When I had finished reading I did not go but sat still until he looked up, when I said to him: 'What Your Highness is now doing is still no more than a palliative measure. I do not under-estimate its importance or I should not have troubled you with it. But it seems to me far more important that Prince Wilhelm, who will be your main ally in the inevitable struggle between you and the Crown Prince's set, should be made as independent as possible, financially independent, that is. I know that your opponents are already counting on making the Prince docile by a mixture of inducements and threats; they will give him extra money if he is a good boy, but not otherwise.' The Chancellor thought this over very seriously and then said with a smile: 'The most I could do would be to say to the Kaiser: "Put your grandson in such a posi-tion that your son cannot avenge himself on him for the ill-treatment he himself received from you."' I replied: 'Perhaps there is another way. The Crown Prince is most eager for his civil list to be increased when he becomes Kaiser, and if possible doubled. Field-Marshal Manteuffel and Miquel, in order to curry favour, have both advised him to press for it: Miquel told me he had recommended the Prince to have the motion brought before Parliament immediately after his accession in the first flush of enthusiasm which usually fades later on. The Prince replied to Manteuffel: "Oh, the Chancellor would never agree to that." This increased civil list is a trump card', I went on, 'which you will presumably not allow them to snatch out of your hand. If you proposed the motion you could give as one of your reasons the fact that the Kaiser must make the Crown Prince (the present Prince Wilhelm) a substantially increased allowance.'

His Highness replied: 'The Prussian civil list could be increased. But it would not be possible to create a Reich civil list as the Crown Prince's followers desire. The other German Princes, or most of them at any rate, are as poor as church mice and you can't expect them to levy a tax on their countries to pay for the Kaiser's civil list.'

So then I went on my way. Late that evening I met Herbert returning home from the Bismarck family celebrations. He said, speaking thickly: 'Well, you seem to have dragooned my father into writing to the Crown Princess. And he did—a most charming letter, whose only reply was a short note to me from Seckendorff, which my father called "dry and business-like".' I remarked that the Chancellor's letter was itself a letter of thanks; if the Crown Princess was expected to thank him in turn for his letter of thanks, there was no reason why this constant exchange of thanks should ever stop. But in any case I had the feeling that the Bismarck family, especially the Rantzaus and Princess Bismarck, had fastened on this point to make Prince Bismarck feel he had overdone things by sending this letter.

So I went to see Seckendorff yesterday and discussed the matter. It then became clear that the Crown Princess had originally wanted him to go and deliver her message to Herbert in person, but Seckendorff was not keen on doing that, because the day before when he had called on Herbert with some inquiry or other, he had been coolly received and hastily dealt with, because Herbert happened to be engaged on something else. That is unfortunately a vice of Bismarck's family. Up to now they have seen how their father surmounts all difficulties, and so they think it not worth while to consider any one's feelings, but behave just as their fancy takes them.

Seckendorff was annoyed at first to think his note to Herbert, which he thought most elegant, had not been fully appreciated, but he finally promised to see that Herbert or Bill were invited soon.

The Crown Princess would probably take that opportunity of saying some kind word about the Chancellor's letter.

The person who actually decorated the picture frame, and who had the idea originally, is, of course, Seckendorff, as is usual in cases like this.

Now that Busch and Herbert Bismarck are working side by side in the Foreign Ministry we are having too many sources of authority. This hampers the conduct of business, and annoys no one more than the two men themselves. When I asked Herbert recently how long it would go on, he said irritably: 'I don't know, but I'd be very glad if you would tell Hatzfeldt to have a word with my father.'

Hatzfeldt conferred with the Chancellor yesterday, but was told that Busch must stay with us 'a few more weeks' until Herbert had become more broken in to the work. He has been breaking in for three months now. Herbert is an efficient worker and has an open mind, but is too vehement. In disputes with foreign governments his communications are too apt to assume the form of an ultimatum. His father, however, fears nothing so much as vehemence in diplomatic relations. He is bound to make Herbert Under State Secretary because the affair is now in train, but the directorship of the Foreign Ministry as State Secretary or as Under State Secretary without a State Secretary will not be handed over to him just yet, as many people expect, and as Bernhard

184

Bülow (St Petersburg) hopes, for he would like to become Under State Secretary and the Egeria of the Foreign Ministry.

Of course Bismarck would have preferred all along to have had his son at his disposal year in year out as Minister in some minor Legation such as Darmstadt or Weimar. Now that Bill is getting married,[1] Herbert will probably have to go and live in the country with his father until he too grows tired of it and takes a wife so as to break away. Bill is asking to be transferred to some provincial administration, which really surprises me. I should have thought his wife would have wanted him to enter diplomatic life.

5 *April* 1885

Friedberg told me to-day that a comment the Chancellor passed many years ago on the Crown Prince—'If only he had a nose a little more like the Great Elector's, but he hasn't'—naturally reached the ears of the person concerned, who bitterly resents it to this very day.

Friedberg thinks the Crown Prince has no other plan but that of keeping on the Chancellor. Whether Friedberg knows about the Geffcken correspondence, I cannot say.

Courcel told me to-day that the Chancellor, whom he was sitting next to at the Kaiser's birthday celebrations, spoke to him appreciatively of Hatzfeldt: *C'est un ambassadeur idéal, il ne gâte jamais rien*, but said he was ailing and therefore fought shy of the thick files in the Ministry.

Courcel concluded from this that the Chancellor wished by gradual stages to push Hatzfeldt into an Embassy, and to keep Herbert here alone, but not in the near future, perhaps in a year's time.

6 *April* 1885

Herbert called this morning to say goodbye. He is going with his father to Schönhausen until to-morrow evening. Herbert still knew nothing of Hatzfeldt's conversation with his father yesterday about postponing the change of Under State Secretary. I told him: 'The relations between father and children in your family are such as are usually found only in royal households. You never find such a lack of intimacy anywhere else.'

Lord Rosebery,[2] an English Cabinet Minister, is arriving here

[1] On 6 July 1885 Wilhelm von Bismarck married Sybille von Arnim-Kröchlendorf, daughter of Malvine von Arnim, Bismarck's sister.
[2] Archibald Philip Primrose, fifth Earl Rosebery. Lord Privy Seal in the Gladstone Cabinet, March–June 1885; Foreign Secretary, February–August 1886, August 1892–March 1894; Prime Minister, March 1894–June 1895.

to-morrow evening in a private capacity to visit Herbert Bismarck who stayed with him during his last trip to England.[1] Lord Rosebery is married to a Rothschild; has suffered from financial trouble in the past and is an intelligent, ambitious man.

He is certainly coming to ask us to mediate, i.e. prevail on Russia to give way.[2] After his experiences in '78 Prince Bismarck will be reluctant to do so. I wonder whether the Crown Prince and Princess will try to prejudice him in England's favour or whether they will keep quiet. The Crown Princess is already wildly excited. A few days ago, speaking of Russia, she said: 'I ask you, how *can* one trust people who never keep their word? They swore never to enter China, but they did; never to march on Merv, but now they have done so.[3] How can England depend on it if they now swear they will not march on Herat?' It is a good thing we still have the Kaiser and Bismarck, otherwise we should be waging a war for Gladstone. Yet the Crown Princess cannot be moved from her opinion that Gladstone, whose whole tenure of office has been a series of foolish and humiliating acts, at least in foreign policy, is a great statesman. For this to be possible the lady must be more obstinate than intelligent. I have heard so often of her unusual skill at lying and pretence that I may well have mentioned it [in] these pages. It is typical of her intellectual powers that she always advances abstract principles, but never ventures upon a discussion of their application to concrete instances. She always evades the issue.

8 *April* 1885

Two people I observe with a certain amusement are Count Berchem, the newly appointed Director,[4] and Bernhard Bülow, Counsellor at the Embassy in St Petersburg. Both are great place-seekers, both would very much like to be Under State Secretary when Herbert becomes State Secretary, and each has recognized the other as his rival. The attitude of both men is in keeping with this. Berchem told me: 'Bülow can't look anyone straight in the eye, and when he does, *il fait un effort sur lui-même*.' (A perfectly true judgment, I may say.) Bülow on the other hand tells you when you are alone with him: 'Berchem

---

[1] Rosebery's visit was postponed until May. See Marquess of Crewe, *Lord Rosebery* (London, 1931), vol. i, p. 235. See below, p. 201, note 4.

[2] In the course of Russia's penetration into Afghanistan, Russian troops on 30 March 1885 attacked Afghan forces in Penjdeh. The repercussions of this incident brought England and Russia to the brink of war.

[3] The occupation of Merv in 1884 had brought Russia to the frontier of Afghanistan.

[4] Of the Economic Policy Division of the Foreign Ministry.

keeps up a correspondence with Schweinitz and tells him everything that goes on here. Schweinitz keeps it secret, but I found out the other day by accident.' And so it goes on, hack, hack.

Berchem's mother came of a Jewish family called Eichthal, from Munich. Together with a considerable fortune, he has also inherited from her more brains than fall to the lot of the average Bavarian nobleman. And for this very reason Berchem has inherited a feeling of uncertainty—one could hardly call it snobbishness —which comes out in his anxious avoidance of all but the most genteel society, and in the way he sometimes draws attention to the status conferred on him by birth rather than by position. Consistently enough he married in Vienna a Pallavicini, poor, faded, but noble. Despite his ambition I cannot believe he would ever knowingly commit a mean act.

I would not be so sure of Bülow in this respect. I have in the past had all kinds of experiences with the Bülow family.

In the autumn of 1872, when I was still on good terms with Harry Arnim, I once wrote him a letter in which I made some remark about Bülow,[1] at that time Minister for Mecklenburg [in Berlin] ; I said he always knew on which side his bread was buttered.

Arnim had this letter read out during the trial, in secret session. The same thing would probably have happened in public session too if the defence had not been in such a hurry to get me out of the witness box. Two years later, when I was Bülow's immediate subordinate at the Foreign Ministry, he did all he could to plague me, right up to the end. But after he had had a stroke he sent for me, bade me farewell and entrusted his sons to my care. I have done for them what lay in my power because they are really very competent.

The second son,[2] a captain and former adjutant to Prince Wilhelm, on whom he had a good influence, is the most intelligent. He is energetic, clear-minded, rather heartless, perhaps dishonest, but not so aggressively insincere as his eldest brother Bernhard.

The latter's character can best be shown by the following story. In the spring of '75 when the Arnim feud was at its height, the well-known journalist Beckmann returned to Paris, bringing with him a collection of secret personal details relating to the Foreign Ministry. Hohenlohe or Wesdehlen[3]—no, it was Lindau[4]—

[1] Bernhard Ernst von Bülow, the father of the Bernhard von Bülow in the St Petersburg Embassy.   [2] Adolf von Bülow.
[3] Ludwig, Count von Wesdehlen. First Secretary in the Embassy in Paris, 1873–80.
[4] Dr Rudolf Lindau. Attached to the Paris Embassy to deal with Press and commercial affairs; from 1878 *Legationsrat* in the Foreign Ministry.

asked him: 'Where did you get all this?' He said it was from Henning Arnim,[1] who goes drinking every evening with young Bülow. Bülow told Arnim there was no reason for them to carry on their fathers' quarrel, which was moreover in *his* father's case purely a professional necessity. Arnim agreed.

On the contrary Bülow senior carried the affair far beyond mere professional necessity, for instance he pressed the Chancellor to bring the charge of high treason. But to other people father and son laid the blame on the Chancellor.

Bernhard Bülow is clean-shaven and pasty, with a shifty look and an almost perpetual smile. Intellectually plausible rather than penetrating. Has no ideas in reserve with which to meet all contingencies, but appropriates other people's ideas and skilfully retails them without acknowledging the source. In this way he often flatters the originator of the idea. Bülow has wormed his way into Herbert's favour, whom behind his back, and perhaps even to his face, he compares to Achilles.

When Bülow wants to set one man against another, he says with his insinuating smile: 'He doesn't like you.' A simple and almost infallible method.

Bülow can hardly wait for the day when Herbert becomes State Secretary and he becomes Under State Secretary, and is therefore scheming against Hatzfeldt, who annoys him in any case by his rather condescending treatment. I can tell Bülow is behaving insincerely, because the opinions he expresses to me about the relations between Herbert and Hatzfeldt are totally different from those he expresses to other people.

It is hard to say what effect this secret scheming will have on Herbert because he is unfortunately most susceptible to flattery.

Incidentally, once in his life Bülow met a more skilful intriguer than himself. This was little Countess Dönhoff-Camporeale,[2] who after a marriage lasting sixteen years, of which there are two or three children, divorced her husband about a year ago in order to marry Bülow. The eldest daughter is about sixteen. Amongst her mother's earlier love-affairs the one with the painter Lenbach caused an unusual amount of talk. Just over a year ago another divorcée, with whom Lenbach had carried on an affair for years, took her own life, and in the farewell letter she wrote to Lenbach she mentioned 'his Countess'—this very Dönhoff, who has been

---

[1] Henning, Count von Arnim-Suckow. Harry von Arnim's son.
[2] Marie, Countess Dönhoff-Camporeale. Divorced from Count Karl Dönhoff on 31 March 1883; daughter of Prince Domenico Camporeale and Donna Laura Minghetti, whose second marriage was to Marco Minghetti, the Italian Minister-President.

living in Rome since her divorce. Lenbach has also been there about two years.

Bülow is certain that the little Countess has never given a thought to any one but him. If Bülow goes through with this marriage it will be a help rather than a hindrance to him in his career under the future Kaiser; the little Countess is very much a *protégée* of the Crown Princess. Indeed the Crown Princess would welcome anything that might cause offence in Berlin society.

The marriage plans are still a secret. Bülow trusts me[1] but he would not be averse to seeing me go.

12 *April* 1885

Herbert said to me yesterday evening after returning slightly tipsy from his mother's birthday party: 'I've been trying to persuade my father for a year now to recall that hopeless idiot Hohenlohe from Paris. He replies: "The other chaps aren't any better." But I think in that case he should turn to the younger men, even if they're only twenty-four years old. That's what Frederick the Great did. He sent Goltz to St Petersburg to end the Seven Years War. The King wrote afterwards to him: "*Vos coups d'essai sont des coups de maître.*" '

In other words, Bülow has managed to convince Herbert that Hohenlohe can do nothing without Bülow, and that Bülow would be the right man to be Ambassador in Paris. Both men constantly discuss a little scheme to get rid of all the older Ambassadors and Ministers (not a bad thing in itself) and to put young men in their place. The beauty of it is that Bülow keeps up a continuous and friendly correspondence with Hohenlohe.

That reminds me of Bülow's behaviour to Wesdehlen once in Paris. The latter had made the acquaintance, through a Swiss female relative, of a Count Royer du Nord, who sometimes asked him to dinner—a rare occurrence under conditions then obtaining. When Bülow arrived in Paris, Wesdehlen introduced him to Count Royer, but noticed after some time that the latter had stopped inviting [him], Wesdehlen, but that Bülow dined there far more often. Wesdehlen, somewhat puzzled, sent his Swiss relative to find out why. Scarcely had she uttered the name Wesdehlen in the family circle than the ladies of the house pounced upon her: '*Oui, parlez-en, de votre M. de Wesdehlen.* Herr von Bülow tells us Wesdehlen is a Gallophobe and that Bülow's father, the State Secretary, was repeatedly alarmed by Wesdehlen's pessimism.'

[1] Bülow informed Holstein of his understanding with Marie Dönhoff in a letter of 18 April 1884 (*Correspondence*).

Dear old Wesdehlen expressed no opinion at all, let alone one that could alarm anybody. The tale was invented by Bülow *pour les besoins de la conte*, so as to be without a rival in the Royer household, where one could often pick up items of news.

You cannot call Bülow a bad diplomatist; for example he has succeeded in winning Herbert over completely to his side and will try to use him to further his ambition and his vindictiveness.

I shall be interested to see what comes of this. Herbert probably met with a setback to his personal plans right at the start, for he told me that he has not said a word to His Highness on personnel matters for some time, but lets everything go through Hatzfeldt. Herbert may have been too insistent, and the old man is perhaps afraid of finding a rival Chancellor in his son. In spite of this I think Herbert's influence will prevail in the long run.

There is great resentment amongst the people against the Crown Prince for holding so aloof from Bismarck's birthday celebrations and for staying away from the torchlight procession. Of course his wife carries the blame for all this. I am told that expressions such as the following can often be heard among the ordinary folk lately: 'The Crown Prince won't make a good ruler. We want Prince Wilhelm; *he*'ll be a second Frederick the Great.'

Herbert dined with the Crown Prince and Princess on Thursday. The Crown Princess sent for him afterwards and, somewhat to his amazement, had a long conversation with him. I told him: 'That was no doubt to show her gratitude for your father's letter.' Bravo Seckendorff!

16 *April* 1885

The Crown Prince and Princess gave a little ball on Monday to celebrate Princess Victoria's birthday. When Radolinski suggested inviting the Kaiser, the Crown Prince replied: 'Oh, no, why should we? Everything would have to be formal.' In the end he did invite his father, but may have done so without cordiality, for the old gentleman, who is usually fond of watching dancing, did not come.

The Crown Princess stated again recently that in the coming transformation of society there would be no more room for 'powerful' monarchs. Power was superfluous; it was enough for the sovereign to secure personal influence. In England, for example, where the Queen possessed no real power, she did nevertheless wield unusual influence and was also generally loved and respected.

The Princess went on to speak very bitterly about universal suffrage and in particular about tariffs; free trade, she said, was the only right policy.

Waldersee came to see me yesterday and asked me to find out secretly what the Chancellor's present attitude to the *Kreuzzeitung* was, and whether he would have any objection if Waldersee took steps to have it circulated more widely than at present amongst the army officers. At the moment the *Norddeutsche* and the *Post* were much read. In Waldersee's view it was a good thing to introduce in the army a newspaper that always remained conservative, under any regime.

I passed on his inquiry and received the answer: No. The Chancellor said he could not regard the *Kreuzzeitung* as conservative, but that its constant flirtation with the Centre Party, sometimes concealed, sometimes open, obliged him to regard it as subversive, for the Centre Party, whose sole and hitherto undisputed leader was Windthorst, pursued subversive aims. A moderate regime would always be able to come to terms with a Centre in which no one stood farther to the left than Schorlemer and in which men like Franckenstein,[1] Wendt[2] and Schalscha[3] formed the decisive majority. But, said the Chancellor, these elements were being terrorized and pushed to the wall by Windthorst, who is now ousting Schorlemer, thus severing or loosening the ties between the Centre and the Free Economic Association,[4] and making the passing of the tariff bill[5] doubtful.

The *Kreuzzeitung*, which was firmly united with this Party on most questions, did not deserve to be specially recommended to the army.

18 *April* 1885

Herbert Bismarck told me yesterday: 'Radolinski has invited me to dinner next Monday. I was going to decline at first, thinking there would be people from the Crown Prince's entourage, and I've nothing in common with them. But his servant informed me the dinner party was for Prince Wilhelm, so I accepted. I've already a dinner engagement with him at Potsdam to-morrow.

---

[1] Georg Arbogast, Baron von und zu Franckenstein. Centre Party Reichstag Deputy from 1872; Party leader and first Vice-President, 1879–87.

[2] Karl, Baron von Wendt. Member of the Reichstag, 1874–93.

[3] Alexander von Schalscha. Member of the Reichstag, 1877–87, 1890–3; of the Prussian Chamber of Deputies from 1889.

[4] An inter-party union of 204 protectionist Reichstag deputies.

[5] On 8 January Bismarck brought before the Reichstag a supplementary tariff bill raising the duty on grain, pulse, malt, flour, spirits, honey and timber. The bill was adopted by the Reichstag with certain amendments on 13 May.

Yesterday evening at Launay's[1] I was standing in a corner when Prince Wilhelm, catching sight of me from a distance, pushed through the crowd to reach me. We had a long conversation.'

It is clear from Herbert's whole behaviour that he thinks he will never succeed with the Crown Prince (i.e. his wife) by fair means, but only through bringing pressure to bear. But it is a regrettable exaggeration on Herbert's part to lend his connexion with Prince Wilhelm an even stronger air of antagonism by cutting the Crown Prince's court. But persuasion has no effect on Herbert's self-assurance and self-will. It is easier to persuade his father. The latter wants to retain every means, the soft as well as the harsh, at his disposal, whereas Herbert always tends towards violence. In addition Rantzau incites him against the Crown Prince's court, as I have already mentioned.

And it cannot be denied that the Crown Princess likes to employ a policy of pinpricks when she dares. She did admittedly invite Herbert to dinner at Seckendorff's instigation, and made some courteous remarks to him about his father's letter, saying she 'would incorporate it in her collection of autograph letters', but on the other hand she did not invite Herbert, only Bill, to Princess Victoria's birthday ball three days later, which caused great offence to Herbert. Thus people's tempers are being strained by these minor irritations, in readiness for the final clash.

The porter of No. 76[2] looks after Hatzfeldt's little pug bitch for him. It appears that the peace of mind of Prince Bismarck's dogs next door was disturbed by the proximity of this little creature, for Bismarck sent the following message to the porter this morning: if the dog belonged to him, then he had no right to keep one; if it belonged to Count Hatzfeldt, it must be removed to his flat. Hatzfeldt, to whom the porter passed on this message, was of course extremely indignant and said it was unheard of for such a message to be sent by the Chancellor to a Minister by a servant; a step like this undermined all authority.

He is quite right. The lack of consideration shown by the Bismarcks, father and sons, increases daily, particularly towards those who have swallowed an insult in the past. Business suffers from it and enmities are increased and exacerbated.

Even so there is no denying that Hatzfeldt does compromise his position by laziness. Berchem has just called on me to complain that he *never* succeeded in getting hold of Hatzfeldt to confer with

---

[1] Eduard, Count di Launay. Sardinian Minister, then Italian Minister and Ambassador in Berlin, 1856–92.
[2] No. 76 Wilhelmstrasse. The Foreign Ministry.

him; the inevitable result was that business was transacted without Hatzfeldt and that his prestige in Division II suffered from this. Hatzfeldt is in fact only interested in policy and certain major issues; to the rest, particularly the personnel of the consulates, he is completely indifferent, and tries to shake it off his shoulders.

6 *May* 1885

War between England and Russia has been averted for the moment. A great misfortune for Germany, because when the Crown Prince becomes Kaiser and Bismarck finally goes, Germany will be dragged into the war as England's vassal. The Crown Princess was half demented at the idea that the war might break out now. The people who wish to be on good terms with her later on behaved accordingly. Schweinitz used his influence in St Petersburg for peace as far as he could, and Hatzfeldt, anti-Russian in any case both on principle and because of his instincts as a Catholic, spoke of the danger of allowing Russia to become even stronger. She would not have become stronger, just fatter.

Bismarck said last week: 'The Russians would take a far more vigorous line in the Afghan question if they were not afraid our Kaiser may suddenly die overnight.'

It was nevertheless folly on the part of the Russians to postpone the issue. Present risk would have been preferable to future certainty.

Münster, the old blockhead, thought war was inevitable.

Plessen showed more judgment than I had credited him with. He remained firmly convinced the affair was not to be taken seriously.

Extracts from or copies of Plessen's letters to Herbert Bismarck were shown to the Kaiser. One letter[1] ended with the sentence: 'Münster regards anyone who does not think war is inevitable, as an immature child.' His Majesty wrote in the margin: 'But does not Councillor of Embassy von Plessen inform his chief of his opinions, as the concluding sentence of his letter almost obliges one to suppose?'

This little reproof was well deserved. Herbert's system aims at playing off the Councillors of Embassy against the Ambassadors and showing from his correspondence with the former that the latter are incompetent, which can be objected to less from the standpoint of factual accuracy than of professional etiquette. If

---

[1] Of 30 April. In the Foreign Ministry files.

Arnim had been no more than a blockhead, I should never have written about him.[1]

The close friendship between Herbert and Prince Wilhelm will no doubt also contribute towards prejudicing the Crown Princess against Bismarck's regime.

Count Hohenau recently gave a small banquet for Princess Victoria. Prince Wilhelm complained to Herbert that he and his wife were not invited. 'I conclude that the Crown Princess has probably drawn up the list', said the Prince. Herbert dropped a hint to Hohenau, who naturally hastened to send the Prince and Princess a belated invitation.

'When the Crown Prince comes to power, the Crown Princess will be Kaiser', said good old R[adolinski] a couple of days ago. The previous day the Crown Prince had wished to promote a coachman, whom she detested, to the rank of head groom I believe. At this she spat out: 'I see I have no say in this house, for which *I*'ve done *everything*. If you go on like this I shall leave the house.' He began to dither and tremble, and of course she had her own way.

Lucius, to make himself popular with the Crown Prince and Princess, has raised the rents on the Oels estates[2] so high and brought down the salaries and wages so low, that there is resentment on all sides. People in the beer houses publicly congratulate or commiserate with each other according to whether they are employed on the Saxon estates or the Crown Prince's. R[adolinski] recently brought to the notice of the Kaiser and Kaiserin, and also informed the Crown Prince, that his tenants had decided no longer to greet him with an ovation when he visited them. R. said it was not right for a Crown Prince to drain his estates like a 'milch cow' (Lucius' term).

The Crown Prince ran round his room wailing: 'There you are, now there's somebody else who hates me! It's dreadful! But where am I to find the money? We *must* have it.' And she observed: 'Yes, a milch cow, that's just what it is.'

Prate to them of political liberties as much as you like, but don't touch their money. If the monarchical principle emerges alive from the Crown Prince's reign, if the Crown Prince can still hand on a monarchy to his son, then Prince Wilhelm can count himself lucky. But he realized long ago that his *own* inheritance was at stake; he may be expected to show fight.

[1] See *Memoirs*, p. 95.
[2] After the death of Duke Wilhelm of Brunswick on 18 October 1884, the Principality of Oels, with the castles of Oels and Bernstadt and fifteen estates, were made over to the Crown Prince of Prussia to hold in fee.

In the opinion of all the initiated, in so far as they are honest, it is absolutely inconceivable that the Crown Prince should ever, no matter what the circumstances, assert his own will in opposition to his wife's. 'You only have to look what she's made of him', S[ommerfel]d said recently. 'But for her he'd be the average man, very arrogant, good-tempered, of mediocre gifts and with a good deal of common sense. But *now* he's not a man at all, he has no ideas of his own, unless she allows him. He's a mere cipher. "Ask my wife" or "Have you discussed the matter with the Crown Princess?"—and there's no more to be said.'

7 *May* 1885

I do not know whether I have mentioned already that Prince Hatzfeldt-Trachenberg and Prince Carolath-Amtitz were to be dismissed from their post as officers in the royal suite because they had voted against an army bill introduced by the War Minister. Hatzfeldt, hearing of this in time, wrote a letter of apology to the Lord High Chamberlain, Stolberg, in which he said he had completely misunderstood the situation and very much regretted it, etc. It was a more serious matter in Carolath's case because this was his second offence; he had already voted the same way once last year and has the general reputation of being prepared to come to terms with Richter at the crucial moment. His nickname in the Reichstag is 'Caro'; most apt, for he looks like a tubby little spaniel and behaves like a fawning toady. His mother, Guido Henckel's[1] sister, was a fickle woman, which explains why it is uncertain whether Caro's father was a waiter or a coachman, but he was certainly either one or the other.

And so after the voting the War Minister went to the Kaiser and demanded the dismissal of both Princes. The Kaiser approved in principle. Albedyll called on the Chancellor and asked whether he had any objection to Carolath's dismissal. His Highness replied: 'On the contrary, go ahead.' The Kaiser then ratified the dismissal; rather unwisely the reason for it was hinted at in the Imperial order. Carolath then called on Herbert and declared he would go over to the Progressives, and would read out the Imperial order from the rostrum, to show the scant respect paid to the clause in the Constitution whereby no one may be persecuted on account of his voting in Parliament.

This dismissal was deplored by the Conservative Party because in the next elections it would probably be used against all those

---

[1] Guido, Count von Henckel-Donnersmarck. Member of the Prussian Council of State; leading industrialist.

Conservative candidates who are officers of the reserve. People would be sure to say: 'Don't elect an officer of the reserve, because he's *bound* always to vote with the Government.'

The Crown Prince was furious: 'Why don't they shut up shop straight away if a man's to be punished for voting as he thinks.'

Puttkamer was furiously angry with Bronsart. Carolath, he said, was nine-tenths *Landrat* and only one-tenth officer. His dismissal would also affect his civilian status, and for that reason the War Minister, i.e. Albedyll, should not have taken steps without prior agreement with the Minister of the Interior.

Meanwhile Herbert had laid the matter before his father, stressing the point that the dismissal, together with a hint as to its cause, was a political blunder.

The Chancellor drove to see the Kaiser, who began by angrily snapping at him: 'I have made my decision.' But then, as usual, he gave in to Prince Bismarck's arguments and said he agreed that Carolath should in the near future be restored to his former status in the royal suite. Luckily his dismissal had not yet been published in the weekly army gazette.

This affair later provoked violent disagreement between Albedyll and Puttkamer and Albedyll threatened to resign. But the Chancellor invited him to a meal and calmed him down by telling him it was enough for Carolath's reinstatement to be under consideration in a general way. Meanwhile he could still be kept dangling for a while.[1]

I doubt whether Albedyll's departure would have been a disadvantage. It might have been so politically, but most certainly not militarily. His system of protection must be without parallel both in Prussian history and in the armies of the other great Powers to-day. Lieutenant-Colonel von Lignitz, Military Attaché in St Petersburg, wrote recently: 'The quality of the supreme and high commanders in the Russian army has improved in recent years, because the present War Minister, Vannovski,[2] acts as objectively as possible when filling new posts; the former system of protection has almost completely died out.'

I read his report in all innocence and had no idea that both Albedyll and Waldersee would see in this statement a covert criticism of *their* methods. But so it was; they both took occasion to write a disagreeable letter to Lignitz, not on this subject but on some other pretext.

Lignitz is an infantry officer of the line recently elevated to the

---

[1] Compare Waldersee, *Denkwürdigkeiten*, vol. I, pp. 257–8.
[2] General Peter Vannovski. Russian War Minister, 1881–97.

nobility, who was with the Russian army in the Russo-Turkish War and greatly distinguished himself. He won the Order of St George and the *Pour le Mérite*. I am not in a position to judge his specifically military achievements but I regard his intellectual capacity and his energy as far above the average. His defects, and at the same time the obstacles to his success, lie in his character, at least so I am told. An unreliable friend, he is said to be of the stamp of those commanders who don't attack until their neighbour has taken a sound beating; they then become heroes and are decorated.

Lignitz's successes in the Russo-Turkish War had made him many enemies among the General Staff, where there is more envy even than among the diplomatists. In addition neither Schweinitz nor Werder liked him, for they found this goat among the sheep most embarrassing. If Bismarck had not insisted on Lignitz's remaining in St Petersburg for as long as our relations with Russia were strained, he would have been removed long since.

Werder suppressed a number of Lignitz's dispatches when they were too anti-Russian.

And now Lignitz is leaving, and is to be put in command of a regiment somewhere or other. I wonder if we shall hear of him again. His failure to be promoted aide-de-camp, as is usual for Military Attachés in St Petersburg, is an undeserved insult whatever his character may be.

I am very much afraid that Waldersee sets greater store by industry and elegance than intelligence. As for Albedyll, he is only interested in people's connexions; he affords his particular protection to his wife's tea-party cronies.

12 *May* 1885

I did not stay long at the beer-party for the Reichstag to-day because I wished to avoid contact with the Kröchlendorf family, who were of course pushing themselves very much to the fore.

Tyras was, as usual, the object of the greatest attentions. Some-one remarked: 'It is instructive for the study of mankind to watch how differently the same people behave towards humble men's children and great men's dogs.'

Berchem told me he had a row with the Chancellor yesterday. The latter, white with rage, asked him which *Rat* had drafted the document he had in front of him. Herr von Lindenfels.[1] At which the Chancellor burst out: 'How dare the man write nonsense

[1] Gustav von Lindenfels. *Vortragender Rat* in the Economic Policy Division of the Foreign Ministry, 1885–97.

like this?' Berchem replied: 'I am responsible for the final version; I cast it in that form after *you*, sir, instructed me to do so yesterday.' The Chancellor calmed down immediately. He tends to forget what he has said more often than he used to.

Stumm, who has been transferred from Darmstadt to Copenhagen, was invited out yesterday evening by the Crown Prince and Princess, and went in some trepidation, because he had not met them since the Battenberg incident.[1] But the Crown Princess was most affable saying only: 'There are certain things we won't discuss', which was the last thing Stumm wished to do. The Crown Prince on the other hand seized a moment when he was alone with Stumm to pour out his heart to him on the subject of the Battenbergs, of whom he spoke in the most disparaging terms. He was particularly annoyed at the thought of a Battenberg becoming the Queen of England's son-in-law. 'The Marquess of Lorne[2] is a distinguished man, but what of the Battenbergs?'

Despite all this phrase-making I think the danger of a marriage between the Prince of Bulgaria and Princess Victoria is still present so long as he has not married somebody else.

Stumm's way of flattering Herbert is quite different from Bülow's. His attraction may well lie in this very difference. Bülow employs the smooth approach, Stumm the affectionate approach. 'Herbert's really a wonderful person; I love him like a brother', and so on.

But I do not think Stumm tells lies, whereas I am certain Bülow does. For example, after his recent audience with the Crown Princess, he told Herbert that the conversation had turned on the Afghan affair and that in order to hint to the Princess that he did not take England's war threats seriously, he had quoted the oriental proverb: 'The caravan (Russia) is on the move, the dogs are barking.' At this she leapt to her feet saying: 'I will not hear my compatriots spoken of in that way.'

I am prepared to bet that Bülow did not put it in those words and think it argues great faith in people's credulity to pass off such tales as true. But Herbert believes it, so Bülow had judged his public correctly.

16 *May* 1885

A couple of days ago Schweninger informed the Chancellor that Hatzfeldt was suffering from a troublesome appendix which

---

[1] See *Memoirs*, pp. 135–6.
[2] John Sutherland-Campbell, Marquess of Lorne. From 1900 Duke of Argyll. In 1871 he married Princess Louise, Queen Victoria's fourth daughter.

required treatment, because if it grew worse the patient might be carried off within three days. Struck, who used to be Hatzfeldt's doctor, never thought his condition was so serious; it is therefore not impossible that Schweninger was being used as the mouthpiece of the Rantzau clique in order to get Hatzfeldt away from Berlin.

The Chancellor said yesterday that he intended to turn Hatzfeldt's state of health into a 'coup' directed against Münster. He said the Kaiser thought highly of Hatzfeldt, and the prospect of Hatzfeldt's being unable to remain here and having to be accommodated elsewhere would perhaps cause His Majesty to get rid of Münster.

Some time ago now a shrewd lady told me the Chancellor found Hatzfeldt's presence here an embarrassment because of the excessively high regard he enjoyed at court, particularly with the Crown Prince.

If they succeed in sending Hatzfeldt to London (or to St Petersburg, moving Schweinitz to London), they will look for a mere figurehead to fill the post of State Secretary. No one occurs to me but Stirum, who might possibly feel inclined to accept this almost ludicrous post. All the important negotiations both with the Chancellor and with the ambassadors, all the influence in personnel matters, would fall to Herbert's share. Even now the ambassadors seek out Herbert rather than Hatzfeldt because the latter is cautious and the former is talkative and informative, and he tells them more than is good for us. The way to loosen Herbert's tongue is to invite him to a morning meal or lunch and serve exquisite wines. No one has ever been so good at this as the Russian Kapnist,[1] who was here as a delegate to the Congo Conference. Kapnist's very, very strong point is that he is a courtier—his weak point is that he is a diplomatic snob. But vulgar characters are acceptable to Herbert provided they humble themselves before him.

Herbert's character is unevenly developed. He has, alongside some outstanding qualities, others which hold down his *achievements* to the mediocre level, and will easily compass his downfall when his *position* has raised him above this level, whereas a mediocre but tactful person would muddle through. His defects are violence, arrogance and vanity. These first two qualities of his repel almost everybody, with the exception of the few who are clever enough to flatter him in the right way. Towards these latter he behaves with unlimited credulity, and believes what they say

[1] Count Peter Kapnist. Russian Minister at The Hague, 1884–92.

199

about him and what they say about other people. Hence a very capricious handling of personnel matters, which creates much bad feeling and will create much more. At the same time he always acts in the best of faith, striving to do what is right, but always convinced he is doing so.

Someone told me yesterday that Bismarck has held a slightly lower opinion of Herbert since they have been working together here. Prince Bismarck may have somewhat exaggerated to himself both the quantity and the quality of Herbert's work; only the day before yesterday he said: 'It's a fact that my two sons take things very easy.'

And His Highness told Berchem only recently: 'Herbert likes his liquor; too much hard work on top of it might be bad for his health.'

I have myself been in a position to observe that Bismarck is afraid of his son's vehemence. During our disputes with England over colonial affairs, Herbert once wrote Münster a dispatch which, though skilfully framed, was in tone simply an ultimatum. Bismarck laid the document on one side, remarking that it was a bit early to adopt that tone. The Chancellor nearly always waters down the factual content of his son's dispatches. On the other hand he thinks him a good judge of men because he is even more mistrustful and pessimistic than his father—*et ce n'est pas peu dire*. In the evenings Herbert is in a state of alcoholic excitement, in the mornings before lunch he has more or less of a hangover; after lunch he likes to take a refreshing nap with a newspaper on his knees. Drink is impairing his energy for work—he never used to be like this.

Herbert has already stated that even after his father has retired he wishes to remain in the service of the state, because he has no interest in anything else.

Both father and son are at present pursuing the aim of making the son State Secretary, not just yet, but as soon as possible. Bismarck, as I learned from B[erchem?], has the remarkable notion that under the new reign his son is more likely to be kept on as State Secretary here than as an ambassador abroad. I think the reverse would be more probable.

1 *June* 1885

The Chancellor sent for the French Ambassador last Thursday and told him the Kaiser's health gave grounds for anxiety. They must be prepared for the succession at any time. When that happened he, Bismarck, would probably not remain. When the

Crown Prince became Kaiser he would want to act in concert with England at once on matters of foreign policy. It was therefore advisable for France to come to an immediate agreement with England on Egypt. He requested Courcel to inform Freycinet[1] of this in confidence.

The Ambassador, somewhat taken aback, called on Hatzfeldt and told him what had happened. Hatzfeldt was also rather shocked.[2]

I for my part see it as yet another stroke of real genius. Not everything Bismarck says is to be taken at face value, but honesty is his guiding principle. When Bismarck says he will not remain under the new regime, I do not believe him. He will stay on if he can decently do so. To improve his chances he will restore his former good relations with England. He has been provided with a plausible pretext for doing so by the Freycinet Cabinet, which is behaving towards England with a vague ambiguity over the Egyptian question, but is showing complete ruthlessness towards Germany in colonial questions—Dubreka and Little Popo.[3]

And so Bismarck has given the French Government due warning of the ending of co-operation. To express his thoughts with un-diplomatic candour he need only have said: 'I myself, if I do stay on, shall have to adopt a different attitude towards England during the new reign from my attitude hitherto', instead of merely saying: 'My successor will pursue a different policy towards England.' But he was not obliged to go so far; as it was he went far enough. I should like to see any other Minister who would have done the same. Not every one knows how to be adroit and dignified at the same time.

And so there has been a policy switch. I do not think we shall follow the English line entirely as long as Bismarck remains. But even he will make sure that in future we run parallel both with France and England, and that these two lines never cross, as they sometimes did in recent years.

Lord Rosebery was given a very good reception here.[4] He asked us to treat England better. The Chancellor pointed out that

---

[1] Charles de Freycinet. Foreign Minister in the Brisson Cabinet, 1885–6. Compare Bernhard Schwertfeger, *Die Diplomatischen Akten des Auswärtigen Amtes*, 1871–1914 (Berlin, 1927), vol. I, pp. 428–30.

[2] See *Documents Diplomatiques Français*, Première Série, vol. VI, no. 29, pp. 40–47.

[3] Compare *Documents Diplomatiques Français*, Première Série, vol. VI, p. 53, note 1. On 3 June 1885, Freycinet sent a telegram to Courcel, saying: '*Le Ministre de la Marine verrait de graves inconvénients à laisser l'Allemagne s'établir soit au Dubréka, soit au Petit Popo, soit même à Porto Seguro.*'

[4] Lord Rosebery had been visiting Bismarck in Berlin from 22–26 May 1885. See also *Grosse Politik*, vol. III, no. 704, pp. 449–50.

we had materially assisted England at the Congress of Berlin and at the beginning of the Egyptian disturbances, but that in colonial affairs we had only reaped ingratitude, and had come up against England at every turn. Lord R. took note of this and held out hopes of remedying the situation. He expressed the wish to Herbert that he might receive sympathetic treatment from the German Press. An article of the most flattering kind was drafted, and was looked through by the Chancellor himself.

There is a feeling of antagonism towards the Chancellor at the Crown Prince's court. Friedberg told me he had the impression that another wedge had been driven recently between the Chancellor and the Crown Prince. It was regrettable that the Chancellor's behaviour was not more considerate; for example the Crown Prince had felt very hurt that he had not been previously informed of the Prussian proposal to the *Bundesrat* relating to the exclusion of the Duke of Cumberland.[1] 'I count for nothing now, and I shall count for nothing later on. That man holds all the power', His Imperial Highness said.

The Crown Princess once said: 'Now Bismarck governs not only the German Reich, but also the eighty-eight-year-old Kaiser. But how will it be when Bismarck is faced with a *real* Kaiser?' Her words sound like a jest when one thinks of the Crown Prince's personality. She is the only possible *real* Kaiser.

Bill Bismarck said yesterday: 'Why doesn't the Crown Prince come to see my father more often?'

He was annoyed when I replied that perhaps His Imperial Highness expected the Chancellor to call on him occasionally too. The feeling of absolute power which has spread throughout the Bismarck family constitutes a serious danger.

Moreover the two sons are determined not to go when their father eventually resigns.

Friedberg said that when the Chancellor does retire the Crown Prince will certainly choose as head of his government the most distinguished man he can find, if possible a Prince. 'No mere Müller, Schulze or Friedberg'; this sentiment, he said, is all of a piece with the Prince's enormous dynastic arrogance.

4 *June* 1885

Incredible! Yesterday before he left, the Chancellor told Bleichröder the same story he had told Courcel, about the imminent change of ruler and regime. Bleichröder's impression was that the Chancellor regarded an understanding with England as

[1] See p. 166.

only one of the ways of remaining in office. When Bleichröder observed that this would not clear away all difficulties, and that his main difficulties would be encountered rather in domestic policy, the Chancellor replied that he would be able to co-operate with the National Liberals, though not with Forckenbeck, Rickert and company. The Chancellor had gone into full details of the Crown Prince's household, had asked about Seckendorff's relations with the Crown Princess, and had remarked that you could never tell how long it would all last before someone else replaced him.

What can be the explanation of Bismarck's discussing all this with such a gossip as Bl.? Bl., who cannot bear Seckendorff, is bound to repeat everything. Not only will this intensely annoy the Crown Princess yet again, but Seck., who was hitherto well-disposed towards the Chancellor and often put himself out for him, may be driven into the enemy camp.

Moreover the English will of course now learn *why* the Chancellor is suddenly so co-operative. But they cannot be expected to be grateful to him. On the contrary, he is in great danger of falling between two stools—England and France.

In view of the talkativeness of both father and son I fail to see how we are going to keep any political secrets now. What is the use of the best fencing tactics if one's opponent knows in advance which thrust to expect?

Bleichröder also told me the Chancellor embraced him when he took his leave; he seems to be doing that a good deal lately.

Courcel told me that Prince Bismarck said he was anxious about Herbert's suitability for the post of State Secretary. He would carry on negotiations with diplomats very well, but it was less certain whether he would be any good at running the internal affairs of the Ministry. Apart from Bucher and myself the *Räte* were either young or lacking in *esprit politique*.

Courcel was left with the impression that the Chancellor is in a great hurry to make Herbert State Secretary.

The Crown Princess cannot bear Herbert. And there is a very lively hatred between her and Princess Bismarck. The Crown Princess tells how the latter said in '70 that it was disgusting to nurse wounded French soldiers in our military hospitals; they ought to be left to die.

I have heard Princess Bismarck talk like that often enough. She has the excuse that Herbert had just been wounded. But that does not make it any better. In any case the real reason for the royal hatred is that dear Princess Bismarck with her customary lack of restraint has for many years said the most venomous things about the Crown Princess that could possibly be imagined.

A few days ago Bernhard Bülow, the future Under State Secretary, sent me a letter to Herbert, unsealed, to be passed on to Herbert sealed. Dear Bülow is full of attentions towards me—to my face. His covering letter to me[1] is a good example of trouble-making. He assumed I would show this letter to Herbert, but I did not. Schweinitz and Berchem should be grateful to me.

Herbert's susceptibility to flattery, together with his volubility when he has been drinking, are grave defects. [...]

6 June 1885

The Crown Princess recently stated her opinion that Prince Bismarck must of course remain in office during the new reign, and that agreement would be reached with him on most points, though not on all. Why should it not be possible to bring about a general agreement between all parties favourable to the monarchy, including the Liberals, to form a front against the Republicans and Socialists?

On his most recent trip to Königsberg the Crown Prince said: 'It's a scandal that the State doesn't put on a special train for me.' That is one way of looking at it, but hardly a liberal way. Money, pomp, cheering. But *not* power, because power means work.

Otto Stolberg, the Lord High Chamberlain, has not a very happy turn of phrase, least of all in French. He was speaking the other day of the Grand-Duchess Vladimir, Countess Stolberg's niece. '*Ce qui me plaît chez ma nièce*', he told a Russian lady, '*c'est que d'un côté elle est Grande Duchesse, et de l'autre elle est femme.*'

'*Oh*', replied the Russian lady, '*alors elle s'assied sur la Grande Duchesse.*' [...]

9 June 1885

Radolinski, who took over the Crown Prince's household barely a year ago with a debt of 30,000 marks, has wiped out this debt and saved 82,000 marks, which he has invested in deeds of mortgage. That will materially strengthen his position.

Bismarck wanted to take the sum of eleven or twelve hundred thousand marks to be set aside from the Bismarck fund for an endowment to benefit teachers, and invest it in mortgages on his estates, so that he could repay Bleichröder the sums on which he

---

[1] Letter of 28 May 1885 (*Correspondence*).

has for many years been paying four per cent. Very safe investments too. But Bleichröder declined 'for fear of a second *Reichsglocke*'.[1] So his mortgages remain.

Yesterday the Crown Princess expressed her opinion of her daughters' marriages. She did not agree that the hereditary Princess of Meiningen had made such a bad match—her husband was intelligent, and Duke of Meiningen was a very respectable position. All the difficulties arose from her daughter's extremely difficult character.

They had intended marrying their second daughter[2] to a Portuguese prince,[3] but the condition had been laid down that she should become a Catholic as soon as she was married. The condition was unacceptable and the match was now definitely off.[4] Her daughter's marrying the Prince of Bulgaria, *particularly* if he continued as ruler of Bulgaria, was absolutely out of the question.

For her younger daughters[5] she hoped to find husbands of moderate rank in Germany, whom she preferred to foreign royalty.

This latter remark is certainly directed against the plan of marrying one of the younger Princesses to the heir to the Russian throne.[6]

18 *June* 1885

[...] The day before yesterday someone asked the Crown Prince: 'Why does Your Imperial Highness so hate the Chancellor?'

[1] See p. 23, note 3.   [2] Princess Victoria.
[3] Crown Prince Carlos, son of Louis I. King of Portugal, 1889–1908.
[4] The King of Portugal brought up the possibility of a marriage in a personal letter to the Crown Princess in the autumn of 1884. The Crown Princess turned it down, giving as her reason that the change of religion was unacceptable. On 4 June 1885 Herbert von Bismarck had an interview with Penafiel, the Portuguese Minister. According to his memorandum of the same date, he took the opportunity of re-opening the marriage question as he had been instructed. Penafiel explained that the wife of the Portuguese Crown Prince must be a Catholic when she entered the country. Herbert von Bismarck arranged with Penafiel that the latter should write to the Prime Minister, a close friend of his, and say that the German Crown Prince was raising insuperable objections on account of the condition requiring a change of religion, but was otherwise very much in favour of the marriage. The Chancellor noted here: 'I cannot affirm this; I only *presume* he would *agree* to the marriage if there were no conditions relating to religion. Once the Princess becomes Portuguese, her doings no longer concern us. I am by no means *certain* of the Crown Prince's opinion.' On 22 June Penafiel informed Herbert von Bismarck that the Crown Princess had requested the King of Portugal, through his sister, '[to] take no steps in the wooing of the Princess Victoria, because she was promised to another, *son cœur était pris*'. The King, he said, now sought the Chancellor's advice as to his further conduct. The Chancellor issued instructions to inform Penafiel that this other engagement was a thing of the past. On 23 June the Chancellor informed Kaiser Wilhelm as follows: 'I have learnt from confidential sources that the Portuguese Court intends to send an official request to Your Majesty for the hand of H.R.H. Princess Victoria, in which there would be no mention of the religious question. I can only respectfully repeat that I should be glad if such an alliance with a person of equal rank would put a stop once and for all to any other plans.' (From the Foreign Ministry files.)
[5] Princess Sophie and Princess Margarethe.   [6] See pp. 153–4.

'Because', replied H.I.H., 'he's done things to me which can never be forgotten. I still remember, for instance, how he called on me after Nobiling's assassination attempt with the document conferring on me the status of "deputy".[1] I can see him in front of me now, with his arrogant bearing. We began arguing at once about the expressions "deputy" or "regent". He flushed an angry red, picked up his helmet and stood up. I asked him: "Who gives orders here? Do you or do I?" He replied: "I am your obedient servant." I said to him: "If you are my servant, then sit down and give me a clear account of the situation." He wept. Such crocodile tears. He said he was still so much affected by his interview with my father. But that was all a lie. They were tears of rage.'

I still remember clearly that the Chancellor returned from the above-mentioned interview in a state of extreme annoyance; but from his account he had had the best of the argument. He told me the Crown Prince had said: 'You are forgetting in whose presence you are.' To which he replied: 'It is Your Imperial Highness' fault if people forget.'

The Crown Prince has a great reputation for truthfulness and exact verbal accuracy when repeating conversations.

When one hears that kind of story one may well feel worried about the two men's future relations. Unfortunately there is now Herbert as an additional element of provocation. I have already spoken of his demonstrative behaviour towards Prince Wilhelm, who grows daily more abusive about his mother. Naturally his parents lay all this at Bismarck's door. What is more, Herbert's undoubted arrogance in his official and unofficial dealings is already the talk of the town. The Crown Prince has noticed it too, and said, typically: 'He behaves as if he were of the blood royal.' On another occasion H.I.H. said: 'I detest both the sons. You can come to an understanding with the father, but if he thinks I'm going to be saddled with his sons as well, he's making a mistake.' Major-domoism is a household word in the New Palace.

These are minor irritations. But how necessary the old Chancellor still is as an insurance against the follies which the Crown Prince would otherwise commit, especially to begin with.

He will be hard put to it to prevent the Battenberg marriage. The moment the Kaiser is dead, the whole thing will probably come to the fore again. The Crown Prince himself speaks of the

[1] On 2 June 1878 Dr Karl Nobiling shot and badly wounded Kaiser Wilhelm I. The Crown Prince was not made regent, which would have vested in him full sovereign power, but only deputy, obliged to carry on his father's policy.

Battenbergs with the utmost contempt and Prince Wilhelm is furious, but in spite of this I rather think the Crown Princess will push the marriage through unless Bismarck prevents it, at least so long as the Prince still rules in Bulgaria.

A few days ago Prince Wilhelm was talking to Hatzfeldt about it and in particular made fun of his sister, to whom his mother always referred as 'that poor child'.

Hatzfeldt observed: 'The Prince of Bulgaria is certainly a very handsome man.' 'Yes, yes', replied H.R.H., 'but if you gave her someone else she'd fall in love with him too. The trouble is, she doesn't see anybody else.'

I can understand, incidentally, why Herbert and Prince Wilhelm get on well—they share the same rather crude attitude to life.

The Conservative Ministry has been formed in England. As early as March the Chancellor had instructed Herbert to call on Salisbury[1] in London to reassure him on Germany's attitude. We were by no means hostile to England on principle. We had supported England not only at the Congress of Berlin but also during the first phase of the Egyptian affair. But at every point in our colonial policy we had met with hostile resistance from England which had obliged us to take reprisals. Our claims in that respect were very moderate and as soon as they were satisfied, our attitude towards British policy would revert to what it was in the days of Beaconsfield.[2] If, therefore, Lord Salisbury were faced with the possibility of forming a government, he should not allow himself to be deterred through fears of friction with Germany.

There is no doubt that this disclosure materially contributed towards persuading Salisbury to form a cabinet.

Salisbury will have to show initiative at some point in his foreign policy, either in Egypt or Afghanistan. The former is more likely. If he simply does nothing, he is sure to be defeated in the elections. Even at best his party's prospects are not bright. [...]

Yesterday afternoon I had called on Radolinski in the New Palace. He accompanied me to the railway station. Travelling in my compartment were Seckendorff and Sommerfeld. As the train pulled out, Sommerfeld remarked thoughtfully, as he gazed after Radolinski: 'He gets fatter every day.' 'Yes', Seckendorff chimed in, 'it's a wonder he still likes his food, with the weight of all Europe on his shoulders.'

[1] Robert Cecil, third Marquess of Salisbury. British Foreign Secretary in the Disraeli Cabinet, 1878–80; second delegate at the Congress of Berlin; Prime Minister, June 1885–February 1886, August 1886–August 1892, 1895–1902; Foreign Secretary, June 1885–February 1886, January 1887–August 1892, 1895–1900.

[2] Benjamin Disraeli, Earl of Beaconsfield. British Prime Minister, 1868, 1874–80.

Radolinski has carved out a splendid position for himself with the Crown Prince and Princess, and contrary to expectation allows no one to meddle in his work. It remains to be seen whether at the crucial moment of the accession his rivals will succeed in getting rid of him. Seckendorff would then like to push his cousin, Ompteda, into the post.

I am curious to see how Seckendorff will intercede for the Chancellor at the critical moment. And he will need all the support he can muster. Friedberg told someone to-day that he had always hoped hitherto that the new Kaiser and the Chancellor would co-operate, at least to begin with, but this hope was steadily fading.

The main mischief-maker is of course the Crown Princess; that is why Seckendorff is so important.

He may be spurred on by the information I can give him from a reliable source, namely that it is the intention of the future Kaiser and Kaiserin to bring Normann back to Berlin in one capacity or another, the moment they have got rid of the Chancellor. Seckendorff has not much interest in factual questions, but feels the more keenly anything touching him personally and the name Normann almost gives him an electric shock.

But these are all paltry expedients to set against the harm done by all the Bismarcks with their tongues. Here is an example: just now four of us, including Herbert B., were lunching in the hall of mirrors at the Kaiserhof. It came up in conversation that the Crown Prince and the King of Saxony had been in danger of being trampled to death by horses yesterday. 'It would have been a pity about the King of Saxony', remarked Herbert, so loudly that the whole room heard him. [...]

28 *June* 1885

Before leaving for Oels the Crown Prince summoned Herbert to the Palace. Herbert had taken with him all kinds of dispatches on the Egyptian and Afghan questions etc., but he told me it was a deplorable fact that the Crown Prince had no interest at all in politics but only in personnel matters. H.I.H. had spoken exclusively of Manteuffel's successor[1] and the *revirement* it might cause.

It appeared from Herbert's statement that the Chancellor in his eagerness to get rid of Hatzfeldt and replace him by Herbert (during this Kaiser's lifetime), had immediately taken advantage of Hohenlohe's visit to Kissingen to sound him as to his willingness

---

[1] As Governor of Alsace-Lorraine. Manteuffel died on 17 June 1885. Compare Bismarck, *Die gesammelten Werke*, vol. VI c, nos. 312–13, pp. 318–21.

to assume the governorship.[1] Of course Hohenlohe consented; in Paris he gets 150,000 francs, which is more than he needs, and in Strasbourg he will get 262,000 francs. A dispatch was sent at once to the Kaiser, whose reply is still awaited.

Meanwhile the Crown Prince had also written to the Chancellor on the same subject. But, since his proposals did not fit in with Prince Bismarck's plans, the latter had made him wait, with the pretext that His Majesty must first be given the opportunity to express his opinion.

That is why the Crown Prince had sent for Herbert, but I imagine all he got out of him was the idea that the Chancellor was pursuing his own designs and keeping them secret.

Herbert could not conceal from him that Hohenlohe might be going to Strasbourg. 'Oh, and who'll go to Paris?' 'Well, Münster maybe.' 'Incredible. But who'd go to London?' 'Alvensleben perhaps.' 'Alvensleben! Do you think that dreary Junker from the Altmark, who's never been to England, would do for London?' Herbert gave an evasive reply. The whole thing was a feint, to avoid mentioning Hatzfeldt by name.

All this does no good, for it makes the Crown Prince even more embittered against the politics of the Bismarck family.

My guess is that Hatzfeldt will have to go, because Bismarck is firmly resolved that the post of State Secretary shall fall vacant, come what may. The strength of his resolve, and his willingness to go to any lengths, is obvious from the fact that Hohenlohe, of whom Herbert said to me six weeks ago: 'I'm vainly trying to persuade my father to dismiss this utterly incompetent Ambassador', is now to be pushed into a position which makes far more varied and exacting demands than the Paris Ambassadorship. What is aimed at is a reshuffle of ambassadors in which something reasonable will be found for Hatzfeldt!

But it is important for Hatzfeldt *which* embassy he is sent to. That is why I wrote and told him to be here without fail when the Chancellor passes through Berlin on the second of next month.

Hatzfeldt's reply is enclosed.[2] The idea that *he* ought to have been offered Strasbourg is thoroughly naïve and shows he has not been following events closely. The Chancellor will *never* send a man of outstanding intelligence to Strasbourg. That is the *only* reason why he bore with Manteuffel's follies so patiently.

Waldersee came to say goodbye to me to-day. He is off to

[1] Compare *Denkwürdigkeiten des Fürsten Chlodwig zu Hohenlohe-Schillingsfürst*, 2 vols. (Stuttgart and Leipzig, 1906), vol. II, p. 358.

[2] Letter of 26 June 1885 (*Correspondence*).

Switzerland. He also spoke of the Crown Prince, with the greatest bitterness. I can understand that, after hearing from Friedberg recently that Waldersee was 'not the Crown Prince's man'.

That is one point on which I agree with the Crown Prince. Waldersee is lazy. Herbert told me in amazement that Waldersee had recently said to him: 'Don't trouble to put yourself out to come and visit me. You have a lot to do and I have *nothing*.' Even so, he still persecutes Lignitz as vigorously as ever. To-day, when I asked him what Lignitz was doing now, he replied with a sneer that he had been temporarily ordered to the Alexander Regiment. He now flattered himself that he would be put in command of the regiment. But that was out of the question; he would be given a regiment of the line.

I was reminded of Lignitz's saying: 'The horse's tail commands in Prussia to-day.' It is a fact that the cavalry forms a disproportionate majority of the General Staff. It is to be hoped we do not live to regret it.

30 *June* 1885

A letter from the Kaiser to the Chancellor, written in his own hand, arrived yesterday evening enclosed in a second envelope addressed to Herbert. It was sent on to Kissingen by express post, and news of its arrival was also telegraphed.

Herbert said: 'That's the answer at last to my father's letter of the 22nd. My father is waiting for it like the Jews awaiting the Messiah. I sent a telegram announcing its arrival because my father has already threatened to go to Ems himself to settle the matter.'

I asked no questions and changed the subject, because I disagree with the whole procedure. For it can only be the matter of appointing an ambassador—presumably Hohenlohe—to Strasbourg as soon as possible, and the ensuing shift of Hatzfeldt–Herbert.

The fact that the Chancellor thought of going to Ems himself shows his desire to push Herbert to the fore with all the means in his power, during this Kaiser's lifetime.

Caprivi is suffering from varicose veins. Yesterday I tried to persuade him to see Schweninger, but so far without success. He must change his routine, for a sedentary life in itself has a harmful effect on his health. His varicose veins are a sign of poor circulation. I told him that if he was not better by Friday I should nag him again.

It would be a grievous loss if his capacity for work deteriorated now. A character like his is so refreshing in this dreary existence.

He spoke of Waldersee with great fairness, although the two men dislike each other: during the operations of 1870, Waldersee was for a time with General Voigts-Rhetz,[1] whose Chief of Staff was Caprivi. Since Waldersee had for some time past enjoyed the complete confidence of this utterly senile General, he might have been in a position to make Caprivi's task more difficult by giving contrary advice, but instead of this Waldersee behaved with perfect propriety and restraint.

Some time ago now Waldersee once spoke to me about Caprivi in a far more vehement tone, reproaching him with obstinacy, vanity etc. When I compare these two appraisals, I have the impression that one man is criticizing from above, the other from below, and both involuntarily. In Waldersee's case there was a decided streak of vanity.

5 *July* 1885

The Crown Princess has recently held several hour-long conversations with her entourage to discuss relations with the Chancellor. It was repeatedly pointed out to the Princess that when she became Kaiserin she would have to bear a heavy weight of unpopularity and suspicion because of the un-German sentiments attributed to her.

'Your Imperial Highness', said one of them, 'just imagine your situation if the Chancellor sits sulking in Varzin and Prince Wilhelm deserts to his camp with beat of drums and flourish of trumpets—as he undoubtedly will. *Such* an opposition would be stronger than Your Imperial Highness' government.' The Crown Princess protested that she simply could not imagine how it could possibly come about that Prince Bismarck should retire from politics.

'Yes, Your Imperial Highness', Radolinski said to her one day in reply to this, 'but the Chancellor's remaining depends on your final renunciation of people like Forckenbeck and Löwe.'[2] 'Yes', she said, 'I can see that.' In short, she is at the moment more amenable than her weak husband, because she sees the dangers of her position more clearly than he.

The night before last, on my return home, I found a telegram from Sommerfeld which he had sent off in duplicate, one copy to

[1] Konstantin Bernhard von Voigts-Rhetz. Prussian General; Commander of the Xth Army Corps, 1870–1.
[2] Dr Wilhelm Löwe. Member of the Reichstag from 1867; in 1874 he left the Progressives and formed a pro-government Party (Löwe-Berger); in 1884 he joined the National Liberals.

my flat and the other to the Ministry. He urgently requested to see me.

Next morning S. disclosed the following: The Crown Princess wished to bring about a rapprochement with the Chancellor. Not that she intended giving up her principles, but she was anxious to convince him that even in matters on which she did not share his convictions she would not place obstacles in his path, any more than she had done during the regency. She therefore wished to thrash things out at length with Prince Bismarck, either verbally or in writing.

She had originally chosen the latter method and had drawn up quite a long memorandum to Friedberg and a shorter one to Albedyll, so that they could inform the Chancellor of the contents. But the Crown Prince vetoed this, saying it was too artificial and would arouse comment. She was now sitting there wishing to speak to the Chancellor before he left, if it were at all possible. Sommerfeld asked me whether Bismarck was coming to Berlin again after the Kröchlendorf[1] wedding, and whether he might again be prevailed upon to send the Crown Prince and Princess a telegram announcing his arrival, as he did three days ago. He would then be invited to the New Palace; the rest would follow naturally.

I called on the Chancellor whom I had last seen on 2 April on the same subject. 'Permit me', I said, 'to start with a question. Did the Crown Prince, when he visited you yesterday evening, speak to you of the Princess's wish to have things out with you?' 'No.' 'Well, this wish is present nevertheless. She desires a rapprochement and would therefore like to discuss things with you.' He said: 'We've had no quarrel needing to be settled. The only thing I reproach the lady with is that she's remained an Englishwoman and exerts a pro-English influence on her husband. She's got no feeling for Germany.'

I said: 'And no religion either, none whatever.'

He replied: 'Well, that's her own affair. All I object to is her bad political influence. Yesterday evening the Crown Prince behaved more cordially towards me than usual, but he was not forthcoming on the burning questions of the future, although I gave him the opportunity to express his views on possible ministerial appointments. In reply to the compliments he paid me I said: "I do indeed possess a certain capital which I cannot bequeath, namely the experience of very many years and my credit abroad. I am prepared to turn this capital to good account, pro-

[1] See p. 185, note 1.

vided it is made possible for me to do so, and provided the greater part of the work is taken from my shoulders. The only field in which I am to a certain extent indispensable is foreign policy, in the immediate future. I shall in fact still be able to direct foreign policy, but I must be relieved of all other German and Prussian responsibilities. I am in good shape for a man of seventy, provided I do little or nothing. But besides the question of my health there are also the concrete problems of the future. I confess I am enough of an idealist to set store by a good epitaph. I refuse to run the risk of having mine spoiled at the very last minute."

'At this point the Crown Prince could have seized the opportunity to raise immediately the question of planning for the future, and in particular the composition of his cabinet. But he steered clear of all this and kept to generalities.'

From this the Chancellor concluded that the Crown Prince was contemplating a cabinet of a very leftish tinge. He spoke of that Jewish extortioner, Löwe, and said: 'I refuse to serve with Ministers I despise.' He suspected that the sole aim of the Crown Princess's co-operation was to trap him into demonstrations which would make it appear to her that he was clinging to his position.

I will not repeat my arguments. They worked. Now that I no longer look upon him as an oracle but reckon with his weaknesses, I am far more successful than I used to be.

After a forty minutes' discussion, during which he threw out many striking ideas but was also more tedious than he used to be, I departed with the assurance that he would return to Berlin on the actual evening of the wedding, the 6th, and would be at Their Imperial Highnesses' disposal on the 7th. They themselves have an appointment in Boitzenburg on the 8th and this narrow margin of time did not make my task any easier. I had the same feeling I used to have when I had passed an examination.

Prince Bismarck's face is remarkably shrunken, but he looks very well. He is noticeably proud of his eyebrows, which he strokes to make them stand out and look unnaturally formidable. But despite these minor reservations I left him with the impression: he can still do more than the next man.

I was struck by his indifference in religious matters; Rottenburg's influence.

I forgot to mention that one of his main reproaches against the Crown Princess is her project of the Bulgarian marriage. 'This descendant of the Haucke-Bozaks[1] is to be brought here as an English spy. But the Portuguese will probably approach us in the

---

[1] See p. 123, note 2.

near future with an official proposal from the Crown Prince of Portugal.[1] There's no need for the Princess to become a Catholic at once, she can do it gradually. And she'll probably earn her salvation just as well in the Catholic Church as by following her mother's religion.'

Politically right. I should try to do the same. The tone is rather reminiscent of Frederick the Great.

When I entered, Prince Bismarck had in front of him his quarterly bank statement from Bleichröder.

6 *July* 1885

After my conversation with the Chancellor I called on Sommerfeld again and told him part of what had passed. He said: 'The Crown Princess has certainly forbidden the Crown Prince to talk about his future Ministers, and so on. *She* wants to discuss that with the Chancellor. The worst is the Bulgarian marriage. The Princess will not be dissuaded from it.'

Sommerfeld remarked in conclusion: 'When I come back from leave, I'll have another talk with you to see what the Chancellor can do for me. The prospect of becoming one of six aides-decamp does not satisfy me. I'd like something else.' Cash payments only, *quid pro quo*. And he is far from being [the] worst.

I was talking to Seckendorff yesterday morning about the Chancellor's forthcoming interview with the Crown Princess. He said:

'The Chancellor must above all continue to impress her; he must still appear to her as *Jupiter tonans*. What she needs is powerful contradiction. Anyone who handles her with kid gloves is lost. Malet, for example, is in his present scrape because he does not occasionally treat her to a piece of his mind as Ampthill used to. The Princess responds to rough treatment; she resigns herself when she sees she is up against a brick wall. But she refuses to be passed over entirely. She can endure being told she is still an Englishwoman with no enthusiasm for Germany, provided it is conceded that she has political talent and was reared in the classical school of politics. But any hint of doubt as to her political sagacity would infuriate her.

'You cannot in fact by-pass the Crown Princess, because the

---

[1] In a letter of 8 July, Bismarck informed the Kaiser that the Portuguese Minister had just delivered a letter from the King of Portugal to the Crown Prince. The Crown Prince had asked for three or four days in which to think over the Portuguese proposal. Bismarck supposed that the Crown Prince would consult the Kaiser, and requested the latter to 'further this marriage between people of equal rank, particularly since there has been no more mention of a change of religion'. The prevention of the Bulgarian marriage would avoid a serious blow to the monarchical principle. (From the Foreign Ministry files.)

Crown Prince is no more than a screen for her. It makes life easier for *him* if you tell *her* the way *he* should go.

'I disagree entirely with the view that there is nothing more to be done in the Bulgarian affair. I can't do anything, still less can Sommerfeld, but the Chancellor can. But he really must be firm. He must not play any card in vain. "You wish me to help you bear the burden of unpopularity, responsibility and suspicion; at the same time you are afraid I shall want to bring pressure to bear on your decision. Far from exerting pressure, I have come here to learn what your commands will be. I shall be able to judge from them whether *I* am the man to carry them out. Above all I demand to see your cards on the table. I must have the truth. The truth was concealed from me in this Bulgarian business; I learnt it by other ways and means. I must formally protest against this marriage for the future, because objectively, quite apart from political misgivings about Bulgaria, the marriage of one of the German Kaiser's daughters to a man of such humble origins would harm the prestige of the Royal Family and would in particular be imputed to you as an English intrigue." '

Seckendorff continued:

'The question whether the Crown Princess or the Chancellor wins the day is crucial for their future relations. The whole of the English clique is pulling at her skirts. They want to get the Bulgarian Prince here at any price. If the Crown Princess is obliged to give up the project—for fear of public opinion—she will not give *that* as the reason to her family. And so the relations between our Court and London will be slightly strained, and the Crown Princess's stock will rise ten per cent.

'The Crown Princess certainly does not object to the Crown Prince of Portugal. She has actually told Penafiel[1] that he could not be considered for Princess Victoria, but might do for one of the younger princesses. This means that the change of religion is not an obstacle provided it is not required immediately. But the English clique is violently opposed to the marriage. Morier[2] has worked hard to prevent it.

'Above all, the Chancellor's conversation with the Crown Princess must produce some definite result. If it comes to nothing, it will have failed. And the Chancellor won't be seeing the Princess again for some time. Meanwhile all kinds of things may happen.'

As he was leaving S. said again: 'The Chancellor must insist on having specific assurances, because the Crown Princess is a twister.'

[1] Portuguese Minister in Berlin.
[2] Sir Robert Morier. British Ambassador in St Petersburg, 1884–93.

I think Seckendorff's views are right. When one sees the astonishing candour of the Crown Princess's entourage towards her one feels certain that the Chancellor would do well not to mince matters.

Seckendorff does not, I think, want anything from the Chancellor. His aims lie in other directions.

7 *July* 1885

I have just informed the Chancellor of the foregoing. By 9.30 he was already sitting at his desk in his dressing-gown, looking sallow and bad-tempered. I could tell from the hesitant way the chancellery clerk went in to announce me that Bismarck was in a bad mood. A hangover from the wedding and probably uneasiness on account of his forthcoming conversation in Potsdam.

The news I brought interested him sufficiently to drive away all trace of ill-temper. I pointed out that the advice to treat the Crown Princess firmly had already been vindicated, because her entourage falls into two categories only: those who simply do as they please and those she ill-treats.

When I observed that the interview would be a failure if it produced no definite result, he asked: 'What would count as a "definite result"?' I told him: 'Your pushing through the Portuguese marriage.'

When I left, the Chancellor rose from behind his desk, a thing he rarely does after conferences. There was an odd touch of formality in his bearing, and no doubt in mine too. I suppose he was not used to people giving him advice, and disliked it. Even so, he had let me have my say, and I asked for nothing more.

He asked me one more question about what he should wear. I told him Hatzfeldt had sent a telegram to Radolinski to find out and would bring the reply along to his conference. We then bowed, and I left. The Chancellor's leave-taking bow has often struck me as strangely frigid. Its purpose is to make the departing visitor feel yet again the great gulf between great and small. This intention of impressing was more noticeable to-day than usual. He was obviously annoyed at being given advice. If everything turns out well, he will forgive me, but he will not let pass any opportunity which may arise for snubbing me.

Hatzfeldt and I have often had the experience of seeing the Chancellor, once he has acknowledged some achievement (more often Hatzfeldt's than mine), seize on some opportunity to remind the person concerned of his own insignificance.

When the Chancellor went to see the Crown Prince recently he was met at Wildpark station by Radolinski. I had told the Chancellor: 'If there's anything risky you wish to impress on the Crown Princess, you must tell her yourself, because the weight lent to your ideas by your personality cannot be delegated to any one else.' In spite of this His Highness failed to hold his tongue this time and to Radolinski's amazement tried out on him, as soon as they were in the carriage, the speech he intended for the Crown Princess: English influence a misfortune—forcing us to accept the Bulgarian as her son-in-law—on the other hand, Portuguese marriage an advantage, etc.

Radolinski, whom the Chancellor had never before favoured with such a burst of confidence, came to the conclusion that he was only being told all this so that he could secretly inform the Crown Princess. So he went and told her all he had just heard. Her Imperial Highness, upon this timely, or rather, untimely, warning, flew into a rage saying that she would not dream of selling her child (and yet, if the diplomatic dispatches are to be believed, the Prince of Bulgaria is in reality a man of the utmost depravity). At the same time she instructed Radolinski to tell the Chancellor on the way back to the station that the Portuguese marriage was completely out of the question.

She avoided every opportunity of being alone with His Highness, sheltered behind her daughter, and, as soon as the meal was over, packed him off into the garden with the Crown Prince 'to smoke'. Half an hour later she sent the carriage after them because it was 'high time to set out for the station'. On this return journey Radolinski was to deliver his message.

The Crown Prince was very friendly to Prince Bismarck, told him that he must of course stay on, and that the other Ministers would be able to remain too, at least to begin with.

Prince Bismarck then made his speech about English influence and about marriage projects. The Crown Prince pursed his lips and said nothing, which Bismarck interpreted thus: 'The poor devil agrees with me, but he daren't say so.'

He told Hatzfeldt, to whom he had expressed his general satisfaction with the outcome of the interview: 'I had a lot of trouble with the present Kaiserin too.'

But the present Kaiser was at all events a different man from what his son appears to be.

The only result I have achieved by my exertions in this affair is to arouse Herbert's jealousy. His main reason for sending

Hatzfeldt away was the latter's connexion with the Crown Prince and Princess. It does not suit Herbert to see yet another person acting as go-between for the Crown Prince and the Chancellor.

His somewhat childish resentment broke out behind my back over a very trifling matter. Berchem was talking to Herbert about substitutions for men going on summer leave, which was none of his business. I had previously stated that I did not wish to substitute for anyone unless I was ordered to do so. Berchem unintentionally distorted this, saying I refused to take on temporary duty at all. Herbert flared up: 'If Holstein refuses to do temporary duty, he must go.' Berchem, rather alarmed, told this in confidence to Hatzfeldt, who told me. Only a few years ago I should have taken it greatly to heart that a person like Herbert, whose father, like himself, I have done my best to help and support for twenty-three years without any reward, should speak of me in this way to someone else. Nowadays I know the crude behaviour of the Bismarck family too well to be surprised. I found the incident psychologically interesting and useful as a pointer.

I was returning from a walk when Hatzfeldt met me in the garden and told me of this. I went straight to Herbert, who had been looking for me in the meantime, behaved as though I knew nothing and, after talking about one or two other things, simply told him I had been asked by a colleague to take over his duties, but had declined until I was officially requested to do so.

I then turned the conversation on the Chancellor's journey to Potsdam (the Chancellor was actually on his way), and saw from Herbert's half embarrassed, half surly reply, that his father had in fact said not a word about it. The old man is quite right; people who drink *do* talk too much; but he should hold his tongue himself and, for instance, say [nothing] to Bleichröder. He informed him just recently that the Russian strategic railway to Serachs was to be completed, not in two years, as is generally believed, but in one year or less—one of our top diplomatic secrets—and that he certainly expected war between Russia and England within a year. Bleichröder, who has considerable financial interests in Russian bonds, and therefore in the preservation of peace, will no doubt pass on this information to the English. The English and the Russians, as soon as they realize that Bismarck 'expects' them to go to war, will of course be doubly careful not to do so. Bismarck will thus have frustrated his own ends.

But to return to Herbert. I told him the main outlines of my talks with Sommerfeld and Seckendorff, omitting everything which might compromise them with the Crown Princess. When I remarked casually that this role of go-between had been forced upon me, and that one could expect nothing pleasant by undertaking it, he said curtly, 'No'. Otherwise he was very cordial. I have let no one, not even Berchem, see that Hatzfeldt passed on to me Herbert's remark which was made to him *sub sigillo*.

In withholding my information from Herbert the Chancellor may have intended to sow discord between us. He enjoys that. When I was recalled to the Foreign Ministry over nine years ago, His Highness said one evening in front of a dozen people: 'I've recalled Holstein so that I can have someone on whom I can completely rely.' Bülow[1] and Radowitz, as was natural, heard of this remark and were from that moment my enemies.

Herbert will meet with very different types from me in his future path, some who to-day are best at cringing before him.

Rittmeister Bülow,[2] brother of the Bülow who is Counsellor of Embassy,[3] called on me yesterday. He always comes when he wants something. He soon turned the conversation on Prince Wilhelm. Herbert had advised the Prince to ask for a transfer from Potsdam to Berlin to broaden his horizon and avoid one-sidedness. This, Bülow said, was unnecessary and impracticable. Berlin would be dangerous ground for him; he might easily form dubious, perhaps even democratic (!), connexions. He could obtain all the political education he needed in Potsdam, if some suitable person from each department in Berlin had a few hours' conversation with him once a week. For instance the Foreign Ministry could send some staid middle-aged person like me or Bülow, his brother, who would carefully expound things to the Prince without making them seem boring. And at suitable points a joke should be introduced.

I replied with a laugh that I had no intention of doing anything of the sort. I said Bülow's brother would certainly be eminently suited to the task, but I could not see what post he could be offered here. The post of a mere *Vortragender Rat* in exchange for St Petersburg would not suit him.

'Hardly', said B.

I went on to point out that the Foreign Ministry was kept in excellently close touch with Prince Wilhelm through Herbert. 'Yes', said Bülow, rather impatiently, 'because Herbert is just as lively as the Prince.'

The aim of his visit thus became clear: B. wanted to create an

---

[1] Bernhard Ernst von Bülow, the former State Secretary.
[2] Adolf von Bülow.   [3] Bernhard von Bülow.

atmosphere unfavourable to Prince Wilhelm's transfer to Berlin and favourable to the recall of his brother. The seeds of both ideas were sown in my mind; they might take root, I might perhaps drop a useful hint to someone or other.

This was the first symptom of an antagonism I had long guessed at, but which will not be fully realized until Bismarck has disappeared from the scene. But then these different Bülow brothers, as a group, will carry far more weight than Herbert standing alone. One reason is that they painstakingly and perfidiously seek out and cultivate connexions, and are prepared to be agreeable to people of whom they expect the same in return, while Herbert will then be surprised at the isolation he is now carefully laying up for himself.

I have not said a word about Hatzfeldt yet.

When he greeted the Chancellor on his return from Kissingen, the Chancellor told him that Hohenlohe's name had been proposed to the Kaiser for Alsace-Lorraine and had been approved by him. 'A quiet man who never makes a mess of things. In any case his task consists in tactfully waiting upon events. We can expect a real improvement in conditions there only as a result of German education and compulsory military service, that is, very gradually. If it were possible to achieve more, Manteuffel would have done so.' (!)

Hatzfeldt refused to commit himself, and took refuge in generalities.

So the Chancellor went one step further and came to his main point. Paris was falling vacant—would H. like it? In Schweninger's opinion H. should take care of his health. And the Chancellor added that in the new reign, if he stayed on at all, he would be satisfied with the skeleton of his present position, and would confine himself to the Foreign Ministry (which His Highness had already told me). Hatzfeldt's scope would then become too narrow and limited. His Highness had certainly no intention of making his son a Minister yet. And so, if it suited Hatzfeldt, he would be able to resume his post later if he liked (!). The Chancellor fully appreciated that Hatzfeldt could have been very [useful] to him in the forthcoming crisis because of his connexions with the Crown Prince's court. But it would be selfish to keep H. waiting in suspense until another embassy fell vacant; it did not happen every day. The Chancellor would prefer to send him to London rather than Paris, where politics would be less lively in the next few years than in London, but it was doubtful whether the Kaiser could be brought to approve Münster's transfer to Paris.

Hatzfeldt, who had been prepared for what was to come, asked without further ado to be given London rather than Paris if that were at all possible.

Hatzfeldt told me afterwards that he had the impression the Chancellor was in earnest when he said he would like to have taken advantage of H.'s good position with the Crown Prince. And that is why the Chancellor said there was no hurry, and the Kaiser could be given a few months in which to decide. But Herbert is pressing for a quick decision. This is in fact what happened.

At the Chancellor's dinner table the other day (Berchem was present), the discussion turned on whether it was permissible to hit someone for any kind of insult, or whether a challenge should be offered immediately, before coming to blows. Herbert and Rantzau upheld the first view, the Chancellor upheld the latter.

'But', said Rantzau, 'if someone calls you a fathead, surely you've got to hit him.'

'Sometimes', replied His Highness, 'you feel privately that the other fellow is right.'

Berchem says the effect was worth seeing.

Despite the serene contempt expressed in the Chancellor's remark, R. does nevertheless exert a certain harmful influence through his wife and mother-in-law.

I was very sorry to learn from that very shrewd man Kr.[1] that the Chancellor has recently been less proof against the influence of his entourage than he used to be. If ever we reach the stage at which other people trade on his name and his power, we shall be in *very* great danger, especially from abroad. Let us hope it will not come to that just yet.

13 *July* 1885

I enclose:

(1). A letter from Hohenlohe,[2] obviously elated at the prospect of his great organizing mission in Strasbourg. If he only knew the whole story, and that he was picked because they wanted a nonentity!

(2). A letter from Sommerfeld,[3] to whom I had sent a brief cautious note on events in the New Palace (Chancellor and Crown Princess).

The term 'farce' used by Seckendorff gives me pause, because Se. knows the Crown Princess far better than So. Ah well, I can

[1] It is uncertain to whom these initials refer.
[2] Of 11 July 1885 (*Correspondence*).
[3] Of 12 July 1885 (*Correspondence*).

await further developments the more calmly in that I shall no longer be acting as go-between.

I shall inform So. of this by word of mouth as soon as I see him. He still thinks great rewards await him. Naïve fellow.

Two days ago I brought Hatzfeldt and Caprivi together over a picnic meal in Wannsee. Both came with the best intentions and it all went well. As a result Caprivi is invited to dine with Hatzfeldt to-day. Twice on Saturday I had the impression that they were both privately criticizing each other.

To begin with, Caprivi related that some person who had been in Paris in 1814 had told him that Blücher and Gneisenau had looked more distinguished than all the Princes. Hatzfeldt said nothing, but I know his face well enough to realize that the idea that a man who is a mere General can be, or appear to be, more distinguished than a *Grand Seigneur*, does not fit into his scheme of things. Shortly afterwards a *Vortragender Rat* from the Foreign Ministry walked past our table and bowed to us. 'Wasn't that one of our men?' Hatzfeldt asked me. 'Yes, Lindenfels.' Caprivi pricked up his ears. The possibility that a Chief might not know the senior officials of his staff was probably a new idea to him.

Since neither of the men concerned had any feeling they had given offence, both incidents passed unnoticed.

Herbert wrote to me to-day from Bad Königstein asking me to send Plessen a copy of a letter written by the Chancellor to Salisbury,[1] the English version of which I had been responsible for, and insisting it should go to him personally. Münster must know nothing about it.[2] Strange professional behaviour. Naturally I sent off the copy to London at once.

20 *July* 1885

The anxiety and haste displayed by the Crown Princess in her attempts to come to terms with the Chancellor have been explained in a way I had not thought of.

A few weeks ago the Prince of Wales wrote his sister a rude letter, saying she was to blame for the strained relations between England and Germany. By her foolish and incessant flaunting of her English nationality, regardless of German susceptibilities, she had inflamed the German nation and in particular the Chancellor

---

[1] Letter of 8 July 1885 (*Grosse Politik*, vol. IV, no. 783, pp. 133–4.)

[2] Herbert von Bismarck wrote on 12 July: 'Will you please have a copy of my father's letter to Salisbury sent to Plessen, personally. Since his name appears in it, S. will probably discuss matters with him confidentially, so Pl. must be put in possession of the facts. Please ask Brauer whether he has written to Münster yet to give him his instructions for which that letter prepares the ground; we arranged this the day I left. [...] '

against England. The whole of England must now suffer for her folly, and so on. The Prince said he had been told all this by Lord Rosebery. The Crown Princess (so she says) replied to the Prince in the same uncivil tone, saying he must be quite mad. There was not a word of truth in it. She had never done anything which could give offence, and so on.

But shortly afterwards she made these overtures to the Chancellor.

I feel sure she will never forgive Herbert for stirring up her brother against her through his friend Rosebery.

Whether it was fear of German public opinion or of her English relatives which made her more amenable (to all appearances), she is still pursuing these tactics.

She has written a plausible letter to Radolinski, in which she says it has come to her ears that the Chancellor went away disappointed from the New Palace because he had had no opportunity of discussing with her the question of the Portuguese marriage, among other things. Nothing had been further from her intentions than to avoid him; she had thought it was wrong to force herself on him, because the Crown Prince had a great deal he wished to discuss and was in fact exceptionally satisfied with this interview. She had also intended to make good this missed opportunity on the Chancellor's next visit, which she hoped he would make longer by arranging to stay overnight.

Radolinski sent this letter to the Chancellor, who replied with a long four-page letter in his own hand. He had never expected her to touch on the Portuguese question during such a brief visit. He was left with nothing but the most agreeable impression of his visit. The opposite view may have arisen in 'more intimate circles at the Foreign Ministry' because, when asked upon his return whether the Portuguese question had been discussed, he had simply replied that there had been neither time nor opportunity to do so. He was most especially glad to hear that His Imperial Highness was satisfied with the interview, and would for his part not fail to make use of the gracious permission to pay Their Imperial Highnesses a further visit as soon as he returned to Berlin.

Both of them as sweet as sugar. What a farce.

The way he involved the 'more intimate circles at the Foreign Ministry' in this business was not exactly pretty. The impression given is that these 'circles' were inquisitive beforehand and gossiped afterwards, whereas he himself was the soul of discretion. This reveals the unattractive side of Prince Bismarck's nature.

I know no one in the world among those who are highly regarded by their fellow-men who so seldom espoused the cause of others and so frequently let others bear the blame. This thrust can only have been aimed at Hatzfeldt because, apart from the family, he was the only person who had seen Prince Bismarck on his return from Potsdam and had asked about his visit. But I am sure from my knowledge of Prince Bismarck that he was less concerned to throw the blame on one definite person than to clear himself.

Radolinski came out with an idea to-day which I had been expecting for some time: why did I hold aloof from the Crown Prince and Princess? Didn't I at last desire a rapprochement, and so on. He said they often spoke of me.

I replied that I thought it best to persist in my attitude of reserve. I was not one of those members of the Foreign Ministry whose duties involved *official* contacts with the royal family, and I was afraid that my private relations with them would be regarded as a superfluous accompaniment of legitimate official relations.

Radolinski said: 'It's all the same to me, but you'll be pushed out just as Hatzfeldt has been pushed out.'

Radolinski is annoyed, not with the Chancellor whom he always stands up for, but with Herbert. And I do agree that Herbert with his cool egoism would push me aside if he thought I was in his way at any point. He has the power to do so. But I fail to see why he should if I am *not* in his way.

Herbert will now try, with his usual passion and tenacity, to bring the Chancellor and the Crown Prince together by acting as confidant to both. He will not succeed, because the Crown Prince and Princess positively detest him. 'I'm not vindictive (!) but— ship him to China!' the Crown Princess told someone yesterday.

When Herbert realizes, as he must one day, that his success is purely superficial and that they receive him but do not take him into their confidence, he will cast about suspiciously to see who may be to blame.

That the Chancellor himself is prepared to leave to his son the entire business of mediation with the Crown Prince is shown by his behaviour to me—or rather the behaviour of both father and son—when I had my second interview with Bismarck on this matter.

This morning the Chancellor sent us a letter he had received from the Kaiser, in which the latter asks whether the Chancellor knows what the Crown Prince replied to the King of Portugal's recent proposal of marriage. Notwithstanding his double capacity as head of the family and sovereign, the Kaiser said he had been told nothing by his son.[1]

In fact the Crown Prince turned down the proposal and a King's messenger took the letter with him to Lisbon two days ago. We shall see what happens now.

24 *July* 1885

The Chancellor instructed Hatzfeldt to ask the Portuguese Minister what was in the letter sent by the King of Portugal to the Crown Prince.

Penafiel said that although he did not know the contents of the letter he was certain of one thing, namely that it had been stipulated that the Princess should become a Catholic immediately upon her marriage, because it would not have been possible in view of public opinion to allow her to enter the country as a Protestant Crown Princess.

This lets the Crown Prince (i.e. ours) out nicely. For the Chancellor had assumed that the Portuguese would allow time and affection to effect a conversion instead of making it a preliminary condition.

At the same time it has dawned on the Crown Princess that the question of her daughter's marriage has been under negotiation for months between the Bismarcks, father and son, and the Portuguese Minister, without the knowledge or consent of the girl's own mother. Her Imperial Highness is fuming with rage. 'I absolutely refuse to let him meddle in my family affairs.'

Three days ago the Crown Prince wrote a letter to the Kaiser about this offer of marriage, i.e. he informed His Majesty after the event that he had turned it down. His reason—the religious question.[2]

The Crown Princess drafted the letter; he merely copied it out. [...]

[1] The Kaiser's letter to Bismarck was dated 17 July. The Kaiser was not informed about the Crown Prince's intended reply until 22 July, when Bismarck sent him a report from Hatzfeldt of the previous day. Hatzfeldt had been informed by Radolinski that the King of Portugal, in his letter to the Crown Prince, had again made a change of religion a condition for the marriage. The Crown Prince therefore thought 'he should reject the proposal in his reply to the King of Portugal, and in doing so believed he could count on His Majesty's assent, since they were already agreed that any condition relating to religion was unacceptable'. (From the Foreign Ministry files.)

[2] The Crown Prince's letter to the Kaiser of 23 July 1885 contains the following passage: 'In itself it seems incomprehensible that the King should try again after the answer he received at that time [in the autumn of 1884, see p. 205, note 4]. I am therefore inclined to think that someone or other has committed an indiscretion and urged him to make a further attempt.' (From the Foreign Ministry files.)

The Portuguese Minister called on Hatzfeldt a couple of days ago to announce that the Crown Prince's letter (declining on religious grounds) had arrived in Lisbon. He requested Hatzfeldt to inform the Chancellor '*puisque c'est lui qui a pris l'affaire sous sa direction*'. The Minister wanted to know what was to be done now. Hatzfeldt told him there was really nothing more that could be done.

Hatzfeldt passed on to Prince Bismarck this announcement *without* the query, which would only have annoyed His Highness needlessly.[1]

The Minister also told Hatzfeldt that Bismarck had said of the required change of religion: '*Ça, ce n'est pas une affaire.*'

It is worth noting, incidentally, that our Princesses have indeed gone over to the Greek Orthodox Church but not to the Roman Church. The mother of the present King of Bavaria, Queen Marie,[2] became a Catholic only a few years ago.

The Russian Government had intimated officially in the spring that it would not invite any foreign officers to this year's Russian manœuvres. They intend to practise all kinds of tactical innovations which they do not wish to be observed. As a result of this communication Albedyll wrote and told the Foreign Ministry that under these circumstances H.M. also wished to abstain from inviting Russian officers to the German manœuvres. A few days later the Russian Military Attaché, Prince Dolgoruki, called on Herbert to request that Russian officers should in fact be invited. Dolgoruki had already met with a refusal from the War Minister. But Herbert, without consulting anybody, arranged that Schweinitz should be instructed to invite the Russian Government to name the officers it proposed sending to this year's manœuvres.

A communication arrived yesterday from Schweinitz to the effect that the Russians are sending General Radetzky and two staff officers.

And yet the Kaiser decided that no Russians were to be invited.

A letter has been sent to-day to Albedyll in Gastein informing him that Schweinitz has given notice of the arrival of three Russians. Fortunately Dolgoruki is himself in Gastein and will

---

[1] Hatzfeldt's memorandum of 2 August on his talk with the Portuguese Minister is in the Foreign Ministry files. In a communication to Kaiser Wilhelm, dated 17 August, Bismarck again expressed his regret at the breakdown of negotiations on the Portuguese marriage, and at the fact 'that as a result the difficulties which may arise from other possibilities have not been definitely removed'.

[2] Marie, Princess of Prussia, daughter of Prince Wilhelm of Prussia (the brother of King Friedrich Wilhelm III), was married to Maximilian II, King of Bavaria, 1848–64.

probably set things right. And the Kaiser will probably not even ask how the matter was raised. But these are things which, during the coming reign, may cause a crisis overnight between the Hohenzollern and the Bismarcks. Warnings do no good. Megalomania.

5 *August* 1885

I visited old Bleichröder to-day. He spoke as follows:

'I inquired to-day when I could call on the Chancellor during the next few days. I had a medal struck for his birthday, with his portrait on one side and his coat of arms on the other. When Prince Bismarck saw the portrait he exclaimed: "That's by far the best that has ever been done of me. How did the artist manage to catch such a likeness? I've never sat for him." I replied: "No, but he was present in the photographer's studio on the last two or three occasions when Your Highness was being photographed; he completed a sketch there while you were sitting for the photographer." Then I told Prince Bismarck I would present him with ten gold medals (each one costs twenty-four ducats), twenty-five in silver and twenty-five in bronze, to distribute among the family and friends. And then I pointed out to him that the value of these sixty medals would be very high if no further ones were struck. One could, on the other hand, have a considerable quantity of bronze medals struck and sold for the benefit of some charity. Prince Bismarck seized eagerly on this last idea, asked me if I thought people would buy them, and when I said certainly, gave his consent for the medal to be circulated among the public. And so I have had ten thousand of them struck. I'm taking Prince Bismarck his sixty now.'

The medal is a masterpiece of flattery; it shows Prince Bismarck as he was twelve years ago.

Bleichröder went on:

'I want to talk to Prince Bismarck about the economic situation, which is gloomy.

'The raising of our corn duties[1] has caused our neighbour states to raise the duty on German exports by about twenty per cent. As a result our industry can no longer export. It is thrown back on the home market, itself suffering from over-production. It is a sad state of affairs, but nothing can be done about it.

'The second regrettable case is the Stock Exchange tax[2] which is driving investments abroad. Prince Bismarck knows that as

[1] On 22 May 1885 the Reichstag passed a tariff bill providing for a considerable increase in the duties on corn.

[2] On 8 May 1885 the Reichstag passed the Stock Exchange Bill, which raised the duty on stock exchange transactions.

well as I do, and was equally opposed to the Stock Exchange tax, but when the *Kreuzzeitung* and the *Reichsbote* hinted that Prince Bismarck was showing undue deference to the financiers, he deemed it wiser to stop protesting. I said to him: "Your Highness need not say a word. I understand Your Highness; I have the same idea. Sometimes in my dreams I see a second *Reichsglocke*[1] rising before my eyes." Prince Bismarck said nothing, but I could see I had hit the nail on the head.

'The third abuse is the Law on Corporations.[2]

'As long as that exists new enterprises are impossible. Perhaps something may yet be done in that direction. I will try to raise the question.

'Perhaps we can still work on opinion in Austria and Hungary in particular; that's why I should very much like to see Prince Bismarck before he sees Kálnoky next week.'[3]

Bleichröder also said:

'The *Norddeutsche* article two days ago attacking France did not surprise me.[4] The Chancellor told me six weeks ago: "It is impossible to make a political *volte-face* at the moment of succession. You must do it beforehand." This article makes it perfectly clear that his *volte-face* is now a fact. By turning away from France we are turning towards England. But by turning towards England we are rather giving Russia the cold shoulder. In a word, we are now pursuing a see-saw policy calculated to make us suspect in every quarter. There is only one man who may succeed in playing this game several times without coming to any harm. But I'll tell him what I think too, when I have the opportunity.'

I agree with Bleichröder entirely. This vacillating policy at home and abroad, on the official and the human level, corresponds to the Chancellor's innermost attitude to people: not friends, just tools, like knives and forks which are changed after each course. Such are his skill and power that he can play this game longer than anybody else unharmed. In former days he did not play it so often as he does now, impelled by his increasing sense of power.

8 *August* 1885

The Russian dislike of Hatzfeldt is quite in character. Its

[1] See p. 23, note 3.

[2] The so-called first Corporation Law of 11 June 1870 introduced a series of standardizing measures whereby, among other things, the formation of limited companies was made conditional upon their entry in the trade register. On 28 July 1884 the Reichstag passed an amended Corporation Law, the main purpose of which was to introduce stricter control over the foundation of new limited companies.

[3] Kálnoky visited Bismarck in Varzin from 12–16 August.

[4] On 3 August the *Norddeutsche Allgemeine Zeitung* had pointed out that German attempts at bringing about good relations with France had so far met with no success. Compare *Grosse Politik*, vol. III, no. 706, p. 451.

causes are both public and personal. Public in that he was sent to Constantinople just at the time when Gorchakov's dislike of Bismarck had, through Gorchakov's fault, acquired a national colouring. Thus, in the summer of 1878 Hatzfeldt received anti-Russian instructions which he carried out so effectively that Lobanov, at that time Russian Ambassador in Constantinople (now in Vienna), became and has remained his bitter enemy. In addition—and this is the second public reason—Schweinitz and Werder did their utmost in St Petersburg to harm Hatzfeldt.

The more personal cause is, I believe, the antipathy felt by every one brought up as a Catholic (even though, like Hatzfeldt, he has lost his faith) towards members of the Greek Orthodox Church. In short, the dislike is mutual and if, as the Crown Princess recently said to him, Hatzfeldt is the future Foreign Minister of the German Reich, then the Russians had better not expect any special favours from him when in office.

Some time ago Hatzfeldt was to receive a Russian decoration. The Tsar conferred on him the White Eagle, the lowest of those which could be considered. When Giers remarked that it was not much, the Tsar replied: 'It's enough.'

A short time ago Dolgoruki, the Russian Military Attaché, called on Herbert and asked him to prevent Hatzfeldt from being sent as Ambassador to St Petersburg. I think he unintentionally did Hatzfeldt a great service. I have for years suspected that the Chancellor's long-standing intention of sending Hatzfeldt from Berlin to St Petersburg some day only arose from his conviction that Hatzfeldt would find it the most *un*favourable sphere from the purely personal standpoint. This possibility vanished the moment the Russian Government itself refused to accept Hatzfeldt.

It seems to be the order of the day in Russian court circles to ignore Hatzfeldt.

In the course of a long conversation I had with Peter Shuvalov[1] some time ago now, I asked him whether he would like to call on Hatzfeldt. He simply answered: '*Je ne le connais pas*', and changed the subject.

Giers behaved in the same way when he was passing through Berlin last year. His only reason for going to see Hatzfeldt this year is that when the Russian Ambassador, Shuvalov[2] (Peter's brother), called on Bleichröder to announce that Giers would be passing through, Bleichröder asked whether Giers would be visiting Hatzfeldt. When Shuvalov replied that Giers would be

[1] Russian Ambassador in London 1874–9; representative at the Congress of Berlin, 1878.
[2] Paul, Count Shuvalov. Russian Ambassador in Berlin, 1885–94.

seeing nobody, Bl. declared that in that case he himself could, of course, not call on Herr von Giers either. Since Giers was anxious to see Bl., he called on Hatzfeldt at eleven and received Bl. at half-past eleven for a long talk. Since Bl. has realized Hatzfeldt has a future he has become a staunch supporter of his.

The impression Bl. gained from his talk with Giers was that the Russians were certainly intent on acquiring Herat, if possible without going to war. Further, that they regarded us with suspicion. Giers asked Bl.: 'Is Prince Bismarck on very good terms with the present British Government?'

11 *August* 1885

Bleichröder is back from Varzin. The evening he arrived there, Prince Bismarck had a talk with him in his room before dinner. Afterwards, both during and after the meal, Rantzau refused to stir, despite the fact that Prince Bismarck showed by his choice of indifferent topics of conversation that he wanted to be alone with Bl. Prince Bismarck even discussed Goethe, but still Rantzau sat there, presumably so that he could report the conversation to Herbert. Next morning before Bleichröder left, Prince Bismarck had another talk with Bl., introducing it with the words: 'Rantzau is still asleep.'

Bl. has the impression that Prince Bismarck is treating Rantzau with marked coolness and keeping him at arm's length, and says Rantzau looks depressed.

Prince Bismarck told Bl. that the Crown Prince had requested him to remain in office under the new reign. Bismarck added: 'In that case I shall of course permit no change in Germany's foreign policy.' Bl. interrupted to remark that he had the impression that war between Russia and England was inevitable. His Highness replied that he thought so too. It would break out in the late autumn or the spring, unless something happened to prevent it. The next morning[1] His Highness reverted to this topic and said: 'As I have already observed, something or other may yet occur to prevent war.' And when Bl. asked: 'What sort of thing?' he said: 'Either the death of our Kaiser, in which case the Russians will immediately moderate their claims, or else an outbreak of nihilism, which would make it difficult to take troops out of the country.'

The Chancellor inquired after Hatzfeldt's health, and praised him 'as an Ambassador'. 'The best horse in the stable.' But far

[1] The foregoing statements were presumably made to Bleichröder on the evening of his arrival at Varzin.

less suitable as a Minister. He said it was a good thing he was leaving Berlin.

Bl. had intended suggesting to the Chancellor that it might be a good idea to leave Hatzfeldt in Berlin over the winter even after his appointment as Ambassador, to serve as mediator with the Crown Prince. But Bl. suppressed this idea when he noticed from the Chancellor's last remark that he was itching to get rid of Hatzfeldt and to install Herbert during the present Kaiser's lifetime.

To return to foreign policy, the Chancellor said in reply to Bl.'s question that it was very wrong of the Russians to be suspicious of us at the moment. So long as he was at the helm Germany would never depart from the strictest neutrality towards Russia.

The French Government, he said, was wrong to feel insulted by the recent article in the *Norddeutsche*. On the contrary, the article had been intended to strengthen the hand of the government, i.e. the Conservative-Republican Party, in the election campaign against the Radicals and Royalists, both of whom were chauvinistic. In any case the present French Government—Freycinet's—had no claims on us. In the Egyptian affair, when we had been prepared in the spring to support her claims against England's, the French had required us, with our tiny interests there, to act *first*, and had meanwhile tried to reach an understanding with England behind our back.[1] And so, he said, we would not trouble any more about the Egyptian question (i.e. we would leave England a free hand).

Bl. had a detailed conference on the grave economic situation. The Chancellor listened to everything but made little reply.

When Bl. asked whether it would not be advisable to enter upon a customs union with Austria-Hungary, His Highness said he would gladly do so, but unfortunately it was impossible because of the Peace of Frankfurt, which conferred most-favoured nation rights on France. And we could not enter upon a customs union with France.

The fact that Giers, when passing through Berlin, had not expressed a wish to see the Chancellor seemed to be on his mind. (Since then His Highness has himself taken the initiative and informed Giers that if he felt it was too far to come to Friedrichsruh, he, Bismarck, would willingly travel to Berlin.)[2]

[1] Compare *Grosse Politik*, vol. III, no. 702, pp. 445–7.
[2] Giers stayed in Berlin from 6 to 7 August on his way to Franzensbad, and had a conference with Hatzfeldt (see above, p. 229). In a communication sent by Rantzau from Varzin on 6 August, Hatzfeldt was instructed to find out from Shuvalov whether Giers wished to

The Chancellor also said it made no difference to him whether the Conservatives remained at the helm in England or the Radicals came to power.

Bleichröder interpreted this as meaning that Prince Bismarck would prefer to see Lord Rosebery as Prime Minister. R. has gone to stay in Homburg for the period when Herbert is in Königstein and Princess Bismarck in Homburg; the Princess sees Lady Rosebery (*née* Rothschild) every day and thinks her the most charming woman she has ever met. Money makes up for beauty.

My own view is that Prince Bismarck would prefer Salisbury, but that he can foresee a Radical victory.

21 *August* 1885

Herbert wrote to me a few days ago and asked me to take his mother out to a meal somewhere when she was passing through Berlin; when she was left alone she ate nothing.[1]

It was not difficult to see what this meant: it was a way of bringing us together again. I had not sat at Princess Bismarck's table for fourteen months, but had declined her invitations. If she wished to dine with me, it was a different matter. So I wrote to her in Homburg inviting her to dinner. She accepted by telegram. I also invited the Berchems, Lindau and a young Herr Meister, whose family has been friendly with Princess Bismarck since Frankfurt days.

I did not go to the station, to avoid meeting Keudell. Perhaps he had the same idea; although he had only been in Berlin forty-eight hours, obviously to meet Princess Bismarck, he left the morning she arrived. I heard this from Schlözer, who added scornfully: 'Whenever she's not in Varzin, Keudell daren't go see her.' Well, no doubt it had all been settled in writing between Princess Bismarck and K., or else verbally in Homburg. In any case I had the pleasure of not seeing him. I ordered all kinds of unwholesome dishes for Princess Bismarck because I know they are what she prefers. And in fact she ate and drank a good deal. She had two helpings of princess potatoes and stuffed artichokes.

To my surprise she spoke with affection and kindness of her old enemy, the Kaiserin, whom she had visited in Wiesbaden from Homburg, praising her energy and immense devotion to duty, and

visit Bismarck while he was in Germany. This communication did not reach the Foreign Ministry until after Giers' departure. On 10 August Rantzau informed the Foreign Ministry that Bismarck had not intended suggesting to Giers a visit to Varzin, but instead a meeting at some place which Giers found convenient on his return journey to Russia. (From the Foreign Ministry files.)

[1] Letter of 14 August 1885. Not printed.

saying she would have been dead long ago if she had not been determined to stay alive.

She has a deep dislike of her daughter-in-law, which is probably further increased by the way that young lady, having caught her man, now shows scant ceremony to her mother-in-law. That is how I see it, because they met in Homburg. Princess Bismarck told me she felt certain that Sybille didn't really love her husband at all and was entirely frigid.

We dined at seven; from ten until half-past eleven Meister and I sat talking to Princess Bismarck, and this morning I went to the station. After what she had done, I wanted to do the handsome thing. [...]

22 *August* 1885

Berchem came to see me to-day in great excitement to tell me that Prince Wilhelm was corresponding with the St Petersburg Bülow. Now that Berchem is deputizing for the Under State Secretary he sees the check list of the mail sent by courier.

Two days ago a letter from the Prince to Bülow had been entered.

This affair is causing a stir in the very small circle in which it is known. And in fact, whatever made the Prince do it? If he wants Bülow to carry out small commissions for him, such as silver cigarette cases, an adjutant can write the letter. I connect this with statements made by Adolf Bülow, which I have probably noted somewhere. He said it would be a good thing if people like me (!) or his brother Bernhard remained in continuous official touch with the Prince so as to keep him always on the right path.

It is my guess that Adolf Bülow, perhaps in concert with Herbert, had already secretly arranged this association. I think the Bülows are running a great risk: the present Crown Prince will take very ill this systematic alienation of his son. Mainly as a result of Herbert Bismarck's persuasion, Prince Wilhelm has now been driven so far into the opposition camp that even Caprivi expressed to me severe criticisms of H.R.H. the other day. He said he was still a callow youth but imagined he was goodness knows what and despised the people whose job it was to teach him anything. For example, a naval officer had been assigned the task of teaching the Prince the general rudiments of his career. But the way these 'lectures' had been held aroused Caprivi's indignation; the instructor had been treated like a booby.

Prince Wilhelm undoubtedly possesses some good qualities for a ruler—he is hard and obstinate. But he is spoiled by this exaggerated resentment against his father. The people behind Prince Wilhelm are assuming that the Crown Prince's inflamed caecum will shorten his life. And the first thing they will do when they are 'in' will be to squabble. There will never be room for Herbert and Bernhard Bülow at the same time, once the 'great' Bismarck has gone. Bülow is lying low at the moment, but he will take care not to do so later on. Herbert will one day be torn to pieces by his 'friends'; that is the kind of friend he chooses. But that may not happen for a long time. The Kaiser is said to be very well again, which does not prevent the whole of his entourage from always carrying about in their pockets the strongest smelling-salts and other restoratives in case of emergency.

23 *August* 1885

A peculiar trait of character in the Chancellor. When all the fuss about the Carolines broke out,[1] Hatzfeldt, acting on the Chancellor's instructions, informed the Spanish Minister[2] that Germany had no intention of encroaching on existing rights. If Spain could show proof of prior occupation, or other titles, we would even give up places where the German flag had already been hoisted.[3]

Simultaneously with this declaration of Hatzfeldt's a telegram was received in Berlin sent by the Spanish Minister-President

[1] In January 1885 the Hamburg firm of Robertson and Hernsheim suggested to Bismarck that 'the German flag should be hoisted on the West and East Carolines, the Marshall, Kingsmill, Pheasant Island and Ellice groups, to protect the dominant German trade interests on these islands' and make the islands secure against English or Australian occupation. The suggestion was not acted upon immediately, because reports of a planned English occupation turned out to be false. On 3 June 1885, Solms was instructed to investigate rumours of a possible Spanish occupation, because on 3 March 1875 Germany and England had lodged joint notes of protest against Spanish claims on the Carolines. Solms replied on 9 June that Spain probably did intend to annex the Carolines. In a marginal note on a letter from Herbert von Bismarck of 23 June, the Chancellor gave orders that Germany must anticipate a Spanish annexation. On 21 July Kaiser Wilhelm expressed his approval, upon which the Admiralty took the necessary measures. The announcement of an imminent Spanish annexation, which reached Berlin on 1 August 1885 from the Consul in Manila, did not cause Bismarck to modify the measures already decided on. On 4 August Count Solms was instructed by telegram to inform the Spanish Government of the German occupation of the Pelew and Caroline Islands. At the same time the German Embassy in London was instructed to inform the British Government and to state that by reason of the Anglo-German agreement on colonial questions Germany counted on British co-operation to resist possible Spanish claims. On 7 August the London Embassy telegraphed that Salisbury had informed the British representative in Madrid of Germany's wishes. When Solms reported that he had carried out his instructions, received on 4 August, Bismarck noted: 'We shall have to respect anything Spain did in fact possess *before* our occupation, or occupied in the same way as ourselves by hoisting their flag. But we need not make that the starting-point of the negotiations.' On 12 August the Spanish Minister delivered a note to Count Hatzfeldt stating that the Carolines had been a Spanish possession since 1543. (From the Foreign Ministry files.)

[2] Count Benomar. Spanish Minister in Berlin, 1875–88.

[3] This statement was made on 19 August. On the same day Count Benomar delivered an official protest against the German occupation. (From the Foreign Ministry files.)

Canovas[1] direct to Hatzfeldt, whom he has known for many years. The telegram, couched in very conciliatory terms, expressed the hope that the affair would be settled in a way consonant with the friendly relations between the two countries and their joint monarchical interests.[2]

Hatzfeldt sent this telegram to the Chancellor. He ignored it and gave express orders for his original conciliatory remarks to be passed on to London by our representative there, but not to Madrid. In other words, His Highness took no notice of the telegram addressed to Hatzfeldt and not to himself. That should teach Canovas to address himself in future to God rather than to one of the saints. Without authorization from the Chancellor, Hatzfeldt was of course unable to reply and so the Spanish Prime Minister, proud and vain as they come, was subjected to an affront such as he has probably never suffered since he has been Minister-President.[3] Moreover, this want of consideration in a matter of etiquette was bound to give rise to the assumption that we were heading for an open break. Hatzfeldt's declaration to Benomar was thus pushed in the background; if our hope of reconciliation was meant seriously, why did we not repeat it to the Minister-President?

As a result there has been wildly mounting excitement over the last three days; there was particular agitation from government newspapers which had hitherto exercised restraint.

Solms telegraphed this morning to say that all kinds of unpleasant incidents were to be feared.[4] Whereupon Hatzfeldt inquired in Varzin whether he might reply to Canovas and at the same time in the name of His Highness repeat the declaration he had made to Benomar. His Highness replied without the customary opening: 'Reply to Tel. no. ...', i.e. he ignored Hatzfeldt's question and simply said: 'I request you to insert in one of tomorrow morning's papers the announcement that we have proposed submitting the Carolines question to the arbitration of a friendly Power.'[5]

---

[1] Antonio Canovas de Castillo. Leader of the Conservative Party; Minister-President, 1883–5, 1890–2, 1895–7.

[2] The telegram in question was sent by Canovas to Benomar on 17 August and ended with the request that Count Hatzfeldt be informed of its contents. Benomar sent him a copy of the telegram. (From the Foreign Ministry files.)

[3] It is clear from the Foreign Ministry files that Bismarck was of the opinion that Germany had no interest in maintaining the Canovas ministry.

[4] Solms had reported the possibility of popular anti-German demonstrations. (From the Foreign Ministry files.)

[5] In a telegram sent the same day (23 August) Bismarck gave instructions that Count Benomar be informed of Germany's willingness to accept arbitration; the question was not important enough to affect the existing good relations between Germany and Spain. (From the Foreign Ministry files.)

That is a sensible idea. Only it would have been better to have said so, or said something similar, a week ago; now it looks as though we had been intimidated by Spain's anger. But the main point is that Canovas is to get no answer, as a punishment for not addressing himself to His Highness.

What a sinister degree of vanity.

25 August 1885

The idea of annexing the Carolines was raised, so Herbert tells me, in April by *Legationsrat* Krauel,[1] now in charge of colonial affairs, an intelligent man but an ambitious climber. Krauel won Herbert's support for the idea and as a result the Chancellor also agreed to it. We are now approaching a situation in which we may deal a grievous blow to the Spanish monarchy, which we have hitherto supported in every possible way. Prince Bismarck, in contrast to his attitude hitherto, to-day expressed his view that it made no difference to us if the Conservative Ministry in Spain, or even the King himself, were overthrown and a republic proclaimed. We should never get anything out of the Spaniards anyway.

In that case I should like to know what the point was of the Crown Prince's trip to Spain two years ago which cost so much and raised so much dust?

Hatzfeldt is well disposed towards Spain and Canovas, consequently His Highness is opposed to them: age, success and contempt of mankind all combine to make Prince Bismarck allow his moods to influence public affairs more than he used to. The Carolines affair is a bad omen.

Hatzfeldt conferred with the Kaiser on the Carolines yesterday.[2] The old gentleman was dissatisfied, and said he had always been afraid that no good would come of the Chancellor's violent behaviour in colonial affairs. Any adventurer could ask for German protection and be granted it at once, without Bismarck's troubling to find out beforehand whether this act would land him in conflict with friendly Powers.

The Kaiser said he was also afraid that Herbert Bismarck, for whom he had generally the greatest esteem, would encourage the Chancellor still further along this course. Also the Kaiser had never imagined the Chancellor would insist on employing his son in Berlin itself.

[1] Friedrich Richard Krauel. Temporarily attached to the Foreign Ministry, 1883, 1884–5; official in charge of colonial affairs, May 1885–90; Director of the Colonial Division of the Foreign Ministry, April–July 1890; Minister in Buenos Aires, 1890–4; in Rio de Janeiro, 1894–8.
[2] No memorandum of this conference was found in the Foreign Ministry files.

Herbert feels perfectly confident of his influence on his father and regards himself as co-ruler. Yesterday he saw a document written by Hatzfeldt himself. 'I don't like that', he said, 'I don't want to correct what Hatzfeldt has written, but I'll talk to him and get him to alter it.'

Hatzfeldt feels happier every day to think he is leaving; the position of a man standing between the two Bismarcks, father and son, is 'half ridiculous, half contemptible'.

I am sincerely sorry about all this, first because of the result on the conduct of affairs, but also for Herbert and for Prince Bismarck whom his son will gradually compromise in the eyes of the public. Their blind faith in him will be lost. The many people whom Herbert offends will take good care to let the world know how affairs are now conducted here. 'Our Ministry—I don't just mean the bricks and mortar—hardly bears living in now', Berchem said yesterday. 'Some of the staff have been around too long and do not take so firm a stand as they used to—the rest are too recent. Two extremes.'

Our first diplomatic setback for twenty-three years will be a critical moment. The Chancellor himself feels this too and therefore would rather King Alfonso went under than himself. Let us hope some middle way will still be found.

I told Herbert that if we acquire the Carolines or even part of them we must call them the Krauelines.

27 *August* 1885

Kopp, Bishop of Fulda,[1] was hitherto the one German Bishop who was always ready to stake his entire position on working in Rome for a reconciliation between Church and State. Ambitious and energetic, completely beyond reproach, he was the man the Government needed for the archbishopric of Cologne. The Minister for Ecclesiastical Affairs suggested that the Chancellor should support Kopp's candidature. Schlözer said it would probably be pushed through in Rome, but the Chancellor said no, we must be satisfied with the candidate nominated by the Curia, the harmless and useless Krementz.[2] First the urge to go against Gossler's wishes, and secondly the fear that the world might think Kopp played an essential role in the peaceful settlement of the *Kulturkampf*. No one must take any credit except His Highness.

Since Krementz's appointment Kopp has become a different

[1] Georg von Kopp. His activities as a mediator contributed to the settlement of the *Kulturkampf*.
[2] Phillipp Krementz. From 1867 Bishop of Ermland; Archbishop of Cologne, 1885–99 (Cardinal from 1893).

person. Formerly it was he who more or less held in check Korum[1] (Manteuffel's French protégé), who is the disintegrating element in the Prussian clergy. Now Kopp says to himself: 'Why should I make enemies who can harm me when I have no friends who will help me.' So he quietly sat by when Korum, at the Bishops' conference in Fulda, formed the Prussian episcopate into a united league against the Government. As a result the ecclesiastical problem is far worse now than three months ago. The Bishops, led by Korum, are putting fresh claims before the Government, instead of mediating between the Government and Rome, as Kopp had done *until then* and not without success.

Before the Fulda conference met, Gossler had written to Kopp, with whom he had corresponded regularly for many years, and had expressed the hope that Kopp would again prove a champion of reconciliation. Bismarck had made Gossler write this letter. In consequence Gossler has just sent in Kopp's reply. The gist of his four pages is: 'Leave me alone. You can expect nothing further from me.' A cold douche.

Bismarck, as a result of Monts'[2] letter from Rome,[3] is now asking very innocently whether Kopp ever expressed the 'wish' to become Archbishop of Cologne, or whether it was not more likely that 'they' had been afraid of harming him by recommending him in Rome? 'They' means H.H. himself. Gossler's instinct was right, so was Schlözer's.

The Spanish 'Krauelines' affair is not improving.

The Spaniards, in their anger, are now beginning to insult the Crown Prince. The President of the Independent Law Society of Madrid barely succeeded in preventing a motion from being deliberated (and presumably passed) in public session, which would have struck the Crown Prince's name from the list of members.

General Salamanca, whom the Crown Prince had decorated with the Red Eagle, First Class, declared his desire to return it, and wrote an insulting accompanying letter to the Crown Prince. The

[1] Michael Felix Korum. Professor of theology at the Strasbourg Seminary for Priests, Preacher for the French-speaking congregation, Canon and Archpriest at the Cathedral; Bishop of Trier, 1881–1921.

[2] Anton, Count von Monts. Secretary of the Prussian Legation to the Holy See, 1884–6; First Secretary in the Embassy in Vienna, 1886–90; later Ambassador in Rome.

[3] A letter to Holstein of 18 August 1885, the major portion of which Holstein had copied and sent to Bismarck. Monts quoted a letter from Kopp of 12 August expressing concern about an article in the *Norddeutsche Allgemeine Zeitung* praising Cardinal Melchers (who had been deposed as Archbishop of Cologne because of his bitter opposition to the Government during the *Kulturkampf*). 'Does the Government by any chance have similar illusions?' Kopp asked. 'Well, hardly a month will be out before it will realize to what hollow illusions it has abandoned itself in the course of the year. The disillusionment will be thorough. [...]'

Government intervened energetically, reprimanded the General and prevented the dispatch of the decoration and the letter to H.I.H. But the General published the letter.

As for Bismarck, he persists in saying that a republic in France, Spain *and* Italy could do nothing but good to the solidarity of the Three Emperors' Alliance, because those sovereigns would then realize 'that they would lose more from a republic than they would gain from each other'.[1]

And up to now we have done our utmost to uphold the monarchy in Spain and Italy! We pursue a policy of moods nowadays. In addition the Chancellor has instructed Solms by telegram to tell the King of Spain 'that the remaining in office of the present Ministers can do nothing but harm to the German-Spanish negotiations'.[2]

In contrast to this, the Chancellor always used to hold the view that one should never interfere in another country's domestic affairs, e.g., cabinet questions.

I asked Herbert, to whom I expressed my opinion in no measured terms: 'How do you think the King of Spain will react to this request to change his cabinet? If he does so, and we publish in a month's time a White Paper on the Carolines question containing the relevant telegram, the whole Spanish nation will see that their King changed his cabinet by command. You see, that's what comes of living in complete isolation and seeing no one but Rantzau. Even a genius cannot live like that with impunity.'

Herbert is also beginning to feel depressed at the way things are going. Since yesterday he has been toning down his communications to Varzin as much as possible. But neither he nor Hatzfeldt dared to hold back the telegram to Madrid.

But that is not the end. The English have requested our support for Drummond Wolff[3] in his negotiations with the Sultan in Constantinople.[4]

[1] By order of the Chancellor, Count Solms was sent telegraphic instructions to this effect. The simultaneous order to publish an article on these lines in the *Kölnische Zeitung* was not immediately carried out, and was then countermanded in a telegram from Bismarck. (From the Foreign Ministry files.)

[2] Telegram of 26 August. Solms was to inform the King on Bismarck's behalf: 'Our intentions are conciliatory, but the remaining in office of *these* Ministers is against our interests and, I believe, the King's interests too.' (From the Foreign Ministry files.)

[3] Sir Henry Drummond Charles Wolff. Envoy extraordinary to the Turkish Sultan; High Commissioner for Egypt, 1885–6.

[4] On 19 August the British Chargé d'Affaires delivered the following *note verbale* to the Foreign Ministry: 'Sir Edward Malet is instructed to make the following confidential communication to the Imperial Government. It is impossible for Her Majesty's Government to fix any date for the withdrawal of their forces from Egypt. In fact they consider that to fix such a date at present would be to destroy their power to re-establish order in that country. They desire however to create confidence that they have no intention of separating

Hatzfeldt, who is by no means a Russophile, said to me at once: 'We can't do that. Wolff's main task in Constantinople is to pave the way for an alliance aimed against Russia. If, as England desires, we advise the Sultan to come to an agreement with England over Egypt, then we shall be taking sides against Russia.'

But the Chancellor decided we must support Drummond Wolff. Hatzfeldt was given the pleasant task of making this seem plausible to the Russian Ambassador. Of course Shuvalov behaved like a cat with its tail on fire and refused to be calmed down. 'What you are prepared to promote is an Anglo-Turkish alliance against Russia', he shouted.

Hatzfeldt was completely in command of the situation and gave a masterly reply, but he closed his report to the Chancellor with these words: 'I do not think the mistrust which has recently revived in St Petersburg will be lessened by Count Shuvalov's report.'[1]

So first of all we welcome the idea of the establishment of a republic in the Latin countries because it will strengthen the Three Emperors' Alliance; we then shake the foundations of the Three Emperors' Alliance by flirting with England over the very point on which Russia is most touchy.

Egypt from the dominions of the Ottoman Empire or to take any course which would be contrary to the Treaty Law in Europe. They desire accordingly for the above reasons and also for those of convenience to obtain a small Turkish contingent at Shakni and on the southern frontiers of Egypt proper on the Nile [...] and they would for the same reason also like to station a small Turkish detachment at Alexandria and Cairo. These Turkish detachments would stay in Egypt as long as the British troops stay there and leave with them.' On 20 August Plessen, Chargé d'Affaires in London, reported that Lord Salisbury had requested the German Government's support for Sir Drummond Wolff's negotiations in Constantinople. Even before this dispatch arrived, Bismarck had decided on 21 August that Germany would further England's wishes, in so far as this was possible without damaging her relations with France and Turkey. In a marginal note of 23 August Bismarck gave instructions that Russia was to be informed that Germany 'would no longer operate *against* England in Egypt'. On 24 August detailed instructions were sent by Bismarck to Hatzfeldt, asking him to have talks with Sir Edward Malet and Count Shuvalov along these lines. (From the Foreign Ministry files.)

[1] Hatzfeldt's interview with Shuvalov took place on 26 August. Hatzfeldt's account of it concludes with the words: 'My impression is that the very lively mistrust existing in Russia since Lord Salisbury assumed office will not be diminished by Count Shuvalov, judging by his behaviour to-day.' Bismarck appended the following comment: 'I am still of the opinion that England will lose power as compared with Russia if she aggravates her relations with France by introducing Turkish troops into Egypt. French sea power counts more with England than any continental power. If St Petersburg does not believe this, we can so arrange things that our support of Sir D. Wolff is merely a consequence of our publicly proclaimed attitude on Turkish relations with Egypt. If we further the Sultan's designs on Egypt, I believe this will not harm Russian policy but favour it; we can, however, drop the idea and restrict ourselves to assuring Malet that we will refrain from opposing England in Egypt, but cannot further English interests in Constantinople as long as the dispute between England and Russia is not settled; it would violate the law of neutrality. Malet can be told all this, if they fail to see in St Petersburg that my view is right. Vlangali [Aide of the Russian Foreign Minister] will have no opinion in the matter, but Giers will, and I hope to see him.' (From the Foreign Ministry files.) See also entry for 3 November 1885.

28 *August* 1885

The Chancellor has decided that I am to be in charge of the Carolines affair from now on, instead of the official in charge of colonial affairs.[1] A pleasant task, now things are in such a mess. It might have done some good three months ago.

29 *August* 1885

The Kaiser has disagreed with the Chancellor's views on Spain, and voiced grave doubts about a republic in Spain. He said the Austrian monarchy was tottering on its foundations. Kaiser Franz Joseph was obviously at his wits' end how to govern his heterogeneous territory, and the Hungarians were tending more and more towards separatism and a republic. The setting-up of a republic in Spain would be a bad example for such aspirations. H.M. hoped the Chancellor would not handle the Spanish affair too roughly. H.M. would also be grateful if the Chancellor would hold a further exchange of ideas with him over this question.[2]

In my opinion the old Kaiser is behaving like a statesman and the Chancellor is not. I find this sudden swing towards republicanism incomprehensible. I wonder whether His Highness also has the notion that the more republics there are, the sooner the Crown Princess will feel alarmed?

Herbert, too, is privately not very happy about this sudden change, but he does as he is told and feels depressed.

His Highness has shown his displeasure at the way the 'Krauelines' question has been bungled by giving orders for colonial questions to be passed to the Political Division the moment they acquire any political significance. He wished to have submitted to him the draft of an order, which he will sign himself.

But His Highness himself has done as much as Krauel to make a mess of things: if he had sent a courteous reply to Canovas' telegram to Hatzfeldt, the present outcry would not have arisen. The official Spanish Press did not begin to behave aggressively— a stupid policy anyway for the weaker side—until Canovas felt he had been insulted. And the Chancellor's antagonism towards the Canovas Ministry dates from that unfortunate telegram.

---

[1] Bismarck had written on the margin of a draft submitted to him on this question: 'This is not a colonial question but a political one, and is the province of the Spanish Section. The Carolines are incidental to the main issue, namely our relations with Spain.' (From the Foreign Ministry files.)

[2] The Kaiser expressed these views in a conference with Herbert von Bismarck on the Carolines question.

1 *September* 1885

[...] Prince [Wilhelm] called on Herbert to-day to be informed about the political situation, and his comment was: 'It won't matter in the least if the King of Spain gets chucked out. Why does he run after the women instead of attending to his business?'

3 *September* 1885

Prince Wilhelm told Herbert Bismarck that while the Crown Prince was in Spain the King of Spain suddenly descended one day on General Blumenthal to hand over personally a high-ranking Spanish decoration. His Majesty was accompanied by his Chancellor in charge of decorations, and they were both wearing full regalia, with pumps and cloak. The King, who speaks fluent German, delivered an address to the General which closed with these words: 'Permit me, then, to introduce myself, Clown no. I and (pointing to the Chancellor) Clown no. II', to which the General replied: 'Then I can only ask to be enrolled as Clown no. III.' But on reflection the General must have realized what offensive behaviour this was. At any rate it would appear from the army list that he has never sought permission to wear this decoration.

A king who makes his dignity and its attributes seem ridiculous has nowadays very little prospect of dying a king. Prince Wilhelm thinks so too.

The Kaiser of Austria has spoken unfavourably of Prince Wilhelm, calling him a surprisingly self-satisfied young man for his age, with far too decided views.

No, thank you, we have not the slightest wish to exchange him for skinny Crown Prince Rudolf, bursting with author's vanity because of his books on travel and hunting and striving to emulate Joseph II. To imitate Joseph II he poses as a free-thinker. He once said to Count Wedel, pointing at a couple of priests: 'Once I'm on the throne I'll show these chaps where they stand.' What a fool. The Catholic Church is not an implacable foe of the Austrian Kaiser, as it is of our Kaiser, but rather the main bulwark against the Greek Orthodox Slavs. [...]

7 *September* 1885

Well, Bismarck's foreign policy has suffered its first setback. We have meekly accepted a slap in the face from Spain and are retiring from the fray. Other people will be encouraged by this example.

First of all the Bismarcks, father and son, treated the Spaniards badly. Canovas received no reply. Solms was told to state in Madrid that so long as the present Ministry was in power our negotiations had no prospect of success. The same thing was said in the Press, with the additional comment that Sagasta's[1] party would conduct the negotiations more skilfully, and it was to be hoped they would soon come to power. Herbert treated the unfortunate Benomar abominably, saying the cruellest things to him which he submitted to almost in tears.[2]

The picture changed suddenly two days ago. Mobs in Madrid and Valencia defaced the coat of arms on our Legation and our Consulate; almost all Spaniards who possessed German decorations returned them. Sagasta, feeling he had been compromised by praise in the German Press, declared publicly that, should the King entrust him with the formation of a cabinet, he would only accept on the condition that war was declared on Germany immediately.

As soon as the Chancellor in Varzin realized the Spaniards were in earnest, he climbed down. Count Solms had to give soothing assurances in Madrid, among others, that we should not have sent a single ship to the Carolines had we known that the Spaniards had claims on them! And all this will be published—has probably been published already. The old Kaiser is far more dignified than the Chancellor. 'I agree that, as the Chancellor suggests, we should *for the present* ignore the attack on our Legation, because the Spanish Government is powerless at the moment and because the King called out both police *and* troops, i.e. he did what lay in his power. But I certainly expect his Government to make amends to my Government with the least possible delay, as soon as order has been re-established.'[3]

Canovas' Government, which the Chancellor hoped to overthrow, now represents his only hope of coming out of this business even *reasonably* respectably. Canovas feels that his opponents, the Republicans, wish to use the opportunity to break him and so, instead of declaring war, he will probably suspend the constitution

[1] Praxedes Mateo Sagasta. Leader of the Liberal Party in Spain; Spanish Minister-President, 1881–3, 1885–6, 1886–90, 1892–5, 1897–9, 1901–2.

[2] In an interview with Benomar on 30 August, Herbert von Bismarck, representing Count Hatzfeldt, used very harsh language and refused to discuss the Spanish Government's offer to grant Germany freedom of trade and a naval base in the Carolines. (From the Foreign Ministry files.)

[3] Reproduced almost verbatim from a marginal comment made by Kaiser Wilhelm on a report to him of 5 September describing the incidents in Madrid. Count Solms was instructed to state in Madrid that the action of the German gun-boat (hoisting the German flag on the main island of the Caroline group) did not prejudice the legal question. The Admiralty was instructed to prevent further action by the gun-boat. (From the Foreign Ministry files.)

for a time and indulge in some sharp-shooting. He may succeed by this means in retaining the King, who has been almost overthrown by this Caroline affair and has expressed his bitterness that it should be none other than Germany that was responsible.

The Chancellor had already let it be known in many quarters, and had actually had the Kaiser informed in conference, that a republic in Spain was more to our advantage than the monarchy. But to-day His Highness instructed Solms in a personal telegram to prevail on the King, our only friend in Spain, to take energetic measures.[1] I still have in my file a directive which came in from Varzin yesterday morning instructing me to write to Hohenlohe and tell him to make it clear in his conversations in Paris that we set no store whatever by King Alfonso and his monarchy, and that a Spanish republic would be acceptable to us. I have asked Herbert to query this to-day, and to see whether this dispatch is still to go.[2]

There is no longer any coherence between Prince Bismarck's various orders. And his nerve has completely gone, so that the main thing he thinks about is that the export of spirits would suffer from a war with Spain.

Having gone so far, we should have accepted the risk of a war with Spain; in no time at all we should have wiped out the Spanish navy, which is deplorable, and captured the Philippines, the Canaries and so on, and we should not have emboldened the whole world by our setback. This may cost us dear one day, and quite soon.

Herbert is very careworn and looks a most bilious colour. It is a bad start[3] for him, because he and Krauel stirred up this trouble.

9 *September* 1885

Herbert read an extract from Wedel's letter about the Prince of Bulgaria,[4] first to the Kaiser and then to the Crown Prince. The Crown Prince was beside himself with rage, particularly when it referred to 'declarations' on the part of Princess Victoria.

'But who's been demanding declarations from my daughter? Who's been climbing up the back stairs to the second floor? What on earth is going on behind my back? It's just like a medieval romance.'

[1] The telegram was sent off on 6 September. (From the Foreign Ministry files.)
[2] The dispatch was sent off the same day (7 September). (From the Foreign Ministry files.)
[3] Herbert von Bismarck had become Under State Secretary in the Foreign Ministry on 10 May 1885.
[4] Letter to Holstein of 2 September 1885 (*Correspondence*).

When Herbert observed it was very painful for him to read out such things to His Imperial Highness, the Prince exclaimed: 'Not at all, I am most grateful to you. It is at least one way of learning what goes on. You must imagine I'm pretending, but I give you my word this is all news to me.'

H.I.H. was furious with the Prince of Bulgaria for discussing the affair with Count Wedel, whom the Crown Prince hardly knows. 'Do you know whose fault it is that this Bulgarian is giving himself such airs? It's His Majesty the Kaiser's fault. Why does he make this Prince, who scarcely has a right to be called "Highness", a General *à la suite* in the *Gardes du Corps*, an honour held previously only by old Prince Wilhelm[1] and Prince Albrecht (senior)?[2] I don't even hold it myself. I've only got one Guards uniform, whereas my son Wilhelm already has two and the Grand-Duke of Schwerin actually has three.

'If I have any say in the matter I'll take good care that my Battenberg brother-in-law[3] only appears in the court lists as Royal Highness of Great Britain. It is a scandal that the Queen [Victoria] has made him a Royal Highness; it's as if we wanted to do the same for the Marquess of Lorne.'

H.I.H. kept the extract so as to forward it to the Crown Princess that same evening when a courier was due to leave for Rome via Baveno. That will be a pleasant correspondence. I wonder whether he will have the last word?

Meanwhile I have told Herbert that someone (I did not name Seckendorff) had indicated that the only way of preventing the Bulgarian marriage was for the Kaiser to obtain a definite promise from the Crown Prince never to give his consent to it; the Crown Prince would keep his promise. I suggested the Chancellor might write to the Kaiser suggesting this. The answer arrived to-day: The Chancellor proposed to write the letter to H.M. Something useful has been started there, because an alliance with a valet's grandson would certainly damage the royal family in the eyes of the people.

The Spaniards are willing to make any amends which lie in their power, i.e. which the Government can push through without being thrown out.[4] The Chancellor is alarmingly moderate—too moderate. Caprivi said to me to-day: 'It would be a pity if the Chancellor were to suffer a set-back. His domestic policy meets

[1] Wilhelm, Prince of Prussia, the later Kaiser Wilhelm I.
[2] Albrecht, Prince of Prussia. Brother of Wilhelm I.
[3] Heinrich von Battenberg, the husband of Princess Beatrice of England.
[4] Solms telegraphed on 8 September that Canovas had given him this assurance. (From the Foreign Ministry files.)

245

with no approval. He only scrapes together majority votes because people think that in foreign affairs he is infallible and irreplaceable.'

I do what I can to ensure that we stick to a firm line.

12 *September* 1885

[...] Have I already said that the quarrel between Gossler and the Chancellor has been made up? I went to see Lucanus and advised him to let his Minister get in touch with Herbert. He did so, and Herbert set things right.

Rottenburg told me this, said how glad he was and added: 'And I have written to tell Rantzau that the matter has been dropped until after the elections.'

Aha, I thought, so it's only a truce. The very next day I called on Lucanus, who expressed his gratitude to me for my first piece of advice, and I then advised him to see that his Minister kept in touch with Herbert and sought his opinion in cases when it was desirable to know in advance Prince Bismarck's opinion and mood with some certainty.

Similarly I advised Stephan to apply to Herbert in his troubles. He, Stephan, had informed the Chancellor that a reduction in telegram rates had been decided on at the Telegraph Conference,[1] particularly for telegrams between Germany and Austria. The first few years would show a slight deficit which would, however, be subsequently made good. Stephan had used the unfortunate expression: 'Your Highness can rely on my experience.' The idea that anybody should set himself up as an authority against Bismarck annoyed him. He replied that he missed being offered any evidence, that he was not a public meeting that could be put off with fair words and promises. A reply from Stephan received a still ruder rejoinder. Rantzau wrote to Rottenburg: 'Tell Stephan to keep quiet. *We* are not in the habit of keeping up disputes beyond this point.' Stephan talked of resigning. I advised him to go and see Herbert. The affair will be decided on Monday. I put it to Herbert, who despite his many faults is a man of honour, that he will greatly enhance his status here with those people who are at present jealous of him because of his youth, if they realize that he supports their case with the Chancellor when they are in difficulties.

The Chancellor is working hard, i.e. he issues a lot of instructions, but he is superficial and contradicts himself. He makes decisions without consulting the files and without much reflection.

[1] The International Telegraph Conference in Berlin, 19 August–17 September.

Hence the contradictions. Yesterday morning, for example, a memorandum came through saying it was unnatural that the French Press should suddenly, without exception, side with us in the German-Spanish dispute; there was treachery behind this; probably they wanted to entice us into a war with Spain, only to unite with Spain later to attack us. Courier sent to Paris to ask Hohenlohe.

A second directive arrived in the afternoon: we must publish an article in the *Kölnische Zeitung* pointing out that several of the most influential French dailies, precisely those with government sympathies, were agitating against us in the Spanish dispute. A Press cutting was enclosed on both occasions; in the first he had read that the French Press was friendly towards us and in the second, that the Government Press organs were attacking us.[1]

13 *September* 1885

I wonder what His Highness will say. I mentioned yesterday that he had a dispatch sent to Paris to find out what the French were really plotting, and what lay behind the failure of the French Press to abuse us more roundly than it was doing in this Caroline question.

I replied that the French Government was probably afraid of arousing the animosity of the German Government by open support of republican propaganda against King Alfonso.

I then quoted him word for word a passage from a two-year-old dispatch, signed by him, which stated that Spain could count not only on our sympathy in her dealings with her republican neighbour, but also, if necessary, on an energetic proof of it; the Spanish Minister was to be told so. Something similar, I wrote, was also hinted to the French at that time, and they imagined that King Alfonso still enjoyed the good will of our gracious Majesty to-day.[2]

The reminder of this period two years ago will not please His Highness; *now*, in his annoyance over the Carolines dispute he has declared in Paris, Vienna, Rome and London that we attach not

[1] On 25 September Herbert von Bismarck had an interview with Courcel. The latter was instructed by Freycinet to express his regret at the doubts cast on France's loyalty in the German-Spanish dispute by the German Press. These doubts were without foundation. It was M. Freycinet's wish to maintain and foster the good relations with Germany which were entered into in the summer and autumn of the previous year. (*Grosse Politik*, vol. III, no. 708, pp. 453–4; *Documents Diplomatiques Français*, Première Série, vol. VI, no. 72, pp. 88–90.)

[2] The reply Holstein describes here was sent off to the Chancellor over Herbert von Bismarck's signature. The declaration he mentions was communicated to Under State Secretary Busch on 5 October 1883 to be passed on to Count Benomar. (From the Foreign Ministry files.) See also Hatzfeldt's letter to Holstein of 6 October 1883 (*Correspondence*).

the slightest importance to the Spanish monarchy, but that we think a republic a good thing, not only for France but also for Spain *and* Italy; the more republics existed, the more firmly would the monarchies close their ranks! Logic the handmaid of passion. I am told they say in ministerial circles that His Highness just lives from day to day and has no longer any guiding principle.

In expelling Polish labourers (Russian as well as Austrian) he is also going too far. Puttkamer is wringing his hands. We risk a similar expulsion by the Russian and Austro-Hungarian Governments of many thousands of German nationals now living in prosperity abroad. But *that* is exactly what the Chancellor wants; all he sees is the question of agricultural wages. He wrote in the margin of a document to-day: 'I am not afraid of these counter-expulsions. When abroad, all those Germans are useless to their country. Their capacities can only be utilized when they are back here.'

But in what frame of mind will these people return to their mother country which has reduced them to beggary abroad so as to exploit them at home? I am convinced that checking emigration is just as dangerous as checking diarrhoea; you keep the poison in the system. Charles I of England also forbade emigration. The day when this command was put into execution an emigrant ship was anchored in one of the English ports, with a full cargo. One of the people prevented from leaving that day was Oliver Cromwell. But emigration has always been one of the Chancellor's *bêtes noires*; he regards it not as a natural necessity of the age but as an intrigue of shipping agents. Puttkamer wants to persuade the Chancellor to mitigate the severity of our measures so that German nationals abroad shall also be treated less harshly, so I have again advised him, through Berchem, to use Herbert as a go-between. Herbert is sensible about this matter, and realizes his father's approach is too one-sided.

The Spanish General, Salamanca, had returned his Red Eagle to General Loë and included an impertinent letter to the Crown Prince with the request that both might be sent to H.I.H. Salamanca had simultaneously published his letter to H.I.H.

Loë replied that as a Prussian officer he regarded this as an insult and demanded that Salamanca should take back the letter or give satisfaction. Loë's Chief of Staff, Colonel Planitz, was sent to Madrid with this message. The duel was to be fought on neutral soil, possibly in Genoa.

Salamanca took back his letter and proffered satisfactory explanations.

Waldersee is infuriated, because he is afraid his 'friend' Loë will now acquire immense status in the eyes of the Crown Prince and the Chancellor. He called on me twice to inquire, mentioning at the same time that Loë has been an enemy of the Chancellor's for a very long time, personally and through his family. Most amusing to see them all (or nearly all) at each other's throats. At any rate Loë has behaved splendidly.

27 September 1885

Sommerfeld came to see me a few days ago and told me the Crown Prince was quite extraordinarily angry with Herbert Bismarck. H.I.H. had said with great venom that Herbert had meddled like a tactless intriguer in family affairs which were no concern of his, and so on. (Presumably the Bulgarian affair, in which the Princess has proved to her husband that every one but herself was a liar.) And so, Sommerfeld went on, it was quite pointless to try to bring Herbert and the Crown Prince together; the Crown Prince had categorically refused to have anything further to do with Herbert. It was therefore necessary to find some other person suited to mediate between the Crown Prince and the Chancellor. Sommerfeld said he had suggested me to H.I.H., who welcomed the suggestion.

I told Sommerfeld to drop the idea. I said if I became a party to going behind Herbert's back, I should be thrown out of the Foreign Ministry in a few months, and that I had not the least desire to be bored to death in some petty Legation or other.

He said somebody else must be found, because Herbert would not do.

I heard yesterday from Herbert himself, who was rather annoyed about it, that Albedyll was with the Chancellor on the Crown Prince's instructions. 'Albedyll has already wormed his way so far into H.I.H.'s favour that he is used at every turn for all sorts of things', said Herbert.

Of course, *he* is now marked out as go-between and is outstandingly well suited to that kind of diplomatic work, although I think him a pernicious influence in his military capacity on account of the traffic in offices which he and Waldersee practise. Only yesterday a most capable General Staff Officer told me our army was going backwards (age of its leaders, ossification of the troops in constant parades, choice of unsuitable people for the General Staff), whereas all the other armies were going forward.

This conversation Albedyll had with the Chancellor concerned

Brunswick.[1] The Crown Prince had been asked whether he felt inclined to let his son Heinrich be made Regent. Under his wife's influence he replied that from the legitimist standpoint he would prefer a descendant of the Duke of Cumberland to be given the Dukedom, but if the Chancellor thought it necessary, Prince Heinrich was at his disposal. As a result of this indeterminate attitude Prince Albrecht[2] will probably be recommended for election as Regent to the regency council.

I find the Crown Prince's sudden change of attitude towards Herbert psychologically interesting. Sommerfeld has probably had a hand in this, apart from the Crown Princess; he was recently deeply insulted by Herbert's haughty behaviour.

7 *October* 1885

Bismarck's suggestion of the Pope as arbitrator was another very clever move;[3] the idea was first mooted by a Spanish Ultramontane paper, naturally in the firm belief that Germany could never accept *him* as arbitrator. But when we did come forward with the idea, the Spaniards hedged and said, no, not an arbitrator, just an intermediary. And they would very much like to get out of mediation, too, because they are beginning to understand that their legal rights look dubious. The Ministers in Madrid and their Minister here have expressed their urgent desire to reach direct agreement without an intermediary.[4]

But Bismarck justifiably attached importance to affording the Pope the pleasure of a successful piece of negotiation. But, as I said above, the Chancellor is giving way too much, perhaps with an eye to the export of spirits to Spain. I have had to write a secret dispatch to Schlözer[5] instructing him to tell Jacobini[6] in confidence that we were prepared to compose our differences with

[1] See p. 166, note 1.

[2] On 21 October 1885 Albrecht, Prince of Prussia, was elected Regent of the Duchy of Brunswick by the Brunswick Parliament.

[3] On 21 September Bismarck reported to Kaiser Wilhelm that in order to make it impossible for Spain to persist in refusing arbitration, he had proposed to Count Benomar to make the Pope arbitrator. 'At the same time I intend this as a show of courtesy to the Pope, the effect of which on our ecclesiastical controversy will be, I hope, to render the Pope less susceptible to the influence of the Catholic Democrats who are led by Windthorst.' (Bismarck, *Die gesammelten Werke*, vol. vi c, no. 317, p. 324.)

[4] On 24 September Count Solms reported that the Spanish Government accepted the Pope as mediator. On 25 September Solms telegraphed that the Pope would be very glad to undertake this mediation. The Foreign Ministry files show that Bismarck declined the Spanish offers of direct agreement out of consideration for Germany's relations with the Pope

[5] Holstein's draft was cancelled by Herbert von Bismarck, who himself prepared a dispatch which after extensive alterations by the Chancellor was sent off on 10 October. (From the Foreign Ministry files.) See below, pp. 256–7.

[6] Ludovico Jacobini. Papal Nuncio in Vienna, 1874–80; from 1880 Cardinal State Secretary.

Spain on the following basis: we would concede them sovereignty over all the Carolines in exchange for the granting of the freedom to trade and settle (offered by the Spaniards weeks ago) and the granting of a coaling station.

The Curia was requested to offer this suggestion as its own.

The day on which the draft for this dispatch was sent to Varzin, Herbert after consulting with me wrote a memorandum pointing out: (1) that the Spaniards had obviously no documentary proof of their claims, (2) that the *Albatros* had now taken possession of the eastern part of the Carolines and that it was therefore worth considering whether we wished to cede *all* the Carolines to the Spaniards or to keep the eastern islands in the group.[1]

That wretched Rantzau on some pretext or another did not submit this extremely competent memorandum to the Chancellor. Herbert, considerably annoyed, sent it a second time, but it will probably be too late now. It might have produced its effect *before* Prince Bismarck had corrected the draft of the secret dispatch to Schlözer and thus taken up his attitude towards the mediation question; but once he *has* stated an opinion, even if it is merely to tell the Foreign Ministry he thinks such and such a condition practicable and satisfactory, he never moves an inch.

If we cede the *whole* of the Carolines, German public opinion will hardly be satisfied. And I for my part regret all the drudgery I've had over it.

In my French translation of our most recent note to Madrid which was dispatched yesterday I reproduced the sense rather than the actual wording. His Highness has gone over it substituting a number of appalling Germanisms—but he thinks he knows French.[2]

His German is unexcelled, but as regards foreign languages he knows English better than French. He does not think so at all, however, and has had sent to England not only the German text but also the [French] translation, which now contains one or two real howlers.

12 *October* 1885

Courcel was talking to me recently about Alsace-Lorraine. He deplored the number of expulsion orders now being made. I told

[1] The memorandum is dated 5 October and was entered in the Foreign Ministry journal on 7 October. Bismarck saw the document on 8 October. In a marginal comment to Herbert von Bismarck's argument about the impression that would be made on public opinion by the cession of the eastern section of the Carolines, Bismarck observed: 'That does not depend on our policy but on the attitude of the [political] parties. Even if we were pure as angels we should not win over Richter and Windthorst.'

[2] This note, dated 1 October, was published in the *Reichsanzeiger*

him a certain reaction was only natural after the exaggerated weakness of Manteuffel's regime. We chatted about it in a friendly way, until Courcel finally said: 'I make no secret of the fact that I wrote myself to my Government immediately after Manteuffel's death, warning them to be prepared for a reaction.'[1] Naturally, the French are sure to have been the first to make fun of the old fool while exploiting him for their own ends.

13 *October* 1885

I think it more probable that a couple of Balkan States will open fire on each other, than that nothing will happen at all.[2] The Powers are not united: Austria and England are moving closer together, while the Tsar of Russia would like to rule the world from Denmark, as sole despot.[3]

Herbert went to Friedrichsruh this morning, probably to influence his father in favour of Russia and against Austria. This afternoon I sent him a telegram which may upset his plan.[4] Herbert's method of always forcing Austria to do what he wants by ill-treating her seems to me impracticable. And in the present instance the Russians are really the more shameless.

I wonder whether old Bismarck will preserve peace. It hardly looks like it, but he has already achieved some remarkable feats. It would be no great misfortune if the Bulgars and the Serbs fought each other, provided His Highness can prevent the Powers from intervening.

To show he is concerned with small things as well as great, His

[1] See *Documents Diplomatiques Français*, Prèmiere Série, vol. vi, no. 44, pp. 64–6.

[2] On 18 September a revolution broke out in Philippopolis with the aim of uniting Eastern Rumelia with Bulgaria. Prince Alexander was obliged by strong nationalist pressure to accept the leadership of this movement.

[3] Since late September Alexander III had been in Copenhagen. On 3 October he received a delegation from Eastern Rumelia.

[4] Holstein telegraphed to Herbert von Bismarck, in Friedrichsruh: 'Extract from Vienna dispatch. Count Kálnoky finds Prince Lobanov's explanations unsatisfactory, fails to see *definite* basis for diplomatic action by Powers and talks of resigning if Russia's present attitude wrecks his pro-Russian policy. Report follows.' In this report (of 11 October) Reuss wrote: 'He [Kálnoky] had expected and urged the Russian Cabinet to enable him to reach agreement with it on the handling of the [Eastern Rumelian-Bulgarian] question. Instead, Prince Lobanov has been unable to give him any definite information on the way Russia intended to put into execution her vague general ideas.' Reuss said Kálnoky believed 'that the removal of the Prince of Battenberg was the only real [Russian] objective, and this was of a personal nature; after this, however, came the political objective, the aim of which was to recover by this means Russia's lost influence in both Bulgarias'. Bismarck commented here: 'Of course, and that corresponds to the aims of the Berlin and the later treaties. But it is unlikely that the Russians will succeed.' According to a later report from Reuss of 13 October, Kálnoky had particularly emphasized that Austria must know Russia's real intentions. Bismarck made it plain by means of caustic marginal comments that Austria must also make clear-cut proposals to Russia. In Bismarck's opinion the vital thing was that the three Imperial Powers should act in concert. But time must be gained for this; evrey claim now for an immediate clear-cut solution rendered an agreement impossible. (From the Foreign Ministry files.)

Highness decreed two days ago that a circular should be sent to our Imperial missions and consulates throughout the world directing them not to number the *first* page of their dispatches. This directive cancels a previous one of six months ago which laid down that every page of a dispatch should be numbered.

Herbert Bismarck asked Rottenburg a couple of days ago how he could bring himself to receive Bleichröder. Rottenburg, who always tries to be pleasant to everybody and is particularly pleasant to Bleichröder, explained, in order to save his face, that Bleichröder had offered the porter, Manthey, twenty marks if he would show him in to see Rottenburg. Of course it is all a lie. Overestimation of his own worth and also a lack of moral courage.

15 *October* 1885

A short time ago I read the dispatches which Herbert sent to Vienna yesterday evening as a result of his interview with the Chancellor.[1] They are excellently written; the son has inherited a good deal of his father's sense of style and learnt much from him. But Herbert has not hit on exactly the right tone—far from it. He slates the Austrian Government as if he were addressing a subordinate official, and actually talks of 'finessing'. If Reuss, as is his custom, simply submits these dispatches to Kálnoky instead of telling him the general contents, then this tone will provoke deep resentment. The son is now doing what his father has so far always avoided; he is making the Austrians feel they are dependent on us. In addition he speaks of 'my knowledge of the situation', 'my personal experience', as if he were his father. If we continue to adopt *this* tone, we shall not improve our relations to the other Powers—on the contrary.

I regard as dangerous the way Bismarck leaves his son to handle even the most vital affairs. His son has the young man's preference for an ultimatum style. [...]

The Chancellor is keenly interested in the project of a canal linking the North Sea and the Baltic.[2] The idea is to come before the Federal Council very soon. Estimated cost, 153 million marks, of which Prussia would pay 50 million.

The army is opposed to the plan, saying the canal would be of no importance in a war on land, but would in time of war require at least a division to protect it. The navy was not in favour either. They said that in order to make the canal useful in time of war

[1] In two of Herbert Bismarck's dispatches to Vienna, nos. 589 and 590 of 14 October, the German attitude towards Kálnoky's opinions as reported by Reuss was made clear. Dispatch no. 590 is printed as Appendix I, pp. 385–7.

[2] Later named the Kaiser Wilhelm Canal, constructed between 1887 and 1895.

there was still need for very considerable construction of fortifications and canalizing of coastal waters as far as Wilhelmshaven. Only after great insistence by the Chancellor did Caprivi agree.

Moltke, on the other hand, has declared that he will go away if the question comes up for discussion in the Federal Council and the Reichstag, because he does not wish to speak in support of it.

But why is the Chancellor so much in favour?[1]

16 October 1885

Yesterday, Herbert was summoned to Prince Wilhelm's presence immediately after his arrival. The Prince told Herbert that while he was hunting in Mürzsteg the Prince of Wales telegraphed him from Pest to say he urgently wanted to talk to him. Prince Wilhelm replied he was not free until 11 October, so the Prince of Wales said, very well, he would wait until the 11 October. Meanwhile he led such a fast life in Pest that even the Hungarians shook their heads.

When Prince Wilhelm arrived in Pest the Prince of Wales informed him in great embarrassment that he must forego the pleasure of seeing Prince Wilhelm at Sandringham this year as he had hoped. For it was impossible to pass through Windsor without calling there. But the Queen (Prince Wilhelm added: 'the old hag') had said that in view of the attitude adopted towards the question of the Bulgarian marriage by Prince Wilhelm and Prince Heinrich she did not wish to see them.

Prince Wilhelm told Herbert he was very glad he now had a weapon he could use against his mother if she should reproach him with not being sufficiently well-disposed towards the Queen of England. His mother, incidentally, was more eager than ever for his sister to marry the Prince of Bulgaria who is now, moreover, regarded by all the women as a matchless hero. To hear them you would think Battenberg had led an assault party up the ladders with a sabre in one hand and a revolver in the other. This unjustified prestige would be lost immediately if the Bulgarian were sent back to Sofia from Philippopolis like a whipped cur; it would in fact be best if he were driven right out of Bulgaria, because that would make him look ridiculous to the ladies.

Herbert's close friendship with Prince Wilhelm makes his relations with the Crown Prince's court more and more difficult.

The Chancellor has achieved one thing temporarily: a momentary agreement between Austria and Russia. But the whole affair is delicate and still remains so.

[1] See Bismarck, *Die gesammelten Werke*, vol. vi c, no. 315, p. 323.

Someone very familiar with conditions in the Crown Prince's household told me recently the Crown Princess had a great passion for intrigue and energy in carrying out intrigues, but she had no *courage* at all.

18 *October* 1885

[...] I had advised Hohenlohe to replace Hofmann,[1] the State Secretary, by Puttkamer,[2] the Under State Secretary, as soon as possible and in addition to appoint a vigorous senior *Landrat* as his *Chef de Cabinet*. I enclose his evasive reply.[3] If he retains the present stick-in-the-mud he will do badly, but I wash my hands in innocence. [...]

24 *October* 1885

In the enclosed letter,[4] Radolinski bids me state that the Crown Princess has expressed the wish to see Hatzfeldt before his departure for London.[5] She wants to win him over to supporting Battenberg, and will probably promise to receive and reinstate Countess Hatzfeldt provided Hatzfeldt keeps Battenberg in Bulgaria. His official duty will more likely be the exact opposite. The Chancellor is perfectly prepared to oblige the Russians by supporting their policy in Bulgaria; on the other hand he will not be at all sorry if the *English* adopt a stiffer attitude which involves them in a quarrel with the Russians. Hatzfeldt can to that extent oblige both sides, however odd that may sound.

In my reply to Radolinski I said I was a man of too little account to pass on such a request, and anyway I thought it probable that Hatzfeldt would in any case be recalled to Berlin to receive his instructions. I shall take care not to get my finger crushed between these two millstones; I saw in the spring where that leads to. But the Crown Prince and Princess seem to have picked on me for that very purpose. Besides Radolinski, Sommerfeld also reproached me recently for not making any advances to the Crown Prince and Princess and said I owed it to my position. We shall see which side is the more obstinate.

The Crown Princess told Radolinski that Battenberg could perfectly well become King of Bulgaria now, which would make

[1] Karl von Hofmann. State Secretary for Alsace-Lorraine, 1880–87.

[2] Max von Puttkamer. Under State Secretary for Alsace-Lorraine; State Secretary, 1889–1901.

[3] Hohenlohe wrote on 14 October: 'Wilmowski urged me not to make any change in the Ministry of State so early as this, and since the Chancellor also advised me to carry on with Hofmann for the present, I shall have to try to do so. [...]'

[4] Letter of Friday evening [23 October 1885] (*Correspondence*).

[5] Hatzfeldt had been appointed Ambassador to Great Britain.

things easier for the marriage. Had he not behaved magnificently and heroically? And the young Princess had confessed to her mother in Venice that if anything happened to him she would jump into a canal. 'Fancy my poor child jumping into a canal',[1] said her mother to Radolinski, with tears in her eyes.

The whole thing is rather amusing. Far more serious is Herbert's increasingly apparent inclination towards Russia and aversion to Austria. The son is not a trapeze artist like his father, who constantly kept the balance between them. Whereas the father's preferences may privately lie with Russia, the son makes no attempt to conceal his feelings. If this is not changed we shall in a couple of years have not a Three Emperors' Alliance, but a Two Emperors' Alliance, and Austria will seek support elsewhere. That will certainly not accord with the Crown Prince's policy.

I fail to understand the Chancellor at the moment. Three months ago, when the Kaiser was so feeble, His Highness spoke of the need for a political *volte-face*, and consequently dropped France and turned to England. But if we now consistently ill-treat Austria to please Russia, that will hardly be a change of policy which will suit the next Kaiser.

I heard again yesterday how completely out of favour Herbert is with the Crown Prince and Princess. Two days ago they gave a dance for Princess Wilhelm.[2] When Their Imperial Highnesses saw Herbert's name on the list of guests, they said: 'Oh no, we don't want him; we'd better just invite people from Potsdam.'

27 *October* 1885

When the documents were sent to Rome recently for the information of Schlözer and the Pope, they were accompanied by a secret dispatch to Schlözer which said we would accept 'a proposal for mediation *based on the most recent Spanish proposals*'. The gist of these proposals was to grant us freedom to trade and settle, a port and a coal depot, in exchange for recognition of Spanish sovereignty over the entire Caroline and Pelew archipelago.

I had drafted this confidential dispatch quite differently, but Herbert scrapped my version and composed the dispatch himself. His father signed it.

It is on the basis of this confidential dispatch that the Pope has now put forward his proposal for mediation: he thinks Spain should claim complete sovereignty over both groups [of islands]

---

[1] In English in the original.
[2] Augusta Victoria, wife of Prince Wilhelm of Prussia and later Kaiserin of Germany.

and should grant us liberty of trade etc.—everything which was suggested in the dispatch.[1]

That means the affair has been decided against Germany. The Pope is not to blame. He had put forward the suggestion written by the junior Bismarck and signed by his father. Those two are to blame for this loss of face. The son's handling of this affair has been hot-headed and injudicious; the father's has been thoughtless and superficial. When we sent the dispatches from Rome, together with the mediation proposal, to Friedrichsruh, the Chancellor wrote a long marginal note which contained a contradiction! On the one hand he said we must inform the Pope that we would negotiate with Spain *on the basis of the mediation proposal*, i.e. recognizing Spain's historic sovereign rights. But then, to spin out the affair, we were to add that we could not make a definite statement until we had received reports from the *Albatros* (which is still cruising round the Carolines and annexing them!).[2] What is the point? If we recognize Spain's historic sovereignty over the group, we do not need the *Albatros*'s reports. What does it matter where she hoists our flag if we concede that the entire group has been under the Spanish flag since 1526? The most such a reply would do would be to make us ridiculous and contemptible in the eyes of the world, as imitators of Haugwitz's ambiguous policy.[3]

I have asked Krauel, the originator of all this Carolines business, to draft this disgusting dispatch to Rome[4] so that no one can reproach *me* afterwards with overlooking any of the arguments at my disposal. Now that the Bismarcks, father and son, have bungled the affair there is nothing more to be done. All my efforts, to which I sacrificed my leave, have been rendered useless by *one* sentence in the confidential dispatch to Schlözer. The Pope is acting in good faith. He believes we want to show him a kindness by granting *him* a concession we are unwilling to grant the Spaniards directly.

Herbert works really hard, but his self-confidence exceeds his gifts. His father, on the other hand, is only interested in the export of spirits to Spain and spends the rest of his time ruminating on his fame. His vanity increases as his achievements

---

[1] The Pope's proposal for mediation was communicated to Berlin in a dispatch from Schlözer dated 22 October. (From the Foreign Ministry files.)

[2] Bismarck's marginal note stated: 'We would negotiate with Spain on the basis of the Pope's mediation proposal, as soon as we possessed the naval reports we needed to justify our decisions to the Reichstag, and to obtain a basis for our detailed negotiations with Spain.' (From the Foreign Ministry files.)

[3] The policy of the Prussian Foreign Minister in 1805–6 which vacillated between support of Napoleon and the anti-Napoleon coalition.

[4] The dispatch drafted by Krauel, dated 1 November, was sent off on 2 November. (From the Foreign Ministry files.)

diminish: in this growing vanity, this jealousy of every idea of which he is not the father or at least the grandfather, therein lies the danger, namely the paralysis of all activity.

Both father and son are now convinced that the Pope will bear the blame for the bad outcome, not the Chancellor. Let us hope so, but I do not believe it.

The enclosed letter from Hatzfeldt shows clearly how embittered he is deep down at having been shown the door.[1] But it is a good thing both for him and for Hohenlohe that Manteuffel died. Otherwise one or other of them would have been out of a job. Either Hatzfeldt here, or Hohenlohe, to make room for Hatzfeldt. Herbert would never have endured Hatzfeldt here; at the moment Herbert is in a foul temper because Hatzfeldt goes to Friedrichsruh instead of being satisfied with Herbert's instructions. I must say I do not blame Hatzfeldt.

If it is true—as I believe from Hatzfeldt's definite statement— that the Chancellor promised him the Grand Cross of the Red Eagle, I think it typical that Herbert's objection (for it *was* Herbert) was enough to cause his father to break his promise. The father is indifferent to everything and in addition he has lost his nerve, particularly where his son is concerned.

His son will make a good ambassador some day, but *here*— I am curious to see what fresh trouble he will cause here, half intentionally and half unintentionally.

3 *November* 1885

I have taken three weeks' partial leave, i.e. I am free until two and have given up one part of my work. My aim was to be rid of the Carolines once more. Now that the Bismarcks, father and son, have declared that we shall take the Spanish proposals as a basis for further negotiations, and Spanish sovereignty is thus recognized, we ought to have done with the affair as quickly as possible. Instead we are again finessing and corresponding endlessly. And at the same time the Chancellor told Hatzfeldt in Friedrichsruh that 'the fellows at the Foreign Ministry still had eyes bigger than their stomachs, but that *he* was sick of the whole thing'.

Then why does he not say so? Instead he indulges in undignified cavilling. The tendency Prince Bismarck has always had of taking the credit for himself and blaming others for things that go wrong must often cause great bitterness. The Carolines affair was stirred up by Kusserow, Krauel and Herbert. The father followed suit

---

[1] Letter to Holstein of 25 October 1885 (*Correspondence*).

because his son led the way, and he is thus one of those primarily responsible. Now he behaves as if the whole thing had nothing to do with him.[1]

The conflict between father and son over the Bulgarian affair is permanent. Whereas the son, to please the Russians and Prince Wilhelm, wants to drive out Battenberg at all costs, his father told Hatzfeldt, and also telegraphed yesterday to Radowitz, that he would 'rather have Battenberg in Sofia than in Berlin'.[2]

Whereas Herbert would go through thick and thin with Russia and would gladly sacrifice to Russia every other alliance, his father told Hatzfeldt that the links now being forged between the House of Orleans, Denmark and Russia[3] combined with the increased royalist temper in France were such as to make us cautious. We should have to arrange things so that, if the worst happened, we could play off an Austro-Anglo-Italian alliance against a Franco-Russian alliance. Well, we will not remain in a position to do so for very long if Herbert has his way.

And what do we gain by giving way to Russia? That Russia thinks our attitude unnatural and suspects us.

When Drummond Wolff went to Constantinople the English asked us to support him. Thereupon we asked the Russians if they objected. They replied, certainly, they objected very strongly; Drummond Wolff's mission was aiming at an Anglo-Turkish alliance, and that would be most unwelcome to them. We said

---

[1] On 17 December 1885 Schlözer and the Spanish Ambassador to the Holy See signed an agreement based on the Pope's proposal for mediation. Germany recognized Spain's rights over the Carolines and received in return the right of free trade and permission to set up a coaling depot for the fleet. The secret files on the Carolines question show that during the month of September 1885, the German Foreign Ministry and the Admiralty believed in the possibility of a war with Spain and were considering the measures to be taken in that event. Bismarck, convinced that a war with Spain would develop into a Franco-German war, wished to avoid a conflict, but if that should be impossible, he thought in terms of a defensive and colonial war against Spain. (From the Foreign Ministry files.)

[2] In telegram no. 158 of 30 October 1885 Radowitz had reported: 'Redish Bey told me today *in confidence* but apparently on the Sultan's instructions: the Sultan has recently been strongly influenced against Prince Alexander. His Majesty's attitude to this personnel question could now be formulated in this way: he would meet the wishes of the Imperial Powers whether they wanted to maintain the Prince on the throne or to depose him. In the latter case, however, he must have previous guarantees for his successor, who must be a Prince with no connexions with any other royal family in the Balkan peninsula.' Bismarck replied by telegram on 1 November: 'I know that His Majesty the Kaiser prefers to keep the Prince of Battenberg in Sofia rather than have him in Berlin, not for political reasons, still less from sympathy with the Prince and his policy, but because his presence in Germany and especially in Berlin would for a variety of reasons be inconvenient to him personally. Will you please bear this in mind during your conversations, but remember also that any German co-operation in maintaining the Prince of Bulgaria in Sofia would annoy the Tsar of Russia.' (From the Foreign Ministry files.)

[3] On 22 October 1885, Prince Waldemar of Denmark, son of King Christian IX and brother of the Tsarina of Russia, had married Princess Marie of Orleans, daughter of the Duke of Chartres.

in that case we would not support Wolff. Our representative in Constantinople, who had already been instructed to support Wolff, received fresh instructions saying neither one thing nor the other.[1]

D. Wolff has now attained his object and knows we did not assist him,[2] but the Russians believe we exerted our influence in secret. A humiliating policy. What I set down here is thought and felt by others in the Foreign Ministry.

3 November 1885

Since Hatzfeldt has been here[3] he has been the centre of interest in the diplomatic world. Kaiser, Crown Prince, Crown Princess, Ambassadors, everybody wanted to talk to him. And so Herbert is pressing his hardest for Hatzfeldt's departure. The Kaiser, who was alleged formerly to have expressed impatience with Hatzfeldt's delay, and similarly the Chancellor in Friedrichsruh had both told Hatzfeldt personally that it did not matter about a few days.

But Herbert must now have requested his father to get Hatzfeldt away. And so His Highness, in contrast to his verbal assurance, telegraphed to-day: 'Has Count Hatzfeldt not gone yet? If not his departure is urgently desirable.'

This incident, amusing in itself, gives one food for thought. What kind of a future awaits us?

[1] See p. 239, note 4.

On 31 August 1885 the German Chargé d'Affaires in Constantinople was briefly informed by telegram of the aim of Sir Drummond Wolff's mission and instructed to find out the Sultan's objections to Turkey's military co-operation in Egypt. The telegram went on: 'If Sir Drummond Wolff should ask you for your support, you are to counter by inquiring what England's plans are and what the English programme consists of.' Bismarck commented on a further request from Salisbury for support of Sir Drummond Wolff, delivered by the English Ambassador on 9 September: 'It will be an advantage if Thielmann [the German Chargé d'Affaires in Constantinople] expressly establishes the Sultan's unwillingness to send the "small body" [of troops] and to ask his vassal, the Khedive, to allow them to march through his territory. The English will not win the Sultan's confidence by such demands—on the contrary. If they offer him a *large sum of money*, they may succeed. The instructions are too foolish to be supported *vigorously*. That would only arouse the Sultan's mistrust.' On 14 September Muraviev informed the Foreign Ministry that Russia was opposed to German support of England's wishes in Constantinople. Bismarck then decided there should be no support. The same day Herbert von Bismarck informed the English Chargé d'Affaires that his father thought England's desire to see Turkish troops stationed in Egypt was mistaken since it brought the Sultan into a vassal's relationship with England, but that Germany was prepared to support the Egyptian interests of the present British Cabinet. On 23 September Thielmann was instructed to support England's present wishes in regard to the recruitment in Turkey of troops for Egypt and the dispatch of a Turkish Commissioner to reorganize the Egyptian army and restore order, especially in the Sudan. (From the Foreign Ministry files.)

[2] The Anglo-Turkish Convention was signed on 24 October 1885. On 26 October Sir Edward Malet informed Count Herbert von Bismarck that he was instructed to 'express to the Chancellor Lord Salisbury's most particular thanks for the help afforded his Egyptian policy'. (From the Foreign Ministry files.)

[3] In Berlin, before taking up his post in London.

The *Chancellor's* intellectual and nervous energies are drying up. Sometimes he has isolated ideas that give a pleasant sound but have no supporting harmony; major and minor are utterly confused. His nerves can no longer stand a powerful strain. Like Frederick the Great in the Potato War just before his death.[1] At the same time dominated by material personal interests, hostile to everything savouring of a temperance society, e.g. the restriction of the sale of spirits on the open sea (North Sea Fisheries) desired by *all* the other nations.

Herbert, with a quite unusual mastery of official routine for his age, but without any perception of what is difficult or easy, near or far, or simply unattainable. Jealous of his independence, and therefore not easily accessible to advice from senior officials, but an easy prey to flatterers, domestic or foreign, who tickle his vanity over a glass of wine. In the same way a married man will often ill-treat his wife and in return submits to ill-usage from a *concierge's* daughter. Perhaps he will become Chancellor under Prince Wilhelm—then there will be great wars. He is unlikely to come to power under the Crown Prince. The Crown Princess's hatred of him dates from Wedel's letter about the Prince of Bulgaria.[2] She thinks Wedel wrote the letter to me on Herbert's instructions. I do not really think so, but neither can I affirm the contrary. Herbert does sometimes like old-fashioned methods. For instance to-day's telegram about Hatzfeldt's departure was definitely prearranged.

Hatzfeldt, incredibly able intellectually but devoid of any solid basis, a weak nature destined to be dominated. For his lioness he has the *Crown Princess,* a foreigner. Only to-day a Secretary of Legation who had dined with Her Imperial Highness told me that he had not known at first what she meant by 'we' and 'our interests'. It could not mean German interests. He soon realized it meant 'the English' and 'England'.

And yet I am inclined to think that a good many things will turn out better under the new reign than people fear; similarly a good many things will be far worse during the remainder of the Bismarckian era than people expect. No consistency, no coherence.

5 *November* 1885

Have just accompanied Hatzfeldt to the station. So ends another chapter in my life. We have worked together for four

---

[1] Unlike Frederick's earlier mobile campaigns, the war with Austria over the Bavarian succession (1778–9) was one of position. During the winter the troops are supposed to have been reduced to a diet of potatoes.

[2] See entry for 9 September 1885.

years. I have often felt irritated by his folly in private and family affairs, but never, so far as I remember, by his professional conduct; there, on the contrary, I have often admired him.

His predominating sentiment is good-natured indolence. The way he said farewell to the people who had been associated with him here at the Foreign Ministry was not exactly filled with feeling—I have never seen a more indifferent leave-taking. The only people who saw him off at the station were Courcel, Berchem, Redern and I.

Herbert, whom I saw in the course of the evening, was visibly relieved at H.'s forthcoming departure. Friedberg incidentally told someone that he knew for certain Herbert had already had enough of the job here and longed to become an ambassador. He may want to, but the old man will not let him go, certainly not without a row. But if it did happen, the old man would break three or four of his successors and then tell his son: 'You must come back, I can't work with the others, they're too stupid.' Herbert probably knows this, and when he talks of leaving it is mainly a pretence.

The Kaiser, urged on by the Chancellor, now wants to exact from the Crown Prince a promise that he will *never* agree to his daughter's marriage with the Prince of Battenberg. Seckendorff raised this idea three months ago and I passed it on to Herbert at his request. The affair has been dragging on for so long now that the Crown Princess has probably got wind of the plan in the meantime and will have forbidden her husband in advance to make any such promise. This will cause a further rift between Kaiser and Crown Prince, Crown Prince and Chancellor.

The marriage between the St Petersburg Bülow and la Dönhoff is soon to take place. They will be a dangerous couple: she, the Crown Princess's favourite, he, the world's worst intriguer.

Redern told me to-day that his brother-in-law, Count Zichy, had made Battenberg's acquaintance in Pest; the latter had suggested that Zichy should accompany him to Sofia. Fighting would break out there very soon. The Russians had organized a conspiracy to make Waldemar of Denmark Prince of both Bulgarias. But he, Battenberg, would get in first and spring the mine ahead of time. The whole thing would pass off bloodlessly and gaily.

But now Battenberg denies having known of this affair so long beforehand.

Striking his name off the Russian army list was a stupidity on the part of the Tsar. I wonder if he will get away with it.

The Chancellor has sent the Kaiser another report stating yet again how impolitic a marriage between Princess Victoria and the Prince of Battenberg would be.[1] The pretext for this expression of opinion was a dispatch from Busch in Bucharest[2] stating that Bratianu,[3] the Minister-President, had expressed fears that this marriage would come to pass.

Since the Chancellor knows the Kaiser shares his views, it was pointless to worry the old gentleman again. But the worst of it was that His Highness had decided that Herbert was to read this dispatch aloud to the Crown Prince. On my insistence Herbert decided to hand the documents to the Crown Prince for him to read himself, instead of reading them to him with commentaries. The audience took place this afternoon. Herbert gave H.I.H. the documents to read; the Crown Prince swore and said he did not understand why 'Ministers' interfered in his family affairs and expressed the hope 'that he would now hear no more of the matter'.

This Bulgarian business coming after the Brunswick affair[4] will cause a great rift between the Crown Prince and Princess and the Bismarcks. For both sides it has now become a question of vanity—shall there be a marriage or not? I can do nothing more about it. Last week the Bismarcks, father and son, were surprised that the latter had not yet been summoned to see the Crown Prince since his return, so I saw to that at once. Herbert has been there twice since then and will also be invited to the soirée on the 21st. But it seems to me that the irritation grows on each occasion. Herbert obviously fails to strike the right note.

It is typical of the Chancellor that he has dragged third parties into this affair: first Wedel, then Busch. The Princess is unlikely to forgive either of them.

Last week Rottenburg told Lindau the following:

The Chancellor thinks he will not last long once the Crown

---

[1] On 3 November 1885 Bismarck explained in a report to the Kaiser that Prince Alexander, ruling in Bulgaria with English support, could be nothing but an advantage to German policy, in view of the Anglo-Russian tension which would result. A marriage between Prince Alexander and Princess Victoria would oblige Germany, on dynastic grounds, to pursue an anti-Russian policy in which there was nothing to be gained for Germany. Bismarck proposed that the Kaiser should obtain a promise from the Crown Prince that he would never allow this marriage. Kaiser Wilhelm, who showed his agreement with Bismarck's statements in his marginal comments, observed at this point: 'should be attempted'. (From the Foreign Ministry files.)

[2] Busch's dispatch of 6 November was sent to the Kaiser on 10 November with a report by Bismarck in which the above arguments were again put forward. (From the Foreign Ministry files.)

[3] Joan Bratianu. Rumanian Minister-President, 1876–88. [4] See p. 166, note 1.

Prince becomes Kaiser. He foresees a break, and intends to found a newspaper afterwards. £100,000 sterling with which to found it are at his disposal at any time. A German in England, the man who made a great fortune in the sale of Apollinaris Tonic Waters,[1] is advancing the money. The paper is certain to have a great future.

So says Rottenburg. There is certainly something in this story. I am less inclined to believe that the Chancellor really intends to go into the opposition camp as a newspaper editor. Probably he wants to use the story as a threat to the Crown Prince and Princess. No doubt it was told to Lindau so that it could percolate to the New Palace. Realistically conceived.

Lenbach has painted a magnificent portrait of the Chancellor, better than any so far. He has been offered 20,000 marks for it. But Lenbach turned down the offer and presented the portrait to the Bismarck family. 'It's a good thing at least they're so glad to receive presents', said L., who feels that the Chancellor's portraits have contributed considerably towards increasing his (Lenbach's) fame, and would therefore like to show his gratitude.

Yes, they accept presents all right.

Bernhard Bülow is a most interesting presage of the future. He writes letters to Herbert with quite a Russian tinge, and yet the Crown Princess told Radolinski only a few days ago: 'Oh, Bülow entirely shares my views.' It is quite conceivable that Bülow is thus currying favour with them both.

As for the Chancellor, the world of fact is becoming increasingly indifferent to him and personal matters are occupying him more and more. A few days ago the War Minister had stated in a communication to His Highness that His Majesty had taken such and such a step 'on the basis of a report from the Foreign Ministry'. This elicited from the Chancellor a reply of several pages. It was not the Foreign Ministry but he, the Chancellor, who was responsible for that report; only the actual framing of it had been entrusted to the Under State Secretary. His Highness thought it necessary to make this point clear. And yet H.H. asserts his health is not strong enough to sustain the demands made on him. But he has time for such puerilities. It must be the effect of age—although he was always rather like that. I can still remember, many years ago, his stream of abuse at some official demand made on him. I was listening and said afterwards to Bill, who had also been listening: 'He could have dealt with

[1] Edward Hermann Steinkopf. In 1888 he acquired a London paper, the *St James's Gazette*.

the affair in half the time he's spent cursing.' 'Of course', said Bill. 'But don't you see, he prefers cursing.'

17 *November* 1885

General Caprivi, who is seeing visitors from a chaise-longue, told me yesterday: 'Albedyll is a misfortune for the army, and so is Waldersee.'

I learnt to-day that when the Grand-Duke of Baden requested the promotion of a lieutenant of the Horse Guards, a native of Baden, to the rank of adjutant, Albedyll turned down the request 'because Lieutenant von Chelius is the most junior officer in the regiment and therefore his military education is still too incomplete'.

It is obvious that if a German Prince requests that one of his own subjects be made an adjutant etc., this request must be granted for political reasons, particularly in the case of such a loyal member of the Reich as the Grand-Duke. He was infuriated at this treatment. He had already sent official intimation to Chelius' father that his son was to become an adjutant and as a result he felt he looked a fool in the eyes of all his subjects.

Subsequently he requested two more promotions to the rank of adjutant which were also refused! He was made to feel what a fool he had been to conclude a military convention with Prussia.

Either Albedyll has a personal grudge against the Grand-Duke or else the Grand-Duchess has not been friendly enough towards Frau von Albedyll. Frau von A., sister of the Duchess of Manchester and Countess Bludow, is said to be the most arrogant woman in Berlin. She is much younger than her husband (his second wife) and has him completely under her thumb.

I find this an appalling piece of tactlessness.

Godeffroy[1] told me to-day (though I knew already) that through Herbert's personal letters, Bülow in St Petersburg is far more accurately informed on the situation than Schweinitz, and that Schweinitz pays court to him so that he will read out isolated passages from the letters. An unnatural state of affairs.

Waldersee, who came to see me two days ago, told me with some annoyance that the Kaiser, acting on a suggestion of Herbert Bismarck's which Albedyll presented, had detailed Waldersee's personal adjutant, Captain von Hüne,[2] to attend the Indian manœuvres which take place in January. In addition the Crown Prince asked for Captain (or Major) von Hagenow, and thus both

[1] Attaché at the German Embassy in St Petersburg, 1885–6.
[2] Ernst, Baron von Hüne-Hoiningen. Military Attaché in Paris, 1886–91.

officers were appointed, without Waldersee, acting Chief of the General Staff, being consulted.

Hüne's absence will be particularly unwelcome to Waldersee, whose only reason for choosing him as adjutant was that Hüne is on good terms with the Crown Princess and Waldersee feels the need of support in that quarter.

Yesterday Caprivi expressed great disapproval of the North Sea-Baltic canal project. Friedberg, whom I saw beforehand, said it would not go through the Reichstag.

27 *November* 1885

In spite of a triple warning by the Chancellor to show greater restraint, Radowitz is behaving in Constantinople as though present-day Germany were a vassal of Russia; his behaviour is reminiscent of the days of Friedrich Wilhelm IV and Gerlach. There is only *one* explanation: Radowitz is receiving contrary instructions in personal letters from Herbert. Herbert is completely taken in by the Russians. He dines with Shuvalov two or three times a week, is served (as he says himself) seven different kinds of wine and is grossly flattered. But on the diplomatic level Shuvalov treats him like a callow youth, as can be seen from his demands.

When the Turks during a session of the Conference[1] raised the question of renewing the fortifications along the Balkan passes and manning them with Turkish troops, which the Peace of Berlin entitled them to do, Shuvalov proposed to Herbert that *we* should oppose the idea, because it was too ticklish a matter for the Russians.[2] Another time, when there was talk of the possibility of a Russian march into Bulgaria to restore order, Shuv. said to Herbert: 'You must let us have two companies, no more, because every one is afraid of you, and if there are German troops involved, only a few, we shall meet with no resistance. Without your help

---

[1] See p. 386, note 1.

[2] On 10 November, Herbert von Bismarck wrote a memorandum on a conversation he had had with Shuvalov on the previous evening. According to Shuvalov, Nelidov had asked Giers: '*Faut-il continuer à s'opposer complètement contre occupation Balcans si les Turcs l'exigent?*' Giers had replied: '*Les Traités de Berlin donnent ce droit à la Porte; concertez-vous avec collègues d'Allemagne et d'Autriche sur besoin de l'application.*' Count Shuvalov termed it madness for Russian policy to allow fortification of the Balkan passes directed against Russia, and asked Count Bismarck to do him the 'personal favour' to empower Radowitz to cast his vote against the occupation of the Balkan passes. Prince Bismarck's decision in the matter was as follows: 'We can by no means ally ourselves with Shuvalov against his Tsar and be more Russian than the Tsar himself. [...] We can, as a result of this apparent "indiscretion", give Radowitz no other instructions than the ones he has already: when Russia and Austria agree, to vote as they do; when they disagree, to wait and to ask for further instructions.' (From the Foreign Ministry files.)

we should run into great difficulties during this march and we might as well not attempt it at all.'[1]

I did not fail to say to Herbert: 'He underestimates you because you're so young', which he surlily admitted. Nevertheless he is still as much under Shuv.'s influence as ever.

I have no doubt that Herbert is giving policy a different slant from the one his father intended.

Herbert's arrogance towards his staff is unspeakable. He delights in telling the ladies at social gatherings that the whole of the Foreign Ministry, from the highest to the lowest, trembles before him. He makes himself look ridiculous.

It is natural that my status with him should be different from other people's, but I keep well in the background to avoid provoking his jealousy. That is also the reason for my refusing to visit the Crown Prince's court.

Herbert is particularly jealous of Hatzfeldt. He remarked recently to Wilhelm Redern: 'A dispatch has come in from Hatzfeldt, eighteen pages long, but we're no wiser now than we were before.' On the contrary, the dispatch was most interesting.

28 November 1885

The Chancellor called on the Crown Prince to-day, expressed his approbation of Battenberg's achievements and explained how his interests could best be served, namely by a dilatory policy.

So he has veered right round. H.H. now realizes that he cannot push Battenberg out and is making the best of it.

The good Crown Prince was most edified by this conversation and commented afterwards: 'It is really remarkable the way the

---

[1] In a dispatch from Sofia on 3 November Saldern had reported that a peaceful surrender by the Bulgarians in the Eastern Rumelian question was at present out of the question. In sending it to the Foreign Ministry Rantzau enclosed a note dated 10 November stating: 'The Chancellor requests you, when passing on this document [i.e. Saldern's dispatch] to Count Shuvalov, to put to him quite confidentially the suggestion that it might be very useful if Russia and Austria tried to reach an agreement on the question of a Russian entry into Bulgaria in case the Bulgarians resist the Conference's decisions. We would gladly sound the Cabinet in Vienna on this idea, and would give it our support if only we were sure Russia was contemplating such a step.' On 11 November Herbert von Bismarck informed the Russian Ambassador of this. In an interview of 18 November at which Muraviev was also present, Shuvalov informed Herbert von Bismarck that M. Giers had declined the suggestion. Shuvalov further stated that he thought Giers feared English intervention if the Russians marched in. The undertaking would be safe only if Germany followed up her advice by armed support. Prince Bismarck here wrote the following marginal comment: 'We gave no advice, we merely recommended reaching agreement beforehand with Austria on this eventuality, assuming there is no other course. And even if we, i.e. *I* personally, do give Russia advice, it is not with the intention of giving her armed support, but because of our interest in the transaction and our good will towards the parties concerned, to which category *we* hardly belong. All we want is peace between the *monarchies* in Europe!' (From the Foreign Ministry files.)

Chancellor has shared my views on every important question of foreign policy since Nikolsburg.'[1]

I do not blame Bismarck for sailing with the wind—I find it most entertaining. But it was a mean act to try to blacken Hatzfeldt in the eyes of the Crown Prince by asserting that the Countess was again with child. I am certain it is untrue, but the Crown Prince, who is very strait-laced, was extremely angry.

The Crown Princess issued a warning to Hatzfeldt that his imprudent behaviour had given rise to this rumour. She also said she would be very sorry to see H. ruin himself, because he was the only Foreign Minister she would feel able to trust later on, meaning, I imagine, after the older Bismarck has gone.

But it is clear from this slur on Hatzfeldt how jealous of him the Bismarcks are.

I have, unfortunately, known for a long time that Bismarck, the man, possessed a mean nature, but this fresh proof of it has rather shaken me. Hatzfeldt, who gave up an agreeable post as Ambassador in Constantinople to come and slave in Berlin as State Secretary, deserved better of Bismarck than to be treated like this.

I observe to my regret that one after the other of his father's qualities is coming out in Herbert; I mean his father's character, not his genius. Both father and son are liars.

I observed an amusing little detail just recently. Herbert and Rantzau had always worked in adjoining rooms. Three days before Rantzau arrived Herbert moved into the State Secretary's office and pushed a young Secretary of Legation, whom he uses to deliver oral messages, into the room between himself and Rantzau. Herbert, in fact, wants to reign in lonely grandeur; Rantzau's familiar bustling in and out did not suit him. People might otherwise have imagined Rantzau had influence. I can picture Rantzau's fury, since he is just as vain and haughty, but has to disguise the fact somewhat.

1 *December* 1885

No one could say that our foreign service is now being efficiently run. To-day, for example, we are still without news of the terms laid down by Bulgaria for the conclusion of peace.[2] The terms are printed in the newspapers already. Our representatives abroad are cowed, and yet it occurs to no one at this end to tell

---

[1] The preliminary peace between Austria and Prussia of 26 July 1866.

[2] In the war between Serbia and Bulgaria. Peace was concluded on 3 March 1886 on the basis of the *status quo*. See *Memoirs*, p. 134, note 4.

them occasionally which problem or which object should occupy their attention.

The Chancellor's ideas have lost all coherence—he changes his mind overnight. During the recent colonial debate he began by saying it was legalistic casuistry to regard the German colonies as foreign territory.[1] But the previous day he had written with his own hand in the margin of a document: 'The colonies are foreign territory.'

The trouble is not that he sometimes confuses or forgets things —any one else would do the same—but that no one dares to point out his mistakes.

The Chancellor told Bleichröder that it would be our duty to collaborate more with England now. And yet Salisbury tells Hatzfeldt that the two proposals at the conference which England finds unacceptable were introduced not by the Russian delegate but by Radowitz.[2] I think, indeed I know, that Radowitz is vain, and easy game for the shrewder Nelidov;[3] even so R. would not go so far unless he had secret instructions from Herbert, who pursues a policy of his own behind his father's back.

We are now entering upon a critical phase: Russia and Austria are extremely incensed against each other. I wonder how the Chancellor will extricate himself from the difficulty. If he entrusts the affair too much to his son, it may turn out badly.

9 December 1885

A few days ago Count Khevenhüller[4] told Bray[5] that the Prince of Bulgaria had said he was giving way to Austrian pressure for an armistice[6] only out of personal regard for Kaiser Franz Joseph, because the latter had afforded asylum to his father, Prince Alexander of Hesse, at a time when he had been cast off by his Russian relations.[7]

Bray reported this. And the report was sent on from Berlin to St Petersburg with instructions to Schweinitz to point out to

[1] In the Reichstag on 28 November. (Bismarck, *Die gesammelten Werke*, vol. XIII, pp. 79–102.)

[2] Hatzfeldt reported this in a telegram of 30 November. See also *Grosse Politik*, vol. V, no. 961, pp. 18–20.

[3] Alexander von Nelidov. Russian Ambassador in Constantinople, 1883–97.

[4] Rudolf, Count Khevenhüller-Metsch. Austro-Hungarian Minister in Belgrade, 1881–6.

[5] Hippolyt, Count von Bray-Steinburg. Consul-General, later Minister in Belgrade, 1879–91.

[6] Austria's diplomatic intervention in the war between Serbia and Bulgaria had prevented a Bulgarian invasion of Serbia.

[7] In 1851, Prince Alexander was obliged to leave the Russian Court because of the infatuation with Countess Julie Haucke, a lady-in-waiting to Prince Alexander's sister, the wife of the heir to the Russian throne. After leaving Russia, Prince Alexander joined the Austrian army and married Countess Haucke.

M. Giers the Prince of Bulgaria's attitude towards Kaiser Franz Joseph.[1] Russia and Austria are thus being set at loggerheads, while the Chancellor, on the contrary, is striving to prevent them from coming to blows.

Herbert's personal hatred of Battenberg drives him to extraordinary lengths. After the Russians had, out of consideration for Austria, withdrawn a threatening clause in the Eastern Rumelia affair, Herbert telegraphed in his father's name (in the name of His Highness *in mundum*), but without showing him the telegram, that the threat could in fact be inserted in the protocol[2] in a different form; the Russians were thus obliged to take back the concessions they had already made to Austria.

We are trouble-makers, not peace-makers. Herbert wants to get rid of the Prince of Bulgaria at all costs; he has probably promised Prince Wilhelm he will do so. In addition Herbert hates the Austrians because he was badly treated as an Attaché in Austria in 1877; the countesses gave him the cold shoulder; some of them did not wish to be introduced to him. Such personal considerations make a lasting impression on him. I have only just heard of this from Berchem. It explains a good deal.

I believe I mentioned some time ago that Rottenburg said the Chancellor wished to found a big newspaper on his retirement. The capital would be put up by a German living in England who had made a great fortune out of Apollinaris Water.

I treated the affair as a threat against the Crown Prince and Princess.

An anonymous pamphlet has now appeared in Zürich, entitled *Co-rulers and foreign influences in Germany*, in which the Queen of England and her 'female agents' are sharply attacked. The pamphlet is being sent to newspapers and Members of the Reichstag. The Crown Princess has also received a copy. I have just been reading it. I am certain that Bucher wrote it, on instructions of course. Bucher is enjoying six months' leave, on full pay, somewhere in the Tyrol or in Switzerland. One can understand the Chancellor's reluctance to let him go.

The idea is not bad, because the Crown Princess is a coward in the face of public opinion.

To outward appearance the Chancellor is on good terms with

[1] Bray's dispatch of 1 December was received by the Foreign Ministry on 7 December and was forwarded to St Petersburg the same day with an accompanying note which tallies with Holstein's account of it. (From the Foreign Ministry files.)

[2] This was a declaration by the representatives of the three Imperial Powers in Constantinople to be handed to the Porte. It was never delivered. See *Grosse Politik*, vol. v, no. 961, enclosure, p. 20.

her. He dined there yesterday and stayed on talking to her alone for an hour and half. Both of them expressed their extreme satisfaction with the discussion, which concerned Battenberg.

25 *December* 1885

A vignette. My colleague Brauer, who is in charge of Near Eastern affairs, came to see me to-day in my office. While he was there we heard from the Chancellor's garden next-door the crack of a small-bore rifle. Brauer said with a laugh: 'Perhaps they're shooting senior officials.' After a few moments he left, but dashed back immediately and called me into his office. 'I didn't know how right I was when I said officials were being shot', he said.

One of the windows in his office, which is on the same corridor as mine and looks out on to the Chancellor's garden verandah some fifty yards away, was pierced with five bullet holes. The force had been such that the panes were not splintered, but simply had small round holes. Two bullets, the size of buck-shot, had flattened themselves against the wall, and I found them on the floor. Brauer had installed a costly ventilation apparatus in two double window-panes. That too was shattered.

When I had returned to my room I heard noisy footsteps in the corridor followed immediately by laughter from Herbert and Rantzau. Herbert had come to examine the shots and was pleased about their power. 'It shoots extremely well.' When asked what he had aimed at, he replied: 'The window sash.'

When Lindau observed: 'You might have hit someone, you know', Herbert replied easily: 'Oh, no, because the first time I aimed at the upper panes and waited to see if any one came to the windows. When no one appeared I knew that the room was empty.'

Brauer remarked: 'But, Count Bismarck, you might have hit a clerk bringing in files.'

'Yes', laughed Herbert, 'and what silly faces the chaps would have made when the bullets went singing round their heads.'

The feelings of Brauer and Lindau (who works next-door to Brauer) can well be imagined. Furious, but they do not show it.

Brauer said, half jesting, in his Baden dialect: 'It reminds you of the darkest days of Nero.'

N.B. Herbert had not proffered *one word* of apology for letting the wintry air into the room through five holes—intentionally too.

I have described this scene, my dear Ize, because it explains to you a good deal about myself which you may not have understood until now. With rough types like Herbert and his family there is only *one* way of avoiding the alternative between degradation and conflict, namely to withdraw of one's own accord. That is what I have done, and at first it gave me rather a jolt. But when I see how others are treated I am glad I made a clean break. I hardly think they would shoot through *my* window. [...]

29 *December* 1885

On the 21st of this month, for the first time for a year and a half, I dined with the Bismarcks, and again on the 27th.

Princess Bismarck had sent Rottenburg to see me and to put it to me that Prince Bismarck was ill and lonely, and did not want to see any new faces. It was a pity I had stopped coming. Would I feel able to meet Rantzau in the Bismarck's drawing-room without making difficulties for him?

I told R. to take his message to Herbert who knew all the circumstances. (Some months ago I was in Herbert's room when Rantzau came in and delivered a message without acknowledging me. When he had gone I said to Herbert: 'Tell your brother-in-law that if he does that again we shall fight a duel.' Herbert thought this perfectly proper and delivered my message; Rantzau has acknowledged me ever since.)

Someone came in at that point so Rottenburg replied: 'No, I don't want to see Herbert, I must have a detailed conversation with you. I'll come back this evening.'

I went straight to Herbert, told him what had happened and asked him to tell his mother to invite me once, and then she would see. I said the idea that I should not behave politely to Rantzau in her drawing-room was quite monstrous. Whether I could amuse the Chancellor was a very different matter. I had the feeling I had never amused him. Lehndorff or Dietze would be better for that purpose.

With that I had said all I wanted to, and when Rottenburg called back once or twice in the evening, anxious to create an impression as a mediator, I was not in.

A few days later I received an invitation. There were only Bill and his wife and the old people. We all greeted one another as if we had met the previous day. The meal lasted scarcely half an hour. Afterwards the Chancellor lay down on the chaise-longue and smoked four pipes, and the conversation between the two of us was quite lively. It was the same the day before yesterday, when I was invited again. He has grown older and more feeble. He still sees things clearly, but his glance is directed towards selfish considerations and interests more than it used to be. His memory and more particularly his energy and self-confidence have declined. I think Bleichröder is right when he says that the Chancellor, who used to declare openly that he allowed no one, not even the Kaiser or his wife, to influence him, now suffers under Herbert's pressure. The latter is applying to his father his own precepts, in which considerateness never figured. I am afraid that in foreign policy Herbert already leads his father wherever he wants.

The antagonism towards Austria which the old man has repeatedly expressed comes no doubt from his son.

Prince Bismarck was furious with the Kaiserin who had requested that Patow be given the Black Eagle. 'That filthy scoundrel, who has ruined everything he's undertaken, and most recently the province of Saxony.' He spoke of this at some length.

He then inveighed against beer which he said was unnecessary, if not harmful, because it made people fat, lazy and dull, and sang the praises of brandy which he said was indispensable to man.

The total impression on me was unpleasant: a man no longer able to perform the varied tasks attaching to his position, but hampering other people in their work, except for Herbert, who tyrannizes over him.

Sometimes his father's maxims come out very naïvely in Herbert. He said to someone the other day in a bar: 'Officials have to be kept in a permanent state of irritation and alarm; the moment that ceases, they stop working.' It is the old man all over again.

The day after the shooting affair Herbert fired at Brauer's window yet again; when Brauer showed himself he was received with Homeric laughter from Herbert and the Rantzaus. When they told the story to Prince Bismarck later on he inquired with great interest what the range had been and remarked: 'Yes, those things have a terrific impact. It might have shot a man dead if it had happened to hit him.'

What extraordinary people.

1886

Bismarck and Herbert. Holstein mistrusts Bismarck's foreign policy. Shuvalov's demands on Herbert von Bismarck. Courcel's views. Hatzfeldt's success in London. Threat to disavow Hatzfeldt. Rantzau wants Werthern's post. Difficulties about Bulgaria and Prince Alexander. Holstein's memorandum for Queen Victoria. Dangers in Alsace-Lorraine. Prince Wilhelm to go to Skierniewice and work in the Foreign Ministry. The Crown Prince's opposition to this. The situation in the Balkans. Holstein and Hatzfeldt's attempts to stiffen Britain and Austria against Russia. Bismarck against Prince Alexander. Holstein working for Italian alliance. Hatzfeldt letters. Austrian fears of Russia. Bismarck's anger at Russia. Russian distrust of Bismarck. Holstein and Herbert von Bismarck. Proposed Franco-Russian alliance. Hatzfeldt on British policy. Germany's Russian policy. Lord Randolph Churchill's views.

10 *January* 1886

I have been invited to dine with the Bismarcks several times recently, with only Herbert present, and yesterday Schweninger was there too. I am confirmed in my original impression that Prince Bismarck is losing his grip.

It came up in conversation that there was no Secretary of Legation in Dresden. 'Why not?' asked Prince Bismarck. 'We haven't got any', replied Herbert. 'Then create some', said his father. 'No', said his son, 'the young men we've got now don't know enough, they've still a lot to learn.' 'Bah', said the old man, 'I expect you can find someone.' 'No', said his son, 'they must pass their exams first.'

Herbert was right in this matter. The old man's caprice has spoiled a good many things. But the way he meekly submitted to this rebuff showed me he was not the man he used to be. He has now a kind of dread of his son's violence. Therein lies a serious danger, for Herbert has lost his sense of balance.

Yesterday we were discussing health and long life. Prince Bismarck, who took part in the conversation with a certain melancholy, observed in conclusion: 'Yes, if they let me stay in the country year in year out, I would promise to serve to the end of my days and never to retire. I could go on directing the Foreign Ministry from there, and I would leave the other departments to look after themselves for the most part.'

Herbert warmly supported this plan of living in the country. His father's presence makes his work more difficult.

Prince Bismarck went on to discuss the other Ministers, praising Maybach but criticizing all the rest, Gossler in particular, who, he said, was doing nothing in the religious sphere and neglecting the *Kulturkampf*, and was pursuing a stupid educational policy. Rottenburg has certainly been busy there; he wants to get rid of Gossler. I shall tell Lucanus to-morrow to advise Gossler always to remain in close touch with Herbert. That is the only conceivable way of countering Rottenburg's machinations.

Prince Bismarck told us the other day that the Director of Archives had submitted to him some secret memoirs of Frederick the Great with an inquiry whether they could be published. Prince Bismarck was obliged to say no, on account of the observations on Austria and Russia. The King, he said, made all kinds of criticisms of Austria. But at one stage—1768—he had noted that he had been obliged to place himself on good terms with Russia and as a result, to afford her his help. The time might come when he would regret having contributed to the aggrandizement of the colossus. He must therefore consider the possibility of an alliance with Austria.

While Prince Bismarck was telling me this he obviously had the same ideas as Frederick the Great. But will Herbert hold to that course? He lacks his father's balance wheel.

13 *January* 1886

On New Year's Eve the Chancellor was extraordinarily depressed. 'Another year gone', he said to Bill. 'Yes', Bill replied with a laugh, 'we grow cleverer each year.' 'Oh, no', said the old man. 'I used to be cleverer than I am now. I can feel it; I have far greater difficulty in grasping things, and I have lost my control of affairs.' Bill told me this.

Berchem, who is to introduce the Foreign Ministry estimate, had a talk yesterday with Franckenstein and Maltzan-Gültz.[1] Franckenstein declared the estimate would certainly go through provided the Chancellor did *not* attend the debate. 'If he does I'll answer for nothing.' Maltzan agreed.

The Chancellor's credit in all non-diplomatic questions is very small, as is clear from the foregoing. His procedure in Parliament is usually as follows: he introduces an intrinsically sensible proposal, defends it in such an aggressive fashion that Parliament

[1] Helmuth, Baron von Maltzan-Gültz. Conservative Member of the Reichstag from 1871; State Secretary in the Treasury, 1888–93.

rejects it purely from anger, and then he writes newspaper articles attacking parliamentarianism. He treats this like a sport, perhaps with the thought at the back of his mind that the more indignant people become, the more difficult it becomes to govern them without him.

But the trend in foreign policy is far more dangerous. Herbert's behaviour is such that not only I, but Brauer, the Near Eastern expert, and Berchem, too, have the feeling that he wants his own little war too, so as to become a famous man. That would be the Bismarckian war of succession.

Herbert hates the Prince of Bulgaria and hates the Austrians. He would prefer anything to Battenberg's remaining in Bulgaria, if only because he, Herbert, told Prince Wilhelm that Battenberg would be driven out.

As a first step towards this goal Austria is to be urged to have a demarcation line drawn between herself and Russia in the Balkan peninsula, i.e. she is to recognize that Bulgaria belongs to the Russian sphere of interest, and that Russia may do what she wishes there.

When I told Herbert to-day I did not think the Austrians were disposed to accept this view, he replied in his usual way: 'In that case it's all up with Austria.'

I should not attach any importance to such childish behaviour if I did not see more clearly every day *how* weak the old man is in the face of his son. And the cause is also partly physical. The Schweninger cure has weakened his heart.

For the first time in twenty-five years I mistrust Bismarck's foreign policy. The old man is led by his son, and the son is led by vanity and the Russian Embassy.

Our greatest guarantee of peace is the fact that the other Powers have already noticed German policy is no longer what it used to be, and the more we push forward, the more they hang back. But Bismarck's prestige is being ruined in the process.

Minor scandals occur almost daily. Recently the Bismarcks, father and son, jointly released a paragraph in the *Norddeutsche* concerning the Carolines, in which the whole affair was, without any justification, treated as still undecided.

Immediate alarm in the Spanish Press and official inquiry in writing by the Spanish Minister.

Herbert sent for him, blustered at him and simply commented afterwards that in the end the Minister had expressed his gratitude for what had happened.

Dear Herbert thinks he can obtain anything by rough treatment.

Radolinski gave a small dance yesterday. On my advice Herbert had been invited. The Crown Princess had a long talk with him. On leaving she said to Radolinski: 'Wasn't I nice to H.B.? But, do you know, he is not a clever man.'[1]

Unfortunately true, and will become more so. He has many petty traits, and his greater qualities are overshadowed by his immense vanity.

All the petty squabbles at Court or in the Foreign Ministry etc. now recede in face of the danger I perceive from the direction of our foreign policy. But I can do nothing about that. Just look on. As I have said, other people's fear is our greatest safeguard. The more we push them to bold acts, the quicker they draw back. So far at any rate.

23 January 1886

Bleichröder and Dietze both told me yesterday that the Chancellor was less active and did not show his former vigour.

Bleichröder had requested the Chancellor to reconcile him with Herbert, who hates him. The Chancellor had declined and complained that Herbert's violence created all sorts of difficulties both in the Foreign Ministry and with the Crown Prince. In short, the Chancellor hinted that he had no influence over Herbert in cases where his passions were aroused.

'An odd state of affairs', Bleichröder said to me. 'The family has *me* to thank for Schönhausen, Herbert will inherit it one day, and yet I risk being thrown out if I want to visit him.'

The Italian papers are carrying the news that the German-Austrian alliance will not last much longer. The last Near Eastern crisis tore a rent in it that can never be patched up.

The German Press laughs at the story; I think there is a good deal of truth in it. Austria cannot put up with Herbert's treatment indefinitely. Kálnoky has already told Reuss, in anger: 'Austria must look about for a different ally.'

Herbert dangles on the end of Russia's strings like a puppet. In addition he gave someone to understand only yesterday evening that he bears the Austrians a grudge for the bad treatment he suffered at their hands as Secretary of Legation in 1876.

Herbert informed Berchem yesterday that the Chancellor had said he intended to send for Franckenstein and speak to him as follows: if the motion for the state brandy monopoly[2] were

---

[1] In English in the original.

[2] The state brandy monopoly was intended as an aid to big landowners, but especially as an added source of income for the Reich. Bismarck hoped that this added income would make the Reich less dependent on direct taxes, and consequently on the representative bodies within the Reich which voted those taxes. The motion was defeated in the Reichstag in March 1886.

defeated, it would have demonstrated that the German Reich could not continue in its present form, for sixteen million Catholics, through their representatives, were making any kind of government impossible. The Chancellor would then make preliminary arrangements for surrendering the south German states, notably Bavaria, to Austrian suzerainty.

Berchem had very properly replied: 'If the Chancellor tells Franckenstein that, he will laugh. In the first place the Bavarians do not want Austrian suzerainty and in the second place the Hungarians and the Austrian Slavs would go to war to prevent any strengthening of the German element within Austria.'

The whole idea is childish and reminiscent of childhood days, when one was told: 'If you aren't a good boy at once, I'll sell you to that stranger.'

The political prestige of the Bismarck regime is rapidly declining.

7 *February* 1886

I write less frequently now, my dear Ize, not because there is less to observe but because I find it painful to set down the things I see: the Bismarckian era is drawing to a close—I wish it were *already* over, for God only knows what may yet happen.

An example will explain my anxieties.

The Italian Ambassador[1] informed me yesterday that Count Robilant[2] urgently desired the Turkish-Bulgarian agreement[3] to be approved by the Powers as soon as possible, so that at least *one* of the three unresolved Balkan questions—Turkish-Bulgarian, Serbo-Bulgarian and Greek—might be settled. Robilant also sent word that the French Government had suggested to St Petersburg that those three questions should be decided *together* by means of a conference in Constantinople, i.e. simply a revision of the Treaty of Berlin. The interesting point about this suggestion was less the fact that the French made it, than the secretive behaviour of the Russians towards *us*.

I had summed up Launay's communications in a memorandum.

[1] Count Launay.

[2] Nicolis, Count di Robilant. Italian Minister and Ambassador in Vienna, 1871–85; Foreign Minister in the Depretis Cabinet, 1885–7.

[3] On 1 February Turkey and Bulgaria reached agreement over Eastern Rumelia. The Sultan intended to invest Prince Alexander with the office of Governor-General of Eastern Rumelia every five years. But Russia required that this office should be conferred on the Prince of Bulgaria as such, and not on Prince Alexander. See p. 279, note 2. The Powers accepted this compromise and on 5 April an agreement was signed, whereby the Prince of Bulgaria was appointed Governor-General of Eastern Rumelia for a period of five years.

To my astonishment Herbert *withheld* this from Prince Bismarck.[1]
Herbert does not want to approve the Turkish-Bulgarian agreement; he wants to support the Russians, who would like to overthrow it. When Radowitz announced three days ago that the
Russians had made counter-proposals to the Turkish-Bulgarian
agreement aimed at preventing Prince Alexander from taking
root, the Chancellor wrote in the margin of the telegram: 'The
Turks are unlikely to accept the Russian amendment which departs even further from the Treaty of Berlin than does the Turkish-
Bulgarian agreement.'[2] But Herbert telegraphed to Radowitz
asking him to try to reach agreement with the Austrian Ambassador on the amendments, and then to support the Russian amendment.[3]

Robilant's views did not fit into this programme. And so the
Chancellor was simply not informed of them. We are no longer
pursuing Bismarck's policy, but Herbert's. Herbert is prepared to
go through thick and thin with the Russians. And in return they
treat him like a simpleton; I think I have already mentioned this.
Shuvalov descended on him to-day, accompanied by Muraviev,[4]
the Counsellor of Embassy—which runs counter to all etiquette—
and proposed in the latter's presence that Germany should submit
to the other Powers the idea *d'écarter le Prince de Bulgarie*!
Shuvalov added that it was just an idea of his. But that was too
much even for Herbert. He said we could not do that. At which
Shuvalov asked whether he might write to St Petersburg stating
as Herbert's opinion that Battenberg's removal should be proposed. (Muraviev was sitting there as a witness.) Herbert
replied quite skilfully that we could not do that either; Russia
must first make sure of Austria's consent, then we would give
ours too.[5]

[1] According to the files of the Foreign Ministry, the contents of Holstein's memorandum
were communicated to the Embassies in London, Vienna, St Petersburg and Rome for their
information and to be used as they thought fit. The memorandum was not submitted to the
Chancellor.

[2] In telegram no. 28 of 4 February Radowitz had reported: 'According to a confidential
statement by my Russian colleague, St Petersburg is demanding that the administration of
Eastern Rumelia should be entrusted, not to Prince Alexander personally, but to whoever is
Prince of Bulgaria at the time, and that there should be no time limit.' Bismarck observed
here: 'In itself better for Bulgaria; questionable whether acceptable to the Porte; departs
further from the Treaty of Berlin than the present agreement.' (From the Foreign Ministry
files.)

[3] Herbert von Bismarck telegraphed to Radowitz on 4 February: 'If Russia's consent to
the agreement can be obtained, then she should be met half-way in the interests of peace',
because the essential point was that the Powers should be united. It seems probable that
Bismarck saw the telegram before it was sent off.

[4] Michael, Count Muraviev. Counsellor of Embassy in Berlin, 1884–93.

[5] According to Herbert von Bismarck's memorandum on this interview, Shuvalov said:
'You could most easily rid us of the Prince [of Bulgaria] *si vous l'écartiez. Il serait coulé et*

The Russians really imagine they can make use of us for anything.

Vanity produces disastrous effects in both the Bismarcks, father and son.

The father showed it in the way he attacked the Austrian Government in his otherwise excellent speech on Poland,[1] and afterwards published expressions of agreement by anti-Government German-Austrian bodies in the *Norddeutsche*.

Count Wedel writes that the Viennese are shattered, and think this means the end of good relations with Germany.[2]

The son, by posing publicly as Lord Rosebery's protector and counsellor, has already made the latter's position wellnigh impossible in the eyes of the European and particularly the British public, and yet he is the very man who could be useful to us if properly treated.

The main point on which father and son part company at present is that His Highness wants to keep Battenberg in Bulgaria as a wedge between England and Russia, while H.B. is quietly scheming, as he has done from the start, for Battenberg's removal, to earn the Russians' approval and Prince Wilhelm's admiration.

But Bismarck himself, as I am convinced afresh each time I see him, no longer holds the reins of power.

It is fortunate that the outside world does not yet know this, but it is bound to notice it gradually. The embassies must realize it merely from the change of style. H.B. writes diffusely and at length and expressions occur like 'this measure is intempestive' or 'the fleets must concur' (meaning 'collaborate') etc.

9 *February* 1886

Courcel called on me to-day before he left. He seemed in a particularly pessimistic mood, both as regards French internal affairs and also relations between France and ourselves. Courcel is a frank, excitable person who says a good deal when roused.

He deplored the internal weakness of the present Government.

obligé de quitter la Principauté: il s'agirait seulement pour l'Empereur Guillaume de prendre l'initiative.' Prince Bismarck commented in the margin: 'Why and how?' The memorandum continues: 'I [Herbert von Bismarck] replied by an evasive phrase, saying that in all these questions which did not affect German interests we kept ourselves in the background. Since the accompanying Counsellor of Embassy [Muraviev] showed signs of uneasiness at this time, Count Shuvalov did not make his question any more precise. [...] ' Count Bismarck's suggestion of an Austro-Russian agreement referred to the Bulgarian question in general and appeared at the beginning of his long memorandum. (From the Foreign Ministry files.)

[1] On 28 January 1886. (*Die gesammelten Werke*, vol. XIII, pp. 144–66.)

[2] No relevant letter or official report by Wedel was found among Holstein's papers or in the Foreign Ministry files.

He said it was thus obliged to follow the current of public opinion, which was anti-German. A strong government would be able to ignore it. The kind of government he had in mind was revealed shortly afterwards when he attacked the *Kölnische Zeitung*, calling it *un brûlot*. The chief reproach he levelled against it, amongst other things, was that it attacked the Prince of Orleans.

After some time he said, rather contradicting the foregoing: 'We don't hate the Germans. *Comment pourrions-nous revendiquer l'Alsace, si nous haïssions les Allemands?*' He complained of the way Germany pursued the principle of nationality, whereas France gladly absorbed any kindly-disposed races or individuals. '*La plupart des frontières aujourd'hui sont des frontières factices; la frontière que vous nous avez donnée est factice.* You have glory now, you have wealth, you have a stable government. We have the opposite of all that. You have taken from us provinces which we loved, and from which we drew a useful influx of Nordic people. Now that they are severed we have lost our balance. We have been governed ever since by Gascons, Provençals and similar impossible types.

'The Germans now rate themselves higher than the rest of mankind; I differentiate between mankind and Germans', and so on.

Behind everything Courcel said one could sense the unspoken thought: 'Things can't go on like this much longer, or France will be ruined.'

Of course it was not my business to convert him; I just said what seemed calculated to make him more informative.

I note this conversation in view of possible events. I find it another ominous sign that Courcel is talking of giving up his post here. When he came here some years ago he said his one endeavour was to bring about good relations; if ever war seemed likely he would leave without waiting until the very last minute. He is now saying his wife longs to be back in Paris.

I realized to-day that the French were very offended at our refusal, in view of the progress made by the agitating activities of Déroulède[1] and his friends, to take part in the Exhibition of 1889. As a result Russia, Austria and Italy are also declining, so it will be a fiasco. The Exhibition can now only be national instead of international. Who knows what may happen before '89?

---

[1] Paul Déroulède. President of the French League of Patriots.

14 *February* 1886

Copy of a letter from Hatzfeldt.[1]

London, 11 *Feb., evening*

Well, Rosebery *has cold feet*; that is the explanation of my silence.

He came in the end yesterday evening. He *insists* on my sending a telegram: first, to ask for advice about Serbia. So I explained to him that he must neither ask for advice nor shelter behind others, but should act for himself, and then he would get support. He then asked me to telegraph that he wished to request Vienna to exercise moral pressure on Serbia, and would like our support. I expressed my willingness; he then became . . .[2] and said he must ask the old man[3] first, and that he would write to me in a couple of hours.

The evening went by, to-day ditto. At last at eight p.m. a letter from him in which he said Vienna seemed calmer about Serbia, and it would therefore probably be better to wait. Which means that the old man has wriggled out of doing anything. This evening I sat down again and replied by private note. I thanked him for his information, regretted I was unable, on the strength of the news reaching me to-day, entirely to share his confidence in reports from Vienna, and said I could not help fearing that things would not take a satisfactory course if they were left to themselves. Full stop; no requests; did not ask to see him. Nothing. Just now, at ten p.m., back came another note: he felt convinced I had better information than he, and would *try* to come to-morrow.

I give you all these details so you can see what stupidity I am struggling against at the moment. I shall not report officially about it—at most I shall write a private letter or get Plessen to write, since he knows about this business anyway.

If Rosebery comes to-morrow I shall make a final attempt at putting life into dead bodies, but I have not much hope. If I succeed in arousing anything resembling energy and a definite attitude, then you may get a telegram before these lines reach you.

So much for Hatzfeldt. He was trying to urge the Gladstone cabinet to take vigorous measures against Greece. Since Salisbury's defeat the Greeks had been more insanely convinced than ever that their old friend Gladstone would never side against them but always support them.

But peace in the Near East, i.e. in Europe, depends on Greece's attitude. Unless England intervenes, no one will intervene, and war will break out.

---

[1] The original of Hatzfeldt's letter was not found among Holstein's papers.
[2] Dots in the text.　　　　　　　　　　　　　　[3] Gladstone.

Hatzfeldt's problem was thus a very difficult one. He solved it with that superior skill he possesses in persuading people by elucidating and marshalling the facts. A telegram arrived yesterday to say that England wished to confer with the Powers by telegraph on suitable means to bring about an *immediate* disarmament of Greece.[1]

Hatzfeldt had persuaded Rosebery, and through him, Gladstone.

All the thanks he got was a telegram[2] which roused my indignation; it was inspired by Herbert and dictated by the Chancellor. First, blame for a point of detail, then all kinds of petty instructions and reservations; *not one word* in acknowledgement of his really great diplomatic achievement. Those two exude envy through every pore.

I wrote to him at once yesterday evening, telling him to keep his chin up and go on working for peace. My letter will arrive in time because no diplomatic business is done in London on Sundays.

Old Bismarck really desires peace, but, as I noticed again yesterday when I dined alone with him, His Highness is fast shrivelling up: lonely, nervy, suspicious, lacking his former grasp of affairs and thus open to every suggestion coming from his favourite son. The latter, as I said before, would not be averse to a war, no matter what the pretext. He said to me a few days ago: 'If only we could keep Russia and Austria from each other's throats, I shouldn't mind a war between Greece and Turkey.'

In *that* case we should not have sent the *Friedrich Karl* into the Mediterranean.[3] Now it has been sent, the affair must be taken seriously, as the Kaiser and the Chancellor wish.

But rather than let Hatzfeldt score a diplomatic success, Herbert would dash everything to pieces.

I had a visit to-day from *Hofrat* Wollmann, Head of the Central Bureau, a quite outstanding official; he complained that he found it hard to maintain his staff's enthusiasm for work in view of the

[1] According to Hatzfeldt's telegram of 13 February, Lord Rosebery had linked the proposal with the condition that a German warship (the *Friedrich Karl*) should shortly appear off Crete. (From the Foreign Ministry files.)

[2] The telegram of reply began by stating that Hatzfeldt could already have confirmed the early arrival of the *Friedrich Karl* off Crete. Prince Bismarck further stated that any disarmament of Greece should only refer to the Greek fleet. Whatever action was to be taken on land could be left to the superior Turkish power. 'Acts of aggression against objectives other than the Greek fleet, particularly a bombardment of inhabited areas, such as the bombardment of Alexandria [11 July 1882], ought in my opinion [i.e. Bismarck's] to be entirely avoided and left to the Turkish army.' (From the Foreign Ministry files.)

[3] Towards the end of January an international fleet was concentrated in Suda Bay in Crete to lend weight to a note by the Powers warning Greece not to embark on a war with Turkey.

treatment they had to endure from the Under State Secretary. However keenly they worked, from morning till night, they were still slated for being idle.

What Wollmann says is true. In his evening rages or his morning hangovers Herbert ill-treats his subordinates and the Chancellery clerks. Recently he attended a drinking-party given by the Bonn 'Prussians', but had said he would look in at the Ministry later. As a result the staff of the Central Bureau waited for him until a quarter to one. He was drunk long before then, as I learned next morning from Lerchenfeld.[1]

I wonder what will be the end of it all. That is the way to ruin a staff of officials. Hitherto our people have been incorruptible.

18 *February* 1886

The Sarauw[2] trial in Leipzig has proved that almost *all* our most important military secrets—mobilization plans, plans for 'screening' the forts, new ammunition for destroying fortifications—have been betrayed to the French. The traitors cannot all be people in a humble position.

The centre of the French spy network was and is Berlin. A former Prussian captain, O'Danne, who was cashiered in 1870 for corruption, travels to and fro between Paris and Berlin and makes no secret of his relations with the French War Ministry. There may be several such people. A few years ago, when fire broke out in the General Staff building, the view was heard that the sole purpose of the fire was to conceal the disappearance of secret plans.

Sinister omens. And when you see at the same time in whose hands the direction of our army is: that gossiping courtier Albedyll and that jellyfish, Waldersee . . .

A few days ago I was invited to dine with the Chancellor again. His servant did not bring the invitation until a quarter to four; when I asked who had cried off he said: 'No one, Their Highnesses are alone.' And in fact I found only the two old people. When Prince Bismarck appeared his wife said to him, still visibly annoyed: 'I thought we should be dining alone. But Herbert didn't want that. He asked: "Who's coming?" I said: "No one." At that he said: "Then invite someone." I said: "It will give your father a rest to dine alone with me." But he said: "No, that wouldn't give father a rest." '

---

[1] Hugo, Count von Lerchenfeld. Bavarian Minister in Berlin, 1880–1919.

[2] On 11 February the *Reichsgericht* condemned the retired Danish Captain Sarauw to twelve years' imprisonment on a charge of high treason. Sarauw had passed on German military information to France.

'Oh, what a rude young man', said His Highness, laughing. The story amused me too despite its discourteous intention.

During the meal Princess Bismarck spoke little, and afterwards she rummaged around or else went to sleep. That suited me very well, because I had thus one and a half hours alone with His Highness and was able to put forward several things I wanted to, and in particular a few points in favour of the hard-pressed Gossler.

But apart from this I had, unfortunately, further occasion to note that he is not the man he used to be. He is weaker, and, I am tempted to say, more commonplace.

The Kaiser, old as he is, still sometimes cracks his little joke.

The other day at the court ball the Italian Ambassador, whom he has known for more than thirty years now, was expressing to him his pleasure that the Reichstag, after rejecting the steam tender the first time, had at length approved it. 'Oh, yes', said His Maj., 'the Reichstag suffers from intermittent fever—now hot, now cold.'

22 February 1886

Copy of a pencilled letter from Hatzfeldt.[1]

London, 19 *February*, 11 *o'clock*

That's all very fine, but don't forget that this wretched situation continues. The man (Rosebery) is like india-rubber. If you seize hold of it, it gives; if you let go for a moment (and I can't sleep with him) it returns to its original shape.

His standpoint is: 'If it is *inevitable* we will do it (blockade); but I should prefer if it were not *necessary*.' Hence all this vacillation. Etc. etc.

Why in heaven's name am I left without news from Vienna and Rome in such circumstances? If I could say to-day that there is agreement in both quarters, I could behave quite differently. Instead of which Rosebery was able to confront me with a telegram from Rome according to which Robilant has certainly said the most foolish things.

Why did I not receive a telegram announcing the arrival of our ship?

Please see that I get some *facts* by telegram. That is the only way I can do my work, and find a pretext for constantly calling on him; even that is not easy here. He is playing the harried, over-worked man, and I must have *information*, so that I can see him every day. And that is the only way of keeping hold of him.

Haven't our people advocated this matter in Vienna and Rome?

---

[1] The original of Hatzfeldt's letter was not found among Holstein's papers.

There must be an *answer*! Why don't I get it? I find this completely incomprehensible and most inconvenient.

Etc. etc.

So much for Hatzfeldt. I have copied out this fragment to give a picture of his situation. Of all our diplomats, he is the one most often under fire, but Herbert purposely leaves him without information. I am convinced that Herbert (in opposition to his father) only wants a war between Greece and Turkey to prevent Hatzfeldt from registering a further success in the cause of peace, as he did in 1880.

All kinds of strange things are happening. Some time ago a few English fishermen, who were drunk, committed acts of violence against German fishermen in the North Sea (*Dietrich* and *Anna*). The British Government stated it would punish those responsible if we would take part in a conference of North Sea Powers with the intention of considering the restriction of the sale of spirits on the open sea. (Cooper Conference.[1]) We agreed. The English punished the men involved and then required us to attend the Conference. Bismarck, who is reluctant to restrict trade in spirits in any way, has declined *four times* already. The English are now threatening to print in the Blue Book the original note containing our promise alongside the subsequent refusals. Herbert replied to this threat to-day or yesterday by stating that the note containing our promise was signed by Hatzfeldt. If it were published we should repudiate it and state that he had acted without instructions! (And yet there are in the files two sets of the Chancellor's written orders giving Hatzfeldt these instructions.) The English, Herbert went on, must consider whether they would like Hatzfeldt's position to be made untenable so soon after his arrival in England.

The English are now willing to alter the document in question from 'we shall then be glad to attend the Conference' to 'we shall then be glad to consider attending a Conference'.[2]

Comment is hardly necessary.

23 *June* 1886

Dear Ize,

The enclosed packet[3] may interest you in parts and show

[1] 'Cooper' was the English expression for ships which sold spirits on the high seas. The *Dietrich* and the *Anna Helene* were regarded as 'coopers' by the English.

[2] An international conference which the Germans attended took place at The Hague from 10 to 26 June 1886, to remedy the abuses resulting from the sale of spirits in the North Sea. (*Accounts and Papers*, 1888, xcviii, C. 5263.)

[3] A collection of letters to Holstein. Not printed.

you that business is flourishing as usual. There would also be enough material to write up if I were not so tired of constantly criticizing. I have lost my former confidence in the supreme direction of our policy. Father and son are not at one. The father said to Berchem six weeks ago: 'If Russia and Austria come to blows, we shall have to support Austria; we can't let her be crushed.' The son, on the other hand, said to me three weeks ago: 'We can do business with Russia, but not with Austria. We will help Russia smash Austria.' And there is no denying that the son, with his almost morbid vehemence, is gaining a greater hold over his father every year, simply because the old man grows daily more indifferent to his work. Vanity and self-seeking are what interest him mainly. Even so, there would be a crash if he went. Our loss would not lie in the things he really does but the things the outside world still imagines he does. But this prestige of ours, both diplomatic and military, has feet of clay. If only Waldersee were replaced by a more competent person! However, I do not think we shall have international complications this summer.

27 *June* 1886

Rantzau, who dislikes Berlin now because he was not made Under State Secretary,[1] is asking for the well-paid post in Munich, which is completely unsuitable for an arrogant personality like his. All the same, old Werthern is to be done in to make room.

2 *July* 1886

The question came up recently for discussion whether Prince Luitpold[2] should visit the Kaiser at Ems, and further, whether the Kaiser, on his way to Gastein, ought to appear in Munich or be greeted by Prince Luitpold at some other Bavarian railway station.

Lerchenfeld supported the particularist case: Prince Luitpold not to go to Ems; the Kaiser to be received at Kempten or Rosenheim, not Munich.

Berchem, who is honest but under Lerchenfeld's influence, sent a report in this sense to Bülow[3] for the Kaiser.

Bülow replied that His Maj. wished Werthern to be requested to report (a thing which should have been done beforehand) on

[1] On 1 May 1886 Herbert von Bismarck was made State Secretary in the Foreign Ministry. The new Under State Secretary was Count Berchem.

[2] Luitpold, Prince of Bavaria. Prince Regent, 1886–1912. Ludwig II, King of Bavaria, had died on 13 June 1886.

[3] Otto von Bülow. Minister in Berne, 1882–92; frequently Foreign Ministry representative in the Kaiser's retinue.

the suitability of the one or the other project with regard to Bavarian popular feeling.

Werthern reported that Prince Luitpold had intended to visit the Kaiser at Ems, but Lerchenfeld had dissuaded him (!) because it would fatigue the Kaiser. The only suitable place to greet the Kaiser in Bavaria was Munich; not the station, but the town Palace, so that the entire populace could see the Kaiser.

Berchem submitted Werthern's dispatch to the Chancellor with a memorandum stating that Werthern's dispatch was hardly suitable for submitting to the Kaiser. The views put forward in it were unsound and in addition it contained an accusation of Lerchenfeld. He asked whether Werthern should be requested to send in another dispatch with more orthodox views.

His Highness, whose sole concern now is to replace Werthern by Rantzau as soon as possible, glossed Werthern's dispatch most unfavourably and followed Berchem's suggestion of requesting him to send in a fresh dispatch along indicated lines to be submitted to His Maj.

Quite something. However, since I am fortunately not the responsible official I shall not interfere. But in a *tête-à-tête* with Berchem, whom I rather like, I warned him not to draw the bow too tight. [...]

10 *July* 1886

The Prince Regent of Bavaria had told Werthern: 'During the long time you have been here you have earned general confidence; I hope, therefore, that your Government will continue to leave you here. Please report this.'

So Werthern did report. The Chancellor replied saying he was glad that His Majesty's representative had earned the Prince Regent's confidence. No change of representative was contemplated by us.

The Kaiser was not shown this laudatory dispatch. The Chancellor said in private: 'I've never seen this clumsy manoeuvring aspect of Werthern before. But what can I do about it? I must say something courteous in reply.'

This attempt to supplant Werthern by Rantzau is one of the most despicable and arbitrary acts I have ever seen. So this mole-like activity will go on. The sinister thing about it is that it endangers the existence of the loyal Lutz[1] Cabinet. Lutz's enemies, headed by Lerchenfeld and Berchem, are now whispering in the right quarter that Werthern will never be got rid of

_____
[1] Johann, Baron von Lutz. Bavarian Minister-President, 1880–90.

while Lutz remains Minister. I am very doubtful how old Bismarck will behave when faced with a choice between Lutz and Rantzau. I prefer to hope that Herbert, with whom I have spoken very freely on the subject, possesses sufficient objectivity to realize how harmful Rantzau would be in Munich with his arrogant, touchy, vindictive character. It would surely be better to create a vacancy at Brussels where he can do no harm.

22 July 1886

There has been much ill-feeling about the Prince of Bulgaria during the past few weeks. First, the Rumanian Ministers claimed that during his recent stay in Bucharest the Prince stated that he must launch an immediate attack on Macedonia; he wished to shake off the tutelage of the Great Powers; and finally, his action was secretly approved in Berlin. This last statement was the worst.[1]

Secondly, the Prince of Bulgaria advanced a claim to be made a German Lieutenant-General now, on the grounds of seniority. The Kaiser and the Chancellor were opposed to it, because it would be a slap in the face for Russia. The Crown Prince's court supported the idea, of course. There is in fact no necessity whatever to promote the Prince; foreign Princes are given a rank corresponding to their status at home, and then are not promoted any further.

The simultaneous occurrence of both grounds for complaint (Bucharest conversations and promotion) was unfortunate. While Bismarck, through little Saldern, demanded from the Prince of Bulgaria an explanation of those statements, particularly the one concerning alleged German support, the Crown Prince and the Prince of Bulgaria complained that the latter was not promoted.[2] Newspaper articles appeared stating that, to please Russia, the

[1] Prince Alexander visited Bucharest at the beginning of June. The information about his conversations originated with Bratianu and Sturdza and reached the Foreign Ministry in dispatches from Bucharest and Constantinople. According to them, Prince Alexander had stated in Bucharest that 'Prince Bismarck knew and approved of his plans and would help him with them. He did nothing without contact with Berlin.' In a dispatch of 5 July Saldern, in Sofia, was instructed 'to ask Prince Alexander cautiously but unequivocally how these falsehoods could have arisen'. On 12 July Saldern telegraphed to say Prince Alexander had told him that the news reaching Berlin of his conversations in Bucharest was untrue. As early as 3 July Prince Alexander had dictated a memorandum to Saldern covering these talks. This contained no mention of German support. (From the Foreign Ministry files.) See *Aufzeichnungen und Erinnerungen aus dem Leben des Botschafters Joseph Maria von Radowitz*, edited by Hajo Holborn (Berlin and Leipzig, 1925), vol. II, p. 264; Corti, *Alexander von Battenberg*, pp. 296-7.

[2] In a dispatch of 4 July, Saldern communicated the following dictated statement from Prince Alexander: 'He said he had learnt he was to be passed over in the matter of promotion; he could not help expressing his bitter disappointment at the fact that despite all his efforts he had not yet succeeded in being treated by the German Government as anything but an unfeeling *objet de compensation*, and it was infinitely hard for him always to be given stones instead of bread by the land of his birth.' (From the Foreign Ministry files.)

Prince of Bulgaria would soon be struck off the Prussian army list altogether; such servility was deplorable. The Chancellor, extremely annoyed at these articles, instructed Le Maistre to represent to Prince Alexander of Hesse in Darmstadt—where His Highness thought these publications originated—that this behaviour prejudiced the Bulgarian cause.

Prince Alexander and the Grand-Duke, who had also been involved in the affair, replied in writing, the former calmly and with dignity, the latter sharply, almost impertinently.[1] The idea was expressed in both letters that too great submissiveness to Russia was in fact not approved by the German people. The Crown Princess had received letters similar in content and instructed Radolinski to send them to the Chancellor.[2] The Chancellor replied to Rado. with the venomous letter I sent you yesterday.[3] However—all this took effect.

Three days ago Shuvalov had made all kinds of shameless requests, one of which was that the *Norddeutsche* should print an article attacking the Prince of Bulgaria. Berchem had given an evasive reply and sent a report to the Chancellor. The latter wrote in the margin: 'If we did this we should provide justification for the Darmstadt phrase that we were making German policy subservient, i.e. subordinate to Russia.'[4]

His Highness, as a commoner, still respects genuine Princes.

This memorandum written at the Crown Princess's request for the Queen of England, 6 Aug. '86.

If the gap caused by England's withdrawal from over-all world politics remains unfilled, Austria will be well advised to reach agreement with Russia on the Black Sea question.

Such an agreement, though difficult, is nevertheless possible even if Russian troops occupy Bulgaria. The danger to Austria from this kind of action on the part of Russia is that it makes Bosnia and Herzegovina difficult to hold in check.

[1] The Foreign Ministry files contain only a communication by the Grand-Duke of Hesse to the Hessian Minister of State, Finger, dated 5 July, which Le Maistre passed on to Berlin. The communication states *inter alia*: 'I understand the annoyance felt in Berlin at being accused of taking a step which insults an officer's military honour through servility to or fear of Russia. But I cannot think that there was the slightest belief that Prince Alexander or his father had anything to do with spreading the rumour.'

[2] The Foreign Ministry files contain the copy of a letter from the Grand-Duke of Hesse to the Crown Princess, dated 30 June, in which he enclosed a note written to him on 28 June by Prince Alexander of Hesse; both letters sharply criticized the attitude which the Imperial Government had adopted to Prince Alexander of Bulgaria through undue consideration for Russia. The documents were sent to the Foreign Ministry by Rottenburg on Bismarck's instructions.

[3] Bismarck's letter to Radolinski of 18 July 1886 (*Correspondence*).

[4] The interview between Count Berchem and Ambassador Shuvalov took place on 20 July. (From the Foreign Ministry files.)

Agreement with Russia is *easy*, provided Russia simply advanced from Batum towards the northern entrance of the Bosphorus. The Black Sea would then become a Russian Sea, and Russia would exercise hegemony over all the coastal regions, including the remnants of the Turkish Empire. In Bulgaria the Pan-Slav agitation would then do the rest without Russian troops.

Russian hegemony would thus be felt even in India; the Sultan, as Caliph, would bring his influence to bear on the Indian Mohammedans to support the Russian agitation.

The conflict between England and Russia can be postponed by an English retreat, but it cannot be avoided. After each retreat England's position becomes weaker because more isolated.

An Anglo-Russian agreement whereby Turkey and the Slav Balkan countries together with the Black Sea were left to Russia, which in turn promised not to attack the English in India—such an agreement would naturally suffer the fate of former agreements over Khiva.[1] When one sees with what gigantic strides the Russians have drawn closer to the frontiers of India in the last twelve years, and with what American haste they are laying the trans-Caspian railway, one cannot for a moment assume that the struggle for India can be postponed for another decade, whatever concessions England may make.

Russia would enter upon this struggle in the most favourable circumstances, England in the most unfavourable: Russia with the prestige of invincibility and backed by the Mohammedan influence of the Sultan, who would by that time have been mediatized. England completely isolated, disgraced in the eyes of the Asiatics because of her concessions and without allies in Europe; for no European parliament or people would sit by and allow its government to embark on a major war to confirm England in her possession of India.

England's position is totally different if she fights to defend the Turkish Empire. This winter Turkey assigned 300,000 troops to Europe, which the Austrian Military Attaché, Manéga, an outstanding specialist, called the best army Turkey has ever had. If England paid the Turks, 500,000 men could easily be mustered. The superiority of the Turkish soldier over the Russian soldier was proved afresh in the last war in the Balkans. England's only difficulty will be to convince the Sultan that England is *really on*

---

[1] On 8 January 1873 Count Shuvalov had given Earl Granville assurances that the forthcoming Russian expedition against Khiva in the spring was not intented to annex Khiva or even to occupy it for a long time. He informed him of the Tsar's opinion that there were no problems in Central Asia likely to trouble the good understanding between Russia and England. (*Accounts and Papers*, LXXXV, C. 699, no. 3.) In the spring of 1873 the Russians captured Khiva and extorted far-reaching concessions from the Khan Muhammed Rahim. All the territories on the right bank of the Oxus were annexed by Russia and heavy war reparations imposed on the Khanate whereby the country was in fact reduced to a Russian dependency.

his side. He no longer has any faith in her and so prefers to reach agreement with Russia, no matter what the conditions, since he prefers amputation to death.

England with Turkey in her pay is superior to the Russians. For the Russians would have to use a good half of their army to man the Austrian frontiers, even if Austria did not enter the war at once.

In any case, Austria could hardly keep out of a Russo-Turkish conflict for long. For the moment the Russians and the Turks are at war, it is mathematically certain that the Prince of Montenegro[1] will also declare war; Bosnia and Herzegovina will join forces with him, thus leaving Austria with the choice either of ceding both provinces or of declaring war on Russia's ally. Before 1878 Austria's position was more secure, and that made it possible for her to stand back and watch the Russo-Turkish war.

To sum up: events in the Balkan peninsula may follow one of two patterns.

Either England drives the intimidated Sultan to act by taking action herself; Turkish action would bring in Montenegro, and this would in turn bring in Austria in her own defence.

Or else England gives up the idea of active intervention. The Sultan would then accede to *every* Russian demand. Austria, who has only subordinate political or rather trading interests in the Black Sea, would in particular be able to declare herself in accord with any Russo-Turkish agreement, if the Russians advance on the Bosphorus from the Asiatic side. The possibility of a duel between Russia and Austria is thus forestalled.

Germany stands firm and keeps watch on the Vosges. As long as the present relations with France continue, *no* German Government will be able to justify itself to the people if it disperses the forces of the Reich. In these circumstances Germany could not give *direct* expression to her good intentions towards England, but could at the most give proof of it by the influence she exerted over Austria's attitude at the crucial moment. This influence could take one of three forms: urging, restraint, or letting things take their own course. Letting matters take their own course would probably suffice to involve Austria with a Hungarian *avant-garde* in any Anglo-Turkish action.

8 *August* 1886

Conditions in Alsace-Lorraine are less satisfactory than they need be. Hohenlohe and Hofmann, instead of complementing each other, are alike in their aversion for stern measures.

The military men in the Imperial Provinces have gradually become uneasy at the conditions which have resulted from letting

[1] Nicholas I (Nikita). Prince of Montenegro, 1860–1910; King, 1910–18.

things drift. They are strongly urging the commanding General, Heuduck,[1] to make representations to higher authorities.

I learnt this from a Colonel of a regiment in the Imperial Provinces, and had his information checked and supplemented by an agent of the political police. I then sent Hohenlohe the enclosed *exposé* and advised him to tackle the affair vigorously and also to discuss one or two points with the Chancellor.

I enclose Hohenlohe's reply.[2] I shall now advise him to get in personal touch with the commanding General, and request him to communicate all complaints coming to his knowledge direct to Hohenlohe. This would take the sting out of the complaints. He must, in addition, request Hofmann not to cancel any expulsion order given by the local authorities without prior consultation with Hohenlohe.

[Enclosure]

Alsace-Lorraine is swarming with French officers both on the active and reserve list.

The former usually go about as commercial travellers. Their main rendezvous are: in Strasbourg, Hotel Pfeifer; in Colmar, Ville de Nancy; in Türkheim, Hotel Meyer; in Markolsheim, Hotel Miss; in Schlettstadt, Hotel Aigle et Mouton; in Zabern, Bœuf Noir; in Saarburg, Hotel Ackermann; in Saargemünd, Lion d'Or. None of these hotels so much as enter Frenchmen in their register, particularly suspicious types.

This absence of any check is, however, not the exception but the rule. It never occurs to the *maire* of a town or village to report French officers, or people who may be officers, to the police. On the contrary, both the local authorities and the populace give these travellers every possible aid and lie to the gendarme if he happens to make inquiries.

An immensely demoralizing effect is produced on the German authorities and encouragement given to French sympathizers by the sight of the State Secretary, Hofmann, cancelling three-quarters of the expulsion orders given by the district authorities. As a result, French officers in the Imperial Provinces carry on their activities openly, covered in glory, and with no danger of unpleasantness for themselves and their adherents. The most effective and most dangerous type of propaganda is put about by the firemen's organizations. These organizations cover every township, great or small, in the Imperial Provinces. [...]

[1] Wilhelm von Heuduck. Commander of the XV Army Corps in Alsace (Strasbourg).
[2] Hohenlohe replied on 6 August that he was acquainted with the officers' grounds of complaint and was taking steps to remedy the situation. 'I think that when the army realizes that we mean business, they will calm down. [...]'

One aim of the firemen's organization, which is under military leadership, is presumably to send men of military age to France the moment war breaks out, perhaps also to set fire to barracks at places left unguarded, and to destroy bridges and railway lines.

In order to stamp out this cancer, which continues to spread under the present regime as it did under Manteuffel's, and in order to remove the great danger it constitutes, energetic measures are needed over the next few years. 1. Expulsion of French reserve officers from the Imperial Provinces. 2. All *maires* in the villages and all hotel-keepers in the towns to be obliged to report to the gendarmerie immediately all foreigners, even those who are members of their family. This command to be made known by public posters, to ensure that everyone knows it and to increase the fear of denunciation. 3. Identity documents of all commercial travellers to be carefully examined, and perhaps only *German subjects* to be admitted to this calling.

The Alsace-Lorrainer is a prudent person. When he realizes he is up against the law and that the law is to be applied in earnest, his ardour will cool.

16 *August* 1886

Radolinski summoned me to Potsdam this morning by telegram 'to discuss an important matter'. This is what had happened.

In Gastein, presumably at Herbert's suggestion, the Kaiser, the Chancellor and Prince Wilhelm had agreed that the latter should go to Skierniewice in the middle of September to greet the Tsar. On the 10th a telegram arrived here from Gastein instructing us to announce Prince Wilhelm's coming via the Russian Embassy here.[1] On the 11th the Crown Prince heard of the affair *after it had been arranged* in a letter from Prince Wilhelm, who told him at the same time that on the Kaiser's decision he would be working in the Foreign Ministry next winter.

The Crown Prince, perceiving in this behaviour the endeavour to draw his son away from him and play him off against his father, wrote to the Chancellor that he thought *both* arrangements undesirable.[2]

The Chancellor replied by telegram that the Prince's coming had already been announced and that the arrangements could not now be altered. It was necessary for one of the royal family to go, and it would have been somewhat excessive to send the Crown Prince. No mention of working in the Foreign Ministry.[3]

[1] See *Grosse Politik*, vol. v, no. 981, p. 55.
[2] Letter of 12 August. (*Grosse Politik*, vol. v, no. 982, pp. 55–6.)
[3] Bismarck to the Foreign Ministry, 15 August. (*Grosse Politik*, vol. v, no. 983, p. 56.)

We sent for Radolinski yesterday and told him the telegram's contents so that he could break the news gently to the Crown Prince and Princess.

So when Rado in his turn sent for me quite early this morning, I feared a complication. This was so, and it had been brought about by Prince Wilhelm. The latter had sent the following telegram *en clair* to his Court Chamberlain, Liebenau, who had written to him to say how offended his parents felt at being passed over. 'As regards your observation on my failure to inform the New Palace of my plans for travelling to S[kierniewice], I asked His Majesty's permission twice—because I foresaw what would happen—but he required me on my word of honour not to say a word to **any** one. Make use of this fact.'

This communication and the thought of having been humiliated even in front of the telegraph officials finally made the pot boil over. The Crown Prince, in a fit of rage which weak characters sometimes display, declared he would now simply forbid his son's journey. The Crown Princess, though probably even more indignant, had the idea that the Crown Prince should put himself at the Chancellor's disposal for this journey. Rado met me at the station with a very long face, and told me that this time there was no prospect of making the Crown Prince change his mind. He had called in my help to find some formula for the Crown Prince's telegram that would cause the least possible offence. We drove to the Bavarian cottage in the Wildpark and there drew up more or less the following telegram:

'In view of the state of health of my son, who was recently prevented on his physician's advice from attending the celebrations here in memory of Frederick the Great, I regard the more exacting and nerve-racking journey to Skierniewice as dangerous, and it is therefore my wish at all events that it shall not take place. However, to comply with your intentions as far as possible, I am myself prepared to undertake this journey, because in addition I think it a good thing to make my own contribution towards emphasizing our wish of maintaining correct relations with Russia. I request you therefore to prepare His Majesty and the Russian Government for the change of plan made necessary by my son's health. I shall be glad to see you on your way through Berlin so as to obtain information on political matters.'

We both thought we could not sugar the pill more than this, so I returned to Berlin. By six the messenger from Potsdam was here with the telegram, which was to be ciphered in the Ministry.

The Crown Prince had accepted our entire draft, except for the addition of 'at all events'.[1]

We must now wait and see what His Highness replies.[2] Rado is gloomy because he regards a serious quarrel as inevitable if the Chancellor fails to comply with the Crown Prince's wish, and shelters behind the Kaiser. I think everything depends on whether Herbert is still in Gastein or already in Lugano. The former possibility would be unfortunate.

In any case it is not pleasant to see the *modus vivendi* which one has so long devoted all one's efforts to restoring being endangered by such outbreaks of puerile megalomania.

But it did not surprise me personally, since I have said I expected something of the sort would happen. *Et nous en verrons encore bien d'autres*, particularly if the Kaiser, now an unresisting tool and wanting to be left in peace, lives a long time.

Herbert is one of the Furies. He flatters his old father's pride and vanity, but occasionally intimidates him by his violence, whichever is required.

17 *August* 1886

A telegram arrived this morning from the Chancellor stating that His Maj. should be recommended to substitute the Crown Prince for Prince Wilhelm.[3]

Six hours later a second very secret telegram from the Chancellor to His Majesty:

On account of Prince Wilhelm's state of health the Crown Prince has expressed the wish that he should travel to Poland himself instead of his son. The *formal* courtesy shown will thus be greater, but on the other hand there is the danger that Tsar Alexander and the Crown Prince may quarrel over the Prince of Battenberg, whom the former hates and the latter loves. The Chancellor therefore requests H.M. not to reach a decision before having a personal interview with the Chancellor, who wishes first to discuss the matter with M. Giers.[4]

Berchem went to Babelsberg at once and conferred with H.M. on the matter.

The Kaiser spoke with delight of Prince Wilhelm, but harshly and unfavourably of the Crown Prince.

Prince Wilhelm, he said, had an excellent influence on Tsar

---

[1] The draft of the telegram prepared by the Crown Prince, which contains one or two other insignificant alterations from the text given here, is in the Foreign Ministry files.

[2] Bismarck's reply to the Crown Prince of 17 August is printed in the *Correspondence*.

[3] The telegram instructed Count Berchem to inform the Kaiser of the Crown Prince's wishes, and to support them.　　　　[4] See *Grosse Politik*, vol. v, no. 984, p. 57.

Alexander, whom he had already influenced in our favour during his earlier Russian trip.[1] Tsar Alexander, who had formerly spoken only of a Two Emperors' Alliance, was not favourably disposed to the Three Emperors' Alliance until after Prince Wilhelm's visit, and so forth.[2] (While Berchem told me this I felt I was listening to Herbert's own words.) The Crown Prince, H.M. had continued, mentioned Prince Wilhelm's health, but it had not yet been proved to him, the Kaiser, that his health was really so delicate. The Kaiser said he required first a *doctor's certificate* (!). He would in any case put off his decision until he had spoken to the Chancellor.

The Crown Prince, said H.M. in a very harsh tone, with his liberalizing tendencies (which had admittedly somewhat diminished of late) was not suitable society for Tsar Alexander. Prince Wilhelm had also actually complained to his grandfather about his father, because the latter constantly felt offended.

To sum up: The Chancellor, influenced either by Herbert or Rottenburg, does not want the Crown Prince to go to Russia, but in order to prevent it he is now sheltering behind the Kaiser. We shall probably hear all kinds of unpleasant things in the next few weeks, for this business will cause a good deal of ill-feeling.

When the Kaiserin arrived in Potsdam recently, Perponcher[3] sent a verbal message by court courier that the Kaiserin was exhausted and did not wish to be met at the station. The Crown Princess was therefore not to trouble; the Crown Prince could go if he wished.

18 *August* 1886

Courcel, during one of his customary frank conversations, said recently: 'You see, if we had the Rhine frontier, our *natural* frontier, both our peoples would live in harmony. But for us it is a question of security. *Nous ne faisons plus d'enfants et nous n'avons pas de frontière, comment voulez-vous que nous vivions? Au lieu de frontière nous avons construit un tas de bicoques, qui nous seront peut-être plus nuisibles qu'utiles à la prochaine guerre—que Dieu écarte'*, he added. I disputed nothing, but regarded the remark as an ominous sign. When I expressed to him my sincere regret at his departure,[4] he said: '*Je serai peut-être plus utile plus tard.*' In

---

[1] In May 1884. See p. 153, note 3.   [2] See *Grosse Politik*, vol. v, p. 57, note *.

[3] Friedrich, Count von Perponcher-Sedlnitzky. Prussian General; Court Chamberlain to Wilhelm I.

[4] Courcel had resigned as Ambassador to Germany, and was recalled on 24 August 1886. On 9 September Jules Herbette, Director in the French Foreign Ministry, was appointed in his place.

conjunction with what he had said earlier, it sounded almost as if he meant: 'As a mediator after the war.'

Our best safeguard now lies in the hatred and contempt felt by the Tsar for the French Republic.

19 *August* 1886

Extract from a letter from Herbert to Berchem, dated Gastein, the 16th:

I urgently request you to represent to His Imp. Highness that this kind of work (i.e. letter to H.I.H. on his inquiry about the Polish journey) does *great* harm to my father during this strenuous cure, and also to prevail on His Highness to refrain from any further correspondence which is after all completely unnecessary. Up to three days ago my father was quite cheerful and was also sleeping well. Then came the letter written by the Crown Prince, which caused a lot of mental exertion, depression etc. and since that day my father has been exhausted, over-excited and red in the face, and has been sleeping less well, in fact last night he slept deplorably. It is indeed thoroughly irresponsible to harass my father in this way at his age and in his state of health.

Then follows a remark that the whole affair doubtless originated in England, where they do not trust Prince Wilhelm.

The tone of the letter is indicative. What it really means is: 'After the Crown Prince's letter arrived I had untold difficulty in holding my father to his intentions; he almost did what the Crown Prince demanded, instead of doing what I think right.'

It will be quite interesting psychologically to see what happens next.

14 *September* 1886

Caprivi and Le Maistre, who have been talking to the Chancellor, both tell me he is in a state of almost morbid irritation about Battenberg, whom he already imagines as Governor of Alsace-Lorraine, and then as Chancellor, i.e. under the coming reign.

In his fear and rage Bismarck resorts to quite preposterous methods. The anti-Polish agitation which he is organizing against Battenberg in the inspired Press is only doing the Chancellor harm amongst the people, even those who are otherwise loyal.

The foreign policy we are now pursuing is thoroughly wretched and decrepit. Bismarck worries about everything and wants to be left in peace; his son on the other hand, constantly impelled by personal motives and experiences, would like to join with Russia and Prince Wilhelm in pursuing a policy directed against Austria and the Crown Prince, and would like to sacrifice Austria completely to Russian interests. In particular he would like to prevent Austria from going to war if England and Turkey declared war on Russia. If Austria did this, if she stood by and did not take part in the war between England and Russia—which is, moreover, still a long way off—she would be lost beyond hope.

All Hatzfeldt's letters[1] are concerned with the fact that the English, convinced that the three Emperors have already settled the Near Eastern question amongst themselves, dare not take action alone. It is therefore Austria's duty to give England privately to understand that this is not the case; of course, *if* England continues to do nothing, Austria *will* feel obliged to reach agreement with Russia, but she will gladly consider the possibility of co-operation with England if England will bestir herself. Tentative approaches between Vienna and London are taking place at this moment.[2] I told Tavera,[3] the Austrian Chargé d'Affaires (an old acquaintance from Copenhagen days), that I was not at all curious to learn how things were going. I could not very well suppress any information he gave me, but my Government would find itself in a false position *vis-à-vis* Russia if it had knowledge of negotiations for an anti-Russian alliance. It was better to allow us to remain impartial. Tavera did however beg to be allowed to consult me occasionally. I told him: 'I'd rather not if you can manage without.'[4]

I also wrote to Hatzfeldt telling him to report nothing, if possible, about the negotiations between Austria and England, for which he is also pressing.

The very interesting conversation with Salisbury in the letter I enclose to-day[5] is concerned with this topic. Hatzfeldt endeavoured to rid Salisbury of the suspicion that if England declared war she would have all *three* Imperial Powers against her.

The policy I am pursuing together with Hatzfeldt is the Chancellor's policy. Only two months ago he wrote: 'Austria can *support* England but never act *instead* of her.' But Herbert would like to prevent Austria even from supporting England. That is why we must quietly carry out the father's intentions without his or his son's knowledge. Otherwise Herbert will tell the Russians everything.

[1] See *Correspondence*.   [2] Compare *Grosse Politik*, vol. IV, chapter xxv.
[3] Schmit, Ritter von Tavera. Austro-Hungarian Counsellor of Embassy in Berlin, 1885–6
[4] On Holstein's relations with Austrian diplomats during this period see Helmut Krausnick, *Holsteins Geheimpolitik in der Ära Bismarck 1886–1890* (Hamburg, 1942).
[5] Letter of [12 September 1886] (*Correspondence*).

Morier, the British Ambassador in St Petersburg, is working for an alliance between Russia, England and France. He would like Russia to guarantee India to the English, but in return hand over to the Russians the entire Balkan peninsula and also Austria, while France and Italy would take from Germany and Austria anything that suited them. A nice little plan, but things will doubtless turn out differently. Above all, the English, unless they are mad, cannot allow the Sultan, who as Caliph wields authority over 85 million Indian Mohammedans, to become a vassal of Russia, or else her rule in India will soon be over.

But Morier is as busy as a bee working for his idea, was hostile to Battenberg from the start and has done his utmost to harm him in St Petersburg. He has kept this fact out of his dispatches, of course. I had written to ask Hatzfeldt to have another word with Salisbury about Morier.

Malet, the Ambassador in Berlin, is on the right track. He says that although Germany herself will not attack Russia, she will not prevent anyone else, and so it was desirable that Salisbury should speak to Malet.

We must now wait and see.

Letters from Hatzfeldt.[1]

London, 14 *Sept.* 1886

Saw Salisbury and just have time to drop you a line before the post leaves. Cannot report before to-morrow's post, in any case wish to think over at leisure what I should say, and how.[2]

Result: he is still as willing as he was, but thinks he must wait until people here have been roused by facts. We are proving an appalling embarrassment to him, not because we are unwilling to co-operate, but *parce que nous donnons à chaque instant des coups d'épaule aux autres qui empêchent les faits qui pourraient échauffer ici de se produire.* You see? It is not help in itself that annoys him, but the fact that we thereby prevent what would help *him* here.

His difficulty is therefore purely *domestic*, not caused by a lack of courage. This is even less the case in that he has no doubt that energetic action here would bring the others to a standstill.

He is *waiting* for facts which will stir up people here. He would therefore have welcomed an invasion of Bulgaria. It is for that very reason that he deplores our *coups d'épaule* with which we have

---

[1] The originals of Hatzfeldt's letters were not found among Holstein's papers.

[2] In his dispatch of 15 September reporting this interview Count Hatzfeldt stated that Salisbury, in view of the domestic political situation in England, was adopting an attitude of wait-and-see, but did not give up the hope that the development of the situation would rouse popular opinion in England, and thereby enable him to adopt a diplomatic position opposed to Russia. Hatzfeldt added that he did not think there would be serious opposition to Russia from England so long as Salisbury felt himself isolated. (From the Foreign Ministry files.)

prevented Prince Alexander from punishing the guilty, because this would have precipitated a crisis and, forcing Russia to act, would have produced the necessary mood *here*.[1]

For the moment he is just waiting. Things will *not* go quite smoothly; difficulties will be raised because of the candidate,[2] but particularly because of the mood of Eastern Rumelia, as I foresaw. Salisbury now maintains that the Treaty of Berlin must be upheld. The protocol on Eastern Rumelia does *not* state, at least not clearly, that it passes to the successor, although no name is mentioned.[3]

All this is *manœuvring* to gain time, and will produce no serious results in itself. But he hopes that *other* things will happen in the meantime whose effect will be felt here, and also that Austria will change her mind by then.

White[4] is leaving for his new post in a few weeks' time.

More to-morrow.

14 Sept. '86

Just received your letter of yesterday morning. By now you will have received my letter of this evening which was written in a great hurry. I wish to add straight away something important which you may be able to turn to advantage. When Salisbury complained again to-day that nothing could be done with Austria, I said: 'If I were an Austrian, I should also feel great misgivings, first because you showed no energy, but also because I should not be at all sure, if I did co-operate, whether you might not subsequently leave me in the lurch and reach agreements alone. The latter consideration may carry great weight.'

Salisbury seemed very struck by this, said: 'Do you really think so?' and became obviously thoughtful. He then said: 'I thought you meant that what deterred them particularly was their conviction of our weakness.' I replied: 'No, I don't think that at all, because it would be inaccurate. You can still achieve results if you seriously want to. But in addition you still enjoy great prestige, and the extremely cautious behaviour in St Petersburg shows best the value they place on it there, and how highly you are rated despite your weakness hitherto.'

[1] After the revolt against Prince Alexander and his kidnapping by a group of pro-Russian officers on 21 August, a provisional government was formed in Sofia from the Russian party, led by the Metropolitan Clement of Tirnova, Zankov, and Major Gruev. In the counter-revolution of 24 August, Clement, Zankov, and Gruev were arrested. On 1 September the Russian Chargé d' Affaires in Berlin, Count Muraviev, expressed the hope of his Government that there should be no acts of violence in Bulgaria and that the Powers would instruct their representatives in Sofia accordingly. In a telegram of the same date, Saldern was instructed in Sofia to prevent executions, since a peaceful solution of the crisis would otherwise be made difficult. (From the Foreign Ministry files.) Prince Alexander abdicated for good on 7 September 1886, and Bulgaria was left under a Regency led by Stefan Stambulov.

[2] For the throne of Bulgaria.   [3] See p. 278, note 3.

[4] Sir William White. British Ambassador in Constantinople, 1886–91.

Salisbury and I have agreed to talk to each other just like private individuals and not to make [official] use [of the conversations]. Bear this in mind when you make use of my information!

I also asked him to allow 'us' our freedom of action; he could rely on me.

We also reverted to Morier. Salisbury is obviously struck by his behaviour and said he would very much like to get at the truth. He had heard nothing and the dispatches were above reproach. I said that from all I had heard there could be no doubt, but he could of course *not* base himself on that, but must investigate for himself.[1]

Just one more point. It is clear that both in London and Vienna a subtle game is being played. Here they are intimidated by the various refusals. If it really is the fact, as you say, *qu'on ne demande pas mieux*, then [Vienna] must show some sort of willingness to co-operate, some inclination towards an exchange of views, or at the very least a willingness to open discussions if approaches were made from this end. It would be even better to know what Vienna would regard as capable of being discussed. A hint to Hengelmüller,[2] who is most eager for it, would suffice, but—and you can hint at this if necessary—he must go and see Salisbury, not Iddesleigh,[3] who is an idiot.

As a parting gift to Malet, who went to Balmoral yesterday, I gave him the idea that the re-election in Bulgaria was purely a matter of money.

As regards Egypt, I think the right tone to adopt to make an impression here would be for the *Köln. Ztg.* to say: once you have lost the Bosphorus you will inevitably lose Egypt also, because it will not be long before Russia and France jointly raise this question, and then, given the present state of affairs, you will not be able to do anything about it.

I was very struck by the controversy in the *Köln. Zeitung* with the Austrian newspapers about the value of the alliance. So we've already reached that stage! The impression this is bound to produce here is that the calculation whereby Austria must in the end make overtures to the English side was correct.

Just received your letter of Monday evening. It is just another *coup d'épaule*; weak.[4]

[1] Bülow had reported from St Petersburg on 21 August about Sir Robert Morier's sharply hostile attitude towards Prince Alexander of Bulgaria. This dispatch was communicated to the Embassies in Vienna and London on 1 September. (From the Foreign Ministry files.)

[2] Ladislaus, Baron von Hengelmüller von Hengervár. Austro-Hungarian Counsellor of Embassy in London.

[3] Sir Stafford Northcote, from 1885 Earl of Iddesleigh. British Foreign Secretary in the second Salisbury Cabinet, August 1886–January 1887.

[4] Note by Holstein: 'We had advised the Austrians to support a Russian demand regarding Bulgaria.'

In a detailed dispatch to Vienna dated 6 September, Bismarck had instructed Prince Reuss

Normann called on me to-day. After talking of official matters we naturally discussed the Crown Prince's court. N. defended the Crown Prince, but seemed deeply embittered against the Princess. The intention of influencing the husband without, or *against*, his wife was evident in all N. said. That was the handle once used by Seckendorff to get rid of Normann. That, incidentally, was not the worst thing Seck. ever did.

Norm. said that if Seck. were suddenly struck down by a flash of lightning, the Princess would exult from sheer relief; she felt bound to him either because of past incidents or letters. Herbert persists in his intention of training Prince Wilhelm in the Foreign Ministry this winter. After the Crown Prince's written declaration that he is flatly opposed to it, this overriding of a father's wishes is an unmistakable omen. The Crown Prince is simply passed over. I should think this proper if it concerned a vital political question. But for a triviality of this kind, when the only aim is to satisfy Herbert's vanity and love of power, such behaviour seems to me deplorable. As Bismarck's achievements diminish, so the pretensions of Bismarck's son increase.

Letters from Hatzfeldt.[1]

16 *Sept.* '86

Just received your letter of two mornings ago. This news about Montebello[2] seems to me *far more important* than *anything*

to make clear to Kálnoky that it was not in Austria's interests to create difficulties for Russia about Bulgaria, even in case of a Russian entry into Bulgaria. A Bismarck dispatch to Vienna of 13 September, only partially reproduced in the *Grosse Politik* (vol. v, no. 987, pp. 62–3), states: ' [...] Austria came very near to invading Serbia last autumn. Because of the constant threat there of upheavals of every kind, Austria may easily find herself very shortly obliged, by the outbreak of a revolution, actually to occupy this country against her will. In view of the fact that Austria may very soon find herself in a position in Serbia analogous to Russia's position in Bulgaria, and may experience the imperative necessity for occupying it, she should in my opinion come to some reciprocal arrangement with Russia about Bulgaria; if this does not happen, then one must assume that Russia would in such an eventuality react in exactly the same way as Austria would react to Russian influence in Bulgaria [...].' On 12 September the Russian Government suggested to Berlin that the three Imperial Courts should recognize the existing Bulgarian Government and that the representatives of the Imperial Powers should superintend the elections to the Bulgarian National Assembly. Bismarck passed on the suggestion to Vienna the same day, recommending acceptance. (From the Foreign Ministry files.)

[1] The originals of Hatzfeldt's letters were not found among Holstein's papers.

[2] Adrien, Count Montebello. French Ambassador in Constantinople, 1886–91.

Note by Holstein: 'France declares her readiness to defend Turkey against England in Mediterranean questions, if necessary in co-operation with Russia, should the Sultan call on the English to evacuate Egypt.'

Radowitz had reported this information from Constantinople on 6 and 11 September. Bismarck ordered both dispatches to be communicated to London. The dispatches sent to London were dated 10 and 17 September. (From the Foreign Ministry files.)

that has happened hitherto and gives *us* food for thought in particular.

Compare with Giers' letter to the Russian representative here which I reported yesterday, with its obvious resentment against England.[1] If things become difficult here this resentment may lead to Russia's putting into effect Montebello's mention of an *accord*—perhaps directed only against England at first—but once things have reached that stage we shall *have* to go along through thick and thin, even to the detriment of Austria, otherwise we shall have to risk what we have hitherto avoided—war. Could we count on England *then*?

It all looks very serious, if this is the real situation.

But I still think, even at this late hour, that a really serious word from England would bring things to a standstill—and I still think that things will happen, unless we again prevent them, which will make the thick blood of the English boil.

I will see what use I can make of your information, although it can be done only with the greatest caution. I am now in a difficult position *vis-à-vis* Rustem,[2] because although it certainly does not correspond to his wishes, he will say to me: 'What are we to do? You have proclaimed loudly in all the newspapers that you do not even care what happens to Constantinople, you have dropped us and even intimidated us here to such an extent that we dare not speak!' But I will try to use my influence as far as possible.

Why am I not officially informed of what you have told me to-day, so *that I can make use of it*? Surely we do not have to show France any consideration, and it can do nothing but good if people here are enlightened. I find this incomprehensible.[3]

Hengelmüller has heard *nothing* from Vienna, as he told me before—so there is apparently no question yet of any approach.[4]

I am lunching with Randolph Churchill[5] to-morrow and shall see, if possible, how he regards the situation.

19 *Sept.*

Had a talk with Rand. Churchill[6] after luncheon which confirmed what I already knew of his attitude and views. He is *decidedly* in favour of agreement with Russia which he does not consider difficult, since the English can enter into any agreement provided

---

[1] In a dispatch of 15 September Hatzfeldt reported that the Russian Ambassador in London had received a personal letter from Giers. 'The letter says, so the Ambassador informs me in confidence, that he will soon be receiving news [of the situation in Bulgaria]. The position is still so confused that the Russian Government itself has to wait for news. Then follows the comment: "*les Anglais sont très mauvais pour nous*", from which the Ambassador deduces a certain resentment against England.' (From the Foreign Ministry files.)

[2] Rustem Pasha. Turkish Ambassador in London, 1885–95.

[3] Note by Holstein: 'I do not.'   [4] Note by Holstein: 'There is.'

[5] Lord Randolph Churchill. Chancellor of the Exchequer in the second Salisbury Cabinet, August–December 1886.

[6] See *Grosse Politik*, vol. IV, no. 865, pp. 269–71.

India is secured (!). The only weak point in his argument was Egypt. He refuses to believe that anyone—Russia or France or anyone else—will try to bring this up. But if they did, then England would have to go to war without hesitation.

3 October 1886[1]

At the moment the Chancellor is completely obsessed with fear of Battenberg. He sees him already as a candidate for the Chancellorship. A dictated document came in yesterday, *thirty* pages long, a personal report to the Kaiser,[2] in which Battenberg is branded as a coward and goodness knows what else. The Chancellor intends to send the report to the Crown Prince afterwards and then to publish it. I have advised Herbert urgently not to take these two steps, and he sees I am right. Even the newspaper articles which have already been published harm the Chancellor far more than Battenberg. The unfortunate thing is that the Chancellor lacks the *slightest* trace of magnanimity. That is why he does not understand that attacking a man when he is down makes a bad impression on the nation and particularly on decent people.

We have another similar case with regard to Spain. The Spaniards have just extended a trade agreement which assures us of an annual export to Spain of over 100 million marks. The Spanish Government had gone to immense trouble over this, even endangering its political existence. Now, a few days later, the Spaniards approach us with the request that we support in Paris their proposal for the expulsion of Zorilla from France.[3] Herbert refuses their Minister's request, adding: 'Do not imagine we shall ever forget the Carolines affair.'[4] This reply is not only unmagnanimous, it is also unwise. Of course we could not act in

---

[1] Holstein mistakenly dated this entry 3 September.   [2] See Appendix II, pp. 388–93.

[3] Manuel Ruiz Zorilla. Spanish politician; President of the Cortes, 1870; Minister-President, 1871, 1872; he left Spain when King Amadeo I abdicated, February 1873; later he supported the Republic, opposed the restoration of the monarchy and conducted active republican propaganda from Paris.

The Spanish proposal was reported from Madrid by Tattenbach in a dispatch of 24 September 1886. Bismarck commented as follows on a telegram of 26 September stating that the Spanish Minister was returning to Berlin from Baden-Baden to seek Bismarck's advice on the question of Zorilla's expulsion: 'How kind! After the Carolines business we shall not put ourselves out for Spanish interests.' (From the Foreign Ministry files.)

[4] In Count Bismarck's memorandum on his interview with Benomar on 29 September there is no mention of the Carolines affair. Nor was there a direct refusal of the Spanish request. It appears from the Foreign Ministry files that Bismarck tried to handle the incident in dilatory fashion. Only the advantage which might possibly result from joint action by the three Imperial Powers and the consequent consolidation of their alliance induced Bismarck, in the event of agreement between Austria, Russia and Germany, to instruct the Ambassador in Paris to support a Spanish move in Paris, and thus to risk alienating or even overthrowing Freycinet. On 16 October Münster telegraphed from Paris that the representatives of the Imperial Powers had supported the Spanish move. The request was dropped by Spain after its rejection by Freycinet.

isolation, but only in concert with the two other Imperial Powers. The Tsar of Russia, because of his abhorrence of republicanism, and Austria as a relative of Spain,[1] would have co-operated immediately. Then if Freycinet, who is completely under the thumb of the Radicals, refused this expulsion after all, knowing that war would not be waged on that account, the tension between Russia and France, which is vitally important to us, would thereby have been decidedly stiffened.

But no, the satisfaction of hitting the Spaniards over the head was greater than political interests.

I will have another try to-day to put in a word for good sense, but am doubtful of success.

The Crown Princess, on Radolinski's sensible advice, is striving to keep in touch with the Chancellor by all kinds of trifling correspondence on marriage plans.[2] It will not do her much good. Bismarck's plan is to repress the next Kaiser with Prince Wilhelm's help. Whether this will succeed, I doubt. Herbert thinks his father's prestige, like the Kaiser's, will grow with advancing age. But the case is different. What people admire in the Kaiser is his truly noble character. That is hardly the case with Bismarck; but rather one relies on his acumen which nearly always used to hit on the right solution. But now even well-meaning people are beginning to have their doubts about him. He is in fact rapidly deteriorating.

I must add to my earlier remarks that when Herbert replied to the Spanish Minister he was acting on his father's instructions. The old man had said it was all the same to us whether Spain and even Italy became republics!

It really does not seem possible that he can say such things. One of his greatest political achievements was that he hampered France's two attempts at becoming a monarchy; as a result France has remained an isolated republic to this very day. But if Spain and Italy also become republics, the three of them would form a dangerous, solid bloc. He overlooks all this because of his grudge about the Carolines.

The period of greatness is over, as I have long realized. The decline began with Schweninger's cure. But for Schweninger he might perhaps be dead, but he would have died great. Schweninger marks the dividing-line between hyper-tension and ossification. His breadth of vision and his energy are gone, he is an unperceptive, unfeeling, timid old man, without memory, easily

---

[1] Maria Cristina, Regent of Spain, was the daughter of Archduke Karl Ferdinand of Austria.   [2] See *Correspondence*.

swayed; all he has left is a considerable dialectical skill in putting forward his often wrong-headed, constantly shifting views.

Caprivi said yesterday: 'The Russians and the French are moving forward and continuing to develop. But we are wearing blinkers.'

Quite true. In politics too Bismarck is still playing the same old cards, Russia and Austria. He finds the new cards, Italy, Spain and the Balkan States, inconvenient and unpleasant. He pushes them away. That shows he is an old man.

5 *October* 1886

Dear Radolinski thinks that Herbert Bism. could carve out a good position for himself with the Crown Prince and Princess if he persuaded his father to bring the Kaiser to agree to the marriage of Battenberg and Princess Victoria.[1]

I wrote and told Rado not to meddle with *that*.[2]

Bismarck *père* becomes more furious with Battenberg every day. He is also getting more and more annoyed with the Austrians, presumably because Herbert's letters are stirring him up. According to a letter from Rantzau to Herbert yesterday, His Highness wants to make the Austrians regret their alliance with us.[3] I am not sure what is meant by that, but I expect very little good will come of our present policy. We make every possible diplomatic concession to the Russians, and then the Chancellor dictates an article for the *Norddeutsche* inviting the English to look around for allies; they would not look in vain. No wonder the Russian Press has treated us since then with the utmost insolence and contempt, maintaining that our friendship with Russia springs merely from fear. Yesterday when Herbert was saying that Prince Wilhelm was to work in the Foreign Ministry during the winter, I told him that in my opinion he, Herbert, would derive more harm than good from the arrangement. I said his influence on Prince Wilhelm was already as great as it could ever be. If the Prince worked here against the declared wishes of his father (the Crown Prince),[4] then not only the latter but the general public too would side against Herbert. They would accuse him of lust for power.

H. went red in the face and said: 'I'm not doing anything; I

---

[1] See Radolinski's letters to Holstein of 2 and 4 October (*Correspondence*).

[2] Letter of 4 October. See also extract from Holstein's letter of 5 October, footnote to Radolinski's letter of 4 October (*Correspondence*).

[3] This letter was not found in the Foreign Ministry files, but see *Grosse Politik*, vol. v, no. 1014, p. 136.

[4] See the Crown Prince's letter to Bismarck of 28 September (Bismarck, *Die gesammelten Werke*, vol. xv, pp. 455–6).

don't want anything. Prince Wilhelm made the arrangement with his grandfather and then informed my father.'

That is nonsense. Without prompting from Herbert the Prince would never have thought of it. The whole affair was settled at Gastein where they were all together.

The way the Crown Prince is being treated at the moment is bound to make him look ridiculous in the eyes of the world, and perhaps is intended to. Some degree of influence, even a strong influence, has a salutary effect on a weak nature like his; but external appearances must be preserved. Things cannot go on long like this.

2 *November* 1886

Berchem is back from leave; positively fawning. He finds his status diminished in various respects. Has only himself to blame.

Russia and France are drawing closer together. That is the result of our policy of finessing. No one trusts us.

I have been working hard recently and, as I can see, not without success, to ensure that at least no offence is given to Italy, who would very much like to ally herself with Germany and Austria.[1] First I won over Herbert and then he won over his father to the idea.

Germany, Austria and Italy form a sizeable bloc which probably weighs as much as Russia and France put together. The policy of the two Bismarcks is, or was until recently, a most wretched one: they *refuse* to see that Russia is massing her strength against us, or rather mainly against Austria. Can we let Austria be smashed? No. Then we must fight it out with Russia and look around for allies, great and small. Instead the Chancellor went on attempting to caress Russia—rather like stroking a mad dog that bites you anyhow.

The Chancellor is just beginning to change his mind. Bleichröder, who was in Varzin last week, told me: 'I'm very surprised. Prince Bismarck has suddenly lost faith in the permanence of our good relations with Russia.'

I am glad that at least we have a competent Military Attaché in Paris to replace Villaume.[2] Hüne has many defects of character, but he is clear-sighted and level headed.

Münster and Redern are both suffering from softening of the brain. Redern maintains that the French are not contemplating a

---

[1] See *Grosse Politik*, vol. IV, chapter XXIV.
[2] Karl von Villaume. Prussian Lieutenant-Colonel; Military Attaché in Paris, 1882–6, in St Petersburg, 1887–93.

revanche, and in addition he would like to ally Germany with France against England.

People here are laying modest bets on how many years it will take before he becomes a Catholic. [...]

Radolinski is suffering badly with sciatica but he is going to have treatment. A few days ago Lyncker[1] said to me: 'If Radol. retires we may as well all go home.' [...]

9 *November* 1886

Copy of a letter from Hatzfeldt dated 7 November.[2]

I didn't write because there was nothing happening here. They are waiting to see how things will develop in Bulgaria, what, if anything, happened in Vienna, and what White accomplishes. Kaiser Franz Joseph's address[3] is naturally being interpreted as meaning that all the conditions are being accepted in Vienna, and so they will not lift a finger at this end.

The Duke of Cambridge,[4] whom I have just met in the country, tells me that Kaiser Franz Joseph told him personally in Galicia how desirable it was for White to go to Constantinople —his private wishes are apparently at variance with his public attitude.

Your most recent letters, for which I send you warm if belated thanks, interested me very much, particularly His Highness' statements to Shuvalov.[5] You will agree that they are aiming at the very thing I used to preach years ago, at that time in opposition to Herbert B. So of course I agree with it, but I am sorry it has happened *so late*, and I entirely share your view that we are thereby forfeiting yet again all the benefit gained by our former labours of love in St Petersburg. And the net result seems to be the settling of the Ambassador question between St Petersburg and Paris![6] But what have we gained?

[1] Moritz, Baron von Lyncker. Court Chamberlain to Crown Prince Friedrich Wilhelm.

[2] The original of Hatzfeldt's letter was not found among Holstein's papers.

[3] At the reception of the Delegations on 6 November. The Kaiser said that his Government was endeavouring in the final settlement of the Bulgarian question to create in the autonomous principality a legal situation which, while doing justice to the legitimate wishes of the Bulgarians, would also be in line with existing treaties and correspond to the interests of Europe.

[4] George, Duke of Cambridge. British Field-Marshal; Commander-in-Chief of the British army, 1856–95.

[5] See Holstein's letter to Hatzfeldt of 26 October 1886, describing this conversation between Bismarck and Shuvalov (*Correspondence*). See also p. 313, note 3.

[6] The French Ambassador in St Petersburg, Félix Appert, had been recalled by his Government in February 1886 because he had attempted to prevent the liberation of the nihilist Prince Kropotkin, who had been arrested in France. Tsar Alexander was annoyed at the recall of an Ambassador he liked, and instructed his own Ambassador in Paris, Baron Mohrenheim, to go on leave. In October, Mohrenheim was ordered back to his post in Paris and Antoine de Laboulaye was appointed to succeed Appert. See *Grosse Politik*, vol. vi, nos. 1203, 1209, pp. 96–8, 104–5; *Documents Diplomatiques Français*, Première Série, vol. vi, p. 206 and *passim*.

I am positively horrified at to-day's dispatches concerning colonial questions,[1] and so is Krauel. All this suspicion is unjustified: there was certainly no need to go as far as reaching agreement on Zanzibar.[2] The assumption that the agreement is unwelcome to people here and that they are reluctant to inform the Sultan (of Zanzibar) is completely false, as are all the conclusions drawn from it. The only thing that is true is that old Iddesleigh is reluctant to provoke France's annoyance in this way unnecessarily, which may be stupid but is fairly understandable. If we show annoyance or even ill-will over the Egyptian question —after the assurances we have given![3]—just when they think they have met us half-way, they may become extremely stubborn. So I urgently request you to do everything in your power to calm down the Chancellor and prevent him from making any unpleasant statements.[4]

12 *November* 1886

Letter from Hatzfeldt.[5]

10 *Nov.*

What does His Highness think of Salisbury's speech?[6] It is certainly most forceful in style, perhaps too forceful if they are not bent on action.

My conversation with Károlyi[7] was interesting. He said further that Austria wanted an agreement between Vienna and London and [he] had urged it often enough. But where was the guarantee here? In certain circumstances—which you know—one might be obliged to draw the sword, but one would need allies in that case. How did we feel about it? Surely we could not wish to leave them in the lurch then, and so forth. You may be sure I gave nothing away, but took refuge behind time-honoured formulæ. I shall be seeing Salisbury to-morrow because there is trouble over

[1] The editors did not have access to the files of the Colonial Division.

[2] On 1 November England and Germany concluded an agreement on the frontiers of the Sultan of Zanzibar's territories and the delimitation of mutual interests in East Africa.

[3] Bismarck had informed Hatzfeldt in a telegram sent on 16 October: 'In view of France's attempts to make England's position in Egypt difficult and to enlist the support of other Powers for this purpose, England can count on a friendly policy from Germany. We are also prepared to implement this promise.' (*Grosse Politik*, vol. IV, no. 800, pp. 153–4.)

[4] Note by Holstein: 'Rantzau had stirred up the Chancellor against Hatzfeldt quite without reason, for H. achieved everything we had set out to achieve in the Zanzibar negotiations.'

[5] The original of Hatzfeldt's letter was not found among Holstein's papers.

[6] Lord Salisbury, at a banquet in honour of the new Lord Mayor of London on 9 November, had made a speech in which he expressed England's readiness to uphold the provisions of the Treaty of Berlin with regard to Bulgaria, but only in collaboration with other Powers holding similar views.

[7] Alois, Count Károlyi. Austro-Hungarian Ambassador in Berlin, 1871–8, in London, 1878–88. Hatzfeldt reported on the same day that the Austrian Ambassador had told him that in the present situation Austria was obliged to try to maintain peace. On the other hand Austria could not accept a Russian occupation of Bulgaria without a protest, and would in that eventuality be obliged to look round for allies. (From the Foreign Ministry files.)

Samoa[1]—I may see Randolph Churchill too if he is back. We shall of course discuss other matters too, and I shall write to you afterwards.

The Russians seem to have a candidate[2] at last, whose installation is to create that 'legal' status which will pacify the other Powers. But who is the lucky man?[3]

I still think things will go on like this until the spring—but then anything may happen at any time. Let us hope that by then we shall have sold a great many Russian bonds; even at a considerable loss it would still be a sound transaction.

Do you think Kálnoky will manage to stay in office? If not, we may see a decided change of policy.

14 *November* 1886

Letter from Hatzfeldt.[4]

11 *Nov.*

Many thanks for your most interesting letter of two days ago.[5]

I realized long ago the very serious danger of Bülow's dispatches and others of a similar nature, and entirely agree with you. In Bülow's case they can be explained quite simply by ambition and the certainty of earning the approval of the Chief (second generation), as in fact he has done for a long time.

But I should like to probe more deeply into the matter and to make the melancholy statement that we could have foreseen all this. Remember our discussions and the observation I repeatedly made; namely that we could expect no thanks unless we were resolved to go through thick and thin *whatever happened*, and that one refusal, one moment's hesitation would be enough to nullify *all* our previous labours of love.

That *must* have been the effect produced by Bismarck's statement to Shuvalov,[6] as I told you in my last letter.[7] And to a certain extent this is even justified, since the Russians can say they would never have gone so far or committed so many follies if we had dealt more openly with them earlier and had told them frankly *how* far we could go. For them to withdraw at this stage is an *ignominious defeat*—and therein lies the danger to peace which *could* have been avoided by an open and *friendly* statement at the *right* time. Such a statement would not have provoked more resentment against us, probably less, than it is *bound* to provoke now.

So what have we gained? A most dangerous over-all situation

---

[1] The conflicting interests of Britain, the United States, New Zealand, and Germany, and the support these countries afforded the rival native princes, had brought about serious disturbances in Samoa.   [2] For the Bulgarian throne.

[3] Prince Nicholas Dadian of Mingrelia. The *Sobranje* refused to accept his candidature towards the end of November.

[4] The original of Hatzfeldt's letter was not found among Holstein's papers.

[5] Hatzfeldt means Holstein's letter of 10 November 1886 (*Correspondence*).

[6] See p. 309, note 5, and p. 313, note 3.   [7] Hatzfeldt's letter of 7 November. See above.

in which we may easily be involved even if we exercise the greatest caution; and we have failed to achieve our goal of preserving Russia's friendship.

We shall overcome this difficulty too, and His Highness will find a way out, but it might have been avoided. I know of only one satisfactory explanation for it all. Some higher authority had to be handled with consideration.[1]

As regards people here, I do not entirely agree with your judgment. They are far from being heroes, we agree on that. But they are the inevitable product and expression of present-day democratic developments in England, which, I am afraid, have not been followed closely enough in Germany. At any rate I did not realize the situation on arriving here, and since then many signs from Berlin have shown me that people there are still underestimating the evil, i.e. the democratization of English society. The result of this regrettable development, which can only be checked, not reversed, is that here even the greatest statesman is *obliged* to subordinate himself to considerations of so-called public opinion and the party situation. In foreign policy he must wait on events and let them work for him. Thus we may say that it is difficult to have any dealings at all with a democratic country, but we cannot hold the individual statesman responsible.

Meanwhile Salisbury's speech has shown you that he, taking advantage of his opponents' mistakes and realizing their effect on a considerable section of British public opinion, has taken yet another step forward. Further than that he could not go, without aggravating the attacks already being made on him and actually providing a basis for them. Public opinion is not yet ripe for any positive action which might cost money, and Parliament is probably not ready either. It can only be brought about by further mistakes on the part of his opponents, and, to a lesser degree, by the realization on the part of the nation that England would not stand alone. Thus everything will depend on whether [the Russians] really resort to occupation and a manifest act of aggression, and on the effect this produces in Vienna. In this respect I am rather in the dark and can only judge by Károlyi's remarks with which you are familiar, without knowing how accurate they are. If they are justified, then I must assume that England, as I assumed previously, would not quietly condone certain acts, in which case she would look round for allies—casting glances very much in our direction in the process.

In my opinion you will get nowhere with Italy alone. She would not act without England[2] and Vienna would not find such a dubious friend sufficient.

---

[1] Note by Holstein: 'No, not a bit of it. It was a love of finessing on the part of Bismarck and love of Russia coupled with hatred of Austria on the part of his son.'
[2] Note by Holstein: 'Not true.'

One of Raupach's plays, *Maria Magdalena*, ends with the father, having been made miserable by his family's misconduct, exclaiming: 'I understand the world no longer.'[1] The Chancellor reminds me of this father. He has been striving for years to make the Austrians realize, first, that the eastern half of the Balkan peninsula is set apart for Russia and the western half for Austria (theory of spheres of interest), secondly that Russia will be weakened if she is allowed to advance as far as Bulgaria, or even Constantinople.

Neither of these views has been well received in Austria.

The Austrians regard *those* spheres of interest as an illusion because Montenegro would never fall to their share, and in any case they could never digest it. The Austrians do not believe Russia would be weakened if she advanced as far as Constantinople—neither do I. I am reminded of Lamartine's words from the tribune in 1848: 'Gentlemen, the guillotine is no longer to be feared. Even if it were erected, the populace would destroy it within a week.' At which a listener called out: 'But what would happen *during* that week?' It is the same with Russia. After capturing Constantinople she might perhaps slowly disintegrate; but *at first* this exploit would confer on her a prestige and an increase of power that would assure her of any alliances she wished, and make her the arbiter of Europe—Germany included.

In their attempts to spread these two theories, both Bismarcks have involved themselves in contradictions, thus arousing the suspicions of the Russians. First of all they told the Russians: 'March on Bulgaria.'[2] Shuvalov, on the instructions of his Government, then asked: 'If we *do* invade Bulgaria, will you, Germany, keep Austria off our backs?' To which the Chancellor replied: 'No, we cannot do without any of the present Great Powers. If you Russians are intending to humble the Austrians, we shall be obliged to take steps against you.' The Chancellor informed Vienna of this statement a fortnight ago.[3] This provoked

[1] The author of *Maria Magdalena* is not Raupach, but Friedrich Hebbel.

[2] Herbert von Bismarck told Count Shuvalov on 15 October that Germany would not oppose a Russian invasion of Bulgaria. But he urgently recommended that Russia should come to an understanding with Austria beforehand. (From the Foreign Ministry files.) See also *Grosse Politik*, vol. v, no. 989, pp. 65–8.

[3] The above-mentioned conversations between Bismarck and Shuvalov took place on 19 and 20 October. Bismarck gave orders for his dictated memorandum to be sent to Vienna. In his accompanying dispatch of 23 October, Herbert von Bismarck stated that he had informed the Austrian Chargé d'Affaires of the interview and had at the same time emphasized that Germany would deplore threats or military action on the part of Austria if the Russians invaded Bulgaria. (From the Foreign Ministry files.) See *Grosse Politik*, vol. v, p. 78, note *.

a most forthright speech by Kálnoky, in which he informed the Russians that occupation of Bulgaria, whether in whole or in part, would constitute a *casus belli*.[1]

Naturally the Russians lay the blame for this on Bismarck's encouraging advice and Shuvalov says: 'The Austrians are counting on your willingness to side with them and against us, if necessary.'

The Chancellor's last interview was most unpleasant. Afterwards the Chancellor roundly cursed the Russian Ambassador's importunity and instructed Herbert to tell him *'que son père avait eu l'impression que le Cte Shuvalov avait voulu le mettre dedans'*. Herbert repeated this word for word, not only to the Ambassador but to Muraviev as well.[2]

What impression can be made by this kind of behaviour? In the long run only a deplorable one. The Russians for their part think *we* are trying to deceive *them*, by urging them to march on Bulgaria—which Herbert has been doing for a long time with the utmost zeal.

The Chancellor's vanity in this matter is conspicuous. He expects the Tsar to have complete confidence in him in spite of it all. Bülow's dispatches have harped on this theme the whole summer, and the Chancellor liked the idea.

Recently, however, Reuss (Vienna) came here and informed us that Grand-Duke Vladimir[3] had told him the Tsar was deeply suspicious of the Chancellor and his policy.[4] This piece of information was kept very secret because it offended the Chancellor, who has felt a lively dislike of the Grand-Duke ever since. 'His statements are not to be relied on', His Highness wrote only three days ago in the margin of a document in which the Grand-Duke was mentioned.

And yet the Grand-Duke acted very decently in giving Reuss this information. He wanted to make the Chancellor collaborate honestly either with Russia or Austria, whereas all His Highness enjoys is vacillation and intrigue.

[1] In the Hungarian Delegation's budget committee, on 13 November. See *Grosse Politik*, vol. v, p. 70, note * * *.

[2] On 27 October Rantzau wrote to Herbert von Bismarck from Varzin: 'Papa is extremely angry with the Russians; he says they are pursuing a dishonourable policy of bringing things to a climax, only to let us down with Kaulbars' fantastic policy (see p. 316, notes 1 and 2).' Prince Bismarck was prepared, if necessary, to support a Russian invasion of Bulgaria in Rome in the name of the three Imperial Powers; nor would he hinder any action by Russia on his own responsibility. 'But he does not wish to take part in a repetition of Dulcigno and Zorilla.' Herbert von Bismarck was instructed to inform Muraviev of this. The letter bears a note in Count Bismarck's handwriting: 'Discussed this with Count Muraviev. 29/10.' (From the Foreign Ministry files.)

[3] Brother of Tsar Alexander III.

[4] See *Grosse Politik*, vol. v, p. 68, note * *; no. 992, pp. 75–84. See also Holstein's letter to Hatzfeldt of 10 November 1886 (*Correspondence*).

Schweinitz, with his flair for style, expressed the Tsar's mistrust of the Chancellor in these words: 'His feelings towards the Chancellor are a blend of admiration and fear.'[1]

The way His Highness encourages Russians and Austrians alternately is by no means a sign of genius. I think he is sinking rapidly in the general estimation. His main political objective now seems to be to levy on the Russians prohibitive duties on grain, wood, and fatstock. We shall see what happens next.

1 *December* 1886[2]

Herb. Bismarck recently told me Prince Wilhelm would soon be working in the Foreign Ministry. Herbert said that whenever he was too busy to give the Prince instruction he would send him to me. I replied: 'Since this is an official request I cannot refuse, but I should find such association with the Prince highly undesirable. In the first place, he gossips about everything he hears —we have had examples of this very recently.' (I cited several instances.) 'But in addition my love of the truth would get me into trouble. You see, if he asks me my opinion I shall have to tell him; and my opinion differs from yours in quite a few essentials. In particular I think the time for a Russo-German alliance is past. We *cannot*—and your father *will not*—satisfy the demands our friendship with Russia would make with respect to Austria. We cannot and will not participate in or be spectators of Austria's destruction by Russia. If we *did* participate (which is in fact what Herbert wants), we should then, after Austria's annihilation, be trapped between Russia and France, who would prescribe any conditions they liked. They would probably revive Chateaubriand's programme from the time of Charles X: France would allow Russia a free hand in the Balkans, while she, in return, would aid France to regain the Rhine frontier. Our dear friend Tsar Nicholas had agreed on this with Charles X when the July Revolution broke out. The only reason for the Tsar's rage and his contempt for Louis-Philippe was that the latter, a timid man, did not want to have anything to do with this plan of action. Whatever one may think of Austria, at least she is useful because she prevents us from having to face Russia and France alone. Instead of wasting our time on Russia, with whom we shall never be reconciled, we ought to do our utmost to conclude an alliance between Germany, Austria and Italy as soon as possible. The

[1] Report by Schweinitz of 9 November. (*Grosse Politik*, vol. VI, no. 1206, pp. 99–101).
[2] This entry was probably written on two consecutive days, or else it should be dated 2 December. See p. 317, notes 1 and 2.

three of us would then form a sizeable bloc and it is probable that, according to circumstances, England, Spain or Turkey would ally themselves with us at the crucial moment. Those are the lines on which I should speak to Prince Wilhelm.'

Herb. replied: 'I am in favour of an Italian alliance too. And I do not share Prince Wilhelm's view that Russia, if only because of old memories of 1815, would never embark on a war against Germany.'

I have in fact gradually brought Herbert to the point of supporting the idea of an Italian alliance now and of trying to bring his father round to it as well—he dislikes the Italians. Only two months ago His Highness told Keudell that an Italian alliance was of no importance whatever!

Old people are like that. The Austro-Russian alliance suits him and he would like to stick to it.

The old Kaiser, so often underrated, sees the situation more clearly. He has a lively mistrust of Russia and is outraged at the way Russia got rid of Battenberg—whom, incidentally, Kaiser Wilhelm dislikes; he is also scandalized by Kaulbars'[1] entire behaviour.[2]

With Herbert everything is based on personal impressions and influences. Recently—and it was high time—he was beginning to feel annoyed with Russia. But just then Grand-Duke Vladimir passed through Berlin together with his wife. Herbert thinks very highly of them both, and the Grand-Duke, who is very shrewd, took him in completely![3] When I pointed out to Herbert that one or two fallacies had crept into the argument, he turned a deaf ear.

And yet we have been repeatedly warned just lately that the Grand-Duke is a Frenchman through and through. He even looks it. His real grandfather was not the Grand-Duke of Hesse but the latter's Master of the Horse, Baron Grancey, who came of an *émigré* family.

At the wedding in Weimar in November[4] the Grand-Duke, who is Commandant of our 12th Hussar Regiment, wore Russian uniform exclusively. So did the Grand-Duke [of Hesse] much to

[1] Nikolai, Baron von Kaulbars. The Tsar's Plenipotentiary Extraordinary in Bulgaria, 25 September–17 November 1886.

[2] Kaulbars had required from Bulgaria unconditional obedience to the Tsar and had decreed a number of arbitrary regulations in his name. His failure to extort Bulgaria's obedience convinced Kaulbars that nothing could be done with the present rulers in Bulgaria (the Regency Council installed after Alexander of Battenberg's abdication.) He left the country, together with all the Russian consuls.

[3] Compare Herbert von Bismarck's memorandum of 22 November 1886. (*Grosse Politik*, vol. v, no. 992, pp. 75–84.)

[4] On 6 November Princess Elizabeth of Sachsen-Weimar-Eisenach married Johann Albert, Duke of Mecklenburg-Schwerin.

the Crown Prince's fury. When the deputation from the 12th Hussar Regiment was presented to the Grand-Duke, he received them smoking a cigar. I told Herbert all this. 'Oh', he said, 'I don't expect it's true.'

This summer has had the most unfortunate effect possible on relations between the Chancellor and the Crown Prince. In every question that arose the Chancellor disregarded the Crown Prince's wishes.

In the Bulgarian question he kept up a ruthless persecution of Battenberg in the *Norddeutsche Zeitung*, thereby damaging his own reputation in Germany;

with regard to Prince Wilhelm's trip to Warsaw,

with regard to Prince W.'s work in the Foreign Ministry.

On these last two points the Chancellor could have given way. He was adamant because he and Herbert wanted to demonstrate their power.

The pitcher goes so often to the well that it is broken at last.

We heard through Robilant to-day that, according to a dispatch from the Italian Ambassador in Paris and information from another reliable source, it was Grand-Duke Vladimir who proposed in Paris a Franco-Russian alliance.[1] I wonder what Herbert will say to that. Probably: 'It's all a lie.'

The French have definitely turned down the proposal. The introduction of the automatic rifle and the re-fortification of the frontier forts mean that they are not really ready for war this coming year.

The Crown Prince has written the Chancellor a letter complaining of Prince Wilhelm's appointment to the Foreign Ministry, and in particular that the Chancellor had submitted the proposal to the Kaiser without first consulting the Crown Prince as he had promised.[2]

[1] Keudell telegraphed this information from Rome on 2 December. See also *Grosse Politik*, vol. VI, chapter XXXIX.

[2] A copy of this letter of 2 December, in the Crown Prince's own handwriting, is in the Foreign Ministry files. Bismarck's reply of 5 December states that Kaiser Wilhelm reached no decision during his audience with Bismarck; the ultimate decision had apparently been communicated to the Crown Prince, but not to him, Bismarck. A report for the Kaiser by Bismarck dated 15 December states: 'According to the contents of Your Majesty's most gracious note of the 13th of this month [not in the Foreign Ministry files] I may regard His Royal Highness Prince Wilhelm's employment in the Foreign Ministry as an official command. [...] It will accordingly be the Foreign Ministry's task to acquaint His Royal Highness with the working and organization of the Ministry, which he will visit once or twice a week, and also to familiarize him with official routine by submitting to him documents from the files accompanied by an appropriate commentary.' (*Die gesammelten Werke*, vol. VI c, no. 343, pp. 347–8.) In a communication to the Kaiser of 17 December the Crown Prince upheld his protest against employing Prince Wilhelm in the Foreign Ministry in view of his immaturity. (From the Foreign Ministry files.)

This trivial affair is a deplorable revelation of Bismarck's arrogance. It was a completely unnecessary arrangement. I doubt whether it serves any purpose. Prince Wilhelm is far too immature.

Little Saldern was requested by the Chancellor to explain what had induced him to inquire here after the Sofia revolution whether he [ought] to take charge of Prince Alexander's private property.[1]

The little man justified himself as best he could, in writing.[2] He said among other things that he had also aimed at removing Prince Alexander's private correspondence from the hands of the insurgents because it was rumoured that it contained letters from members of our royal family. All the Prince's secret correspondence had been successfully burnt while the soldiers supposed to be keeping an eye on the consular officials were busy in another room.

His Highness refuted Saldern's excuses one after the other, dealt him a reprimand and remarked, especially in the case of the secret correspondence: 'The private correspondence of a prince is no doubt a serious political danger. But if royal personages indulge in that kind of thing they must take the consequences.'[3]

In other words His Highness is furious with little Saldern for having spared the Crown Prince's family from appearing ridiculous in the eyes of the public. Saldern was quite right, as I told him when he called on me to-day in a depressed state of mind.

2 December 1886

Letters from Hatzfeldt.[4]

23 Nov.

For *your* information. Randolph Church. is deeply indignant

---

[1] Saldern had made this inquiry in a telegram of 25 August. On 27 August the Chancellor at Bad Elster commanded the following telegram to be sent to Saldern: 'I have agreed with Giers that, in common with your Russian and Austrian colleagues, you should strive to promote and support the liquidation of Prince Alexander's private affairs, but you must do nothing on your own.' (From the Foreign Ministry files.)

[2] In his memorandum of 29 November, Saldern referred to the fact that Prince Alexander had once more become a German subject as a result of his abdication. (From the Foreign Ministry files.)

[3] According to a communication written by Rantzau from Friedrichsruh on 1 December, the remark mentioned here by Holstein ran as follows: 'Moreover His Highness is out of sympathy with the goals which Herr von Saldern has set himself. There were no official documents which might have compromised us, and the private correspondence between members of royal houses is one of the greatest evils in existence; we should be hard put to it to protect such correspondence from being compromised and it can be protected from abuse only by the prudence of those involved, which leaves much to be desired.' (From the Foreign Ministry files.)

[4] The originals of Hatzfeldt's letters were not found among Holstein's papers.

and disappointed over our attitude in the Egyptian question.[1] He said he had expected we would give the French a clear and positive assurance that we had no interests in Egypt and were convinced that England would fulfil all her obligations. But our attitude would inevitably *encourage* the French, being the type of people they were. I have had *great* difficulty even in calming him down a *little*. Get them to send me some reassuring message for him if you can.

Just seen Salisbury. He tells me the Russians invited Italy and France to join forces with them, but received a refusal from them both; the French said they were not ready yet.

Salisb. takes a calmer view of the over-all situation now; he does not expect any precipitate decision in St Petersburg. In his opinion the Russians could be allowed to hold *fresh* election to a *Sobranje* which would, however, *not* elect the Russian candidate, i.e. people here would see to that; so that is no way out. I think it would be far better for the old *Sobranje* to elect the candidate; that ought to be possible unless I am completely deceived.

Kálnoky's proposal—European commission—will hardly be agreed to. What do you think?[2]

24 Nov.

Many thanks for your most interesting letter, received yesterday evening. I was not the least bit surprised by what happened, mad though it is.[3] That is what we must expect of people we have flattered and made a fuss of, the moment we depart from established custom.

My only comment on Herbert's observation on Bernhard Bülow's dispatch:[4] 'There's nothing new in that', is that I and many others never expected anything else. But there was nothing strong enough to support this point of view, and the kind of place-seekers Germany alone fosters were of course *obliged* to support the contrary view.

Salisbury, as you know, took a calmer view of things two days ago, and he may be right if his information is correct. In my view

[1] See Hatzfeldt's telegram of 24 November (*Grosse Politik*, vol. iv, no. 807, pp. 163–4).

[2] Note by Holstein: 'Has already been turned down.'

[3] Note by Holstein: 'The transfer to France of protection of Russian interests in Bulgaria, after we had been approached first.'

Bismarck commented on the telegram from St Petersburg of 19 November containing the request that Germany should take over the protection of Russian interests in Bulgaria: 'Unfortunately this cannot be refused.' On 23 November the French Ambassador in Berlin communicated the information that France had undertaken to protect Russian interests in Bulgaria. (From the Foreign Ministry files.)

[4] Of 15 November. Bülow confirmed Grand-Duke Vladimir's disclosure to Reuss (see p. 314) and furnished much additional evidence of the Tsar's anti-German attitude. (*Grosse Politik*, vol. v, no. 990, pp. 68–73.)

the course of events depends entirely on the development of *our* relations with Russia. If they become more strained, if we speak out more firmly, the others will take heart immediately and will probably hold Russia in check—how long is another question. But if we really want to preserve peace, the first condition is to find some way out of the appalling confusion in Bulgaria which would be acceptable to Russia. That is only possible *si nous nous en mêlons*. The solution which Kálnoky himself is advocating strikes me as unsuitable. It gets rid neither of the Regency nor the *Sobranje*, nor does it ensure the election of a Prince. But Russia must have partial fulfilment of all three conditions if she is to be kept quiet.

Further developments here—apart from what we do—will depend to a large extent on the attitude of Parliament next January. The Government does not feel quite safe yet, and is therefore treading very carefully. If Hartington[1] stands firm, a majority is assured, and England will be able to take a firmer line.

I see signs that the Grand Old Man[2] is flirting with the Russians. At the moment he is of no importance. It is an established fact, which was confirmed to me only today, that in the provinces the liberal Press is rapidly gaining confidence in Salisbury's foreign policy. Here only the *Daily News* opposes it—*Pall Mall* is of no importance at all.

I am very much afraid that His Highness, under Herbert's influence, underestimates Randolph Churchill's importance here. I am indifferent to him as a person, in fact I do not even like him. But, unless things change considerably, he is the man, as things stand now, who may be expected to take positive and far-reaching action. I should therefore deeply deplore it if he were discouraged or alienated from us. You will be doing a worthwhile action if you can prevent that. . . .

Thus Hatzfeldt.

As regards R. Churchill, it is personal politics again.

Herbert is annoyed that his friend, Rosebery, has had to resign, he is annoyed that Hatzfeldt is on good terms with Churchill, and is particularly annoyed that Churchill recently passed through Berlin without calling on him. As a result instructions approved by the Chancellor were sent to Hatzfeldt three days ago, telling him not to have too much to do with Churchill because he could not be relied on. No importance must be attached to anything

---

[1] Spencer Compton Cavendish, Marquess of Hartington. As leader of the Liberal Unionists, who had left the Liberal party over the question of Irish Home Rule, Hartington controlled the decisive votes in the House of Commons.

[2] Note by Holstein: 'Gladstone.'

Churchill might say about supporting Austria.[1] Most encouraging for Hatzfeldt.

In addition, the Italians are now making quite definite offers to support Germany and Austria against Russia and France.[2] We shall see what His Highness thinks of this new state of affairs.

Letter from Hatzfeldt.[3]

4 Dec. '86

Many thanks for your most interesting letter of last Thursday which I have just received.

R. Churchill is far more a man of action than Rosebery, and people's blindness to this fact is most deplorable. But it cannot and ought not to prevent me from writing an account of my most recent conversation with him. This must be submitted to His Highness, who will separate the grain from the chaff.[4] Times are too serious to let opportunities slip, if I can help it.

If we negotiate with Italy, what in the world prevents us from doing the same with England? The ground is prepared and all we need is the will to do so. The only demand R. Churchill makes— to use our influence in Constantinople, if necessary, so that their way of retreat is not cut off—is not unreasonable. All he really requires of us is 'connivance' which might be defined as: agreement without visible signs.

When we parted, he said: 'If you only represented Austria as well, how quickly we should reach agreement. But what with

[1] A dispatch of 27 November, dictated by Bismarck, states: 'If Lord Randolph is intimating that Austria is certain of English support if she takes up the challenge, then I can only regard this assertion as insincere, judging by what we know from Vienna and from Your Excellency through Count Károlyi, and that its intention is to induce Austria to act and then to let her down, or else to refer her to us for support while England would remain neutral. Lord Randolph himself is not in a position to give any guarantee on this matter. For, as soon as he leaves the Cabinet, voluntarily or otherwise, the situation becomes totally different and every guarantee he has given becomes void.' (From the Foreign Ministry files.) See *Grosse Politik*, vol. IV, no. 873, pp. 283–5.

[2] In a memorandum of 30 November, Herbert von Bismarck quoted from a personal letter from Count Robilant to Count Launay: 'Within eighteen to twenty days after mobilization orders we shall have 150,000 troops on the north-west frontier, ready for a *défense offensive* against France. 200,000 troops, i.e. 6 army corps, 4 cavalry divisions and one division of Alpine troops, will be available at the same time, either to cross the Alps and make for the Rhine to support the Germans, or else to march through Austria to attack the Russians.' (*Grosse Politik*, vol. IV, no. 836, appendix III, p. 208.)

[3] The original of Hatzfeldt's letter was not found among Holstein's papers.

[4] Hatzfeldt's telegram of 5 December about his conversation with Churchill was submitted to the Chancellor. Churchill had told Hatzfeldt 'that if Austria wished, with the connivance of Germany, to adopt a decisive attitude with regard to the Near East, England would co-operate and throw all her weight into the scale. He then expressly repeated that a powerful British fleet which might have to force the Dardanelles would appear in the Black Sea. In addition England could equip 60,000 crack troops in six weeks and send them to the theatre of war. [...]' Churchill had added: 'The only thing we should then expect of a friendly Germany would be that she should exert her influence in Constantinople so that our Black Sea fleet should not find its way of retreat through the Dardanelles blocked.' (*Grosse Politik*, vol. IV, no. 874, pp. 285–7.)

Károlyi, who dislikes us, and our old blockhead (Iddesleigh) who is either asleep or dithering, it's impossible.'

I think, by the way, that he is now seriously aiming at getting rid of the 'old blockhead'. May he soon succeed.

Just think what a long way Germany has come since Gastein[1] and Franzensbad,[2] in the direction you and I desire What an immense difference between the views and attitude adopted then, and His Highness' most recent communication to me![3] And are we prepared to stop at that while it lies within our power to assemble such a formidable coalition that it will either ensure peace or else crush any disturber of the peace so that he will not rise for decades?

Just let me have the points they want here and which they may perhaps concede, *et je me charge du reste.*

A propos, I must just add this. Krauel's 'praise' for my colonial activities here amused me greatly. If there were any sense of justice in the Foreign Ministry they would have realized long ago, even without Krauel's help, that I am the only person who understood that aspect of the situation here and that they would never have achieved anything without me: that is actually a fact, however conceited it may sound.

Yours etc.

6 Dec.[4]

You can see from my to-day's dispatches that people here are furiously angry with Turkey.[5] Salisbury was fuming against the Sultan to-day, saying he should simply be removed. The *Daily Telegraph* article, inspired by R. Churchill, has deeply affected the Turkish Ambassador here, and he is drawing the attention of his Government to it. We must now wait and see what effect these threats will produce in Constantinople—it would be a really serious matter if they were carried out. What do you think of the crisis in Paris?[6] Do you think it will cause any change in French foreign policy? I don't think so.

[1] On 8 and 9 August a meeting had taken place at Bad Gastein between Kaiser Wilhelm and Kaiser Franz Joseph, in which Bismarck and Kálnoky took part. There are no detailed memoranda of these conversations. (*Grosse Politik*, vol. v, p. 55, note ***.)

[2] See p. 390, note 2.

[3] Bismarck's dispatch of 27 November, quoted on p. 321, note 1, began with the statement: 'If it were definitely established that Austria, if attacked by Russia in connexion with the Near Eastern question, whether on account of Bulgaria or the Dardanelles, can count on England's support, and if we had a dependable guarantee of that in Berlin, it would not be our duty to discourage Austria from resisting Russia.'

[4] The original of Hatzfeldt's letter was not found among Holstein's papers.

[5] Hatzfeldt reported that day a conversation with Lord Salisbury. In order to preserve peace, Salisbury was considering whether to inform Russia, by means of a calculated indiscretion, that a Russian attack on Austria with the help of Turkey would provoke England to adopt the severest measures against Turkey. Hatzfeldt gained the impression from this interview 'that a threatening tone is now to be adopted against the Sultan, since he is apparently abiding by his agreement with Russia'. (*Grosse Politik*, vol. iv, no. 875, pp. 287–9.)

[6] The Freycinet Ministry had been overthrown on 3 December.

People here seem reassured now about our attitude in the Egyptian question. Salisbury thanked me to-day. They are still as firm as ever about evacuation.

Write again soon.

Thus Hatzfeldt. When he makes the point about reaching agreement with England he is not quite right. England can only incur treaty obligations by act of parliament, and opinion in England has not yet reached that stage.

By that I do not mean I admire our present policy. The Chancellor stands in front of the Tsar, cap in hand, trying to console him with fine phrases for the fact that in the sphere of political interests we are already Russia's opponents. This attitude, which dates from September '84, does nothing but harm because it degrades us and makes the Russians overbearing. *Everyone* can see that, even the old Kaiser, whom it was very difficult to win over to granting concessions to Russia on one or two occasions, e.g. last September when we took steps to prevent the condemnation of the conspirators who had captured Prince Alexander.[1] Only Herbert is in favour of this Russian policy, and so every one regards him as responsible. He does this less from a love of Russia than from hatred of Austria, Randolph Churchill and Hatzfeldt.

On the other hand I am bound to acknowledge that he did give way to my insistence in the Italian question. Whereas the Chancellor told Keudell only two months ago that we regarded the extension of the Italian agreement as completely unimportant, Herbert has managed the affair in such a way that it is to be hoped we shall accomplish something towards the New Year.

The extent to which the old man has lagged behind the march of events is shown by the remark he has been fond of repeating for years: 'I set no store whatever by the Italian alliance because without it Austria will be more submissive towards Russia.'

But it is not a question of Austria's 'submissiveness' towards Russia; the question is whether Austria, together with others, is strong enough to resist Russia. If *we* should have to help in the east, we shall be too weak against France.

Even Bismarck will not succeed in forcing Russia and Austria to love each other, or even to keep the peace for long; he is about the only person who thinks he can. He would see things more clearly if it were not for Herbert.

[1] See p. 301, note 1.

323

Letter from Hatzfeldt.[1]

Rando. Churchill, who wanted to talk to me about Egypt, rushed up to me brandishing White's telegram in my face. (N.B. it stated that Radowitz is supporting the Russians in Constantinople, thus preventing the English from achieving anything at all with the Sultan.) I had to battle with him for an hour and a half. He was boiling with indignation. He said England had compromised herself in the eyes of the Russians and was now being left in the lurch by Austria and Germany. All he had asked us was to exert our influence in Constantinople and now we were supporting Russia there and making White's task impossible. We were trying to embroil England while standing aloof ourselves. Well, he wasn't playing. He had Parliament to consider. If pushed to extremes, he would resign, and then the whole affair would come to nothing. But he said there was still time and England might yet reach agreement with Russia, leaving her a *completely* free hand in return for a guarantee in Asia.

I am not reporting this because it would only cause ill-feeling.[2] You can imagine what a struggle I had. In the end he calmed down but criticized us most severely. He supposed we must know what we wanted. He said there were after all only two courses open to us: either to go all out in support of Russia and thus purchase peace—which we should not succeed in doing in view of Russia's hatred of us—or else to form a powerful quadruple alliance, which could come into existence at any time if we so desired.

I need not tell you what I think of all this. *Je ne comprends plus*. Even so I do think I might be kept informed of our policy—and I know *nothing* about our attitude during the last few days.

Write soon.

Thus Hatzfeldt.

He is right, but I do not admit it entirely to avoid embittering him still further.

---

[1] The original of Hatzfeldt's letter was not found among Holstein's papers.

[2] Hatzfeldt telegraphed that day to the Foreign Ministry: 'Telegram from British Ambassador in Constantinople to-day stated Herr von Radowitz told him he had instructions to support endeavours aimed at modifying the Regency Council in Bulgaria, and that Your Highness was of the opinion that the Bulgarians would do better to reach agreement with the Sultan than to send a deputation to the Powers. Lord Randolph Churchill, who informed me of this telegram in confidence, complained bitterly that Germany, according to this, was using her influence in Constantinople to frustrate, and indeed nullify, Sir W. White's task.' Bismarck wrote these instructions on the margin: 'Inform London Embassy that we cannot take an anti-Russian line in the *Bulgarian* question; that is for England and Austria to do. Our connivance is limited to *passive* assistance; if one expects *more* from us and does nothing oneself, we should as a result only be pushed still closer to Russia, because in addition to an *inevitable* war with France we could not face having Russia as an enemy too, in view of the weakness of the Austrian army and England's reluctance to act.' (From the Foreign Ministry files.)

Italy, England, even Spain[1] are in favour of an alliance, and Turkey could be brought in as well. Faced with such a bloc, Russia and France would be powerless.

Instead we discourage the others by our hesitation *entre la brune et la blonde*, now Russia, now England—we even make tentative advances to France.

Instead of flattering Russia we ought to stand up to her. After all we cannot *satisfy* the Russians; we only make them still more arrogant. This is no longer Bismarckian policy but Haugwitz's policy of 1805.

Letter from Hatzfeldt.[2]

14 Dec.

You will believe me when I say that I myself expected no results from the telegram.[3] But I could not suppress such a forceful inquiry, based on the wording of a telegram, whatever the effect might be. And I do *not* think it has seriously annoyed His Highness, judging by a most courteous telegram for Rand. Churchill concerning the other problem (Egypt), which I received to-day direct from His Highness.[4]

On the *facts of the case* we are of course agreed, as usual. Only I do not think you fully understand people's motives here yet. Never think the other fellow is too stupid—that is a good old precept, and so, in order to judge him aright, one must try to put oneself in his place and enter into his thought processes.

Rand. Churchill argues as follows: Two courses are open to me, either to take a firm stand against Russia or else to seek agreement with Russia with a guarantee for Afghanistan. I prefer the former, and will go to any lengths. But, apart from public opinion here, the respective strength of the Powers makes this impossible unless Austria co-operates and Germany does not oppose us. But Austria makes excuses and, like Germany, would like me to face the music alone. The latter is actually exerting her influence against me in Constantinople. What, in these circumstances, will be the result if I, e.g. by issuing a statement in St Petersburg, show my hand and thus completely forfeit Russia's good will? Peace in Europe would no doubt be assured, but

---

[1] The collection of Foreign Ministry files entitled *Spain's Adherence to the Treaty of Alliance between Germany, Austria and Italy*, shows that in the autumn of 1886 Spain wished to join the Triple Alliance. The German Government took no interest in this suggestion owing to the instability of conditions in Spain.

[2] The original of Hatzfeldt's letter was not found among Holstein's papers.

[3] See p. 324, note 2.

[4] In reply to Hatzfeldt's dispatch on his conversation with Lord Randolph Churchill on 11 December about Egypt, Bismarck telegraphed to Hatzfeldt on 14 December: 'I am prepared to give diplomatic support to any acceptable plan put forward by the British Government concerning Egypt, but in particular this one which is financially practicable.' (From the Foreign Ministry files.)

pressure would be diverted towards my most vulnerable point, Afghanistan, where it is certain no one would help me. In these circumstances I should be a fool to meddle in the affair.

The situation is different if Austria co-operates. But that can only be hoped for if Germany really *wants it*. So long as she dissuades Austria we shall get nowhere.

So that if I, England, am to commit myself any further, Germany must stop dissuading Austria. Further, she must not exert her influence against us in Constantinople, which, as things stand, is bound to be decisive for the Turks. For *there* lies my only possible base of operations. If I cannot get into [the Black Sea], or cannot get out again, I can do nothing at all.

Résumé: If A. co-operates, as a result of Germany's friendly attitude, and if the latter refrains from supporting the Russians in Const. and harming me, then I can see my way clearly ahead and am prepared to reach a *complete* agreement, at once.

That is my little friend's argument, and if you put yourself in his place you will agree it makes sense. That is why I see no prospect of changing the situation unless we lend a supporting hand or else things become so serious that the two parties mainly concerned draw closer of their own accord.

The contempt with which Germany chooses to regard this little man is *quite absurd*. Here he is almost the key figure and, if I am not completely deceived, will become so more and more. Moreover Salisbury knows every word that passes between us, and that suits him very well because the little man can speak more frankly.

But, knowing which way the wind is blowing at home, I did not report my most recent conversation with him; I think you agreed with this? I shall not write until I can say something *new*.

I saw him again to-day about the Egyptian question. We also discussed the most important problem (Bulgaria). He rejects out of hand any doubts as to England's *ability* to act. He says the navy, in particular, is more powerful than ever. The Mediterranean fleet could be on the spot in ten days. It would be replaced in the Mediterranean by the Home Fleet in the same length of time, and the Home Fleet would be replaced by the North Sea Fleet. 40 to 60 thousand troops could be on the spot, perhaps within four weeks. At home they could be replaced at once by the perfectly organized militia. Money in plenty as soon as it was needed, even for the Turks if they joined in. He just laughs at the French navy. Scepticism produces little effect on such self-assurance as this, as you can imagine.

I am leaving here on the 22nd or 23rd. Here everything will just come to a standstill. I am of course not coming to Berlin unless I am summoned there. But it would in fact be a good thing if I could see His Highness himself.

I have not discussed Italy with any one. Don't you think some one was just trying to get you to talk?

Is there no prospect of Plessen getting a post soon?

Good night.

27 December 1886

It is remarkable the way the Chancellor changes his mind; to-day it is yes, the next day no. Only a week ago he informed the Kaiser and the Ministers that he foresaw a war with France in the very near future. Two days ago he wrote and told the War Minister that war would not break out next year.[1]

About ten days ago he informed Bleichröder that he was on no account to participate in the projected 500-million Russian loan. Yesterday he told Bleichröder it was impossible for him *not* to participate in the loan, or else it would look as though the Chancellor was opposed to it. That would cause resentment in Russia.

The army chiefs all agree that next year would be the most favourable year in which to make war, because we have developed the high-explosive shell and the repeating rifle, and so they think *we* ought to precipitate a war. The Chancellor, who has lost the initiative he had in 1866, says for his part that the Generals want a war because of the endowments they would get.

I myself have no opinion in the matter, or rather I think our superior armaments could be cancelled out by our inferior leadership. The Albedyll-Waldersee regime.

I grow more convinced every day that the Bismarcks will not last long when the Crown Prince is Kaiser. They presume too far.

The Crown Princess recently upbraided her son for the offence he had given his father by allowing himself to be drafted into the Foreign Ministry against his father's wishes. After one or two evasions Prince Wilhelm said: 'The only thing that matters to us Princes is the Kaiser's command. And it's the Kaiser who pays me, not my father. When my father becomes Kaiser I shall obey him in the same way.'

The resentment which inevitably results from scenes like this is naturally directed against Herbert, who is regarded as the originator of the whole idea.

The Crown Prince always refers to Herbert as 'that callow youth'. Even the Kaiser, though he puts up with him, is not very

[1] Bismarck to Bronsart, 24 December 1886 (*Die gesammelten Werke*, vol. VI c, no. 346, pp. 349–51).

fond of him. Berchem has just told me that at some ceremony the other day the Kaiser shook hands with Berchem but not with Herbert.

Bill, who observes events with his customary philosophic detachment, again censured His Highness' behaviour more than once on his recent passage through Berlin; he also blamed H.H.'s persecution of Battenberg (which he said only served to increase the victim's popularity), and his vacillation in matters of high policy.

I did my best to get him to influence his brother [away from] his blind aversion to Austria and his equally blind inclination towards Russia.

I may already have mentioned in these diaries my refusal to give Prince Wilhelm political instruction here. Herbert told me three or four weeks ago that he had chosen me to do the job whenever he had not time himself.

I replied that I begged to be excused. In the first place, I said, the Prince was most indiscreet and repeated everything, even the most secret matters, to any one who cared to hear. Secondly I felt obliged to draw Herbert's attention to a fact he already knew anyhow, namely that my views on our policy towards Russia and Austria differed from his. I then explained carefully, yet again, that we cannot let Austria be destroyed by Russia because we should then stand helpless between Russia and France; but that *if* we hinder Russian designs on Austria we must *as a result* be prepared to face her hostility instead of flattering her in a way that disheartens the other Powers—Engd. as well as Austria—and increases Russian arrogance.

Herbert listened in silence. Prince Wilhelm has now been sent to Berchem, but for the most part Herbert himself talks to him.

I have had one or two quite long conversations with Gossler recently. He had heard that I had occasionally taken his part. He said: 'I had been wondering for a long time what was the real cause of the Chancellor's incredible attitude towards the Protestant Church. Now I know. Again and again he utters these words: "The Protestant pastors are my bitterest enemies. A great number of them once signed the statement attacking me in the *Kreuzzeitung*."[1] When I put it to him that Catholicism was

---

[1] In June 1875 the *Kreuzzeitung* attacked Bismarck, Delbrück and Camphausen in a series of articles and reproached them with corrupt conduct in financial matters. On 9 February 1876, in the Reichstag, Bismarck called on all decent people to withdraw their support from the newspaper at once. A great number of prominent persons, including many members of the Protestant clergy (mainly Conservatives), approved the newspaper's attitude in a public statement.

everywhere gaining ground because of itinerant Catholic workers, the Chancellor, instead of considering my suggestions, said: " If the pastors have no hold over their people, let them become Catholic." '

For a long time now I have thought Gossler an excellent Minister and have done what I could to support him without knowing him.

Peter Shuvalov's negotiations. Holstein and the renewal of the Triple Alliance. His criticism of German policy. His successes. Advocates bringing Bulgarian matters to a decision. Hohenlohe's position saved. The Schnäbele affair. Publication of the Russian-Austrian negotiations in 1876–7. The Crown Prince's illness. Prince Wilhelm's character. Letters from the Crown Princess' entourage. Mounting resentment against Herbert von Bismarck. Crown Prince's illness fatal. The Tsar's visit.

8 *January* 1887

The enclosed letter from Eulenburg[1] (Munich) is full of human interest. E. wanted to keep Werthern in Munich, partly because he is an easygoing Chief and also because Eulenburg himself was hoping to be considered as Chief in a few years' time. But he now realizes that Werthern *must* go, and wants to curry favour with Bismarck by himself advising Werthern to leave.[2] I have dissuaded him from playing this dubious role because Bismarck will get rid of Werthern without Eulenburg's help, if that is what he intends.

The Queen of England, who cannot bear Churchill, has written and told the Crown Princess she mistrusts Hatzfeldt because he is too intimate with Churchill.

The friendship between the two men sprang up partly because Lady Randolph, an American, is a close friend of Countess Hatzfeldt. But quite apart from that I believe Churchill will come into prominence again sooner or later.[3]

Peter Shuvalov is here on a secret mission with the aim of winning us over.[4] Without going into details I should just like

[1] Philipp, Count zu Eulenburg-Hertefeld. Secretary of Legation in Munich, 1881–8; Minister in Oldenburg, 1888–90, in Stuttgart, 1890–1, in Munich, 1891–4; Ambassador in Vienna, 1894–1901.

[2] In a letter to Holstein dated 5 January 1887 Eulenberg wrote: 'I should be glad to do him [Werthern] a final service by persuading him to hand in his resignation at a time when *no dispute* is in the air.'

[3] Lord Randolph Churchill had resigned as Chancellor of the Exchequer on 20 December 1886.

[4] On 6 January Peter Shuvalov informed Herbert von Bismarck that he had not come as a *simple particulier*, but on behalf of the Tsar, who was uneasy about the possibility that the Prince of Battenberg might return to Bulgaria. Moreover, during this interview Count Shuvalov prepared the way for the negotiations which were to lead to the conclusion of the Reinsurance Treaty. (*Grosse Politik*, vol. v, nos. 1030; 1062, pp. 160–3; 212–14.)

to state briefly my view that Russia would like to involve us in a war with France so that she herself can attack Austria. The Russians realize that, except for France, Europe is turning away from them. They would therefore like to risk the great throw before the anti-Russian bloc is linked together by a system of treaties—the sooner the better.

Herbert has fallen completely under the spell of Peter Shuvalov's considerable charm of manner and would like to do everything he asks. Let us hope the Old Man does not give way all along the line.

Schweinitz told me to-day: 'There are young men here (Prince Wilhelm and Herbert) [who think] we can count on Russia's neutrality in a Franco-German war. I doubt whether the Tsar could remain neutral even if he wished. We are only secure against Russia if she is committed elsewhere.'

Schweinitz also alluded to the fact that the Russians see through our two-faced policy; on the one hand we behave as if we were Russia's best friends, on the other hand we secretly advise Austria, England and Italy to form an alliance against Russia.[1] It would look better if we did all this openly, and we should then find we had formed an alliance against Russia and France in no time.

11 *January* 1887

The wind has again shifted strongly against Austria here. Peter Shuvalov is here negotiating. I do not want to give you details, but I do wonder what will be the verdict of history on this policy of the later Bismarck period. Herbert controls his father completely.

'When I concluded the alliance with Austria', Bismarck told Shuvalov,[2] 'I thought I was allying myself with a powerful Kaiser, instead of which I see I have allied myself with the Hungarian Parliament.'

Mere phrases aimed at justifying His Highness to himself.

Peter Shuvalov said a remarkable thing to Herbert after a few stiff drinks. Herbert spoke of Tsar Alexander's *caractère simple et loyal.*

'*Peuh*', said Shuvalov, '*qui sait? Je ne vois pas jusqu'au fond, personne ne le connaît. Il n'est peut-être pas si simple ni si loyal que vous pensez.*' Exactly what I think. [...]

Instead of concluding an alliance with Austria, Italy, England and Turkey—who are all willing—and then quietly waiting to

---

[1] Holstein is referring to the negotiations which led to the First Mediterranean Agreement of 12 February 1887 between England and Italy, to which Austria adhered on 24 March and Spain on 4 May. (*Grosse Politik*, vol. IV, chapters XXV–XXVII.)

[2] Probably at a dinner party on 10 January. (See *Grosse Politik*, vol. V, p. 214, note *.)

see what Russia and France do, the latest plan is to fight France and allow Russia, as the price of her neutrality, a free hand in the Near East, no matter whether Austria is destroyed in the process or not. 'We'll turn our attention to France and for a time we won't look at what is going on behind our back', says Herbert. A wretched arrangement, because if the Russians crush Austria we shall stand alone between Russia and France, and even if we have conquered France we shall have to go to war all over again.

I cannot prevent this rapprochement with Russia: the magnetic force pulling Herbert and therefore his father in that direction is too strong. But I am pushing as hard as I can to bring about an Austro-Italian alliance. England would then come in as the third member, and the three of them, with Turkey into the bargain, would be too strong for Russia.

Robilant, in a personal letter to Launay which the latter read to me, said: '*Nous ne voulons pas profiter sans rien faire. Nous sommes tout prêts à nous lancer dans la bagarre, et nous pourrons beaucoup faire. Mais la politique des mains nettes, nous ne la ferons pas. J'espère que l'année qui commence sera bonne pour l'Italie, et Vive le Roi!*'[1]

The Italians want payment and the Austrians think the price too high, but I am persuading them to agree. The enclosed letter from Reuss[2] refers to this. I hope we achieve something soon. The Russians realize something is afoot and will therefore, in my opinion, wish to hasten events. Preparations in the Black Sea region are also going forward very secretly.

Our policy with its criss-cross of commitments, as I told Bill yesterday, resembles the tangle of lines at a big railway station. The chief pointsman thinks he can click everything into its proper place and hopes particularly that the greater the confusion the more indispensable he is. Many people are now reproaching him for this.

As regards domestic policy, Herbert would like to bring about a constitutional conflict. I am no judge of domestic matters, but I do not think the Chancellor is now the man to *weather* a conflict; and I said so to Herbert and Bill.

20 *January* 1887

Austria will have nothing to do with the Italian proposals recommended by us, because she mistrusts us too much.[3] This

---

[1] This quotation from Robilant's letter is also in the Foreign Ministry files in a memorandum by Herbert von Bismarck of 6 January.   [2] Of 9 January 1887 (*Correspondence*).
[3] See *Grosse Politik*, vol. IV, no. 845, pp. 231–7; p. 240, note ***.

Austrian refusal springs from the fear that the moment there exists a sufficiently strong anti-Russian bloc we shall bring about a war between Russia and Austria so as to have a free hand towards France. This suspicion has perhaps some foundation. But the question is whether Austria will in fact be able to avoid such a war, i.e. whether she will decide to give way to Russian claims on the Balkan peninsula. If not, then it is madness on the part of the Austrians not to have secured Italy's co-operation, at any price.

However, this setback does show how mistaken our dishonest policy is. We could already have united Austria, Italy, England and Turkey in a single alliance if we ourselves had openly proclaimed our intentions. Russia and France would have been powerless against us. They were all ripe for this alliance. But our present attitude of friendship towards Russia is preventing *any* anti-Russian grouping. Austria, Italy, England, are all becoming suspicious and hanging back because they are saying to themselves: 'What is behind this? Germany is a close friend of Russia's and is inciting us *against* Russia!'

We may still have to fight it out with France, alone, with Russia as *unoccupied* spectator. Or else we come to an arrangement with Russia and possibly Italy and as a result Austria will be crushed by them both, while we settle our accounts with France. We shall then stand *alone* between Russia and France.

Oh well, things usually do not go so badly as they might. But it is a pity so much work has been wasted.

21 *January* 1887

Psychologically interesting.

The day before yesterday at 9.30 p.m. President Tiedemann called on me in my office and poured out his troubles. He is now Head of the Administration in Bromberg and the whole of our present Polish policy—colonization etc.[1]—was worked out by him. The Chancellor was very pleased with his work and informed the Ministers last year that he intended to put forward Tiedemann as candidate for the post of Head of the Administration in Posen. In fact Count Zedlitz[2] was appointed. Puttkamer, Bötticher and Rottenburg had opposed Tiedemann, and the Chancellor, who has never stood up for any one in his life, dropped

[1] To check the spread of Polish nationals, a settlers' law was promulgated on 26 April 1886 by the King of Prussia which provided for a settlers' commission to purchase Polish estates in Posen and West Prussia and install German settlers.

[2] Robert, Count von Zedlitz-Trützschler. Head of the Administration in Posen from 1886; Prussian Minister for Ecclesiastical Affairs, 1891–2.

Tiedemann, although he had in private already held out hopes to him of the most definite kind. Now His Highness is ashamed to meet Tiedemann and when Tiedemann was in Berlin for the Landtag H.H. did not invite him or otherwise see him.

In his profession Tiedemann is far more outstanding than Rottenburg and Bötticher, who are consequently afraid of him and keep him at arm's length, although it was Tiedemann who formerly brought Bötticher to the Chancellor's notice.

Yesterday, when I mentioned in passing to Frau von Bötticher that I thought Tiedemann looked depressed, she replied—she is a good-natured goose who gets her ideas ready-made from her husband: 'Well, that's because he wasn't made Head of Adminis-tration', then she added with a sneer: 'Do you think he's suited for it?' Tiedemann lacks the servile diplomacy of Rottenburg and Bötticher, and it must moreover be admitted that he is not always entirely tactful. But he has other qualities instead, and those three—Puttkamer, Bötticher and Rottenburg—persecute him more because of his qualities than his defects.

Similarly another most able man, Bödicker[1] of the Bureau of Insurance, was harried and persecuted by Bötticher and Rott. for fear he might become too important; for instance he, the only man with a thorough knowledge of the insurance system since its inception, was *not* invited to sit on the commission which is deliberating the further development of the insurance system[2] under Schelling's[3] chairmanship. It really does not seem possible. But the Chancellor does not worry about such 'trifles' and leaves Bötticher and Rottenburg to deal with domestic matters. These two little men have learnt from the great man that it is better to put lesser men into the higher positions.

14 *March* 1887

Dear Ize,

As I write the date I am reminded that it is now thirty-nine years since that 13 or 14 March when we, my parents and I, were in Karlstein[4] after selling Trebenow.[5] I can still see the lean old

---

[1] Anton Bödicker. Head of the Imperial Insurance Bureau, 1884–97.

[2] The commission discussed the draft bill concerning the delimitation and organization of trade associations, so as to give effect to the law of 5 May 1886 concerning accident and sickness insurance. The draft bill was passed in the Prussian Landtag on 9 March and 28 April 1887.

[3] Ludwig Hermann von Schelling. State Secretary of the Ministry of Justice, 1879–89.

[4] Karlstein near Zehden on the Oder. The estate belonging to Ida von Stülpnagel's mother, Minna von Holtzendorff.

[5] Trebenow was the Holstein family estate, which August von Holstein, Friedrich's father, sold in 1848.

fellow in his high black cravat with no collar, who on 20 March brought us the first news of the Revolution. And to-day? To-day we can say with the huntsman in Wallenstein: 'And what else shall I live to see!' I think we shall have trouble. Whether it will be this year is not certain, but it is possible.

In the sphere of diplomacy we are prepared for it.

Two days ago ratifications of various treaties between Austria, Italy and Germany were exchanged. Above all, we now have a defensive alliance with Italy against France.[1]

There is in addition an agreement between England and Italy, loosely knit it is true, concerning 'Attempts to preserve the *status quo* in the Black Sea'. Hatzfeldt telegraphed yesterday evening that Austria had adhered to this agreement.[2]

Thus my exertions of the past six months have been crowned with success.

Only last autumn the Chancellor told Keudell: 'I'm not interested in Italy.' First I won over Herbert to the idea of an Italian alliance, then he persuaded his father.

After a long gap I have been seeing the Chancellor a good deal in recent weeks. He has become an *old man*. The days when he could claim to think of everything are past: now one has to try to help and support him whenever possible.

To my great regret Hohenlohe will probably be thrown out. The ostensible reason is the election fiasco,[3] but the real reason is, I suspect, that the Chancellor wants to allow the post of Governor to fall into abeyance together with its salary of 70,000 taler, because he knows the Crown Princess has earmarked it as a marriage portion for her intended son-in-law, Battenberg.

Keudell's temporary transfer to the retired list was signed yesterday. He had asked for it himself after a quarrel with two officials in the Italian Foreign Ministry but probably never imagined he would be taken seriously. Robilant, however, had asked for a change of ambassador[4] twice already, and so we seized this opportunity. When someone asked Herbert this morning: 'But whatever will your mother say?' he replied: 'Oh, it's a

[1] Holstein is referring to the renewal of the Triple Alliance on 20 February. The defensive alliance with Italy against France differed from the original Triple Alliance in that Germany also assured Italy of her support even in the event of her being threatened in North Africa. *Grosse Politik*, vol. IV, no. 859, pp. 258–9.

[2] Holstein is mistaken. This news was announced in a telegram of 13 March sent by Reuss from Vienna. (From the Foreign Ministry files.)

[3] Hohenlohe had urged the electors of Alsace-Lorraine to support those candidates who favoured the seven-years' military budget of the German Reich (*Septennatsvorlage*). The elections to the Reichstag of 21 February resulted in a heavy defeat for the candidates in favour of the government measure.

[4] See *Memoirs*, pp. 75–7.

splendid thing for her; Keudell can come here and play the piano to her.'

There was a lot to tell you these last few months. But I was too busy.

Yours affectionately,

Fritz

Ciphered letter to Thielmann.[1]

Reply enclosed.[2]   sent 22 March

Private and Confidential

Only for your information; for want of communication by courier.

The Chancellor has threatened St Petersburg[3] with your recall unless the lies in the Press concerning your behaviour during the recent *putsch*[4] are denied. Giers censures and deplores the attitude of the Russian Press and is willing to issue a denial.[5]

The mistrust between Russia and ourselves is increasing in Germany, perhaps in Russia too. There is no longer room for doubt that highly placed Russians in Paris have repeatedly put out feelers for an alliance which have found no response there on the grounds that they were *premature*. Russian restraint during the recent *putsch* may well have some connexion with this. However, Freycinet has stated he does not think this restraint will last long.[6]

Meanwhile a strong group of Great Powers, not including Germany, has very recently combined to form an 'Alliance of Principles', i.e. a statement of principles with a view to the protection of the *status quo* in the Black Sea region and along the coast

[1] Max Franz Guido, Baron von Thielmann. First Secretary in the Embassy in Paris, 1880–2, in Constantinople, 1882–6; Consul-General in Sofia, 1886–7; Prussian Minister in Darmstadt, 1887–90.

[2] Thielmann wrote on 29 March 1887: 'I send you my most humble thanks for your kind information of the 21st inst., so flattering to me. I impressed it firmly on my memory and then consigned it to a place which makes any subsequent indiscretion impossible, namely the fire. [...]'

[3] In a dispatch to St Petersburg of 13 March. (From the Foreign Ministry files.)

[4] On 28 February and 3 March military insurrections against the government broke out in Bulgaria which were quickly suppressed. The Bulgarian Government gave out that the revolts had taken place with the foreknowledge of the Russian Government.

[5] Schweinitz telegraphed on 19 March that, with the approval of the Tsar, a correction of the Press slanders against Thielmann would be published in the *Regierungsbote*. It appeared on 21 March. (From the Foreign Ministry files.)

[6] Münster had telegraphed from Paris on 8 March: 'Met Flourens, Freycinet and Baron von Mohrenheim when visiting Minister Goblet. Flourens said it now seemed certain to him that the Russians had given up the idea of occupying Bulgaria and wished to wait and see what happened. M. Freycinet thinks the Russians would wait for about five or six weeks. He said everything was being done here to avoid complications. He admitted that about a fortnight ago the Russians had made proposals here which had been turned down. Baron von Mohrenheim gave a definite assurance that Russia did not wish to intervene.' (From the Foreign Ministry files.)

336

of the Aegean and the Mediterranean. Independently of this we have a firm alliance with Italy for the defence of our mutual interests. Everything is ready,[1] favourably arranged, and even the question of *Italia irredenta* has been temporarily buried or locked away. How long this favourable situation will last, how long Robilant and Salisbury will remain in office, no one can say.

Thus, there could not be a more opportune time for the Bulgarians to establish themselves definitively on their present geographical basis.[2] On the other hand it would be harmful and would serve only Russian interests if, as is feared in England, the Bulgarians fomented a disturbance in *Macedonia*. This would spread confusion among friendly nations and would, in particular, drive the Turks back into the Russian camp, whereas at present, as we are assured by Goltz Pasha,[3] now in Berlin, the Sultan would gladly give up Eastern Rumelia if he could thereby obtain a powerful Bulgaria as a bulwark against Russia.

Our arch-enemies in Russia would like to postpone a Near Eastern conflict until after the war between Germany and France, in which they hope to intervene. It would therefore be a good thing for Germany if the inevitable war in the Near East broke out as soon as possible.

The foregoing is of course only the expression of my personal opinion. If you share it you may be able to exert a *negative* influence by avoiding as far as possible any pronouncement which might *discourage* the Bulgarians—provided you have no definite, unequivocal instructions to the contrary. But it seems to me that *positive* advice in the above sense might have unpleasant consequences for your position and for the Cabinet here, because you are of course surrounded by Russian spies and other unreliable persons.

The surest way to set the ball rolling would be for the Bulgarians to re-elect Prince Alexander, although there is the *remote* possibility that the Russians, in view of the superior force that would gradually be arrayed against them, may do nothing, at least for the moment. You can, of course, say nothing definite *in favour* of his re-election, but in my opinion you need not work *against* it unless you have definite instructions to do so.

As regards your reports, I would merely observe that we find it convenient if we can simply send on your dispatches to St Petersburg, particularly those dealing with ticklish questions.

---

[1] At this point in his draft Holstein crossed out the words: 'for the fray' [*zum Gefecht*].

[2] At this point in his draft Holstein crossed out the sentence: 'Also the re-election of Prince Alexander would be convenient because it would bring things to a decision.'

[3] Kolmar, Baron von der Goltz. Prussian officer serving with the Turkish army, 1883–95.

Draft them accordingly, and particularly avoid giving the Russians any legitimate grounds for complaint.

The alliances I mentioned at the beginning are secret. If they are mentioned in your hearing, be reserved rather than deny them.

I rely on your honour not to let one word of this information reach the Embassy in Constantinople.[1]

5 *April* 1887

I have pulled Hohenlohe through, against His Highness, Bötticher and others.[2] When I became convinced that Hohenlohe could expect no good from any of them, I told him: 'Don't consider them any more, don't worry about them in the least; go direct to the Kaiser, which is your prerogative as Governor.'

Hohenlohe did so, pushed through the desired changes in his staff and obtained a promise from the Kaiser that he would now be granted a period during which no new legislation concerning Alsace-Lorraine would be introduced.

When the Chancellor proposed to the Kaiser the abolition of the governorship, H.M. gave him a decidedly negative answer.

In spite of this the Council of Ministers, at the Chancellor's suggestion, decided to prepare this draft bill. So the Kaiser, a few days later, sent Wilmowski to Bötticher to say H.M. was astonished to find them troubling about a bill after he had stated he did not wish it!

Bötticher, in great embarrassment, said they were still at the stage of preparing the material.

The Kaiser, whom no one now dares to treat firmly because he is so feeble, wields more power to-day than ever before. And so Hohenlohe has at least a period of grace. He must put it to good use.

I have thus repaid him for the kindness he showed me twelve years ago.[3] His Jesuitical mother-in-law, old Princess

---

[1] At this point in his draft Holstein crossed out the words: 'otherwise we might just as well tell Nelidov'.

[2] See Hohenlohe, *Denkwürdigkeiten*, vol. ii, pp. 416 et seq.

[3] Holstein was Second Secretary at the German Embassy in Paris, 1871–6; from 1874 he served under Ambassador Prince Hohenlohe. In a letter to Bismarck of 23 May 1875, Hohenlohe wrote: ' [...] I now hear that proposals for personnel changes are being drawn up in the offices of the Foreign Ministry and that the question will be discussed whether Count Wesdehlen [the First Secretary] is to be given an independent post or is to remain here as senior *Rat* with the title and status of Minister. Now, I should have no reason whatever to complain if Count Wesdehlen remained here. He is a calm tactful man whom any head of a mission would be glad to have at his side. But in this case I should be sorry for Holstein who would thus see his hopes of moving up into first place disappear, whereas members of the diplomatic service who are more junior have already been promoted to higher position. I know that Your Highness appreciates Holstein's good qualities and therefore I have no hesitation in recommending him to Your Highness' consideration. If Count Wesdehlen went from here to an independent post I should for my part have no objection if Holstein were given the top post here. Your Highness knows him better and will

Wittgenstein, who was friendly with the Kaiserin and with Arnim, agitated against me with all her might. So did Reuss, though he now writes me most cordial letters. He informed Hohenlohe, through the latter's brother-in-law Peter Wittgenstein, that *he* would not tolerate a Secretary like me in *his* Embassy. For years afterwards I treated Reuss abominably. But he will not be turned away—provided I can either be of use to him or harm him. At the moment official requirements oblige me to correspond with him, although it does very little good; he is a great coward and does nothing without instructions. As Herbert says: 'A demobilized corporal made postman.'

29 *April* 1887

We are giving way over the Schnäbele affair.[1] Schnäbele is being set free. I was against handing him over, Bleichröder was in favour.

If the Chancellor intended to give way, he should have stated right from the start: '*Provided* it is shown that Schnäbele was *enticed* over the frontier, he will be set free.' But H.H. did nothing of the sort; he declared verbally and in writing: 'The *guet-apens* is less serious than the fact that Schnäbele has for years abused his official position for purposes of espionage.' Not until a few days later, when Bleichröder informed him that Rothschild thought the political situation was serious, did H.H. state that Schnäbele would be released, since his position as customs official conferred on him a certain international immunity.

So once again we give way as soon as our opponent stands up to us. Like the Carolines affair. Other nations will soon realize what I have known for two years, namely that H.H. has lost his nerve.

In addition he is now suffering from a positive mania for secret treaties. For instance, after concluding treaties with Austria and Italy which are directed against Russia and France, he now wants to conclude a treaty *with* Russia.[2] I am not saying that

therefore be more able than I to judge of his suitability for the position here. As far as I am concerned I cannot but give the best possible report of his abilities and his zeal. [...]' Bismarck replied on 26 May: '[...] I was very glad to hear your favourable opinion of Holstein, in which I concur; no changes of staff in your Embassy will be undertaken without your previous knowledge, and your wishes and suggestions will be given primary consideration. [...]' (From the Foreign Ministry files.)

[1] Guillaume Schnäbele was a French customs official who had promoted espionage activities in Alsace-Lorraine. He was arrested on 20 April but released on 28 April when it became clear that he had crossed the frontier at the invitation of a German colleague. See *Grosse Politik*, vol. VI, nos. 1257–64, pp. 182–9.

[2] Holstein is referring to the negotiations which led to the Reinsurance Treaty of 18 June 1887.

these various agreements contradict each other—but they do provoke a general mistrust of us, precisely because they are secret. A does not know what arrangement we have come to with B and naturally assumes the worst.

Prince Bismarck's dominant qualities used to be cunning and energy (which seldom go together); his chief defects were vanity and a lust for power. His energy has gone. His cunning, on which he now relies exclusively, spends itself in tortuous exaggeration. His vanity and his lust for power have also increased. I see evidence of this in what Bill told me the other day: 'I'm afraid Herbert's becoming too independent for H.H.'s taste. H.H. told me yesterday that Herbert was working himself to death here and that it would be best if he left to take up an ambassadorship. When I asked him who would replace Herbert here, H.H. said he had thought of Berchem. So I suppose I'm to become Under State Secretary, but I don't wish to, if only because my mother cannot bear my wife.'

Bill's information is in every respect typical. The old man is growing jealous of Herbert. H.H., whose memory has completely gone and who is too lazy to study the files, still insists on making his marginal annotations as before, usually without consulting any one, and as a result often contradicts himself; Herbert then has the unpleasant task of pointing out these contradictions. H.H. is annoyed every time, because from the very start he refuses to entertain the possibility that he can *ever* be mistaken. He would never put up with such criticisms from a stranger—he would be dismissed at once. Hence it is unavoidable that for the duration of the Bismarck regime one of his sons *must* be here. I said so to Bill, but he replied that Herbert was more suited to the post because he, Bill, was even more headstrong.

As a Protestant I find Bismarck's attitude towards the ecclesiastical question most sinister. It seems to me quite possible that H.H. thinks that if the whole of Germany, both Government and governed, had only one religion, namely the Catholic religion, the Government would the more easily obtain a Conservative majority. He may also have considered the future, when Germany might possibly acquire German-speaking Austria and when a Protestant Imperial Government would be permanently in the minority.

Bill, referring to the new religious laws,[1] said: 'We shall all end up as Catholics, but that won't do any harm.'

---

[1] On 27 April a new law was passed in the Prussian Landtag removing many of the restrictions which had been imposed on the Catholic Church during the *Kulturkampf*. The law aimed at reconciling the Prussian State with the Curia.

H.H. once said to me many years ago when we were talking of the sack of Magdeburg by Tilly: 'The inhabitants of Magdeburg were rebels against their Kaiser.'

H.H. sets politics rather too far above religion. [...]

8 *May* 1887

On New Year's Eve '76/'77 Herbert, Bucher and I transcribed three highly secret documents. They were the so-called Reichstadt agreements between Russia and Austria which prepared the way for the Russo-Turkish War.[1] Andrássy had communicated them to Berlin without the Russians' knowledge because it went against his conscience to keep such a secret from us, in view of Austria's good relations with Germany. At that time the best possible personal relations existed between Bismarck and Andrássy. Bismarck used to tell any one who cared to hear it that his relations with Andrássy were those which obtain between neighbouring country squires rather than neighbouring Ministers.

Now, as a result of the latest publications in the *Norddeutsche Allgemeine Zeitung*,[2] Andrássy has been politically ruined by no other means than those very documents he had communicated to us in good faith.

Two days ago the Austrian Kaiser expressed his wish, through Széchényi, that these disclosures should be discontinued.[3] Herbert replied that this wish would be complied with as far as possible

[1] See p. 5, note 6. Holstein means the drafts of the Budapest Convention of 15 January 1877. These were communicated to the German Government on 30 and 31 December 1876 by the Austrian and by the Russian Governments. The Austrian Ambassador also handed over to the Foreign Ministry a series of documents relating to the negotiations between Austria and Russia which preceded the Convention. See *Grosse Politik*, vol. II, p. 91, note *; no. 265, pp. 111–14.

[2] In a dispatch to Vienna of 18 April 1887, Bismarck had proposed that the attacks of Pan-Slav politicians and newspapers, representing Austria's occupation of Bosnia and Herzegovina as the result of an Austro-German intrigue at the Congress of Berlin, should be countered by publications on the Austro-Russian negotiations of 1876–7. According to a dispatch from Vienna of 26 April, Kálnoky declined to take this action, not least because of the difficulties such a disclosure would cause in the Hungarian Parliament after Andrássy's repeated statements that the occupation of the provinces had not been 'premeditated'. Kaiser Franz Joseph also had the gravest misgivings against such a disclosure and feared Alexander III's displeasure. Alexander III on the other hand, when approached by Germany, had agreed to the action desired by Bismarck. (Dispatch from Bülow in St Petersburg, 22 April 1887.) On 30 April 1887 Vienna was informed of Alexander III's agreement. It was assumed in Bismarck's dispatch that the Austrian Government would now have no objection. Articles appeared in the *Norddeutsche Allgemeine Zeitung* on 20, 27 and 28 April and on 2, 3, 5 and 6 May, containing certain disclosures relating to the Austro-Russian negotiations of 1876–7. (From the Foreign Ministry files.)

[3] In a dispatch dated 4 May which reached Berlin on 6 May, Reuss stated that Kálnoky had expressed the request that no further disclosures be made now that the existence of the Austro-Russian Convention and its date had been made known. (From the Foreign Ministry files.)

but that we might nevertheless be obliged to furnish further evidence to justify allegations already made.[1]

Such behaviour leaves me speechless. If anything were still needed to prove to me that to the Chancellor *nothing* is sacred, this behaviour would do so. The Chancellor imagines the Russians will hate him less after these disclosures. He is mistaken. The Russians, the one nation he is running after, do not hate him, they despise him. This feeling will be intensified by these latest disclosures. And where is the sense in ruining Andrássy? There is no political advantage in it—on the contrary. Now that the Austria-Italy-England bloc has been welded together, the sooner this grouping comes to blows with Russia the better. And a clash is more probable with Andrássy in power than Kálnoky.

Thus the motive for this behaviour towards Andrássy can in fact only be personal. Andrássy was an outstanding personality, and the Chancellor would like to see nonentities like Kálnoky in power all over Europe so that he can be the only prominent figure. We shall experience more of this kind of thing. A curious policy. And who can trust us now?

17 *May* 1887

I have just learned, while writing this, that the doctors—Bergmann, Gerhardt[2] etc.—diagnose the Crown Prince's throat trouble as cancer. Bergmann insists on sending for a Dr Mackenzie[3] from London—the greatest cancer speciality [*sic*]—to give his opinion. The operation must be performed from the *outside*; part of the larynx must be removed. Bergmann 'knows a case' of a patient who was permanently cured by a throat operation of this kind.

[1] See *Grosse Politik*, vol. v, no. 1101, pp. 271–2. The section of Bismarck's dispatch to Vienna on 8 May not published in the *Grosse Politik* sets forth the reasons why these disclosures helped Russo-German relations, particularly by strengthening Giers' position against Pan-Slav attacks, and states that Germany could not be expected to sacrifice Russo-German relations to 'the parliamentary interests of individual Hungarian Ministers'. On 8 May Prince Reuss reported to Berlin Andrássy's complaint that these disclosures were directed against him or at least admitted of that interpretation. In a dispatch of 12 May Bismarck again explained the political advantages of a clear statement of the background to the Austrian occupation of Bosnia and Herzegovina. The controversy that raged between the German and Austrian Press as a result of the articles in the *Norddeutsche Allgemeine Zeitung* had not been of Germany's seeking. In the section of his dispatch from Vienna of 11 May 1887 not published in the *Grosse Politik* (vol. v, no. 1102, pp. 272–3), Prince Reuss again stated the reasons why Kaiser Franz Joseph and Kálnoky raised objections to further disclosures. The effect on the Balkan States and the Sultan would be most unfortunate. Despite Bismarck's insistence (dispatch to Vienna of 16 May), Austria's consent to a publication of the documents could not be obtained. The incident was closed by a statement in the Hungarian Parliament by the Hungarian Minister-President Tisza who confirmed the existence of the Austro-Russian agreements of 1876–7. (From the Foreign Ministry files.)

[2] Karl Gerhardt. Professor of medicine at Berlin.

[3] Dr, later Sir Morell Mackenzie. Throat specialist.

God moves in a mysterious way. The relentless course of world history is unexpectedly altered. Prince Wilhelm may be Kaiser at thirty. What will happen then?

If the Prince were ten years older *or* the Chancellor ten years younger, I should, from the purely political and impersonal point of view, regard this as a propitious event.

But now, when a young Kaiser will join with Herbert in sometimes forcing old Prince Bismarck's hand, the situation is fraught with great danger.

On the other hand, what role might the Crown Princess have played in the regime of Kaiser Friedrich Wilhelm I? She has many bad qualities, [she is] sensual, false, cowardly and heartless. Their children love their father and feel sorry for him, but they dislike their mother. Whether *he* would ever have been able to shake off her influence was the riddle of the future, which may now never be solved.

For the Kaiser, the Crown Prince has simply ceased to exist, so W.[1] said yesterday. H.M. has often said: 'I have no son now; the Crown Prince is a stranger.' The Kaiserin is said to have agitated a great deal out of hatred for the Crown Princess.

20 *May* 1887

Mackenzie, the Scotch specialist, has made a suggestion the other duffers should have had [*sic*] already, namely that a tiny fragment of the tumour shall be painlessly removed with cocaine and examined under the microscope to see whether it is cancer or not. Whether or not it turns out to be cancer, I think it is a reflection on the quality of the Berlin doctors that they never thought of doing so before.

The Chancellor drove to see the Kaiser this afternoon to inform him that the Crown Prince must undergo an operation in which his life would be in danger. His Majesty's consent must be obtained for this operation. Would His Maj. care to see the doctors to-morrow, beforehand?

H.M. replied: 'Oh, to-morrow is most inconvenient for me, because I'm inspecting the troops at Potsdam.'

When the Chancellor insisted, H.M. said: 'Very well, the doctors must come early so as not to upset my inspection.'

Only once in the course of the conversation did the Kaiser say: 'Oh, my poor son', but even then he showed no emotion.

This helps one to understand the kind of thing that went on in medieval times between crowned kings and their heirs.

[1] Probably Wilmowski.

343

The Crown Princess has behaved in such a way as to drive Friedberg and her entourage into paroxysms of fury. Friedberg said he thought Her Imp. Highness would greet a catastrophe as the gateway to freedom.

When Rado[linski] informed her that the doctors said it was cancer, she replied: 'Oh, it won't be as bad as that. But it's a pity Fritz hasn't made a will. Vicky should have the income from Öls to be able to marry Prince Alexander.'

On another occasion: 'If the worst happens I shall have no one's feelings to consider, *je jette mon bonnet par-dessus les moulins* and I shall give all my money to Vicky so she can marry the Prince of Bulgaria.' And again: 'Couldn't we just get the Crown Prince to rush through a will in Vicky's favour?' Radolinski, Kessel[1] and Friedberg are agreed that the Crown Princess is *completely* indifferent. The idea that Seck[endorff] is her lover is regaining ground. She seems to be picturing the charms of leading a bohemian life with him in Italy. 'I shan't stay *here* an hour longer than I must', she said yesterday.

22 *May* 1887 (*evening*)

The microscope examination has yielded nothing. As the fragment was so tiny, to-morrow a somewhat larger piece is to be removed for a fresh examination.

Mackenzie still thinks it is not cancer.

Schweninger, who of course joins in the talk though he knows nothing of the case, says cancer cannot be determined microscopically.

People like me cannot form any opinion, but must wait patiently. I find it a bad sign that, in addition to Gerhardt and Bergmann, Tobold[2] also diagnoses cancer. On the other hand Gerhardt and Bergmann called in Mackenzie as the greatest living authority on diseases of the throat.

23 *May* 1887

Virchow,[3] who made the microscope examination, thought it furnished, if not entire proof, certainly a favourable pointer to the absence of cancer. The Britisher seems to be proved right. Our Berlin oracles, Gerhardt, Bergmann etc. seem to be diminished in stature already. Mackenzie claims he will completely cure the Crown Prince in a few months. He also says that the operation

---

[1] Gustav von Kessel. Aide-de-camp to Crown Prince Friedrich Wilhelm.

[2] Dr Adalbert Tobold. Throat specialist.

[3] Rudolf Virchow. Professor and Director of the Institute of Pathology in Berlin; Member of the Reichstag (Progressive Party), 1880–93.

Bergmann wanted to perform has been tried repeatedly by Langenbeck,[1] but that all the patients died under the knife.

The replies I received from Herbert and Bill to my first unfavourable report on the Crown Prince are quite in character.[2]

27 *May* 1887

They are not at all easy in their minds about the Crown Prince. The doctors here, particularly Bergmann and Tobold, persist in their opinion that it is cancer. Even the Crown Prince regards himself as a dead man. Mackenzie will be back in a fortnight's time. He wishes the throat to be left alone for the present. Gerhardt has moved over to Mackenzie's opinion and will send him reports during his absence.

The enclosed letter from Hohenlohe[3] shows a certain aversion to stern measures;[4] they just go against the grain. In those circumstances there is no point in writing to him, so I shall shelve the correspondence for the present.

1 *June* 1887

The letter from B.[5] is typical of the clear-sightedness and sceptical attitude of its writer. This very scepticism prevents him from making any serious effort. It just is not worth it.

Since Bill has some influence on Herbert, I had written to him setting forth my anxieties in detail. Our constant affectation of mystery and our endlessly vacillating policy have brought us to the point at which every one mistrusts us. I have spoken my mind about that often enough already.

Count Tornielli,[6] to whom Goltz[7] refers,[8] is the Italian Minister

[1] Dr Bernhard von Langenbeck. Professor of medicine; co-founder of the German Society of Surgeons.

[2] Herbert von Bismarck wrote on 20 May 1887: 'This is certainly most important news, unless it turns out that the Berlin doctors have made a mistake, which has often been the case. It was stated some weeks ago that it was cancer, but then the statement was denied. [...]' Wilhelm von Bismarck wrote on 18 May 1887: 'Many thanks for your news, which naturally interested me very much. I do not think it can possibly be kept secret. I heard the *rumour* from Paul Lindau at the beginning of April. The Press, needless to say, is anxiously hushing it up, but it is sure to be spread by word of mouth. [...]'

[3] Hohenlohe's letter of 25 May 1887. Not printed.

[4] The reference is to the proposed introduction of compulsory passports in Alsace-Lorraine.

[5] Wilhelm von Bismarck's letter of 31 May (*Correspondence*).

[6] Count Giuseppe Tornielli Brusati di Vergano. Minister in Bucharest, 1879–88; Ambassador in London, 1889–95, in Paris, 1895–1908.

[7] Karl August, Count von der Goltz. First Secretary of Embassy in Vienna, 1884–6, in Rome 1886–90.

[8] Goltz wrote on 25 May 1887 that he had spoken to Malvano (Director-General in the Italian Foreign Ministry) according to Holstein's instructions. 'If I may permit myself to state my personal impression of my interview with Signor Malvano, I would say that Count Tornielli's chances of being considered for a position of any importance while the present ruling group remains in power here have been completely wrecked. I am firmly convinced that the aim Your Excellency designated to me has been realized to the fullest extent. [...]'

in Bucharest. Shrewd, anti-German, pro-Russian and pro-French. Had the prospect of becoming Foreign Minister. That had to be prevented.

As for the Crown Prince's health, we are back where we started, i.e. the doctors cannot agree. It will certainly become evident whether the inflammation decreases or increases over the next few weeks. In the latter event it would be a clear case of cancer.

The Chancellor has said that the Crown Princess's behaviour gave him the impression she wished to be free. And that is what Friedberg said.

28 *June* 1887[1]

Before leaving [Berlin],[2] the Crown Princess was straining every nerve to extort from the Crown Prince a will drawn up exclusively in her favour. She asked Radolinski, Kessel and Friedberg in turn to suggest this to the Crown Prince. When all three refused she tackled the Prince herself, and, as usual, got what she wanted. The amount concerned was relatively small, three or four hundred thousand marks, about the same as a figure in the Crown Prince's household budget representing unpaid bills. This latter circumstance was seized on by Friedberg, who was furious over the affair and had said to me: 'She's not going to get that will.' So when the Crown Princess, in her husband's presence, requested Friedberg to draw up a will along the lines mentioned above, he replied: 'Certainly, nothing could be easier. But Your Imp. Highnesses must first make a declaration that the estate which is to be disposed of is unencumbered by debts.' Friedberg said later that at that moment the Princess looked at him like a serpent. But the plan for making a will came to nothing.

Caprivi said the other day: 'The Crown Prince has never been held in such high esteem as now.'

Caprivi is one of many people who regard the Crown Prince as less dangerous than Prince Wilhelm because the former can be led, but not the latter.

I was very struck by a talk I had two days ago with Herbert about Prince Wilhelm. Herbert told me that the famous Hungarian painter Koppay (who rose to fame with his death mask of King Ludwig II) has said of Prince Wilhelm, whose portrait he was then engaged on: 'Nothing pleases him for long.' Herbert

[1] In a letter to Ida von Stülpnagel of 28 June [1887] Holstein wrote: 'I am sorry I have made so few entries over the last few months. There was plenty of material. But although I am physically fit I am mentally tired.' (Rogge, *Friedrich von Holstein*, p. 144.)

[2] The Crown Prince and Princess left Berlin on 13 June for London to attend the celebration of Queen Victoria's Golden Jubilee.

said this judgment was unfortunately only too correct. The Prince had no staying power—he simply wanted to be amused. And all that really interested him in army life was wearing a handsome uniform and marching through the streets to music. He fancied himself as Frederick the Great, but had neither his gifts nor his knowledge. And Frederick the Great, as a young man, had ceaselessly worked and exercised his intellect, whereas Prince Wilhelm allowed his talents to deteriorate by constantly consorting with Potsdam Lieutenants. And as cold as a block of ice. Convinced from the start that people only exist to be used—either for work or amusement—and that even then they only do duty for a given period, after which they may be cast aside. Herbert said the Prince was impressed by no one, except, it was to be hoped, the Chancellor. If the Prince were to ascend the throne now, many blunders would be committed. His views on domestic policy were those of a Potsdam Lieutenant and would, if acted upon, easily plunge Germany into a jolly civil war. It would really be catastrophic if the Prince remained in Potsdam any longer; he should be given a Berlin infantry regiment, not the First Regiment of Guards as was intended. The Chancellor has spoken to the Kaiser on the matter but H.M. declared the Prince must command the First Regiment of Guards simply because his father and grandfather had done so, and also because it would cost 200,000 marks to fit out Schloss Bellevue. The Chancellor told Herbert: 'I've exhausted all my arguments and there's nothing more I can do; I don't want to annoy the old gentleman in his feeble condition.'

(Incidentally, it is remarkable how rarely the Chancellor gets his own way with the Kaiser on matters towards which the old gentleman is not already favourably disposed. Formerly H.H. always resorted to pressure, but that method is now impossible with the old gentleman, and he has no idea how to 'manage' the Kaiser.) Herbert's last hope was Albedyll, but he had already made one vain attempt, and it is doubtful whether his personal interests do not cause him to sympathize more with the Potsdam clique.

I found Herbert's changed attitude towards Prince Wilhelm particularly interesting psychologically in that it revealed that *he* does not enjoy that status with the Prince which he desired and imagined he had.

The character sketch he gave me of the Prince—heartless, superficial, vain—has been confirmed from the most varied quarters. A Major told me that when the Prince was informed that in the opinion of the doctors in Berlin, his father was suffering from cancer, he exclaimed: 'The officers must be informed of this immediately', and actually tried to be as good as his word, probably with the intention of having himself proclaimed at once as 'the coming man'. An attractive feature. Waldersee and the Bülow set have a bad influence on him.

Kissingen, 7 August 1887

I am going to London to-morrow. Hatzfeldt wants to talk to me. He is beside himself because the English have recently been turning towards Russia. But we cannot do much to change the situation; it depends on circumstances beyond our control. More about this another time.[1]

12 September 1887

Warmest greetings, my dear Ize. Returned home yesterday evening;[2] but am going to stay with the Radolinskis until Friday, when Herbert will probably be back. In very good health, and all set for another stretch.

F.

28 September 1887

The Crown Prince is in a poor way. He looks wretched and has difficulty in swallowing. And I regard it as a bad sign that Mackenzie is in such a hurry to obtain recognition for his services. He was knighted because he insisted that Radolinski should see to it; similarly he would also like a Prussian decoration double quick.

The Crown Princess's behaviour is typical. Gay and carefree, with but one idea—never to return to Prussia. I persist in my view, which is now shared by others, namely that from the very beginning she accepted the idea that the worst would happen. Judging by all I have heard of her in recent months, I am tempted to call her a degenerate or corrupt character. Nature and pressure of circumstance have combined to produce this effect. She came here thirty years ago, her father's spoiled darling, convinced she was a political prodigy. Far from acquiring influence here, she saw herself obliged to renounce any kind of open political activity and to conform to the restraint of the Prussian Court which she hated. She has always despised her husband. She will greet his death as the moment of deliverance.

[1] See Holstein's letter to Ida von Stülpnagel of 10 August 1887. (Rogge, *Friedrich von Holstein*, pp. 146–7.)

[2] From leave in Pontresina.

When I was talking to Caprivi about the possibility of the Crown Prince's death in the near future, he said: 'Good Heavens, whatever will happen if Prince Wilhelm becomes Kaiser as early as this? He thinks he understands *everything*, even shipbuilding. We launched a cruiser recently, fitted with the so-called "turtle-back armour plate" [*Schildkrötenpanzer*]. The Prince sat opposite me during the meal, spoke very optimistically of all that might be expected from this model, and asked my opinion. I told him the experts still had certain doubts, some of which would not be dispelled until a cruiser of this type had seen some fighting. The Prince said nothing. A few moments later he rose to propose the toast of the day. In conclusion he expressed the hope that he would very soon see the launching of another cruiser of this type. He's as obstinate as a mule, and so is Prince Heinrich.'

It must be mentioned here that Prince Heinrich is set against Caprivi by his adjutant, Seckendorff,[1] and then stirs up Prince Wilhelm against him too.

It seems a pity that Prince Wilhelm, along with many desirable qualities in a monarch, e.g. cold-blooded detachment, has also inherited his mother's self-will and duplicity.

The old Kaiser appears to be completely heartless towards his son. On Radolinski's return from England His Majesty spoke bitterly to him of all the money his son needed; he scarcely referred at all to the latest bulletin about his illness.

Verbatim extract from a letter written by a member of the Crown Prince's entourage (not to me).[2]

Toblach, 24 September 1887

I should like to reply to your letter, even if I have not very cheerful news. First of all the Crown Prince. What am I to say? I can see that as long as we stay here his voice is slowly deteriorating. I know that the Crown Prince has been itching to get away for the last ten days, and wants to go to Gries, but he has not succeeded. The Crown Princess has fixed their departure for the 28th and no power on God's earth can alter her decision. It has gradually become really chilly here; naturally this has affected the Crown Prince's throat. Not the slightest consideration has been shown him in either the daily routine, the excursions, or the insistence on open windows. First of all it was said one of his vocal cords was inflamed; next day, thank God, the inflammation had disappeared, but had unfortunately been followed by slight

[1] Albert, Baron von Seckendorff. Naval Captain.
[2] The letter was probably sent to Radolinski, who was in Berlin at the time. Presumably it was written by Lyncker.

tonsillitis. Then the Crown Prince was given a cocaine injection because his throat caused him pain. That night he could not go to sleep; he was probably worried too, because during the evening, after the injection, his voice failed completely for five or ten minutes, but then it came back. Then during that same night he took some cocaine, probably too much, because now he could not sleep a wink, was completely exhausted next morning and looked ill. Nevertheless we took our walk as usual and had lunch out of doors where, in spite of quite a warm sun, we were frozen the moment it went behind a cloud, so we had violent alternations of temperature the whole time. Naturally he caught cold, did not appear at dinner, and went to bed early. That was yesterday.

This morning, after a good night's rest, he looked well again, but his voice is now as hoarse as it was in the New Palace on his return from Ems. Dr Mackenzie still says: 'I am satisfied. The Crown Prince is doing well; this extreme hoarseness is the result of this momentary chill and will soon pass.' Even so he has advised us to leave here at once, so the Crown Prince, Dr Hovell[1] and I are going tomorrow to Trent, while the Crown Princess, of course, will stay on until the 28th, and then, with Seckendorff and Countess Perponcher,[2] will hurtle across the mountains direct to Venice, probably taking Princess Victoria with her. The two young Princesses with all the baggage will join us in Trent, and then we go to Venice, Hotel Europa, where we are due on the afternoon of the 28th. The Crown Princess intends to arrive there on the 29th, but I shall believe that when I see her. Once she starts travelling around with S. she is unlikely to land in Venice on time. S. asked me to-day whether it might not be better for the Crown Prince's health if he stayed in Venice alone. So they have probably hatched their little scheme already.

Oh, this Crown Princess   I am glad for the Crown Prince's sake that he will be alone for a few days. But it is a real rest-cure for me too. I cannot tell you how that woman gets on my nerves. Now, when it is so bitterly cold that all our teeth are chattering with the frost and the Princesses are going around with blue noses and their hands in mittens, she declares the weather is unbearably hot and has the windows opened; then, mark you, she puts on a great thick shawl. It froze during the night and was still bitterly cold this morning. As usual, I had cursed the loudest about the cold, so she greeted me this morning at breakfast with: 'Isn't it a wonderful warm summer day?' During our walks she runs ahead like a mad thing until the Crown Prince comes to a standstill, exhausted, and says: 'I can't go any further. My wife is racing ahead again.' I stay with [him] then, but the Princess just walks on, saying with a soft upward glance: 'You will walk

---

[1] Dr Mark Hovell. Throat specialist.
[2] Countess Wanda Perponcher. Wife of the Court Chamberlain to Wilhelm I.

really slowly, won't you, dear Fritz, so that you don't get too hot?' and so on.

I cannot bear to see that everlasting smile on her face—the woman has driven every good genius out of her house with that smile.

One afternoon, a few days ago, the Crown Princess, with Countess Perponcher and Seckendorff, had climbed three-quarters of the way up a mountain and there spent the night in a kind of hut so as to reach the summit next morning. After they had come down again we were all to pick them up at a certain village, have lunch there and drive home together. During this trip Countess Perponcher seems first to have realized for herself what a particularly warm understanding existed between the other two; she returned from the expedition in great astonishment, to put it mildly. And down below on the mountain-side stood our dear Crown Prince consumed with anxiety and longing for his faithful wife's return. When at last she did appear his delight was really moving, and was equalled only by her indifference. Even in the carriage he still held her hand. There is nothing to be done about him; if he *refuses* to notice he is simply incorrigible. And it is impossible to help him; as soon as you come to the rescue he changes sides immediately and champions his wife's cause, which he was attacking a moment ago. In any case it is impossible to achieve anything here in the face of such a tangle of selfish desires. In your letter, my dear sir, you state your most decided opinion that the Crown Prince should, if at all possible, choose to reside in Germany this winter. I think I can assure you that this will not be the case. Even so I did make an attempt to persuade him. I took advantage of the morning when the Crown Princess was up the mountain and, referring to a conversation I had with the Crown Prince in Buckingham Palace on this same subject, I told him that the impressions I had carried back from Berlin to London at that time were now confirmed by you, and that in view of the Kaiser's condition people in Berlin were more uneasy than before and regarded it as more than probable that his presence would be required in Berlin this winter; pressure of circumstances would then oblige him to travel and suddenly to exchange the climate of the Riviera for that of North Germany. I then asked him to take advantage of Mackenzie's presence here now to discuss this more than likely event and to consider whether in the circumstances it was not preferable to hold court this winter in one of the palaces in West Germany.

The Crown Prince replied with some heat, and said first of all that the Kaiser had far too strong a constitution and, though ninety, must be treated like a man of seventy. He then became very bitter, saying the Kaiser would outlive him etc. In the end it came out that the whole situation had in fact already been considered by the Crown Princess with the result that, if it became necessary, the Crown Prince would travel to Berlin with a respirator and would return as quickly as possible. In conclusion a point of view came to light which was new to me and greatly surprised me, and which was conceived, not in the Crown Prince's brain, but in the Princess's. I realized he ought not to have said it, but it just slipped out. The Crown Prince has no intention of acting as a mere deputy, should illness render the Kaiser incapable of governing for a time; he would come in only if he were created Regent, i.e. absolute power or *nothing at all*. This was already his intention, or more accurately his wife's intention, when the Kaiser lay severely wounded after the attempt on his life. It is obvious that the Crown Prince has to this day never forgiven the Chancellor for frustrating his plans, and for confronting him on his return from England with a *fait accompli* in the shape of an order drawn up by the Kaiser and appointing the Crown Prince as deputy.[1] Then followed more bitter remarks: Bismarck had ruled for twenty-five years and would continue to rule under him; he was too old now to have any duty but that of keeping things going until his son could come fresh to the task.

I listened to all this with feelings of profound and sincere grief, and realized how unfortunate the Crown Prince is; such a noble character by nature, he has been driven by his wife's constant intrigues into a position in which he feels unhappy and whose artificiality must be apparent to him at times, but which he has now neither the courage nor the strength to abandon.

Verbatim extract from a letter written by a member of the Crown Prince's entourage.

Venice, 28 September 1887

The doctors are unanimous in saying that this fresh chill has had no harmful effects on the malady itself, but it will take ten or twelve days for the effects of the chill on his general condition to wear off. Winterfeld[2] is here and a *good thing* too. I told him everything I wrote to you; he was outraged and had a long and serious conversation yesterday with Mackenzie who arrived in Trent last evening. Winterfeld repeated to me this unhappy conversation, and assured me, when I asked him, that Mackenzie regarded the Crown Prince's original complaint, the tumour which had been operated on, as cured, since it showed no signs of developing again; on the other hand the Crown Prince was unfortunately so delicate and his throat and larynx so liable to swell, that if this did not stop soon it would constitute a very grave danger. He now exhibits the kind of swellings which at first gave

[1] See p. 206, note 1. [2] Major-General von Winterfeld. Aide-de-camp to the Crown Prince.

rise to the fear that the tumour was growing again. M. says that if these swellings could be successfully got rid of without fresh ones developing, he could in several months' time bring the Crown Prince to the point at which he would be out of danger. But if the Crown Prince caught one or two more chills like the one caught in Toblach, with consequent swellings, Mackenzie could not give him more than three months to live. If the Crown Prince insists on speaking and runs the risk of catching fresh chills, it will not merely delay his recovery, it will be a matter of life and death. So Winterfeld spoke very seriously to Mack., so seriously that he felt obliged to offer a few words of apology to M., who was not in the least offended, however, shook hands with him and promised to write very seriously to the Crown Princess. M. complained bitterly of the Crown Princess's selfishness which wounded the Crown Prince so deeply; for example he mentioned to W. what happened during walks and how she rushed along so that the Crown Prince was out of breath each time, and when he was finally forced to a standstill he felt morally broken, and felt he was a feeble invalid not even equal to going for a walk. You see, other people have the same impression as I have. M. has quite definitely forbidden the Crown Prince to talk much and pointed out the danger of doing so, without telling him the whole truth about the dangerous condition of his throat. On the other hand he will write and tell the Crown Princess all this, and W. will speak to her on the same lines when she arrives to-morrow. I wonder whether it will do any good? I hardly think so.

10 *October* 1887

The release of that young idiot Schnäbele[1] has given rise to an acrimonious correspondence between Wilmowski and Herbert.

According to the files,[2] so I am told—I did not have time to check the facts myself—Herbert had written to Strasbourg: 'The Chancellor wishes that Schnäbele's pardon be recommended to His Majesty.' Whereupon Puttkamer, the Under State Secretary, who was deputizing for the Governor at the time, immediately released Schnäbele. The Kaiser learned of his release from the newspapers. The Grand-Dukes of Baden and Saxony, the Kaiserin and the Grand-Duchess of Baden seem then to have stirred up His Majesty as they usually do, telling him his authority

[1] Gustav Schnäbele, sixteen-year-old son of Guillaume Schnäbele (see p. 339, note 1), was arrested when crossing the frontier into Germany on 19 September on a charge of displaying subversive slogans and endangering the public peace. The *Landesgericht* at Metz condemned Schnäbele on 29 September to three weeks' imprisonment and a 20-mark fine. The sentence was suspended and Schnäbele was released from custody. (From the Foreign Ministry files.)

[2] Holstein's account which follows here tallies with the Foreign Ministry files.

was being flouted, etc. An inquiry was made of Puttkamer. He said the release had taken place 'at the instigation of the Foreign Ministry', and then came to Baden to whitewash himself. Then followed a letter from Wilmowski to Herbert: 'H.M. is most displeased.' Very stinging reply from Herbert. Further reply from Wilmowski arrived yesterday; Herbert's rejoinder was sent off yesterday evening. I do not expect we have heard the last of this.[1]

If the Foreign Ministry did in fact write to Strasbourg that the Chancellor wished Schnäbele's pardon to be recommended to H.M., then we are technically in the right. I regret all the more that Herbert is endangering his favourable position by the vehemence of his replies, but even so he has not laid himself open to any particular charge.

The incident is, however, an important symptom of Herbert's position and the resentment accumulated against him. Wilmowski and Bülow[2] could have warned Herbert in time, as soon as the Kaiser first expressed his annoyance. But they just stood by and allowed the storm to gather and then break. H.M. was giving vent to the resentment Berchem referred to. H.M. feels neglected. The late State Secretary, Bülow, used to send him at least one memorandum a week on foreign policy, whether anything was happening or not. Unfortunately Herbert does not imitate this habit and of course never acts on advice he is given, but thinks that everyone, even the Kaiser, must be pleased to accept the treatment Herbert deigns to accord him. I think I have already said that in 1873 his father said of him: 'Herbert is a tormentor both of man and beast.' And in fact domineering (i.e. hectoring other people) and drinking are his only two pleasures in life. And the way he pursues them earns him general contempt. Rottenburg told me yesterday he was horrified by 'the clouds banking over Herbert's head!' This disapproval was general, first because it was felt that the Chancellor's name was being taken in vain and thus a great many things were being embarked on which H.H. would not have allowed to go through if he had known about them; secondly because Herbert was to be seen far too often in beer-cellars where he prated about everything under the sun and even made disrespectful remarks about H.M.

Rottenburg said Bill should come back to Berlin for good, because he was the only person whose advice Herbert heeded. That is true. The only other people Herbert listens to are flatterers.

When he was eighteen years old he once said: 'I never follow

---

[1] On 10 October, at Wilmowski's suggestion, Kaiser Wilhelm declared the matter closed. Schnäbele was pardoned. (From the Foreign Ministry files.)   [2] Otto von Bülow.

other people's advice because I find their ideas are even more stupid than my own.'

But Bill will not want to come here. Perhaps Sybille may.

5 *November* 1887

The enclosed letter from Bill[1] with all kinds of interesting reflexions is the answer to mine in which I told him Herbert's position was threatened by his own behaviour and that he needed someone here to give him advice. Bill was the only person whose advice Herbert would follow. Bill does not wish to come.

The Kaiserin has dropsy. The swelling is already quite severe.

The Kaiser may *perhaps* pull through this time. He is very weak.

It is impossible to form an opinion about the Crown Prince.

Radolinski has set up an entail. In the event of his own and his son's death the entail is to pass to Prince Heinrich, as second son of the royal house.

Recently Prince Wilhelm spoke to Radol. about this and explained to him that Prince Heinrich would be a rich man in any case, but he, Wilhelm, had nothing to live on, did not know how he would pay his travelling expenses, etc. Briefly, Radol. ought to bequeath everything to him. Radol. said with a laugh: 'He behaved as though my son and I were as good as dead already.'

Extraordinary people.

When Radol. was dining recently with Prince Wilhelm, the Princess told him her eldest son is always saying: 'Do you know, Mama, Papa is a gypsy. He's so restless and is always travelling around.'

That is true. He has no perseverance. He seems to have had enough of his 'job' in the Foreign Ministry already. He has been here *once*, and he did not even see Herbert, but made an appointment with Radolinski.

For *one* reason I could wish that the Kaiser's career would end now; because otherwise Bismarck, who is an old man, will compromise himself with Russia yet again. And the result would be that, like all persons of dubious reliability, we should stand *alone* at the crucial moment because there would be no one left who trusted us.

If only I were mistaken!

9 *November* 1887

It is all up with the Crown Prince. The German doctors are proved right.

[1] Of 20 October 1887 (*Correspondence*).

The Crown Princess's behaviour has been incredible.

In Toblach Mackenzie said the Crown Prince was dangerously ill and must go at once to Cairo or Madeira. When the Crown Princess heard this she exclaimed: 'That will never do. Where am I to stay? It would be all right if I could spend the winter in Rome, but not otherwise.'

Despite the doctors' request she refused in Toblach to alter the time for lunch. As a result, just when the midday sun was at its height, the Crown Prince was sitting at table instead of being out of doors.

When the Crown Princess was returning to the Continent on the English royal yacht, either the *Osborne* or the *Victoria and Albert*, she said to Wegner,[1] the personal physician: 'Twenty-nine years ago I came to Germany in this very ship; I wish I'd never seen it!'

In Munich she received a telegram from the hotel proprietor in Toblach advising them not to come because the climate was too harsh for the Crown Prince. She took no notice; she had there, as the Crown Prince himself put it, good subjects to paint, she wanted to go for walks and grow slimmer.

General Count Waldersee asked me to-day: 'How long do you think the Chancellor and Prince Wilhelm would work in harness? Not long, I imagine. The present Kaiser is an old man; it does not affect him if he happens to read somewhere: "Prince Bismarck does everything. He is the ruler and the Kaiser is only a puppet." In the poor Crown Prince's case it would have been rather more difficult, because that was his sore point. But when Prince Wilhelm is Kaiser he will insist on appearing as the man who really rules—that is why I don't think he and the Chancellor will agree for long.'

I think Waldersee is right. But both the Bismarcks may tone down considerably once Prince Wilhelm becomes Kaiser. They both stand in awe of him.

Herbert is so pleased about the Crown Prince's approaching end that every one in the Foreign Ministry notices it. He told me his father once said to him years ago: 'If the Lord means well by Germany, he'll never let the Crown Prince ascend the throne.'

11 *November* 1887

According to an official bulletin sent to the Kaiser the doctors have unanimously informed the Crown Prince that he is suffering from cancer of the larynx, but that they would hardly advise him to

[1] Surgeon-General; doctor to Crown Prince Friedrich Wilhelm.

undergo the operation for removal of the entire larynx, because it was most uncertain and even when it succeeded the patient suffered acutely for the rest of his life. The Crown Prince took the news heroically and after thinking things over he declared in writing that he did not wish his larynx to be removed and would only consent to undergoing a tracheotomy if he started having fits of suffocation. The Crown Prince is staying in Italy for the present. I have not yet inquired how long this state of affairs can last. Fränkel[1] said it would be months, not years.

It looks as though they are trying to suppress the truth. I think that is a bad thing. If the Kaiser dies overnight it seems to me unavoidable that the dying Crown Prince shall be made to renounce his claim to the throne, because under present conditions his wife could do all manner of mischief in a few months. But if the people are to understand his abdication they must be informed of his illness.

The Chancellor arrives on Tuesday, the Tsar on Friday.[2] I wonder what mood the latter is coming in. The recent Press campaign against Russia and the financial measures taken against Russian bonds[3] must have annoyed him intensely. According to reliable sources he stated recently in Copenhagen that he would be glad to see Kaiser Wilhelm but could not bring himself to receive Prince Bismarck, because he had not told him the truth at their last meeting.[4] This pronouncement was passed to H.H. and I think that when the two men meet they will neither of them feel inclined to give way.

Bill helps me to strengthen Herbert's resolution, and he in turn sees that his father stands firm. In spite of this I am worried, because an old love is never forgotten.

14 *November* 1887

The Crown Princess and her democratic adherents are spreading barefaced lies about the Crown Prince's health. The aim is to prevent the Crown Prince from being made to renounce his claim to the throne on the grounds of incapacity.

The enclosed letter from Radolinski[5] makes it clear that the outlook is in fact hopeless. He also says that the Crown Princess torments and upsets her husband by lamenting her own and her

---

[1] Dr Bernhard Fränkel.   [2] 18 November 1887.

[3] Shortly after the conclusion of the Reinsurance Treaty a campaign was launched in the German Press against Russian state bonds. In November Bismarck prevailed on the *Deutsche Reichsbank* and the *Preussische Seehandlung* to take the decision to stop loans on Russian securities. See *Grosse Politik*, vol. v, chapter xxxvi, Appendix 1.

[4] 15–17 September 1884, in Skierniewice. See p. 161, note 1.

[5] Of 10 November 1887 (*Correspondence*).

daughter's fate. They are still contemplating the Battenberg marriage. There will be a really violent conflict between the advocates of abdication and the Crown Princess's following. The democrats think, quite rightly, that a dying monarch with the Crown Prince's character, completely dominated by his wife, could do great things in a few months, i.e. he could destroy or severely damage the monarchy. The next step would be for him to hand over to the representatives of the people various monarchical rights 'which his successor would only abuse'. If he had remained in good health I feel certain he would have kept on the Chancellor for several years more. As things are his one aim is to ensure for himself in a few months undying fame as a liberal friend of the people and, unconcerned about the more distant future, he will probably part company with Bismarck.

To put an end to this democratic agitation we ought to publish both of General Winterfeld's cipher telegrams about the decisive consultation of the doctors and their disclosure to the Crown Prince, together with his reply.[1]

Princess Victoria wrote to a lady-in-waiting, Countess Perponcher, that her father had been really ill again, but he was better now, and the excellent Mackenzie would put everything right. The Countess was not to believe any of the nonsense she read in the papers. That really is the last straw.

Hohenlohe is going downhill. He treats important matters lightly and vice versa.

18 *November* 1887

The poor Crown Prince is now more than ever under the Princess's thumb. Two letters from him arrived the day before yesterday, one to Friedberg and one to General Mischke. They are both full of biting scorn for the German doctors. One of them reads: 'Admittedly Schrötter[2] comes from Vienna, but he is still a German.' The other letter ends with these words: 'I trust in God and Sir Morell Mackenzie.' L[yncker], who informed me of this,[3] said out of the bitterness of his heart: 'Perhaps God still means to deal kindly with us, since he has spared us from such a reign as this.' Friedberg and Mischke, who have both known the

---

[1] On 10 November Winterfeld telegraphed from San Remo that the doctors thought the only chance of saving the Crown Prince's life was an operation for the removal of the larynx, but even this chance was very slim. According to a telegram of 11 November, the Crown Prince had received the news that he was suffering from cancer of the larynx with great composure, and had stated that he did not want to be operated on. (From the Foreign Ministry files.)

[2] Dr Leopold Schrötter, Ritter von Kristelli. Throat specialist.

[3] In a letter of 8 November. Not printed.

Crown Prince for many years, raise their hands to heaven and say they would never have believed it of him. He seems to regard himself as an Englishman who has landed in Germany by accident.

But what will happen if the Kaiser dies before the Crown Prince? That would be terrible. He would feel inclined to renounce his claim, but she would never let him.

Meanwhile the outlook in foreign affairs is gradually becoming really serious. War fever is increasing in the French army because they feel—justifiably—that their rifle is better than ours. And the Russians judge that the time is ripe for a war with Austria because the Austrians are at this very moment engaged on the manufacture of a new rifle.

To-day's visit by the Tsar will not improve the situation. The thing I originally feared, i.e. that we would try yet again to flirt with Russia and should then fall between two stools, England and Russia, will not come to pass, thanks to the Russians' insolence. First of all they continue to mass troops in Poland, and then we received private information about ten days ago that the Tsar was really furious with the Chancellor and intended to refuse him audience. I shall believe this when I see it.[1] Even so, these various factors provoked a wholesome indignation in the Chancellor, who published scathing articles and adopted all kinds of measures certain to annoy the Russians.[2] Thus the acrimony has increased on both sides over the last week.

[1] The Tsar had a talk of more than an hour with Bismarck, who once more made it clear that if Russia attacked Austria, Germany would be obliged by her treaty commitments to come to Austria's help, and that Germany's diplomatic attitude in the Bulgarian affair was determined, as it always had been, by the provisions of the Treaty of Berlin. (*Grosse Politik*, vol. v, no. 1129, p. 324; see also no. 1057, pp. 203–5.)

[2] See p. 357, note 3.

1888

Prince Wilhelm critical of the Bismarcks. The Stöcker affair. The Imperial family. Bismarck threatens resignation over the Battenberg marriage plan. Prince Wilhelm's intervention. Queen Victoria's visit. Bismarck and Crown Prince Wilhelm. Danger of war. Bismarck and Kaiser Friedrich. Kaiser Wilhelm's conversation with the Pope. Herbert Bismarck's plans in case of war. Kaiserin Friedrich and her son.

11 *January* 1888

Scarcely a year and a half ago Herbert brought Prince Wilhelm into the Foreign Ministry so as to have him more under his influence. Things went swimmingly at first. When the Crown Prince fell ill in the spring, Herbert told me: 'My first thought on learning that it was cancer was a selfish one. I said to myself, now I'm in harness for the rest of my life. Under the Crown Prince's rule I should have found a pretext for retiring and having a rest, but under Prince Wilhelm I shall be hard put to it to find an excuse.'

Things are totally different now, although Prince Wilhelm is not yet Kaiser. Liebenau, the Court Chamberlain, said three days ago: 'Herbert Bismarck, by behaving too much like the Prince's bosom friend, has forfeited all the authority and influence he had over him.'

That must indeed be so. I heard several months ago that Herbert's tippling, boisterous behaviour and frequenting of taverns was giving rise to a good deal of comment, even in court circles. Even Prince Wilhelm, who likes encouraging other people to have a drink though not drinking himself, is said to have passed remarks on it. I wrote and told Bill so that he could warn his brother. But Bill with his usual insensitiveness said it was Herbert's only pleasure, after all.

Now things are in a fine mess. Herbert himself has recently begun to realize that Prince Wilhelm has ceased to value his opinions, and is not exactly in a good mood as a result.

They both dined with Lerchenfeld yesterday and Herbert was so little able to conceal his bad temper that all the other guests noticed it. People were talking of a 'break' between Herbert and the Prince.

But Prince Wilhelm is annoyed with the Chancellor too. He said a few days ago: 'I have ceased to understand the Chancellor's policy; he will yet succeed in estranging us from Austria.' And after yesterday's dinner party the Prince spoke his mind on this subject more fully: 'The Chancellor, for purely selfish reasons, doesn't want another war, although he and my grandfather between them have a moral value of 250,000 men so long as they live. I shall have to pay the interest on this delay later on. I shall have to bear the brunt of the crisis, though I shall be young and weak.'

Unfortunately I cannot entirely disagree with the Prince. The Chancellor's present policy can only be compared with Frederick the Great's policy during the Bavarian war of succession—it lacks drive. And he makes it only too clear that he would like to push others forward while sitting still himself. That is why people have lost their trust in him and in Germany. The Chancellor has no need whatever to make war in order to have his way. In concert with Austria, Italy, Rumania, Turkey, England and Spain he could to-day obtain a good deal from Russia and France even without making war. Instead of which, he first of all harries the Austrians into rearming though they have neither the desire nor the money to do so; scarcely have they given way to his insistence and started rearming cautiously and economically than he cries out that Austria wants to drag us into an aggressive war against Russia. Naturally the Austrians are outraged and feel they have been duped.[1] Prince Reuss' letters contain more on this subject.[2]

And so Prince Wilhelm, in the statement noted above, is not so far wrong. I am curious to see whether the Prince's attitude has any effect at all on the Chancellor; he has already realized that he will not be able to deal so easily with him as he has with his father and grandfather.

The Chancellor has achieved one thing that no civilian in world history has ever achieved. The fame resulting from three victorious wars attached to *him*, not to the army leaders. The explanation probably lies in the impersonality of the military leadership. In a fourth war things might have been different, and I regret to say that for a character like the Chancellor's this consideration carries great weight.

If I seem to be talking lightly about war, it is because I regard it as inevitable. The only question is whether it will break out at a moment favourable to us or to our enemies.

[1] See *Grosse Politik*, vol. VI, chapters XXXVII and XXXVIII.
[2] See *Correspondence*.

I am told that the Chancellor is now taking morphia almost every evening as a cure for insomnia. That explains his changes of mood. He told Bleichröder in October: 'If I have ever been firmly convinced of anything during my political career, I am convinced now that war with Russia is inevitable in the near future.' Last Monday he said to Bleichröder: 'I tell you, so long as I am Minister we shall not make war on Russia, come what may.' And last Thursday, also in conversation with Bleichröder, his tone was again more bellicose.

But the things he tells Bleichröder, his confidant for many years, are mild. About ten days ago he spoke as follows to two Italian General Staff officers, Colonel Albertone and Count Da Bormida, whom he had never seen before in his life: 'It is my settled conviction and firm intention that we shall have peace for three or four more years. However, we have a military party intent on waging war quite soon. Prince Wilhelm belongs to this party. The only question is whether he will find a Minister to carry out this programme once he is Kaiser.' Incredible. The Italians were struck by the way Prince Bismarck's hands shook as he spoke.

There are two factors to be considered in all the Chancellor does or neglects to do from now on: morphia and Prince Wilhelm.

The Stöcker affair[1] has rather increased Prince Wilhelm's prestige.

The Chancellor was right as to the *facts*—it was unsuitable for the future Kaiser to become identified with Stöcker. The King of Prussia can take a good many liberties, particularly if he is a soldier king. But the German Kaiser must do nothing to alienate the moderate parties of the centre, because outside the old Prussian provinces these parties are the only ones we can count on. The Chancellor said: 'A Kaiser entering on his reign under Stöcker's auspices will find that the elections to his first Reichstag will rule out the existence of Kaiser and Chancellor.'

H.H., as I have said, was right as to the *facts*, but not in the *method he adopted*. It was incredible that he should subject the young Prince, whose ignorance had involved him in this affair,

---

[1] At a meeting in support of the Berlin City Mission on 28 November 1887, the Court Chaplain, Adolf von Stöcker, made a political speech. Stöcker was the founder of the anti-Semitic Christian Socialist Party and violently opposed to the Social Democrats and Progressives. Prince Wilhelm, who attended the meeting with his wife, was sharply criticized in an article inspired by Bismarck which appeared in the *Norddeutsche Allgemeine Zeitung*. The basis for the attack was that the Prince's name was being coupled politically with Stöcker's as a result of the meeting. See *Memoirs*, pp. 137–9.

to censure in the columns of the *Norddeutsche*, instead of explaining his point of view in a letter or private interview. Rottenburg agitated a great deal in the affair. This behaviour made the Prince exceedingly indignant. He told his former tutor Hinzpeter:[1] 'For the sake of the Chancellor I have, so to speak, for years locked myself out of my parents' house. So I did not deserve such treatment from the Chancellor, of all people.'

Then followed angry outbursts. The Prince exclaimed: 'The Chancellor cannot go on enjoying the power he wields at present; he simply must realize there's still a Kaiser.' Or else, striking the table with his fist: 'He'd better remember that I shall be his master.' Or else: 'I shall not manage without the Chancellor at first. But in due course I hope the German Reich will be sufficiently consolidated to be able to dispense with Prince Bismarck's co-operation.'

Just at this period, when the young man was already inclined to be critical, came that discreditable episode in our foreign policy, when we first urged Austria to rearm in November and December, so that we could subsequently accuse her of secretly desiring war and of hatching ambitious Polish-Jesuit schemes. Prince Wilhelm had watched all this closely, and Waldersee, who had been intensely annoyed by the Stöcker affair, no doubt saw to it that H.R.H. was kept informed. The latter said one day to Eulenburg, the Grand Master of Ceremonies: 'Can you still follow the Chancellor's policy? I can't. He will cause a rift between Austria and ourselves before he's finished.'

The reason the Prince came out well from the Stöcker affair is that the Liberal parties in the Reichstag also signed the appeal,[2] thus giving it the stamp of political impartiality. In the earlier correspondence between the Prince and the Chancellor, the young man tenaciously maintained his point of view, namely that the incident had been artificially exaggerated beyond its original significance until it had become a major political question.[3]

His adherents are now telling him: 'You have shown the Chancellor for the first time that you have got backbone, and you've done yourself no harm. Keep it up!'

However strange this may sound coming from me, I hope sincerely that the Prince's 'backbone' will also make itself felt in our foreign policy. We may perhaps strike a good middle course between his policy and the Chancellor's policy of backing down.

[1] Georg Ernst Hinzpeter. Prince Wilhelm's tutor, 1866–77.
[2] The appeal on behalf of the Berlin City Mission, and missions in other cities, was signed by prominent members of the nobility, top civil servants, clergy and professors, and, among Members of the Reichstag, by Bennigsen, Miquel, Benda and Marquardsen.
[3] See Bismarck, *Die gesammelten Werke*, vol. xv, pp. 460–70; vol. vi c. no. 382, pp. 382–5.

When Radolinski informed the Kaiser on Thursday that the Crown Prince was to be operated on, the old gentleman wept a good deal, said 'my poor, poor son', but slept well all night. In all three generations of that family warmth of feeling is very under-developed.

When the Kaiser celebrated his birthday recently the Crown Prince arrived a quarter of an hour before he was expected. The Kaiserin asked him in a hectoring tone: 'What are you doing here? Why, the Kaiser is not ready yet'—and the Crown Prince had to wait outside.

The Crown Prince, although he is the only man of sensibility in the whole family, did not refrain from making waspish remarks about his parents' longevity. 'You'll see', he said in great irritation to someone the day the corner-stone of the Reichstag building was laid, 'my father will live to see the building dedicated.' On another occasion he said: 'I was standing in the White Room yesterday evening'—a ball had been held—'when I heard something behind me rattling. I looked round, it was my mother. She's so skinny now that her old bones fairly rattle. But that does not keep her at home. She must put in an appearance even though she's got one foot in the grave.'

Prince Wilhelm's attitude to his father's illness is purely businesslike. Between him and his mother there is fierce hatred. Recently on her son's birthday she refused to drink to his health.

Except for a few fanatics no one now imagines that the Crown Prince has anything but cancer. And if it is cancer, then, so the doctors think, it will probably be all over by the 1st of April. His strength has declined very rapidly during the past four weeks.

The Chancellor's speech[1] is a masterpiece of rhetoric. Its contents are admittedly open to criticism in places by the specialist, whether he is a soldier or a diplomatist. The Chancellor felt that himself, which explains why he flattered the officers, the non-commissioned officers, the muscular stalwarts of the reserves, the whole nation in fact. As a result his speech has been a great success at home, and has done less harm abroad than I had feared.

It has made no difference to the general situation. The hatred and mistrust in certain quarters remain as strong as ever. Perhaps we shall keep the peace this year, during which we shall be exposed to the danger of seeing our alliances dissolved.

---

[1] Of 6 February. (*Die gesammelten Werke*, vol. XIII, pp. 326–48.)

When Bergmann returned from Charlottenburg yesterday he told the Grand-Duke of Baden that he expected the final catastrophe in May provided there were no complications, otherwise in the middle of April.

All kinds of stories are current about the general lack of affection in the Imperial family. When Prince Wilhelm telegraphed from Karlsruhe early this month announcing his intention of visiting his father in San Remo, the present Kaiserin[1] submitted to her husband a telegram of refusal, observing: 'The visit would exhaust you too much.' But the father wished to see his son. Whereupon his wife stamped her foot and exclaimed: 'Then you can't be so ill as you think.'[2]

On the last day of Kaiser Wilhelm's life, when news of his death had been telegraphed prematurely, Princess Vicky asked someone: 'Tell me, is the old man dead or is he alive still?'[3]

The Kaiserin is now trying to bring about the marriage between Princess Vicky and the Prince of Battenberg. The latter does not wish it and has in fact replied that even if the Kaiser commanded him to marry her he would say no, so long as the Crown Prince[4] withheld his consent. But the Crown Prince to-day sent Battenberg the following message through Prince Heinrich: 'If he dared so much as to become engaged to her, the Crown Prince would banish him from the country the moment he became Kaiser and would renounce all further responsibility for his sister.' When H[erbert] B[ismarck] observed that it was not unknown for an engaged couple to be locked together in a room so as to extort the family's consent, the Crown Prince replied: 'That wouldn't make any difference to me—I'd make the break.'

An affectionate family. [...]

Prince Wilhelm, the Crown Prince, is the riddle of the future. 'He is not an attractive character', someone told me who knows him intimately. But he possesses some of the qualities requisite in a monarch: a passion for the army (much of which is still play-acting); ruthlessness, also that quality referred to by Maria Theresa when writing to her daughters' tutor: '*Il faut qu'elles sachent dissimuler.*' Heartless.

The Bismarcks, both father and son, stand in wholesome dread of him. The Chancellor is fond of telling his intimates that he feels sure of the Crown Prince. I do not believe that and I rather

[1] Kaiserin Victoria. Kaiser Wilhelm I had died on 9 March 1888.
[2] Compare Sir Frederick Ponsonby, *The Letters of the Empress Frederick* (London, 1928), p. 279.
[3] In English in the original.   [4] Prince Wilhelm.

doubt whether the Chancellor believes it himself. The Chancellor's military opponents tell the Crown Prince that Frederick II would never have become Frederick the Great under the political tutelage of a Minister like Bismarck. In addition they keep telling the Prince that the Bismarcks, father and son, are not over-scrupulous about the truth, and try to take him in.

The conflict will arise over the war question. Bismarck wants to put off making war while he remains at the helm. The generals, regardless of their views on other matters—Waldersee, Bronsart, Verdy, Loë, Caprivi—think time is running *against* us, that 1889 will be a particularly unfavourable year, and that we ought not to allow certain military preparations along our frontier or the Galician frontier. If those measures are in fact adopted in the course of this summer, then we shall see who is master. I hope for many reasons that Bismarck remains at the helm for a few more years, but on the other hand I feel: 'Cobbler, stick to your last!' An intelligent general is surely better able to judge of the *military* necessity for defence than a civilian in uniform.

31 *March* 1888

The Battenberg struggle is in full swing. When the Chancellor arrived at Charlottenburg to-day for an audience, the Kaiser told him (or wrote down) that he wished to give Battenberg an army post and confer on him the *Pour le Mérite*, as the first of several measures he had in mind for the Prince.

The Chancellor explained to him that such a procedure would strain our relations with Russia so severely that he would refuse to accept the responsibility; he, the Chancellor, would resign if that happened. The Kaiser gave in and instructed Radolinski to send Battenberg a telegram requesting him not to come here the day after to-morrow as arranged. The Kaiserin, who had been waiting at the door for the Chancellor to go, came in just as Radolinski was receiving these instructions. Then the sparks flew. 'But that's outrageous, it will be the death of my poor child', and so on. The poor helpless Kaiser wrote down: 'I cannot plunge this country into a war with Russia on account of her marriage.' She became more and more violent. Radolinski said to her: 'But, Your Majesty, I implore you to think of the Kaiser's health.' She did not even hear him, she kept talking. The Kaiser rent his clothes, wept, tore his hair, gasped for breath, but stood firm about Battenberg's visit. Radolinski telegraphed to Battenberg: 'By order of His Majesty I request you to postpone your visit.' But these scenes will now continue. Radolinski is in despair about the Kaiser, and has just called on the Chancellor (9 p.m.). The Kaiserin will stop at *nothing* to bring about this marriage.[1]

I am not particularly impressed by the Kaiserin's behaviour in this affair. On the other hand the danger of such a marriage so far as Russia is concerned is not so great as the Chancellor makes it appear. The Chancellor wants to use this opportunity of winning back the position of trust he formerly enjoyed with the Crown Prince, before the Stöcker affair.

3 *April* 1888

To-morrow morning the Chancellor's memorandum to the Kaiser will be dispatched which states that if H.M. were to persist in his 'plan of conferring distinctions on and making advances to the Prince of Battenberg', the Chancellor would, to his profound regret, feel obliged to ask to be relieved of his functions. He explained the reasons for this standpoint at great length by pointing out the part Battenberg might yet play in Bulgaria's *future*, and the consequent jeopardizing of our relations with Russia.[2]

An hour before I read this, Radolinski, quite ill with exhaustion, had told me that the Kaiserin is determined to make the Kaiser accept Bismarck's resignation. All she wants is to force through this marriage, and she is indifferent to everything else. 'If the Chancellor wants to resign on that account, public opinion will say he is in the wrong. He once told me himself that this marriage would cease to be a political question as soon as the Prince of Battenberg ceased to be Prince of Bulgaria; after that only family interests would be concerned.'

I have already noted that the good Chancellor is somewhat exaggerating the matter; the Russian danger is not so serious as all that. He wants to curry favour with the Crown Prince. Meanwhile, as things are at present, we must try to prevent disaster.

First of all Rado. must prevent the immediate acceptance of Bismarck's resignation to-morrow by saying to the Kaiserin: 'Be careful not to fall between two stools; don't let the Chancellor go before making sure that Battenberg really wants this marriage.' (He has in fact behaved up to now as though he did not, unless he had the consent of his future brother-in-law, Prince Wilhelm.) The Kaiserin will then send an inquiry to Darmstadt, probably adding that the Kaiser commanded Battenberg to come to Berlin.

[1] See *Memoirs*, p. 141.
[2] Memorandum of 3 April 1888. (*Grosse Politik*, vol. VI, no. 1331, pp. 282–7.)

Meanwhile I will get Liebenau to suggest to the Crown Prince the idea of writing a thoroughly offensive letter to the Grand-Duke of Hesse, as head of the family, declining the honour of having Battenberg as brother-in-law. Since his accession is so imminent, his letter is likely to produce its effect.

11 *April* 1888

On Wednesday, 4 April, the Chancellor dictated to the Crown Prince a very biting letter to Battenberg, culminating in the declaration that, if B. pursued this marriage project any further, the Crown Prince would regard him as his enemy and the enemy of the Reich.[1]

On Thursday the Chancellor had audience, first of the Kaiser, who made no mention of the two memoranda hinting at Bismarck's possible resignation and stared at the ceiling as soon as H.H. referred to the subject.[2] He then had audience of the Kaiserin. She got round the Chancellor completely. He told her he was obliged to adopt this attitude towards the marriage project. As far as he was concerned the two young people could marry, provided *he* knew nothing about it. Above all the Kaiserin must see that she inherited from her husband a suitable sum, say nine million marks for her three daughters' dowries.

The Kaiserin for her part said His Highness could curse her up hill and down dale and lay all the blame on her afterwards.

On Friday the Chancellor sent for Friedberg and Stolberg and it was agreed, much to the two men's amazement, that the Kaiser should be allowed nine million marks from his father's estate to dispose of as he wished.

Yesterday, Tuesday, H.H. again had audience of the Kaiserin. He advised her, among other things, to invest this money safely *abroad* as soon as she received it, and not to purchase a palace in Berlin for the young couple as she had intended, 'because you never know whether Their Highnesses will like it here afterwards'. But they both agreed that the appearance of a quarrel must still be kept up. So the Press battle still goes merrily on.

Meanwhile the Minister for Baden, Marschall,[3] was sent with the Chancellor's instructions to Darmstadt last Thursday or Friday at the suggestion of his Grand-Duke, to terrify the other Grand-Duke[4] with the consequences this marriage would entail—

[1] See Corti, *Alexander von Battenberg*, pp. 404–5.
[2] Memoranda of 3 and 4 April 1888. (*Grosse Politik*, vol. vi, nos. 1331–2, pp. 282–8.)
[3] Adolf Hermann Marschall, Baron von Bieberstein. Minister representing Baden in Berlin, 1883–90; State Secretary in the German Foreign Ministry, 1890–7; Ambassador in Constantinople, 1897–1912.   [4] The Grand-Duke of Hesse.

the Chancellor's resignation, war, etc. The Grand-Duke, a frivolous man at heart, was so impressed by his interview with Marschall that he seriously set about persuading Battenberg to give up the idea.[1] The Prince, who had told him formerly that he would never marry without the Crown Prince's consent, suddenly became more obstinate. Probably his future mother-in-law, the Kaiserin, had written and told him his darling was now a rich woman too. But the Grand-Duke insisted, and was supported by our Minister, Thielmann. The latter has just reported by telegram[2] that while the Grand-Duke was granting him audience this morning, he received a letter from the Kaiser telling him not to meddle in things which did not concern him. The letter had been written yesterday evening between six and eight, that is, *after* Prince Bismarck's audience with the Kaiserin.

Poor weak Kaiser. Three days ago he wrote on a sheet of paper that he did not want to hear any more about this marriage; Battenberg could at best contract a morganatic marriage, 'but my wife gives me no peace'.

The deciding factor in this affair is the nine million marks grant. The Chancellor thus made the marriage possible. Why? Simply because he is afraid of dismissal. Similarly, his apparently furious opposition to the marriage springs from his fear of the Crown Prince. It is the same double game he plays in foreign policy, between the Russians on the one hand and their enemies on the other. It is a measure of Bismarck's immense prestige that such behaviour did not render his position impossible long ago.

Does H.H. imagine, then, that Prince Wilhelm will never hear of this later on?

Speaking of Prince Wilhelm. He now puts on fine autocratic airs. Herbert told me to-day that he had an appointment with H.I.H. yesterday at the palace at a quarter to one. When Herbert, as he states, drove up just two minutes late, the Prince was already driving past him on his way to the station; he would have had exactly two minutes to spare for this audience. He had left orders behind for Herbert to be at Potsdam station at ten past

---

[1] Neither Bismarck's instructions nor any dispatch from Marschall were found in the Foreign Ministry files. A dispatch from Thielmann in Darmstadt of 9 April contains the following passage: '[...] Meanwhile I was able to confirm that the Minister for Baden in Berlin, Herr von Marschall, who arrived here last Saturday morning [7 April], was received in audience by the Grand-Duke immediately, and left Darmstadt the same Saturday afternoon. The Grand-Duke has maintained complete silence about Herr von Marschall's message to him from his sovereign; but according to a hint I obtained from a reliable source I may assume that Your Highness has received direct information about the contents of the Grand-Duke's interview with Herr von Marschall. [...]' See also Corti, *Alexander von Battenberg*, p. 407.

[2] This telegram is in the Foreign Ministry files. Holstein's summary of it is accurate.

five. When he arrived, the Prince told him he had no time to discuss political matters. He only wanted to express his wish that Philipp Eulenburg should prolong his spell of temporary duty in Munich; he thought it would be a very good thing if Eulenburg became Minister in Munich later on.

I should love to have seen Herbert's face when he heard this, and still more Rantzau's face when Herbert told him. The way they axed old Werthern was despicable. And now it looks as though Rantzau will not even be able to enjoy the prize.

As I was sitting writing towards ten o'clock, Herbert sent for me to discuss a telegram to London. He was slightly tipsy and felt talkative. With the candour he shows at such times he said that, if he should outlive his father, he would not get on long with Kaiser Wilhelm II, and will probably not do so even during his father's prolonged absence in the summer. I think this most likely.

Herbert also showed me a note which the Kaiser had handed to the Chancellor to-day on his arrival, already written out. It read: 'You will have realized from your interview with the Kaiserin yesterday that the fullest consideration has been given to all the points raised in your memorandum.[1] I therefore regard the matter as settled.'

What a farce! Each bent on tricking the other, but the poor Kaiser is tricked the worst. I am not at all sure that Herbert knows exactly what his father said to the Kaiserin. In any case I hardly think any one can have such a rounded view of the affair as I have, because every one confides in me—i.e. the few who know anything about it.

To sum up: I do not think the Chancellor will strengthen his position with the future Wilhelm II by his present double game. Surely the Prince must be aware of it—Waldersee sees to that.

17 *April* 1888

In the opinion of the doctors the Kaiser has only a few days to live. Professor Bergmann, who recently explored the tubal aperture with his finger, discovered that the œsophagus was also affected, and so he thinks an early death as a result of an affectation of the lung would be the best thing.

The way the English doctors treat the Kaiser defies description. No doubt we shall hear enough about this after his death.

I was in Charlottenburg yesterday visiting Radolinski, who is completely broken-hearted. He seems the only one of the whole

---

[1] See above, p. 367.

set who feels any grief. While I was with him a butler announced that the Crown Prince had ordered dinner at seven o'clock for eight persons: himself, his wife, Prince Heinrich, Prince and Princess von Meiningen, etc. The Kaiserin and her other daughters are dining at eight in another part of the castle.

The appearance of Waldersee walking across the courtyard on his way to the Crown Prince's apartment caused a stir amongst our group. 'There he goes', said Lyncker and Reischach.[1]

Yes, there he goes, despite the Chancellor, who tried his hardest to have him transferred as Commanding General to Hanover. But the scheme failed because Moltke declared he would resign if it went through. Waldersee, who knows all this,[2] will presumably take his revenge. He has indeed already begun by shattering the Crown Prince's confidence in the Bismarcks' regard for truth, as I mentioned above. The effects of this damage will soon be evident.

At the moment it strikes one with unaccustomed strangeness to see how full of attentions the two Bismarcks are for the Crown Prince. And to think how inconsiderately they treated the noble old Kaiser. But his grandson, I feel sure, will pay off many an old score. The Chancellor is striving desperately to make people think he is the object of the Crown Prince's deepest respect. We shall see how long that will last. During the recent Battenberg crisis the Crown Prince needed him to prevent the marriage.

Prince Heinrich is furious because the four Princesses have each received two million marks (and Mama has yet another million with which to do what she likes) and he has received nothing. The Chancellor has thus made an enemy of him.

Yesterday at midday the Crown Prince summoned the Commandant of Charlottenburg, a Major, to come to him in the palace courtyard and commanded him: 'The moment you hear the news of the Kaiser's death, man the entire castle and let no one go out, without exception.' At that very moment the public started to shout: 'Hurrah!' The Kaiser had appeared at a window to take a look at his people.

The Kaiser will not have a priest for his last moments. The Kaiserin said: 'We come into the world without a priest and we can go out of it without a priest.'

The Kaiserin, incidentally, is now said to be looking really exhausted from weeping. Her daughters take the affair lightly,

---

[1] Hugo, Baron von Reischach. Court Chamberlain to Kaiser Friedrich.
[2] See Waldersee, *Denkwürdigkeiten*, vol. I, p. 374.

go for rides with Seckendorff and Dr Hovell and enjoy themselves to the full. There are good and bad men and princes. When you see how they all behave amongst themselves one wonders what the man in the street is to expect from them. I am glad I have always kept strictly aloof.

The rapid development of the Kaiser's illness and also, I really believe, opposition from Queen Victoria, have for the moment put a stop to the Battenberg marriage.

18 *April* 1888

The Kaiser's illness is said now to have assumed the character of galloping consumption. Opinions vary as to how long it will last. They say it could last a few weeks but they think it more probable that it will all be over within a week.

Battenberg has written the Kaiserin a letter earnestly imploring her to allow the marriage to take place quietly during the Kaiser's lifetime. He would not like 'to be set back against his brothers'. 'Have pity on me, who have endured insults rof many years.' A contemptible letter which clearly reveals the adventurer. He is trying to influence the Kaiserin by stating that *after* the Kaiser's death he would under no circumstances marry without Wilhelm II's consent. He said he regards a marriage entered into without consent or marriage contract as a sort of concubinage. So it is now or never.[1]

The Kaiserin and Princess Vicky were extremely excited. Once more Radolinski had to step into the breach. He discussed the matter with the Kaiserin until half past eleven one evening, with the result that she turned down Battenberg's urgent request.

But this morning a further difficulty arose. Prince Heinrich, the buffoon in this farce, who had no doubt instructions from Darmstadt, came and requested that *he* too should be married in haste before his father died. In Darmstadt of course. The Kaiserin and Vicky would then have gone there, and the *other* wedding would have taken place at the same time, very secretly. Rado had a hard task to prevent this too. But he finally prevailed on the Kaiserin also to refuse this request. Rado has to defend the positions the Chancellor abandons.

This evening at nine Reischach telephoned Rado. to say the Kaiser had been worse again during the last two hours: no attacks of suffocation, but a very high fever.

---

[1] See Corti, *Alexander von Battenberg*, pp. 414–15.

There were lively apprehensions here about the Crown Prince's encounter with his English grandmother,[1] so on the one hand I set Liebenau to work on the Prince, and on the other hand I telegraphed to Hatzfeldt: 'Cannot Salisbury send the Queen a telegram advising her to treat the Crown Prince decently for political reasons?' He replied: 'The Duke of Rutland[2] has been instructed to work in that direction after the Queen's arrival.' I replied: 'The first meeting is the decisive one. The Duke ought to go and meet the Queen and prepare her.' He replied: 'Have succeeded in getting Ld. Salisbury to influence her by different method on way through Leipzig. Please treat this as strictly confidential at his request.'

Various people called on me to-day to tell me how extraordinarily gracious the Queen had been to the Crown Prince and vice versa.

Let us hope this will somewhat lessen the Prince's foolish hatred of England.

I got Radolin to suggest Herbert's appointment as a Minister of State, much to the other Ministers' fury. Some time ago now Gossler said to me when we were discussing this: 'Oh, no, don't. At the moment, whenever the big bow-wow is not actually attending a session, we can at least grouse to our hearts' content. But that will have to stop if his son is listening.' However, I thought the appointment necessary on objective grounds.

The day following Herbert's appointment Waldersee called on me and said with obvious satisfaction: 'Caprivi has been passed over by Herbert's appointment.' I sensed at once what lay behind this—the hope of a quarrel between the Chancellor and Caprivi—and so I wrote to Herbert that very evening suggesting that something should be done for Caprivi, but that he should not be made a Minister of State since he was of course due to return to the army.

To-day Caprivi was appointed General of Infantry.

Friedberg told me yesterday evening that during yesterday's sitting the Chancellor made a speech in praise of Caprivi such as he (H.H.) had never yet made for any one.

That was for fear Caprivi might feel hurt by Herbert's promotion. I know my old Chief.

If only I knew how we could manage to keep Caprivi and Rado.

---

[1] Queen Victoria visited the German Kaiser and Kaiserin in Berlin from 24–26 April.

[2] Lord John Manners, from 3 March 1888 Duke of Rutland. Chancellor of the Duchy of Lancaster. He was in Berlin at this time, and met Queen Victoria on her arrival.

in Berlin as Bismarck's allies in the struggles of the coming regime. But I have not enough power and H.H. not enough tact; Herbert is intimidated by the Crown Prince.

13 *May* 1888

Highly confidential

Kálnoky told Reuss recently that it would perhaps have been better after all if war had broken out last autumn. Reuss reported this;[1] the Chancellor refuted that view immediately with the usual arguments: 'Nothing to be gained by war, public opinion against war of aggression', etc.[2] He sent the dispatch itself, together with his refutation, to the Crown Prince.[3]

At the same time all kinds of grave reports came in from the General Staff about Russian plans, purchasing of provisions, etc., which, however, were not to be put into effect before next winter. When the Chancellor then went to confer with the Crown Prince, the young man seemed bent on war and could not be turned from his opinion. The Chancellor, much disturbed, wrote the Prince an *exposé* of sixteen tightly packed pages opposing war with Russia.[4] The Prince sent for Waldersee, held a long conference with him and Major Bissing, and then sent the Chancellor a written reply,[5] which H.H. thought weak, reiterating the Prince's former opinion.

The Chancellor told Radolin: 'That young man wants war with Russia, and would like to draw his sword straight away if he could. I shall not be a party to it', and so forth.

When I went to thank H.H. for my decoration[6] he replied when I asked how he was: 'Not particularly well, I didn't sleep because the Crown Prince's wishes were going round and round in my head. That young man wants to pursue a policy which would cause me to resign after our first three months together.' That was on Thursday. The same day he said to Herbert over lunch, with reference to Prince Wilhelm's policy: 'Alas, my poor grandchildren.'

I went and told Bleichröder I thought the Chancellor was annoyed at Prince Wilhelm's warlike tendencies, and was talking of resigning. I requested Bl. to go and see H.H. and then, if

[1] Reuss to Bismarck, 28 April 1888. (*Grosse Politik*, vol. vi, no. 1339, pp. 301–2.)
[2] Bismarck to Reuss, 3 May 1888. (*Grosse Politik*, vol. vi, no. 1340, pp. 302–3.)
[3] See the footnotes to the documents cited above.
[4] See *Grosse Politik*, vol. vi, no. 1341, pp. 304–7.
[5] See Bismarck, *Die gesammelten Werke*, vol. xv, pp. 554–7; also Waldersee, *Denkwürdigkeiten*, vol. i, pp. 395–9.
[6] On 5 May 1888 the Red Eagle Second Class with oak leaves was conferred on Holstein.

H.H. spoke on those lines, to ask him: 'Your Highness, when a pair of horses stampede, is it better for the coachman to be hurled from his box or to remain in his seat where he can still control them a little?'

Bl. wasted no time, but went on Friday to call on H.H., who spoke of the Crown Prince with great restraint and without criticizing him—a sign he is afraid of the young man. He merely said: 'The Crown Prince does not want war, but if war is forced upon him by the other side he will greet it most joyfully.' When H.H. went on to speak of possible differences of opinion and of his resigning, Bl. produced the simile of the coachman, which H.H. accepted without demur. Bl. summed up his impressions as follows: 'Prince Bismarck wants to avoid war if at all possible, but if it is unavoidable he will go along and not resign.'

H.H. suddenly summoned the Ministry of State to-day, to discuss the introduction of compulsory passports in Alsace-Lorraine for the border with France.[1] Hohenlohe had declared himself unwilling to accept responsibility for this measure, which would arouse great resentment and might eventually lead to war.[2] The Chancellor spoke alone for nearly two hours.[3] If the worst came to the worst, he said, war with France would not be a disaster. Russia was not yet ready, and certainly needed time to become so. France's attitude showed that war could not be avoided in the long run. With a Kaiser of ninety-one years of age, as well as with a Kaiser who is mortally ill, one had to pursue a policy different from that required by a young man craving for action. The Chancellor said he would handle a case like the Schnäbele affair differently now from the way he handled it at the time.

Whether or not passports were made compulsory, we must, he said, be prepared for incidents which might easily lead to war. Even the question of succession that would arise in Luxemburg after the King of Holland's death might lead to all kinds of developments.[4]

[1] Hohenlohe wrote in his diary for 8 May 1888: ' [...] Prince Bismarck [has now] put it to me to introduce compulsory passports for the border with France, which present legislation allows me to do on my own responsibility. He also informed me that the Ambassador in Paris may not issue a visa without making a preliminary inquiry, which would lead to interminable delays.' (Hohenlohe, *Denkwürdigkeiten*, vol. II, p. 432.)

[2] See *ibid.*, vol. II, pp. 432 et seq.

[3] See *Bismarck-Erinnerungen des Staatsministers Freiherrn Lucius von Ballhausen* (Stuttgart and Berlin, 1921), p. 452.

[4] After the extinction of the male line of the royal house of the Netherlands (King Wilhelm III died in 1890 and was succeeded by his daughter Wilhelmine) the former Dukes of Nassau succeeded to the throne in Luxemburg.

One of the Ministers told me that he and his colleagues had the impression that the Chancellor would now welcome a war with France. They had all left the session in a very grave mood.

I too regard this as a serious sign, but it takes two sides to make a war. Unless Boulangism[1] causes the French to lose their heads entirely they will not start a war *this* year, and *we* shall not start one, according to H.H.

I am curious to see how much consistency and vigour he will show in carrying out his programme. These are not his strong qualities at the moment. But in any case a good deal has been gained in that he is resolved in principle to co-operate in a war.

I have spent many, many hours thinking about this war question and I think our chances would be best this year, both as regards alliances and armaments. Caprivi expresses it thus: ' *Time is running against us.* '

I wrote and told Hohenlohe that since he had been instructed by the Imperial Government to introduce compulsory passports, his responsibility had been discharged. I wonder whether he will stay. He is not really the man for times of stress.

I forgot to say that if Hohenlohe does resign, Caprivi is to go to Strasbourg as Governor-General.

My general impression is that Prince Bismarck, despite his spirited speech, which was no doubt aimed at H.I.H., is not likely to force matters to a crisis.

15 *May* 1888

A strange chapter of human history could now be written by any one taking as his theme the powerlessness of the dying Kaiser and of his wife.

I am not one of the Kaiserin's adherents—rather the contrary. But I am bound to admit that her unpopularity is now used by many as a *pretext* for turning away from the Kaiser and towards his successor.

It is shocking for royalists to see how completely powerless the Kaiser is. It is very gratifying that he has not been able to realize his liberal fantasies. But surely he should now be deferred to in *minor* matters. But no. Their Majesties are actually the object of a wanton sport. The other day Radolin asked the Chancellor

---

[1] Georges Boulanger. French General. Champion of the *revanche* idea in France; as War Minister he pressed for war in the Franco-German crisis in the spring of 1887, and was dropped from the Cabinet soon after; in 1888–9 he gathered together a national opposition party in the Chamber and worked for a military dictatorship. In 1889 he was accused of high treason and fled the country.

whether he would object if Virchow, Bunsen and Schrader[1] were decorated. The Chancellor replied: 'Of course not; I don't mind. What disquiets me is the Crown Prince's lust for war. I shall have no hand in that.' And so Radolin wrote on Their Majesties' instructions that the Kaiser wished those three men to receive decorations. The Chancellor summoned the Council of Ministers, introduced for form's sake the question of these decorations, with many innuendos aimed at the Kaiserin, accepted Virchow as being an eminent scholar, but refused the other two, whom he had accepted by word of mouth. He then brought up the question of passports and talked war policy to please the Crown Prince.[2]

What harm would a few minor decorations have done? Hardly noticeable. But the people who sit on the Council of Ministers want to take their revenge on the Kaiser and Kaiserin because of all the anxiety they have felt at times. Herbert is one of the most violent. If I had just become a Minister of State, like him, *contre vents et marées*, common decency would prompt me to do the other side a favour in return.

I hear that the Russian Ambassador has been complaining to his friends of Herbert's unfriendly treatment. That is no sort of diplomacy, even if we do make war on Russia. But it is all done to curry favour with the Crown Prince, who is opposed to Russia.

To-day the Kaiserin is reaping what she formerly sowed with her ostentatious contempt of everything that is German. But the people who are now gratuitously insulting the Kaiserin will get their own back under Wilhelm II; he will show them what a monarch is. That is the nemesis of world history.

22 October 1888

The Kaiser[3] is an excellent dissembler. Albedyll thought himself so well in favour that he decided to ruin Stolberg, convinced that he, Albedyll, need only say the word to become Minister of the Royal Household. So he told the Kaiser that Stolberg's indolence was to blame for the publication of Louis Schneider's memoirs.[4] His heirs had offered the Ministry of the Royal Household to make cuts in them in return for compensation, but Stolberg had simply let the matter slide. This publication had damaged the

---

[1] Karl Schrader. A director of the Berlin–Anhalt railway from 1872; of the German Bank from 1883; National Liberal Secessionist, later Radical Member of the Reichstag, 1881–93; 1898–1912.

[2] See Lucius von Ballhausen, *Bismarck-Erinnerungen*, p. 453.

[3] Wilhelm II. Kaiser Friedrich III had died on 15 June.

[4] Louis Schneider. Actor and author; reader to Wilhelm I. Two sets of memoirs were published after Schneider's death: *Aus meinem Leben*, 3 vols. (Berlin, 1879), and the work to which Holstein refers: *Aus dem Leben Kaiser Wilhelms, 1849–1873*, 2 vols. (Berlin, 1888)

Kaiser Wilhelm legend. The Kaiser, furious, dismissed Stolberg straight away and appointed Wedell,[1] who was recommended by Bismarck.

Lehndorff was another who imagined himself on the best of terms with the Kaiser. The Kaiser was so gracious to him that Waldersee asked His Majesty: 'Has Your Majesty revised his opinion of Count Lehndorff?' 'Not at all', said H.M., 'but I treat him kindly because I should like to find out what he's really after.'

Rottenburg pulled strings right and left in his attempt to make the Chancellor accompany the Kaiser on his tour, at least through South Germany. It would have done a great deal of harm because the ovations would have been divided between the Kaiser and the Chancellor in such a way as to arouse the Kaiser's jealousy and thus to harm the Chancellor. But Rottenburg would have been given three decorations. After the idea had fallen through, mainly as a result of Herbert's representations, Rottenburg went and nagged the Chancellor, suggesting to him that many people already regarded him as a back number, and making the old man quite confused. Herbert and I have had to pay for this ever since, as is clear from the enclosed reprimand[2] I received for having carried out one of the Kaiser's commands which reached me through Herbert—a completely harmless one—without first obtaining the Chancellor's consent. I have accordingly broken off relations with Rottenburg, who will be the loser in the long run.

22 *October* 1888

We are now allowing the Press to discuss the Pope's conversations with the Kaiser and Herbert as though they were satisfactory, whereas in fact they were not in the least satisfactory.[3]

The Pope wanted to go the limit: restoration of temporal power. We were to help him in this by an alliance with Russia, Austria and Spain against Italy and France. The Kaiser made a spirited reply and said, among other things, that when Rome ceased to be the capital, Italy would also cease to be a monarchy. It would then turn into a Radical republic, and during the first hour of its existence the Pope and all his Cardinals would be thrown out of the Vatican.

The Pope told Herbert that if Germany made no attempt to

---

[1] Wilhelm von Wedell-Piesdorf. German Conservative Member of the Reichstag; President of the Reichstag, 1884–6; Minister of the Royal Household, 1888–1907.

[2] Bismarck's letter to Holstein of 3 October 1888 (*Correspondence*).

[3] The Foreign Ministry files contain a long memorandum on these conversations written by Herbert von Bismarck on 15 October. The main points are summarized by Holstein below. See also Raschdau to Holstein, 13 October; Herbert von Bismarck to Holstein, 15 and 17 October; Solms to Holstein, 2 November 1888 (*Correspondence*).

restore his temporal power he would be obliged *de traiter l'Allemagne avec hostilité*. Herbert had the impression that a member of the Jesuit faction was concealed somewhere behind a tapestry to make sure the Pope repeated his lesson properly.

I forgot to add that the Pope told the Kaiser that if the Curia was satisfied it would use its influence to ensure that the German Catholics performed their duty towards the Government.

To which the Kaiser replied that so far as *Prussian* Catholics were concerned, he, the Kaiser, would see to it himself that they performed their duty.

Schweninger told me a couple of days ago that the effects of alcohol on Herbert's constitution—brain and kidneys—were gaining ground. If Herbert were to go, the old man would very soon commit a blunder because there would be no one left to turn him back from a mistaken decision. Only last week he revoked an important order which he had approved four days previously at my suggestion.

The old man is like a hysterical old maid. A week after he had, quite unjustly, reprimanded me in writing, he told Lindau: 'Give my best wishes to H. and tell him I am satisfied with his reports and hope this work[1] is also proving satisfactory to him'—which I can hardly say is the case. Herbert went straight to Friedrichsruh yesterday to reverse one or two of the old man's absurd decisions. Rottenburg, quite apart from his ill-will, knows nothing about foreign policy.[2]

24 October 1888

The Kaiser does not appear to have had a very great personal success in Italy. The Italians thought him somewhat imperious and brusque. He hardly spoke to the Lord Mayor of Rome or to the Presidents of the Senate and the Chamber of Deputies. Only on the army did he create a good impression, and he got on well with Crispi too. A *frondeur* in his retinue said: 'His Majesty can afford to be free and easy with an old conspirator like him.' On the whole I think it quite a good thing that H.M. has somewhat broken away from customary etiquette. It is better for him to impress people than to flirt with them.

Herbert, it seems, gave way once or twice to his habitual outbursts of rage, once, for example, in front of the Italian Grand Master of Ceremonies, Count Gianotti.

[1] At the beginning of October, while Herbert von Bismarck was accompanying the Kaiser on his journey and Count Berchem was on leave, Holstein acted for a time both as State Secretary and as Under State Secretary. (See Rogge, *Friedrich von Holstein*, p. 150.)

[2] Rottenburg was in attendance on Bismarck at Friedrichsruh.

The story is told in Stuttgart that when the Kaiser was driving through the town with the King[1] and asked him the name of a certain building, the reply was: 'I'm very sorry but I'm a stranger here myself.' The joke does at any rate show the King's standing in his country.

That reminds me of an incident in 1870. At the outbreak of war Radolin was Chargé d'Affaires in Stuttgart. St Vallier was the French Minister. St Vallier told Radolin later that in July 1870 the King and Varnbüler[2] had asked him, the French Minister, for introductions to the French Generals.

I am delighted to hear that the King of Württemberg was hissed at Nice. I shall use that as a pretext for publishing a little article in the *Köln. Zeitung* attacking the practice of German Princes of going to France.

Our young Kaiser has rather too great a passion for travel. He would like to go to Spain and then next summer to Athens for the wedding.[3] The Kaiserin and the Kaiserin Friedrich also want to go to Athens. The latter is trying to prevent the former from going, so as not to take second place. I most earnestly wish that the whole trip were off. This is overdoing it.

Roggenbach has been seriously compromised by the search of Geffcken's[4] house. Letters from R. were found from which it is clear that he knew beforehand of the intended publication of the diary. Also crude outbursts against the present Kaiser. Finally a memorandum to this same Kaiser, attacking Bismarck's policy.[5]

29 *October* 1888

[...] Herbert is mainly responsible for the Kaiser's remarkable address to the city deputation by provoking his indignation at articles in Progressive newspapers in which Kaiser Friedrich's reign and personality are always contrasted favourably with the present.[6] I rather doubt whether the speech will have a

[1] Karl I, King of Württemberg, 1864–91.

[2] Karl von Varnbüler. Württemberg Minister of State.

[3] The marriage of Princess Sophie, the Kaiser's sister, and Prince Constantine of Greece. The wedding took place on 27 October 1889 in the presence of Kaiser Wilhelm II.

[4] Professor Geffcken was responsible for the publication of extracts from Kaiser Friedrich's war diary in the *Deutsche Rundschau*. He was arrested on 30 September 1888 on a charge of high treason, but proceedings were suspended soon afterwards.

[5] See *Im Ring der Gegner Bismarcks. Denkschriften und politischer Briefwechsel Franz von Roggenbachs mit Kaiserin Augusta und Albrecht von Stosch, 1865–96*, edited by Julius Heyderhoff (Leipzig, 1943), pp. 294 et seq.

[6] In an address of 27 October, replying to an offer from a deputation from the city of Berlin to erect a fountain in front of the Castle, the Kaiser complained of the shameless way in which a section of the Berlin Press discussed his family affairs.

favourable effect. Moreover, the timing was extraordinary: the city had just purchased Begas'[1] fountain for two or three thousand marks, to please the Kaiser.

The day before yesterday the Chancellor sent Herbert yet another letter thanking me for the services I had rendered him during my spell of temporary duty. This is the third time he has thanked me, and this behaviour is quite typical. H.H. knows perfectly well that he has offended me. Now he feels uneasy about it.

1 *November* 1888

Things are looking more serious again. The French Ministers and Generals are starting to make warmongering speeches; I have never known the Ministers in particular do such a thing since 1871. The Russians just go on moving their troops closer to their western frontier. Secret reports to this effect have kept coming in during the last few weeks.

Herbert has an impossible idea. He thinks that if war breaks out we should fling all our weight against France, if possible in combination with Italy. Against Russia we should use only the reserves or similar 'new formations', thus leaving the Austrians entirely to their own devices. Herbert, of course, is pre-eminently dominated by his passions. The Taaffe incident[2] increased his former resentment against the Austrians, whom he would like to see annihilated. The fact that we should then stand alone between Russia and France does not alarm him. He thinks France is to be crushed in this coming war. He actually told me the following story in this connexion: he was walking through the Museo Borbonico in Naples with the Kaiser. The Kaiser stood for a few moments in front of the statue of Julius Caesar, examined it closely and then walked on, without saying a word. But later, on their return journey, he said to Herbert: 'I think I have a mission to destroy Gaul, like Julius Caesar.'

Herbert told this to his father, who commented: 'If that's what he wants, he'll need all the most favourable circumstances assembled at the same time. One such factor is that we should be the attacked party.'

When Herbert told me this I said: 'I am convinced that H.H. really does not want another war so long as *he* is in office.'

[1] Reinhold Begas. German sculptor.
[2] The Kaiser, during his visit to Vienna in the autumn of 1888, had hoped to weaken Taaffe's position by conferring the Order of the Black Eagle on the Hungarian Minister-President Tisza, but not on Taaffe. The attempt failed. Taaffe's Ministry was in fact strengthened by this slight.

'Well', said H.B., 'he now inclines to the view that France will attack us one of these days.'

The most serious factor in all this is, I think, not the prospect of war in itself, but H.B.'s idea of leaving Austria unprotected. We must strive to prevent *that*, whatever the risk.

11 *November* 1888

Launay told me the Kaiser had spoken most virulently to King Umberto of Kaiserin Friedrich: '*Cette petite boulotte qui vise à avoir de l'influence: mais je veux être seul maître dans ma famille.*'

Kaiserin Friedrich has only herself to blame for the present state of affairs. She speaks, curses, sulks, as if she were still dealing with her husband, instead of her son, who resembles her too much to put up with such treatment.

Kaiserin Friedr. told someone recently: 'He—the Kaiser—is no longer my son. My curse upon him; may his children cause him untold sorrow.'

In this way she is playing straight into the hands of her enemies, who want her to be forced right out of the country.

Personally I could wish she had some influence over her son, to prevent his being entirely exposed to the influence of crude characters. In some respects the Kaiserin could exert a humanizing influence.

The young Kaiser's excessive frankness is sometimes a danger. He told Launay: 'After the French, the people I hate most are diplomats and deputies.' And to King Umberto: 'At home when we see a black coat at a social gathering, and when in answer to our question "Who is that?" we are told he is a deputy, we turn our back on him.'

Meanwhile I hear from observant people that the Kaiser is gradually becoming less boyish and behaving more like a monarch.

His liveliness is invaluable to us as a corrective to the Chancellor's increasing apathy. I do not like to think what would become of us if the latter were still the only influential figure, as he was in the two preceding reigns. *Après moi le déluge*, H.H. thinks, and does his utmost to resist any innovations.

For example, the French have eighty more field batteries than we have. The General Staff is therefore demanding that our artillery should also be increased. H.H. is unwilling. Why was this not done last year? It would now be difficult to justify the proposal. But the Kaiser insists. Yesterday after the hunt he brought Herbert and Waldersee together over supper. Waldersee ('who was in this respect perfectly sensible' according to Herbert) put forward his point of view,[1] and Herbert went to Friedrichsruh on the 12th [sic]. We must try to maintain harmony between the Bismarcks and Wald.; they will just have to reckon with each other now, under the present Kaiser.

[1] See Waldersee, *Denkwürdigkeiten*, vol. II, pp. 17–18.

Herbert von Bismarck to Heinrich VII Reuss[1]

Secret   *Berlin*, 14 *October* 1885
No. 590

Now that your reports nos. 335 and 337 of the 11th and 12th instant[2] have just returned from the Chancellor, I have the honour to append to my dispatch no. 589 of to-day's date[2] the following résumé of His Highness' observations on your reports.

When a Power like Russia refers her friends to treaties, and merely demands that they be upheld, Prince Bismarck sees no possibility of saying no or of replying to Russia that, out of consideration for Serbia and Bulgaria and Parliamentary Delegations, we deemed a violation of the treaties advisable and ignored the appeal of our co-signatory, Russia, to uphold them, because we were afraid that if we did so Russia would exercise the influence in Bulgaria which she had retained by the provisions of the Congress of Berlin and which had also been readily granted her up to now in the transactions of the three Imperial Courts, but which has been diminished and perhaps actually destroyed by the Prince of Battenberg and by radical Bulgarian revolutionaries like Karavelov.[4] To the Chancellor it seems impossible that we should, for fear of this eventuality which we foresaw and acknowledged, resist Russia when she invokes the treaties which Bulgaria has undoubtedly violated. The entire attitude of the three Imperial Courts has hitherto been based on the idea that Serbia and Bosnia fall within the Austrian sphere of influence and Bulgaria within the Russian sphere of influence. If we honestly abide by this arrangement we shall probably never see the outcome which Austria fears but which Russia is fully entitled to expect. The Russians will be just as unsuccessful in their further attempts to assimilate Bulgaria as they are in Serbia and Rumania, where they have been constantly losing ground since the last war.[5] The Chancellor thinks that there will be a change of attitude even in Montenegro when the time is ripe. If things are left to take their course, Prince Bismarck does not think the Russians will succeed even in getting rid of the Prince of Battenberg; the moment the maintenance of the *status quo ante* is proclaimed, the continued reign of the Prince in present-day Bulgaria is implied. The Chancellor greatly regrets that Count Kálnoky has threatened Prince Lobanov with his resignation, because he is afraid M. Giers

---

[1] From the Foreign Ministry files.   [2] See p. 252, note 4.   [3] See p. 253, note 1.
[4] Peter Karavelov. Bulgarian politician; member of the Bulgarian Regency, 1886–7.
[5] Serbia and Rumania had joined Russia in the war against Turkey of 1877–8.

may counter with the same move; but the latter must after all show greater consideration to his Tsar than Count Kálnoky need show to the Delegations, whose interference in foreign policy, if recognized or even permitted by the Minister, would make foreign policy completely impossible. It is not M. Giers but Tsar Alexander who commands the situation in Russia; the Tsar wants to get rid of Battenberg, and M. Giers dares not tell him what is possible and what is not possible. How he proposes to carry out what Count Kálnoky calls his very vague general ideas is not yet known even to the Russian Minister.

It is in this sense that one is to understand Prince Lobanov's remark that it was still too early to express an opinion on the attainment of the aims pursued by Russian policy. Even if the Ambassadors in Constantinople[1] should fail to find a practicable solution, time will still be won by the continuation of their deliberations, and that is a great deal. All the suggestions and queries put to you by Count Kálnoky will be discussed in Constantinople, and whatever the Powers agree on will be done; but at present they are not yet in agreement, and anyone who demands an immediate clear-cut solution, i.e. who raises difficulties, thereby blocks the way to agreement.

Russia has not yet proposed the removal of the Prince of Battenberg; whether she will succeed in achieving this remains doubtful. That Russia should be striving to recover her lost influence in both Bulgarias is, as has been said, natural, and corresponds to our agreements: but it is unlikely that Russia will succeed in so doing. Even so it must be remembered when determining one's attitude to this question that Austria has hitherto regarded a united Bulgaria as depending on Russia's good pleasure. When Count Kálnoky goes on to say he desires an understanding with Russia, it is worth noting that it takes two sides to reach an agreement, and that this becomes difficult when Austria reneges and departs from the former agreements by trying to draw Bulgaria into the Austrian sphere of power.

It is natural for Count Kálnoky to be eager to know Russia's views soon; but Russia is no doubt equally anxious to learn Austria's: Count Kálnoky was wrong to become suspicious as a result of Prince Lobanov's journey: he expects of M. Giers more than a far more independent (and more clear-minded) Minister could achieve under *these* circumstances.

As regards the doubts expressed by Count Kálnoky, according to your dispatch no. 337, on the possibility of restoring the *status quo*, the Chancellor observed that this must nevertheless be attempted; six Powers in agreement carried more weight than the Austrian Minister appeared willing to attribute to them.

[1] A conference of the Ambassadors in Constantinople had been convened to discuss problems arising from the revolution in Eastern Rumelia.

When Count Kálnoky speaks of Kremsier[1] and of the safeguarding of *mutual interests*, his present interpretation of them seems to be that Bulgaria is to be absorbed into the Austrian sphere of influence. The impression inevitably gained from the total contents of your dispatches is that it is rather Austria who is trying to finesse.

That M. Giers should have reserved His Majesty's consent for his 'further ideas' is not strange, but only natural. This very point constitutes his main difficulty, and when one reflects with what anxiety and lack of independence he now acts and how precarious his position already was in the spring, one realizes the great probability of M. Giers' resignation. The Chancellor is, however, very doubtful whether this resignation would correspond to Austria's wishes and interests: if Count Ignatiev succeeded him and if in the course of the coming weeks Mr Gladstone were returned to power in the English elections, that would be a future situation which ought to weigh heavier than worry about the Delegations. That it is best 'to leave the small Balkan states to their own devices' is certainly Prince Bismarck's view; this will come about if we can gain *time*. The idea of a personal union under the Prince of Battenberg was only a last resort; the *status quo ante* is better, if *all* the Powers desire it; it was not to be expected that Russia would desire it, because she would thereby antagonize Bulgarian national feeling and the Pan-Slavists. This last is more important than all the rest. Count Kálnoky's statement which you reproduce on p. 5 of dispatch no. 337, 'that he did not want to begrudge the Russians *their legitimate influence* over the territory to which they lay claim' does not accord with his opposition to a 'Russian Pashadom' quoted a few lines further down. This contradiction seems to indicate that Austria still aspires to make her influence felt in Bulgaria and to cut across Russian influence there. As I have already made clear in the beginning, this is directly opposed to the provisions of our secret treaties and might tend to arouse mistrust of the aims of Austrian policy.

I request you to have a confidential talk with Count Kálnoky along the lines suggested above and to draw his attention to the grave consequences which would result from pressing M. Giers too hard. The main thing for us now is to gain time. Whether we shall obtain the consent of all the Powers to one form or another of Bulgarian union remains to be seen; if not, then no harm will be done; any time gained has the effect of restraining the Powers from intervention in Serbo-Bulgarian affairs.

H[erbert von] B[ismarck]

[1] A reference to the meeting between Francis Joseph and Alexander III on 25 August 1885 in that town.

Reich-Chancellor Bismarck to Kaiser Wilhelm I[1]

Varzin, 30 September 1886

While most humbly submitting to Your Majesty the enclosed dispatch from Your Majesty's Minister in Darmstadt of the 24th of this month,[2] I am taking the liberty of respectfully appending to its contents one or two considerations on the former Prince of Bulgaria and his future.

Already some years ago Your Majesty foresaw the possibility that in case Prince Alexander left Bulgaria he would return to Germany and endeavour to create a position for himself here. Your Majesty described this possibility as undesirable, and in consequence our diplomatic activities have been directed towards unobtrusively counteracting all endeavours in Bulgaria aimed at the Prince's overthrow. However, his overthrow has been effected, not because Russia's endeavours in this direction have proved irresistible, but because the Prince himself made his position so untenable that he finally lost all courage and desire to retain it.

When the Prince of Battenberg came to power in Bulgaria, it was assumed in every quarter that the new Prince would ally himself and Bulgaria with the Russians, to whose protection alone he owed his election, and who were until then the actual masters in Bulgaria, which they held under military occupation. The Prince's close kinship with the Russian Imperial family justified the assumption that this relationship would be lasting and would contribute to mutual satisfaction and trust. This assumption was proved mistaken; the Prince was soon intent on shaking off his dependence on Russia; whether he was thereby following English influences or his own ambition need not be decided. That he had no intention of being satisfied with the modest mission of hereditary Russian governor may be concluded from the anxiety with which he sought support, now from the other Balkan states, including Greece, now from the Porte, which might enable him to free himself of his dependence on Russia. The Prince's youth and inexperience explain his inept overestimation of his own prospects and claims, and of the importance of Bulgaria and the Balkan States as a whole which he suggested should form a coalition, and will explain why he set himself unattainable goals. The final result of his ambitious endeavours was that he forfeited

---

[1] From the Foreign Ministry files. See p. 305.

[2] Le Maistre had reported that Prince Alexander would remain in Germany for the time being and would not accept an invitation from Queen Victoria to go to England.

the confidence one after the other, not only of his relatives at the Court of the Tsars, but also of the neighbouring Balkan States, then of the Porte, and in the end even of Austria; this year he finally lost England's confidence too. True to his character, which derives its qualities and defects more from his Polish than his German ancestry, he had in the end created the impression on every one with whom he associated that they could count neither on his discernment nor his reliability. Nevertheless, his abdication resulted not from any pressure at home or abroad but from his own free decision. The idea of abdicating must have been present in him for years, not indeed constantly, but at repeated intervals. He had for years toyed with the idea of giving up his position in Bulgaria in exchange for a financial settlement which would serve as a basis for his future position in Germany.

For a person accustomed to the social life of the great European capitals, life in Sofia could offer few intrinsic attractions. Even with more modest demands on life, a person accustomed to European polite society could hardly find any compensation for his isolation in Sofia in the satisfaction of exercising constitutional government over an uncultivated people. After the Prince had thrown off his allegiance to Russia but had failed to win the confidence of other Powers or of his neighbours, his restless ambition sought satisfaction in the policy which led to the revolt in Eastern Rumelia a year ago. By secretly participating in this he had deceived not only Russia but also Austria, his friend hitherto, and had not foreseen that this revolutionary conquest would plunge him into war with Serbia.

Although the fortunes of war favoured him at Slivnitza, he found himself as a result in a situation which looked threatening to the Cabinet in Vienna, and obliged them to choose between Bulgaria and Serbia. As Prince Alexander might have foreseen, Austria decided in favour of Serbia, and from that moment Bulgaria could rely on *none* of the neighbouring Powers whose influence on her fate was decisive, i.e. Austria-Hungary, Russia and Turkey, to give the support so urgently needed by that small country and its sovereign. Among these Powers, it was at first only Russia which desired the removal of the Prince, so that the latter, backed by England's good will and the tolerance shown by Austria and Turkey, could have continued to rule as before, had he possessed the necessary skill.

The eight years of his reign had matured his character and his understanding of the country and its people so little that he let himself be persuaded without the slightest basis that he was threatened with fresh attacks by Serbia, and allowed his reliable troops to be spirited away under cover of this pretext; he was incapable of accurately appraising the character of the population he ruled or the troops he commanded. With an assurance bordering on stupidity he attributed to the officers of the Bulgarian militia sentiments such as animate Your Majesty's officers, and in face of the dangers which, as experience has shown, surround every sovereign in Balkan countries, he did not even take the precaution of mounting a trustworthy guard over his castle and his bedroom. If he had known something of the history of those countries and the character of their inhabitants, the Prince could have been in no doubt that the only protection for him or for any of his successors against incidents like those of 21 August lay in *personal vigilance and knowledge of human nature*, and a sufficiently powerful and reliable bodyguard.

The Prince's Polish blood which comes out in this wanton recklessness is shown equally clearly in the discouragement with which he allowed his signature to the abdication document to be forced from him at the point of a revolver. This remarkable change of mood according to circumstances, so typical of the Slavs, is also evident in the grovelling telegram to the Tsar of Russia after his return from Lemberg, which contrasted most violently with the Prince's attitude towards the Tsar over a period of years, and which finally caused him to forfeit even England's confidence.[1] The only psychological explanation I can find for this step and for the humble tone of his telegram is the assumption that the Prince's nerves were shattered by the nocturnal attack of 21 August and that he could not bear to contemplate continuing an existence which would require him to be prepared daily for similar incidents. He is one of those people who, like all officers, advance unflinchingly in the face of danger in open battle, but cannot endure the feeling of being *constantly* in danger. If I assume that this, and not love of the Bulgarian people, was the deciding factor in his abdication, then I find the telegram to Tsar Alexander, and its tone, perfectly explicable.

The Foreign Minister, M. Giers, had already told me at Franzensbad that Russia was prepared to disburse a considerable sum if the Prince would abdicate and pave the way for Russia in Bulgaria.[2] I suspect M. Giers of entertaining this plan without the knowledge of the Tsar, his master, at any rate without any consideration of the Tsar's burning hatred of his cousin. If Tsar Alexander had accepted M. Giers' plan, the servile telegram and the subsequent abdication might well have prepared the ground for a more generous settlement. That is the only explanation that occurs to me of the violent change in the Prince's attitude towards Russia and of his completely unsolicited abdication immediately

---

[1] See Corti, *Alexander von Battenberg*, p. 334.

[2] Bismarck and Giers had met at Franzensbad on 26 and 27 August 1886. Giers emphasized Russia's determination not to intervene in Bulgaria. Both statesmen regarded the possibility of Prince Alexander's return to Bulgaria as dangerous and discussed the advisability of a financial settlement to be paid by Russia to Prince Alexander. (From the Foreign Ministry files.)

after the acclaim of the army and the nation in Sofia had assured him that in spite of Russian hostility, which was after all nothing new, he could continue to rule as before. For seven or eight years the Prince had not doubted his ability to govern Bulgaria without or in opposition to Russia; indeed, he had not shrunk from any act liable to increase the Russians' hatred of him. Although a mutiny by some of his officers had dealt a blow to his exaggerated confidence in their reliability, this damage was completely atoned for and wiped out by the unanimity with which all the rest of the army and the people demonstrated their loyalty. With this support the Prince could perfectly well have gone on reigning for another eight years, in spite of Russia, just as he had done before. But he had lost both the courage and the desire to endure any longer his isolation in Sofia, a place with no intrinsic attractions for a pleasure-loving young man, once he had realized that this isolation did not even afford him the luxury of a safe night's rest. He preferred to return to Germany to see whether he could embark on a more satisfying, more agreeable and more secure existence in Your Majesty's Reich or elsewhere.

His first step towards this goal was a publicity campaign in the German, Austrian and British Press, conducted with great skill and, judging from its scope, at considerable expense. All the German opposition newspapers, Jesuit, Guelph [Hanoverian], Radical, Polish, and Social Democratic, at once recognized in the Prince and his cause a useful weapon with which to attack the Government and its foreign policy. All parties and individuals working for the overthrow of the existing order realized with unerring instinct that Prince Alexander, with his connexions with influential circles in Germany and England, could under certain conditions be used as a figurehead by the 'malcontents'. The preliminary basis for this calculation is, first the rank of General held by the Prince in the Prussian army, and, second, his royal relatives. Any man in that position, equipped as well with all the outstanding qualities of heart and mind which the Press attributes to Prince Alexander, justifiably becomes a candidate for an exalted position. I have no opinion of the Prince's talent as a strategist; all I know from the dispatches I have read is that he displayed the same degree of intrepidity as shown by hundreds of thousands of officers and men under Your Majesty's command during wars and major battles, without its being assumed *on that account alone* that each one of them possessed talents that would fit him for a senior post in the High Command. But my long years of experience as a statesman entitle me to pass an opinion on his ability in this field, and I feel I may venture the opinion that the Prince's policy throughout his reign until now offers a striking example of political ineptitude. With one might say an almost childish wilfulness he followed one after the other the mutually

391

contradictory promptings of his personal ambition, and never even went far enough along any one of the paths he had taken to be able to convince himself *for certain* that it was mistaken. But his worst fault in the realm of statesmanship is his lack of loyalty and reliability. A politician who has lost his reputation in this respect can find no one to believe in him, and that means the end of his career, as in the case of my late Austrian colleague, Count Prokesch;[1] he was more gifted by nature and more experienced in politics than Prince Alexander but none of his gifts were of any avail to him because people neither trusted nor believed him.

It is evident from the organs of the Press that since his return to Germany Prince Alexander has the support of all those parties whose representatives form the majority in the Reichstag which opposed Your Majesty's Government on the Polish question last winter, and whose newspapers have been unanimous for the last six weeks in their condemnation of Germany's Bulgarian policy. Thus, if Your Majesty wished to make him Chancellor, for example, he would in that position command a majority in the Reichstag, though he would at the same time be the occasion of a split in that majority, because it is united only by its opposition to Government proposals, not by any positive aims. But apart from this possibility, which I adduce merely as an illustration, the Prince's political friends are working for the idea that an important post should be found for him in the service of the state, if possible the post of Your Majesty's Governor in the Imperial Provinces whether or not the Prince marries one of the royal Princesses.

If the Prince did not scruple for one moment to break faith first with the Sultan, his liege lord by treaty, then with his nearest blood-relation and patron, the Tsar of Russia, to whom he owed his principality, who, after experiences such as these, could guarantee Prince Alexander's fitness to be entrusted with the governorship of Alsace-Lorraine, i.e. the one post which, more than any other in the Reich, demands as its indispensable condition unswerving loyalty to Kaiser and Reich and the belief of the army and the people in this loyalty?

If the Prince broke faith with the Sultan and the Tsar in order to become King of the Bulgars or from any other motive, then where is the guarantee against the possibility of his turning against the German Kaiser if he saw any prospect of becoming, possibly with French assistance, King of the Swabians as Prince of the Confederation of the Rhine? If Prince Alexander shares the Polish sympathies of his mother's family, on which I offer no

---

[1] Anton, Count Prokesch von Osten. Austrian Minister in Berlin, 1849–52. Presiding Minister at the German Federal Diet in Frankfurt-am-Main, where he had violent clashes with Bismarck; Internuncio, then Ambassador in Constantinople, 1855–71; retired since 1871. Died 26 October 1876.

opinion, and if as is possible he feels more Polish than German, as do most sons of Polish mothers and German fathers, then such a betrayal of Germany would by Polish logic be not merely justifiable as a service to the Polish fatherland but actually honourable.

While respectfully submitting to Your Majesty this picture of the anxieties for our future with which the Battenberg question fills me, I take the further liberty of emphasizing that the basis for the possibilities I have outlined lies in the fact that the Prince wears the uniform of a Prussian General and will shortly appear as such when he attends the manœuvres in Hesse. It is unusual, in fact it is unprecedented, for a Prussian General to be regarded as a political figure and raised to the summit of popularity by the sympathies of the entire German opposition, from the Social Democrats to the Guelphs, including the Austro-Hungarian democrats.

I had hoped that Prince Alexander would shortly accept an invitation of the Queen to go to England. Since this does not appear to be the case and since he cannot be expected to spend all his time in Jugenheim, we may expect this General to make contacts in Germany which will result in political connexions, and the importance which the opposition Press has attached to this gentleman is a hint to him that he ought to play a part in the politics of the Reich. I do not think him capable of playing this part, but I do not think he will refuse.

Before most respectfully adding a request to this presentation, I should like to request Your Majesty graciously to state whether he thinks my fears are well founded, and whether Your Majesty will graciously permit me to submit for Your Majesty's approval official proposals for dealing with the question, particularly as regards the Press and the confidential correspondence with German courts, some of which have given a good reception to the legend built up around the figure of the Prince by his Press campaign. Then the winter deliberations of the Reichstag would afford an opportunity of adopting an attitude towards the question publicly.[1]

von Bismarck

[1] Kaiser Wilhelm wrote the following comment on this document: 'Entirely agree with this presentation of the situation, and also agree on the threatening nature of the Prince of Bulgaria's behaviour. Wilhelm. 1.10.86.'

BIOGRAPHICAL INDEX

[*Note.* biog. = biographical sketch]

Abdul Hamid II, Sultan of Turkey (1876–1909): 6, 20 n. 1, 23 n. 4, 179, 181, 239–40, 259 n. 2, 260 n. 1, 278 n. 3, 291–2, 300, 303 n. 2, 322, 324, 337, 342 n. 1, 392

Abeken, Heinrich: xvii, biog. 59 n. 1

Albedyll, General Emil von: biog. 14 n. 3; 15, 17, 32, 34, 36, 47–8, 81, 120, 177, 195–7, 212, 226, 249–50, 265, 284, 327, 347, 377

Alexander II, Tsar of Russia (1855–81): 5, 8, 38, 54, 111 n. 1, 138

Alexander III, Tsar of Russia (1881–94): 9, 16, 37 n. 2, 65–6, 75 n. 2, 92, 96, 99, 144, 161, 171 n. 4, 229, 252, 259 n. 2, 262, 266 n. 2, 294–7, 298, 306, 309 n. 6, 314–15, 316 n. 2, 319 n. 4, 323, 330 n. 4, 331, 336 n. 5, 341 n. 2, 357, 359, 386–7, 390, 392

Alexander, Prince of Battenberg, then Prince of Bulgaria: xvi–xvii; biog. 111 n. 1; proposed Hohenzollern marriage, 112, 122, 125, 134, 143–5, 153, 155, 171, 198, 205, 207, 213, 215, 217, 244–5, 254, 255–6, 259, 261, 262, 263, 271, 335, 365, 366–9, 372; Eastern question, 252 n. 2 and 3, 269–70, 278–80, 289–90, 300, 301, 302 n. 1, 330 n. 4, 337, 385–7; Bismarck, 267, 298, 305, 307, 317, 318, 328; text of Bismarck report to Wilhelm I, 388–93; miscellaneous, 276, 296, 316, 323, 344

Alexander, Prince of Hesse-Darmstadt: 123 n. 2, 138, 269, 290

Alfonso XII, King of Spain (1875–85): 18–19, 44 n. 1, 45, 236, 237, 239, 241, 242, 243–4, 247

Alvensleben, Friedrich Johann, Count von: biog. 136 n. 2; 209

Amadeo I, King of Spain (1871–3): 305 n. 3

Ampthill, Odo Russell, Lord: biog. 15 n. 3; 24, 55, 134, 142, 214

Andrássy, Julius, Count: biog. 11 n. 3; 54, 126, 341–2

Appert, Félix: 309 n. 6

Arnim-Boitzenburg, Adolf, Count von: biog. 70 n. 2

Arnim-Kröchlendorf, Malvine von: 185 n. 1

Arnim-Kröchlendorf, Sybille von: *see* Bismarck-Schönhausen, Sybille von

Arnim-Suckow, Harry, Count von: 63 n. 1, 67, 78, 119, 187, 194, 339

Arnim-Suckow, Henning, Count von: 188

Augusta, Kaiserin (wife of Wilhelm I): 2, 3–4, 24, 59, 111, 136, 140, 171, 194, 217, 232, 273, 297, 339, 343, 353, 364

Augusta Victoria (wife of Wilhelm II): 123 n. 1, 177 n. 1, 182, 256, 362 n. 1, 380

Bamberger, Ludwig: biog. 117 n. 2; 168

Battenberg, Prince Alexander von: *see* Alexander

Battenberg, Prince Heinrich von: 122 n. 2, 198, 245

Battenberg, Prince Ludwig von: 125 n. 2, 132

Battenberg, Princess von (*née* Countess Julie Haucke): 123 n. 2, 137–8, 269 n. 7

Beatrice, Princess of England: biog. 122 n. 2; 132

Bebel, August: biog. 67 n. 6

Behr-Negendank, Ulrich, Count von: biog. 22 n. 6; 23

Bennigsen, Rudolf von: biog. 33 n. 1; 34, 69–70, 74, 102, 112, 116–18, 167, 363 n. 2

Benomar, Count: biog. 234 n. 2; 235, 243, 247, 250 n. 3, 276, 305, 306

Berchem, Maximilian, Count von: biog. 11 n. 2; 100–1, 136; career, 186–7; 192, 197–8, 200, 204, 218, 219, 221, 232, 233, 237, 248, 262, 270, 275, 276, 277–8, 284, 287–8, 290, 296–7, 298, 308, 328, 340, 354, 379 n. 1

Bergmann, Dr Ernst von: biog. 38 n. 2; 39, 41, 342, 344–5, 365, 370

Beust, Friedrich Ferdinand, Count von: biog. 54 n. 1; 141

Bismarck-Schönhausen, Herbert von: xii–xiv, xvi–xvii, xviii, xix; biog. 22 n. 5; family relations, 49, 104, 110–11, 114, 152, 230, 232, 289; character, 55, 57, 158, 198, 199–200, 261, 271–3, 284, 354; career, 100–3, 125, 136–7, 140, 146–7, 184–5, 203, 210; relations with father, 118, 121, 131, 237, 248, 274–5, 277, 287, 297, 306, 340, 357; Crown Prince and Princess, 175–6, 183, 192, 206, 208–9, 223–5, 249–50, 256, 327, 356, 377; Bülow, 188–90, 204, 220, 264, 265; Prince Wilhelm, 191–2, 194, 233–4, 242, 254, 294, 298, 303, 308, 315–16, 328, 343, 346–7, 360, 365–6, 369–71, 378–9, 380–2; Battenberg marriage, 244–5, 263, 307; Hatzfeldt, 217–19, 221, 229, 231, 258,

260–1, 268, 283, 286, 309, 320; Carolines question, 234 n. 1, 236–7, 239, 241, 243–4, 251, 256–8; Eastern question, 252–3, 270, 276, 279–80, 305; dispatch to Reuss on Eastern question, 385–7; pro-Russian views, 256, 259, 266–7, 269, 299, 312 n. 1, 313–14, 316–17, 323, 331–2, 381–2; miscellaneous, 53, 62, 80, 83 n. 5, 92, 95, 96 n. 2, 98 n. 2, 145, 179, 186, 193, 195, 202, 205 n. 4, 207, 222, 226, 246, 247 n. 1 and 2, 276, 296, 311, 319, 321 n. 2, 330 n. 4, 335, 339, 341, 345, 348, 353, 357, 373, 374

Bismarck-Schönhausen, Johanna von (*née* Puttkamer): xii, 3, 7, 22, 24, 35, 38, 48, 57, 64, 65, 93, 94, 95, 97, 102, 110–11, 114, 151, 182, 184, 189, 203–4, 221, 232–3, 272, 284–5, 340

Bismarck-Schönhausen, Otto von: biog. 1 n. 1; Holstein, vii, viii, xi–xix, 65, 182, 272–5, 284–5, 381; *Kulturkampf*, 2–3, 4–5, 7, 91, 237–8; internal affairs, 7–8, 33–4, 56–8, 69–70, 82, 105, 116–17, 191, 248; Hatzfeldt, 10–11, 16, 25–6, 32, 78–9, 89, 120, 173, 175, 184, 192, 198–9, 209–10, 220–1, 260, 283; Egypt, 12–13, 160, 325; officials, 14, 27–9, 61–3, 130, 140–2, 159, 189, 333–4, 338; state of mind, 19, 21, 48–9, 129, 261, 272–3, 327, 339–40, 376; Bleichröder, 18, 23, 56–8, 64, 95, 131, 202–4, 205, 227–8, 230–2; Crown Prince and Princess, 31, 37, 46, 50–2, 68, 71–2, 74, 96–7, 99, 102, 106, 117–18, 121, 149, 150–1, 154–5, 164–5, 167, 174–7, 178–84, 205–6, 208–9, 211–18, 222–6, 249, 267–8, 294–7, 298, 306–7, 317–18, 346, 352, 358, 378; health, 20, 22, 35, 38–9, 41, 48, 103–4, 132–3, 157–8; character, 64–5, 76, 113–14, 197, 274, 284–5; Russia, 9, 66, 197, 359; Bavarian loan, 73, 75, 77, 79–80, 94–5; family relations, 92–4, 103–4, 110–11, 114–15; Council of State, 105, 119, 124; Battenberg marriage, 112, 122–3, 125, 134, 138, 143–6, 245, 263, 305, 366–9; text of report to Wilhelm I, 388–93; Wilhelm I, 120, 142, 196, 210, 343; Army, 126–7, 128–9; Eastern question, 171 n. 4, 252–3, 255, 259, 266–7, 269–70, 279–80, 289–90, 302 n. 4, 324 n. 2, 385–7; general international scene, 160, 186, 193, 228, 308, 311–12, 313–14, 316, 323, 331–2, 335, 364; Herbert Bismarck, 100–1, 136–7, 146–8, 185, 190, 200, 219, 262, 274–7, 287, 354, 373, 379; Prince Wilhelm, 153, 347, 356, 361–3, 365–6, 367–71, 374–5, 377, 378, 382; colonial affairs, 156, 161–4, 169, 310; succession, 167–8, 201–3, 204, 264; Carolines question, 234–7, 239, 241, 242–4, 247–8, 250–1, 256–8; Drummond Wolff, 240, 260 n. 1; Andrássy, 341–2; miscellaneous, 6, 9, 17,

30, 36, 40, 43, 44, 45, 53–5, 59–60, 67, 83 n. 5, 85–7, 90, 98, 107, 108–10, 135, 152, 166, 172, 188, 246, 264, 286, 288, 299, 303, 309 n. 5, 320, 321, 327, 328, 330, 339–41, 353, 357, 364, 373, 379, 380

Bismarck-Schönhausen, Sybille von (*née* Arnim-Kröchlendorf): 185 n. 1, 212, 233, 272, 340, 355

Bismarck-Schönhausen, Wilhelm von (Bill): xii–xiii, xix, biog. 27 n. 2; relations with father, 52, 118, 124; family relations, 93, 96, 114–15, 133, 152, 340, 345, 354–5, 357, 360; character, 202, 328, 332; miscellaneous, 35, 38, 48, 50, 57, 117, 127, 137, 146, 162, 184, 185, 192, 212, 264, 272, 275

Bleichröder, Gerson: biog. 8 n. 3; relations with Bismarck, 18, 23, 58, 65, 94–5, 116, 131, 178, 181, 202–3, 204–5, 218, 227–8, 230–2, 277, 327, 374–5; income tax question, 56–7, 64; Bavarian loan, 73, 75, 77–8, 79–80, 87–8, 94; scandal, 83–5, 93; miscellaneous, 9, 16–17, 19, 20, 22, 31, 101, 103, 104, 141, 156, 214, 229–30, 253, 269, 273, 308, 339, 362

Blücher, Gebhard Leberecht von: 127, 222

Blumenthal, Leonhard, Count von: biog. 34 n. 2; 242

Bodelschwingh, Karl von: biog. 58 n. 1

Bödicker, Anton: biog. 334 n. 1

Bojanowski: biog. 29 n. 1; 124, 125, 129–30, 133, 140–2

Bonin, Adolf von: biog. 127 n. 1

Bötticher, Karl Heinrich von: biog. 13 n. 2; 17, 20, 26, 67, 102, 131, 133, 134–5, 161, 163, 165, 333–4, 338

Boulanger, Georges: biog. 376 n. 1

Brandenburg, Gustav, Count von: biog. 145 n. 2

Brandenstein, Karl von: biog. 129 n. 1

Bratianu, Joan: biog. 263 n. 3; 289 n. 1

Brauer, Arthur von: biog. 3 n. 2; 29, 222 n. 2, 271, 273, 276

Bray-Steinburg, Hippolyt, Count von: biog. 269 n. 5; 270 n. 1

Brincken: biog. 31 n. 4

Bronsart von Schellendorf, Paul: biog. 35 n. 2; 36, 113, 120, 127, 135, 168, 195–6, 226, 264, 327, 366

Brunswick, *see* Ernst August, Duke of Cumberland and Brunswick

Bucher, Lothar: biog. 22 n. 2; 27–9, 39, 63–4, 91, 124, 137, 173, 203, 270, 341

Budberg, Andreas, Baron von: biog. 27 n. 1

Bülow, Adolf von: biog. 47 n. 1; 187, 219–20, 233

Bülow, Bernhard von: biog. 47 n. 2; 156, 185; character, 186–90; 198, 204, 219–20; Prince Wilhelm, 233–4, 348; Herbert Bismarck, 264, 265; 262, 302 n. 1, 311, 314, 319, 341 n. 2

Bülow, Bernhard Ernst von: biog. 13 n. 1; 15, 26, 47, 61, 141, 187–8, 189, 219, 354

Bülow, Otto von: biog. 287 n. 3; 354

Bunge, Nicholas von: biog. 17 n. 1

Bunsen, Georg von: biog. 95 n. 3, 377

Buol, Karl Ferdinand, Count von: biog. 107 n. 1; 108

Burchard, Emil von: biog. 113 n. 1

Busch, Klemens August: biog. 2 n. 9; 13, 14, 16, 22, 23, 24, 28, 55, 62–3, 78, 125, 129–30, 137, 140, 144, 147–8, 160, 184, 247 n. 2, 263

Cambridge, George, Duke of: biog. 309 n. 4

Camphausen, Otto von: biog. 125 n. 1; 328 n. 1

Canovas de Castillo, Antonio: biog. 235 n. 1; 236, 241, 243–4

Caprivi, Leo, Count von: biog. 36 n. 3; 121, 129, 136; colonial policy, 158–60, 161, 162–4, 210–11; Hatzfeldt, 222; 233, 245, 254, 265, 266, 298, 307, 346, 349, 366, 373, 376

Carlos, Crown Prince of Portugal: biog. 205 n. 3; 214, 215

Carolath, Princess Elizabeth von (née Hatzfeldt-Trachenberg): biog. 110 n. 1

Carolath-Amtitz, Prince: 195–6

Churchill, Lord Randolph: biog. 304 n. 5; 311, 318–22, 323, 324, 325–6, 330

Cohn, see Meyer-Cohn

Courcel, Alphonse, Baron de: biog. 5 n. 8; 21, 134; character, 155–7; 160, 169, 185, 200–1, 202, 203, 247 n. 1, 251–2, 262, 280–1, 297–8

Crailsheim, Christoph Krafft, Baron von: biog. 40 n. 2; 135

Crispi, Francesco: 379

Delbrück, Rudolf von: 328 n. 1

Derenthall, Eduard von: biog. 100 n. 2; 136

Déroulède, Paul: biog. 281 n. 1

Dietze-Barby, G. A. von: biog. 116 n. 2; 117, 126, 272, 277

Disraeli, Benjamin, Earl of Beaconsfield: biog. 207 n. 2

Dolgoruki, Nicholas, Prince: biog. 15 n. 5; 80, 91–2, 95, 96, 98–9, 226, 229

Dönhoff-Camporeale, Marie, Countess: biog. 188 n. 2; 189, 262

Dryander, Ernst von: biog. 115 n. 1.

Dufferin, Frederick Blackwood, Marquess of: biog. 60 n. 4

Edward, Prince of Wales, then Edward VII, King of England (1901–10): 134, 144–5, 161, 162, 176, 179–80, 222–3, 254

Eisendecher, Karl von: xviii n. 1; biog. 87 n. 1; 98, 101, 125, 136

Ernst II, Duke of Saxe-Coburg and Gotha: biog. 31 n. 2

Ernst August, Duke of Cumberland and Brunswick: biog. 166 n. 1, 202, 250, 263

Eulenburg, August, Count zu: biog. 1 n. 3; 2, 3–4, 11–12, 149, 150–1, 363

Eulenburg, Botho, Count zu: biog. 4 n. 2

Eulenburg, Friedrich, Count zu: biog. 26 n. 4; 43

Eulenburg-Hertefeld, Philipp, Count zu: biog. 330 n. 1; 370

Fabrice, Oswald: 107

Falk, Dr Adalbert: biog. 90 n. 1

Farre, General Jean Joseph: biog. 17 n. 3

Favre, Jules: biog. 138 n. 1

Ferry, Jules: biog. 160 n. 2; 162, 169

Forckenbeck, Max von: biog. 72 n. 2; 74, 76, 113, 117, 165, 203, 211

Fournier, Hugues: biog. 65 n. 2

Franck, Karl, Ritter von: biog. 25 n. 6

Franckenstein, Georg Arbogast, Baron von und zu: biog. 191 n. 1; 275, 277–8

Fränkel, Dr Bernhard: 357

Franz Joseph, Kaiser of Austria-Hungary (1848–1916): 5, 9, 11, 25, 65–6, 106–7, 241, 242, 269–70, 309, 322 n. 1, 331, 341 n. 2, 342 n. 1, 387 n. 1

Frelinghuysen, Frederick T.: biog. 86 n. 3

Frerichs, Friedrich Theodor: biog 22 n. 4; 38–9, 41

Freycinet, Charles de: 12 n. 3; biog. 201 n. 1; 231, 247 n. 1, 252 n. 1, 305 n. 4, 306, 322 n. 6, 336

Friedberg, Heinrich von: biog. 2 n. 7; 5, 20, 67–9, 72, 83; Bleichröder, 84–5; 90, 117–18, 185, 202, 208, 210, 212, 262, 266, 344, 346, 358, 368, 373

Friedrich II, Duke of Anhalt: biog. 112 n. 3

Friedrich I, Grand Duke of Baden: 40, 121 n. 1, 136, 180, 265, 353, 365, 368

Friedrich III, Kaiser: see Friedrich Wilhelm, German Crown Prince

Friedrich, Kaiserin: see Victoria, German Crown Princess

Friedrich II, King of Prussia (1740–86): 21, 35, 79, 118, 189, 214, 261, 275, 295, 347, 361, 366

Friedrich Karl, Prince of Prussia: biog. 58 n. 2

Friedrich Leopold, Prince: 58

Friedrich Wilhelm, German Crown Prince, then Kaiser Friedrich III (9 March–15 June 1888): xv–xviii; Hatzfeldt, 1–2, 20, 32, 40, 55, 77, 199, 220–1, 260; Bismarck, 9–10, 21, 31, 50–2, 59, 68–9, 79, 96–7, 102, 105–6, 113, 117–18, 121, 146–9, 150–1, 168–9, 174, 177–85, 186, 190, 193, 202, 205–6, 208, 209, 212–13, 214, 217, 224, 230–1, 264, 267–8, 270, 298, 306, 317–18, 327; Wilhelm I, 11–12, 39; Prince Wilhelm, 34, 37, 177–8, 233–4, 294–7; trip to Spain and Rome, 43, 44 n. 1, 45–6, 50–2, 236, 242; Rauchhaupt, 71–2, 73–4; political views, 95–6, 98, 152–3,

196, 201, 256; Crown Princess Victoria, 99, 161, 194–5, 303; Council of State, 105, 119, 164–7; Battenberg marriage, 111–12, 123, 134, 143–4, 198, 244–5, 255, 262, 263, 289, 305, 366–70; character, 47, 154–5, 164, 170–1, 178, 204; Herbert Bismarck, 175, 176–7, 191–2, 218, 249–50, 254, 261, 307–8; Portuguese marriage, 205 n. 4, 214 n. 1, 225–6; last illness, 342–5, 346, 348–53, 355–9, 360, 364, 365, 370–2, 376–7; miscellaneous, 3–4, 5, 8, 15, 17, 23, 29–30, 35, 47–8, 80–1, 83, 89, 100, 104, 139, 158, 189, 210, 223, 238, 248, 265, 299, 380

Friedrich Wilhelm IV, King of Prussia (1840–61): 7, 10, 19, 114 n. 1, 266

Gablenz, Anton, Baron von: biog. 25 n. 3; 26
Gablenz, Ludwig, Baron von: biog. 25 n. 4
Gambetta, Léon: biog. 6 n. 4; 26
Geffcken, Dr Heinrich: biog. 180 n. 1; 185, 380
Gerhardt, Karl: biog. 342 n. 2; 344–5
Gerlach, Leopold von: biog. 7 n. 1; 10, 266
Giers, Nicholas von: biog. 16 n. 1; 44, 55, 66–7, 74, 75, 92, 98–9, 130 n. 1, 229–30, 231, 240 n. 1, 266 n. 2, 267 n. 1, 270, 296, 304, 318 n. 1, 336, 342 n. 1, 385–7, 390
Gladstone, William Ewart: biog. 6 n. 5; 59–60, 98 n. 2, 128, 156, 158, 162, 169, 186, 282–3, 320, 387
Gneist, Rudolf von: biog. 172 n. 3
Goltz, Karl August, Count von der: biog. 345 n. 7; 346
Goltz, Kolmar, Baron von der: biog. 337 n. 3
Goltz, Robert, Count von der: biog. 78 n. 3; 189
Gorchakov, Alexander, Prince: biog. 36 n. 2; 54, 59, 167, 229
Gorchakov, Michael, Prince: 132
Göring: biog. 129 n. 3; 130
Gossler, Gustav von: biog. 71 n. 1; 82, 91, 93, 109–10, 140, 150, 237–8, 246, 275, 285, 328–9, 373
Granville, George Leveson-Gower, Earl: 12 n. 3; biog. 59 n. 3; 60, 158, 162, 175 n. 2, 291 n. 1

Hartington, Spencer Compton Cavendish, Marquess of: biog. 320 n. 1
Hatzfeldt-Trachenberg, Prince: 195–6
Hatzfeldt-Wildenburg, Helene, Countess (née Moulton): 32–3, 62, 88–90, 101, 173, 176, 181, 255, 268, 330
Hatzfeldt-Wildenburg, Helene Suzanne von: 31, 32–3, 88–9, 173, 176
Hatzfeldt-Wildenburg, Paul, Count von: xiii, xiv, xvi; biog. 1 n. 5; Crown Prince and Princess, 2, 20, 50–2, 55–6, 152–3, 181, 225–6, 268; Bismarck, 10–11, 13, 77–9,

118, 120–1, 145–7, 198–9, 208–9, 224, 230–1; career, 16, 25, 26, 62–3, 172–3, 184, 185, 210, 220–1, 258; personal affairs, 24, 32–3, 88–90, 175–6; Kusserow, 27–9, 159; Bavarian loan, 73, 75, 77, 79–80; character, 129, 168, 179, 192–3, 261–2; Battenberg marriage, 134, 142–3, 144, 207, 255; Herbert Bismarck, 100–1, 136–7, 217–18, 237, 260, 267; Caprivi, 158–9, 163–4, 222; Russia, 228–30, 231 n. 2, 240; Carolines question, 234–7, 239, 241; in London, 269, 282–3, 299, 330, 335, 348, 373; letters quoted, 282, 285–6, 300–2, 303–5, 309–12, 318–20, 321–3, 324, 325; miscellaneous, 5, 6, 7, 14, 18–19, 21, 22, 31, 37, 40, 43, 44 n. 1, 45, 49, 66, 71, 76, 98, 99, 102, 119, 124, 130, 135, 154, 156, 162, 169, 188, 190, 201, 216, 219, 247 n. 2, 259
Haucke, see Battenberg, Princess of
Haussonville, Maximilian, Count von: biog. 23 n. 1
Haymerlé, Heinrich, Baron von: biog. 11 n. 4
Heinrich, Prince of Prussia: biog. 100 n. 1; 102, 153, 154, 250, 254, 349, 355, 365, 371, 372
Helldorf-Bedra, Otto Heinrich von: biog. 167 n. 1
Henckel-Donnersmarck, Guido, Count von: 83 n. 5; biog. 195 n. 1
Hengelmüller von Hengervár, Ladislaus, Baron von: biog. 302 n. 2; 304
Herbette, Jules: 297 n. 4; 319 n. 3
Heuduck, Wilhelm von: biog. 293 n. 1
Heydt, August, Baron von der: biog. 43 n. 1; 58
Heyking, Edmund: biog. 3 n. 3
Hinzpeter, Georg Ernst: biog. 363 n. 1
Hirsch, Moritz von, Baron Hirsch auf Gereuth: biog. 18 n. 2, 23 n. 4
Hobrecht, Arthur von: biog. 72 n. 3
Hofmann, Karl von: biog. 255 n. 1; 292–3
Hohenlohe-Schillingsfürst, Chlodwig, Prince zu: 12 n. 3; biog. 61 n. 2; 62, 71, 78, 83 n. 5, 88, 156, 174, 187, 189, 208–9, 210, 220, 221, 244, 247, 255, 258, 292–3, 335, 338–9, 345, 358, 375–6
Hohenlohe-Schillingsfürst, Konstantin, Prince zu: biog. 11 n. 5
Hohenlohe-Schillingsfürst, Victor, Prince zu, Duke of Ratibor: biog. 172 n. 1
Hohenzollern-Sigmaringen, Prince Karl von: biog. 6 n. 7
Holleben, Theodor von: biog. 15 n. 4; 17, 27–8
Holtzendorff, Franz von: biog. 52 n. 1
Homeyer, Gustav: biog. 124 n. 1; 125
Hovell, Dr Mark: biog. 350 n. 1; 372
Hüne-Hoiningen, Ernst, Baron von: biog. 265 n. 2; 266, 308

Iddesleigh, *see* Northcote, Sir Stafford
Ignatiev, Nikolai Pavlovich, Count: biog. 9
  n. 4; 16, 387
Itzenplitz, Heinrich, Count von: biog. 78
  n. 1

Jacobini, Ludovico: 2 n. 10; biog. 250 n. 6
Jahn, Friedrich Ludwig: biog. 36 n. 1
Jasmund, Consul-General von: 105-6

Kálnoky von Köröspatak, Gustav, Count:
  biog. 11 n. 7; 65-6, 155, 161 n. 1, 228,
  252 n. 3, 253 n. 1, 277, 302 n. 4, 311, 314,
  319-20, 322 n. 1, 341 n. 2, n. 3, 342, 374,
  385-7
Kameke, General Georg von: biog. 15 n. 1;
  17, 31-2, 34, 37, 42, 44
Kapnist, Peter, Count: biog. 199 n. 1
Karavelov, Peter: biog. 385 n. 4
Karl, Prince of Prussia: 58, 59
Károlyi, Alois, Count: biog. 310 n. 7, 312,
  321 n. 1, 322
Kaulbars, Nikolai, Baron von: biog. 316 n. 1
Kessel, Gustav von: biog. 344 n. 1; 346
Keudell, Robert von: biog. 45 n. 1; 59, 140-
  1, 232, 316, 317 n. 2, 323, 335-6
Khevenhüller-Metsch, Rudolf, Count: biog.
  269 n. 4
Kiderlen-Wächter, Alfred von: biog. 174
  n. 2; 175
Koch, Robert: biog. 134 n. 2
Kolemine, Mme: 132, 137
Köller, Ernst Matthias von: 34
Kopp, Georg von, Bishop of Fulda: biog.
  237 n. 1; 238
Korum, Michael Felix: biog. 238 n. 1
Krauel, Friedrich Richard: biog. 236 n. 1;
  241, 244, 257-8, 310, 322
Krementz, Phillipp: biog. 237 n. 2
Kropotkin, Prince: 309 n. 6
Krüger, *Polizeirat*: 16, 51, 55
Kusserow, Heinrich von: biog. 14 n. 1;
  27-9, 32, 64, 124, 159, 258

Laboulaye, Antoine de: 309 n. 6
Lasker, Eduard: biog. 67 n. 3; 72, 86, 87,
  98, 101, 103, 172
Launay, Eduard, Count di: biog 192 n. 1;
  278, 285, 321 n. 2, 332, 382
Le Maistre, Rudolf: biog. 78 n. 2; 290, 298,
  388
Ledochowski, Miecislaw, Count: biog. 83
  n. 2
Lehndorff, Heinrich August, Count von:
  biog. 25 n. 1; 56-7, 92, 127, 149-50,
  272, 378
Lenbach, Franz von: 188-9, 264
Leo XIII, Pope (1878-1903): 2 n. 5, n. 10,
  43, 44 n. 1, 51, 82-3, 250-1, 256-8, 259
  n. 1, 378-9
Leopold, Duke of Albany: 112

Lerchenfeld, Hugo, Count von: biog. 284
  n. 1; 287-8, 360
Levetzow, Albert von: biog. 108 n. 2; 109
Lewin, Professor: 41
Lewinstein: 10
Leyden, Ernst Viktor von: biog. 39 n. 1; 41
Liebenau, Court Chamberlain: 47-8, 295,
  360, 368, 373
Lignitz, Lieutenant-Colonel von: 196-7, 210
Limburg-Stirum, Friedrich Wilhelm, Count
  zu: biog. 39 n. 3; career, 60-4; 78, 86, 199
Lindau, Dr Rudolf: biog. 187 n. 4; 188, 232,
  263-4, 271, 379
Lobanov-Rostovski, Prince Alexei: biog. 65
  n. 3; 66, 229, 252 n. 4, 385-6
Loë, Walther, Baron von: biog. 43 n. 3;
  248-9, 366
Lorne, John Sutherland-Campbell, Marquess
  of: biog. 198 n. 2, 245
Louis I, King of Portugal (1889-1908):
  205 n. 4, 214 n. 1, 224-5
Löwe, Dr Wilhelm: biog. 211 n. 2; 213
Lucanus, Hermann von: biog. 71 n. 2; 246,
  275
Lucius, Robert, later Baron Lucius von Ball-
  hausen: biog. 67 n. 4; 69-70, 84, 102, 114,
  194
Lüderitz, Adolf: biog. 159 n. 1; 163
Ludwig IV, Grand-Duke of Hesse-Darmstadt: 131-2, 134, 137, 146, 290, 316, 368
Ludwig II, King of Bavaria (1864-86): 30,
  40; Bavarian loan, 73, 75, 77, 80, 87-8,
  94, 95 n. 1; 178, 287 n. 2, 346
Luise, Grand-Duchess of Baden: 100-1, 136,
  265, 353
Luitpold, Prince of Bavaria: biog. 287 n. 2;
  288
Lutz, Johann, Baron von: biog. 288 n. 1; 289
Lyncker, Moritz, Baron von: biog. 309 n. 1;
  349 n. 2, 358, 371

Mackenzie, Dr Morell: biog. 342 n. 3; 343,
  344-5, 348, 350, 351, 352-3, 356, 358
Madai, *Landrat*: biog. 72 n. 1
Malet, Sir Edward: biog. 169 n. 2; 214, 239
  n. 4, 240 n. 1, 260 n. 2, 300, 302
Maltzan-Gültz, Helmuth, Baron von: biog.
  275 n. 1
Manteuffel, Edwin, Baron von: biog. 49
  n. 2; 50, 183, 208, 209, 220, 238, 252,
  258, 294
Manteuffel, Otto, Baron von: biog. 10
  n. 3; 27
Maria Cristina, Regent of Spain: 306 n. 1
Maria Feodorovna, Tsarina of Russia: 92;
  biog. 154 n. 3; 259 n. 3
Marie, Princess of Prussia: biog. 226 n. 2.
Marschall von Bieberstein, Adolf Hermann,
  Baron von: biog. 368 n. 3; 369
Maybach, Albert von: biog. 26 n. 3; 67, 70,
  93, 100, 102, 113, 118, 275

Meiningen, Bernhard von: 112, 122, 205, 371
Meiningen, Charlotte, Grand-Duchess of: 153, 205, 371
Melchers, Paulus: biog. 83 n. 3; 238 n. 3
Mendelssohn: 130 n. 1
Mendelssohn-Bartholdy, Ernst: biog. 181 n. 1
Mensdorff-Pouilly, Alexander, Count: biog. 25 n. 5
Meyendorff, Peter, Baron von: biog. 26 n. 6
Meyer-Cohn, Baron von: biog. 1 n. 4; 11, 73, 75, 76–7
Miquel, Dr Johannes: biog. 112 n. 4; 116–18, 167, 183, 363 n. 2
Mischke, General: 80–1, 83, 99, 149, 358
Mohrenheim, Baron von: 309 n. 6, 336 n. 6
Moltke, Helmuth, Count von: biog. 15 n. 2; 17, 126–7, 254, 371
Montebello, Adrien, Count: biog. 303 n. 2; 304
Monts, Anton, Count von: biog. 238 n. 2
Morier, Sir Robert: biog. 215 n. 2; 300, 302
Mühler, Heinrich von: biog. 140 n. 2
Münster, Georg Herbert, Count zu: biog. 51 n. 2; 59–60, 86, 140–1, 145, 175, 193, 199, 200, 209, 220, 222, 305 n. 4, 308, 336 n. 6
Muraviev, Michael, Count: 260 n. 1, 267 n. 1, biog. 279 n. 4; 301 n. 1, 314

Napoleon III, Emperor of France (1852–70): 6, 107, 114
Nelidov, Alexander von: 266 n. 3; biog. 269 n. 2; 338 n. 1
Nicholas I, Prince, later King of Montenegro (1860–1918): biog. 292 n. 1
Nicholas Alexandrovich, Grand-Duke of Russia, later Tsar Nicholas II (1894–1917): 153–4
Nicholas I, Tsar of Russia (1825–55): 107, 138, 315
Nicholas of Nassau, Prince: 32, 173
Nobiling, Dr Karl: 206
Normann, Karl von: biog. 30 n. 2; 36, 45–7, 51, 59, 68, 69, 72, 76, 78, 81, 83, 99, 106, 146–9, 150, 151, 208, 303
Northcote, Sir Stafford, Earl of Iddesleigh: biog. 302 n. 3; 310, 322

Orlov, Nikolai, Prince: biog. 8 n. 5; 9, 48, 74–5, 80, 83, 92, 96, 98

Palmerston, Henry John Temple, Viscount: biog. 60 n. 2
Patow, Erasmus Robert, Baron von: biog. 52 n. 2; 273
Penafiel: 205 n. 4, 215, 225–6
Perponcher-Sedlnitzky, Friedrich, Count von: biog. 297 n. 3
Perponcher, Countess: biog. 350 n. 2; 351, 358
Pfister, Bavarian Privy Councillor: 77, 80, 88, 94, 95 n. 1
Plessen, see Scheel-Plessen

Poschinger, Heinrich, Ritter von: biog. 19 n. 1
Prokesch von Osten, Anton, Count: biog. 392 n. 1
Puttkamer, Max von: biog. 255 n. 2
Puttkamer, Robert Viktor von: biog. 2 n. 6; 23, 35, 44, 48, 56–7, 71–2, 74, 84, 93, 102, 109, 196, 248, 333–4, 353–4

Radetzky, General: 226
Radolin-Radolinski, Hugo Leszczyc, Count von: xvi–xvii; biog. 11 n. 1; 16, 24, 88, 146, 148, 150, 190, 191, 194, 204, 207–8, 211, 216, 217, 223–4, 225 n. 1, 255–6, 264, 277, 290, 294–6, 306, 307, 309, 344, 346, 348, 349, 355, 357, 364, 366–7, 370–1, 372, 373, 374, 376–7, 380
Radowitz, Joseph Maria von: biog. 18 n. 1; 20, 27, 61, 62, 63, 75, 101, 103, 150, 219, 259, 266, 269, 279, 303 n. 2, 324
Rantzau, Marie, Countess (née Bismarck-Schönhausen): xii, 35, 93, 96–7, 111, 114, 132, 151, 182, 184, 221
Rantzau, Kuno, Count zu: xii–xiii; biog. 24 n. 2; inefficiency, 44, 49, 251; relations with Bismarck family, 72, 78, 80, 96–7, 103–4, 110–11, 114–15, 132, 192, 221, 230, 268; relations with other officials, 93–4, 95, 100–1, 199; quarrel with Holstein, 151–2, 272; character, 271–2, 273; Munich post, 287–9, 370; miscellaneous, 28–9, 35, 57, 65, 73, 77, 182, 184, 231 n. 2, 239, 246, 267 n. 1, 307, 310 n. 4, 314 n. 2, 318 n. 3
Rauchhaupt: biog. 71 n. 3; 73–4, 171
Redern, Heinrich, Count von: biog. 53 n. 2
Redern, Wilhelm, Count von (Court Chamberlain): biog. 24 n. 1
Redern, Wilhelm, Count von (diplomat): biog. 15 n. 6; 262, 267, 308–9
Reischach, Hugo, Baron von: biog. 371 n. 1; 372
Reuss, Heinrich VII, Prince: xix; biog. 155 n. 1; 252 n. 3, 253, 277, 302 n. 4, 314, 319 n. 4, 332, 335 n. 2, 339, 341 n. 3, 342 n. 1, 361, 374, 385–7
Reuss, Heinrich XXII, Prince: biog. 106 n. 3
Richter, Eugen: biog. 67 n. 5; 117, 176, 195, 251 n. 1
Richthofen, Oswald, Baron von: biog. 133 n. 1
Rickert, Heinrich: biog. 69 n. 1; 203
Robilant, Nicolis, Count di: biog. 278 n. 2; 279, 285, 317, 321 n. 2, 332, 335, 337
Roggenbach, Franz, Baron von: biog. 121 n. 1; 380
Roon, Albrecht, Count von: biog. 5 n. 2; 26, 43, 65, 127
Rosebery, Archibald Philip Primrose, Lord: biog. 185 n. 2; 186, 201–2, 223, 232, 280, 282–3, 285, 320–1

Rotenhan, Wolfram, Baron von: biog. 174 n. 1; 175
Rötger: 84, 131, 150, 172
Rottenburg, Franz von: biog. 21 n. 1; 22, 35, 49, 56, 67, 79–80, 91, 93–4, 95, 102, 110, 114, 115, 117, 124, 131, 172, 213, 246, 253, 263–4, 270, 272, 275, 290 n. 2, 297, 333–4, 354, 363, 378, 379
Rudolf, Crown Prince of Austria: 21, 242
Rustem Pasha: biog. 304 n. 2
Rutland, Lord John Manners, Duke of: biog. 373 n. 2

Saburov, Peter von: biog. 35 n. 1; 66–7, 74–6, 80, 83, 92, 98–9, 100
St Vallier, Charles, Count de: biog. 156 n. 2; 380
Sagasta, Praxedes Mateo: biog. 243 n. 1
Salamanca, General: 238–9, 248
Saldern, Konrad von: biog. 171 n. 3; 172, 267 n. 1, 289, 301 n. 1, 318
Salisbury, Robert Cecil, Marquess of: 86; biog. 207 n. 1; 222, 232, 234 n. 1, 239 n. 4, 240 n. 1, 260 n. 1, n. 2, 269, 282, 299–302, 310, 312, 319–20, 322–3, 326, 337, 373
Sarauw, Captain: 284
Sargent, A. A: biog. 86 n. 4; 87
Schalscha, Alexander von: biog. 191 n. 3
Scheel-Plessen, Ludwig, Baron von: biog. 53 n. 1; 193, 222, 239 n. 4, 282, 327
Schelling, Ludwig Hermann von: biog. 334 n. 3
Schleinitz, Alexander, Baron von: biog. 10 n. 4; 76–8
Schlözer, Kurd von: biog. 2 n. 4; 3, 43, 45, 83 n. 4, 232, 237, 238, 250–1, 256–7, 259 n. 1
Schnäbele, Guillaume: biog. 339 n. 1; 353 n. 1, 375
Schnäbele, Gustav: biog. 353 n. 1; 354
Schneider, Louis: biog. 377 n. 4
Scholz, Adolf von: biog. 26 n. 2; 50; income tax plan, 56–7, 64; 67, 72, 100, 101–2, 113–14, 130
Schorlemer-Alst, Burghard, Baron von: biog. 7 n. 5; 8, 191
Schrader, Karl: biog. 377 n. 1
Schrötter, Dr Leopold, Ritter von Kristelli: biog. 358 n. 2
Schwabach, Julius: biog. 75 n. 1, 141
Schwarzenberg, Felix, Prince: biog. 107 n. 2
Schweinitz, Hans Lothar von; biog. 20 n. 2; career, 53–5; 75 n. 2, 96 n. 1, 98, 126, 130 n. 1, 187, 193, 197, 199, 204, 226, 229, 265, 269, 315, 331, 336 n. 5
Schweninger, Dr Ernst: biog. 48 n. 1; 103–4, 110–11, 115, 129, 132–3, 151, 173, 198–9, 210, 220, 274, 276, 306, 344, 379
Seckendorff, Albert von: biog. 349 n. 1
Seckendorff, Götz, Count von: biog. 1 n. 7; 2, 3–4, 11, 30, 31, 32, 34, 88, 128, 180,

183–4, 190, 192, 203, 207–8, 214–16, 218, 221–2, 245, 262, 303, 344, 350–1, 372
Shuvalov, Paul, Count: biog. 229 n. 2; 231 n. 2, 239 n. 4, 240, 266–7, 279, 290, 291 n. 1, 309, 311, 313–14, 377
Shuvalov, Peter, Count: biog. 229 n. 1; 331–2
Simson, Martin Eduard von: biog. 122 n. 1
Skobelev, Michael: biog. 9 n. 1; 14
Solms-Sonnenwalde, Eberhard, Count zu: biog. 45 n. 2; 78, 234 n. 1, 235, 239, 243–4, 250 n. 4
Sommerfeld, Lieutenant-Colonel: biog. 30 n. 1; 31, 35, 43, 68 n. 1, 177, 195, 207, 211–12, 214–15, 218, 221–2, 249, 250, 255
Sophie, Princess of Prussia: 154, 205, 380 n. 3
Stambulov, Stefan: 301 n. 1
Steinkopf, Edward Hermann: 264 n. 1, 270
Steinmetz, Karl Friedrich von: biog. 127 n. 2
Stephan, Heinrich von: biog. 40 n. 1; 246
Stillfried-Alcantara, Rudolf, Count von: biog. 4 n. 1
Stirum—see Limburg-Stirum
Stöcker, Adolf von: biog. 362 n. 1; 363, 367
Stockmar, Ernst von: biog. 46 n. 1; 106, 148
Stolberg-Wernigerode, Eberhard, Count zu: biog. 80 n. 2
Stolberg-Wernigerode, Otto, Count zu: biog. 70 n. 1; 195, 204, 368, 377–8
Stosch, Albrecht von: biog. 17 n. 4; 34, 37, 39, 40, 46–7, 76, 99, 106, 117, 123, 147, 148, 149, 160, 163
Struck, Dr Heinrich: biog. 22 n. 3; 110–11, 135, 175, 199
Stülpnagel, Ida von: vii–viii, xviii, 42, 271, 278, 286, 334, 346 n. 1, 348
Stumm, Ferdinand, Baron von: biog. 29 n. 2, 134, 146–7, 198
Széchényi, Imre, Count: biog. 23 n. 2, 178, 341

Taaffe, Eduard, Count von: biog. 11 n. 6; 381
Tavera, Schmit, Ritter von: biog. 299 n. 3
Thielmann, Max Franz Guido, Baron von: 260 n. 1; biog. 336 n. 1; 337–8, 369
Thun-Hohenstein, Friedrich, Count von: biog. 108 n. 1
Tiedemann, Christoph von: biog. 65 n. 1; 92–4, 333–4
Tissot, Charles Joseph: biog. 6 n. 1
Tobold, Dr Adalbert: biog. 344 n. 2; 345
Tornielli Brusati di Vergano, Count Giuseppe: biog. 345 n. 6; 346

Umberto, King of Italy (1878–1900): 43, 382

Vannovski, General Peter: biog. 196 n. 2
Varnbüler, Karl von: biog. 380 n. 2
Verdy du Vernois, Julius von: biog. 129 n. 2; 366
Victor Emmanuel II, King of Italy (1849–78): 36
Victoria, Queen of England (1837–1901): xv, 111–12, 122, 132, 137, 139–40, 153,

161, 190, 198, 245, 254, 270, 290, 330, 346 n. 2, 372, 373, 388 n. 2, 393

Victoria, German Crown Princess, then Kaiserin Friedrich: xv, xvi; Hatzfeldt, 1–2, 32, 55, 88–9, 173, 179, 229, 255, 260, 268, 330; Prince Wilhelm, 15, 40, 48, 165, 168, 206, 327, 364, 365, 382; unpopularity, 69, 128, 158, 166; Crown Prince, 96, 99, 155, 164, 167, 195, 303; Crown Prince's illness, 343–4, 346, 348, 349–53, 356–8, 371, 376–7; Battenberg marriage, 111–12, 122–3, 134, 138, 142–5, 153, 198, 207, 254, 255–6, 262, 290, 307, 335, 366–70, 372; Bismarck, 174, 175, 176–7, 180–1, 182–4, 186, 190, 202, 211–19, 221, 222–4, 241, 264, 270–1, 295, 306; Herbert Bismarck, 192, 194, 224, 249, 261, 277; Portuguese marriage, 205, 214–16, 225; miscellaneous, 3–4, 12, 18, 30, 46, 68, 72, 83, 106, 137, 139, 146–9, 150, 154, 161, 171, 189, 190–1, 193, 203–4, 208, 250, 297, 355, 380

Victoria of Hesse, Princess: 125 n. 2; 132, 134

Victoria, Princess of Prussia (daughter of Friedrich III): xvi, 89; Battenberg marriage, 111–12, 122, 125, 134, 143–5, 153, 171 n. 4, 198, 207, 215, 217, 244, 254, 256, 262, 263, 307, 344, 358, 365, 366, 372; 190, 192, 194; Portuguese proposal, 205, 214, 225; 350

Villaume, Karl von: biog. 308 n. 2

Virchow, Rudolf: biog. 344 n. 3; 377

Vladimir, Grand-Duke of Russia, 314, 316–17, 319 n. 4

Voigts-Rhetz, Konstantin Bernhard von: biog. 211 n. 1

Wagner, Emil von: biog. 61 n. 1

Waldemar, Prince of Denmark: 259 n. 3, 262

Waldemar, Prince of Prussia: 97

Waldersee, Alfred, Count von: xviii n. 1; biog. 14 n. 2; 15, 17, 21, 31, 34, 36, 40, 49, 92, 123–4, 126–7, 129, 145, 159, 180, 191, 196–7, 209–11, 249, 265–6, 284, 287, 327, 348, 356, 363, 366, 370, 371, 373, 374, 378, 382–3

Wallenberg, Marie von (née von Rochow): 38, 115

Wedel, Karl, Count von: biog. 25 n. 2; 107, 242, 244–5, 261, 263, 280

Wedell-Malchow, Friedrich von: biog. 39 n. 2

Wedell-Piesdorf, Wilhelm von: biog. 378 n. 1

Wegner, Dr: 356

Wehren, Colonel von: 151–2

Wendt, Karl, Baron von: biog. 191 n. 2

Werder, Bernhard von: biog. 55 n. 2; 126, 197, 229

Werther, Karl, Freiherr von: biog. 12 n. 1; 78

Werthern-Beuchlingen, Georg, Baron von: biog. 30 n. 3; 40, 73, 287–9, 330, 370

Wesdehlen, Ludwig, Count von: biog. 187 n. 3; 189–90, 338 n. 3

White, Andrew D.: biog. 86 n. 2

White, Sir William: biog. 301 n. 4; 309, 324

Wilhelm I, King of Prussia, then German Kaiser (1861–88): xv, xvii; Bismarck, 14–15, 21, 36, 38, 74, 97, 100–1, 117, 118, 126–7, 182, 196, 202, 210, 317, 356; Crown Prince, 39–40, 43, 44 n. 1, 100, 165, 168, 190, 296, 343, 349, 351–2, 364; Bavarian loan, 73, 75, 76–9; Battenberg marriage, 111–12, 122–3, 134, 143, 145, 245, 262, 263, 289, 307, 316, 323; Bismarck report on Battenberg, 305, text, 388–93; Council of State, 119–20, 121, 124; health, 140, 142, 166, 234, 256, 356; succession, 179, 181, 183, 193, 200, 206, 230, 355, 357, 359; Portuguese marriage, 205 n. 4, 214 n. 1, 224–5, 226 n. 1; Carolines question, 234 n. 1, 236, 241, 243–4, 250 n. 3; Prince Wilhelm, 294–7, 347; miscellaneous, 1, 2, 3, 5, 11–12, 17, 19, 23, 25, 32, 34, 37 n. 1, 42, 44, 46, 52, 55, 58, 61, 67, 68, 72, 87 n. 3, 89, 92, 98, 102, 103, 105, 106, 128, 135, 136, 149, 153, 154, 161, 171, 174, 185, 186, 195, 199, 208, 209, 217, 220, 221, 226–7, 260, 265, 273, 283, 285, 287–8, 306, 309 n. 3, 322 n. 1, 327, 328, 333 n. 1, 338, 353–4, 365, 377 n. 4

Wilhelm II, Prince of Prussia, then German Crown Prince, Kaiser (1888–1918): xviii; relations with parents, 15, 34, 37, 46–8, 154–5, 165, 168, 177–8, 294–7, 327, 352, 364, 371; Bismarck, 128, 183, 211, 294–8, 306, 361–3, 365, 367, 374–5; Battenberg marriage, 153, 207, 369, 372; Herbert Bismarck, 191–2, 194, 206, 219–20, 242, 254, 261, 270, 276, 280, 299, 328, 369–70; Bülow, 233–4; character, 346–8, 349, 355, 377–83; work in Foreign Ministry, 303, 307–8, 315–16, 317–18, 360; succession, 343, 356; miscellaneous, 21, 40, 60, 97, 123 n. 1, 167, 190, 245, 259, 331, 373

Wilhelm, Duke of Brunswick: 166 n. 1, 194 n. 2

Wilke: 119–20

Wilmowski, Karl, Baron von: biog. 119 n. 3; 120, 255 n. 3, 338, 353–4

Windthorst, Ludwig: biog. 8 n. 4; 18, 191, 250 n. 3, 251 n. 1

Winter, Leopold von: 106 n. 1

Winterfeld, Hugo von: 99, 352–3, 358

Wolff, Sir Henry Drummond Charles: biog. 239 n. 3; 240, 259–60

Wollmann, Hofrat: 283–4

Wurmb: biog. 171 n. 2

Zedlitz-Trützschler, Robert, Count von: biog. 333 n. 2

Zorilla, Manuel Ruiz: biog. 305 n. 3

SUBJECT INDEX

Afghanistan: 98, 185–6, 193, 207–8, 325–6

Alliances and alignments: France-Russia, xiv, 259, 317, 336; Austria-Italy-England, xiv, 259, 331–3, 342; Germany-Russia, xv, 297, 315, 339, 357; Germany-Russia-Austria, xvi, 239–40, 256, 297, 316; England-Turkey, 240; Germany-Austria, 277, 302, 331; Russia-England-France, 300; Germany-Austria-Italy, 308, 315–16, 321, 331, 335, 337, 339; Germany-Italy, 316, 323, 325, 333, 335, 337; Russia-France-Italy, 319; Germany-England, 325, 331; Germany-Spain, 44, 325; Germany-Turkey, 325, 331; Austria-Italy, 332–3; Germany-Austria-Italy-Rumania-Turkey-England-Spain, 361. (*See also* individual countries)

Alsace-Lorraine: Manteuffel regime, 49–50, 209, 250–1; Hohenlohe regime, 208–9, 220–1, 255, 292–4, 335, 338; expulsions, 250–1; compulsory passports, 375

Army (German): preventive measures against Russia, 14–15; position of War Minister, 17, 31–2, 34; local taxation, 34, 37; payment of troops (1866), 58; leadership, 126–9, 196, 210, 249, 284, 287; voting of reserve officers, 195–6

Austria: German relations, xiv, xv, 10, 22–3, 25–6, 37, 54, 58, 114, 231, 248, 252–3, 256, 270, 273–7, 279–80, 287, 299, 307, 326, 328, 331, 361, 363, 381; Russian relations, 5, 10, 12, 65–6, 254, 269–70, 276, 283, 287, 290, 302–3, 323, 341–2, 359; English relations, 291–2, 299–301, 321–2, 325–7; internal situation, 11, 107–8, 241–2, 278, 299; international position, 312–15, 321–4, 326, 330, 332, 385–6

Balkans: division into spheres of interest, xiii, 15–16, 276, 313, 385–7

Battenberg marriage: international implications, xvi, xvii, 112, 125–6, 134, 143–4, 153, 171–2, 217, 263, 366–70, 372, 388–93. (*See also* Alexander, Prince of Battenberg)

Bosnia and Herzegovina: 5, 9, 15, 290, 341–2, 385

Bulgaria: Russian policy, xiii, 6, 15–16, 252, 255, 262, 266–7, 290–1, 311, 316, 318, 330; crises of 1885–6, 252, 254–6, 259, 266–70, 276, 278–80, 289–90, 300–4,

385–93; international position, 309, 313–14, 316, 318–22, 324, 326, 336–7. (*See also* Alexander, Prince of Battenberg, Battenberg marriage)

Caroline Islands: xiii, 234–9, 241–5, 247–8, 250–1, 256–9, 276, 305

Church: clergymen's pension scheme, 82; organization, 90–1; religious study, 115–16; Catholic, 242, 277–8, 328–9, 340–1; Protestant, 328–9, 340–1

Colonies: German policy, xvi, 17, 138–9, 152–5, 158, 160–4, 169, 175, 181, 200–2, 207, 236, 269; Angra Pequena, 159, 163; Congo Conference, 169, 171, 199; Zanzibar, 310; Samoa, 311. (*See also* Caroline Islands)

Council of State (Prussia): 105, 112, 119, 121, 124, 142, 164–7

Egypt: Anglo-French relations, 5–6, 59, 127–8, 152–3, 156, 160, 162, 200–2, 231, 239–40; Anglo-German relations, 207–8, 310, 319, 324–6; international position, 302–3, 323–5; crisis of 1882, 12; conference of 1884, 127–8, 152–3, 158; Drummond Wolff mission, 239–40, 259–60

England: German relations (*see also* Colonies), xiv, xv, xvi, 29–30, 69, 98–9, 127–8, 135–6, 145, 152–5, 157–8, 161–2, 168–9, 174–6, 179–81, 185–6, 200–3, 207, 212, 222–3, 228, 239–40, 254–5, 259–61, 269, 286, 308, 318–21, 325, 373; French relations (*see also* Egypt), 127, 157, 162, 169, 200–1, 300; Russian relations, 98, 185–6, 193, 218, 230, 240, 255, 259–60, 263, 280, 290–2, 300, 304, 320, 325, 348; Austrian relations, 299–301, 321–2, 325–6; Turkish relations, 239–40, 259–60, 322; internal situation, 59–60, 98, 231, 312, 320, 326; international position, 282, 290–2, 299–305, 309–10, 322–4, 326, 387; policy, 62, 98, 282–3, 285–6

France: German relations, xiii, 12–14, 21, 155–7, 160, 162, 169, 200–3, 228, 231, 247, 280–1, 284, 297–8, 325, 327, 331–3, 337, 339, 353–4, 359, 376, 381–2; English relations (*see also* Egypt), 127, 157, 162, 169, 200–1, 300; Russian relations, 20, 309, 315, 317, 319, 336; internal situation, 6, 26, 157, 231, 239, 280–1, 322,

403

376; international position, 20–1, 127–8, 298, 322, 324, 300

Greece: dispute with Turkey, 6; Cretan crisis, 282–3, 285–6; international position, 62, 162, 278

Heligoland: 135–6, 175
Holy See: Crown Prince's visit (1883), 43–5, 51; Caroline Islands arbitration, 250–1, 256–9; Wilhelm II's visit (1888), 378–9. (*See also Kulturkampf*)

Italy: war of 1859, 10–12; German relations, 43–6, 50–2, 55–6, 77–8, 259, 307–8, 316, 321, 323, 325, 333, 335, 337, 345–6, 379, 382; international position, 157, 162, 312, 315–16, 319, 321, 323, 325, 331–3, 335; internal situation, 239

Kulturkampf: negotiations with Holy See, xv, xvi, 2–3; law on civil marriage, 4–5; obligatory registration of clergy, 8; school bill, 63; Law of Dispensation, 82–3; Falk legislation, 90; role of Kopp, 237–8; 7, 91, 275

Montenegro: 6, 9, 62, 313, 385

National Liberal Party: Bennigsen and Bismarck, 33–4, 70, 102, 116–17; Miquel and Bismarck, 116–17; Bismarck's willingness to govern with, 112–13, 203

Poland: German colonization project, 333, 392; expulsion of Polish labourers, 248
Portugal: Prussian marriage, 205, 213–17, 223–6

Railways: Turkish, 18, 23; Austrian, 18, 23; Rumanian, 18; South German, 135; Russian, 218
Reichsglocke incident: 23, 205, 228

Reichstadt agreements: 5, 341–2
Russia: German relations (*see also* Bulgaria, Battenberg marriage), xiii–xviii, 5–6, 8–10, 13–16, 37–8, 44, 55, 66–7, 74–6, 80, 83, 91–2, 96, 98–9, 130–1, 153–4, 161, 179–80, 205, 218, 226–31, 239–40, 248, 252, 256, 259–60, 266–7, 269, 277–80, 287, 294–9, 307, 309, 311, 313, 315–17, 319–20, 322–3, 325, 327–8, 330–1, 332–3, 336, 339, 341–2, 357, 359, 361–2, 366–7, 377, 381, 390; Austrian relations, 5, 10, 12, 65–6, 254, 269–70, 276, 283, 287, 290, 302–3, 323, 341–2, 359; English relations, 98, 185–6, 193, 218, 240, 255, 259–60, 263, 280, 290–2, 300, 304, 320, 325, 348; French relations, 20, 309, 315, 317, 319, 336; internal situation, 15–17; international position, xiii, xiv, xv, 6, 15–16, 20–1, 66–7, 259–60, 266–7, 311–16, 322–4, 330–2, 337, 374, 385–7; Turkish War (1877–8), 5, 6, 91, 106, 138, 197

Serbia: 252, 268, 278, 282, 385, 387
Spain: German relations, 43–6, 50–2, 55–6, 77–8, 148–9, 157, 171, 234–6, 238–9, 241–5, 247–8, 250–1, 256–9, 276, 305–7, 325; internal situation, 18–19, 235–6, 239, 241–2, 244, 247–8. (*See also* Caroline Islands)

Taxes: unearned income, 56–8, 64; local and church, 70–1; education, 109–10; stock exchange, 227–8
Turkey: international position, xiii, 5–6, 62, 157, 266, 278–9, 283, 291–2, 299–300, 303, 322, 324–6, 337, 386. (*See also* Egypt, Bulgaria)

United States: Lasker affair, 72, 86–7, 98, 172; official discourtesy, 85–7; pork products, 98, 125; international position, 162

Find